SACRAMENTO PUBLIC LIBRARY
828 "I" Street
Sacramento, CA 95814
05/16

D0953734

ALFRED A. KNOPF

1915 · 100 YEARS · 2015

ALSO BY T. J. STILES

The First Tycoon:
The Epic Life of Cornelius Vanderbilt

Jesse James:
Last Rebel of the Civil War

CUSTER'S TRIALS

CRUSHED STONE

CUSTER'S TRIALS

A Life on the Frontier of a New America

T. J. STILES

ALFRED A. KNOPF   NEW YORK   2015

THIS IS A BORZOI BOOK
PUBLISHED BY ALFRED A. KNOPF

Copyright © 2015 by T. J. Stiles

All rights reserved. Published in the United States by
Alfred A. Knopf, a division of Penguin Random House LLC, New York,
and distributed in Canada by Random House of Canada,
a division of Penguin Random House Ltd., Toronto.

www.aaknopf.com

Knopf, Borzoi Books, and the colophon are registered trademarks
of Penguin Random House LLC.

Grateful acknowledgment is made to the following for permission to reprint
previously published material: The New York Public Library: Excerpts from
Marguerite Merington papers from the Manuscripts and Archives Division.
Reprinted by permission of The New York Public Library, Astor, Lenox, and
Tilden Foundations. · Shirley A. Leckie: Excerpts from *Elizabeth Bacon Custer
and the Making of a Myth* by Shirley A. Leckie. Reprinted by permission of the
author. · Yale University Press: Excerpts from *Life in Custer's Cavalry*, edited
by Robert M. Utley. Reprinted by permission of Yale University Press.

Library of Congress Cataloging-in-Publication Data
Stiles, T. J.
Custer's trials : a life on the frontier of a new America / T. J. Stiles.
pages cm
Includes bibliographical references and index.
ISBN 978-0-307-59264-4 (hardcover) — ISBN 978-1-101-87584-1 (eBook)
1. Custer, George A. (George Armstrong), 1839–1876.   2. Generals—
United States—Biography.   3. United States. Army—Biography.
4. United States—History—Civil War, 1861–1865.   5. Little Bighorn,
Battle of the, Mont., 1876.   6. Indians of North America—Wars—
Great Plains.   I. Title.
E467.1.C99S76 2015   973.8'2092—dc23   [B]   2015002070

Jacket photograph courtesy the Library of Congress, Washington, D.C.
Jacket design by Oliver Munday

Maps by Mapping Specialists

Manufactured in the United States of America
First Edition

To my parents,
Dr. Clifford and Carol Stiles,
to my late mentor,
Richard Maxwell Brown,
and most of all
to my daughter,
Sasha

And how much he suffered merely to appear in his own eyes
what he wished to be!

—LEO TOLSTOY, "The Raid"

Contents

Illustrations

Maps

Preface

T HE STORY BEGINS WITH its ending. On June 25, 1876, George Armstrong Custer led the 7th U.S. Cavalry Regiment to the Little Bighorn River in the Montana Territory, where Lakota and Northern Cheyenne warriors surrounded him and a detachment of more than 200 troops and slaughtered them to a man. Renowned as Custer's Last Stand, it was the greatest defeat inflicted upon the U.S. Army in the late-nineteenth-century Indian wars. Like John Hancock's signing of the Declaration of Independence, it is the one fact about the man that lives in American memory.

For generations of writers about Custer, death defined his life. Since none of the soldiers who accompanied him on his final ride lived to tell about it, his annihilation has been a great mystery. The mechanics of his last battle have been analyzed and supposed in extreme detail in order to solve it. Every accident in his life, every choice, every personality trait has been interpreted in terms of how it led here. In most books he appears as a man on the march to the Little Bighorn, or a glorified corpse thereafter.

Death has defined his significance as well. His personal end brought to a climax a defining narrative of American mythology and American guilt: the conquest and dispossession of the native peoples of this continent. His personal moral character has stood in for the moral character of the United States. As the cultural consensus has shifted, the image of Custer in national memory has changed from champion of civilization, who died to tame the savage wilderness, to arrogant murderer and land thief. "Custer has been shorthand for hubris, ignorance, and had-it-coming," Timothy Egan observed in the *New York Times* on November 30, 2012, "but in earlier decades Custer was a hero."

Well said—though Egan might have specified hubris *with regard to American Indians*, a hero *on the Great Plains*. For posterity, Custer's death seals him into the single role of frontier soldier. We remember him as a man of one region, the West, and one conflict, the Indian wars. The judicious Robert M. Utley devoted all but twenty of the 209 pages of narrative in his seminal biography, *Cavalier in Buckskin,* to the frontier years.

That's fair enough. The Little Bighorn was a landmark event, and Custer played a high-profile role in Western history. And much of the writing about him has been very good, whether by Utley, Evan Connell, Richard Slotkin, Paul Hutton, Shirley Leckie, Jeffry Wert, Louise Barnett, or others. I also greatly respect the researchers with no other credentials than their passion who have uncovered a wealth of information. (Fascination with Custer is such a phenomenon that there is a fascination with the fascination, as seen in Michael Elliott's fine book *Custerology.*) I did not write this book as a rebuttal, or because previous work is substandard.

Rather, I want to change the camera angle—to examine Custer's life as it was lived, in order to better grasp the man, his times, and his larger meaning. If we can escape the overshadowing preoccupation with his death, a critical fact stands out: he captured the American imagination long before the Little Bighorn, even before he went west. That means he had a significance independent of his demise. But mere chronological balance is not enough. Other, worthy books emphasize his earlier role in the Civil War, when he first won national attention. I am telling his story in a particular light, with a particular sense of context. The result, I hope, is not simply an addition to a familiar story—he was famous for *this* as well as for *that*—but something larger and more comprehensive. I want to explain why his celebrity, and notoriety, spanned both the Civil War and his years on the frontier, resting on neither exclusively but incorporating both.

Something was going on in the country that included the Civil War, westward expansion, and much more. *Something* about the man resonated with Americans as they experienced it. He caught the public imagination because his life spoke to that something.

The search for this unifying theme is complicated by the astonishing number of roles he played. How do we reconcile the buckskin-clad outdoorsman and Indian fighter with the Midwesterner, college graduate, and professional writer? Or the battlefield emancipator with the avowed white supremacist? The widely admired military professional with the malefactor who was court-martialed twice in six years? The loyal friend, loving brother and son, and devoted husband, with the oversensitive, sarcastic gambler who craved attention and intrigued with other women? Then there was the entrepreneur, political partisan, and urbane theater lover. How do we integrate all these conflicting parts?

It is not news that he was contradictory. But we have to grasp the nature of his contradictions to see the man in his totality and understand his significance for the public of his day. Getting at them requires a fresh look at the intimate details of his life, but also a new sense of context. We must see him less in terms of *place* than of *time*.

George Armstrong Custer lived on a chronological frontier even more than a geographical one. He and his contemporaries experienced the greatest wave of change ever to strike American society, a tsunami that ripped out and reordered everything. *This* is what his life spoke to, wherever he went.

This moment is when the modern came. The emerging new order was industrial, corporate, scientific, and legal—diminishing the individualistic, the romantic, and the heroic in American culture. The rise of impersonal institutions, governmental bureaucracies, and national markets began to overshadow everything local, traditional, and customary, imposing organization, rationalization, standardization, and centralization.

Such a brief description sounds overly schematic, because it is. America has never been locked into a steady state, but has always been dynamic. Even before Custer's birth the public embraced the rowdy marketplace, celebrating its virtues of competition and entrepreneurship as the spirit of "go-ahead." Monetary transactions already edged in among traditional relationships of Southern master and slave or the Hudson Valley gentry and his tenant farmers. Nepotism and personal patronage would linger long after the rise of the corporation and professionalization. A dust cloud obscures any historical movement; clear distinctions blur on close inspection.

Yet Custer's contemporaries felt themselves caught in a great transformation. The antebellum economy of personal relationships, of independent merchants, artisans, and farmers, had provided the basis for Jacksonian laissez-faire populism and the Republicans' Free Labor philosophy. During Custer's adult life, Americans saw themselves falling under the shadow of capital, concentrated in gigantic corporations. Before the war, working for hire was seen as only a temporary stage on the way to working for oneself. By 1868, writes the historian Heather Cox Richardson, the "ideal of self-sufficiency" began to give way to the reality of "a permanent class of wage earners."[1] The nation's informal, improvised quality (Lincoln was a self-taught lawyer) faded as large institutions and expanded government bureaucracies rationalized their operations and professionalized their staff. Inherited distinctions, particularly the distinction of race, were dismantled in law if not in effect, replaced with at least technical equality. Taken together, all this looks like the birth of modernity.[2]

This wave of change defies the impulse to tell a story of good versus evil. The Civil War slaughtered three-quarters of a million people and devastated much of the South, yet it freed four million slaves and preserved the Union. The Indian wars crushed the independence of indigenous peoples, yet the central government acted out of similar motives as in the Civil War, asserting national unity and federal authority. The new corporate economy concentrated wealth and power, creating vast disparities, yet also brought development, individual mobility, and new opportunities. The media became national in scope, fostering a distinctively American literary culture; but the Civil War gave rise to a darker, more modern sensibility in intellectual circles.

Custer lived his entire adult life on the crest of this transformation—yet he was personally unreconciled to it. Of the many contradictions in his life and personality, this is the overarching theme: he never adapted to the very modernity he helped to create. His ambivalence toward his times mirrored the mixed feelings of the American people. Like so many of his fellow citizens, he celebrated old virtues even as he supplanted them, and thrilled to innovations even as he struggled with them.

His life intertwined the old and new from the beginning. He was the son of an artisan, a poor blacksmith, who championed the Jacksonian ideal of a producers' republic of equal and independent white men. But Custer went to West Point, the first school of professional education in America, and entered the hierarchical Regular Army, the pioneering institution of rationalization and systemization. The Civil War, though, spawned a different army, reflecting antebellum American society. It gave him room to indulge his romantic, individualistic impulses, and allowed him to rise through connections as well as merit. Promoted to general at an astonishingly young age, he showed that he understood mass, industrialized warfare, yet anachronistically fought with a sword at the head of cavalry charges. He helped to destroy slavery, and implemented emancipation and civil rights acts in Texas and Kentucky after the war. But he never accepted the equality of African Americans or the federal role in protecting civil rights. Indeed, race and politics largely defined his worldview—and he did not look forward to the nation we know today.

Custer battled American Indians ruthlessly, yet wrote that he would resist too were he one of them. He protected the advancing transcontinental railroads, bringing the business corporation and its industrial technology to the frontier, yet he affected the role of the rustic, individualistic frontiersman, wearing buckskin and escorting visiting dignitaries on hunting expeditions. His heroic style of leadership did not serve him well in peace, in an era that required managerial skill and tact.

Even when Custer tried to profit from the new America, he never quite mastered the times. He spent months on Wall Street, with alarming results. He plunged into politics, alienating much of the public. He became something of a public intellectual and popular writer, but his romanticism left him far from the advancing early modernists, such as Mark Twain or Ambrose Bierce.

In an era when women increasingly demanded equality, he married Libbie (Elizabeth) Bacon, an intelligent, highly educated woman. His biography is inevitably hers as well. She played a critical role in his career and did much to create his posthumous myth; yet she carefully cultivated a persona of vulnerable femininity, as society still expected of her. For many years the couple employed an escaped slave, Eliza Brown, to manage their household. She was a central figure in their lives, an independent, outspoken, and formidable young woman. The larger story of upended race relations played out in the privacy of their home, in the sometimes fraught relationship among these three.

Custer's contradictions spoke to the millions of Americans who also failed to root themselves in the new world. They were anxious, uncertain, and divided. When they looked to Custer, though, his admirers saw the Boy General of the Civil War, the gallant soldier who fought like a medieval knight, the daring frontiersman. He seemed to represent the country's youth as it slipped away, the nation as it had been and never would be again. His critics saw him as a sympathizer with slave owners and reactionaries, an egotistical tyrant of an officer who did not care for the equal dignity of his citizen soldiers. Custer became an icon because he embodied the times in a heightened, dramatic way. He was the exaggerated American.[3]

A man out of time with his times makes for instability. One moment Custer would show skill, judgment, loyalty, selflessness, courage, and love; the next he would veer into self-indulgence, impulsivity, sarcasm, self-justification, lies, even betrayal. This is true to some extent of most people, but Custer would pivot with stunning speed, lunging from one extreme to another, often in public.

The popular imagination today sees him as arrogant in his flamboyance—a *Glory-Hunter*, to cite the title of an influential biography. But his dramatic self-regard flowed in large part from deep insecurity. He never stopped trying to escape obscurity. His blacksmith father, Emmanuel Custer, reared him in a stern evangelical Christianity. Much has been written of Emmanuel's playfulness with his sons, but more should be made of his fixed opinions and glowering judgment. He expected Armstrong, as he called his oldest son, to undergo conversion, and implored him to submit to divine authority. Custer's family whispered to him eternally about his soul.

Fleeing obscurity, dreading condemnation, craving approval, he went toward whatever might distinguish him from the crowd, to better appeal to the crowd. Custer imagined a self and sought to make others believe it. What has confused observers is the fact that his ability was real, his courage genuine. The axiom that a big show hides a hollow man does not apply to Custer. The truth is much more complex. He worked to present himself as the man he wished to be—but the effort could make him brittle and defensive. His long practice of conjuring a Custer for public view helped him attract girls and women; he lured them with his living portrait of the reckless hero. But even after he finally won his bride, Libbie, he never felt entirely at ease in marriage. He encountered modernity in a series of trials—some of them in actual courts—and lost. Again and again he saved himself with his gift for fighting. He finally failed at that, too.

From a twenty-first-century perspective, Custer's contradictions make him morally perplexing at best, abhorrent at worst. Many identify him as a willing perpetrator of genocide against American Indians. His admirers note that he didn't make policy, but executed it; if he had died in 1865, another would have carried out the same missions in the West. This is true, though he was responsible for his own decisions and beliefs. He acted out of principle at times and self-interest at others; he believed in the rights of some, but not all, despite a new chorus for equality.

He's a tricky subject for a biographer. For me, he calls to mind chapter five of the Gospel According to Mark. It tells how Jesus encountered a man possessed by demons, who said to him, "My name is Legion: for we are many." With this transposition of singular and plural pronouns, Legion identifies with his evil spirits, and even speaks on their behalf. "And he besought him [Jesus] much that he would not send them away out of the country. Now there was nigh unto the mountains a great herd of swine feeding. And all the devils besought him, saying, Send us into the swine, that we may enter into them. And forthwith Jesus gave them leave." Rather than cast the demons into hell, Christ takes pity on them.

Theologically it is a confusing passage, blurring the boundary between good and evil. In literary terms, it is a piece of pure wisdom. A biographer must sympathize with demons. We cannot be separated from our devils; they define us as much as our goodness and grace. That does not mean we should ignore them or apologize for them—they are still demons, after all. But they are integral to our existence.

Custer's demons were his own, but also his contemporaries', and ours as well. So were his angels. His achievements shaped our past and present, as did his failings. To reduce them all into his final failure—catastrophic though it was—is to turn away from ourselves, to refuse to see the worst in American history or how hard it was to achieve the best. In his own bedeviled way, he confronted questions still asked in the twenty-first century: What do equality and humanity mean? Is there room for the individual in an organizational society? When does individuality become mere selfishness? How can a minority's distinctiveness and autonomy survive amid a mass-market, globalized culture? How to cope with a time of dramatic change? Does the hero still live?

The violence that suffused his life shadows ours. The ambivalence of his contemporaries is our ambivalence—toward our time as well as theirs. Custer's story begins with its ending, and it never ends.

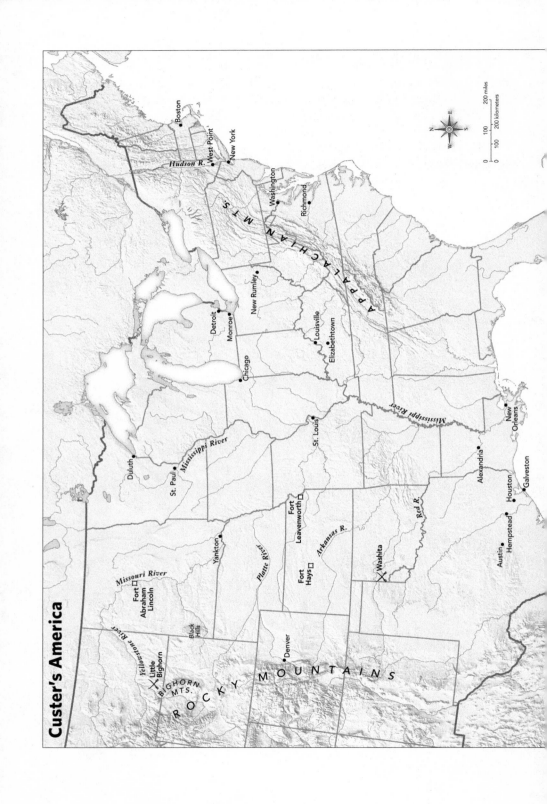

Custer's America

Part One

RISE
1839–1865

I am as full of mischief as ever.
—George Armstrong Custer, November 13, 1858

Custer—the light-hearted and gallant fellow, I cannot mention his name without swimming eyes!
—Morris Schaff, *The Spirit of Old West Point*

The great difficulty is that he is too clever for his own good.
—Tully McCrea, January 19, 1861

I saw him plunge his saber into the belly of a rebel who was trying to kill him. You can guess how bravely soldiers fight for such a general.
—Victor Comte, July 16, 1863

Generalship is bad for people.
—John Keegan, *The Mask of Command*

One

THE ACCUSED

G EORGE ARMSTRONG CUSTER'S GUILT was never in doubt. The question was how harshly he should be condemned for being Custer.

His trial began on the morning of July 5, 1861, at the United States Military Academy, West Point, New York. The designated court-martial room was in the academic building, a stone, neoclassical structure, three stories high and striped with red sandstone pilasters, with a clock tower rising from its northwest corner. The trial chamber occupied the center of the building, along with the gymnasium, and shared the first floor with the Chemical Department in the south wing and the Fencing Department in the north.[1]

Custer entered the room before ten o'clock on July 5. He came without counsel. He wore the gray, single-breasted uniform of a cadet: brass buttons in rows of three across the chest, each row linked by a dark line of embroidery, stacked and widening like a fan from waist to clavicle; and a white collar folded over the rim of gray wool at the neck. Dark piping ran down the outside of his gray pant legs above black shoes. The boy looked younger than his twenty-one years. His blond hair curled at the top when cut short, as it was now. He had clear blue eyes, a long nose with a bit of a bulb at the end, a rather narrow mouth with a pronounced lower lip. His ears stuck out. At seventeen he had already grown to nearly five feet ten inches. Even if he did not grow after entering the academy, he stood taller than the average man. But he was thin.

As Custer waited, eight of the officers who comprised the court listened as the minutes of the previous session were read. A ninth member arrived late. Custer was asked if he objected to any of the men sitting in judgment of him. He did not.[2]

The crime that brought him before the court amounted to little in itself. The military often held courts-martial for the kinds of minor offenses that would be handled administratively in centuries to come; conviction need not end an officer's career. Yet this trial threatened Custer with serious trouble. It might deny him a part in a great civil war, the culmination of a long-brewing national crisis. A new president, Abraham Lincoln, had taken office; much of the slave-owning South had seceded and organized into the Confederate States of America. As Custer sat in the court chamber, a federal army faced a rebel army in northern Virginia. Everyone expected a great battle—today, tomorrow, next week—that would decide the fate of the Southern rebellion. And he might not see it.

The trial also presented a crisis in his understanding of himself. Custer had just graduated from the U.S. Military Academy, but his four years of professional education had not gone smoothly. Almost from the day of his arrival he had grated against the school's regimentation, on a course toward the reckoning in this room. The court could only address the facts of a single violation. In a sense, though, it would pass institutional judgment on Custer's character.

Maj. George Nauman presided. An 1823 graduate of West Point, he had fought in the Seminole War from 1836 to 1838 and served in combat in the Mexican War. To reward his valor, this army without medals had promoted him to brevet lieutenant colonel. Brevets were honorary ranks; they formed a hierarchy of distinction parallel to the functional one, the organizational one. Soldiers treated brevets with enormous respect. Nauman led the court because his brevet predated the actual rank of lieutenant colonel held by William Hoffman.[3]

Hoffman, another West Point graduate, also had fought in a variety of conflicts: the Black Hawk War of 1832, the Seminole War, nine separate battles and skirmishes in Mexico, and an expedition against the Sioux in 1855.[4] Most members of the court had led men under fire, and knew the necessity of discipline.

And yet, they did not serve as judges because of personal experience or merit. They represented the *institution* of the army. With the cherished exception of brevets, their professional identities were organizational. Service ranks were moored to specific posts in particular regiments; an officer was captain *of the 1st Infantry*, major *of the 3rd Artillery*. Men waited years for positions; Custer himself remained technically a cadet, despite having graduated from West Point, as he waited for an opening. Promotion often followed behind a funeral. At fifty-eight, Hoffman could hardly hope to become a full colonel, let alone a general.[5] Their careers moved in grooves cut into the deep-laid stones of the permanent military establishment. They were Regular Army.

First Lt. Steven V. Benet, the judge advocate (the prosecutor), swore in the court and read the charges. First, "Neglect of Duty." Custer, "being officer of the Guard, did fail to take the proper steps to suppress a quarrel between two Cadets near the Guard Tent, in his presence. This at Camp

Anderson, West Point, N.Y., on or about the evening of the 29th day of June 1861." Second, "Conduct to the prejudice of good order and Military discipline," in that Custer "did give countenance to a quarrel between two cadets near the Guard tent, in his presence, by saying, 'Let there be a fair fight,' or words to that effect."

The accused pleaded guilty. Then he called witnesses.[6]

Custer did not challenge the facts of the charges, but hoped to minimize them. He questioned Cadet Peter M. Ryerson, a participant in the brawl, who testified, "The fight was not very serious. It was more of a scuffle. There was only two hard blows given, the first he struck me and the next I struck him. Neither of the parties received any serious injury." Ryerson did not mention that his opponent, Cadet William Ludlow, was an upperclassman who had been harassing him. Ludlow had called him a coward, then hit him in the face. Ryerson had struck back. Someone had stepped in to hold Ryerson. It was then, apparently, that Custer had called for a fair fight. Ludlow confirmed Ryerson's account, though he sneered at the underclassman's prowess. "It was of no serious nature, and I received no injury whatever."[7]

Custer called 1st Lt. William B. Hazen. "Since February I have occupied the position of Assistant Instructor of Tactics, Commanding a Company of Cadets," Hazen said.

"Was the accused a member of the company you commanded, and if so, state what his character has been during that time?" Custer asked.

"Yes, he has been a member of the company commanded by me until recently—and so far as I have seen, his conduct has been perfectly proper, and I have only had occasion to report him for trivial offences [sic], until the one for which he is now on trial. And during that period he has held a good character for conduct."

Hazen himself had arrested Custer for failing to halt the fight, and his testimony helped the prosecution. By contrasting the charges with Custer's past "trivial offences," he underscored the seriousness of the matter at hand. The army could hardly maintain discipline if soldiers engaged in fistfights, let alone with the approval of their superiors.

Custer had often been punished before, but it seems he never grasped the reason. Military discipline serves a larger purpose than merely balancing the scales of justice. It must teach soldiers to follow orders and abide by regulations, in order to create a force that responds to commands predictably and efficiently. Discipline is the very point of the institution, the difference between an army and a mob. But Custer never admitted the necessity of his own prosecution.

His fear of being left behind preoccupied him. His academy class had graduated a year ahead of schedule. His friends had all rushed to Washington, D.C., and Virginia, where they trained troops or joined regiments for the imminent battle. But he remained, detained, facing the consequences not merely of one misdeed, but of four years of transgressions.

He asked for a recess until the next morning to prepare a final statement to explain himself. The court granted his request and adjourned.[8]

ALL OF CUSTER'S ADULT LIFE beamed through the aperture of his first day at West Point. It was not a lens, focusing him on an inevitable fate, but a prism that established the spectrum of what might come. In the years ahead, he would face potentially fatal decisions—some avoidable, others less so—all of which resulted from where he went in early June 1857.[9]

He arrived alone. All the new cadets did. They boarded Hudson River steamboats at Albany docks, Manhattan slips, New Jersey piers, or the Erie Railway terminal at Piermont, New York. The boys wandered the decks between paddlewheels that churned in arching wooden cowlings, ordered drinks from the bar and dinner from the kitchen, chatted in parlors, or watched the Palisade shore from the rail.[10]

Seemingly every traveler described the Hudson Valley as stunningly beautiful—especially in the Highlands, the region above Stony Point, New York, about thirty miles north of the uppermost tip of Manhattan. "The passengers had gathered in the forward part of the boat," Morris Schaff recalled, writing of his initial voyage to the academy, "and what a scene of river and mountains lay before us!" One observer claimed that it was impossible to "give an idea of the sudden darkening of the Hudson, and the underground effect of the sharp, overhanging mountains as you first sweep into the highlands." Schaff remembered the thrill, as his boat steamed south, when "I heard a passenger nearby observe, 'There is West Point!' "[11]

"I think it is the most romantic spot I ever saw," Custer wrote on August 7, 1857.[12] The features that had led the Continental Army to fortify the site during the Revolution—the narrowing of the great river, the perfect forty-acre plateau 160 feet above water level, shelved into the Highlands—made it a destination for tourists, artists, and foreign dignitaries.

Down on the river, the steamboat slowed to moor at a dock beneath the bluff. Would-be cadets boarded a horse-drawn omnibus or threw their bags into a cart and walked up a steep, winding road cut into the bluff. Finally they reached the Plain, rimmed by twin rows of elms. "The library, chapel, and turreted, four-storied, granite barracks [stood behind the trees] on the south side," Schaff wrote, "and on the west the unpretentious quarters of the superintendent, the commandant, the professors and instructors, all overlooking the velvety sward of the extensive parade [ground]."[13]

George Strong arrived during a dress parade by the Corps of Cadets. He vividly remembered the "hundreds of eager spectators, the stirring music—and then the dead silence, broken at length by the voice of the officer in charge, as by seeming magic he put in motion the gray clockwork of the manual of arms."[14]

When the clockwork stopped, Strong crossed the Plain to find his place, as Custer and all the others did. These bewildered boys ran from the adjutant's office to the treasurer to the quartermaster, signing the register, handing over their money, receiving the few things allowed in the barracks: a dipper, tin washbasin, bucket, slate, stationery, mathematics book, and two blankets that reeked of lanolin gone foul, a scent that new cadets carried for weeks.[15]

Adjutant, quartermaster, barracks, blankets: these were elements of the official West Point, the formal institution that would test, grade, and assign demerits. But Custer found another West Point within the barracks—the internal hierarchy of boys that defined daily life far more than written rules, recitations, and professors.

This inner reality was not entirely unofficial. In the barracks, the new arrivals met cadet officers—upperclassmen assigned to take charge of them. Schaff vividly recalled how older boys surrounded him on his arrival, shouting at him to take off his hat and stand at attention, in a torrent of derision and fury. A new cadet heard that he was lowest of all creatures. A "plebe." An "animal."[16]

The cadets' world existed largely within the barracks, the academy's largest building. Its stone walls rose four stories above the south side of the Plain, 360 feet long and 60 wide; a wing extended another 100 feet to one side. Completed in 1851, it resembled a Tudor manor house, or perhaps a hotel that had been converted into a fortress. Crenellated battlements of red sandstone ran across the top between the hexagonal towers at each corner. A large passageway called the sally port pierced the center at ground level; above it was a large hall with chapel-like windows reaching nearly three stories in height. Eight separate doors perforated the front; they opened into the eight divisions, or separate blocks of rooms. Altogether they contained 136 cadet rooms, with desks, chairs, and simple beds with thin mattresses. Gaslight was installed the year Custer arrived. He would shift from division to division over the years, but this building would be his home until he left West Point.[17]

He had to pass two examinations to be accepted, physical and academic. The latter merely tested basic reading, writing, and arithmetic. Even so, each plebe received a tutor and studied four hours each day. Even if Custer were to fail, he could try again in August. Real attrition would come later, when classes began.[18]

In the meantime, Custer's life was dominated by older boys. By day, he faced constant scrutiny. Day and night—especially at night—he faced "devilment." He might be startled out of his sleep to find himself in a blanket held by six older cadets and tossed helplessly in the air. He could be ordered to report to a man he believed to be a doctor, who would diagnose a terrible illness and force him to drink a disgusting concoction to cure it. He might be confined in a tent or room as older cadets blew smoke in his face until he got sick—a torment called "smoking out."

In writing or conversation, Custer never dwelled on the devilment he endured. Yet he inevitably suffered with the others. The ritual forced the plebes to acknowledge the stratification of cadets—the supremacy of their own, unofficial rules. "It was a mighty leveler," Schaff wrote. "The fellow who got it worst and most frequently . . . at least courted it by some lofty manner or resented witticism."

As for Custer, one trace of his torment would endure. "His bright locks gave him a girlish appearance," one soldier later wrote, "which . . . procured him the nickname of 'Fanny.' . . . The name 'Fanny' stuck to Custer through his academic life and long after." In a world of boys struggling to be young men, in a constant battle for dominance, he was mocked with the name of a girl.

Custer passed his tests.[19]

"I LIKE WEST POINT as well if not better than I did at first," Custer wrote in a letter on August 7. "We have about three more weeks of camp life for this year." He referred to the encampment, the summer military training program.[20]

The cadets spent the Hudson Valley's hot and humid weeks in rows of tents on the Plain, learning the practical business of being a soldier. They awoke at five thirty each morning for drills that took up much of the day, until five o'clock in the afternoon. In later years, Custer would study tactics for infantry, cavalry, and artillery, maneuvers for companies and battalions, siege techniques, and pontoon bridging, as well as the manufacture and firing of rockets, explosive shells, and other artillery munitions. In his first summer he entered the "school of the soldier." As a member of one of four cadet companies, he trained as the lowest-ranking infantryman: formation marching, cleaning and firing a rifled musket, standing guard, and suffering "fatigue" duty, the military term for labor.[21]

He did so under orders from fellow students. The first class—the senior class—provided the captains and lieutenants for the student companies. Sergeants came from the second class, and corporals from the third. Fourth classmen were all privates, as were fifth classmen. The five-year system began in 1854. Often attributed to Secretary of War Jefferson Davis, it actually originated with Chief Engineer Joseph Totten. It increased the size of the Cadet Corps, placing greater responsibility on student leaders to maintain discipline and lead the training.[22]

"There is something so ludicrous, when once it is seen through, about the airs of some cadet officers," wrote Schaff. Perhaps that's because their authority came from outside the society of boys. They were picked by the tactical instructors—that is to say, the institution. But some cadets held unspoken ranks, earned from their peers.

In the athletic world of the encampment, prowess won respect. So did "spirit and honor," as Tully McCrea called a willingness to fight. Once he saw a diminutive boy react to an insult with a punch that staggered the larger cadet. "He is a spirited, gentlemanly little fellow," McCrea concluded, "and I like him very much."[23]

What separated an admired few from the more awkward and insecure cadets was a natural self-confidence. Herman Melville witnessed this in a nautical setting; he described a type he called the "Handsome Sailor," who, "with the offhand unaffectedness of natural regality, . . . seemed to accept the spontaneous homage of his shipmates." At West Point, Peter Michie recalled, "[h]e who was fearless, outspoken, generous, and self-sacrificing became the leader among his fellows."[24]

There was a third set as well. These boys did not excel in academics or drill; they scorned the institutional favorites as cadets who "truckle and cringe to those in power," in McCrea's words. Nor were they necessarily noble or self-sacrificing. Yet they won standing. If some cadets were "careful in behavior and attentive to discipline," Michie recalled, "others, on the contrary, [were] quite the reverse."[25] For the latter, the highest accomplishment was not getting caught in an exploit known to the entire corps.

"Occasionally some of the cadets have the boldness to cross the sentinels' posts at night," Custer wrote on August 7. He described how they would go to the village of Buttermilk Falls, a couple of miles south, for illicit pleasures. He detailed the method (changing into civilian clothes), the penalties ("occasionally persons are dismissed"), and a foray two nights before by "one of my class mates in company with two elder classmen. . . . Both are now in confinement in their tents. One is in the tent next to mine and neither of them can leave their tents and when they go to their meals they are marched under a guard of eight cadets."[26]

Custer always had a keen eye when something interested him.

HE COMPLETELY MISREAD WEST POINT before he arrived. On December 12, 1856, he assessed his plans to enroll in a letter to his half sister, Lydia Ann Reed, who lived in Monroe, Michigan. "Mother is much opposed to me going there but Father and David [his older half brother] are in favor of it very much. I think it is the best place that I could go," he wrote. He listed one reason: money.

"I will get $28 per month for five years and be getting a good education at the same time and when I come out I will get 5 years pay ahead," he calculated. "I think I am lucky in getting the appointment which I think I am certain of now." He was indeed lucky to get it; it had been extremely unlikely. But the kind of luck he had in mind was financial. "John McNutt . . . is worth upwards of two hundred thousand dollars now which he has made in the Army."[27]

It was only natural that he thought of money first. He had been at work since the age of nine, off and on. It was the way of the time, and the way of his family.[28]

In 1824, his father, Emmanuel H. Custer, had moved from Maryland to what became New Rumley, just north of Cadiz in eastern Ohio. The village was closer to Virginia than Michigan or even Cleveland. Emmanuel was a blacksmith. He struggled, but he believed in struggle—both as a devout evangelical Methodist and a partisan Jacksonian Democrat.[29]

A man with a long nose and wide mouth, sporting a long sheaf of a beard that would turn white with time, Emmanuel married, had a daughter, lost a daughter, had two sons. His wife died in 1835, after they had been married for not quite seven years. On February 23, 1836, he married again. His second wife, Maria Ward Kirkpatrick, already had a son, David, and a daughter, Lydia Ann. Maria too had been widowed in 1835, after twelve years of marriage.

A parent dreads a child's death more than anything else. It is the gravest of all struggles of the spirit. Emmanuel had lost one, and he lost more. In 1836, his son John died at the age of three. Maria gave birth to another, James, who died soon after. In 1838, she delivered another, Samuel, who died soon after. On December 5, 1839, she brought George Armstrong onto the earth in a room in the rear of the ground floor of a two-story log house on the corner of Main and Liberty streets in New Rumley. They called him Armstrong, or (in time) "Autie," after his mispronunciation of his name as a toddler. He would always be Armstrong or Autie to those close to him.[30]

Emmanuel tried to improve his fortunes by moving the family to Monroe, Michigan, in 1842, where his brother George (Armstrong's namesake) had his own metalworking business. He moved them all back after a few months. In 1849 they settled on a farm, which he operated along with his blacksmith shop in New Rumley.

For a Jacksonian man in 1849—north of slavery's border, at least— the highest aspiration was to make his own way in the world, with his own hands and his own skill, on his own farm or in his own shop. Armstrong was only nine when Emmanuel tried to equip him for the effort by apprenticing him to Joseph Hunter, a furniture maker in Cadiz. Hunter failed to turn the boy into a craftsman, despite three years before the lathe. In 1852, Emmanuel sent Armstrong to school in Monroe, where Lydia Ann Reed—Ann, as Armstrong called her—now lived. She had married David Reed, a farmer and drayman (in the business of transporting freight by wagon).

Armstrong grew close to his brother-in-law and even closer to Ann. He made friends in Monroe, and came to regard it as his other hometown. But he returned to New Rumley in 1855, just fifteen, to teach school, first in a private academy and then in a public school outside of Cadiz. (His youth was not exactly unusual; in the era's improvised, rapidly growing education system, poorly paid teachers rarely held college diplomas.) There he applied to Congressman John A. Bingham for an appointment to West Point. Each member of the House of Representatives could name a young man to the military academy; usually he would choose someone of the same political party. Bingham, a Republican, knew that Armstrong came from a Democratic family, but nominated him nevertheless, impressed with the sincerity of the young man's request.[31]

And so he came to the academy with dreams of $28 per month and five years' pay in advance. He never spoke of these figures again. He met such cadets as Henry Algernon du Pont, of Delaware's famous gunpowder dynasty, and George Washington Vanderbilt, son of the fabulously wealthy shipowner "Commodore" Cornelius Vanderbilt, who had taken George and the rest of his family on a grand tour of Europe in 1853 in a yacht the size of an ocean liner.[32]

The Corps of Cadets included "the sons of some of the greatest men in our country," Custer wrote during his first year. The remark speaks to how deeply such boys impressed him, rather than the demographic facts. Few of the nation's old patrician families sent their sons to West Point.

"There were no Byrds, Randolphs, Carters, Boylstons, Peabodys, Winthrops, De Lanceys, De Peysters, Schuylers, or others of their status," the historian Morrison observes. The Adams family, which gave America two presidents, would have been appalled if Henry or Charles Francis Jr.—Custer's contemporaries—had chosen the Plain of West Point over Harvard Yard. Academy records show that not even 5 percent of the cadets in this era had affluent parents. Most of the students were sons of farmers, others of merchants, lawyers, and other professionals.[33]

The military academy served not as a school for the elite, but rather as a nationalizing force. Cadets came from every congressional district. Custer studied alongside Edward Buchanan, nephew of President James Buchanan; Adelbert Ames of Maine, who had sailed the globe on his father's ship; and Thomas Rosser, who had left behind several hundred acres of cotton land in Texas, worked by slaves and haunted by alligators. They impressed Custer, who was pleased with himself for joining them.[34]

Having traveled from humble New Rumley to this great national institution, Custer experienced conflicting feelings. As his third year at West Point drew to a close, he wrote to a hometown friend and contrasted their childhoods with the present. "We were happy then because our minds were free and had no care for the future, but now it is different." As he prepared for a professional career, he explicitly recognized that he had responsibility for himself, that "our dependence must be on our own abilities and on these we must rely for all we expect to be or have in future."

Ironically, though, the academy's rigid rules and supervision released him from responsibility. Before he first stepped off the steamboat at West Point's landing, he had struggled alone in the marketplace, earning his living and managing his own affairs. Here his superiors told him when to get up, what to wear, and when to wash. They freed him to be a boy again, in the company of boys.[35]

"BETWEEN NINE AND TEN HOURS DAILY in class or studying": That, writes James Morrison, was how a cadet's time went when the academic year began. The remains of the day included "approximately three hours in military exercises, two hours in recreation, and two hours at meals."[36]

Custer had little ground for comparison. He had embarked on an extraordinarily rare thing in antebellum America: a professional academic education. Few Americans attended even an ordinary college; just 1 percent of working-age men at the time graduated from one. There were only 136 colleges in 1850, increasing to just 209 in 1860. They were small, averaging under 100 students. Studies were limited, since higher education was intended to create gentlemen, not scholars or technical experts.

At West Point, as at other schools, the course was the same for every student, with classes in such subjects as chemistry, ethics, and French, relying on memorization and daily recitation. What distinguished West Point was practical military coursework, as well as its emphasis on engineering. Custer studied fortification drawing, bridging methods, siege techniques, and much more.[37]

"Our January examination is over now and I am glad of it," Custer wrote to his half sister, Ann, and her husband, David, on January 27, 1858. "I passed my examination very creditibly [sic] but . . . a great many [were] found deficient and sent off among them to be found the sons of some of the greatest men in our country. . . . My class which numbered over 100 when we entered in June is now reduced to 69. This shows that if a person wants to get along here he has to study hard."[38]

He did not say that he barely survived. He put his performance in the context of those who failed, not those who excelled. He did it smoothly, a magician pulling a coin from his sister's ear. *Look how many were sent off*—distracting from the many more who scored higher. It's impossible to know if he could have done better. His fellow cadets thought he didn't care to try. Peter Michie recalled, "Custer said that there were but two positions of distinction in a class—head and foot; and as he soon found that he could not be head he determined that he would support his class as a solid base."[39]

Michie's was a polished formulation, in keeping with a legend that would vine its way around Custer's tomb—the Prince Hal of West Point, carousing until the moment for greatness came. But it is difficult to believe that Custer deliberately planned each daily recitation, each twice-a-year examination, with the goal of skimming just above failure without sinking in. The consequences of low standing could last for an entire career, since class ranking determined a graduate's place on the promotion list. Yet Michie's recollection contained an essential truth. Custer analyzed the United States Military Academy and calculated his place—more precisely, his audience. He would perform not for the officers and professors of the official institution, nor even for the cadet officers, but for the society of boys. Poor grades were the unfortunate result.[40]

Conduct as well as academic grades affected class ranking. Demerits drove down the conduct score, and could lead to outright dismissal. Starting in 1855, cadets were limited to 100 demerits every six months; fifth classmen had up to 150 for the same period. A cadet would be "skinned" with a demerit or two for being late to roll call, and as many as ten for an unauthorized absence. He could face punishment as well, since a demerit was an academic mark, not a disciplinary action in itself.[41]

The relatively light weight given to conduct saved Custer. Year after year, he kept a clerk busy recording his demerits, page after page after page. Two adjectives repeat: *Boyish. Trifling.* August 8, 1857: "Boyish conduct" while cleaning up the camp. September 29: "Trifling in ranks marching in from parade." October 21: "Trifling in Ethical section room" while the instructor was busy at the chalkboard. December 19: "Highly unmilitary & trifling conduct throwing stones on post." He laughed in class, talked in ranks, played cards, threw snowballs, lobbed bread across the mess hall.[42]

It was boyish, yes, but not all trifling, not from Custer's perspective. Infectiously, winningly exuberant, he cared very much about his fellow cadets' esteem. He performed for them even in what he did not do. He was appointed a squad marcher, a first rung on the ladder of authority, charged with keeping a small section of cadets in line during the endless formations, reviews, and marches. The Register of Delinquencies describes the inevitable result. February 13, 1858: "Gross & willful neglect of duty as sqd marcher, in not keeping his [section] at attention after having been twice ordered to do so by the [officer] in charge." Also February 13: "Not marching section from Dialectic hall." February 18: "Not dismissing his sectn at proper place." February 20: "Not preservg order in his section." He and three other squad marchers were cited for "allowing gross violations of military propriety." Superintendent Richard Delafield took away the "military trust confided in him."[43]

As the months went by, Custer's antics grew more active, calculated, and funny. During a sermon in the chapel, he sat behind a boy with bright red hair. He stuck one hand in the hair, pantomimed a blacksmith putting metal in a fire, and pretended to hammer his hand on an anvil, to the amusement of cadets next to him. In Spanish class, he asked Professor Patrice de Janon to translate "Class is dismissed." The professor did so; Custer stood and led the rest of the class out the door. De Janon, a Colombia native who previously taught fencing at the academy, was "a poor disciplinarian," writes Morrison, "who could easily be diverted from the subject at hand by questions on dueling etiquette." He did not report Custer, and the incident became a legend.[44]

Custer would always love pranks, a form of humor that combines creativity, energy, and cruelty in nearly equal parts. At West Point they played a social role. As soon as he ascended to the fourth class, he began to devil plebes with enthusiasm. Some of it was simple harassment—yanking them out of bed at night or collapsing their tents on them in the summer encampment. More tellingly, he mocked anything unusual or distinctive. Jasper Myers arrived with an enormous beard, fit for a biblical patriarch; Custer earnestly told him that the government had made a mistake—the appointment to West Point was intended for Myers's son;

the old man should go home and send the boy. A plebe from Maine owned "a huge double-cased silver watch," Schaff recalled. The affectation drew close scrutiny from Custer and his friends, such as Alonzo Cushing from New York and John "Gimlet" Lea of Mississippi. They "would gather about," Schaff wrote, and bombard the animal with questions about it, "asking how he dared to risk his life through New York with it; insisting daily on taking him to the sun-dial . . . and threatening at last that if he didn't bring it to running accurately with the dial, they would have to report him for carrying a timepiece that discredited the official time."[45]

Deviling asserted Custer's superior status, but so did kindness to plebes he liked. "Fellows, come here and hear my fellow Buckeye laugh," Custer exclaimed when he heard Peter Michie's "natural and infectious" guffaws, Schaff wrote. It was a friendly act, but it established Custer as the senior Ohioan, as Michie's patron, revealing his growing deftness with the rules of this strange little society.[46]

"A whole-souled generous friend, and a mighty good fellow, and I like him," his roommate Tully McCrea wrote two years after Custer left West Point. During their cadet years, though, he offered a more nuanced assessment. "The great difficulty is that he is too clever for his own good," McCrea wrote in a letter. "He is always connected with all the mischief that is going on and never studies any more than he can possibly help. He has narrowly escaped several times."[47]

Confident in his ability to avoid disaster, Custer took greater risks in more elaborate performances. Lt. Henry Douglas, an instructor, lived behind the barracks, below Custer's window in the tower room. A beautiful buff rooster ruled Douglas's garden; he would "crow defiantly from the top of the fence to all the roosters down the line of the professors' quarters," Schaff recalled. He also crowed at night—"too often." Custer stole into the garden, snatched the rooster, and killed it. But he needed to do more if this were to be a prank of legend. So he plucked its feathers on a spread of newspapers, put a pot of water on to boil over his room's gaslight, and dropped the bird in. When it was cooked, he ate it. The authorities never learned who did it. The cadets knew, though, and they remembered.[48]

HE NEVER FORGOT THE WORLD outside of West Point. He worried, rather, that it would forget *him*. Those who loved Armstrong knew that he loved them fiercely—and that his affection had an underside of defensiveness, resentment, and fear of neglect.

"For months I have been anxiously and patiently waiting the reception of a letter from you in answer to one that I sent you several *months* ago," he once wrote to a friend. He used the same tone with Ann—wounded, snide, even mocking. "I had been looking for your letter for some time . . . but I guess it is more trouble for you to write than for me," he wrote on October 2, 1859, at a time when he felt overwhelmed with duties and classwork.[49]

In the same letter, he mentioned that he had written to his parents about how sick he had been—sick enough to enter the hospital at the beginning of the fall term in 1859. "They wrote back that Mother had had dreams which made her think that I was sick. You know what a great person Mother is for dreams." He scoffed at being the subject of supernatural news, but he remembered and repeated it.[50]

He wrote incessantly. He wrote with passion. He wrote with manic energy. "Give me the news and particularly of the young folks" in Monroe, he begged, a constant refrain in his letters. He routinely included special greetings, jokes, and stories for his sister's children. When Ann's young daughter died, he wrote, "I thought that nothing that I could say would be of any interest to you."[51]

He fretted endlessly about his parents' poverty and his mother's poor health. He urged them again and again to move to Michigan, closer to the Reeds. "If they were only in better circumstances and were able to get along without working as hard as they have had to, I would have nothing whatever to trouble me," he wrote. He felt motivated by the thought "that after I have graduated I could help them very much."[52]

He helped himself by physically escaping. The cadets' tight restriction to academy grounds loosened for few exceptions. They received a leave of absence for the entire summer at the beginning of the third year. They could obtain a short leave, three days or so, as a reward for going three months without any demerits. And they could leave the campus on Saturdays after morning classes ended, as long as they returned by 10:45 p.m. the same day. "As punishment," Custer recalled, he often had "to perform extra tours of guard duty on Saturdays—times which otherwise I should have been allowed for pleasure and recreation. If my memory serves me right, I devoted sixty-six Saturdays to this method of vindicating outraged military law during my cadetship." Still he made his way out, in a manner he had studied.[53]

He often stole off the grounds to Benny Havens's famous tavern, "in a little cabin under a cliff," as an old soldier wrote, about a mile south of West Point. "The forbidden locality of Benny Havens possessed stronger attractions than the study and demonstrations of a problem in Euclid," Custer remembered. In the spring of 1860, for example, Custer organized a graduation party at the tavern for Stephen Ramseur, Wesley Merritt, and Alexander Pennington. He shared hosting duties with Adelbert Ames, John Pelham, and Thomas Rosser. His life would intersect theirs again and again in the decades to come, giving a lasting significance to such lighthearted evenings.[54]

And Custer would sneak out to meet girls from the small civilian society that fringed the academy, consisting of locals and officers' families. In November 1859, a girl invited him and his friends to a Thanksgiving Day ball. That night he put out the gaslight and went to bed, but not to sleep. At ten o'clock, an officer walked through the barracks, checking each room. After he passed, Custer dressed in civilian clothes and stuffed his bed, arranging the blankets to make it look as if he were sleeping there. He and his confederates slipped out of the barracks, sneaked past the sentries, and walked to the ball. He spent the night dancing, returning sometime after four in the morning, and "reached home a few minutes before reveille [at 5:00 a.m.], changed our citizen's dress for our uniforms, and were then safe," he wrote to his cousin Augusta Ward. "I was in poor humor for hard study during the next day . . . and under the circumstances I was almost (*but not quite*) sorry I had gone to the ball."[55]

This was a picture of intense pressure seeking release. West Point compressed scores of teenage boys and young men within the Plain—the barracks, the wool uniforms, the even more uncomfortable code of conduct—yet they did not cease to be who they were. "'Wet dreams,' 'jerking off,' and such are common conversation, and never excites any surprise [sic] anymore," wrote Custer's roommate, Tully McCrea. Cadets talked endlessly of sexual escape—discussing the best brothels in New York, for example, all nodding in agreement at the pleasures of Mercer Street.[56]

What distinguished Custer was his success at finding that release. "He is a handsome fellow, and a very successful ladies' man," McCrea wrote of him a few years later. "Nor does he care an iota how many of the fair ones break their hearts for him."[57]

McCrea could have been writing specifically about a girl named Mollie. In 1856, when Custer taught outside of Cadiz, he had boarded in the home of Alexander Holland, superintendent of an infirmary. Holland had a teenage daughter named Mary Jane; Custer began to call her Mollie. They were attracted to each other. He wrote her letters, and even composed her a poem. It began:

> *I've seen and kissed that crimson lip*
> *With honied smiles o'erflowing*
> *Enchanted watched the opening rose*
> *Upon thy soft cheek flowing*

He called himself her "true and faithful lover, 'Bachelor Boy.'" He spoke of marrying her. He wrote of "when I see you next at the trundle bed."[58]

After he arrived at West Point, he wrote, "Does [sic] your father & Mother know that we correspond now. What do they say of me. You once promised to tell me what they had said about me but you never did." Another time he begged, "Tell me what objections your Parents make against me." It has been said that her father, a Republican, lobbied Congressman John A. Bingham to appoint the Democrat Custer to West Point just to get rid of him. Bingham's biographers think it plausible. But the relationship, and Holland's disapproval, lingered long after Custer left.[59]

"You say you used to flatter yourself that we were well enough acquainted for me to tell you anything," he wrote to her on November 13, 1858, "so we were and as far as I am concerned we are yet. . . . I am as full of mischief as ever. If there is any change in either of us it is in you." He boasted of how well he jumped his horse in training, and turned the page ninety degrees to scribble a postscript: Are we, he asked, "not well enough acquainted to have a 'sleep' when I come home. Please say yes to it in your next and *you may impose any condition upon me*."[60]

He allowed for limits because she had declared that she would never be one of the "baby factories," as she called married women. Her independence did not deter him; it may even have attracted him. As his summer leave in 1859 approached, he pressed her to let him into her bed when he returned. "What room do you have as your own, and tell me what plan you can make up so that we can have that great 'sleep,'" he asked. "Now do not put me off by saying that you cannot think of any."

He teased her, even taunted her. "You wished to know whether I had any lady lover here or not. Of course I have." He described a petite, black-haired, black-eyed beauty who danced gracefully and "has a *very* pretty foot & ankle. . . . But I suppose that I have given you a description sufficiently long for you to form an opinion of her and one which I should like to know." Was he describing Mollie herself, making her jealous, or a bit of both? Was it cruelty or their characteristic banter?

Then came cryptic references to "Miss Lizzie." He wrote, "I think that I know more about her than any other person and have done more with her or *rather to* and she to me than any other one not excepting your many days acquaintance with her and if she had a husband he could not have done but one thing more than I did and I shall leave you to guess what that was. (Can you guess? If you cannot I will tell you.)" In a letter signed "Your true and devoted H——d," Miss Lizzie, it seems, was the most intimate part of Mollie herself.[61]

When summer came, he was free for two months to search for the "great sleep" wherever he wished, in nearby New York, in towns on the way home, in Mollie's room. On August 29, 1859, the day after he reported back to West Point, a surgeon recorded that he was suffering from gonorrhea. This was the illness that kept him in the hospital at the beginning of the fall term, that his mother had dreamed of without knowing what it was. He must have caught it during his leave. He endured agonizing urination, possibly injections of mercury and solutions of other heavy metals, perhaps permanent damage. His romance with Mollie ended.[62]

CONGRESSMAN BINGHAM's appointment of Custer to West Point led the cadets to assume that he, too, was a Republican. To varying degrees, the confusion over his politics would continue for years to come, sometimes generated by Custer himself. The truth mattered to others. When he arrived at West Point, he could see politics tearing the country apart. Before he graduated, the destruction would be complete. And the question of how politics might rebuild the ruins would overshadow the rest of his life.

Custer's politics began at home. To his father, the Democratic Party was life itself. "Our father Custer was of the most intensely argumentative nature," a daughter-in-law would recall. "He was the strongest kind of politician . . . and grows excited and belligerent over his party affairs." He held dear the Jacksonian ideals of individualism and equality. But the individuals and equals he had in mind were all white men. This was a general truth in American politics, but a particular truth about him. The same daughter-in-law would one day write in a letter, "You are well aware how father Custer feels over the 'nigger' question," and, "You know well father Custer's antipathy to the negro."[63]

The Custers belonged to border-state culture. The Marylander Emmanuel had joined a broad migration from the upper South across the Ohio River. But Bingham was a Republican and an open abolitionist as well, casting suspicion on Custer. The congressman was close to Joshua Giddings, despised in the South for his vehemently antislavery views, and lodged in the same boardinghouse with him in Washington. Southern cadets noticed such things, and demanded that plebes state their political views. "It required more than ordinary moral and physical courage to boldly avow oneself an abolitionist," Custer recalled.[64]

This hostility reflected a rolling revolution in American politics. For a generation, the Whig and Democratic parties had shared power nationally and in virtually every state. In broad terms, Whigs believed in a partnership between wealthy interests and active government to harmonize society and develop the economy. They celebrated banks, public works, and government-sponsored corporations. The Democrats organized behind Andrew Jackson, who vilified "monopoly" and "aristocracy," as they called those who benefited from government favoritism. Democrats wanted fierce and fair competition between individuals, who would rise on their merits.[65]

A battle over the West exploded this system. The struggle centered on whether slavery would be expanded into the unorganized lands west of Minnesota, Iowa, Missouri, and Arkansas, or into the territory acquired from Mexico in 1848. The Missouri Compromise of 1820 barred slavery north of a line roughly equal to Missouri's southern border (except in Missouri itself), and California was admitted as a free state as part of the Compromise of 1850, but the debate continued. "Fire-eating" Southern politicians battled slave exclusion with rising militancy. The Territories and unorganized lands belonged to all the states, they argued; barring slavery discriminated against the South's labor system.[66]

The decisive moment came just three years before Custer entered West Point, with the Kansas-Nebraska Act of 1854. Drafted by Illinois senator Stephen A. Douglas, it organized the Nebraska and Kansas territories west of Iowa and Missouri, opening these lands to white settlement. The act allowed slavery if settlers voted for it, in what was called "popular sovereignty." It shattered the Missouri Compromise prohibition. Outrage swept the North. The Whig Party disintegrated along sectional lines, and the Republican Party arose from its remains. Its reason for existence was opposition to the spread of slavery. It staggered Democrats, winning elections across the North.

Republicans officially opposed abolition, but that mattered little in Dixie. The white South grew increasingly intolerant of *any* criticism of its "peculiar institution" as a cycle of militancy, paranoia, and anger sabotaged routine politics.[67]

In this tense environment, Custer put suspicious Southerners at ease. He roomed with cadets from the South or who had ties there; he made friends with Texans, Mississippians, and Georgians. And he belonged to a largely Southern company, out of the four in the battalion of the Cadet Corps. Traditionally the cadets were sorted by height, since it looked better on the parade ground, but a cadet adjutant made company assignments. Peer pressure led to the Dixification of D Company, where Custer found a home.[68]

Timing helps explain Custer's success in cultivating Southerners. In his first year or two, cadets could still joke about sectional tensions. Virginian Thomas Rowland wrote to his mother that he had liked his sister's letter about "the irrepressible conflict," a phrase made famous by the antislavery senator William Henry Seward of New York in 1858. "I hope, though that Disunion is not so near at hand as she represents it; it might interfere slightly with my commission."[69]

Then, on the night of October 16, 1859, John Brown and eighteen followers seized the federal armory at Harper's Ferry, Virginia, hoping to spark a slave revolt. Instead Brown was captured and sentenced to hang. "Now, if it is deemed necessary that I should forfeit my life for the furtherance of the ends of justice," he said in his final oration, "and mingle my blood further with the blood of my children and with the blood of millions in this slave country whose rights are disregarded by wicked, cruel, and unjust enactments, I say, let it be done."[70]

"How little we cadets at West Point foresaw what the death of that tall, gaunt, gray-bearded and coldly gray-eyed man meant," Schaff reflected. "That trap of the gallows creaking beneath him was the first dying wail of an age; that civilization was facing about." In the North, Brown became a martyr in the cause of freedom; in the South, a symbol of the viciousness of abolitionists. Southern cadets hanged Brown in effigy outside the barracks. Custer's friend from Georgia, P. M. B. Young, said he wished he could behead every last Yankee. Wade Hampton Gibbes of South Carolina commented on Emory Upton's "intimate association with negroes, of a character keenly offensive, and such as no self-respecting cadet could stand for a moment," Schaff wrote. Upton challenged him to a fight. The result was a bloody match, carefully staged in a barracks room, with cadets crowded in the hall and stairs and stoop outside to watch or merely listen.[71]

"I suppose you are a 'Seward' man. If you are I am really sorry for you," Custer wrote to an old New Rumley friend on April 7, 1860. He spent the first part of this letter in a discussion of cavalry exercises, the "Spring Drill" in infantry tactics, and practice with howitzers, mortars, and mounted batteries. But he was more interested in the next election and Brown's impact. It's striking that Custer, who preferred pranks or the novels of James Fennimore Cooper to studying, grew intensely serious when it came to politics. "One thing is certain, democracy [i.e., the Democratic Party] is sure to come out victorious in the next national contest," he wrote. "The victory will be gained by the votes of the conservative masses of the north who hitherto have manifested no interest in the elections but who now will be called out by the desire to repudiate . . . the treasonable foray of John Brown."[72]

On May 5, he composed another letter to his friend on the same themes. He complained about being punished with extra guard duty in the unusual heat, and praised the balls that cadets held during the summer. Then he made a remarkable declaration of his politics, showing how thoroughly he identified with the South.

He admitted that the Democratic Party had suffered a *"temporary* division" at its convention in Charleston. Hardline Southern "fire-eaters" had stormed out, and the orthodox remnant had adjourned to Baltimore. But Custer predicted that all Democrats would unite behind "a sound national & conservative man as their standard bearer who by advocating *equal rights* to the citizens of every section of our Republic will put down and defeat any candidate who holds to the doctrine and principles of the, so called, Republican Party." By "equal rights," he meant the right of white slave owners of the South to carry their slave "property" into the Western Territories—that the South's "peculiar institution" should not be discriminated against in favor of free labor. He went on to argue that Republicans represented only the North; if they won the presidency they would either oppress the South or "produce a dissolution of the Union." He seemed to be eating the same fire as the most militant Southern leaders. "The South has insult after insult heaped upon her but when such acts as the John Brown raid at Harper's Ferry are committed . . . they determine no longer to submit to such aggression but demand that northern abolitionists shall not interfere with their constitutional rights." Custer blamed the growing national crisis on aggression, writing of Southern rights being "invaded" and "trampled." Since he was writing to a Republican, he comes across as sincere, believing that his was the "national" and "conservative" cause.[73]

It was not. Ever since the Northwest Ordinance, predating the Constitution itself, Americans had accepted limits on slavery. Southern politicians broke with that tradition. They made unprecedented, nonnegotiable demands: slavery had to be allowed in *all* new territories, and the Republicans could not be allowed to win the presidency. If these terms were not met, the South would secede from the United States. National politics had become a hostage negotiation, the hostage being the Union. Most Northern Democrats refused to go so far; they wanted respect for popular sovereignty, which meant abiding by Kansas settlers' rejection of slavery. That was why the Charleston convention split in two. Yet Custer embraced Southern extremism.[74]

THE DEMOCRATS DID NOT UNITE. Once Southerners withdrew from the convention, the remaining, largely Northern Democrats reconvened in Baltimore and nominated Stephen A. Douglas of Illinois for president. Southern fire-eaters held their own convention and nominated then vice president John C. Breckinridge and, as his running mate, Senator

Joseph Lane of Oregon, father of one of Custer's friends. Old border-state Whigs, proslavery but Unionist, formed the Constitutional Union Party. And the Republican Party nominated Abraham Lincoln.

"Politics are 'raging high' here now and we hear nothing but talk of disunion," Tully McCrea, a Republican, wrote on October 27, 1860. "Some of the cadets from the southern states had a disunion meeting last night and are going to go home if Lincoln is elected." He added two weeks later, "It has been the cause of much ill feeling among cadets for the last few weeks."

Lincoln won. McCrea was ecstatic. "As we rejoiced the other parties mourned," he wrote on November 10; "the southerners swore and (as is customary with a great many of them) they threatened to do all kinds of terrible things and blustered around at a great rate."[75]

On December 20, South Carolina withdrew from the United States. Secession conventions met across the South. Mississippi went next, followed by Florida, Alabama, Georgia, Louisiana, and then Texas. At West Point, Southern cadets began to resign, draining out over the months that followed Lincoln's election.[76]

"I remember a conversation held at the table at which I sat during the winter of '60–'61," Custer later wrote. He took a place next to P. M. B. Young. The conversation turned to the political situation, as it always did these days. Young turned to Custer and said, "in a half jocular, half earnest manner . . . 'Custer, my boy, we're going to have war. There's no use talking; I see it coming.'" One day soon, he predicted, they would face each other in battle.[77]

By implication, Young told Custer that he belonged to the North whether he liked it or not. After years of edging in among Southern cadets, Custer found that he could never be one of them. He discovered his intrinsic loyalty to the Union and his fellow Northerners. One day Schaff argued angrily with a much bigger Southern cadet. "On my return from recitation," he recalled, "Custer and [Elroy] 'Deacon' Elbert of Iowa, who had heard about the row—and were about the size of the Southerner—met me . . . and said, 'If he lays a hand on you, Morris, we'll maul the earth with him.'"

On February 22, 1861, Washington's birthday, the full cadet band followed tradition by performing as the flag was lowered and darkness fell. As the music struck up, cadets gathered at the barracks windows to watch. At the end of the ceremony, the band marched in formation toward the sally port, and began to play "The Star-Spangled Banner." Custer started a cheer. In another window, his friend Tom Rosser led a cheer for "Dixie" among the Southern cadets. "And so cheer followed cheer," Schaff wrote. "Ah, it was a great night! Rosser at one window, Custer at another."[78]

Custer remained loyal to the Union—but did his underlying politics change? It was a question that important men would try very hard to answer in the years ahead.

"HE HAS NARROWLY ESCAPED several times before but unluckily did not take warning, and now it is too late," McCrea wrote about Custer on January 19, 1861. The midyear examinations were at hand. With expectations of war intensifying, the Academic Board at West Point decided to make the test harder than ever before. Custer, as usual, lagged behind in his studies. He doubted that he could survive the questioning. So he resorted to burglary.

Each class was divided into sections according to students' standing. The top section was taught by the professor, the rest by junior instructors, often young officers. At the examination, the Academic Board watched each instructor quiz his cadets, one by one. Custer knew he would fail one class unless he learned the questions in advance.

The instructor lived in the post hotel, where, McCrea wrote, "bribing one of the servants" was possible. With money or stealth, Custer broke into the instructor's room. He found the examination notebook and started to copy the test. He heard footsteps. He ripped out the sheet of questions and slipped out before he was caught. "But in doing this he spoiled everything, for as soon as the instructor discovered that the leaf was missing he knew that some cadet had it," McCrea observed in a letter. The instructor "changed all the subjects and the risk and trouble was all for nothing." Custer failed the test, along with more than thirty other cadets. The board allowed a reexamination. Custer flunked again, as did all but a few. After three and a half years at West Point, with war seemingly inevitable, his army career was over.

Then he was reinstated. Out of dozens who were dismissed, he was the only one to be saved. He had no idea why. Not for the first time, not for the last, an extraordinary, inexplicable turn of luck had saved him from himself.[79]

And so he remained at West Point in that cascade of days in early 1861, studying, drilling, practicing "cutting heads"—slashing with a saber at leather balls stuffed with straw while riding a horse.[80] There was a new girl, too, named Mariah. McCrea warned Custer that a rumor had swept West Point and its civilian fringe, "generally believed, that you are engaged to Mariah. It is thought so by the ladies as well as cadets. I do not believe it myself, and for your sake I hope that there is no foundation in the report."[81]

He said good-bye to most of his Southern friends as all but a few resigned and went home. He was fond of them still. One Saturday, he recalled, he was yet again serving guard duty as punishment when he saw two of them headed for the steamboat dock amid a crowd of cadets. They "raised their hats in token of farewell," Custer recalled, and he saluted them the only way he could on duty, "by bringing my musket to a 'present.'"[82]

By the time Lincoln took the oath of office on March 4, the secessionists had already organized the Confederate States of America and selected Jefferson Davis as president. Federal troops withdrew from the South or were taken prisoner. In April, the question of war came to rest on Fort Sumter, an island bastion in the harbor of Charleston, South Carolina. Its commanding officer, Maj. Robert Anderson, refused calls to surrender it to the state. A company of engineers stationed at West Point left for New York to join a resupply flotilla sent to sustain Sumter. Everyone wondered if the Confederates would fire on it.

"No one speaks of anything but war," Custer wrote on April 10, 1861. "I feel confident that we will have war in less than a week, and if we do I never expect to graduate here, neither does any one of my classmates nor the class above me, as we would be ordered to join recruits, etc. This is what the officers and professors say."[83]

The first of Custer's predictions came true at 4:30 in the morning on April 12, when Southern gunners opened fire on Sumter. Two days later they pulled down the U.S. flag flying over the fort. On April 15, Lincoln asked for 75,000 militiamen to put down the South's rebellion. The North responded with mobs of volunteers, patriotic mass meetings, and red-white-and-blue bunting from Iowa to Maine.[84]

"The effect was instantaneous," McCrea recalled. On the night when the news of the attack reached West Point, Northern cadets crammed into a room in the barracks. "One could have heard us singing 'The Star Spangled Banner' in Cold Spring [a town across the Hudson]. It was the first time I ever saw the Southern contingent cowed. All their Northern allies had deserted them, and they were stunned."[85]

Custer stood firm for the Union. He wrote to Ann on April 26, "The excitement here is intense. We can scarcely study in consequence of our thoughts being elsewhere." He wrote ponderously of his obligations. "Every good loyal citizen should feel it his duty to support the government to the full extent of his power and if this is obligatory upon all citizens how much more so it is upon me."

But already he was calculating. He had written to Ohio's governor, he said, to ask that he might serve in one of the regiments of volunteers being formed in the state. Such state-organized units, known as the U.S. Volunteers, formed the vast bulk of the forces that would prosecute the war, yet they remained organizationally separate from the standing Regular Army. "I would prefer serving with the troops of my native state. Besides I could get a much higher office [than] in the regular army." The latter mattered most to him. "I would be a Lieutenant but in the volunteers I could be certain of being at least a Captain and probably higher." But the governor made no promises.[86]

The end of Custer's stay at West Point came into view. The first class had graduated early, on May 6. Custer's class would follow seven weeks later, a year ahead of schedule, to supply officers to meet the crisis. He told Ann he was determined to pass his finals on June 18. "I . . . have only averaged four hours sleep in twenty-four during the last two weeks," he wrote on May 31. "Everything is uncertain, life is always so and at no time was it ever more so than at the present," he added. "It is useless to hope that the coming struggle will be a bloodless one or one of short duration. It is certain that much blood will be spilled and that thousands of lives will be lost." Armstrong told Ann he was willing to die, but had a feeling that he would live through the war. "I shall certainly like to."[87]

Custer survived the examination. On June 24, he graduated thirty-fourth in a class of thirty-four. His tally of demerits for the year, 192, was eight short of the annual limit, out of 726 for all of his West Point career—the most of anyone in his class.[88]

On June 29, Custer remained at West Point as the War Department tried to find places for the new graduates, either in Regular Army regiments or as instructors for the U.S. Volunteers. Still treated as a cadet, he served as officer of the guard during the summer encampment. After a quiet morning, he heard "a commotion near the guard tents"—the cadets Peter Ryerson and William Ludlow were having a fistfight, surrounded by a crowd. Custer reacted—not as he had been trained, but as who he was.

"I should have arrested the two combatants and sent them to the guard tents," Custer later wrote. "But the instincts of the boy prevailed over the obligation of the officer of the guard. I pushed my way through the surrounding line of cadets, dashed back those who were interfering in the struggle, and called out loudly, 'Stand back boys; let's have a fair fight.'"[89] After surviving failed examinations, escaping expulsion for his misdeeds, and actually graduating with hopes of "much higher office," he found himself under arrest. He finally faced the consequences of being Custer.

AT HALF PAST NINE in the morning of July 6, the court-martial reconvened. There were no more witnesses. There was only Custer left to speak for Custer. He read his final statement, written the night before.

"Mr. President and gentlemen of the court, the case now presented for your examination and judgment, from the character of the charges, from the nature of my plea, and from the conciseness and conclusiveness of the evidence will need but a simple analysis and a brief statement of the facts on my part before I submit it to your final consideration." He was always wordy when insecure, and he could hardly be more insecure than after pleading guilty before a court-martial. Yet he made a simple case: he was guilty, but not of much. The witnesses had demonstrated that the matter was "trifling." The so-called fight was "merely a scuffle." He certainly would have intervened if it had seemed to be "of a serious character," likely to cause injury.

Then he asked for something else: pity. Pity for being a soldier held back from war. Pity for being himself. After entering West Point in 1857, he said, "I plodded my way for four long years preparing myself for a chosen avocation . . . one which offers to my ambition the most glorious career." Now he had to watch his classmates, "close friends, companions, and brothers," depart for war. Imagine, he asked, "my grief and disappointment at not being permitted to accompany them from our common Alma Mater." This "chagrin and anxiety at being detained at this place . . . to say nothing of the inconveniences that result from being in arrest with restricted limits . . . far exceed any punishment that could be expected under ordinary circumstances from the offences [sic] with which I am charged." He was willing to endure any penalty the court enacted, he said, but he wished them to consider "the peculiar situation which I occupy."

With these mournful words, he recast himself as a victim of circumstance rather than an admitted violator of military law. Yet, for all his misdeeds, he was never rebellious. He pushed against boundaries, but never questioned them. Having come to West Point in search of $28 per month, he discovered that he loved being a soldier.

The judges listened. When Custer finished, Major Nauman, the president of the court, ordered the room cleared for deliberations. Custer did not wait long before being ordered back in to hear the verdict. The court found him guilty on all counts.

The judges sentenced him to—nothing. His only penalty was "to be reprimanded in orders." Judge Advocate Benet explained, "The Court are this lenient in the sentence owing to the peculiar situation of Cadet Custer as presented in his defense, and in consideration of his general good conduct as testified to by Lieutenant Hazen his immediate commander."[90]

Custer's career would continue. But the trial left a larger question unanswered: What place could he have in the Regular Army? It was one of the largest, most rigidly hierarchical, most systematic institutions in America—but Custer was individualistic, romantic, and impulsive. This contrast would color the rest of his life. He was perhaps the truer representative of the young republic, but the army foreshadowed its future.[91]

He remained in the army, bottom of his class, bottom of the promotion list, a highway of misconduct behind him. Only luck had saved him—the very good luck that the nation was descending into the most brutal war in its history.

A little more than a week later, Custer received orders to report to army headquarters in Washington, D.C.[92]

Two

THE OBSERVER

He went to war alone. He did not board a steamboat full of new graduates from West Point. He did not ride off at the head of a regiment, or even trail behind one. George Armstrong Custer set out for Washington by himself.

War is, of course, a group activity. The personal experience in wartime is one of immersion in crowds, those organized assemblies of men known as armies. In the Civil War especially, the soldier rarely found himself alone. There were marches and messes and drills, shared tents and mass formations. Every feature of his existence was standardized, homogenized—soldiers' clothes are called "uniforms" for good reason—and became more so as the war progressed, as the Quartermaster's Department took over the states' initial pell-mell effort to rush troops and supplies to the front.[1]

But Custer began alone. His court-martial jolted him off the tracks that most of his classmates rode to war. That would emerge as a pattern. For most of the next two years, he would be a soldier apart from his unit, an officer with none to command.

He received his commission as second lieutenant of the 2nd U.S. Cavalry Regiment and boarded a steamer at the West Point pier on Thursday, July 18, 1861. He debarked in New York, entering a city that had changed since his last furlough—though not entirely. Broadway still thronged with people passing in and out of shops, their bonnets and top hats shadowed by walls of flat-faced buildings, four to six stories high. The humid air still stank with the manure of countless horses that dragged rattling wagons, carriages, and omnibuses crammed with food, people, goods, and garbage. Newspaper offices still perched in floors above basement oyster cellars and shared-table restaurants on Park Row. P. T. Barnum's American Museum still offered glimpses of the bizarre, not far from the Astor House hotel as well as cluttered warehouses and textile workshops.

What had changed was the public mood. Only a few months before, New York's leading merchants had lobbied Washington to compromise with the South. Mayor Fernando Wood even proposed that Manhattan secede and become a free city, to protect its cotton trade. Now flags and stars-and-stripes bunting brightened the masonry ravines. Recruiting stations sprouted in parks.[2]

Custer visited a military-supply store to buy the equipment expected of a second lieutenant in the United States Cavalry—"sabre, revolver, sash, spurs, etc.," as he later listed them. A few hours later he returned to the Hudson riverfront to take a ferry to the railroad terminals in New Jersey. The British journalist William Russell made the same trip in 1861, "to a large wooden shed covered with inscriptions respecting routes and destinations on the bank of the river, which as far as the eye could see, was bordered by similar establishments." Custer crossed the river and boarded a passenger car on the evening train to Washington—"with a double row of most uncomfortable seats, and a passage down the middle," as Russell described one, "with an immense iron stove in the centre of the car." Any attempt to sleep was interrupted by the train bell, the conductor, and boys shouting, "N'York *Heddle!*"—referring to the copies of the *New York Herald* they had for sale, along with gumdrops, tobacco, apples, and cakes.[3]

"I found the cars crowded with troops, officers and men, hastening to the capital," Custer later wrote. "At each station we passed on the road at which a halt was made, crowds of citizens . . . received us with cheers and cheered us in parting."

He traveled all night, changing trains twice in the dark. At dawn on Saturday, April 20, he arrived in Washington. The view out the left window was dominated by the Capitol, enthroned in marble on a hilltop, scaffolding and cranes clustered around the unfinished dome. But most of this drab city consisted of "fields studded with wooden sheds and huts," Russell wrote, "rudimentary streets of small red brick houses, and some church-spires among them." Specialized to serve the seasonal gathering of Congress, home to very few year-round bureaucrats, Washington was dominated by hotels, restaurants, boardinghouses, and barbershops. Like a bellows, it expanded when congressmen arrived and contracted when they left for their many months in recess.[4]

Once off the train Custer saw slaves everywhere, driving teams of horses, cooking and serving food, shaving and clipping in barbershops, laboring on the Capitol itself. He had never been in so Southern a place, with such a proportionally large black population. Washington was his gateway not only to the Civil War, but also to a new stage in his life, defined by slavery and its consequences.[5]

He went first to the Ebbitt House, a well-regarded hotel where he expected to find some of his classmates. At the front desk he learned that his old roommate James Parker had checked in. Custer went to his door and woke him up.[6]

Parker told him that the federal army of hastily assembled volunteers, under the field command of Gen. Irwin McDowell, had already marched south from the capital. Any moment they expected to hear of a battle with the rebel army under Gen. P. G. T. Beauregard, posted near Manassas, Virginia. Custer asked what he planned to do. Parker was from Missouri, a border state divided in its loyalties, and had supported secession. He pointed to an official document lying on a table. It was an order from the War Department, dismissing 2nd Lt. James P. Parker from the army "for having tendered his resignation in the face of the enemy." The two friends said good-bye. Parker set out for Richmond to accept a commission as a Confederate officer, and Custer reported to the adjutant general's office.[7]

There he waited in "bewilderment," he recalled, as officials bustled about and messengers rushed in and out with stacks of overstuffed envelopes. It was after midnight when the adjutant general finally called him forward. The officer began to tell a subordinate to write out orders for the young West Pointer, then turned back and asked, "Perhaps you would like to be presented to General Scott, Mr. Custer?"

Custer was the most junior officer in the Regular Army of the United States, having graduated at the bottom of the most recent West Point class. Yet here he was being asked if he would like to meet General in Chief Winfield Scott. Yes, Custer recalled answering, "joyfully."

He followed the officer into another room and saw General Scott "seated at a table over which were spread maps and other documents." Congressmen gathered around it, discussing the approaching battle near Manassas. Scott was old, especially by the standards of 1861, but still impressive. A hero of the War of 1812, mastermind of the daring campaign that won the Mexican War, he was seventy-five and infirm, six feet five inches tall and weighing some 300 pounds. Pleased with fame, accustomed to others' deference, he was almost self-consciously lofty in his fine double-breasted uniform with huge gold epaulets that seemed to be the size of dinner plates.[8]

"General, this is Lieutenant Custer of the Second Cavalry; he has just reported from West Point," the adjutant general said (as Custer later recalled).

"Welcome, my young friend, I am glad to welcome you to the service at this critical time. Our country has need of the strong arms of all her loyal sons in this emergency," Scott said. The adjutant general informed him that Custer was assigned to Company G of the 2nd Cavalry, now with McDowell's army. "Now what can I do for you?" Scott asked. Did he want to join other West Pointers in training volunteers, "or is your desire for something more active?" Custer wanted to join his regiment and face the enemy. "A very commendable resolution, young man," the general replied.

"Go and provide yourself with a horse if possible," Scott said, "and call here at seven o'clock this evening. I desire to send some dispatches to General McDowell."

Custer hurried out onto the street. He went from stable to stable, but found them empty. It seemed as if every quadruped had been taken by the army or congressmen going to see the battle. With a regiment to reach, a battle to catch, and messages to carry from General Scott himself, Custer feared he would fail at everything for lack of a horse.

Dejected, he walked down Pennsylvania Avenue, where he encountered an acquaintance. He served in an artillery battery led by Capt. Charles Griffin, now with McDowell's army, and had been sent back to Washington to retrieve a horse. The man agreed to let Custer ride the horse back to the army with him and, reluctantly, to wait until Custer gathered Scott's dispatches at seven o'clock.

That evening they rode their horses across the Long Bridge over the Potomac and headed south. Hours passed in the darkness. Custer's friend described the camp of tens of thousands of Union soldiers near Centreville, Virginia, and an opening skirmish at Blackburn's Ford. Sometime after two in the morning they glimpsed the scattered campfires and dim shapes that indicated the penumbra of the Union army. Soldiers were already awake, some aligning into columns, some "standing in small groups," Custer recalled, "smoking and chatting," others lying down on the ground, fully dressed, napping. Custer guided his horse through the mass of bodies, following his comrade to General McDowell's headquarters.

They arrived at a cluster of tents, "near which a large log fire was blazing," Custer wrote. He reluctantly handed over his dispatches to a staff officer rather than McDowell himself, whom he glimpsed through an open tent flap. Everyone in Washington was waiting for news from the army, Custer told the officer. "Well, I guess they will not have to wait much longer," he replied. "The entire army is under arms, and moving to attack the enemy today."

Custer sat by the general's fire and ate a breakfast of steak, corn bread, and coffee. It was the last meal he would have for another thirty hours.[9] He remounted, apparently keeping his borrowed horse, and searched for his company under a clear night sky, the moon almost full, its blue light throwing shadows on the dark ground. Finally he found his unit and introduced himself to the other officers.[10]

Slowly, agonizingly, the army moved forward as the sun rose. All but a few soldiers were volunteers; many had enlisted for just three months of service. Scarcely trained, often led by equally inexperienced officers, they took hours to sort themselves out on the marching route and get into attacking position.

This was a fight for infantry and artillery, not cavalry. Custer and the other horsemen held back as the lines advanced. "We could hear the battle raging a short distance in our front," he recalled. "A staff officer of Gen. McDowell's came galloping down to where the cavalry was waiting, saying that the General desired us to move across the stream and up the ridge beyond, where we were to support a battery."

It was Griffin's Battery. Up on Henry House Hill above the cavalry, the artillerymen—including Custer's friend—rolled their heavy dark cannons on great wooden wheels into line with the federal infantry and opened fire.

Roar of battle is a cliché, but *roar* is too weak a word. This was the crackling of thousands of muskets, the booming of dozens of cannons, not to mention countless bugles and drums, shouting officers, creaking caissons (two-wheeled carts carrying artillery ammunition), tramping feet, and thumping hooves. Above the din, Custer noticed "the strange hissing and exceedingly vicious sound of the first cannon shot I heard," as solid metal balls passed over their targets and flew near the cavalry behind the hill's crest. Custer had often heard guns fired in practice at West Point, "but a man listens with changed interest when the direction of the balls is toward instead of away from him."[11]

The cavalry did not stand by the artillery. Instead, the 11th and 14th New York infantry regiments hustled up the hill—the 11th wearing the baggy red pants of Zouaves, patterned after Algerian troops serving in the French army and something of a craze in America in 1861. The federal line moved forward; the Confederates seemed to be falling back. The New Yorkers suffered from enemy fire, but another regiment approached from the right, apparently coming to aid Griffin's Battery.

The oncoming troops were rebels. They halted and fired. The volley killed scores of horses, necessary to haul the guns, and decimated Griffin's men. In Custer's first battle, the battery he was assigned to protect was virtually wiped out before he could fire a shot or draw his saber. As for his benefactor, the man who had given him a horse and guided him to the front, his fate is unknown. Custer never mentioned him again.[12]

The battle turned. Union soldiers panicked and fled, clogging the roads and fords across the stream. They had lost.

———

IN THE ENSUING DAYS, the young second lieutenant rewrote the story of disaster. In August, he wrote a twenty-four-page letter to his old roommate Tully McCrea, who was still at West Point. He narrated his long journey to the banks of Bull Run. Instead of describing the late arrival of a passive witness, he told a saga of courage in the face of peril. His post behind the line became a point of great danger. "He belonged to the cavalry that was General McDowell's bodyguard," McCrea wrote, describing Custer's account, "and consequently was in the thickest of the fight." The Union rout became Custer's personal rear-guard action. He said he was last to leave the field, and narrowly escaped being cut off and captured. As his company retreated, he rode behind the men, between their backs and the enemy, to reassure and inspire them.[13]

These claims range from flatly untrue to greatly exaggerated. And it's doubtful that the professional soldiers of a Regular Army regiment were moved by being trailed off the field by a brand-new second lieutenant who had joined them just before the battle (called Bull Run by the federals and Manassas by the Confederates). He did not even have command of his company; he was a "subaltern," as he called himself. Enlisted men knew which officers deserved respect. They knew nothing about Custer.[14]

In many ways, Custer was living an adventure story. Luck rescued him from his drab existence in rural Ohio; luck saved him from expulsion from West Point; and luck preserved him at his court-martial. Instead of punishment, he met the nation's commanding general, found a horse against all odds, delivered urgent dispatches to the army in the field, and rode toward the battle. But there the adventure ended. He did not even see most of the fighting, but simply listened. So Custer assumed authorship over his own tale. First in letters, later in magazine articles and books, he set out to shape and reshape his life, to impose his imagined self over a reality that was remarkable enough. He would not be content until others regarded him as he wished to regard himself.

ON MONDAY MORNING, July 22, after retreating all night, Custer's regiment finally reached Alexandria, Virginia, just across the Potomac from Washington. Custer had hardly slept since leaving West Point almost four days earlier. He had been in the saddle with only short breaks since Saturday evening. He slid to the ground and collapsed in the mud under a tree, where he slept for hours in a steady rain. "When he was awakened he was so stiff and sore that he could scarcely move," McCrea wrote.[15]

Defeat at Bull Run destroyed the popular notion of a quick war. A new call went out for volunteers to serve for three years. The army based in

Washington was reorganized and retrained.* Custer's 2nd U.S. Cavalry Regiment was redesignated the 5th, though the personnel remained the same. Not that Custer got to know the personnel. Seeing an opportunity, he joined the staff of Brig. Gen. Philip Kearny, who commanded an infantry brigade of volunteers.[16]

Custer's decision surprised some of his friends, including Mariah, the young woman back at West Point who believed she was his fiancée. He had kept her belief alive, sending her a letter about Bull Run and Kearny's staff even before he wrote to McCrea. Mariah was appalled. Accustomed to the company of West Point cadets and Regular Army officers, she had "a holy horror for the volunteers," McCrea told Custer. The sentiment was reflected even among the recruits themselves. "If there was anything we volunteers early in the war had great reverence for," one wrote, "it was a 'regular' officer. We looked on them as superior beings."[17]

This was a natural cultural divide between veterans and greenhorns, professionals and amateurs, but it was also an organizational distinction. As mentioned earlier, the Regular Army remained a separate institution from the U.S. Volunteers, who comprised essentially a second national army, existing only for the duration of the war. Regular officers retained their ranks in a separate roster, attached to specific Regular regiments as before the war. Volunteer officers held rank in their own organization. The system would grow rather bewildering as more and more Regular Army officers began to serve in Volunteer units, taking on a second rank—a Volunteer rank. One could be simultaneously a Regular Army captain and a major general of Volunteers; when the war ended and the Volunteers were mustered out of service, he would still be a captain but no longer a major general. Custer was a second lieutenant of the 5th U.S. Cavalry, but he would spend very little time with his unit.

Proud of his West Point education, Custer was nevertheless ambitious. As he previously explained his request to serve with Ohio's volunteers, "I could get a much higher office [than] in the regular army."[18] But he had hardly taken up his duties with Kearny when he fell sick—so sick that he believed he would die. Though the nature of the illness remains obscure, he made a reasonable supposition. Disease slaughtered far more Civil War soldiers than battle, the result of concentrating tens of thousands of men from all over the country in unsanitary camps. He was fortunate to depart the military hospital in October and return home on leave. For the first time in two years, he went to see his parents, now living

---

* "Army" can mean either the national military organization, the U.S. Army, or a specific field force in a defined theater (e.g., the Army of the Potomac).

in Wood County in northwest Ohio. He narrowly missed his younger brother Tom; just sixteen, Tom had joined the army and departed for a battlefront in the West.

Armstrong recovered sufficiently to travel to Michigan and spend several weeks with Ann and her husband, David Reed. Now that his parents had left New Rumley, Monroe was the only hometown with which Custer still had close ties. He found the place transformed by the war. It was still home to a few thousand people, living on crisscrossing streets near the Raisin River. But many men were gone, serving in volunteer regiments, while their families supported themselves as best they could.

As Custer recuperated at Ann's house, he called on friends who had remained at home in the war. One night, after he went out with them, he returned to his sister's house visibly drunk. Ann was appalled. The next day he swore he would never drink again.

His avowal was not unusual. The early United States was an "alcoholic republic," as the historian W. J. Rorabaugh has called it. That gave rise to a countertrend. "A zestful, hearty drinking people became the world's most zealous abstainers," Rorabaugh writes. Temperance societies distributed millions of pamphlets and held public signing ceremonies for "the pledge"—the oath to abstain from alcohol. At West Point, a cadet could be excused for a drinking offense—grounds for expulsion—if his entire class took the pledge. Virtually every class in the 1850s did so.[19]

But the incident was a painful reminder that he inhabited different worlds simultaneously. His behavior would have won him esteem within the stone-walled barracks at West Point; quite the opposite on the tree-lined streets of a quiet village, where it could be witnessed by his sister and uncle and brother-in-law and niece and nephews and countless others he valued. Whatever self-examination and self-discipline went into his pledge, it was precipitated by shame. His self-awareness was almost always couched in his sense of himself in society; and his standing in Monroe mattered to him. His letters itemized the many local elders he wrote to, the friends with whom he exchanged photographs, the young people he hoped would remember him. He yearned to be accepted, to be admired, to belong. If alcohol interfered, he would do without it.

As he made his way back to Washington, his train pulled into Cleveland, where he would lay over until the next morning. He left his trunk at the depot and checked into a hotel, which was surprisingly crowded. A friend from West Point, now captain of a company posted in the city, came over and shook his hand. He insisted that Custer come to a dinner and grand ball being held that night at the same hotel. Custer agreed.

It was nearly midnight before the meal ended and the band began to play. Custer met "several pretty ladies," he wrote, "and danced nearly every dance until daylight." As he was chatting with his friend, he spotted a familiar-looking man in a sergeant's uniform. His name is McLish, the captain said. Then Custer remembered: McLish had once attended his sister's church in Monroe. He drinks, the captain added.

Custer went over and introduced himself. McLish jovially invited him to raise a glass, but Custer said he no longer drank. Dawn approached; the dance dwindled; McLish got drunk. His humor faded as he hung on the lieutenant and talked, swearing and cursing himself. Liquor had ruined him, he said. If not for that, he would have been rich. McLish asked about everyone in Monroe. Tell them you saw me, he said. Stay another day, he begged; come see my wife. Custer declined.

"Do not tell any of his or her relations in Monroe," Custer wrote to Ann, after recounting the meeting, "as it would only pain them without doing any good."[20]

THE YOUNG OFFICERS RODE OUT on horseback from Camp Cliffburn outside of Washington at 8:30 p.m. on February 20, 1862, with a mounted band trotting behind them. Custer rode beside a West Point classmate, Lt. Leroy Elbert of the 3rd U.S. Cavalry. "He is the best friend I ever had," Custer wrote the next day. "I could not think more of him if he was my brother. He has no secrets from me and I none from him."

They headed into the capital and rode to the home of Elbert's girl-friend. The band played a tune and the young men sang below her window. Afterward the party rode from house to house, serenading young women they knew. At each place, the lady went to the door in her night-gown and invited them inside; the young men crowded in and accepted cups of beer or wine. They returned home at three in the morning.

Custer told his sister that "at no place did I drink a drop, not even of ale." But his self-control did not reflect a new maturity when it came to women. Though Elbert had a sweetheart, he observed, "I am not blessed with such a treasure (?)." He urged Ann to give his love to Nellie Van Wormer and Mary Arnold, and added flirting instructions. He forgot Mariah—if he had ever mentioned her to his family in the first place.[21]

CUSTER LED THE LINE of horsemen at a slow trot, to keep their mounts rested until the last moment. Fifty troopers of the 5th U.S. Cavalry Regiment followed Custer, with a supporting company about 500 yards behind. Halfway to the rebels, now a quarter of a mile away, Custer gave the order to draw revolvers. He reined his horse over to the right of the line to get out of the way of his own men's fire.

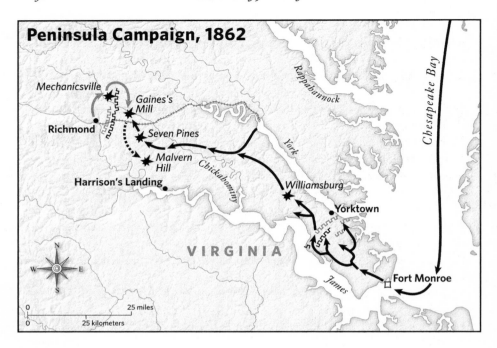

It was the middle of March 1862, near Manassas. The Confederates had remained there since their victory at Bull Run the year before. Now they were withdrawing south. The Union cavalry had followed to a point some eighteen miles beyond Manassas, where they encountered a line of men stationed behind a wall. These were pickets—outlying guards who kept watch on the enemy and screened their own army from reconnaissance. Orders had come to Custer's regiment to drive in the pickets upon the main body of the Confederate army. Custer—still a junior officer, not a company commander—had volunteered to lead the attack.

He kicked his horse into a gallop and launched his men into a charge. It was all over in a few minutes. The rebels escaped to the far side of a ravine, where the cavalry could not easily follow, and opened fire. "The bullets rattled like hail," Custer wrote to his parents. "Several whizzed close to my head." He ordered a withdrawal.

Back in Union camp, he reported to Brig. Gen. George Stoneman, the army's chief of cavalry—and to correspondents for the *New York Tribune*, *New York Times*, *New York World*, and the *Philadelphia Inquirer*. He found it exhilarating to finally battle the enemy after trailing them for a week through cold, steady rain, without more than an hour of sleep on some nights or a single change of his wet, filthy uniform.[22]

The Confederate withdrawal and Union pursuit marked a change,

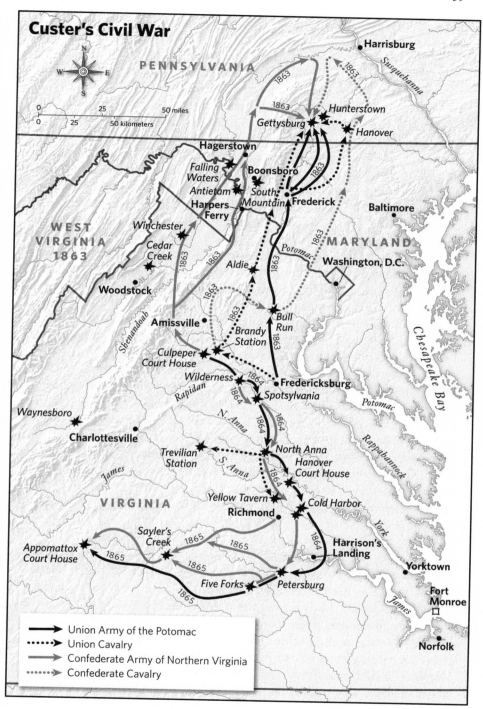

Custer's Civil War

PENNSYLVANIA

Harrisburg

Susquehanna

1863
1863
1863

Hunterstown
Gettysburg
Hanover

Hagerstown

Falling Waters
Boonsboro
Antietam
South Mountain
Frederick

Harpers Ferry

Baltimore

WEST VIRGINIA 1863

Winchester
Cedar Creek

Potomac

MARYLAND

Washington, D.C.

1863

Aldie

1863

Woodstock

Shenandoah

Amissville

Brandy Station

Bull Run

1863

Culpeper Court House

Wilderness
Rapidan
Spotsylvania
Fredericksburg

1864
1864
1864

N. Anna

Potomac

Rappahannock

Waynesboro

Charlottesville

VIRGINIA

Trevilian Station

S. Anna

North Anna
Hanover Court House

1864

James

Yellow Tavern

Richmond

Cold Harbor

Chesapeake Bay

York

Sayler's Creek

1865
1865

Appomattox Court House

1865

1864

Harrison's Landing

Yorktown

Five Forks

1865

Petersburg

1865

James

Fort Monroe

Norfolk

→ Union Army of the Potomac
┈► Union Cavalry
→ Confederate Army of Northern Virginia
┈► Confederate Cavalry

but its nature remained a mystery. During Custer's sick leave, the Union force had been reorganized as the Army of the Potomac, under the command of thirty-five-year-old Maj. Gen. George B. McClellan. He had trained, equipped, and supplied the army brilliantly, transforming it into a potent force. But he had done nothing with it.[23]

At first, it seemed as if Custer's charge might presage a battle. Instead, he and his regiment were recalled to Alexandria. Discontent with McClellan's inactivity had simmered for months in Congress and the press, especially among Republicans; now it came to a boil. On March 17, a motion to censure him only narrowly failed in the Senate.[24] Even Custer's father, Emmanuel, grew uncomfortable with the army's passivity. No friend of Republicans, he wrote to his son, "If the object of the present war is to abolish slaveary [sic] I would say to all the soldiers that was opposed to that do [sic] throw down their arms and go home and let the abolitionist and the rebels fight it out among them selves [sic]." But, he said, "I have been looking for a General move of the army."[25]

"I have more confidence in him [McClellan] than any man living," Custer wrote back. "I am willing to forsake everything and follow him to the ends of the earth and lay down my life for him if necessary. He is here now. I wish you could see him. Everyone officer & privates worship him. I would fight anyone who would say anything against him."[26]

To show that McClellan was "in earnest," he enclosed a copy of his orders, apparently those of March 14, printed and distributed widely to the troops. "SOLDIERS OF THE ARMY OF THE POTOMAC!" the general declared. "For a long time I have kept you inactive, but not without a purpose. . . . The period of inaction has passed. I will bring you now face to face with the rebels, and only pray that God may defend the right. In whatever direction you may move, however strange my actions may appear to you, ever bear in mind that my fate is linked with yours, and that all I do is to bring you, where I know you wish to be—on the decisive battlefield."[27]

"THE GREATEST EXPEDITION EVER FITTED OUT is now going South," Custer wrote to his parents on March 26, 1862. He sat on a wharf in Alexandria, across the Potomac River from Washington, D.C. Tens of thousands of soldiers crowded the waterfront among countless crates, barrels, wagons, horses, mules, cannons, and other freight. Out on the river floated 113 steamers to carry the men and 276 sailing craft and barges to haul the animals, arms, and equipment. Here were fast side-wheel steamers that usually churned the Hudson or Long Island Sound, double-ended ferries from the Delaware and Raritan, not to mention ocean liners—all leased by the War Department. Gathered in a fleet in the Potomac and the upper reaches of Chesapeake Bay, they took turns nosing into the Alexandria wharves.

Bands played "The Star-Spangled Banner" and "Dixie" and steamboat whistles screeched as "the men marched up the gangplanks in steady procession, and steam derricks hoisted aboard wagons and guns and supplies and even artillery horses in slings," writes the historian Stephen W. Sears. McClellan himself went aboard the *Commodore*, the handsome Long Island Sound steamer with first-class accommodations that had been constructed by (and named after) Cornelius Vanderbilt.[28]

The general and his staff embarked from the same dock where Custer sat writing to his parents. The young lieutenant boarded the humbler *Adele Felicia*, which steamed down the river the morning of March 28. Rumors of its destination ran through the boat. Custer had little to do in his cabin except to peer through his binocular field glass at abandoned Confederate batteries and at Mount Vernon. And he wrote letters, as he always did in spare moments. He asked his sister to give his regards to a list of friends from Monroe, and to tell them how busy he had been recently. "I wish you would tell Nellie Van [Wormer] the same thing because I do not want her to think that it is for want of care that I do not write to her. To tell you the truth I think a great deal of Nellie," he wrote. "Give my love to Riley Emma & Aut [Ann's children]. Tell them to be good children and if they never see me again they must never forget me."[29]

He often wrote of the likelihood of his death. In a letter to his friend McCrea, he remarked that he had no idea where the army was headed, but if they went through as much fighting as he expected, "he would probably be in 'Kingdom Come.'" He told his parents that to die for his country would be an honor, "but I anticipate no such result. I think and feel confident that I will go through this war, particularly the coming struggle safely and satisfactorily and that at its close I will return to you all." He scoffed at his mother's premonitions, but he trusted his own.[30]

The rented armada anchored off Fort Monroe, a stone-walled citadel at the tip of a peninsula extending east and southeast from Richmond, between the James River to the south and the York to the north. The ensuing campaign would recast it as *the* Peninsula. Fort Monroe had remained in Union hands, a formidable but isolated outpost that made a convenient staging point for a drive on the rebel capital.

The forest of coal-fired smokestacks and slant-sailed schooner masts jostled as one boat after another moored at the fort's dock and disgorged men, horses, and freight. It took nearly three weeks to transport the entire army: 121,500 men, 1,592 animals, 1,224 vehicles, 44 batteries of artillery, and vast quantities of supplies and equipment.[31]

Like a wet dog emerging from the ocean, the Army of the Potomac shook itself out and trampled a place to lie down outside the fortress walls. Generally speaking, companies of up to 100 men, led by captains, assembled ten to a regiment (later twelve for cavalry regiments), led by a colonel; four regiments to a brigade, led by a brigadier general; three brigades to a division, led by a brigadier or major general; and three divisions to a corps, led by a major general. This was a host of infantry, armed with rifled muskets. Present in smaller numbers were artillerymen, manning four to six cannons in each battery; cavalry, dispersed among the various infantry divisions for scouting and picket duties; as well as engineers, quartermasters, and others.[32]

"Our camp here is really a pretty one," wrote the New York artilleryman Charles Wainwright, "clean white little shelter tents sparkling amidst the young green of the woods for the leaves are just beginning to come out. At night especially when the hundreds of camp fires are lighted the scene more resembles a fairly land or a grand picnic than what one would expect of grim war."[33]

Wainwright's primary impression was of size—size and effort. If the Army of the Potomac were a city, it would be the ninth largest in the United States, ahead of Chicago and just behind St. Louis. Each horse and man was deliberately placed here, assigned a location, fed, sheltered, and clothed. Ammunition was stockpiled and distributed, arms cared for, fortifications dug, waste eliminated. It was a vast machine in motion.

But a blind machine. General McClellan scarcely knew where his own army was, let alone the enemy's. "No one knew the country," wrote François, Prince de Joinville, a French nobleman who served unofficially on McClellan's staff; "the maps were so defective that they were useless." He found this "total ignorance" to be rather remarkable. "We were here twenty-four miles from Yorktown [the town that anchored the Confederate line], and we could not learn what works the enemy had thrown up, nor what his force was within them."[34]

Second Lt. Custer received orders to report to the topographical engineers, the unit that drew maps. If he imagined that he would quietly work at a drafting table, he was mistaken. Quite the opposite: he would scout ahead of the main body of the army in a nearly continual reconnaissance. The topographical engineers were to sneak through woods and swamps, "sketching by the eye and the compass provisional maps, which were photographed at headquarters for the use of the Generals," Joinville noted. Observing the enemy would now be Custer's duty.[35]

THE SCOUTING PARTY HALTED IN THE WOODS some distance in front of the Union line. Custer and the others dismounted and tied up their horses in the brush, where they would not be noticed by the enemy. Their assignment was to find a Confederate gun emplacement somewhere nearby. On hands and knees they crawled through the mud and underbrush of the Peninsula forest, hoping to escape notice. A black man—an escaped slave—led them forward. At the edge of a clearing below a hill, he stopped. The guns are just over the crest, he said. Most of the detachment waited there in the tree line as Custer, another officer, and the guide crawled up the slope to the smoldering ruins of a house, its two chimneys still jutting out of the embers. Custer and his colleague stood up behind one of the chimneys and peered through their field glasses at the Confederate battery, just 500 yards away. Just as they finished their observations, the Confederates spotted them. Custer saw a cannon swivel toward them and fire.

Artillery in the Civil War fired a variety of munitions. For example, there was solid shot—a heavy metal ball that would skip across the ground with enough force to dismember a horse. There was canister (commonly known as grapeshot), a short-range round consisting of a tin can that held many metal balls; they sprayed upon leaving the muzzle, turning a cannon into a giant shotgun. And there was shell. This consisted of a gunpowder charge inside a metal casing, detonated by a fuse; the fuse was cut to different lengths according to the distance to the target.

What the Confederates fired was a shell. At the blast of flame and smoke from the cannon muzzle, Custer and his comrade fell facedown in the mud. The round hummed over their heads, flying on to the edge of the woods. It exploded over the party that had remained behind, where it was supposed to be safe. Metal fragments strafed the soldiers below. One man was hit by a hot, jagged shard that slashed through wool, skin, muscle, and bone, tearing off his arm. Custer, protected from harm by going to the most exposed and dangerous place, scrambled to his feet and ran.[36]

THE BURIAL PARTY TUCKED THEIR SPADES into the ground under the shade of a stand of trees, hollowing out shallow grave after shallow grave. When Custer rode up on the scene, he decided to swing out of his saddle and watch. The detail laid bodies next to their holes, then lowered them into the ground without coffins. Custer counted about 200 dead, killed in a clash with the rebels.

He walked over to a lifeless boy lying next to his grave. "I had never seen him before," he wrote to his sister. "I was struck by his youthful appearance, together with something handsome about his face which even death had not removed." He turned to the other soldiers who stood watching and asked if anyone knew the young man. "They all spoke highly of him and informed me that he had married a beautiful girl a few days previous to his leaving home for the war. I at once thought of the severe shock that awaits her." She would want a memento, he thought. "I took out my knife and stooped down to cut open his pockets. From them I took a knife and a ring. I then cut a lock of his hair off and gave them all to one of his comrades who was from the same town."[37]

On behalf of this stranger, Custer carried out a ritual that became common in the Civil War. It was an attempt to provide a battlefield version of the Good Death, as the historian Drew Gilpin Faust writes in her seminal *This Republic of Suffering:* "a substitute for the traditional stylized deathbed performance," an attempt to "make it possible for men—and their loved ones—to believe they had died well." Custer acted on his own behalf, too. When he singled out a rare still-handsome corpse, he reinforced the illusion that his would be a Good Death as well, his body intact, his looks preserved, his family informed of his valor. Or perhaps the ritual allowed him to more easily forget the wider field of young soldiers, slaughtered in an attack that served no purpose.[38]

He mounted his horse and rode to find the 7th Michigan Infantry Regiment, which had been organized in Monroe. He ran into a group of its officers, many of them his old friends. He joined their circle on the ground, where they ate crackers and drank tea and laughed. One of his Monroe friends "told me he enjoyed the present life and had better health than he ever had before." The war made them happy.[39]

THE SILENCE STRUCK HIM most, the noiselessness of being lifted to heaven. There was none of the yammering of the machinery of modernity—the familiar chuffing and thrashing of the steamboat, the clacking and shrieking train, the brattle of telegraph clicks. Once the hydrogen-producing apparatus finished inflating the great diaphanous membrane, the balloon lifted into the air without a sound.[40]

Custer occupied a shallow basket, only two feet high, attached to the swollen bag above him by cables that were looped by a metal band at chest height. Professor Thaddeus Lowe, chief aeronaut of the Balloon Corps, crammed into the small vehicle beside him. Not yet thirty, with a walrus mustache and a history of adventure aloft, Lowe had pioneered something new in military history: aerial observation. But the army wanted a professional to go up in Lowe's craft, the *Intrepid*, to take a look at the Confederate line. Custer got the job.[41]

Custer had never imagined that he might someday fly. He later admitted that he was reluctant, if not terrified. At first he remained seated as low as he could get in the little basket as men's heads and then rooftops and then treetops sank below him, as he rose 1,000 feet in the air. He asked if the flimsy-looking basket could possibly be safe. Lowe leaped up and down violently. Custer did not ask again.

Then he noticed the view—the forested, wrinkle-edged Peninsula, extending northwest between the wide James and York rivers. He identified the markers of the Confederate line—Warwick Creek on the left, dammed in several places to turn it into a chain of impassable lakes, and Yorktown on the right, on the shore of the York. The wind repeatedly caught the balloon and knocked it about; but when it died down, "with the assistance of a good field glass," he recalled, he could "catch glimpses of canvas through the openings in the forest. . . . Here and there the dim outline of an earthwork could be seen more than half concealed by the trees . . . while men in considerable numbers were standing in and around the entrenchments, often collected in groups, intently observing the balloon."

The young man sketched the enemy line and camps as best he could. A thought occurred to him: Why not go up at night? Campfires would be visible through the forest canopy. So he came down, delivered his map, and went up alone after dark. But in late April tidewater Virginia was already warm, and the rebels lit few fires. He thought of a new approach. Now a veteran balloonist, he went aloft just before dawn, when fires were lit to cook breakfast. This time he saw the encampments precisely, and made an estimate of Confederate strength.[42]

On May 4 he carried out another such reconnaissance in the early hours of the morning and noticed large flames near Yorktown. He heard distant explosions, like cannons, as might be made by abandoned gunpowder catching fire. As the sun rose, he swept the line with his field glass and saw no movement.

The lieutenant descended and reported to Brig. Gen. William F. Smith, a thirty-eight-year-old West Point graduate. He was nicknamed "Baldy," a joke on his vanity as much as his lack of hair, since he carefully combed some thin strands across the top of his head. The chief of the topographical engineers had detailed Custer to Smith, who commanded a division in Gen. Edwin "Bull" Sumner's II Corps.

Custer found Smith with two escaped slaves, known as "contrabands." (The Union army refused to return runaways to their secessionist owners, calling them "contraband of war.") The pair had already delivered the news. The Confederate line, which the Union army had spent weeks preparing to attack, had been evacuated overnight. The enemy was withdrawing up the Peninsula toward Williamsburg.[43]

Custer confirmed the report and joined the stumbling pursuit. Smith's division advanced over rutted roads that snaked through dense woods. The Union column crept forward, halted, crept forward; confusion reigned. Riding at the forefront, Custer came to Skiffe's Creek, spanned by a burning bridge. He shot at Confederate cavalry on the far side and tried to smother the flames, burning his hands. More Union horsemen helped drive off the enemy and save the bridge.[44]

The road Custer traveled was booby-trapped with torpedoes—hidden or buried artillery shells—known to later generations as land mines. The devices killed a handful of Union soldiers and wounded a dozen more. The outraged federals forced Confederate prisoners to clear them.[45]

Smith gave Custer permission to accompany Brig. Gen. Winfield Scott Hancock, who commanded the division's lead brigade. Hancock was a handsome man with thick, dark, wavy hair, a strong nose, and the seemingly inevitable heavy mustache and goatee. A thirty-eight-year-old West Point graduate and Mexican War veteran, he struck virtually everyone as a consummate professional. The next day he turned down a road to the right, diverging from the main Union advance, guided by contraband reports that the Confederates had abandoned the works on the left of their line. Custer rode ahead of the brigade as they advanced through a steady rain. Guns booming to their left told them that they had arrived on the Confederates' flank.[46]

Hancock moved past the abandoned rebel works and deployed his 3,400 men and eighteen guns. Soldiers in sodden blue uniforms spread out into firing lines, two deep, shoulder to shoulder, in open fields. Crews unlimbered cannons, led horses aside, turned muzzles toward the enemy, broke ammunition out of caissons. Bugles blew, drums pattered, regimental flags moved left and right as units took their places. Hancock sent a staff officer to Smith's headquarters to describe his exposed but advantageous position and request additional troops. The man returned with orders to fall back. But Hancock noticed something through the heavy mist that followed the rain—enemy troops moving in his direction. He told his men to stand their ground and dispatched his last aide to plead for reinforcements.

Custer stepped in to assist Hancock. Together they saw the Confederates approach, lines of figures who clutched four-and-a-half-foot rifled muskets waving like marsh reeds in the wind. Hancock's artillery opened fire, blowing holes in the advancing mass. The Confederates reached a rail fence less than a hundred yards away; the obstacle stalled them amid Union fire. They wavered. Hancock ordered a counterattack. His troops fired two volleys and rushed forward cheering.

Custer plunged forward on horseback along with the infantrymen. The enemy line disintegrated in panic. Custer rode up on a captain and five men, who all surrendered to him—a testament to their demoralization. Eventually it became clear that it was over. The Yankees counted the casualties: 500 enemy dead, wounded, and captured, compared to just 100 for themselves. In the otherwise uncoordinated and indecisive Battle of Williamsburg, Hancock had triumphed.[47]

Custer was just twenty-two. He was lean in his single-breasted junior officer's uniform, with a column of brass buttons rising up the center of his torso to his neck, his curly blond hair cut to a moderate length and parted on the left, his chin bare as he cultivated a mustache-and-cheek-whiskers combination that would soon be associated with Gen. Ambrose Burnside. Externally, Custer was the archetype of an eager young officer. Internally, he was many things.

He was a loyal underling. His assignment to the topographical engineers seemed random, yet he carried out his duties promptly and well. His superiors' reports offered no hint of the self-absorbed miscreant of West Point. And he was a serious professional. His letters home often included military analyses, some quite astute. At Williamsburg he studied Hancock's performance—his self-possession and perfectly timed counterstroke. Custer later wrote an account of the battle that showed how much he appreciated the lesson.

In one respect, though, he remained scarcely more than an adolescent. He lacked any real sense that something bad might happen to him. This is not to belittle his courage; moving toward well-armed men who are trying to kill you is a triumph of will, and should never be underrated. But in all his letters home, he never reflected on the terrible juxtapositions of war, on the unpredictability of death.

As the rebel prisoners were gathered in, Custer saw his old West Point classmate and friend John Lea, a Mississippian nicknamed "Gimlet." Once a partner in pranks and deviling plebes, Gimlet now wore an enemy uniform. A bullet or shell fragment had ripped into his leg. He was helpless.

Lea recognized Custer as he approached. He threw his arms around his Yankee friend and wept. "We talked over old times and asked each other hundreds of questions concerning our classmates who were on opposite sides of the contest," Custer wrote to his sister. He attended to the small needs that mattered enormously in the field, giving Lea new socks, hot food, and some money. At the sight of cash in Custer's hand,

Lea burst into tears once more. So much of his recent life had been virtually identical to Custer's—yet here he was, wounded, captured, defeated, and offered charity. He "said it was more than he could stand," Custer wrote. "He had never expected to be placed under such circumstances." Lea asked for Custer's notebook. He scribbled a message that described how well Custer had cared for him, "saying to me that I might happen to be taken prisoner sometime and wanted me to be treated as well as he had been."

Lea's words were well meant, true kindness returned for true kindness—yet they challenged Custer. You *might be gravely wounded*. You *might be taken prisoner*. You *might be placed in circumstances you never expect*. *It may be more than* you *can stand*. Lea compressed into a few sentences the illusion-shattering power of war.[48]

Custer passed over it without comment. He described the encounter to his sister, but did not reflect on any deeper meaning, at least not outwardly. Amid all his avowals of his willingness to die, never had he addressed the possibility of being shot in the leg, forced to surrender, and wagoned off to a prison camp. He had not pictured himself with an arm severed by a random shell, or dying of dysentery after days of having his bowels run out into his pants and boots and blanket and tent. Lea insisted, with his sad fate and friendly words, that Custer face up to the unpredictable death and illness and injury all around him. Custer saw it, he wrote of it, yet he could not bring himself to examine it, at least not in a way that the world could hear his thoughts. He *knew*, and yet he refused to know.

RAIN FELL. "The water comes down most tropically, in sheets instead of in detached drops," wrote one Union officer, "turning the whole country into a sea of mud." For soldiers who tented on the ground and dressed in wool, rain meant misery. Water pervaded everything. It rotted feet in sodden boots amid the pounding patter of continual downpour. Roads turned into creeks, fields into marshes. Carts and gun carriages sank up to their axles in the mire. In the weeks after Williamsburg, the Army of the Potomac splushed up the Peninsula at a plodding pace toward the Chickahominy, a stream that separated the Union force from Richmond.[49]

In the early morning of May 24, Custer came sneaking up to the river through the dense Virginia woods behind the translucent screen of rain. He came with Lt. Nicolas Bowen, his superior in the topographical engineers. Bowen and Custer had been ordered to guide a squadron of cavalry and 500 men from the 4th Michigan Infantry—including some recruits from Monroe—on a reconnaissance in force ahead of the main body of the army. More senior officers came with them, but the two topographical engineers knew the terrain, having slipped out in recent days to probe the depth of the Chickahominy. They led the troops through the trees, moving toward a ford about half a mile above New Bridge, a crossing that would have to be seized before the assault on Richmond.[50]

They reached the edge of the woods near the river. Custer rushed to the bank with thirty men from the 4th Michigan lumbering behind him, burdened with rifled muskets and cartridge boxes. He plunged into the water and emerged on the other side. Finding the ford unguarded, the infantrymen shook out into a line perpendicular to the river. Custer led them on a sweep toward New Bridge, advancing parallel to the troops remaining on the other bank.

About 400 yards from the bridge, they came upon a camp of Confederates, who hardly expected an attack from their own bank of the river. Custer fired first, igniting a volley from his men. The enemy scrambled about in confusion before they finally aligned themselves into a firing line. Back across the Chickahominy, Col. Dwight Woodbury of the 4th Michigan sent part of his force directly across the river to help Custer's detachment, while the rest sprinted down to the bridge to cut the rebels off. The span had been burned, forcing them to wade across. They killed or captured most of the rebels, then spread out in a ditch parallel to the river amid a heavy rain. Accumulated water rose to their knees, turning the ditch into a canal.

Confederate reinforcements arrived and charged forward in a counterattack. The Union troops opened fire and drove them back. The enemy then rolled up artillery and began a bombardment. Colonel Woodbury suggested that it would be prudent to withdraw. They had captured the enemy camp at the bridge along with thirty-seven prisoners, and had killed twenty-eight Confederates. They lost one dead and seven wounded. The men recrossed the river in good order.

The clash fed a hunger for good news in the army amid its long slog through the mud toward Richmond. One of the soldiers from Monroe sent a letter to a hometown newspaper about the fight. "Lieut. Custer deserves praise for his coolness and bravery," he wrote. "It will do his friends in Monroe good to hear that he is already making his mark so soon after graduating." Bowen wrote in his official report, "Lieutenant Custer was the first to cross the stream, the first to open fire upon the enemy, and one of the last to leave the field." General McClellan himself praised the action in a message that evening to Edwin M. Stanton, the secretary of war: "A very gallant reconnaissance made by Lieutenants Bowen and Custer came upon the Louisiana Tigers, handled them terribly, taking some 50 prisoners and killing and wounding very large numbers."[51]

Not long after the skirmish, Custer received orders to report to McClellan. For the second time in his brief career, the second lieutenant met the most senior general in the U.S. Army (Scott having retired). "I thanked him for his gallantry," McClellan recalled, "and asked what I could do for him."

Custer was taken aback. He was acutely self-conscious as he stood in his worn, muddy uniform within the clean white walls of the headquarters tent, before the impeccably dressed general and his aristocratic assistants. He said he didn't want anything—he had done nothing to deserve a reward. "I then asked if he would like to serve on my personal staff as an aide-de-camp," McClellan wrote. "Upon this he brightened up."

Custer said it was the best reward he could imagine.[52]

Three

THE PROTÉGÉ

For the rest of Custer's life, he would revere a man who was his opposite in every way but one. The single trait they shared would wreck one of their careers and nearly ruin the other.

At twenty-two, Custer remained an outsider. To a certain extent, he did not mind. One of his West Point nicknames had been "Cinnamon," from a bottle of scented hair oil he had brought to the academy; even after he stopped using it his roommate Tully McCrea could still write, "He is the most romantic of men and delights in something odd." But he felt his negligible social status. Within the military, his reputation as a careless, carousing cadet lingered. He dragged along at the bottom of the Regulars' promotion list, thanks to his class ranking. He had been placed in the cavalry, the least-respected branch. He had scarcely seen his regiment, thanks to temporary assignments that left him adrift in the Army of the Potomac.[1]

At the opposite end of the officer corps stood Maj. Gen. George B. McClellan. Only thirty-five, he was a bit short—his nickname was "Little Mac"—and stocky, but powerfully built. He parted his great waves of dark hair on the left, above a broad face, large mustache, and a tuft of hair under his lower lip. His stern, arching eyebrows and hot stare gave the impression of disapproval.

It was an accurate impression. A sense of superiority possessed him, the outgrowth of his status as an intellectual leader of the antebellum army. He had entered West Point at fifteen and graduated second in his class in 1846. He became an engineer—one of the army's elite—and served in the campaign that captured Mexico City in 1847. He authored manuals for the cavalry and bayonet and designed the standard military saddle, which still bears his name. Adept with languages, he sailed to Sevastopol in 1855 as an official observer of the Crimean War and published an influential report. Impeccable in dress as in everything else, he often posed with his right hand tucked in his double-breasted uniform above his gold sword sash, in Napoleonic fashion. "Young Napoleon," in fact, is what his admirers called him. He did not object.

McClellan belonged to the inner circles of society, business, and politics. Born to a respectable Philadelphia family at a time when commercial upstarts were challenging social ranking, he brimmed with genteel prejudices. He left the army in the 1850s to serve as a railroad executive, and began to mingle with true patricians—New York's most distinguished financiers. With his connections, list of achievements, and authentic military and managerial expertise, he had seemed a natural choice to organize the Army of the Potomac out of the jumble of regiments defeated at Bull Run in 1861.[2]

Custer described his feelings for McClellan as "worship." More than anything else, that secured his welcome on the general's staff. The twenty or so men who served in headquarters belonged to spheres far removed from New Rumley. Here were foreign noblemen, including the Prince de Joinville and his nephews, Robert and Louis Philippe d'Orleans (the latter the pretender to the throne of France); John Jacob Astor III of New York; and McClellan's own family—his younger brother, Arthur, and father-in-law, Brig. Gen. Randolph Marcy, an 1832 graduate of West Point who served as chief of staff. Yet all these men shared Custer's devotion to their leader. To them, McClellan was power and glory personified, mastery and genius taken to perfection.[3]

After the general rewarded Custer with a promotion, his staff began to circulate a distorted version of how it happened. This account appeared in Connecticut's *Hartford Courant* a few weeks later, recounted by a correspondent who had learned of it from someone at headquarters. "It seems that Lieut. Custer . . . was riding along the banks of the Chickahominy, with Gen. McClellan and staff," the story went. "The General expressed a desire to know the depth of the stream, when Lieut. Custer immediately slipped from his horse and waded across the river and back again. As he emerged dripping from the water, Gen. McClellan said, Lieut. Custer, consider yourself upon my own personal staff, with the rank of Captain."[4]

This rendering stripped the young lieutenant of his actual heroics, his combat leadership in a daylong firefight, in order to place the general at the scene. (Prior to the skirmish Custer had, in fact, tested the depth of the river under the supervision of Brig. Gen. John Barnard, the Army of the Potomac's chief engineer.) The revised anecdote pictured McClellan the way his staff imagined him, the way he imagined himself: the commanding general at the forefront of his army, confronting the enemy and natural obstacles. And it depicted him recognizing and rewarding valor in the field. "Thus you observe that, like Napoleon, our little General sometimes rewards merit upon the instant," the correspondent declared. For

McClellan and his aides, the important thing about promoting Custer was not Custer, but the act itself.[5]

The staff's identification with the general was natural, of course. In the idiom of the time, it was his "military family," making him the father. And he was a genuinely charismatic, magnetic man. But neither he nor his aides tolerated dissent. As the historian Richard Slotkin writes, "McClellan's headquarters was a closed circle, an echo chamber filled with followers and acolytes who praised his every decision as masterful."[6]

They reinforced the general's considerable self-esteem by, for example, stage-managing his appearances before the army. "You have no idea how the men brighten up now, when I go among them—I can see every eye glisten," McClellan wrote to his wife, Ellen. The staff traveled with a portable printing press to distribute his orders and exhortations, which bulged with histrionic phrases and exclamation points.

Awash in praise, McClellan relished his reputation for genius—what a less admiring officer called his "claimed extraordinary judgment." He compared himself to George Washington, noting that he, too, had critics: "All now see that he was right, & I trust that the time will come when it will be equally evident to all that I was right in doing as I did." He even considered himself the hand of God. "I can almost think of myself as a chosen instrument to carry out his schemes," he admitted to General Burnside. "I feel that God has placed a great work in my hands," he wrote Ellen. "My previous life seems to have been unwittingly directed to this great end."[7]

Ironically, his belief that he was a tool of the Almighty reflected fatalism, a sense that he lacked any control over his future. His fears exaggerated his methodical approach to warfare, for he was an engineer by both instinct and training. If Custer never seemed to consider the risks of his actions, McClellan thought of little else.[8]

The movement to the Peninsula looked brilliant on the map—a grand outflanking of the Confederate army that put Union troops within easy striking distance of the enemy capital. But even this maneuver emerged out of McClellan's caution. If beaten, he argued, the Army of the Potomac would enjoy "a perfectly safe retreat down the Peninsula ... with our flanks perfectly covered by the fleet." Forced to take the offensive, he conducted it as an engineering exercise, a methodical advance from one fortified position to another, relying upon heavy artillery.[9]

His aides shared his idiosyncratic combination of technical competence and near paranoia. They organized, equipped, and supplied an army vastly larger than any the United States had operated prior to the Civil War. In this they took advantage of the Regular Army's highly professional Quartermaster's Department.[10]

But dread always lurked. It was personified by the private detective Allan Pinkerton. McClellan hired him to collect intelligence on the enemy. Pinkerton provided plenty of it, all wildly inaccurate. When the rebel army occupied the Yorktown line, it numbered 56,500, but Pinkerton counted 100,000 to 120,000. In late May, reinforcements raised enemy numbers to 75,000; Pinkerton listed 150,000. But all blame cannot be placed on the detective. For McClellan, enemy superiority had become a fixed idea. "All accounts report their numbers as greatly exceeding our own," he wrote to President Lincoln on May 21. Even when promised 41,000 more troops under General McDowell, he felt doomed.[11]

His fears made him angry. All his life he had bristled at those in authority over him; now his very proximity to the highest point of power magnified his resentments. He called Secretary of War Stanton "without exception the vilest man I ever knew or heard of." He scorned Lincoln as "an idiot," a "gorilla," or, when feeling generous, "a well meaning baboon." The day after Custer joined his staff, McClellan wrote to his wife about Lincoln. "It is perfectly sickening to deal with such people & you may rest assured that I will lose as little time as possible in breaking off all connection with them."[12]

Breaking off all connection with them: it was a strange thing to say, as he had no plans to resign. McClellan spent a great deal of time writing furtive letters to certain politicians in New York, even as his inner circle cultivated newspaper editors. They were preparing a second campaign, not against Richmond but against Washington.

Already the results could be seen in the partisan newspapers read by Emmanuel Custer, who once had voiced disappointment in McClellan. They sent a message, and Emmanuel understood it. "I am a Mcleland man," he wrote to Armstrong, "and I want to have him tryumph over all his enemys."[13]

THE CONFEDERATE LOOKS RESIGNED in the photograph. He sits erect in a short, gray, single-breasted jacket with dark piping and shoulder straps—the jacket of a junior officer. His legs are spread apart, feet and calves clad in long cavalry boots, and a forage cap slouches on his head. He looks with sad dignity into the distance. On his left sits a self-consciously jaunty figure in a short, blue, single-breasted jacket with shoulder straps—also the jacket of a junior officer—with a tie tufting out over the collar. One fist rests on the second man's right thigh, elbow up, and he leans slightly forward, his left forearm thrown across the other thigh; he too wears cavalry boots. He sits on a box turned up on its side. He has no hat on his head of curly blond hair, no beard on his chin below a continuous crescent of mustache and cheek whiskers. Looking confident, even cocky, he stares directly at the camera with light blue eyes.

The figure in gray is Lt. James B. Washington, and the man in blue is his West Point classmate, Custer. The photographer, James F. Gibson, an employee of Mathew Brady's famous studio, encountered them chatting after the Battle of Fair Oaks (or Seven Pines, as the Confederates called it). The two were aides to the respective commanding generals—Custer to McClellan, Washington to Lt. Gen. Joseph E. Johnston. The results of the battle could be seen in their faces.

Johnston had tried to cripple the Army of the Potomac before McClellan could move all of it over the Chickahominy and bring his enormous siege guns to bear on Richmond. On May 31, with Union forces still divided by the flooding river, Johnston had attacked the wing on the south side. Union reinforcements had struggled across and stopped the Confederates with heavy losses. A second attack on June 1 did no better. Johnston himself was wounded and his aide Washington captured.[14]

Custer had not made a special friend of Washington at West Point, though he had warm relations with the Southern cadets. One reason for Custer's outrage at John Brown's raid on Harper's Ferry was that Brown had captured Washington's father. And, as with Lea, it gave Custer pleasure to show kindness to a captured classmate.[15]

The image of two officers from the opposing armies, both good-looking young men in smart new uniforms, appealed to the photographer, but he thought something—someone—was missing. Gibson brought this individual over and sat him on the ground between Washington's boots, then took another photograph. This third figure looks uncomfortable; he is enduring this moment. He wears worn, dirty pants and a collarless shirt of coarse cloth. He has his fingers locked around his knees; a second pair of pants pokes out from under the cuffs of the outer pair. He has no shoes or socks. His right foot is bandaged. He looks down at his toes with his brow slightly furrowed, his black hair short-cropped. He looks no older than twelve. He leaves the impression that he has lived through a nightmare.[16]

The third figure is a slave—an escaped slave, to be precise. The photograph of the three would circulate with the title "Both Sides and the Cause," elevating the boy to the central role, but in the image he is no more than a prop. The two officers ignore him. And not merely in this photograph: Custer rarely mentioned black people in his surviving correspondence.

"You must not run them down so they are a '*splendid institution*,' " wrote Marie Miller, a young woman in Monroe, to her friend Custer. Her comment is a fleeting but telling indication of how he viewed slaves, or African Americans in general. Marie no more considered them full-fledged human beings than Custer did. "Why of course I was in earnest asking you to send me a contraband," she wrote, as if they were pets or souvenirs. "I want a *girl*, about 12 or 14, black as black *can be*, with long curly hair etc. in fact a *perfect negress.*"

This was flippant chatter in a lighthearted note, of course. She and Custer teased and flirted, and she wanted to know more about his attraction to Nellie Van Wormer. "*Tell me about her* Armstrong. You know I am your 'confidant' now. *Please* tell me is *she the one.*" Yet her joke about the contraband speaks to the racial attitudes of Monroe and the North in general; she was not the only Northern woman who wrote of shipping a black girl home like livestock. Marie imagined a "negress" as an object, not a child with parents and hopes and needs and ambitions of her own.[17]

Such views were common, even prevalent, in the Army of the Potomac. Enslaved people ran to freedom as soon as they could; they flooded Union camps, "leaving plows standing in the fields," one historian writes. But contrabands often met hostility. There was mockery; in the "game of astonishment" soldiers told wild lies in order to laugh at their credulity. There was exclusion; a newspaper published by the 5th Pennsylvania flatly stated that its "Union" and "Freedom" motto covered "white folks" only. There was cruelty, as seen in the 99th New York, rumored to be selling runaways back to their masters for $20 to $50 each, and in the ads for escaped slaves in soldier-run newspapers. And there was callousness, witnessed whenever troops grabbed a black child and tossed him or her in a blanket, just as upperclassmen deviled plebes at West Point. The men of the 5th Maryland did so one day, and discovered that the blanket was rotten when the boy they tossed fell straight through and broke his neck.[18]

And yet a countertrend slowly gained strength. "I thought I hated slavery as much as possible before I came here," a Pennsylvania soldier wrote, "but here, where I can see some of its workings, I am more than ever convinced of the cruelty and inhumanity of the system." Men from Massachusetts, the great hotbed of abolitionism, proved especially protective of runaways. Even the 8th Michigan "pounced" on a slaveholder, a lieutenant wrote. "He got well frightened, & I presume will think twice before he goes into a Camp of northern soldiers to reclaim biped property."[19]

Sincere compassion contributed to this growing antislavery feeling, but much of it was practical. The flow of contrabands drained the Confederates' labor force and enhanced Union strength; many went to work for the army, freeing troops to fight. They provided valuable intelligence; every time Custer had encountered contrabands with information, they had been proved right. And many Union soldiers were concluding that the war would never end until slavery was destroyed.[20]

But any hierarchical organization adopts the tone set by its leader, especially when that organization was what McClellan called "my army." As Richard Slotkin writes, "The Army of the Potomac was McClellan's hearth and refuge, a perfect social order created by himself, an extension of his identity." *His* army absorbed *his* views, which were blunt. As he later told his father-in-law, "I confess to a prejudice in favor of my own race, & can't learn to like the odor of either Billy Goats or Niggers."[21]

"Help me to dodge the nigger—we want nothing to do with him," McClellan wrote early in the war. "*I* am fighting to preserve the integrity of the Union & the power of the Govt—on no other issue. To gain that end we cannot afford to raise up the negro question." More than a personal declaration, this was a political statement about the goals of the war, one that accepted the legitimacy of human bondage.[22]

It was a dangerous thing to say, though not because Lincoln had a different policy. The South seceded to protect slavery, but the federal government did *not* go to war to destroy it. It fought because one region of the country had rejected the results of a national election and rebelled; Lincoln defended not only America's territorial integrity, but the integrity of the democratic process, the essence of free government itself. And the president had to preserve the loyalty of the border slave states— Missouri, Kentucky, Maryland, and Delaware—and conservative troops in the army. He wished to cultivate dormant Unionists in the South. Artilleryman Charles Wainwright captured the dilemma in his diary: if the president "makes it an abolition war, there will be an end to the Union party at the South, and I for one shall be sorry that I ever lent a hand to it." Lincoln personally hated slavery, but he could not have disagreed with the policy expressed in McClellan's crude statement.[23]

What made McClellan's letter dangerous was the man who received it: Samuel Latham Mitchell Barlow, one of a trio of friends McClellan had made during his years as a railroad executive in the 1850s, all aristocratic financiers who presided over Manhattan's genteel society. Barlow was McClellan's most active contact. Born in 1826, he collected rare books and served as a director and attorney for some of the largest corporations in the country. His specialty was diplomacy and the closed-room negotiation. A more powerful friend was William H. Aspinwall. Born in 1807, he dispatched square-rigged merchantmen over the world's oceans, and was the organizing spirit behind the Pacific Mail Steamship Company, which (thanks to negotiations by Barlow) now shared a monopoly on traffic to California with Cornelius Vanderbilt. Aspinwall built one of the first private art galleries in Manhattan, as did the third member of the group, August Belmont. Born in Germany in 1816, Belmont had come to New York in 1837 as agent for the Rothschilds. A banker, corporate financier, and patron of the arts, he served as national chairman of the Democratic Party. All three men were leaders of the party, which was largely directed from New York.[24]

When McClellan wrote to these men, he intrigued with the political opposition to the commander in chief of the armed forces of the United States. He wanted their help in controlling wartime policy, to maintain a limited conflict between formal armies with as little impact on Southern society as possible.[25]

It's an open question whether Custer, the junior officer on staff, knew anything about McClellan's correspondence with Democratic leaders. He kept busy outside of headquarters, often going aloft in the observation balloon as the army crept closer to Richmond in the month after Seven Pines. His energy won over other members of the staff; the Prince de Joinville later wrote that he "entertained so high an opinion of him, from the first day I met him, that I am proud of his achievements." Custer *was* far enough inside McClellan's circle to see Pinkerton's intelligence reports—and he shared his commander's faith in them. And he and McClellan shared something deep in each of them: politics.[26]

McClellan's hostility to the White House pervaded his headquarters, as did his political intrigue. He "talked very freely of the way in which he had been treated," Gen. George Meade wrote, after Lincoln diverted McDowell's corps from the Army of the Potomac in order to cope with Confederate Gen. Thomas J. "Stonewall" Jackson in the Shenandoah Valley. McClellan dispatched his most trusted subordinate, Gen. Fitz-John Porter, to encourage the editor of the *New York World* to challenge the administration. "I wish you would put the question," Porter said. "Does the President . . . design to cause defeat here for the purpose of prolonging the war." Prolonging the war, he implied, would turn it into an abolitionist crusade.[27]

McClellan, supremely cautious in fighting the enemy, grew reckless in his struggle with his political superiors. What he may not have grasped was that he would have to win on the battlefield to win in Washington. And tied to his future was that of his youngest aide, George Armstrong Custer.[28]

CUSTER ROAMED THE VAST CITY that was the Army of the Potomac, riding alone as his master's voice and his master's eyes and ears. His position in headquarters allowed him to see the entire strategic picture. He grasped the importance of the Chickahominy, which flowed southeast, bisecting the Peninsula until it turned south to the James River, drawing an arc north and east of Richmond. He knew that four of the army's five corps had now crossed to the south side of the Chickahominy, where they were preparing a line of redoubts for the siege of Richmond, and that Brig. Gen. Fitz-John Porter's V Corps remained on the north bank to guard the supply line. When Ann and David Reed came to visit him (a sign of the army's creeping pace), he hinted at his inside knowledge. "You know my rule has always been to disclose nothing whatever connected with *future* movements," he said.[29]

On June 26, he mounted his fine black horse and crossed to the north bank. There trains chuffed and clacked down the Richmond and York River Railroad from landings on the York and Pamunkey rivers, where flotillas of ships unloaded oats and hardtack and boots and belts and cookware and ammunition and all the other countless things an army needed in the field, mountained into Himalayan supply depots. Custer rode through V Corps's sprawling boroughs of dirty white dog tents— inverted Vs of canvas on sticks—until he found the 1st Michigan Infantry camp, where he hoped to see friends.

He heard gunfire. He rode toward it, west to Beaver Dam Creek, which shielded the western front of V Corps. Custer found the Pennsylvania Reserves, a division under Brig. Gen. George A. McCall, dug in on the eastern bank. Union pickets hustled back over the creek. They reported that the Confederates were approaching in force.[30]

"The ball was opened," Custer wrote—soldiers' slang for the start of a battle. He rode to search for McClellan, and found him listening to the gunfire. I know what it means, he told Custer: the start of a rebel counteroffensive. A contraband had come into Union lines with news that Stonewall Jackson had arrived from the Shenandoah Valley with an overwhelming force, ready to attack the Union right flank. *Of course* he would, McClellan thought; without McDowell's corps, he believed he lacked the strength to protect his exposed railroad supply line.[31]

McClellan spoke briefly to Custer, who rode back across the Chickahominy to the Pennsylvania Reserves. He told General McCall that McClellan only wanted his men to hold until dark, and "expected them to maintain the honor of Pennsylvania in that fight." McCall replied, "Tell the general he shall not be disappointed." Custer then galloped to the creek and rode down the line, going from regiment to regiment to repeat McClellan's appeal to their state's honor. Cheers rose in response, cheers thrown up for the commanding general but caught by Custer.[32]

In late afternoon, Confederate soldiers came out of the woods across the creek, stumbling over felled trees, and were slaughtered by Union fire. Wave after wave clambered forward, only to disintegrate in a torrent of bullet, shot, and shell. McClellan eventually joined Custer and McCall on the field and watched a victory unfold.[33]

With the battle still raging, McClellan sent Custer to look for Gen. John Barnard, the army's chief engineer. He found him a short distance to the rear. Earlier in the day, when McClellan still had no idea of how the battle might go, he had ordered Barnard to make plans for a much smaller bridgehead on the northern bank of the Chickahominy. Custer rode up and asked for Barnard's map. With a pencil he drew a line enclosing high ground just past the home of a Dr. Gaines. Here, he said, General McClellan wants you to lay out defensive positions in this location.[34]

What Custer already knew—and most Union generals did not—was that McClellan had decided upon a "change of base." Despite complete victory at Beaver Dam Creek (the Battle of Mechanicsville to the Confederates), McClellan believed that the Confederate Army of Northern Virginia numbered more than 200,000 men, roughly double his own force, enough to smash his supply line. So he elected to switch his base to the James River—to march his army across the Richmond front to the south side of the Peninsula. After a rearguard stand, the north bank of the Chickahominy would be abandoned, the remaining supplies destroyed, and the railroad given up to the enemy.

The truth was that he was allowing himself to be chased off by a smaller army, about 87,000 men to his 105,000. "Change of base" sounded like a step toward a renewed offensive, "yet in truth he was quitting his grand campaign, surrendering the initiative and giving up all hope of laying siege to Richmond from the line of the Chickahominy," writes the historian Stephen Sears. Only the railroad could carry the siege guns that McClellan relied on; abandoning it, he abandoned the offensive.[35]

McClellan ordered Porter to pull V Corps back to the lines Barnard had laid out. Custer remained in the saddle all night as tens of thousands of troops marched and trains whistled and screeched in the darkness, hauling away supplies. The next day McClellan brooded in his headquarters tent south of the Chickahominy. The telegraph rattled with reports from the various corps commanders, especially Porter. At 2:30 p.m. the Confederates again attacked V Corps; the assaults grew heavier. "I am pressed hard, very hard," Porter wired at 5 p.m. But McClellan feared that the rebels would advance out of Richmond and crush him in a pincer. He little realized that Robert E. Lee, now in command of Confederate forces, had taken a huge risk, sending 55,000 men against Porter's reinforced 35,000, leaving only 27,000 rebels inside Richmond, where they put on a show of force to immobilize the 70,000 Union troops south of the river. McClellan ordered a mere two brigades, some 6,000 men, to march to Porter's aid. He sent Custer to guide them. He himself remained at his desk as the crisis unfolded.[36]

The young captain had eaten little more than some hard bread crumbled into his coffee that morning, but he swung up into the saddle on his black horse and rode to find the reinforcements. He led them through the deepening afternoon, across the swaying Grapevine Bridge that sloshed just above the surface of the Chickahominy, into a meadow beyond. They ran into mobs of Union soldiers fleeing the enemy.

The line had broken. Porter's corps was in full retreat. Brig. Gen. William H. French, commander of the reinforcing brigades, marched his troops up to the crest of the plateau that dominated the position. They opened fire on the advancing enemy, halting the onslaught. Custer's own 5th Cavalry charged—without him, of course. Of two hundred enlisted men and seven officers who attacked, he wrote, "only one hundred and forty-five men and *one* officer returned unhurt." One missing officer was a friend from West Point; only his horse came back, and "the saddle was covered with blood."[37]

The enemy attack exhausted itself, but it had shattered the Union position irreparably. Custer spent another night on horseback, helping to get the walking wounded across the river as the V Corps abandoned the north bank. He rode among the clots of bandaged, bleeding men in the lantern-dotted darkness. The bridges would soon be destroyed, he said; they all would be captured if they did not hurry. We're waiting for the ambulances, came a reply. "No ambulances are coming," Custer said.

"Who says no ambulances are coming for us?" someone asked. Custer recognized the voice. It belonged to Julius Adams of Kentucky, a classmate and former roommate from West Point. Custer came over and told him that the battle was lost and they had to cross the river immediately. Adams replied that he was too badly wounded; he could neither walk nor ride. You'll have to leave me behind, he said. "I told him I would not cross the river without him," Custer wrote two weeks later. He swung to the ground, tied his horse to a tree, and ordered four unhurt men to help him break a gate off a nearby fence. They eased Adams onto the gate and carried him over the bridge and a couple of miles to Savage's Station, as Custer rode alongside. Here the V Corps "train"—its herd of supply wagons—was gathered. Custer left Adams, assuming he would be carried along when the wagons moved out the next morning.

The next day Custer came back and found the train gone but Adams still there, alone. "I told him there was now no chance for him," Custer wrote. "He must make up his mind to be taken prisoner. He received this announcement as became a soldier and asked for my little order book to write a few lines to his Mother and to his Sweet-heart." Custer promised to transcribe the notes and mail them. He said good-bye.[38]

The Army of the Potomac's rear guard repelled another Confederate attack, only to continue retreating. McClellan left behind a field hospital with some 2,500 wounded men at Savage's Station, along with doctors who volunteered to remain. McClellan marched his army south, allowing his corps commanders to manage the battles of Glendale the next day and Malvern Hill the day after that—the final clash in what became known as the Seven Days' Battles.[39]

"The success of the movement throughout was all that could be asked and much more than could reasonably be expected," Custer wrote to his sister. But the "change of base," or "flank movement," as Custer called it, confused many of the men. They knew they had repelled every rebel attack except the one at Gaines's Mill, yet after each victory they had retreated.[40]

McClellan had wrung defeat out of victories, at great cost to his men. "The thirty thousand men killed and wounded in the Seven Days' equaled the number of casualties in *all* the battles in the Western theater—including Shiloh—during the first half of 1862," writes the historian James M. McPherson. Two-thirds of those casualties were rebels, but the Union's 10,000 meant grim suffering among survivors and in homes of the dead.[41]

"I lost several friends in the various engagements and lament their loss," Custer wrote to his sister. "It is better to die an honored death than to live in dishonor." These words should not be lightly dismissed. They came from a man who won respect for his courage, who did his utmost to save a badly wounded friend. "In those days Custer was simply a reckless, gallant boy, undeterred by fatigue, unconscious of fear," McClellan later wrote; "but his head was always clear in danger, and he always brought me clear and intelligible reports of what he saw when under the heaviest fire."

Yet even Custer must have known that "death before dishonor" was too neat a formula. Take his friend Adams, for example. There was no clean battlefield death for him, no glorious final moment with an enemy flag in his hand. He lingered, apparently shot through the chest. He either escaped capture or was exchanged and spent most of 1862 on sick leave. Each time he tried to return to duty, the pain and complications of his injuries drove him back to his bed. He went on the line for the first three days of July 1863, then to the hospital; quiet harbor duty followed, then three days with the Army of the Potomac in June 1864, then sick leave again. Knowing he could never fight again, he resigned from the officer corps on June 29. Having suffered for three years from his wounds, he finally died of them on November 15, 1865, at the age of twenty-five.[42]

A VOICE CALLED OUT TO CUSTER, telling him to come see the observation balloon. He stepped out of the large tent that he shared with three other officers and his dogs and looked up. It was aloft, floating over the Union encampment. He found his field glass in his hand, so he put its twin lenses to his eyes. He was stunned to see two young women from Monroe seated in the basket—women in whom he had a certain interest. He dropped his field glass and ran to the balloon's base a short distance away. "*Let me go up too*," he begged the men in charge of it. They agreed. In a moment he somehow reached the basket high above, "but my friends had gone, much to my disappointment."

He awoke. Unusually, he remembered the dream. "I always deal with realities," he wrote to his sister. "I am not a believer in dreams"—unlike his mother—"but on the contrary think it absurd to pay any attention to them."[43] The more he disavowed any significance, the more he implied that the dream haunted him. Two attractive young women appear in his most isolated post, a basket in the air; he suddenly, inexplicably, rises to that great height; they vanish the instant he reaches them. He corners what he desires, yet it escapes him, leaving him bewildered and alone.

When he stepped outside of his tent in the morning—awake, this time—he found himself at Harrison's Landing, the James River bivouac where the Army of the Potomac had retreated after the victory at Malvern Hill. McClellan established his headquarters at Berkeley Plantation, virtually the birthplace of the slaveholding aristocracy in the South. Out of respect, McClellan did not occupy the brick manor house, but ordered tents erected on the grounds. There he brooded on his enemies in the administration.[44]

Just after the Battle of Gaines's Mill, McClellan had sent a remarkable telegram to Secretary Stanton. "If I save this Army now I tell you plainly that I owe no thanks to you or any other persons in Washington—you have done your best to sacrifice this Army." He knew his accusation was shocking, but, he wrote to his wife, Lincoln was "entirely too smart to give my correspondence to the public—it would have ruined him & Stanton forever." His delusion was not tested. In Washington the telegraph supervisor excised that last sentence, and so McClellan's anger grew unchecked.[45]

On July 8, in stifling heat and humidity, Lincoln came to Harrison's Landing. McClellan and staff, including Custer, met his steamer at the pier and conducted him on a review of the army. Afterward the general and the president sat together under an awning on the deck of Lincoln's vessel. McClellan handed the president a letter. Lincoln opened it and read as the general waited.[46]

"I earnestly desire . . . to lay before your excellency, for your private consideration, my general views concerning the existing state of the rebellion," McClellan wrote.

It should not be a war looking to the subjugation of the people of any State in any event. It should not be at all a war upon population, but against armed forces and political organizations. Neither confiscation of property, political executions of persons, territorial organization of States, or forcible abolition of slavery should be contemplated for a moment. . . . Military power should not be allowed to interfere with the relations of servitude, either by supporting or impairing the authority of the master.

He argued that the owners of contrabands should be compensated. And he backed his political lecture with an implicit threat: "A declaration of radical views, especially upon slavery, will rapidly disintegrate our present armies."[47]

Lincoln said nothing, a silence that McClellan took as vindication. The general even saw his defeat as a fine thing, reversing his earlier analysis. "God has helped me, or rather has helped my army & country," he told his wife on July 10. "If I had succeeded in taking Richmond now the fanatics of the North might have been too powerful & reunion impossible." He wrote to Samuel L. M. Barlow, the Democratic Party insider, "I have lost all regard & respect for the majority of the administration, & doubt the propriety of my brave men's blood being spilled to further the designs of such a set of heartless villains."[48]

The self-absorbed general did not see the rising anger at his performance, in the North and even in his own army. Senator Zachariah Chandler of Michigan, an influential Radical on the Joint Committee on the Conduct of the War, wrote to his wife on July 6, "I can hold my temper no longer & *will not try*. . . . McLelland is an *awful* humbug & deserves to be shot." McClellan airily wrote to Barlow, "I do not think it best to reply to the lies of such a fellow as Chandler—he is beneath my notice."[49]

McClellan also misread Lincoln. The recent setbacks had convinced the president that victory required farther-reaching policies. On July 13, he told two cabinet members, "We must free the slaves or be ourselves subdued. The slaves were undeniably an element of strength to those who had their service, and we must decide whether that element should be with us or against us."[50] But McClellan was blind to these shifts in politics—and blind to himself as well.

Custer was more complicated. In the weeks that followed Lincoln's visit, he did two things that illustrated his inner contradictions—actions that were true to himself, yet pointed to two very different possible futures.

One of his deeds was to take part in a Confederate wedding. His old friend John "Gimlet" Lea had been paroled after the Battle of Williamsburg—allowed to go free as long as he did not return to military service before being formally exchanged. Prisoners on both sides obeyed the terms of paroles with remarkable faithfulness. Custer had heard that a family in Williamsburg was caring for his badly wounded friend, and McClellan gave permission to go to look for him.

Custer found Lea restored to health. Lea said that he was engaged to the daughter of his host—"very beautiful to say the least," Custer wrote—and asked Custer to serve as best man. He agreed. During the wedding ceremony they stood together in uniform, one in blue and one in gray, opposite the bride and her attractive cousin Maggie. As Custer escorted Maggie out of the room, he told her she couldn't be a very strong secessionist to agree to take the arm of a Union officer. *"You ought to be in our army,"* she said. "I asked her what she would give me if I would resign in the Northern army and join the Southern," he wrote. She replied, "You are not in earnest, are you?"

He remained with Lea for two weeks, flirting with Maggie. The four spent each evening in the parlor, playing cards or listening to Maggie on the piano, playing "Dixie," "For Southern Rights Hurrah," and other rebel tunes. Custer did not mind; he was more interested in her beauty than her politics. In a sense, though, his very presence was political, in a way McClellan fully endorsed.[51]

The other thing he did set a different tone, an implacable tone. "He vowed that he would not cut his hair until he entered Richmond," Tully McCrea wrote to a friend. "You may think from this that he is a vain man, but he is not; it is nothing more than his penchant for oddity. . . . He is a gallant soldier." He would let his curly blond hair grow and grow until the Union achieved total victory—a sign that he *wanted* total victory, a sign that became more visible with each day.[52]

"CAPTAIN! CAPTAIN!" Custer heard the cry from the far side of some nearby bushes. It was the bugler, still just a boy. "Two secesh are after me!" Custer reined his horse around and found the lad firing his carbine at two Confederates approaching on horseback. Custer drew his revolver and spurred toward them.

It was August 5, 1862, on the Peninsula. Two days earlier he had crossed the James River on a raid with Col. William W. Averell, who commended him for his "impetuous dash."[53] Now he rode with Averell again in a probe of the rebels near White Oak Swamp. He and about 400 Union cavalrymen had charged a few dozen troopers of the 10th Virginia Cavalry, dispersing them. Custer had galloped off to the left after some escaping Confederates, away from the main body, when he heard the bugler.

Seeing Custer, the two rebels turned and fled. Custer rode one of them down; at his call to surrender, the Confederate hesitated, then reined in his horse and handed over his carbine. Custer took him back to the rest of his detachment and put him under guard, then rode out again, accompanied by a lieutenant and ten men. "We had not gone far until we saw an officer and fifteen or twenty men riding toward us with the intention of cutting their way through and joining their main body," he wrote. "When they saw us coming toward them however, they wheeled suddenly to the left and attempted to gallop around us."

Custer picked out the officer and spurred his fine black horse into a gallop. The rebel's mount was at least as fast, so Custer angled to cut him off at a rail fence ahead. The Confederate jumped his horse cleanly over it. Custer followed, his own horse clearing the top rail. He had never felt such a surge of adrenaline—"exciting in the extreme," he wrote. The enemy landed on soft ground, wet after a recent rain, which slowed his progress. Custer guided his horse to more solid footing and rapidly drew closer, hooves thudding the earth, freshly loaded revolver in hand.

Surrender, he yelled. *Surrender or I will shoot.* "He paid no attention," Custer wrote. He fired and missed. "I again called on him to surrender, but received no reply." He cocked his revolver—the six chambers in its cylinder hand-packed with lead balls, powder charges, and percussion caps—and leveled the barrel as he rode. "I took deliberate aim at his body and fired." The hammer snapped down on the percussion cap, sparking the gunpowder, which exploded in a jet of flame and smoke, propelling the ball on a spiraling path through the rifled barrel until it burst out of the muzzle. The other rider suddenly relaxed, sat upright in his saddle for an instant, and toppled heavily to the ground.

Now Custer's strange sense of isolation, his temporary tunnel universe of only him and his prey, evaporated. His party appeared all around him, firing wildly at the rest of the escaping Confederates. The bugle call of "rally"—the command to return to the main force—warbled through the trees. Custer spotted a cluster of five riderless horses. He recognized a bright bay, a "blooded" thoroughbred. An exceptional straight steel sword swung from a black morocco saddle ornamented with silver nails and a red morocco breast strap. It was the horse of his victim, "a perfect beauty." Custer took its rein and led it behind him. "A splendid trophy," he wrote.

He did not see the man he had shot. The lieutenant who fought with Custer "told me that he saw him after he fell, and that he rose to his feet, turned around, threw up his hands and fell to the ground with a stream of blood gushing from his mouth."

Again Averell commended Custer, for his "gallant and spirited conduct." But this skirmish was unique. It was the first time he had killed a man—rather, that he *knew* he had killed a man. He had ridden in charges and ordered at least one himself; he had shot at the enemy and commanded that volleys be fired; but never had he selected an individual and destroyed his life. He had passed through a doorway with no return.

"It was his own fault," he explained to his sister and brother-in-law. "I told him twice to surrender, but was compelled to shoot him." He was answering a silent question—a question no one had asked but himself. Often he had expressed his willingness to die for his country; though not a devout man, his statements reflected the faith in which he had been raised, a religion that worshipped Him who had given His life that others may live. But Custer had never written about killing. It was a soldier's defining function, of course, what set him apart from the civilian, even the constable, detective, or armed guard. Now he faced its reality.

The enemy soldier had been riding away, trying to escape. Custer tracked him, calculated his approach, and took careful aim. He shot him in the back. He had picked a man and erased his memories, canceled his hopes. He had wiped from existence his victim's taste for his favorite food, his habit of how he wore his hat, his superstitions, his most secret fear, the way he laughed. He took the man from his parents and children and friends forever. *I tried not to kill him,* Custer told himself. *I tried twice. And then I had no choice.* Whether the answer satisfied him or not, he never asked the question again.[54]

"I AM WEARY, very weary, of submitting to the whims of such '*things*' as those now over me," McClellan wrote to Samuel Barlow. To his wife, Ellen, he wrote, "I can never regard him [Lincoln] with other feelings than those of thorough contempt—for his mind, heart & morality." The cause of these outbursts was the president's appointment of Maj. Gen. Henry W. Halleck as general in chief. "It is intended as 'a slap in the face,'" McClellan complained. "I do not like the political turn that affairs are taking."[55]

By now Custer belonged to the inner circle. McClellan said that he trusted "the really serious work, especially under fire," only to a handful of professional officers, a few foreign soldiers, and "some youngsters I have caught," including Custer. The young captain and the rest of the staff raged against the formation of the Army of Virginia under Maj. Gen.

John Pope, who launched an overland offensive against Richmond. They hated Halleck's appointment, and stormed against his order that McClellan withdraw the Army of the Potomac from the Peninsula in order to aid Pope. They began to mutter about marching on Washington.[56]

This shocked those outside headquarters. General Burnside visited Harrison's Landing with Halleck in July; as McClellan's old friend, he heard such chatter himself. "I don't know what you fellows call this talk, but I call it flat Treason, by God!" he told them. Gen. Philip Kearny wrote, "McClellan or the few with him are devising a game of politics rather than war."[57]

In August McClellan slowly, grudgingly withdrew from the Peninsula and shipped his men north. He personally set sail on August 23. With the threat to Richmond lifted, Robert E. Lee turned his Army of Northern Virginia against Pope's Army of Virginia with full force. On Halleck's orders, General Fitz-John Porter marched his corps to reinforce Pope, starting a process of whittling down the Army of the Potomac.

McClellan despised Pope, who took a much harder line toward secessionism and rebel civilians. He "will be very badly whipped," McClellan wrote, "& ought to be." With the Army of Virginia fully embroiled in a second battle of Bull Run, McClellan advised Lincoln "to leave Pope to get out of his scrape & at once use all our means to make the Capital perfectly safe." It was a stunning display of self-absorption. Whatever Pope's failings, if reinforced in time he might have avoided the crushing defeat he suffered in the battle. Lincoln called McClellan's delays "unpardonable."[58]

On September 1, McClellan arrived in Washington. There Custer joined him, having left the Peninsula only recently, after tarrying with Lea. Some 20,000 stragglers from Pope's shattered army wandered the countryside. Halleck, now in great distress, removed McClellan from command of the Army of the Potomac and put him in charge of the city's defenses. Stanton wanted him fired. Treasury Secretary Salmon P. Chase privately remarked, "McClellan ought to be shot."[59]

September 1 also saw a flanking attack by Stonewall Jackson on the Army of Virginia at the town of Chantilly. General Kearny died as he led a successful defense. "Unless something can be done to restore tone to this army it will melt away before you know it," Pope reported. The capital itself was in peril. Lincoln saw no choice. He told the cabinet that he could not spare McClellan, not in this crisis. "We must use the tools we have," Lincoln said. "If he can't fight himself, he excels in making others ready to fight." At about seven o'clock on the cold and windy morning of September 2, Lincoln and Halleck walked over to McClellan's rooms on H Street and offered him command again. If he accepted, the Army of Virginia would be absorbed into the Army of the Potomac, which he would lead. He agreed.

"I immediately went to work, collected my staff, and started them in all directions with the necessary orders," McClellan wrote. Word came that Lee's Army of Northern Virginia was marching into western Maryland. If left unopposed, Lee might outflank Washington, capture a major city, perhaps even win foreign recognition of Confederate independence. McClellan's mission changed from simply restoring order and morale to halting an invasion and salvaging the war itself.[60] The crisis transformed young Captain Custer from the servant of a doomed man into the protégé of the savior of the republic—*if* McClellan could save it.

ON SEPTEMBER 14, 1862, Capt. George Armstrong Custer rode alongside Brig. Gen. Alfred Pleasonton, commander of the cavalry division of the Army of the Potomac. They moved west, and they moved up—ascending the eastern slope of South Mountain, a wooded, ravine-split ridge that formed a natural barricade for the Confederate Army of Northern Virginia, located somewhere beyond it. The rest of the Union army marched into the valley behind them.

"The heads of the columns began to appear, and grew and grew," wrote a Union soldier who also stood on South Mountain, looking back at the Army of the Potomac. It was a "beautiful, impressive picture—each column a monstrous, crawling, blue-black snake, miles long, quilled with the silver slant of muskets at a 'shoulder,' its sluggish tail writhing slowly up over the distant eastern ridge." To the north he saw the baggage train. "We knew that each dot was a heavily loaded army wagon, drawn by six mules and occupying forty feet of road at least." In the valley immediately below, about a half mile from his position, the column of infantry "broke abruptly, filing off into line of battle, right and left, across the fields." Pleasonton's cavalry had found a Confederate blocking force on the crest of South Mountain above them.[61]

Custer had been in the saddle almost continuously since Lee crossed the Potomac ten days earlier. McClellan kept him in the field to observe and report. The cavalry handled reconnaissance, so Custer mostly accompanied Pleasonton, often riding back to brief McClellan as the Union army moved north of the Potomac and marched west toward the mountains that shielded Lee's invaders.[62]

It's possible, then, that Custer had not been present in headquarters on September 11, when Col. Thomas Key had approached Nathaniel Paige of the *New York Tribune* with grave news: "A plan to countermarch to Washington and intimidate the President had been seriously discussed the night before by members of McClellan's staff," Paige later recalled. Key claimed that he had stifled any such plot, and said that the general himself knew nothing of it. Did Custer?

Even if there was no real plan for a military coup, the intrigue at head-quarters had only grown more byzantine and insidious. Simply by dis-avowing this talk to a reporter, Key sent a warning to the White House to adopt a conservative course. McClellan himself had considered an ulti-matum, demanding Stanton's resignation as his price for driving Lee out of Maryland, until Burnside dissuaded him.[63]

All this chatter ended abruptly, thanks to the "Lost Order." On Sep-tember 13, McClellan was handed a misplaced copy of Lee's plans. It showed that the enemy divisions were scattered, vulnerable to being destroyed "in detail"—piece by isolated piece. Rarely in history has the fog of war lifted so completely. McClellan's customary fatalism evapo-rated. "Here is a paper," he exulted to brigade commander John Gibbon, "with which if I cannot whip 'Bobbie Lee,' I will be willing to go home."[64]

But McClellan was still McClellan. Eighteen hours passed as he drew up his plans. Finally, at daylight on September 14, he put his men in motion. And so Custer found himself on the slopes of South Mountain. When he rode back to report, he found McClellan well to the rear, con-tent to let his subordinates manage the fighting. Blue-white gun smoke enveloped the crest; by the end of September 14, the Union had won.[65]

At dawn the next morning, Pleasonton and Custer rode together with the 8th Illinois Cavalry Regiment in pursuit of the retreating Confed-erates. The thirty-eight-year-old Pleasonton had graduated from West Point in 1844 and served capably on the frontier and in Mexico. He was a handsome man with a close-cut beard and a mustache that he sometimes waxed into horizontal points. His rather large eyes glinted with intel-ligence and, some thought, a little too much calculation. He was a friend and ally of General McClellan in an officer corps increasingly divided over "Little Mac."[66]

Down into the valley they went. On the edge of Boonsboro, a ham-let with close-built brick houses and storefronts, they saw the backs of the Confederate rear guard, a column of cavalry led by Col. Fitzhugh Lee, Robert E. Lee's nephew. The Union troopers charged, and Custer charged with them. Riding half-ton horses at full gallop, the wave of cav-alrymen collided with the enemy before the rebels could wheel about to face them. Panicked by the bone-breaking momentum of the Union stampede, the rebels scattered in confusion. Fitzhugh Lee was thrown off his horse, leaving it to be captured as he ran for his life through a cornfield. Clouds of dust kicked up on the hot, dry road billowed over the struggling cavalrymen. Finally the Confederates withdrew in disorder.

Pleasonton witnessed the attack. In his report, he cited several Union officers who "were conspicuous for their gallantry on this occasion," including Custer. He was growing fond of the young captain, for his merits as well as his ties to McClellan.[67]

INSTEAD OF RIDING BACK TO speak to McClellan in person, Custer took out a pencil and a small pad and scratched a quick note. He was ebullient after the climactic charge. Around him the people of Boonsboro poured onto the streets, waving flags and cheering the infantrymen of I Corps who marched through town. "We captured between two & three hundred prisoners in Boonsboro," he wrote. "Our cavalry has made several dashing charges. The rebels are scattering all over the country. . . . Everything is as we wish." He signed it, "Custer," but before he could send it back he encountered the I Corps commander, the clean-shaven, hard-drinking, and confident Maj. Gen. Joseph Hooker. He told Custer, "Inform the general that we can capture the entire rebel army." Custer added to his original note, "Gen Hooker says the rebel army is completely demoralized. The rebels are moving towards Shepherdstown. Boonsboro is full of rebel stragglers. Hooker has sent [Maj. Gen. Israel B.] Richardson in pursuit (double quick) and will follow immediately." Custer found a messenger to carry his report back to headquarters so he could ride at the forefront.[68]

Custer caught up to the retreating Confederates by midday. He saw that the Army of Northern Virginia had halted on the north side of the Potomac and deployed in a line that arched across a bend in the river, anchored on the village of Sharpsburg behind Antietam Creek. Again he quickly wrote to McClellan.

> The enemy is drawn up in line of battle on a ridge about two miles beyond Cartersville [i.e., Keedysville]. They are in full view. Their line is a perfect one about a mile and a half long. We can have equally good position as they now occupy. Richardson is forming his line to attack. We are lacking in artillery . . . hurry up more guns we can get good position for two hundred guns. Longstreet is in command and has forty cannon that we know of. We can employ all the troops you can send us.[69]

Oddly, his language removes himself from the general he served: "*We* can employ all the troops *you* can send *us*." To an extent, this reflected his experience with McClellan. In all the battles fought by the Army of the Potomac, McClellan had never taken tactical command, and even Custer assumed he would abdicate that responsibility now.

He was also distancing himself from *himself*—from Custer the junior staff officer, the loyal messenger and passive observer. In the charge at Boonsboro, Custer the warrior—Custer the killer—had emerged supreme. He had cultivated this persona during his months at headquarters, slipping away from staff duties to volunteer for scouts and attacks. This was the part of him that wanted to win, to destroy his enemy—the part that had developed a taste for combat, if not an actual addiction. Keenly wanting a role in the assault, he identified with the vanguard of the Union army.

He did not know that McClellan would finally take field command in person and fight Lee in a set-piece battle. He could not foresee that this was the place where more Americans would die in one day than on any battlefield in history.

Lee had not yet united his army. When Custer scouted his line, he had only 15,000 men in hand. More arrived hourly, but many were completing the capture of the Union garrison at Harper's Ferry, Virginia, several hours' march to the south. Speed could destroy Lee. But his stand on the north side of the Potomac surprised McClellan; as Stephen Sears notes, "McClellan was invariably nonplussed by the unexpected." So the general waited through the rest of that day *and* the next as troops arrived, his artillery rolled up, and he prepared his plans.

The young captain would not belong to a *we* who would win a quick victory ahead of *you*, the main body of the army. Instead, he rejoined the staff that waited on McClellan as he established his headquarters at the redbrick Philip Pry house, on a hill east of Antietam Creek, and deployed his corps left and right along the stream.[70]

September 17, 1862, was the day of battle—a battle named Antietam. (The Confederates referred to it as Sharpsburg.) Custer wrote no more hasty reports, but spoke to McClellan in person, if he spoke to him at all. The general took his staff on a short ride to the headquarters of Fitz-John Porter, where he had a better view. The staff perched a telescope atop a small fortification improvised from fence rails. McClellan peered through it and occasionally spoke quietly with Porter beside him. He kept the staff at bay, unless he called someone to deliver an order or investigate something.[71]

Custer did not join the fighting on the northern flank of the Confederate line, where McClellan ordered the assault to begin. He did not wade into the gunfire that would capitalize with corpses the humdrum features of the landscape: *the Cornfield, West Woods, East Woods, Dunker*

Church, Sunken Road. He did not join the painfully delayed charge on the left under General Burnside, a run through deadly fire across a narrow bridge, a charge that finally crumpled the overstretched Confederate line. He did not fall back with those same men when rebel reinforcements arrived from Harper's Ferry. It was Custer's good fortune to be on McClellan's staff on September 17. He liked to be at the forefront of charges, and, as a rule, such men died that day. About 6,000 men lost their lives and another 17,000 were wounded, counting both sides. It was a tally worse than the losses in the War of 1812 and Mexican War put together.

"It was a good battle plan," James McPherson writes, "and if well executed it might have accomplished Lincoln's wish to 'destroy the rebel army.' But it was not well executed." McClellan still might have won if he had struck the thin enemy center with his reserves. He was unwilling to take the chance. Despite grave losses, Lee taunted McClellan by remaining in place on September 18. McClellan refused to attack again. On September 19, the Confederates marched south, unhindered by pursuit.[72]

Years later, Custer would sit with pen in hand and contemplate the failure of the leader he admired so much. McClellan had "all the natural and acquired endowments sought for in a great leader," he would write. His "mental training and abilities were of a higher order," his "military qualifications and knowledge were superior to those possessed by any officer who subsequently led the Army of the Potomac."

Why then, he would ask himself, did his general not win the war? "McClellan's greatest disadvantage" was that he "was thrust . . . into supreme command of an army without having first had an opportunity to prepare himself by apprenticeship, as his successors had, by working their way up, step by step . . . from colonels and captains to that of general commanding-in-chief [sic]."

But he saw a bigger reason. It showed that he had imbibed the intrigue at headquarters. "The defeat of McClellan was not the result of combinations made either in the Confederate capital or in the camp of the Confederate army, but in Washington," he would claim. "It was the result of an opposition whose birth and outgrowth could be traced to the dominating spirits who at that time were largely in control of the Federal Government." The abolitionist Radicals stabbed him in the back.[73]

THREE JOURNEYS TELL THE STORY of Antietam's aftermath—three treks that reveal the battle's impact on America, on Custer, and on his future.

The first began in Boston. The very night of the battle, a doctor got of out bed to answer a loud knock at his front door. The doctor's name was Oliver Wendell Holmes. He was a fifty-three-year-old professor of medicine at Harvard University, but he was best known as the author of *The Autocrat of the Breakfast Table*, along with other books, and as a contributor to the *Atlantic Monthly*. He had a son by the same name, who was only twenty-one and a captain in the Army of the Potomac. The doctor opened the door and found a messenger with a telegram. It was about his son.

"Capt. H—— wounded shot through the neck thought not mortal at Keedysville," it read. Keedysville was the village nearest Union lines at Antietam. "*Through* the neck,—no bullet left in wound," he pondered, as he would later recall. "Wind-pipe, food-pipe, carotid, jugular, half a dozen smaller, but still formidable vessels, a great braid of nerves, each as big as a lamp-wick, spinal cord,—ought to kill at once, if at all."

He decided to go find his son. Many Americans did the same after battles, especially this one, which left so many wounded, missing, dead, or simply unable to respond to urgent letters. Arriving in Maryland, Holmes traveled over a strange landscape torn up by the passage of armies, "like one of those tornadoes which tear their path through our fields and villages." Asking everywhere for news of his son, he rolled in a hired wagon down a road "filled with straggling and wounded soldiers. . . . It was a pitiable sight, truly pitiable, yet so vast, so far beyond the possibility of relief," he wrote, "it was next to impossible to individualize it, and so bring it home, as one can do with a single broken limb or aching wound."

He arrived on the field at Antietam. Corpses of officers and the affluent were being sealed in iron coffins for shipment home. Dead enlisted men had been shoveled under as fast as possible. "A long ridge of fresh gravel rose before us," he wrote. A sign announced, "The Rebel General Anderson and 80 Rebels are buried in this hole." He looked around. "The whole ground was strewed with fragments of clothing, haversacks, canteens, cap-boxes, bullets, cartridge-boxes, cartridges, scraps of paper, portions of bread and meat. I saw two soldiers' caps that looked as though their owners had been shot through the head. In several places I noticed dark red patches where a pool of blood had curdled and caked." He saw clusters of dead horses, one half buried in the ground, "and his legs stuck out stark and stiff from beneath the gravel."

No record keeping guided him. He asked, asked, and followed leads. Finally he heard that his son was expected to arrive by train at Harrisburg, where Holmes happened to be. He waited at the station, boarded a newly arrived train, and searched. "In the first car, on the fourth seat to the right, I saw my Captain; there I saw him, even my first-born, whom I had sought through many cities. 'How are you, Boy?' 'How are you, Dad?' "[74]

Holmes's hunt for his wounded son captured the collision between civilian and military worlds in this war fought on American soil by armies of citizen soldiers. It hinted at the impact of the carnage, which caused such anxiety as well as loss. It traced the labyrinth into which soldiers disappeared. A wounded man might be lugged into a house or hospital with no record of his location; he might die and be thrown into a hole with seventy-nine others, with no more gravestone than a marker offering a rough tally of the dead below. This was the reality Custer escaped, and yet could not escape.

Custer made the second journey. On September 26, the army released a group of Confederate prisoners on parole. Custer and another young staff officer, apparently James H. Wilson, accompanied them back to rebel lines under a flag of truce. Wilson had graduated from West Point two classes ahead of Custer, and continued to call him "Cinnamon." After reaching the enemy camp, Custer wrote that he chatted for an hour with Southerners who knew his West Point classmates, and scribbled notes for various Confederate friends, including Lea.

In a Virginia town on the route home, Custer and Wilson encountered a young woman whom Wilson knew—"formerly intimately acquainted," in Custer's words. "Why I know you," she said to Wilson. He stared at her for a moment and replied, "Why of course you do. How do you do?" He stepped toward her, "offering to shake her hand, but she was too much of a rebel for this," Custer wrote. She stepped back. "Excuse me Mr. Wilson but I cannot do it."

"My friend was very much surprised after having her make the first advance," Custer wrote. "He blushed deeply and I heard him mutter something . . . about expecting 'to meet with Virginia hospitality on this side of the river . . . but must confess I was mistaken.'" Custer did not consider that she might have made a journey like that of Oliver Wendell Holmes—or that she might have been denied such a pilgrimage to the Union-held battlefield, and was forced to live in uncertainty. He did not ponder whether the war had simply murdered her romantic notions, suffocating them under corpses, shortages, inflation, rebellious slaves, and a ruined countryside. He did not see that many women at home in wartime could not afford gallantry.[75]

LINCOLN MADE THE THIRD JOURNEY—one that determined Custer's future, that carried the entire nation from one era to another. "I think the time has come," he told his cabinet on September 22. "I wish it were a better time. I wish that we were in a better condition. The action of the army against the rebels has not been quite what I should have liked." But Antietam still ranked as a Union victory, terminating Lee's invasion of the North. Lincoln could finally issue the Emancipation Proclamation.

As critics noted, it affected no slaves actually within reach of his authority. Only slaves in rebel-held territory would be declared free as of January 1, 1863. Lincoln could only justify it, in constitutional terms, under his powers as a wartime commander in chief; its legal purpose was to undermine the enemy. Still, it was transformative. As James McPherson writes, "The Proclamation would turn Union forces into armies of liberation after January 1—if they could win the war. And it also invited the slaves to help them win it."[76]

"The Presdt's late Proclamation, the continuation of Stanton & Halleck in office, render it almost impossible for me to retain my commission & self respect at the same time," McClellan wrote to his wife from Sharpsburg on September 25. "I cannot make up my mind to fight for such an accursed doctrine as that of a servile insurrection [i.e., slave rebellion]—it is too infamous."[77]

His fury grew when a second executive order suspended habeas corpus throughout the North for anyone suspected of aiding the rebellion. He wrote to William Aspinwall in New York, "I am very anxious to know how you and men like you regard the recent Proclamations of the Presdt inaugurating servile war, emancipating the slaves, & at one stroke of the pen changing our free institutions into a despotism."[78]

These were dangerous words. He rallied allies within the army and tried to influence the press. A *New York Herald* reporter wrote, "The sentiment throughout the whole army seems in favor of a change of dynasty. . . . There is large promise of a fearful revolution . . . that will startle the country and give us a military dictator."[79]

On October 2, Lincoln went to see the would-be dictator. McClellan and his staff greeted him at the Harper's Ferry train station and gave him a tour of the Antietam battlefield. Custer spent the next day in the saddle, following the general and the president as they reviewed the troops.

Here, in this place of mass death, each of these three men viewed the Civil War in starkly different ways. Lincoln considered it a race to uncompromising victory. He feared that McClellan's reluctance to strike hard would prolong the slaughter indefinitely. McClellan, on the other hand, feared an unlimited war, thinking it far too costly in soldiers' lives and damage done to Southern society. Despite their disagreement, they both saw the war in terms of national policy and military strategy.[80]

And Custer? To him, the war was an experience, more intense than any other. That very evening, he expressed his thoughts in a letter to his cousin Augusta Ward.

You ask me if I will not be glad when the last battle is fought. So far as the country is concerned I, of course, must wish for peace, and will be glad when the war is ended, but if I answer for myself *alone*, I must say that I shall regret to see the war end. I would be willing, yes glad, to see a battle every day of my life. Now do not misunderstand me. I only speak of my own *interests* and *desires*, perfectly regardless of all the world besides, but as I said before, when I think of the pain & misery produced to individuals as well as the miserable sorrow caused throughout the land I cannot but earnestly hope for peace, and at an early date. Do you understand me?[81]

Contradictions and complexities swirl through this passage. He speaks with the romanticism of youth, reflecting a nation that had entered the war as if it were a great adventure; yet already he has witnessed some of the worst of war. He is self-absorbed—addicted, perhaps, to the thrill of running risks, to the visceral pleasure of fighting, defeating, and even killing other men. Yet he is aware of his self-absorption, even if he is unable to move beyond it. Here we see a young man who has yet to be disillusioned, but is intelligent enough to know it. He pleads for understanding, conscious of how terrible he would sound to his cousin, but has no desire to relinquish the pleasure of combat. These feelings set him apart from the lady in Virginia, his hero McClellan, and the tall, sad man who was president. Yet they were not simple.

The next day, October 4, "Little Mac" and staff rode east with the president and his entourage to see the South Mountain battlefield. There they encountered Aspinwall, who was coming from Washington to see the general. "The coincidence was unfortunate for McClellan," writes the historian Richard Slotkin, "because it so clearly exposed the fact that he was in close consultation with the political opposition." Lincoln left and Aspinwall stayed. Speaking for Barlow, Belmont, and himself, Aspinwall stressed "that it is my duty to submit to the Presdt's proclamation & quietly continue doing my duty as a soldier," McClellan recounted to Ellen. He told her that he would "do my best to hit upon some plan of campaign that will enable me to drive the rebels entirely away from this part of the country forever."[82]

The modesty of that last sentence reflected the most fatal of his many flaws: he was no killer. He was still incapable of conceiving a decisive campaign, let alone conducting one. He wrote of merely driving the rebels away, not defeating or destroying them—unenthusiastically at that.

Custer still worshipped his general, but he understood him. Near the end of October, he wrote, "we will then go into winter quarters *somewhere*," and the campaign would stop. Already he was dreaming of dances, sleighing, and good food. "After I get to Monroe I do not intend to eat *'hard bread'* nor *'salt pork'* nor to drink my *'coffee without milk'* although these are the fashionable dishes in the army."[83]

McClellan finally moved south, completing the crossing of the Potomac on November 2. Lincoln, Stanton, and Halleck—as well as newspaper editors and Republicans in Congress—had long since reached the point of exasperation with his political skullduggery and refusal to fight. On November 7, as heavy snow blew through the headquarters camp at Rectortown, Virginia, a messenger brought orders relieving McClellan and assigning Maj. Gen. Ambrose Burnside to take his place.

"On Sunday, November 9, General McClellan began the painful process of bidding farewell to his army," writes the biographer Stephen Sears. "That evening he received the officers of his staff and escort in a highly emotional scene. The side curtains of his tent were raised and the area lit by a large log fire nearby, and as each man entered he greeted him and ushered him inside." The general ordered that each man's glass be filled with champagne. He lifted up his own and said, "To the Army of the Potomac, and bless the day when I shall return to it." The youngest officer present, Capt. George Armstrong Custer, yearned for that day, and believed it would come.

On November 10, McClellan reviewed the troops for the last time, with his staff and General Burnside riding behind him. Afterward Custer stopped by the tent of a young man from Monroe named Henry Clay Christiancy and said he was going home that day. It was not the triumphant return he had imagined. With his patron banished, he faced a future more uncertain than at any time since the war began.[84]

Four

THE PRODIGY

I F CUSTER LEARNED ANYTHING at McClellan's side, it was that the Civil War was political. Military strategy shaped national policy, but so did ideology, constituencies, lobbying, and compromise. Partisanship influenced the appointment of Volunteer officers, as did the personal politics of patronage and nepotism. Politicians and generals alike crafted networks of favorites and supporters in the army.

The irony is that the Regular Army had pioneered the principle of professionalism in antebellum America. It had systematized procedures, set standards for technical proficiency, required competitive bidding for contracts, and virtually invented professional training at the military academy. All this continued during the war; and, as the conflict dragged on, the president and the War Department placed greater emphasis on merit. And yet, a great war for national survival, fought by a mass of citizen soldiers raised by the states, inevitably turned political.

That did not shock Custer. It was the reality he had grown up with; it was the nature of the antebellum era. The American philosophy of government was summed up by New York governor and U.S. secretary of state William L. Marcy: "To the victor belong the spoils." Each new administration fired the postmasters, customs collectors, steamboat inspectors, and other federal employees and appointed political supporters. The economy, too, remained deeply personal, not institutional; the corporate landscape of technical experts, anonymous shareholders, and professional managers did not yet exist. Business consisted of human relationships, from the credit issued to customers by local merchants to the friendships and family ties that held together boards of railroad companies. The Union army was America under arms, functioning much as society functioned. Custer thought that valor might gain him attention, merit might gain him favor, but patronage would save him.[1]

Not long after he arrived at his sister's home in Monroe, soon after McClellan's fall, Lt. Col. Frazey M. Winans handed him a letter. Custer respected Winans, an influential man who had helped to organize the 7th

Michigan Infantry Regiment at the outset of the war. The person who wrote the letter was even more important. His name was Isaac P. Christiancy, an associate justice of the Michigan Supreme Court. Christiancy's duties often kept him in Lansing, the state capital, but he was a Monroe man, owner of the *Monroe Commercial* newspaper. He was also a leading Republican politician, having helped to found the party in Michigan. And he needed a favor from young Captain Custer.[2]

The judge's son Henry wanted an appointment to the staff of Brig. Gen. Andrew A. Humphreys, who commanded an infantry division in the Army of the Potomac. He had made no progress. But Custer knew Humphreys, and had connections throughout the army. Could he help?[3]

For Custer, the letter was timely. Professionally, he was adrift at best, sinking at worst. He found himself not merely without a patron, but tainted by his association with General McClellan. He needed friends— Republican friends.

He might well have offered his assistance even if circumstances were different. He was emphatically loyal—to friends, to his family, to his community, even across the divide of war or politics. Henry was one of the last soldiers he had spoken to before leaving for Monroe on November 10, and they had discussed Henry's quest for a staff position. But the value of Judge Christiancy's friendship was obvious to Custer.

He explained to the judge the particular circumstances that had stalled Henry's quest, adding, "I am particularly anxious that Henry should receive the appointment. I have had experience in company duty and staff duty. The opportunities for improvement are infinitely greater in the latter. Henry would be thrown [into] contact with a class of men whom it would be both an honor and a pleasure to know." The "opportunities for improvement," in other words, were a matter of connections. "I will write a letter tomorrow to one of Gen. [Daniel] Butterfield's staff who is an intimate friend of mine and one to Gen. Humphreys's staff urging that they use their influence." If he was successful, the influential Isaac Christiancy would owe him a favor.[4]

THE YOUNG LADIES' SEMINARY and Collegiate Institute occupied three well-landscaped acres in Monroe, guarded by a handsome iron fence. It was a big building in a small town: an L-shaped, three-story structure with a peaked roof, a colonnade along the first floor, and a one-story extension. The husband-and-wife pair of joint principals, Sarah C. Boyd and the Rev. E. J. Boyd, intended "to furnish Young Ladies as good advantages for a thorough and substantial education as are provided for the other sex by the Colleges of the country," the annual catalog stated. Though the school placed a premium on manners, music, and refinement, its faculty also taught astronomy, geology, English literature, mathematics, French, and vigorous calisthenics. And now and then its doors opened for a party, as they did on Thanksgiving Day, 1862.[5]

Captain Custer attended. He had dreamed of parties during his months in the field, and this event, filled with young women, was irresistible. It is worth repeating what his old roommate Tully McCrea said of him in a letter around this time. "He is a handsome fellow, and a very successful ladies' man," he wrote. "Nor does he care an iota how many of the fair ones break their hearts for him."[6] Custer came despite possible awkwardness with Nellie Van Wormer, a senior in the seminary's collegiate division; already his passion for her had disappeared from his correspondence. It would be well worth paying his respects to junior Mary Christiancy, though the true appeal lay in the young women he may have seen about town but did not yet know. There was the fashionable and flirtatious Fannie Fifield, for example, a recent graduate, and her classmate (and valedictorian) Elizabeth Bacon.[7]

During the party, Custer was introduced to Elizabeth, known as Libbie to her friends and family. Petite and slender-shouldered beneath the acres of fabric and mountain of whalebone that made up a respectable woman's dress, she had a striking face: a quick smile, gray eyes, abundant brown hair that she often parted in the middle and pulled up on the back of her head, leaving stray curls to dangle around her temples, not to mention the softness that comes from being only twenty years old.[8]

The "ladies' man" knew little about her—except perhaps that her father, Judge Daniel Bacon, was a prominent Republican in town. He began to track her. He attended her church, a respectable Presbyterian congregation, whereas his family were evangelical Methodists. He stared at her during the services. He walked past her house, often many times a day, and offered to escort her when she emerged to carry out an errand. He appeared outside her singing school in time to walk her home in the evening. Day by day, they spoke. He learned that she was well educated, shrewd, and quick to laugh, that she was devoted to her sixty-four-year-old father and her stepmother, Rhoda. In mid-December he invited her to a concert; when she declined, citing her family, he said that her stepmother would enjoy it as well, and he "would be very happy of Mrs. Bacon's company too." She still refused, but was clearly pleased.

More than once he began to speak of feelings for her, only to have her change the subject. When he pressed, she said it would be wrong for her to listen. With the new year, he managed to say that he loved her. Nobody else, he told her, could keep him entertained for more than an hour without his feeling "lonely." He would "sacrifice every earthly hope to gain

[her] love," he said. She replied that she would give it to him *if* she could, adding, "Forget me."

I "*never could* forget" you, he said. Libbie responded that she could not forget him either, but wanted simply to be "his true friend through life." He wanted nothing less, he said, than for her to be his wife.[9]

Was he sincere? The boundary between love and lust is not always clear, but it is especially vague in this man who overflowed with both. He spoke fluently a language often regarded as feminine, words of feeling and romance. In each of his previous relationships—with Mollie, Mariah, and Nellie—he had talked earnestly of love and had raised the possibility of marriage. He may have been sincere in each instance, for he was a man who lived fiercely in the present, engaging everything with passion, with aggressive immediacy. On the other hand, he knew that such talk served as an effective means toward an end: the "great sleep," in his words, or getting "spooney," as McCrea and others called it. Just the *impression* of an engagement had induced some women to let him into their beds— and he married none of them. Yet this does not mean he was deliberately manipulative. He wanted love, and may not have distinguished it from sexual attraction. After all, sex itself is not merely a matter of pleasure, but an experience of being wanted, admired, desired. It was an antidote to his insecurities.[10]

His true heart remains opaque. What is known is his response to Libbie's rebuff. He promptly changed his target to her longtime school rival, the vivacious Fannie Fifield. This appealing young woman, with a (heavily draped) figure that men admired, had recently come back to Monroe after a December trip. Custer cultivated her as soon as she returned, perhaps even before he declared his love to Libbie. He occasionally saw another woman as well, but he appeared in the streets and parlors of Monroe mainly with Fannie, the daughter of a prosperous merchant, railway and express agent, and steamboat owner. She reveled in the attention of men—even flirted with them when they were out in public with her friends—and she seemed to enjoy Custer's attention in particular.

Not many days after Libbie told Custer to forget her, he ran into her at a party at a home in Monroe. It was attended by the circle he and Bacon shared, the young men of town, including Jacob Greene, and seminary students and graduates such as Helen and Kate Wing—and Fannie Fifield. The group played blind-man's bluff and other games; all the while Custer flirted with Fannie, even taking her hand. When he had a moment alone, though, he sat next to Libbie. He spoke to her quietly, and she handed him a ring. Afterward he went back to Fifield. In public, Fannie basted him with affection; in private, the town gossiped, she gave him everything he desired.[11]

So the early weeks of 1863 passed as Custer lingered in Monroe, lacking orders. In February he learned that Libbie was going to take a train to Toledo to stay with a friend. He showed up at the station and brushed past her glaring father to carry her bags, daring even to touch her elbow as she climbed the steps into the car. When she returned, he began to hear from her through her friend Nettie Humphrey, whose family owned the Humphrey House hotel in Monroe. Nettie helped to arrange seemingly chance encounters with Libbie in the hotel parlor, and delivered a photograph of Libbie, with instructions to keep it secret.

One Friday evening he took Fifield to an oyster dinner at a family home in town, and saw Bacon there. He found a moment to slip out with Libbie to a side room, and they sat in a love seat facing each other. She seemed self-conscious. Looking in a mirror, she said that the image of the two of them reminded her of "books and pictures I've seen." She leaned into him. He tried to kiss her. She pulled away. She wasn't Fannie Fifield, she snapped, or "Helen W.," another name that came up in gossip about Custer. He replied that he never equated her with such women.

He found her to be increasingly infuriating. She had welcomed his company on the street, then rebuffed his expression of love, then surreptitiously pursued him through her friend Nettie, then refused a simple kiss. She pestered him about her photograph, saying that his niece had been heard talking about it. Was he not keeping it secret, as she had asked? What if her father should learn of their relationship? He denied showing off the picture—unconvincingly, because he had.

In early April, Custer was sitting in the Fifield family parlor when Libbie and Nettie appeared at the door and were welcomed inside. In the presence of Fannie, he could not contain his irritation at Libbie. He criticized her for drinking a little beer at the Humphrey House. She angrily defended herself. Later the party sat at a table to play euchre. With a soldier's proverbial passion for cards, Custer plunged into the game, turning away from his hand only to make sarcastic comments about Libbie.[12]

From the depths of the courageous and loyal Custer, the carefully cultivated Custer, there boiled over the ugly Custer—the self-involved young man who scrawled sarcastic complaints to friends and relatives for neglecting him, who had nearly destroyed his career before it began, who flared in verbose self-righteousness when challenged. In a single evening he terminated his painstaking courtship of Miss Bacon. Orders came to report to Washington, and he departed Monroe as Fanny Fifield's man.

ARMSTRONG ENTERED THE DOMESTIC CIRCLE. Sometime after seven in the evening on Saturday, April 11, he walked into a handsome four-story

town house at 22 East 31st Street, in the fashionable New York neighborhood east of Fifth Avenue. Ellen McClellan welcomed him inside, as did
her husband, George.

The young captain had reported to the War Department on April 10,
only to learn that he had been assigned to assist McClellan in writing his
final, comprehensive report. The report was McClellan's idea. He had
asked for the help of a number of his aides by name, though not Custer at
first. He had added, "It is probable that the services of a few other officers
late of my staff . . . may also be necessary to me."[13]

Custer was flattered to be found necessary. The general said he would
have asked for him long before, Custer wrote to his sister, "but he was
ignorant of my whereabouts & my long letter to him had miscarried."
Now he found himself in McClellan's own home, the gift of the general's
Democratic sponsors, Aspinwall, Barlow, John Jacob Astor, and William
B. Duncan. "I wish you could see the house which was presented to Mrs.
McClellan," Custer wrote. "It is the most magnificently furnished house
I was ever in."

He worked at McClellan's side from ten in the morning until three in
the afternoon. The general's circle of dazzling friends left him feeling
insecure—and poor. "I fear I will be compelled to purchase a new suit
of citizen's clothes," he wrote. "I am living at great expense. My board is
$3.75 per day . . . I breakfast at half past 9 or ten and dine at six. These are
the fashionable hours here." He sent love to his sister's children, and to
someone else. "Tell Rily Em & Aut I send them a kiss and tell Emma to
tell Fannie I send her one also."[14]

At night he returned to the Metropolitan Hotel, an enormous five-
story edifice that stretched for a block along Broadway from a corner on
Prince Street. There ladies sat in "sky parlors" to watch the display of
fashion among the pedestrians in the masonry canyon of Broadway. Next
door was Niblo's Garden, a famous theater. In the morning he joined
the throngs who hailed hackney cabs or clambered aboard horse-drawn
omnibuses or simply walked to work, and he journeyed a mile and three-
quarters to the McClellan house.[15]

Yet each day damaged him. He had planned to survive McClellan's
fall by obtaining command of one of the new cavalry regiments recently
raised in Michigan, in particular the 5th Michigan Cavalry. State governors appointed colonels to lead new volunteer regiments—but Michigan's
Austin Blair was a Republican. Custer sounded out his original Republican patron, Congressman John A. Bingham of Ohio, who still supported
him, but he needed someone with influence in the party in Michigan. He
turned to Isaac Christiancy, who immediately wrote to Blair.

The governor replied bluntly. "Custer is using you to his advantage, just as he used Bingham." The press attention given to the exploits of the young officer now worked against him, for the governor was well aware of his connections. "His people are Rebel Democrats. He himself is a McClellan man; indeed McClellan's fair-haired boy, I should say. Sorry, your honor, but I cannot place myself in such a compromising position, whatever his qualifications. No, I have nothing for him."[16]

Blair was right. Though Custer's family were not "rebels," he *was* a partisan Democrat and son of a partisan Democrat. He *was* a "McClellan man," even his "fair-haired boy." The governor's response reflected his responsibilities, which were not military but political. He had to reward those who desired total victory over the South, an attribute he naturally found in his own party. In his eyes, partisanship was a useful tool in separating reliable Unionists from disloyal "Copperheads" or halfhearted conservatives. Custer's soldierly merits did not enter into his calculation.

When it came to politics, where did the young captain stand? A man so partisan, so opinionated, must have written *something* about the great issues of the day, particularly the Emancipation Proclamation. Yet the public archives contain no contemporary letters on the subject. This conspicuous silence raises suspicions that some letters were deliberately hidden or destroyed in later years, when emancipation would prove far more popular and far less controversial than it was in 1862. Enough material survives to confirm that he shared McClellan's politics—and to suggest that he opposed the proclamation. By Blair's logic, Custer did not deserve a regiment.

FOUR BLANKETS, ONE LINED COAT, and one pair of lined trousers: A quartermaster in Washington handed these items over to Custer on April 22, the tangible signs that the young man was just a first lieutenant once more, with orders to take charge of a company in the 5th U.S. Cavalry. He set out for the Army of the Potomac, camped north of Fredericksburg, Virginia.[17]

Fredericksburg is where the army had suffered a crushing defeat during his absence, on December 13, 1862, under Burnside. By the time Custer arrived, President Lincoln had replaced Burnside with Joseph Hooker, who had revived the army with sweeping reforms. He created a Bureau of Military Information that revolutionized intelligence gathering, introduced a new furlough system, and created badges for each corps to instill pride. He ordered the regular issue of vegetables, fresh potatoes and onions, and soft bread in place of mere hardtack and salted meat. And he united the widely dispersed horsemen into a Cavalry Corps under Brig. Gen. George Stoneman.[18]

On arriving at the army, Custer sought out Brigadier General Plea-sonton. Both men were friends of McClellan's, and they had formed a bond during the Maryland Campaign. Even after the Battle of Antietam Custer had joined Pleasonton on missions until just before his departure in November. The general seemed happy to see him.

Custer's appearance coincided with the start of a Union offensive. On April 29, the Cavalry Corps rode out on a great raid behind Confeder-ate lines. Pleasonton stayed behind with a single brigade. So did Custer. Perhaps he arrived too late, or perhaps Pleasonton contrived to keep him close as Hooker moved against Robert E. Lee's Army of Northern Virginia.[19]

On the morning of May 6, Custer summarized the results of Hooker's offensive in a letter to McClellan. "My dear General, I know you must be anxious to know how *your* army is, and has been, doing," he wrote. "We are defeated, driven back on the left bank of the Rappahannock with a loss which I suppose will exceed our entire loss during the seven days battles." The disastrous battle would be named Chancellorsville, after the crossroads that Hooker occupied after crossing the Rapidan and Rap-pahannock rivers—the crossroads where Lee had launched the boldest counterattack of his career, crushing Hooker's right flank.

Grimly satisfied at Hooker's humiliation, Custer echoed McClellan's earlier hopes for Pope's defeat at Second Bull Run. "To say that every-thing is gloomy and discouraging does not express the state of affairs here," he wrote. "Between Pope's and Hooker's reputation in this army, as a general thing, I would not give a straw for the difference." He even turned to gossip. Reportedly an exploding shell dazed Hooker, he wrote, but Custer doubted it. "If anything except his lack of ability interfered or prevented him from succeeding it was a wound he received from a pro-jectile which requires a cork to be drawn before it is serviceable. I do not know this from personal observation, but two officers . . . informed me that Hooker was '*groggy*' during the fight." Hooker had claimed before the battle that he had the enemy in his "vest pocket," Custer added. "It seems however that he forgot to button his vest pocket."

This was insubordination—the kind of intrigue that had characterized McClellan's own headquarters. "You will not be surprised when I inform you that the universal cry is 'Give us McClellan,'" he wrote. "If I am not mistaken there will be such a howl go up from the conservative press and people of the North which will leave but one course open for the Admin-istration to pursue."[20]

Pleasonton knew of Custer's nearly mutinous letter, which was writ-ten on the stationery of his division headquarters. Custer added, "Genl Pleasonton desires to be remembered to you." Pleasonton had heard the talk that McClellan would return to command, and chose to keep his channels open.

Pleasonton's political style disgusted many of his troopers, who saw through his self-interested maneuvering. "He is pure and simple a newspaper humbug," wrote Charles Francis Adams Jr. on May 12. Grandson of John Quincy Adams, Charles was a captain in the 1st Massachusetts Cavalry. "You always see his name in the papers, but to us who have served under him and seen him under fire he is notorious as a bully and a toady. He does nothing save with a view to a newspaper paragraph." At Antietam, he said, Pleasonton sent his troops into fire while he hid and read a newspaper. "When we came back, we all saw him and laughed among ourselves. Yet mean and contemptible as Pleasonton is, he is always *in* at Head Quarters."[21]

McClellan did not return. Hooker remained in command—which turned out to be a lucky thing for Pleasonton, as Hooker lost patience with his other cavalry generals. On May 22, he placed Pleasonton in charge of the entire Cavalry Corps.

Pleasonton brought Custer onto his staff. On May 16, Custer turned in his company's equipment, from currycombs (for grooming horses) to carbines, and took up his new position.[22] "I live with the General and he is very particular to have a good table when we are not moving," he wrote to his sister Ann. He produced a long list of dishes, including "*ripe tomotoes,*" asparagus, mackerel, veal, pound cake, oranges, gingersnaps, and much more. What really surprised him was Pleasonton's choice of servants. "The General has a *negro woman* and her husband to cook and wait on the table. They go with us when we march. The cook's name is Hannah. I always call her 'Aunt Hannah.' . . . She does not wear hoops and has a red handkerchief tied around her head like all negroes." Custer was taken aback not because Pleasonton had private servants, but because Hannah was black and a woman. He guessed in his letter that his sister's children would not eat the woman's food, knowing her race.

Excitement, delight, and marvel radiated from the page, expressing his relief at so swiftly escaping the drudgery of duty in a line company for the glamor of a general's staff. He boasted of the "fine band" that played every morning and evening. But his joy ebbed as he turned to Libbie. "I am sorry to hear of Mrs. Bacon's illness. It will be a severe blow to Libbie if she should lose her mother [in fact, stepmother]," he wrote to Ann. "*Libbie is the most dutiful daughter I ever knew.* She has a sweet disposition and is the *most sensible* young lady I ever met." Then he abruptly reined in his emotions. "There are not more than a dozen girls in Monroe who I like better than Libbie and that is the truth."[23]

This resoundingly halfhearted praise was more than he usually wrote of her. To his sister, at least, he tended to mention simply that he had heard from Nettie Humphrey, who despite everything remained his conduit to Libbie, who had said she would stay in touch with him. Where it might lead, though, was uncertain at best.[24]

Fannie, on the other hand, aroused his enthusiasm. He reprimanded his sister for not returning Fifield's call. He wanted Ann to sustain his connection to her, whom he wrote of again and again. "This morning I showed Fannie's photograph (the full length one) to General Pleasonton," he wrote on May 27. "He was most pleased with it and paid her some very high compliments."[25]

Having found a staff roost, he resumed his search for a regimental command. On May 17 he wrote a finely calibrated letter to Judge Christiancy, flatly contradicting what he had written to McClellan about Chancellorsville. "The men and officers are united in their refusal to acknowledge the late contest a defeat on our part," he wrote. He criticized Hooker's performance in temperate terms. Union losses would prove heavier than the Confederate, he said, "because, as a general rule, . . . the victorious party aim with much greater care and accuracy at the *back of a man* than at his face, particularly if the latter is aiming also." He wrote from personal experience on the battlefield. He tactfully returned to his pursuit of a regiment. "My position is a desirable one to a person fond of excitement. I would rather be in command of the 5th Michigan Cavalry or the 8th Regiment if that were possible."[26]

He made the most of his privileged position in Cavalry Corps headquarters. He created his own patronage network, for example, helping to place Henry Christiancy on General Humphreys's staff (as he reminded the judge) and bringing a friend from Monroe, Lt. George Yates, onto Pleasonton's staff. Custer pushed his way into a raid behind enemy lines by part of the 3rd Indiana Cavalry—to the annoyance of its commander— and kept for himself the finest horse they captured, named Roanoke. Hooker personally praised his performance. Custer inflated his role in a letter to his sister, claiming he "had command."[27]

The reality of a command eluded him, despite intense lobbying. He visited the camp of the 5th Michigan Cavalry and tried to persuade the officers to petition Governor Blair to appoint him as their colonel. "We all declined to sign such a petition as we considered him too young," wrote one lieutenant. Custer sent detailed, urgent letters to Judge Christiancy about his effort to win over the governor. Blair visited the army, but a chagrined Custer missed his chance to see him. So he gathered recommendations from an array of generals, including Burnside, Stoneman, Humphreys, Pleasonton, and Hooker, who called him "a young officer of great promise and uncommon merit." Custer forwarded them to Christiancy with the comment, "If the Governor refuses to appoint me it will be for some other reason than a lack of recommendations." He already knew there was indeed "some other reason," namely McClellan.[28]

"Everything indicates a protracted stay in this vicinity," he wrote to Judge Christiancy on May 31. "Arbors have been built over the tents, board floors have been laid in them, and other circumstances show that an early advance is not anticipated." Custer added a new pup to the small pack of dogs he kept with him in the field. He picked up his own camp follower, a homeless boy who had wandered into the Army of the Potomac's city of canvas and campfires and attached himself to the young, long-haired staff officer. His name was Johnny Cisco. "I think he would rather starve than see me go hungry. I have dressed him in soldiers' clothes," Custer wrote. One day, returning from his duties, "I found Johnny with his sleeves rolled up. He had washed all my dirty clothes and hung them on the bushes to dry. He did them very well." He let the boy sleep in his tent, curled up with the pup.

Custer's own progress had stalled as well. He dealt with his situation philosophically—though it was a curious philosophy. He identified "a rule which I have always laid down—never to regret anything after it is done." The conventional formula is to *do* nothing which one might later regret, not to dispense with regret no matter what one does. Custer's peculiar approach was both his strength and his weakness. He never suffered from hesitation or second thoughts, which made him a decisive combat officer. But his refusal to regret indicates an indifference to the effects of his actions on others. He refused to admit he was wrong, lashing out sarcastically at his accusers. When cornered by his transparent guilt, he tried to trivialize or dismiss his misdeeds.

By stating this rule in a letter, he showed that he gave it conscious thought. It was a quintessential contradiction for Custer: in a moment of introspection he chose to avoid introspection—he examined himself and decided to shun self-examination. Did he fear the gap between the man he tried so hard to appear to be and the man he actually was? The answer remained locked in a part of his brain where he refused to look, let alone reveal to the world. For whatever reason, he concluded that he could only live by plunging ahead without glancing back.[29]

CUSTER WORKED FOR A MAN under pressure. Alfred Pleasonton had risen in large part by cultivating his superiors, by paying attention to his commanders' moods. And the mood of General Hooker was very bad.

On June 4, 1863, the Bureau of Military Intelligence reported "considerable movement of the enemy." The next day, Hooker told Lincoln that Lee would likely repeat the Antietam Campaign by marching the entire Confederate army through the Shenandoah Valley into Maryland. The looming rebel offensive created intense stress for Hooker, who could not survive as commander of the Army of the Potomac if he lost another battle. He was a man who passed pressure down.

A few days after warning Lincoln, Hooker informed Pleasonton that General J. E. B. Stuart, the Confederate cavalry chief, had concentrated his horsemen to the west, near Culpeper Court House, south of the Rappahannock River. Whatever Stuart planned, Hooker wanted Pleasonton " 'to bust it up' before it got fairly under way."[30]

A photograph taken about this time shows Custer and Pleasonton in the saddle, their horses facing one another. White conical Sibley tents loom in the background, and a trooper stands between them. Pleasonton, his shoulders somewhat hunched, is on a dingy gray animal and wears a high-crowned hat tilted forward and to the right at a sharp angle. Custer sits erect in an elegant saddle on a handsome black horse, hand on his hip, light blue pants tucked into high cavalry boots, dark blue shirt tucked into cavalry gauntlets, with a checked necktie, long curly hair and arching mustache, and a forage cap sloping down to his eyebrows. On his right hip his revolver sits in a holster, butt forward in cavalry fashion, and on his left a long straight sword is visible, the fine blade of Toledo steel he took from the first man he ever killed. He looks content, self-assured, even proud. Pleasonton does not.

It's a subjective matter, judging any person's emotional state from an image of an instant in time. Pleasonton seems grim, unhappy, though the impression may reflect the ultimatum Hooker gave him. But Custer's cockiness is unmistakable. He looks very much like a man determined to regret nothing, and who therefore may do almost anything.

On June 9, the two men splashed their horses across the Rappahannock along with two divisions and reserve brigade of cavalry and an infantry brigade under Brig. Gen. Adelbert Ames, who had graduated from West Point one class ahead of Custer. Pleasonton launched a two-prong attack on Stuart's camp near Brandy Station, starting a messy, hard-fought battle. When it was all over, he praised Custer for "gallantry throughout the fight," and sent him to deliver a captured Confederate battle flag to Hooker's headquarters. He boasted that he had won a great victory at Brandy Station, the biggest cavalry battle in the entire Civil War. The Union horsemen did better than ever before, but Hooker knew it was far from the "bust up" he had demanded.[31]

"We can never discover the whereabouts of the enemy, or divine his intentions, so long as he fills the country with a cloud of cavalry," Hooker complained to Lincoln on June 16. "We must break through that to find him." Somewhere across the Rappahannock to the south, across the Bull Run and Blue Ridge mountains to the west, Lee's army marched—its size, location, and destination unknown. It was Pleasonton's duty to discover all of these. Hooker grew impatient at his continuing failure. "Drive in pickets, if necessary, and get us information," he wrote. "It is better that we should lose men than to be without knowledge of the enemy, as we now seem to be."[32]

On June 17, Custer rode west with Pleasonton toward the Bull Run Mountains. Near the village of Aldie they learned that Brig. Gen. Judson Kilpatrick's brigade had collided with Confederates posted in the Gap beyond. Valedictorian of the West Point class just ahead of Custer, the little Kilpatrick had deep-set eyes, a long ship's-prow nose, and a brick of a jaw fringed with enormous whiskers. He made up for textbook perfection at the academy with recklessness on the battlefield. Custer arrived just as a body of Union troopers fell back from another failed attack, chased by rebel horsemen. Kilpatrick ordered the 1st Maine to counter-countercharge. Custer joined in.

When Frederick Whittaker wrote about this moment more than a decade later, he tried to explain the thrill of a cavalry charge, based on his personal experience as a Union trooper. It was "the fiercest pleasure of life," he wrote. "Horse and rider are drunk with excitement, feeling and seeing nothing but the cloud of dust, the scattered flying figures, conscious of only one mad desire, to reach them, to smite, smite, smite!"

"Mad" certainly described Custer's horse, a beautiful black animal named Harry. It broke formation, streaking ahead of the Union line. Horse and rider plunged into the onrushing mass of enemy cavalry. One Confederate swiveled and fired his revolver; Custer swung his sword and cut almost all the way through the man's arm. Another rebel, saber in hand, galloped after Custer from behind, a position that gave him an advantage, since it was difficult for Custer to twist around to slash or shoot. Custer reined to a stop. His pursuer sped past, reversing the advantage. Custer spurred after him. He swung his blade overhead; the other man raised his to block it. Custer beat down the rebel's sword and finally cut into his skull and brain.

He found himself completely surrounded by Confederate horsemen. But they did not attack. He thought his slouch hat fooled them; when he wore it his fellow soldiers told him he looked like a Southerner. But in the chaos of the fight, amid clouds of dust kicked up by horses and smoke erupting from firearms, the Confederates might never have guessed that a solitary enemy rode among them.

He started for an opening in the enemy ranks. A single rebel discovered him and raised his sword, "but I struck him across the face with my sabre, knocking him off his horse," Custer wrote. "I then put spurs to 'Harry' and made my escape."[33]

The charge that Custer joined finally dislodged the enemy, driving them back into Aldie Gap. But the Union cavalry still did not get a look at Lee's main force. The pressure on Pleasonton increased. He tried to save himself by lobbying Washington behind Hooker's back. He wrote Congressman John Farnsworth, uncle of a young officer on his staff, Elon Farnsworth. In the absence of any real intelligence, he made up a story. "The [Confederate] raid into Pennsylvania appears to be a fizzle, & some of the negroes say, it is reported Gen. Lee is moving his troops back. . . . Tell the President this. Give him my respects & don't forget the medals."[34]

After more fruitless attacks, his scouts finally ascended the Blue Ridge and glimpsed Lee's army massed in the Shenandoah. But Pleasonton's standing remained precarious. On June 23 he wrote again to the congressman. "Our cavalry business is badly managed & will lead us into trouble unless speedily corrected." He wanted a cavalry division under Brig. Gen. Julius Stahel from the Washington garrison, but Stahel's rank predated his own. Stahel, he noted, was a German-speaking Hungarian. "Tell the President from me . . . that I will not *fight* under the order of a *Dutchman*." He attacked Hooker's orders without mentioning his name, saying, "I am sacrificing the lives of gallant & noble men without a purpose or hope of success."

"I am sadly in want of officers with the proper dash to command cavalry, having lost so many good ones," he added. This sounded more like exasperation than a specific request. Hooker seemed ready to fire Pleasonton, in which case Custer would lose a second patron, and drift still farther away from his dream of leading a regiment.[35]

PLEASONTON SURVIVED. Hooker did not. As Lee advanced unhindered into Pennsylvania, Lincoln gave command of the Army of the Potomac to Maj. Gen. George Meade, former head of V Corps. Meade looked a decade older than his forty-seven years, and was as flamboyant as an old scuffed shoe. But he lacked Hooker's or McClellan's ego, and his fellow corps commanders respected him.[36]

When Pleasonton learned of the change on June 28, he left the house he had taken as his headquarters and rode off to confer with Meade. He returned at about three in the afternoon and called Custer into his room. For the young lieutenant, the meeting was ripe with anticipation. Pleasonton had just been promoted; Custer expected to be elevated to captain again, a rank he was entitled to on the staff of a major general. Some time before, Pleasonton told him, he had urged that Custer be promoted—to brigadier general. Now, with Lee marching into the North, Meade agreed to give the brigadier general's star to Custer and two other young officers on Pleasonton's staff, Elon Farnsworth and Wesley Merritt; he had telegraphed Halleck in the War Department to ask for the appointments immediately.

"I almost wished the General had not informed me of the recommendation, as I felt it would only excite hopes and aspirations which, to say the least, could not be realized at present," Custer wrote to Judge Christiancy a few weeks later. It could never happen, he thought, given his age and low rank, and the fact that "I had not a single 'friend at court.'"

That long Sunday afternoon darkened into a long evening as Custer waited for the response from Washington. He was nervous. And yet, he was disingenuously modest in his letter to Christiancy. He had actively pursued more than one Republican "friend at court," particularly Bingham and Christiancy himself. He enjoyed the sponsorship of Pleasonton, which made the promotion possible in the first place. Far from refusing to believe it possible, Custer wrote in the very same letter, "I will be candid enough to admit that my ambition long since caused me to hope in the course of time to render me worth a 'star.' This thought perhaps influenced me not a little in seeking the position of Col. of a cavalry regt." But he never imagined "that in one sudden unlooked for leap" he should go from first lieutenant to brigadier general at the age of twenty-three.

At nine o'clock that night a telegram arrived from Washington. Custer's promotion had been approved. "To say I was elated would faintly express my feelings. I well knew that I had reason to congratulate myself," he wrote.[37]

Custer stayed up with Pleasonton as he reorganized the Cavalry Corps, which officially absorbed Stahel's division, minus Stahel. Pleasonton renamed it the 3rd Cavalry Division and gave it to one of his favorites, Judson Kilpatrick, previously promoted to brigadier general. He made room for his three new brigadiers by firing existing brigade commanders; he explained that he wanted officers "whom he knew."

What should I do with you? Pleasonton asked Custer. "I replied at once that I had but one request to make." He wanted command of the Michigan Brigade, one of two brigades in the newly designated 3rd Division. It comprised the 5th, 6th, and 7th Michigan Cavalry; Custer asked that a fourth regiment, the 1st Michigan, be added to it. Pleasonton told him to take command in the morning.[38]

The promotion of very young men to such high rank occurred many times in the Union army. Examples surrounded Custer, including Kilpatrick and Ames, as well as Merritt and Farnsworth. Still, Custer and others thought his elevation to be rather remarkable. Custer took particular pleasure in outflanking the opposition of Governor Blair, defeating political patronage with military patronage. He wrote to his sister, "The regiment of which I endeavored to obtain the Colonelcy (5th) belongs to my brigade so that I rather outwitted the Governor who did not see fit to give it to me."[39]

The suddenness, not the promotion itself, is what surprised him. He told Christiancy that he had hoped to be a general "in the course of time," though he expected it to be a short course. This was shown by a unique uniform that appeared on him with almost magical speed, just hours after he left Pleasonton's office. It began with his broad-brimmed, low-crowned felt hat, tilted to one side, above his long, curly blond hair, broad, drooping mustache, and tuft of hair beneath his lower lip. He wore a black velveteen jacket rimmed with gold piping. It was double breasted—a distinction reserved to generals—with eight buttons on each side, grouped in vertical pairs. Five parallel lines of gold embroidery looped about the forearm sleeves from wrist to elbow. Underneath he had on a sailor's shirt, its broad rectangular blue collar with white trim draped over the jacket's neck and shoulders, with a star sewn in each corner. A bright red tie, or cravat, puffed out of the neck at the front. He tucked his dark pants into high cavalry boots braced in gilt spurs.

Where did it come from? One unreliable chronicler, Marguerite Merington, attributed its creation to the teenager Joseph Fought, a bugler in Custer's old company in the 5th U.S. Cavalry who stayed with him as an orderly. Fought gave his recollections many years later, claiming that Custer turned to him to find something distinctive for his general's uniform. The boy tracked down a peddler, "an old Jew." But Fought's account identifies only a pair of stars as his contribution. The rest was Custer's. It appears that the lieutenant kept a general's double-breasted jacket stowed in his bags in anticipation, that he had long thought about how he would look with a sailor's collar and red tie flapping at his neck over black velveteen. No one knows when he expected to wear this costume, but he had been planning, or at least dreaming.[40]

Clothing is communication, a message to the world about the person within. The usual point of a uniform is to express commonality—to say a soldier belongs to an army and a branch of service. It deliberately submerges one's identity in the mass. But Custer's outfit declared that he was an individual, not a replaceable part in a great machine. As Tully McCrea said, Custer delighted "in something odd"—something unexpected, distinctive. In this, he reflected the romantic individualism of antebellum America.[41]

By standing out so clearly, Custer insisted that others *look* at him. Whether they found him curious, laughable, or inspiring, they had to stare. "This officer is one of the funniest-looking beings you ever saw," wrote one officer, on seeing him soon after his debut as a general. "His aspect, though highly amusing, is also pleasing, as he has a very merry blue eye, and a devil-may-care style."[42] Custer's *eye* may have been natural and spontaneous, but his *style* was not. He crafted it to serve a purpose. On the battlefield of the 1860s, tactical command and control operated largely through sight and sound. Larger formations—a corps, a division—might be directed by written orders, but the men in companies, regiments, and brigades listened for drums, bugles, and bands; watched for their unit flags; and looked for their leaders on the field. Custer chose to stand out, in part, as a tactical decision, to allow his men to see and follow him, to let subordinates know where their brigade headquarters could be found.

A general who planned in the rear, who received reports and wrote out orders, had no need to stand out. By choosing to attract attention, Custer declared that he would be in the midst of the fighting, that he intended to inspire. Of course, the enemy could spot him just as well as his own soldiers, and target him. His uniform announced his personal courage.

In his black velveteen, Custer tried to shape how his men saw him. He tried to make them believe something about the man inside the uniform, inside his skin. It was a risk. Soldiers in battle saw through false fronts easily. In action, at least, he would have to be the man he tried to appear to be, or he would fail. The test began on the morning of June 29, when he rode off in his outlandish outfit to find his brigade, drenched by rain that poured down from the overcast skies.[43]

IN THE NOVEL *WAR AND PEACE,* Tolstoy wrote that the French invasion of Russia in 1812 did not take place because Napoleon willed it, but because hundreds of thousands, even millions, of Frenchmen desired it. In the midst of this masterwork of storytelling, Tolstoy paused to argue that the mass of humankind drives events, not those few who project the illusion of power, and who believe the illusion themselves.

Perhaps Tolstoy went too far—but he would have been close to the truth if he had been writing of the American Civil War. Yes, high politics and historic issues produced the conflict; yes, decisions by politicians and generals changed the course of events. But it was only a war in the first place because the American people *wanted* to fight. They volunteered by the millions for years of combat; they demanded offensives and decisive battles. Even those who never enlisted applied themselves to logistics, military transportation, and weapons technology—inventing ironclad ships, new pontoon bridges, and repeating rifles, for example. Then there were African Americans, who conducted what one historian has called the greatest slave rebellion in history. They risked death to desert to Union lines by the hundreds, then thousands, then hundreds of thousands. In the end, what happened on factory floors and plantation fields, in town-square meetings and polling places, mattered more than any general's orders.[44]

The deceptively mechanical language of army organization obscures this reality. The term *unit* evokes an undifferentiated mass, a wooden soldier to be moved about. A *company* suggests an institution. A *regiment* sounds like an impersonal clockwork; and it is made up of *battalions* and grouped with others into a *brigade*, hard-edged words evoking blocs of firepower without humanity. And yet, the temporary army of U.S. Volunteers existed only because of individual choice and popular initiative. Citizens had assembled to create these units; initially their officers were voted in by the recruits or appointed by elected officials. Each company or regiment was a village under arms, a county on horseback, one community determined to wipe out another. In such an army, an officer could only command if his soldiers chose to follow.

In detaching from home, though, each unit became a thing unto itself. Each day the men drilled in camp, each hour they spent on an exhausting march, each time they deployed in line of battle, their sense of community separated from their home places. They formed their own expectations, jokes, and jargon. As soldiers they belonged to one another as they never could to civilian friends and kin. At their best, they learned pride and comradeship through what they endured, what they lost, and what they achieved.

But they were not always at their best. In that, their leaders made the difference. The commander made his community work or fall apart. His men united behind him with a common sense of purpose or atomized into a malfunctioning, dissenting horde. A trooper who wrote home of pride in his leader was expressing pride in himself and his unit; when he railed against his chief's incompetence, he himself felt like a failure.

What did the soldier want from the men who led him? Perhaps the question should be reversed: What did he *not* want? He did not want to die, of course, but it would be more precise to say that he did not want his life to be wasted. Aside from the draftee—a late-coming minority in the ranks—he enlisted to fight, and he knew that he could only do so at the risk of his life. He thought there should be good cause for that risk. He wanted leaders who were willing to take the same chances he did.

The soldier was human. In the midst of his suffering, small comforts mattered. He hoped for a furlough, for soft bread and fresh meat, for shoes that did not hurt his feet. To varying degrees he understood the need for discipline, but believed it should be reasonable and fair. In the end, though, all those desires were secondary. In this people's war, what the citizen soldier wanted most from his generals was victory.[45]

IN THE LATE MORNING of June 30, 1863, the 3rd Cavalry Division moved north, searching for the rebel army. Custer led the column with the 1st and 7th Michigan Cavalry regiments; the other two in his brigade, the 5th and 6th, had been detached before he assumed command and remained some distance west. Soon after passing through Hanover, Pennsylvania, the sound of gunfire erupted behind them.

Custer ordered his men to turn about and head toward the fighting. He learned that Confederate horsemen, the advance guard of Stuart's cavalry, had charged the division's rear. At the start of the campaign, Stuart had taken his men on a long raid to the east, riding behind the Army of the Potomac. He had gathered plunder but deprived Lee of his scouting and screening force. Stuart needed to unite with the Army of Northern Virginia; to do that, he had to break through the 3rd Cavalry Division.

As Custer deployed his men and artillery, the missing 5th and 6th Michigan Cavalry arrived on the scene. He dismounted his troops, every fourth man leading horses to the rear. The rest advanced on foot in a loose skirmish line and opened fire.

Theirs was no ordinary fire. The 6th Michigan carried the revolutionary Spencer rifle. (Later the Spencer carbine—a short-barreled version designed for use by cavalry—would be issued in its place.) Unlike the standard single-shot, muzzle-loading rifled musket, it carried seven rounds in a tubular magazine loaded into the butt. A trooper cocked the hammer, yanked a trigger-guard lever that ejected the spent cartridge and loaded the chamber, and pulled the trigger—all in a fraction of a musket's loading time.

Custer loved a mounted charge more than almost anything in life, but he appreciated the Spencer—"in my estimation, the most effective firearm that our cavalry can adopt," he wrote a short time later. Deploying his men on foot allowed them to work their rifles freely and aim accurately. The Confederates, one of Custer's troopers wrote, "were struck dumb with surprise." A prisoner later said "that they couldn't understand how anyone could reload so rapidly."[46]

Stymied, Stuart pulled back and sought an easier route to the Army of Northern Virginia. The Union cavalry continued its own hunt in the intense heat, through a landscape of barns and fields and wooden fences, of low hills and bursts of green woods. Everywhere the armies went, they denuded fences of rails to stoke campfires and trampled the ground into mud and dust. Some of Custer's men were fresh, but not all. "By this time we had become a sorry-looking body of men," one veteran recalled, "having been in the saddle day and night almost continuously for three weeks, without a change of clothing or an opportunity for a general wash."[47]

"Do you know how cavalry moves? It never goes out of a walk, and four miles an hour is *very* rapid marching—'killing to horses' as we always describe it," wrote Capt. Charles F. Adams Jr. to his mother. A company commander dreaded a march.

> You are a slave to your horses, you work like a dog yourself, and you exact the most extreme care from your Sergeants, and you see diseases creeping up on you day by day and your horses breaking down under your eyes. . . . Backs soon get feverish under the saddle and the first day's march swells them; after that day by day the trouble grows. . . . Imagine a horse with his withers swollen to three times the natural size, and with a volcanic, running sore pouring matter down each side, and you have a case with which every cavalry officer is daily called upon to deal, and you imagine a horse which has still to be ridden until he lays down in sheer suffering under the saddle. . . . [The air reeks] with the stench of dead horses, federal and confederate. You pass them on every road and find them in every field, while from their carrions you can follow the march of every army that moves.

It would astonish the civilians back home, Adams wrote, "to see the weak, gaunt, rough animals . . . on which these 'dashing cavalry raids' were executed. It would knock the romance out of you."[48]

On July 1, at the crossroads town of Gettysburg, the Army of the Potomac finally found the Army of Northern Virginia. The vortex of combat sucked in the scattered infantry corps and artillery batteries, as the two sides arrayed themselves in full force on opposing ridges. The climactic battle of the campaign had begun.

On July 2, Kilpatrick led his division far around the left flank of the Confederate army as the fighting raged at Gettysburg. His men drove a small body of the enemy through the hamlet of Hunterstown, northeast of Gettysburg. On the far side, Kilpatrick saw a handful of Confederates out in the open and ordered Custer to clear them away. The young general deployed some of his men on foot to support his attack, and led a small force—just a few dozen riders—in a mounted charge. A Confederate brigade opened fire from cover. "Horses and men toppled into the road," writes one historian. Custer's horse fell, struck by a bullet, cata-pulting him onto the ground. A Union cavalryman rode forward, shot a man aiming at Custer, and pulled the general up behind him. The Yan-kees threw back a counterattack and pulled out after dark.

It has been estimated that Custer led about forty men in his charge. At least twenty-seven of them died, suffered wounds, or were taken pris-oner. The wonder is that as many as thirteen came back unhurt, and that Custer did too. But he was always lucky.[49]

THE THIRD OF JULY was the third day of battle at Gettysburg. The men of the North expected a Confederate assault. The day before, Lee's men had come perilously close to capturing Little Round Top, anchoring the southern end of the Army of the Potomac, and Cemetery Hill and Culp's Hill on the northern flank. Had the rebels seized any of these, they would have unhinged the Union line and won a great victory. Having come so close to success on the second day, Lee seemed sure to attack on the third.

The stakes could not have been more obvious to the soldiers on both sides. The entire Army of Northern Virginia—reinforced to 75,000 troops, including six brigades of cavalrymen—had swept far to the north of the federal capital. Lee and his soldiers were buoyant after their tri-umph at Chancellorsville, confident in their ability to crush the Army of the Potomac. Meade had a lower standard for success—his army merely had to endure and bring the rebel invasion to a halt—but, unlike Lee, he could scarcely survive a failure. Defeat so far north would demoralize the public and perhaps guarantee Confederate independence. With some 90,000 men—15,000 of them cavalry—Meade had an edge in numbers, but not overwhelming superiority.

Custer had spent all night retreating from Hunterstown with the roughly 2,000 men of his brigade (far less than the unit's maximum strength of 4,800). At about four in the morning he and his troopers unsaddled their horses five miles southeast of Gettysburg. A couple of hours later one of Kilpatrick's staff officers rode up and ordered Custer to move with the rest of the 3rd Division to guard the army's far left flank. He roused his men and formed them into a long column. Another staff officer rode up, sent by Brig. Gen. David Gregg, commander of the 2nd Cavalry Division, who ordered Custer to the far *right* of the line of battle, with Pleasonton's approval.[50]

The young general led his men to the intersection of Hanover and Low Dutch roads, almost due east of the northern end of the Union line on the Gettysburg battlefield. From a historical perspective, Custer was in the right place. Since ancient times, horsemen had guarded an army's flanks. Infantry occupied the center and engaged in the heaviest fighting. Firepower made infantry supreme. The rifled musket carried by Civil War foot soldiers had a range of hundreds of yards, visibility permitting; supporting artillery shot still farther. Men on horseback made easy targets, and they lacked firepower. They usually dismounted to shoot even when they used the carbine, the rifle's shorter-barreled sibling—which reduced their numbers by a quarter, since horse holders could not fight. The introduction of the Spencer pointed to a more powerful combat role, but only a few cavalry regiments possessed it.

Cavalrymen on both sides still romanticized the era when mounted charges could shatter enemy lines and win battles. They celebrated medieval knights, royalist cavaliers, and Murat's exploits in Napoleon's campaigns. These all predated the mass use of the rifle. When cavalry charged prepared infantry in the Civil War, they met disaster, as at Gaines's Mill on the Peninsula. A properly controlled charge moved at a slow pace until quite close to the enemy, lest the horses tire out early; when the riders finally spurred into a gallop, they wielded revolvers or sabers, close-range weapons that required them to get almost to within an arm's reach of the foe. Mounted charges could still work, but almost strictly against other horsemen, or foot soldiers who were badly outnumbered, panicking, or unsuspecting. Civil War cavalrymen usually found themselves restricted to raiding, reconnaissance, screening the infantry from observation, pursuing the fleeing enemy after a victory—or fighting enemy cavalry on the flanks of a great battle. And Gettysburg was a great battle.

Custer halted his men facing west, and sent out scouts on a wide-ranging search for the enemy. It was quiet. A little over a mile to the north was a low rise of wooded ground dignified with the name Cress's Ridge, where enemy cannons soon appeared. A heavy skirmish line moved into view, gray-clad troopers edging their way south on foot. The guns began to boom, sending solid shot and exploding shells squarely into the Michigan Brigade. Custer redeployed his men to face the new threat and ordered his skillful artillery chief, Lt. Alexander Pennington, to fire at the enemy guns. Pennington's three-inch rifled cannons soon silenced the better-placed Confederate artillery. Custer sent the 5th Michigan forward in a dismounted skirmish line, and he dispatched scouts to ride around the enemy flanks and investigate the force he now faced.[51]

Unknown to Custer, Lee had decided to win the Battle of Gettysburg with a decisive thrust at the center of the Union line. He had called on General Stuart to take his much-admired horsemen and swing around the Union right flank in a solid mass. He was to get into the rear of the Union infantry during the frontal assault and pursue and destroy the retreating foe. The Michigan Brigade was the last obstacle in his way.

Custer's scouts reported that a heavy force of Confederate cavalry lay to the north. But the rebels hesitated, unsure of what *they* faced. The morning passed amid mere skirmishing. At midday, one of Kilpatrick's staff officers rode up and ordered Custer to follow his original instructions—to go to the opposite flank of the Army of the Potomac. A brigade of General Gregg's 2nd Division soon arrived to relieve him, and Custer reluctantly ordered his men to withdraw. Before he departed, Gregg rode up to confer with him.

At thirty, Gregg was Custer's senior by only a few years, but he looked much older, with dark straight hair and an enormous curly beard. He said that Pleasonton had also ordered Custer to go to Kilpatrick. But he had received a dispatch that "large columns of the enemy's cavalry were moving toward the right of the line"—and here they were. Gregg thought that the Confederates across the field were "evidence that the enemy's cavalry had gained our right, and were about to attack, with the view of gaining the rear of our line of battle," he later reported. They could not risk weakening this critical point by letting Custer's brigade go.

Both men knew that if Custer stayed at Gregg's request, Gregg would be disobeying a direct command from the corps commander. Gregg needed Custer's agreement with his analysis and cooperation in refusing the order.

"General Custer," Gregg wrote, "fully satisfied of the intended attack, was well pleased to remain with his brigade." Just after 1 p.m., as the two generals made their plans, thunder rolled over the field—the concussion of some 150 Confederate artillery pieces all blasting at once, "the largest Southern bombardment of the war," writes James McPherson. For the next two hours, the rebel guns fired shot and shell at the center of the main Union line on Cemetery Ridge, preparing the way for an assault by 12,000 men led by Maj. Gen. George Pickett.[52]

On this field, the battle between cavalry simmered less dramatically. Gregg sent a line of dismounted skirmishers toward Cress's Ridge. A larger rebel force advanced to meet them. Custer dispatched the 5th Michigan on foot to reinforce Gregg's men. They held the line, but fell back when they ran low on ammunition.

The Confederates chose that moment to attack. Two regiments advanced uncertainly on foot. Another rode out of the tree line atop the ridge and down toward the Union skirmishers. It was the veteran 1st Virginia Cavalry.

Custer trotted his horse over to the 7th Michigan, a regiment he had kept mounted and in reserve. Inexperienced, badly understrength (with only 461 officers and enlisted men, less than 60 percent of the brigade's largest regiment), it was the only unit in position to save the endangered skirmishers on the field. Coming up to its commander, Col. William D. Mann, Custer learned that Gregg had ordered the regiment to charge. He said he would go with them. Mann gave the command, and the column rode through the fields at a trot. As the troopers approached the enemy, they sped into a gallop.

Custer rode ahead of them. By now his flamboyant uniform had endured days in the saddle and hours of sleep taken here and there on the ground. It had absorbed dust and rain and mud, not to mention the sweat of a man hard at work in the dense, humid heat without a moment to bathe. Yet he remained distinctive still. Some would remember him flourishing his sword, others, him waving his hat. But all accounts agree that he turned toward his men and shouted, "Come on, you Wolverines!"

With sabers in the air they sped toward the 1st Virginia. They collided with a stone and rail fence. The Union horsemen at the rear crashed into those halted in front; on the other side, the Virginians dismounted and fired revolvers and carbines into the Michiganders' faces. The men of the 7th fired back, over and under fence rails, slashing across the barrier with their sabers. A group managed to tear apart a section of the fence; mounted federal cavalrymen crammed through, only to meet a counterattack.

Custer and a group of men who followed him had kept clear of the fence. He could see a disaster emerging. Amid the confusion, he got the 7th Michigan to disengage from the enemy with assistance from the 5th. They fell back, allowing their artillery crews to fire on the now-exposed Confederates. Then it began again.[53]

Wade Hampton, the richest man in South Carolina, led an oversized brigade of Confederate cavalry. He led it well. He and his men had pulverized the Union charge at Hunterstown, nearly taking Custer's life. Now he led parts of three brigades down Cress's Ridge on horseback—a mass of men, animals, and steel that dwarfed the single-regiment attacks of the fight so far. "A grander spectacle than their advance has rarely been beheld," one Union cavalryman wrote. "They marched with well-aligned fronts and steady reins. Their polished saber-blades dazzled in the sun. All eyes turned upon them." They aimed at Custer's artillery, the key to victory for either side.[54]

"To meet this overwhelming force I had but one available regiment—the 1st Michigan Cavalry, and the fire of battery M, 2d regular artillery," Custer reported. He rode over and found the 1st Michigan mounted and ready to charge, having received orders from Gregg to do so. Col. Charles Town commanded the regiment; despite being very sick, he insisted on being helped into his saddle to attack with his men. "The gallant body of men advanced to the attack of a force outnumbering them five to one," Custer wrote. Once again, he rode at the head of his men.[55]

"On came the rebel cavalry, yelling like demons right toward the battery," wrote the Michigan cavalryman James Kidd.[56] The federal guns blasted them with canister, gigantic shotgun rounds that spread metal balls through the oncoming ranks, slaughtering men and horses. The enemy came faster.

Custer trotted ahead of his outnumbered regiment. At a distance of a hundred yards he ordered a full gallop. Once again he shouted, "Come on, you Wolverines!" The Union troopers roared and smashed their horses into the rebel ranks, "sabering all who came within reach," Custer reported. "So sudden and violent was the collision that many of the horses were turned end over end and crushed the riders beneath them," recalled a witness. "The clashing of sabers, the firing of pistols, the demands for surrender, and cries of the combatants now filled the air."[57]

Custer fought in the center of the struggling mass, immersed in clashing swords, revolver blasts, horses stumbling and colliding. A rallying point and a target, he rode Roanoke, his best horse. "I never intend to ride him into battle," he had written to his sister. "He is too valuable." Now Roanoke took a bullet to the foreleg, and staggered and fell. Custer got clear, pulled himself onto a riderless horse, and rejoined the fight.

He and the 1st Michigan drove into the Confederate formation, splitting it apart. Gregg's division supported the attack; elements of other regiments charged as well. Hampton suffered sword cuts to his head. "For a moment," Custer wrote, "but only a moment, that long, heavy column stood its ground; then, unable to withstand the impetuosity of our attack, it gave way into a disorderly rout." The rebels raced back to their ridge, and did not attack again. The Union cavalry had won.[58]

CUSTER WROTE HIS REPORT more than six weeks after the battle, yet he still could not conceal his pride. "The 1st, being masters of the field, had the proud satisfaction of seeing the much-vaunted [Confederate] 'chivalry,' led by their favorite commander, seek safety in headlong flight," he wrote.[59]

Why wouldn't he be proud? In command less than a week, self-conscious of his youth, aware that he had been promoted through favoritism as well as merit, he found himself at a crucial point at a critical moment—and he had succeeded. The Confederate horsemen had long stood supreme, as Custer acknowledged with his taunt, but at Gettysburg he and his men had defeated them. They did not crush the enemy, of course; as in the infantry battle, it was a defensive victory, yet a victory nonetheless. The rebels had to break the federal line or run back home; by foiling them, the Union won.

The Union cavalry suffered roughly 250 casualties in this fight, nearly 90 percent in the Michigan Brigade. Gregg had commanded, and commanded well, but Custer had *led*, in person and in the place of crisis. Somehow he survived without a wound, despite his plunge into the heaviest fighting and changing horses, too.[60]

The cavalry battle mattered. Stuart was a superb combat leader; if he had been able to reach the rear of the Union line during the rebel infantry attack (known in popular memory as Pickett's Charge), the story of Gettysburg would have taken a different course. This is not to exaggerate: the Union infantry and artillery crushed the main Confederate attack, and if Stuart's cavalrymen had broken through they would have been worn down and short of ammunition after their struggle against the Union troopers. Custer did not win the Battle of Gettysburg. Yet Gregg and others on the ground took Stuart's threat seriously. No army could afford to have a formidable enemy force in its rear during a struggle for its existence. Stuart's arrival there might have had an unsettling impact on Meade's frame of mind, if not his actual line of battle.

Custer's taunt about Southern "chivalry" reveals more than well-earned self-satisfaction. This was the same man who once had repeated the political arguments of secessionist fire-eaters, who had served as best man in a Confederate officer's wedding, who had lingered in a rebel camp to write letters to old friends who now fought against him. In many ways he identified with Southern chivalry—until it came to fighting. Then he wanted to win. With a saber in hand, the killer momentarily negated the conservative in his soul.

But not the romantic. Galloping onto the field, swinging his sword, arrayed in dramatic costume, long blond hair flying from under his rebel hat, he embodied the archaic fantasies of the lads who had marched to war in 1861, dreaming of personal combat with naked steel. Custer's charge succeeded due to the tactical conditions, a battle of cavalry against cavalry. That very success reinforced his illusions—the image of a heedless, dashing hero he cultivated for himself as much as for others. The Yankee press seized on that image, hailing him as the "Boy General of the Golden Locks."

Yet the moment of his triumph was rich—or perhaps we should say heavy—with irony. Another heedless, dashing hero with long curly hair and a carefully chosen costume led an equally dramatic charge almost simultaneously with Custer's—but it ended in disaster. Confederate general Pickett embodied antebellum Southern chivalry; he "looked like a cross between a Cavalier dandy and a riverboat gambler," writes James McPherson. "He affected the romantic style of Sir Walter Scott's heroes and was eager to win everlasting glory at Gettysburg." The attack spearheaded by his division made a stunning display of the traditional martial virtues: 12,000 men stepping in neat lines behind rows of regimental flags, bravely hurling themselves at the very center of the federal line on the aptly named Cemetery Ridge. But massed cannon and rifle fire annihilated them. Just half the rebel host came back; Pickett lost two out of three men from his own division.[61] It was bitterly disillusioning, even for witnesses on the Union side. Valor could not defeat the machinery of war. Firepower crushed courage. What glory could there possibly be amid industrialized slaughter?

This was a lesson the Civil War taught men who endured the hell of pitched infantry combat—men such as the young Oliver Wendell Holmes Jr., shot through the neck at Antietam; or Ambrose Bierce, who later recalled how, in his first fight, his regiment had been marched to just within enemy artillery range and ordered to lie down, where solid shot ricocheted through their ranks, horrifically tearing apart bodies; or William T. Sherman, who after the terrors of Shiloh and other battles declared that "glory is all moonshine." Custer, on the other hand, as a horseman fighting against horsemen, lived within an exception to the rule. The question was whether he would ever understand how, and why, the war darkened some of the best minds of his generation.

Custer's soldiers, though, began to love him for precisely those traits that seemed so obsolete in Pickett's Charge. Only days before, they had laughed at his girlish curls, his foppish outfit, his preposterous youth. But when he plunged into battle, they saw how he fought. Some of his men might well have reflected on the unwisdom of his leading charges. He was a brigadier general, responsible for thousands of lives. He could not control his regiments amid a melee, and if he died in battle, as so many officers did, confusion could prevail and imperil the entire brigade. But the men saw a general who led by example. He "was not afraid to fight like a private soldier," one reflected, and "was ever in front and would never ask them to go where he would not lead." He fought with skill, too, and they admired him for it.[62]

Most important, Custer was not reckless with the lives of his soldiers, however much he was with his own. Though an aggressive commander, he had not attacked blindly. He made the most of the new technology of the repeating Spencer rifle by deploying many of his soldiers on foot, and he put his well-manned artillery to good use. He chose the right moments to charge, essentially counterpunching after his opponent committed himself. At Gettysburg, Gregg confirmed his judgment by ordering charges at the same time he did. Insecure in some respects, he was confident in his own courage and fighting ability, or he never would have worn such an attention-getting getup. Many things may be said about the contradictory Custer, but one of the most important is that he understood the battlefield. There he was at ease.

For the men of the Michigan Brigade, their assessment of Custer came down to one thing. He gave them what they wanted most: victory.

Five

THE WOMEN

Sᴏ GUARDED THE DOORWAY between worlds. On one side was the world of now and on the other the world to come. The passage between them was governed by rules, beliefs, and rituals that Lydia Ann Reed kept for her family, as did many women of her time and place. Dark-haired with wide, sad eyes and a long, thin face, fourteen years older than Armstrong, she stood as sentinel of the faith, reminding her men to mind eternity. Sealed inside a frail frame, denied the powers of the earth because of her sex, she had this one grim dark role to play, beyond the maternal and matrimonial.[1]

"Your vary welcome letter was I was going to say read with much pleasure it made me feel sad to hear that you had to kill that man," she wrote to her brother on August 13, 1862. She had just received his account of the first time he knew for certain he had taken a life, shooting an escaping Confederate officer in the back. She did not write that she was proud of him or grateful for his survival; she said she was troubled. Even in war, killing challenged her faith, in which God alone could determine the end of days and apportion suffering for his own purposes. As a soldier, her brother embodied a conundrum: he did his duty to his fellow men yet invited divine retribution, for as Jesus said, "All they that take the sword shall perish with the sword." Without stopping for punctuation she moved from regret to fear. "I am afraid the next thing I hear you will get shot you are so venturesome," she added. "Oh the horrors of war when will this cruel war be over and many loved ones return home."[2]

Her prayer was a common one in those days. "I feel very ancious about you all the time," she wrote on June 23, 1863, with her customary erratic spelling. "I don't know what day I may have some bad news from you." She feared for his soul as much as his body, uncertain where he would go if he went through the door. She insisted that the invisible was more real than the visible, and called on him to repent. "My Dear Brother O how much I wish you was a christian," she wrote. "You have often said you was happy. I don't think thare is any true happyness in the world with out religion." It would later be said of her, "She cared little for the world's pleasure, but found her chief enjoyment in the church." For Armstrong, the opposite was true, yet he too had been raised on scripture. She gave voice to admonitions that lingered inside his skull.[3]

Armstrong remained a creature of the senses, not the spirit. He filled his heart with temporal things, with fighting, promotion, friendship, music, dancing, gambling, and love—and lust. And he demanded that Ann play a temporal role for him as his intermediary for his romantic affairs. It unsettled her. One Friday morning in June 1863, Fannie Fifield stopped by and mentioned that Armstrong had sent her a letter. Soon after she called again in company with Nettie Humphrey, Libbie Bacon's closest friend. It placed Ann in a difficult position.

Her discomfort surfaced in her letters to Armstrong, as she alternated worries about his health with non sequiturs about the women he desired. She wrote on June 23, "Oh that this cruel war was over. I saw Libbie . . . with a young gentleman and two young ladies. Thare was quite a number of strangers [in town for a Methodist meeting]. Fannie said she had five girls at her house." By juxtaposing Armstrong's love interests with her fears for his safety, she seemed to ramble with inchoate stress at being caught in the middle of his romantic entanglements.[4]

Three weeks after Gettysburg, Ann complained that she had not heard from him despite her many letters. Then she turned to the women. "Fannie has gone east with her Father and Mother," she wrote. "She braught a letter over to send [to Armstrong] with mine. She looked vary nice. She had a beautiful dress on and was as happy as a bee. She enjoys life. There was a concert at the Seminary last Thursday evening. Edward Thurbur the Minister took Libbie." Weary of her role, she complained that she couldn't give him any news about his friends and peers. She was happier describing her children. Her daughter Emma said she wanted to send Armstrong a bowl of gravy; she thought he would like it.

But then she returned to Libbie. Armstrong had recently sent Ann and David Reed a drawing by Alfred Waud, the famous battlefield artist. Waud had drawn Custer himself at the Battle of Aldie, showing him out in front of the charging line of Union cavalry, his black horse in full gallop, long hair and wide-brimmed slouch hat on his head, his sword held high. "Don't you know David took that picture you sent and went and called on Libbie," Ann wrote, "and showed it to her and had quite a talk with her."[5]

Ann's letter suggests that David visited Libbie on his own initiative. In fact, Armstrong had specifically asked his brother-in-law to show the portrait to Fannie *and* Libbie, and to deliver a letter to the latter.[6] But David made a bitter rebuke that Armstrong had not written to *him*, suggesting a growing irritation with Armstrong's assumption that David and Ann should be his agents.

Socially, the Reeds ranked lower than Judge Bacon and his family. To be sure, this small Michigan town was far from the status-obsessed Manhattan fictionalized by Edith Wharton, but ideas of respectability and rank flourished here as well. Ann was the uneducated daughter of a tavern keeper's widow, stepdaughter of a poor and barely literate blacksmith, and wife of a farmer who—though prosperous—hauled stuff around in wagons. She revealed her self-consciousness to Armstrong in the same letter. "You will see I make a grate many mistakes this evening. I don't know how a General can read such a letter as this. Some of the folks think you will hardly speak to common folks now."[7] She didn't really worry about her brother putting on airs, but she certainly classed herself with the "common folks." Fannie Fifield and Libbie Bacon, on the other hand, were daughters of a wealthy businessman and a judge, respectively. Their manners were refined, their schooling elevated, their sense of fashion acute.

Morally, too, Ann felt deeply uncomfortable as her brother pursued two women at once. Her correspondence with him shows that he was sincere in his courtship of Fannie. But his continuing interest in Libbie made things awkward for Ann, especially given the social gap between them. One night in the summer of 1863, Ann went to a shop owned by a woman named Avery. As she turned to leave she came face-to-face with "Miss Libbie B.," as Ann called her. "She bowed vary pleasantly. I don't know wether she bowed to me or Miss Avery. I did not return the bow," Ann wrote. "If she did bow to me she will think I was rather cool."[8] Was she, in fact, being cool? If so, it was not Libbie but her brother's lack of fidelity that left her cold.

After David's visit, Ann seemed to know more about Armstrong's covert communication with Libbie through Nettie Humphrey. She reported to him about Fannie, then grew rather curt, even sarcastic, when it came to Libbie. She heard Libbie's stepmother was going away on a trip, but "I don't know wether Libbie is going or not. Perhaps you know all about it. . . . I suppose Nettie keeps you pretty well posted."[9]

Each letter Armstrong sent to Ann seemed to bear witness to his carelessness and callousness. On July 25, he wrote, "I asked General Pleasonton for a leave of absence in Aug or Sep. He says I can have a leave but only on the condition viz. that I marry Fannie Fifield. Shall I come?" Less than a month after that, Ann was forced to doubt his sincerity toward Fifield. She wrote, "Fannie . . . said she did not know but you was displeased at her. I told her I thought not that you had sent your love to her in my letter. I see I am mistaken you wished to be remembered to her."[10]

Custer was hardly the first man to let opportunism govern his relations with women. "I know girls better than you," he once told Libbie,
and he believed he could manipulate them.[11] His true emotions, though,
remained a mystery to those who knew him best, and perhaps to himself.
The day was coming when he would have to know.

ON NEW YEAR'S EVE, the last day of 1862, Libbie Bacon sat on the floor
of her room with Nettie Humphrey as each read a letter the other had
written the year before. As a band played outside, the two young women
took sheets of paper and wrote new letters to each other, to be opened a
year later. It was their private tradition for greeting the new year. After
they read messages from the past and sent them to the future, they would
sleep beside each other as the calendar turned over.

They were close. Nettie believed that Libbie "belonged to me as much
as to anybody." Libbie talked to Nettie about love and courtship as she
did with no one else. She "raved about Francis C's beautiful mouth," Nettie wrote to her, "and wondered how you *should* dispose of 'that Capt.
Custer!' "[12]

This New Year's Eve showed twenty-year-old Bacon on the threshold
between childhood and maturity, with her schoolgirl's custom, adolescent
attractions, and adult's concern with manners and marriage. In the year
ahead she would face decisions that would direct the course of the rest of
her life, and she was not sure she was ready.[13]

Her existence to that point had been both sheltered and precarious.
She had been born in Monroe on April 8, 1842, to Sophia and Daniel
Bacon, who named her Elizabeth Clift Bacon, though Sophia always
called her Libbie. Daniel, born on December 12, 1798, was a broad, bald-
ing, rather dour-faced man. He had been active in the Whig Party as
long as it existed, serving in the state senate and on the circuit court. He
survived the depression that began in 1837, and invested in real estate and
other enterprises in partnership with Nettie's father.

But death struck the family again and again. When Libbie was three,
her four-month-old sister, Sophia, died. When she was about five, her
older brother Edward fell through a broken step; he spent a year confined
to his bed, then died of illness just after Libbie's sixth birthday. The next
year another sister, Harriett, died when only six months old. Later cholera burned through Monroe, taking many lives. In 1852 she wrote in her
diary about what she planned to do "if I am permitted to live to become a
woman." At ten years old, an early death seemed to her as likely as life.[14]

Beset with these losses, the devout Sophia guided the family into a
deeper engagement with the Presbyterian Church. Piety, she learned,

also made a potent tool for parenting. On one occasion she punished Libbie by sending her to bed early. The girl fell asleep and awoke to find her mother ardently praying for her and *over* her. Sophia had planted shame and it grew. "Oh! I am very wicked. I feel it," Libbie later wrote in her diary, "a typical lament," her biographer Shirley Leckie notes.[15]

In August 1854, Sophia contracted "bloody dysentery." It proved fatal. "I stood by that open grave and felt—oh! God only knows what anguish filled my heart," Libbie told her diary.[16] From that moment onward, she would be sheltered precisely because she had lost so much, because her life had been so uncertain. "My daughter was commited [sic] to my care and protection at the age of twelve years," Daniel Bacon wrote. Her dying mother told him, "I want you to be a mother as well as a father to Elizabeth." Almost a decade later he remarked, "I have ever felt the force of these words. . . . I feel the responsibility beyond anything in my life before or since."[17]

Libbie herself held tightly to childhood. Though she never forgot her grief, she learned how to exploit her loss. "How shamelessly I traded on . . . [being] poor motherless Libbie Bacon," she later recalled. "What an excuse I made of it!" Sent to a boarding school in Auburn, New York, she described her ambivalence about the maturity that seemed forced on her by circumstances. "I like being a *little* girl," she wrote to her father. "I dread being a young lady *so* much. . . . I like acting *free* and *girl like* Not being so *prim* and *particular* about what I say and do!"[18]

In 1859 Libbie's father remarried, wedding a widow named Rhoda Wells Pitts. Over the next few years, he believed, she came to be Libbie's "adviser and protector." Libbie returned to Monroe, underwent the conversion expected of all believers, even those raised in the church, and enrolled at the Young Ladies' Seminary and Collegiate Institute. Two official visitors inspected the school in the spring of 1862, when Libbie graduated as valedictorian, and came away impressed. "The pupils had learned how to study, to obtain control of their own minds, so that their entire energies might be concentrated upon any subject," they reported. "Some schools have too much of the stuffing process—going over a great amount, and crowding into the young brain as much of *this* and *that* as possible. . . . Young girls, especially, are often ruined in health for life by being pressed beyond measure in this way." By contrast, Libbie and her peers were so well taught "that Algebra becomes a plaything. . . . Their essays on commencement day were of great merit." The *Detroit Free Press* praised Libbie's valedictory address as "one of the best."[19]

But she could not escape the internal tides of adolescence and young adulthood. She would later write to her stepmother, "Mother I haven't uttered a cross word [for some time]. Now isn't that pretty well for me?"

She would comment acidly on others, even her own father; when she was talking to him, she noted, he had a tendency to "walk away downtown, leaving me to finish a sentence to the wall."[20]

More than temper, though, her trouble was desire—and being desired. Men admired her thick dark hair and soft dark eyes when she was barely a teenager; she once slapped a doctor who kissed her when she was only thirteen. She pushed men back but also felt a secret pleasure; as Leckie writes, "nothing delighted her more than attracting men."

During an art lesson she had to scramble out of the grasp of her teacher, though not without a sense of triumph. At an exhibition in Toledo, a high school principal "talked and looked me through!" she wrote in her diary. "I guess he knew I had ruffles on my drawers. . . . The exhibition was fine but the Principal finer."[21]

Older men surrounded her in part because the war carried so many young men away. The year 1861 had seen the organization of the 4th Michigan Infantry Regiment in town, mass meetings, flags and bunting everywhere. Libbie and Rhoda sewed and baked for the troops, as countless other women did. The war pulled them into a public role, supporting the military through individual efforts and aid societies, yet mostly in terms that defined middle-class women's lives—the "cult of domesticity," as historians would call it. This was the part that Libbie was expected to fill—to devote herself to domestic and religious chores, regardless of her education, intelligence, and natural independence. She craved love, expected marriage, but dreaded confinement.[22]

In late 1861, Libbie sat in church one Sunday, utterly bored. She sketched a caricature of the man in the pulpit. After the service a minister named Dutton scolded her—then began to call frequently at the Bacon house. He courted her, and her father and stepmother approved. In April he kissed her. "I *knew* then he loved me," she wrote in her diary, "but no love was in my bosom for him, only admiration for his intellect."[23]

She was more taken with her dreams. Two were particularly vivid, coming to her on successive nights, in which she married a soldier, "the dear man who forms the subject of my journal so often." Dutton was not that man. Neither was the lawyer who wooed her before him, nor the railroad clerk who came after.[24]

Thanksgiving of 1862 came. The Boyds, principals of the Young Ladies' Seminary, hosted their holiday party. There she accepted an introduction to a lean young man in a captain's uniform named George Armstrong Custer. He did not look like an ordinary soldier, with his keen blue eyes, red-gold mustache, and curly uncut hair—and he seemed to know it. One reporter wrote that he had "a very slight impediment in his speech," later described as a stammer, particularly pronounced when he grew excited.[25] He was rather excited now. But she was amused as well as attracted by his affectations and swagger; as she had written earlier that year in her diary, "I do so hate [airs] in anybody."

As small as Monroe was, the two did not know each other. He had spent only odd patches of his life in Monroe, between his years in Ohio, West Point, and service in the army. She, too, had spent months away and years cloistered in the seminary. On meeting, a current sparked between them, and Custer felt it. Nettie Humphrey later called her friend Libbie the "spirit of mischief"—echoing Custer's description of himself as "full of mischief." She was not only beautiful, she was *alive.*[26]

So began his siege of her doorstep, his patrol of her routine, his penetration of her diary. "I admire him," she wrote, for suffering sleet and rain "soldierlike" to hold an umbrella for her. He passed by her house "forty times a day," she noted with pleasure. His courtship was "in too much haste tho' I admire his perseverance."

The word "soldierlike" embodied her attraction. He was a creature of duty, discipline, endurance, and strength. Even his aggressiveness appealed to her—though it was "too much." A soldier's virtues and vices did not sit easily in the drawing room. Soldiers gambled and swore among themselves and did worse with women. They killed and they died. In the midst of the great war, soldiers were both the national heroes and the national tragedy. Custer was young, handsome, and far more interesting than the lawyer, railroad clerk, or depressed minister who had pursued her. He was also dangerous. For both reasons he brought intrigue and romance into her life.[27]

Judge Bacon dismissed Custer as "that mustached fellow." The young captain came from the wrong family, the wrong party, the wrong profession. And he had been seen drunk *in the street.* Public standing mattered a great deal to the judge. With Libbie, he later declared, he had "guarded her reputation with intense parental solicitude." A union—even a dalliance—with Custer would do her reputation no good.[28]

Custer's attention flattered Libbie, but she took it no more seriously than the "beautiful mouth" of Francis Chandler. Whenever he snared her on the street, she avoided any discussion of his feelings. Toward the end of 1862, he finally spoke to her with purpose. "Nobody could entertain him but me over an hour without his being lonely," Libbie wrote in her diary. "He tells me he would sacrifice every earthly hope to gain my love and I tell him if I could I would give it to him."[29]

What Custer did not realize was how fiercely Judge Bacon opposed him. After Custer appeared at the train station to see Libbie off on her February trip, Bacon sent an angry letter to her, insisting that she had grown too close to Custer; the whole town was gossiping. She replied that she had repelled his advances. "I did it *all for you*. I like him very well," she wrote. "You have never been a girl, Father, and you cannot tell how hard a trial this was for me." The idea that she was the subject of public talk stung her. "And Monroe people will please mind their own business, and let me alone," she wrote. "I wish the gossipers sunk in the sea."[30]

After her rebuff, Custer turned his attention to Fannie Fifield, Libbie's friend, classmate, and competitor all through her school years. Together with her father's heightened opposition, it had the perverse effect of inciting Libbie to take Custer more seriously. When his attention came easily, she had treated it as a trivial thing; now she wanted it dearly. "Fan is trying to get him to be her devoted and all the time I know how he feels toward me," she reassured herself in her diary. She recruited Nettie to be her secret messenger, supplying an ambrotype portrait of herself for him. Libbie arranged seemingly chance encounters with him at the Humphrey House parlor.[31]

Yet Libbie remained trapped in a quintessential dilemma for a middle-class woman of the mid-1800s. She was to be desired, yet could not desire; or, at least, she could not pursue whom she wanted. She could not break the rules of middle-class respectability. She could not risk her all-important reputation—not only for her own sake but for that of her father. Fannie's disregard for her own public standing was both an advantage and a disadvantage; it gave Fannie more freedom to act, yet made her less valuable. Fannie could see him openly, Libbie told herself, "but I think my reputation is of more account and so I am content tho' the chain frets me often." When Libbie refused Custer's kiss in the love seat before the mirror, she told him that she belonged to a different category of woman than Fifield, and Armstrong hastily agreed. And so she rebounded between furtively expressing affection for him and guarding her reputation—interrogating him, for example, about showing off her picture to his niece.

Unaware of Libbie's turmoil, underestimating the trap that held her, Custer lashed out at her that evening at the Fifield home, when he played cards and ladled her with sarcasm. "I am glad I saw him last night as I did," she wrote in her diary. "I know he fibs, for the matter of the ambrotype shows it." And yet, and yet—"some traits he has are splendid and I have never seen them so fully developed in any other."

Even on the night he turned on her, she still asked him to keep in contact by writing to Nettie. As Custer departed Monroe in the spring of 1863, she told herself that he was not one for "transient love."[32]

This was an argument more than a judgment—an argument with herself. Her diary became an ongoing attempt to persuade herself to disregard his duplicity with Fannie, that her moral superiority was a romantic advantage. Fannie believed they were engaged, but Libbie considered it ridiculous that "C—— knowing the low-minded girl as he does, should wish to *marry* her. He, like others, takes all she gives which I sometimes think is *everything*, but when a man has all he desires in one he rarely desires the girl for his wife," she wrote.

This internal conversation mired her in contradictions and conflicting standards. She never considered that Armstrong was as "low-minded" as Fannie if the two were having sex. Despite the rise of radical "Free Love" advocates, despite calls for women's sexual freedom, Libbie accepted that she must remain chaste but that a single man—especially a soldier— would seize what sex he could. Armstrong described how Fannie sat on his lap and "he kissed her as he liked." Yet he also insisted upon a woman's virginity, often remarking that he would never marry a widow because he refused to have the "left-over remains" of another man.

In the end, the difference she saw between herself and Fannie was less moral than tactical. Libbie wanted what Fannie wanted. She kept Custer at a distance "more from principle than from inclination," she wrote. "I *know* the reason he loved me [was] because I wouldn't let him kiss me and treat me as if we were engaged."[33]

But Armstrong himself kept confounding her attempts to trim their romance to fit the pages of the books she read. One moment she reflected on how "devoted" he was, how interested he was in her, by contrast with her other suitors. "C—— has quite spoiled me," she wrote. "Everything I said or did was remembered or treasured by him." Then Fannie bragged about Custer's romantic letters to her, remarking that he had left a farewell note when he departed Monroe. Libbie replied, "Captain Custer loves me too much to go away and never say good bye to me!"

"Yes, he does like you but I guess he thinks you don't like him much," Fannie answered, making it appear that Armstrong had told her how Libbie had spurned his kiss. Libbie tried to convince herself that Armstrong was "flirting *desperately*" merely so he could "jilt such a renowned flirt."[34]

As the duel between the two women played out, the war approached a crisis. Lee's invasion of Pennsylvania dominated the newspapers, and Custer's name appeared in the *Monroe Commercial*. "We have not a more gallant man in the field," it declared on July 2; "whenever there is a daring expedition to be undertaken or hard fighting to be done, he is ever among the foremost."[35]

Fannie now declared that Custer would marry her that autumn. She even asked Libbie and Nettie to be her bridesmaids. Fannie said that Custer had shown her his photograph of Libbie. She described it and smirked, "You look so careless like."

"He had no business to write the passionate messages he has about me & to me when he has been writing so constantly & lovelike to Fan," Libbie told her diary. "He is nothing to me. He never will be."[36]

But she secretly clung to him as he rose from noted local boy to national hero. His sudden promotion stunned the town. "Upon first appearance of the report that Captain Custer had been made a Brigadier General of Cavalry, we were in some doubt as to its genuineness," the *Commercial* admitted later that month. "He had fairly earned his promotion . . . and it is an honor which Monroe citizens should be proud of." The paper went on to quote the *Philadelphia Inquirer*'s enthusiastic account of his performance at Gettysburg. It called him "conspicuous among the bravest of the brave. Young, dashing, and impulsive, his golden, curly locks, and gay velvet undress jacket, made him a shining mark for the Rebel sharp-shooters; but he came out of the fire unscathed and unharmed. This young officer has a bright future before him."[37]

On July 5, Libbie received a visit from David Reed at her family's home. A bald man with a Lincoln beard, sloping shoulders, and bright blue eyes, he opportunely appeared while Judge Bacon was away, and presented the drawing of Custer at Aldie. The image overwhelmed her. It took the young man she knew only on a quiet street, a domestic parlor, and placed him on the savage battlefield. She noted the wild and dangerous details later in her diary—"an old slouch *reb* hat, a brigand jacket . . . old forlorn pants & boots over them."

Reed told her Custer had insisted that she should see it. He gave her the letter from him and they chatted briefly. As he walked to the door, Libbie remarked that she had heard Custer would marry Fannie later that year. "*Do* you think so?" he said, turning toward her. "If you don't know his feelings, he doesn't know." His manner convinced her, she told her diary, that "C—— loves me devotedly."[38]

Her impression may well have been true. Reed may have been telling her to trust her heart. But his reply can be read in a way Libbie did not consider: "If you don't know his feelings, *he doesn't know*." These same words could mean that Custer himself did not understand his true emotions.

As suggested before, it is too categorical to assume that Custer was being purely duplicitous by pursuing both women, or that he merely used Fannie to make Libbie jealous (as Libbie concluded). Human beings possess an astonishing capacity for believing contradictory ideas when convenient. He could love Fannie *or* Libbie, Fannie *and* Libbie, juggling irreconcilable passions as long as he was not forced to choose. Being desired by more than one woman was a heady experience, and he did not want to let it go. But he was a man now—a general, in fact, and a famous one. Between his family's piety, the judgment of Monroe society, and his new public status, he could not play the cad much longer. He would have to choose between them, which meant he would have to stop fooling himself.

Of course, his true love was the war itself. He was about to choose a woman who would bring him intimately into contact with its true meaning. She was not a family member, not a romantic interest, still less a future wife, but a young woman born into an entirely different world from Monroe, Michigan.

HER WORLD WAS INVISIBLE until the moment she destroyed it. She spent most of her time in the outer world, the white world, where time was not hers at all; it belonged to the man who called himself her owner, or to his wife, their son, or their daughters, for whatever purpose suited them. Only after a long day of serving them—perhaps on Sundays or late on Saturdays—came a precious few hours when she could disappear.

She would later say her name was Eliza Brown. It might not have been a birth name, but one she gave herself after she had washed herself clean of slavery. Whatever it was on July 10, 1860, the census taker ignored it. She went nameless onto the slave schedule on a list headed by the slaveholder Robert H. Pierce, a citizen of Rappahannock County, high in Virginia's piedmont, edged to the west by the Blue Ridge Mountains. Above and below her line came those for two women, aged fifty and thirty; two men, forty and thirty-seven; a boy, sixteen, a girl, twelve, and a boy of one. Eliza was listed as a fourteen-year-old female. She was identified as black, not mulatto, as was the one-year-old boy.[39]

Twenty years later, another census would show her to be thirty-five, living with a husband she had not yet met in 1860, as well as a twenty-year-old black man named John Brown, listed as her son. The boy of 1860 and young man of 1880 may have been the same person, her natural-born child, or they may have been different people—one or both unrelated to her by blood. The life hidden in the single slave cabin on the Pierce farm was often mysterious and always uncertain. The sixty-year-old Pierce may have ordered Eliza, at thirteen, to lift her skirt for his entry; or she may have been raped by Pierce's only son, William, then in his mid-twenties; or she may have been raped by a male slave on that farm or another; or she may have willingly laid down with one; or she may not have been the mother at all, but in later years would take an entirely different boy into her home to raise as her own.

Family was survival for Africans chained in America, but at any moment a family could be rent by rental, sale, or death, so they stretched and adapted the concept beyond their blood kin. The one-year-old boy may not have been born on the Pierce farm, but could have been purchased for investment or taken as payment for a debt. He may have been orphaned by the death or sale of his genetic mother. He may have died soon after the census, since mortality rates among enslaved children ran as high as 45 percent. Only one thing is certain: for a decade after the call of the census taker in 1860, John Brown remained seemingly invisible to the white men and women who saw Eliza Brown. *If* he was there, the outside world never remarked on his presence.[40]

Living on one of the small slaveholding farms that predominated in upper piedmont country, she found little time to withdraw into her own sphere. Unlike the large gang-labor plantations of the Deep South, where scores of slaves formed villages of their own, where the number of hands allowed more specialization by gender, here labor demands were many and varied, and fell upon all. Child slaves went to work at about six years of age. Women as well as men hoed, harvested, and even plowed; they tended livestock, milked, churned butter, and smoked meat as well as cleaned, cooked, sewed, wove fabric, and cared for children. Neighbors comparable to the Pierces sometimes had one or two dedicated house slaves, or else rotated the chores. In this region slaveholders tended to own more adult women than men or children, perhaps because adult male field hands sold for high prices in the Deep South, feeding a busy and heartrending interstate trade. And women still had to perform duties for their own families, from washing clothes to feeding babies to tending garden plots.[41]

African Americans also took advantage of the relative absence of large plantations in Rappahannock County. Instead of being trapped in large, insular fiefdoms, they found opportunities to visit other farms or towns, forming social and kinship networks that spread across the countryside. They met other slaves when sent on errands or when they were rented out—or perhaps when they rented themselves out, as slaveholders sometimes allowed their hands to work elsewhere for wages on Sunday, their free day, and keep what they earned. In this way bond servants built ties to free black communities in northern Virginia as well. Slaves found spouses on other farms; if they received their masters' permission, as they often did, they held ceremonies for these "abroad" marriages (though they lacked any official standing, since a slave could have no legal relationship with anyone but the master). Keenly attuned to those who ruled them, they swiftly discovered and spread news of important events, including the election of 1860, secession, and developments in the Civil War.

The black world, then, was not completely invisible to the white world, but it was wider, more intricate, and more connected than the masters knew. Out of countless African nations, the enslaved made a new people, with distinct customs and dialect. They invented or adapted music, ceremonies, and religious worship for themselves. They abided by their own etiquette with each other, and operated according to their own rules of status.[42]

On the smallholdings of Rappahannock and nearby counties, black women possessed authority. Where they were, their families were. Children remained with their mothers (until death or sale); black fathers often lived on other farms or were sold or rented to distant places, and white fathers rarely acknowledged their slave offspring at all. Women "occupied the least volatile niche available, and so they became the chief keepers and transmitters of the community's culture," writes Steven Hahn.[43]

When Eliza Brown turned fifteen in 1860, she lived under the oversight of the women listed as thirty and fifty years old in the census slave schedule. She later called one of them her mother; the relationship, genetic or not, gave Brown support, but also placed her down the social hierarchy in the slave quarters.[44]

In a stroke of luck, Robert Pierce fell sick. Brown was called in to care for him. She entered the white, two-story house with a high-pitched roof and four columns across the front. Brown now cooked, cleaned, washed clothing, and changed the linens; if necessary, she spoon-fed Pierce and helped him with a bedpan or chamber pot. Such were the ironies, or horrors, of slavery: Pierce might well have raped her or allowed her to be raped, and could sell her or her mother without notice; yet she had to take every care for his recovery.

But the assignment was indeed lucky. With access to the kitchen, she could pilfer food for herself and others. As one female house slave told the white mistress of a different Southern home, "Dey gets a little of all dat's going," referring to her children. Becoming a supplier of food gave her influence and status in the slave quarters, as did her access to information about the white family and news of the outer world. And her growing skill as a cook elevated her in black and white households alike.

Perhaps the most important benefit to working inside the big house was the talent she developed for managing relationships with the master and his family. To a slave, survival depended on knowing how to handle whites, who held the power of life and death. In the kitchen, the master's bedroom, or the parlor, Brown learned subtleties that gave her critical advantages. Her domestic skills, too, gave her a special status among those she served; she pleased them and gained their trust, for every Southerner had heard stories of slaves who poisoned food or contaminated it with shattered glass.

She learned how to manipulate with "a soft, appealing voice," as one

woman later wrote of her, "coddling, crooning," then hectoring or scolding when appropriate. *How* she spoke mattered. "I suppose you take notice
that I has a different way of speaking from the other servants and the field
hands," she later remarked. She would attribute it to her time tending
Pierce, when she listened closely to the white family. By adapting her
speech when among white people she won a degree of respect and could
better negotiate in the countless adjustments of the master-slave relationship. She learned when to drop the "*whar* and *thar*," as she later put it,
spoken in the fields.[45]

No sooner had she found her footing and a little bit of leverage than
the war unsettled her life. The fighting hovered just over the horizon;
Amissville, the nearest village, was less than thirty miles from the battles
of Manassas. Rappahannock County lay directly between Richmond and
the southern end of the Shenandoah Valley, where Stonewall Jackson
marched to distract the Union army during the Peninsula Campaign.
Almost the entire Army of Northern Virginia moved into the valley to
stage its invasions of the North in 1862 and 1863.

At the best of times, the Confederate supply system barely functioned.
So rebel troops stripped the country of grain, horses, chickens, pigs, and
cattle—often with direct orders to do so under the policy of impressment.
Soldiers removed fence rails and even doors for firewood and shelter; polluted wide swathes around their camps with human and animal waste;
swarmed around wells and springs; stirred up streams and ponds as they
bathed and washed clothing; trampled crops and tore up roads. As one
Confederate remarked (albeit in a different location), "They talk about
the ravages of the enemy in their marches through the country, but I do
not think that the Yankees are any worse than our own army."[46]

If hunger were not enough of a threat, slaves faced the possibility of
themselves being impressed. Men in particular were hauled off farms
and plantations to labor for the Confederate forces. Those who remained
faced a subtler problem: their sentiments about the war were the opposite of those of white Virginians. The slave quarters and free black communities had sparkled with news of Lincoln's candidacy and election, of
the outbreak of war. They quickly learned of the escapes to Union army
lines and the contraband policy. The advance of Union armies defined
the boundary between slavery and freedom; all their hopes rested on federal victories in the field.

African Americans had to serve exuberant slaveholders and hide their
dejection after Confederate victories at Manassas, Ball's Bluff, the Seven
Days, and Second Manassas. Sharpsburg, as the rebels called the Battle of
Antietam, promised to reverse the momentum; instead, stalemate ensued.

Yet Antietam also brought the Emancipation Proclamation, which jolted the black South. Some African American leaders saw the previous Union defeats as a necessary prelude in a divine plan. The freedman George Payne spoke to a meeting at a contraband camp near Washington, D.C., on December 31, 1862, moments before the Proclamation went into effect. "Friends, don't you see de han' of God in dis?" he asked. "I shall rejoice that God has placed Mr. Lincum in de president's chair, and dat he wouldn't let de rebels make peace until after dis new year. De Lord has heard de groans of de people, and has come down to deliver!"[47]

The trials continued until Gettysburg, a Union triumph that sent the Confederate army on a rapid retreat into the Shenandoah Valley. This time the Union army followed, not in an annihilating pursuit, to be sure, but still a hard chase. The federal troops, too, consumed the earth as they marched into Virginia. "We are in the land of plenty," one soldier wrote home. "When the army is on the march we have a regiment to drive the sheep and oxen that we pick up on the farms."[48]

The slaves kept each other informed as Union forces drew nearer—crossing the Potomac, marching into Loudoun Valley, moving closer, closer. At five o'clock in the afternoon on Thursday, July 23, 1863, the 3rd Cavalry Division of the Army of the Potomac occupied the village of Amissville.[49] Scores of black men, women, and children fled toward the Union tents, leading federal officers to establish a contraband camp.

It was an opportunity, and Eliza Brown took it. She fled with the others, destroying the world they had made within the world the slaveholders ruled. She hoped to destroy the latter world as well. In later years she found it exasperating that white people from both North and South did not understand that. "Everybody keeps asking why I left," she would say. "I can't see why they can't recollect what the war was for, and that we was all bound to try and see for ourselves how it was. After the 'mancipation, everybody was a-standin' up for liberty, and I wasn't goin' to stay home when everybody else was a-goin'. The day I came into camp, there was a good many other darkeys from all about our place."[50] *What the war was for:* the slaves knew long before political leaders that, in the end, the war was about freedom. Brown knew what she left behind, but she had no idea what lay before her. She soon learned, as Hahn writes, that "when slaves ran away from Southern plantations, they ran toward a war."[51]

TO GET FROM GETTYSBURG to the contraband camp at Amissville, Custer rode over corpses. At least one was a man he killed himself. His soldiers killed others. And, of course, some of the bodies that cobbled the road were *his* men. Custer very nearly joined them under hoof thanks to his insistence on leading charges—and his commander's insistence on foolish charges.

Custer's disobedience on the last day of the Battle of Gettysburg was fortunate as well as wise. When he remained with General Gregg on the right flank of the Army of the Potomac, he kept his brigade away from his division commander, Brig. Gen. Judson Kilpatrick. That day Kilpatrick ordered his other brigade leader, Brig. Gen. Elon Farnsworth, to charge well-placed Confederate infantry. Farnsworth acted precisely as Custer did, riding at the head of his troops. But it was a mounted assault against fortified riflemen and artillery, for no particular purpose. Kilpatrick ordered it over Farnsworth's protests. Farnsworth died with seventy of his men.[52]

"All are glad to be away from the battlefield, where all we could see were dead and wounded," wrote Victor Comte, one of Custer's troopers, to his wife, Elise, after Gettysburg. A small-framed French immigrant in a company in the 5th Michigan filled with Frenchmen, Comte was that most unfortunate of men, a sensitive soldier. "You would have wept if you'd seen 2 or 3 thousand prisoners marching four abreast, three-fourths of whom were wounded and leaving . . . the roads covered with blood. One with an arm missing, another a bullet having pierced his leg, well never has there ever been such wholesale slaughter before." But he felt hope. He believed that the Union would win the war within three months, and then he could come home. "That's what I'm longing for with all my heart."[53]

The Michigan Brigade fought nearly continually in pursuit of the retreating Army of Northern Virginia as the Union infantry trudged behind. On the night of July 4, Kilpatrick pushed Custer and his men against a Confederate rear guard in solid blackness in a ravine at Monterey Pass of South Mountain, southwest of Gettysburg. At about three o'clock the next morning, they broke through and destroyed scores of wagons loaded with supplies and captured some 1,400 wounded rebels. Repeated skirmishing cost lives as they rode through terrain Custer knew from the Antietam Campaign—Hagerstown, Boonsboro, Antietam Creek— racing Lee to the Potomac. The fighting grew so intense that Custer had three horses shot from underneath him in a single day. On July 11, at a place called Falling Waters, the Confederates dug a formidable line with their backs to the river.[54]

Custer and his men splashed onward through "rain which has fallen in torrents for a week without ceasing," Comte wrote. The Union infantry finally caught up behind them, as the rebel army frantically worked to replace a pontoon bridge destroyed previously in a raid. Everyone expected a climactic battle; but General Meade saw the strength of the Confederate position, and hesitated.[55]

Before dawn on July 14, scouts reported to 3rd Cavalry Division headquarters that the enemy had escaped. Custer and Kilpatrick rode ahead with the 6th Michigan, the closest regiment, "as fast as our horses could carry us through mud nearly a foot deep," wrote James H. Kidd, an officer in the 6th. A rebel infantry division still occupied the enemy fortifications. A messenger arrived from Gen. John Buford, commander of the 1st Cavalry Division, asking Kilpatrick to cooperate in a maneuver to capture or destroy those remaining rebels. Instead, Kilpatrick ordered an immediate attack by the single regiment on hand. Wary, Custer ordered 100 men to dismount and approach on foot. No, Kilpatrick said, he wanted them to charge on horseback.[56]

The assault was doomed—only it wasn't—only it was. Mistaking the filthy, unrecognizable Union cavalry for their own men, the rebels allowed this small force to ride up into their works, where the Michigan horsemen began to slash at the defenders with their sabers. The Confederates recovered their wits and killed the officer who led the charge along with twenty-nine of his men, and wounded or captured forty more.

To cope with the mess Kilpatrick had created, Custer deployed the survivors on foot once again and renewed the attack as his other regiments came up. Intense, confused fighting ensued as they finally drove the Confederates out of their works and toward the river. "The 5th Michigan made a charge which released the prisoners and took 52 rebels," Comte wrote to his wife. "General Koster [sic] of Monroe commanded in person and I saw him plunge his saber into the belly of a rebel who was trying to kill him. You can guess how bravely soldiers fight for such a general."

With Buford's men attacking from another direction, they captured hundreds of prisoners and killed Confederate General J. Johnston Pettigrew, "leaving the ground literally covered with rebel dead and wounded," Kidd observed. But the men knew the initial attack had been bungled, and who had bungled it. Kidd wrote home, "Gen. Kilpatrick is called here Gen. '*Kill-Cavalry*' which is about as appropriate as his real name."[57]

Custer faced what might be the soldier's worst conundrum: his superior officer was a danger to his brigade and himself. But the problem disappeared—for a few weeks, at least. On July 15, Kilpatrick went home on leave, and Custer took over the 3rd Cavalry Division. He led it over the Potomac in pursuit of the rebels, who marched south through the Shenandoah Valley.

At five in the afternoon of July 23, Custer took the division into the crossroads known as Amissville in Rappahannock County, Virginia. Lee's army marched by just to the south, on its way back to its fortified position at Fredericksburg. Custer notified Pleasonton that evening, "I will endeavor to annoy the enemy tomorrow morning as much as it is in my power to do."[58]

The result was nearly a disaster. He threatened an infantry corps with just three worn-down cavalry regiments and one battery; in response, the enemy partly encircled his tiny force. "I think our position today the most critical I was ever in," he reported to Pleasonton. He adroitly escaped, but the risk had been entirely unnecessary—a lesson in the dangers of overreaching as a division commander.[59]

The clash (called Newby's Crossroads or Battle Mountain) punctuated the end of the long tale of fighting that began before Gettysburg. Back in camp at Amissville, Custer endured the true tedium of command—in other words, management. "You cannot imagine how completely my time is occupied," he wrote to his sister on July 26. "I am at work night and day usually get up before daylight go to bed late am called up several times during the night." After hard campaigning, the division needed food, new boots, uniforms, and equipment, grain and shoes for the horses, and new horses to replace the many dead. "We have had no forage whatever for three days, not even wheat," he reported. "The grazing is very indifferent. My men are out of rations."[60]

Foraging became a kind of economic warfare that punished local civilians. "The rebels have been collecting and driving off all the cattle, horses, and sheep in this county," he told Pleasonton. Victor Comte and his fellow Frenchmen in the 5th Michigan took pleasure in their own harvest. "While our regiment was chasing the Rebels from Ashby Gap, I was chasing a pig, which I killed," he wrote to his wife. One comrade, he noted, "cooks chickens better than you can get in a hotel. He has fun making coffee and I have fun watching him do it. . . . We make cream sauce twice a day. Fresh beef and pork are not wanting."

But raiding civilians also troubled Comte. "I pity the farmers because if the army stays here another week they'll die of starvation next winter," he wrote on July 30. He and a friend stopped seven soldiers from the 7th Michigan from looting a farmhouse filled with poor women and children, only to see them return with an officer who ordered them to seize the family's flour and cornmeal. "I'm angry to be forced to do things which I detest," he wrote. "I'm fighting and will continue to fight to the end for the Union but they'll never make me cause defenseless innocents to suffer."[61]

Custer might have been inclined to share Comte's sentiments, given his politics. But certain imperatives came with his command position. Anything left behind would supply the enemy. Even worse, white civilians began to turn on his men. A Confederate cavalry officer named Maj.

John Singleton Mosby led a unit of Partisan Rangers in guerrilla raids and ambushes behind Union lines. Soon no officer in the division went without an escort. Custer sent 300 picked men to hunt for Mosby.

They would fail, thanks to the population. Indeed, the partisans *were* the population. Custer complained to Pleasonton that civilians "injure us through bushwhacking, &c. . . . They are bolder and more defiant. . . . I can suppress bushwhacking, and render every man within the limits of my command practically loyal, if allowed to deal with them as I choose." In guerrilla-wracked Missouri, the kind of authority Custer desired led junior officers to burn homes and render civilians "practically loyal" through summary executions. Meade refused the request.[62]

If military logic led to harsh policies, Custer's personal ethics were another matter. They always tended to squirt one direction or another depending on the situation. It was fair enough to capture a fine horse, expensive saddle, and first-rate sword from an enemy in the field, and standard practice to occupy a civilian house as a headquarters. But it was rather unusual to "capture" an expensive private carriage with silver harness. Custer did all of these.

The more successful he was in the field, the more room he allowed for his personal indulgences. He kept his band busy blaring cheerful tunes outside his headquarters as his dogs slept on his bed inside, while Johnny Cisco, the homeless boy, washed his socks and uniform. Custer filled out his staff with young friends from Monroe, including Jacob Greene, boyfriend of Nettie Humphrey. When Custer wrote to his schoolmate John Bulkley on August 2 to explain how he would maneuver him into a position, Greene added a note. "It is just a little more 'bully' than you can think," he wrote. "Come by all means. The thing can be easily fixed. . . . It is delightful."

Custer and his friends were still more boys than men. But Custer's colorful presence and lighthearted air—matched as it was with personal courage and skill—fed his soldiers' pride. The men, too, began to wear bright red neckties.[63]

He also schemed to bring James Christiancy out of a regiment in the West to join his staff. He liked Jim, but continued to cultivate his father, Judge Isaac Christiancy. The United States Senate had not yet confirmed Custer's appointment as a general, and he was worried. On July 26, he sent a letter to the judge explaining how he hoped to get Jim onto his staff. "I wish to speak of another matter and will then close," he added. He feared that a political enemy would lobby Michigan's senators to vote down his confirmation as brigadier general. "If I fail to receive my confirmation from the Senate because I am not worthy to fill the position, well and good. But I do not wish to be defeated in an unfair manner. I speak of this to you hoping and feeling assured that you will do all in your power to aid me and to counteract the influence I speak of."

The judge was inclined to help. As he later told Custer, "Michigan is more proud of your deeds than those of any other man she has sent to the field." But Custer's well-timed offer to help James struck at a vulnerable point, and he felt it. "Poor Jim! I have spent many a sleepless night in consequence of his errors," Christiancy later wrote. Alcoholism—"dissipation"—put him almost beyond help.[64]

As so often in Custer's life, it is difficult to separate opportunism from sincere feeling. He liked Christiancy and his family, and enjoyed being surrounded with Monroe boys on his staff, yet he requested a kind of quid pro quo. Custer undeniably served his country, yet he pursued his own agenda all the while.

As all this played out, Custer remembered the most remarkable luxury he had ever seen in a general's tent—the black cook who served Pleasonton. Sometime before the 3rd Division departed the vicinity of Amissville on July 30, Custer rode over to the nearby camp holding the scores of contrabands who had rushed into Union lines.[65]

"I ALLUS THOUGHT THIS, that I didn't set down to wait to have 'em all free *me*. I helped to free myself." When Eliza Brown later looked back at her teenage self of the summer of 1863, she remembered her march to the Union bivouac at Amissville as an act of will. And it was—a personal rebellion that took her away from the only home she knew, away from the social and kinship networks that supported her, and toward a war. Contraband camps, writes one historian, were "marked by conditions that should have deterred all but the hardiest and most determined of souls."[66]

The escapees often traveled long distances, developing open sores, swollen feet, and hunger. The local food supply had been devoured by both armies, the water polluted. Before Union troops found work for contrabands or transported them out of the battle zone, they put them out of the way. "They have been stowed away in narrow, dark, filthy sheds, old houses, cellars—any sort of places—with scarcely rags enough to cover their persons, or straw enough to sleep upon," a reporter in Virginia wrote in 1863. "Many are lodged in old slave-pens."

On one hand, a historian notes, the camps "became more than mere collecting points. . . . They also became the first great cultural and political meeting grounds that the war produced." For many freed people, the camps reinforced the spirit of freedom, invigorated their sense of their *right* to liberty, to personal autonomy. On the other hand, they became vectors for outbreaks of lethal diseases.[67]

"The day I came into camp," Brown recalled, "there was a good many other darkeys from all about our place. We was a-standin' around waitin' when I first seed the Ginnel." The arrival of the lean young man with a star on each shoulder and an aide beside him drew attention in this holding pen. A general would only come if he had work, and work meant better food, better living conditions, and possibly pay.

He went over to the young women—eighteen of them, by Brown's recollection—and looked them over. Then he came to the teenager Brown, a small woman with a wide mouth, broad, pronounced cheekbones, large, rather sad eyes, a somewhat thin nose, and a face that narrowed sharply from her cheeks down to her chin, almost in the shape of a heart. Clearly she was self-assured. As one woman described her, "She was young though with mature ways."[68]

Custer paused. He looked at her carefully, and asked, "Well, what's *your* name?" Eliza, she said. "Well, Eliza, would you like to come and live with me?" He needed a cook, he explained.

"I waited a minute," she recalled. "I looked *him* all over, too." He was as self-assured as she was, with a cocky air, long, curly hair, enormous mustache, and flamboyant dress. He obviously held high rank, but was perhaps less intimidating because of his youth—and he offered an opportunity to escape the camp. "I reckon I would," she said. "As long as you'll be good to me then I'll be good to you."[69]

"But oh, how awful lonesome I was at fust, and I was afraid of everything in the shape of war," Brown later reflected.[70] The journey to Custer's headquarters took her into yet another world, the military world, a strongly male sphere. Men marched and rode past in regimented columns; they bathed, urinated, and defecated in the open; they gathered in small mobs around card games or pots over fires, shouting profanities and laughing at dirty jokes. Everywhere there were rifles, cannons, caissons, and sabers, not to mention wagons, crates, prisoners, horses, carcasses of horses, and piles of amputated arms and legs outside the surgeon's tent after a skirmish. Most were young, though no one seemed younger than the Boy General and his boyish staff, who constantly kidded one another and played practical jokes.

But Eliza Brown could read white society, even such a strange and artificial one as the 2nd Brigade of the 3rd Cavalry Division of the Army of the Potomac. She learned the tensions and allegiances among the officers, and the significance of the fact that she would run the household of the most important man in the brigade. She would share his power to a small degree—filtered by her sex and race and civilian status, but power enough, provided that Custer himself respected her.

It was a situation that called for assertiveness, and she asserted. The small, teenage girl in a calico dress, hair wrapped in a bandana, took charge of the boy Johnny Cisco, established her authority over the general's mess, and learned how to acquire food and supplies from sources other than the quartermaster's stock. Instead of shrinking before a brigade of armed white men, she often pushed them. "Eliza became mother to the boyish staff," wrote someone who met her a few months later, "advised and scolded if she thought they were too convivial, as if she had been forty. When promotions came it was [she who] sewed on the new shoulder straps." The young men began to seek her out to press their special requests on Custer. She learned of "their joys, their best girls at home, their injuries, their ambitions, their sly suggestions that 'the old man' might consider their case . . . in advance of the others."

It was a role she had trained for on the Pierce farm. As she did then, she acquired news, even secrets, from officers and couriers who, "knowing that a pan of hot biscuits seemed perpetually in the oven, slyly slipped into the kitchen on the way to their horses." She had spent her life learning that information was the key to survival.[71]

Did Custer have sex with her? It is a natural suspicion. Men raped black women throughout the South; and a young woman in an army camp seemed particularly vulnerable. But there is a strikingly total lack of evidence that he did. Indeed, the only real source on this question is Brown herself. "There's many folks says that a woman can't follow the army without throwing themselves away, but I know better," she later said. "I went in, and I come out with the respect of the men and officers." No credible evidence contradicts her. The source as well as the result of her preservation was, as she said, "respect." She earned it.[72]

CUSTER HAD TROUBLE with authority figures in 1863—two, to be precise. The first was Gen. Judson Kilpatrick, who returned from leave on August 4. Back in command, he grew irritated with his flamboyant subordinate, already beloved by reporters. Kilpatrick himself liked to cultivate the press, and wrote official reports notable for their inexact correspondence to reality; even fellow cavalry officers thought him affected and self-serving. It's not surprising that Kilpatrick would find these very traits to be especially reprehensible in someone else.[73]

On August 14, Custer learned a universal truth about life in a large organization: when the boss reprimands you in writing, he is *really* angry. That day Kilpatrick had his assistant adjutant general send a one-sentence letter to Custer: "The General Comdg [commanding] directs me to say that you will under no circumstances forward an Official communication to Major Gen Pleasonton except through Head Quarters." Having risen through favoritism and personal connections, Custer had been too careless about the chain of command.[74]

Then Kilpatrick learned that Custer and his staff had, characteristically, held a friendly chat with a number of enemy officers. The division was stationed across the Rappahannock from Fredericksburg; Custer received a request for a conference with Col. Robert C. Hill of the 48th North Carolina. They met on August 18. Hill asked for an end to the random daily fire because it endangered the civilians still living in Fredericksburg. Custer agreed. "Much was [then] said that had no connection to the business which caused the meeting," Hill wrote. He claimed that he and his staff were guarded, but "Gen. Custer and his staff, all mere youths, branched out extensively, and tried to show us how much they knew." Hill implied that they revealed military secrets.

News of the parley infuriated Kilpatrick, "as such a proceeding on the part of Gen. Custer was most undignified and improper. I spoke to Gen. Custer about it and learned from him that the report was true," he wrote. As we know, it was not the first time Custer had fraternized with the enemy. Samuel Harris of the 5th Michigan later recalled how, shortly before the incident that agitated Kilpatrick, Custer had crossed the river under a flag of truce to pay a social call on Brig. Gen. Thomas Rosser, his friend from West Point, now a Confederate cavalry officer. After a few hours he returned, and said he "had a fine time over there."

Kilpatrick reminded Custer of an explicit order "forbidding all intercourse with the enemy whatever." Custer claimed ignorance but promised to obey it in the future. Kilpatrick took no further action, but the tension simmered.[75]

Custer hoped to influence the other authority figure who vexed him: Judge Daniel Bacon. On August 13 Custer wrote to Nettie Humphrey and asked how the judge saw him since he became a general. As it happened, she had seen much of him recently. "Your name is seldom if ever mentioned between us," she replied. "He is a man of strong prejudices— you & I think some of them unfounded—but—what necessity for me to go over the reasoning I have used so often before!"

The message was clear: he still prohibited Libbie from receiving Custer as a suitor. "He is a truly good man and a fond, devoted Father who would feel ingratitude or deceit on the part of his child, most keenly," Nettie wrote. "An act of disobedience from Libbie, in a matter of importance, would almost kill him, I think." His bias was so fixed that she thought it might be best to abandon "forbidden hopes." She promised to continue to write to Custer, though, because one thing prevented any real harm: Libbie would never disobey her father.[76]

Custer still cultivated Fannie Fifield, but less avidly as summer went on. Libbie aroused more serious feelings in him. On August 27, while Humphrey was still composing her discouraging letter, he had Jim Christiancy write to Judge Bacon in order to have himself put in a better light.[77] "Please pardon this seeming impudence in writing to you uninvited," Christiancy wrote, but he thought that news of the "gallant Michigan Regiments under the command of the no less [gallant] Genl. Custer would afford you some pleasure." He described a recent operation, and praised Custer as a hero and—more important—a serious man. "To say that General Custer is a brave man is unnecessary. He has proven himself to be not only that but also a very cool and self-possessed man. It is indeed very difficult to disturb his mental equilibrium."[78]

But Custer knew he would have to go to Monroe in person to sway Bacon. On September 5 he asked for twenty days' leave to return to Michigan, claiming it was "absolutely necessary . . . owing to the serious illness of my mother." Ann did not mention any illness in a letter she finished the day before—though she did say that his parents had purchased a house in Monroe, had no money, and that "it all depends on you and with your salery you can make them comfortable." It was in this note that she said that Fannie thought "you was displeased at her."[79]

Custer did not get his leave. Orders came from Pleasonton for all three cavalry divisions to move across the Rappahannock. Meade wanted the horsemen to confirm reports that Longstreet had taken his corps west and Lee was retreating to a new position below the Rapidan. Pleasonton's advance led to a battle with Confederate cavalry at Culpeper Court House on September 13, in which Custer led "a really handsome charge," according to Theodore Lyman, who served on Pleasonton's staff. After the enemy was driven back in defeat, Lyman saw Custer approach the headquarters group. "His first greeting to General Pleasonton, as he rode up, was: 'How are you, fifteen-days'-leave-of-absence? They have spoiled my boots but they didn't gain much there, for I stole 'em from a Reb.' And certainly," Lyman wrote in his diary, "there was one boot torn by a piece of shell and the leg hurt also."[80]

So he received his leave after all, once he filed the paperwork, including a surgeon's certificate that he was "suffering the effects of a gunshot wound of the tibial region" from a bullet through his lower leg, almost grazing the bone. He went back to Monroe, having been the subject of more newspaper stories, these praising the "unequalled gallantry" of the "Boy General of the Golden Locks," and another vanishingly narrow escape from death on his record. It hardly mattered that the battle itself hardly mattered.[81]

———

"IT WOULD ALMOST KILL dear Elliot [Bates] to have me finally refuse him," Libbie Bacon wrote in her diary about a smitten West Point cadet. "I tell him over and over again *I do not* love him now enough to be forever. . . . Perhaps I may be able to judge my feelings after a year when my violent fancy for C shall have passed away."[82]

Courtship and fancies and love (or want of it) defined Libbie's existence. She had received as extensive an education as almost any young woman in America—as all but a small number of men—yet she was expected to do nothing with it. Neither her father, stepmother, nor the seminary thought she might lead her life on her own. Her task was to settle on a suitor, one who offered prospects of sufficient income to maintain her station, one of equal or better social standing, and, in particular, one approved by her parents. She did little but read, socialize, go to church, and receive gentlemen callers, such as the reserved Francis Chandler or Elliot Bates. The one area in which she had some control of her destiny—the choice of the man who would overshadow the rest of her life—was confined by her father's judgment. So she tried to doubt her own attraction to Custer, dismissing it as "my violent fancy," an ephemeral thing, hardly the foundation of a stable and respectable relationship.[83]

She had not expected to see Custer for some time, and went to Traverse City on Lake Michigan with her father and stepmother. On September 17 she stepped out of the train onto the platform in Monroe, and saw Custer, who had arrived the day before. "I could not avoid him," she wrote. "I tried to, but I did not succeed."

It would have been impossible to miss his presence in town. Prior to his receiving leave, Nettie had teased Custer, "What sort of sensation do you expect to make if you come here . . . ? I am afraid so much 'brass' will dazzle the eyes of us poor Monroe girls. However we will do our best to endure the blaze of glory." The joke became reality. The local newspapers, the *Monitor* and *Commercial*, quoted glowing articles about him from the metropolitan press, and announced that on September 28 the "Young Ladies and Gents of Monroe" were hosting "a Fancy Dress Ball at the Humphrey House . . . in honor of Gen. George A. Custer."[84]

It was a costume ball. Libbie went. She selected a humble but exotic costume, the persona of someone always ready to pick up and move—a gypsy girl, tambourine in one hand. As the honored party, Custer dressed as Louis XVI. The band struck up at nine in the evening, followed by the unmasking at eleven, followed by dinner at midnight, followed by more dancing.[85]

She saw him as often as three times a day in the Humphrey House parlor during his two-week stay, hiding their romantic intrigue in plain view. Yet she found these moments filled with fresh intensity. He said he wanted to marry her, and she said she wanted to marry him. "I did not know I loved him so until he left Monroe in the spring," she told her cousin Rebecca Richmond. "Try as I did to suppress the 'fancy' for six months it did no good," she wrote in her diary. "I do love him and have all the time. . . . I believe I shall marry him sometime."[86]

But there remained the opposition of her father. Custer had tried to build a relationship with Judge Bacon during his leave, often conversing with him about the war—though he could never quite nerve himself to ask permission to court the judge's daughter. The last opportunity came at the railroad station on October 5, the day he left. Libbie and her father went with Custer, along with many others who came to say farewell. Judge Bacon pulled the young soldier aside before he boarded his train, and spoke kindly about his prospects, and "said he would be disappointed if he did not hear such and such things of me soon," Custer recorded the next day. Custer replied that "I had desired to speak to him, but being prevented from doing so, I would write to him." Bacon said, "Very well."[87]

After Custer departed, emotion overwhelmed Libbie as she opened her diary. "Oh how dear he is. I love him so. His words linger in my ears, his kisses on my lips," she wrote. "Then a thousand doubts come into my mind like tormenting devils and I doubt if I love him. I do tho and I shall sometime be his 'little wife.' "[88]

As the days passed, the tormenting continued. Custer's letters to Nettie showed that he still had not written to Judge Bacon. "My mind has been alternating between hope and fear" concerning how Bacon would react to it, he wrote. "I cannot rid myself of the fear that I may suffer from some unfounded prejudice."[89]

He dreaded being judged—being seen as the poor blacksmith's troublesome son, the womanizing, cursing, gambling, heathen soldier, the Copperhead. Excuses followed. "I would have written *that* letter to *her* father today," he wrote to Humphrey on October 9, "but that I knew I should be interrupted. . . . All my future *destiny* hangs on the answer my letter shall bring."[90]

Finally, on October 16, he finished the letter and mailed it. It arrived two days later. He admitted his failings, but offered a defense for each. He had been a drinker, but had abided by the pledge made to his sister. He had escorted other Monroe girls in public, but merely to divert gossips from his passion for Libbie. He had left home as a teenager and had faced temptation ever since, "but have always had a purpose in life."[91]

"Father is, to my surprise, on my side," Libbie wrote in her diary. "Mother cannot, and will not see him in my light."[92] With a skeptical Rhoda lurking behind him, the judge was guarded in his reply to Custer. "The subject is one of vast moment to me, requiring thought and reflection, that I may require weeks or even months before I can feel to give you a definite answer," he wrote. As a widower, Bacon suggested, he felt more than the typical concern for his child, though he was gratified that Libbie valued education and "moral deportment." He and Rhoda "have guarded her reputation with intense parental solicitude. . . . She is esteemed by relatives and friends as worthy of the hand whose future shall be without spot or blemish." And there was the trouble. Was the "Boy General of the Golden Locks" spotless? For that matter, was he solid, sensible, *moral?* Bacon did not mention Custer's reputation as a ladies' man, but it shadowed his final words—words of caution and concern, but touched with grace. "We are all liable to change in life and are not always our own keeper. Your ability energy and force of character I have always admired, and no one can feel more gratified than myself at your well earned reputation and your high & honorable position." After Custer left Monroe, he wrote, he had held a very open conversation about him with Libbie. The judge said he would "talk with her more upon this important subject which she is at liberty to communicate to you."[93]

"Liberty to communicate": it was not the "future *destiny*" that Custer hoped for in Bacon's letter, but it presented the path to the future. After trying to preserve all opportunities for so long, tugging along Fannie Fifield and Libbie Bacon—and perhaps other women—for nearly a year, Custer had finally committed himself by writing to Judge Bacon. "Liberty to communicate" was as good as an engagement. Custer's bride would have to be Libbie Bacon, or he could never return home without disgrace.

Six

THE GENERAL

H E SAT ALONE IN the dark. It hardly mattered that others filled the seats below him in that theater in Washington, D.C., or that some may have shared the private box he rented. The experience of a play was private, intimate, enveloping. Hidden in darkness in his seat, the stage was all his world, and the players all its people, lit by flames flickering on their footlight wicks.

His love of the theater was both natural and surprising. Natural, because he had constructed his life as a dramatic narrative, told to others in lengthy letters when not acted out in person, rewritten as needed to make a better story than reality could provide. For the past three months, no editing had been necessary. He had been the leading man—adorned in costume on horseback, adorned in costume in a ball held to honor him, adoring his lover in a hotel parlor. Upon his arrival in Washington earlier that day, he had sat very still for an oversized, hand-colored photographic portrait that cost him the extravagant sum of $30. He meant to be admired even when absent.[1]

Then, too, there were obvious similarities between a general and a famous actor. In nineteenth-century combat, a combat leader intended to be seen; he gestured and declaimed for a mass audience. Thousands attended his every movement on the battlefield. His dramatic instincts allowed him to communicate orders with a flash of his sword, to inspire sacrifice with a glance in the right direction.

But the contrasts were stark. The soldier dwelt in war, the most intense reality of all. As a general, Custer altered the course of human events. He killed and he saved. The consequences of his actions reshaped the lives of men, women, and children who never saw his face or heard his name. The actor engaged in verisimilitude, not reality itself, pretending to be someone else. Evangelical Christians steeped in the revival fervor of the Second Great Awakening—such as Custer's father and Ann—derided the theater as worldly, frivolous, and false; they dismissed playacting as superficial, a coarse pleasure performed by questionable types.[2]

Here lies the surprise. Custer knew the pious opinion of the stage, yet the footlight fires hypnotized him. He loved the deliberate performance, the cultivated appearance, the thing that was put on show that it might be admired by the world. Perhaps it was *because* his father's religion disparaged the theater that he embraced it. He was only twenty-three, an age still fat with rebellion, a yearning for excitement and glamor. The phenomenon of stardom itself appealed to him. He wanted those things that were forbidden and pleasurable. He wanted admirers. He wanted embellishment. He wanted to control how others saw him. Like a star actor.

When the performance was over, he purchased a bouquet—presumably to throw onstage—from a vendor who came to his box. Struggling with the flowers and his payment, he placed his pocketbook on the floor. The next morning he discovered that he had left it there. The wallet contained $70. He rushed back, but it was gone.[3]

To lose money in a theater: nothing could have epitomized better his turn off the narrow road of faith, his flight from poverty and provincialism. His family freighted the issue of money with moral obligations again and again. "My Dear Brother I must caution you to be saveing of your money until you get your parents well provided for," Ann had written to him at the end of August. "You know it all depends on you." Emmanuel commented on October 25 on the difficulty of maintaining his new home. "Monroe is a nice place to live in I would like it first rate as Tom says if I had the means to live comfortable," he wrote. "Now I am straped for the present and it seams that we hav not got any thing hardley this is the place to consume Green Backs." Two days later Custer's sister Margaret (or Maggie) wrote that his mother "is very sorry she has to [ask] you (if you have it to spare) to send her five dollars for to get that little building moved that is on the end of the lot. . . . Mother hates to ask you for it if you have not got it."

His mother agonized over asking for five dollars while he spent thirty on a picture of himself and carelessly left seventy on the floor of a private box in a theater. These letters reminded him that each dollar he spent was sutured to the unhealing wound of his family's poverty.[4]

And yet, he deliberately provoked Ann, bragging about his heedlessness. "I am extravagant in many ways," he wrote on November 6. "I lost ten dollars today that I bet on a horserace with Gen. Kirkpatrick. . . . Between you and me I could keep a family with the money I spend needlessly."

Here was Custer the thoughtless youth, and the prankster, the narrator, the dramatist. A prank deliberately attacks sensitivities; it is then defused with a revelation or a conciliating gesture (though only after the explosion). A story requires a change, best preceded by crisis. The reformation of a lead character demands dissipation first. He bragged about his spending both as a painful joke and to prepare for the coming turn in the Prince-Hal-to-Henry-V story he was writing for himself.

"I am going to make a great change some of these days, a change for the better," he added. "I think you will approve of it when you know more about it. Do not let anybody else see this letter. Don't forget it. I must close as I have another letter to write to a young lady in Monroe."[5]

THE CHEERS OF THE MEN rose as dusk fell on October 8, 1863, as soon as they spotted Custer riding into the camp of the Michigan Brigade. The band gathered and began to play "Hail to the Chief." It gratified him. "I wish you could have seen how rejoiced my men seemed to be at my return," he wrote to Nettie Humphrey (knowing Libbie would read his words). "Whatever may be the real sentiments entertained by the world at large, I feel assured that here, surrounded by my noble little band of heroes, I am loved and respected." Everyone was happy to see him, he told his sister, "not excepting Eliza." Eliza was the most likely to rejoice, of course, after weeks without her patron and protector. She was a young black woman alone amid thousands of young white men, shielded only by their respect for Custer and her own force of personality.[6]

The next day the Cavalry Corps broke camp and moved south to investigate reports that Lee was on the march—perhaps to take advantage of the recent departure of two corps to help Gen. Ulysses S. Grant lift the siege of Chattanooga. The Union troopers found the Army of Northern Virginia moving rapidly to outflank the Army of the Potomac—including themselves. The cavalry withdrew north on October 11, but the Confederates cut off the 3rd Division near Brandy Station. Custer led a series of charges that cut open an escape route, losing two horses killed beneath him within fifteen minutes of each other.[7]

Custer did not secure the division's escape alone, but he proved again that he was most adept on the battlefield, where he never lost confidence in himself. He recovered quickly from the surprise of a gaping ditch that halted his first charge, and regained command of his troops after he fell violently from a dying horse. He displayed his fluency with the mechanics of command under fire, smoothly directing the movements of batteries, regiments, squadrons, and companies.

Custer possessed "a gift for combat leadership," writes Robert Utley. He combined keen observation with an intuitive grasp of the meaning of what he saw. A cloud of dust behind a hill might indicate an enemy outflanking maneuver or a retreat; a flicker of gray-clad men in a tree

LEFT: West Point gave George Armstrong Custer a path out of the poverty of his rural Ohio child-hood, and he made the least of it. He befriended Southerners, played pranks, and graduated last in his class in 1861. *National Portrait Gallery, Smithsonian Institution* RIGHT: As a junior officer in the 1862 Peninsula Campaign in Virginia, Custer took advantage of the creeping pace of the Union advance to socialize. Here he reclines on the ground with a dog as he relaxes with members of Gen. Fitz-John Porter's staff. *Library of Congress*

The crisis that led to the Civil War overshadowed Custer's years at West Point, and the city of New York loomed large in his life. This engraving depicts uniformed Republican "Wide Awakes" on parade for Abraham Lincoln on October 3, 1860, on Park Row, center of the newspaper and publishing trade. *Library of Congress*

LEFT: Custer served as a topographical engineer on the Peninsula, scouting enemy lines and drawing maps. He frequently went aloft in this hydrogen-filled observation balloon, developed by Thaddeus Lowe. *Library of Congress* RIGHT: Commander of the Army of the Potomac and mastermind of the Peninsula Campaign, Maj. Gen. George B. McClellan picked Custer for his staff after the young officer took part in a daring raid on May 24, 1862. Custer idolized McClellan and his wife, Mary Ellen. *Library of Congress*

In the Battle of Fair Oaks, or Seven Pines, May 31 and June 1, 1862, Union troops captured Lt. James B. Washington, Custer's fellow cadet at West Point. James F. Gibson photographed the two as they talked after the battle, then included a young "contraband," or escaped slave. This photo circulated with the title "Both Sides and the Cause." *Library of Congress*

On October 3, 1862, after the Battle of Antietam, Lincoln visited McClellan and his staff, shown here, with Custer at far right. Custer imbibed McClellan's rages against the administration and witnessed his intrigue with wealthy Democratic party leaders, and forged his own ties with them after the Civil War. *Library of Congress*

After Lincoln removed McClellan, Custer (left) found a new patron, Gen. Alfred Pleasonton (right), in the spring of 1863. Known for political maneuvering, Pleasonton took command of the Cavalry Corps of the Army of the Potomac under Gen. Joseph Hooker. He knew Custer from the Antietam campaign, and named him to his staff. Custer was already growing his hair long. *Library of Congress*

Custer sought political as well as military patrons. He found one in Isaac Christiancy, a prominent Michigan Republican and state supreme court justice from Monroe. Custer adopted Monroe as his hometown after living there with his older sister after her marriage. *Library of Congress*

On June 17, 1863, Custer participated in an attack near Aldie, Virginia, by Gen. Judson Kilpatrick, who tried to break through the Confederate cavalry to gather intelligence on the invasion of Pennsylvania. This contemporary sketch of the battle by Edwin Forbes depicts the kind of close-range mounted fighting with sabers and revolvers that Custer frequently engaged in. *Library of Congress*

Senator Zachariah Chandler of Michigan wielded great power as a leading Radical Republican, and Custer sought his support as he pursued higher rank. Custer, a Democrat who supported McClellan, misrepresented his views to Chandler and other Radicals, who despised McClellan and his pro-slavery, limited-war philosophy. *Library of Congress*

With the Confederates invading the North, Pleasonton (right) secured Custer's promotion to brigadier general of U.S. Volunteers on June 28, 1863. Custer was twenty-three. As seen here, he wore a black velveteen jacket with gold embroidery, the blue collar of a sailor's shirt tufting out over his shoulders, and a bright red necktie. One witness called him "one of the funniest-looking beings you ever saw" but, like many, admired his "devil-may-care style." *Library of Congress*

Custer helped repel a Confederate cavalry assault at Gettysburg by leading mounted charges. He was not foolhardy, though, unlike his division commander, Judson Kilpatrick. Kilpatrick ordered a handful of Custer's men to charge an enemy fortification at Falling Waters on July 15, 1863, with disastrous results, shown in this sketch by battlefield artist Alfred Waud. *Library of Congress*

During the first half of the Civil War, the gifted Gen. J. E. B. Stuart led the Confederate cavalry to supremacy over Union horsemen on the battlefield. He affected a dashing cavalier style that Custer shared. Custer's men killed Stuart in the Battle of Yellow Tavern on May 11, 1864. *Library of Congress*

Elizabeth "Libbie" Bacon of Monroe, Michigan, met Custer in 1862 when she was twenty years old, her age when this photograph was taken. She graduated that year as valedictorian from the Young Ladies' Seminary and Collegiate Institute in Monroe. Custer pursued her despite her father's disapproval, though he simultaneously courted one of her classmates. *Courtesy of the National Park Service, Little Bighorn Battlefield, Swygert-Smith Collection*

Custer's promotion to brigadier general helped reconcile Libbie Bacon's parents to their courtship. They married on February 9, 1864, in Monroe. Custer cut his hair short for the occasion. She moved to Washington, and adroitly lobbied senators and congressmen to maintain his political support. *Library of Congress*

In July 1863, Custer hired teenager Eliza Brown, an escaped slave, as his cook. Brown "stood supreme as general superintendent" of the household, Libbie Custer wrote. The relationship between the two women combined mutual respect and affection with racial tension and a struggle for control. "Her whole soul was in the wrongs, real or fancied, of her race," Libbie wrote. Libbie thought them largely imaginary. *Courtesy of the National Park Service, Little Bighorn Battlefield, Elizabeth B. Custer Collection*

HARPER'S WEEKLY.
A JOURNAL OF CIVILIZATION.

VOL. VIII.—No. 377.]   NEW YORK, SATURDAY, MARCH 19, 1864.   [$1.00 FOR FOUR MONTHS.
                                                                      [$3.00 PER YEAR IN ADVANCE.

Entered according to Act of Congress, in the Year 1864, by Harper & Brothers, in the Clerk's Office of the District Court for the Southern District of New York.

BRIGADIER-GENERAL GEORGE A. CUSTER.—PHOTOGRAPHED BY BRADY.—[SEE PAGE 187.]

Dubbed "the Boy General of the Golden Locks" by a reporter, Custer received extensive and glowing attention in the press. This cover of *Harper's Weekly* on March 19, 1864, showed him with his freshly cut hair, soon after his wedding—a surprising image for readers familiar with his long blond curls and romantic style. *Library of Congress*

Named general-in-chief by Lincoln, Gen. Ulysses S. Grant came to Virginia to oversee the Army of the Potomac's spring campaign in 1864. Unlike Custer, he was laconic and understated. Custer met him soon after Grant arrived, beginning a long and troubled relationship. *Library of Congress*

Grant put Gen. Philip H. Sheridan in command of the Cavalry Corps. Custer resented the removal of his patron Pleasonton, but soon became Sheridan's favorite subordinate. This staged photograph shows, left to right, Wesley Merritt, Sheridan, George Crook, James Forsyth, and Custer. *Library of Congress*

On September 19, 1864, Custer played a key role in Sheridan's great victory in the third Battle of Winchester (also known as the Battle of Opequon) in the Shenandoah Valley. He timed and led a charge that crushed the enemy flank, a rare instance of cavalry successfully attacking infantry in the war, vividly captured in this Alfred Waud sketch. *Library of Congress*

In the fall of 1864, Custer took part in the burning of fields and barns in the Shenandoah Valley, illustrated here by Waud. This economic warfare seriously injured the Confederate cause, but enraged local guerrillas under Col. John S. Mosby, who targeted Custer and his men. *Library of Congress*

Waud sketched this iconic moment in Custer's career. Just before Custer led the 3rd Cavalry Division in an attack on October 9, 1864, he spotted an old friend from West Point, Gen. Thomas Rosser, across the battlefield. Custer swept off his hat in a salute to his foe. The gesture captured his romantic appeal to a public exhausted by the war. *Library of Congress*

At Cedar Creek on October 18, 1864, Sheridan rallied his men after a surprise Confederate attack and crushed the Southern army. Custer's division played an important role. He went to Washington to present captured flags to the War Department, shown in this sketch by Waud. Custer's status as a national hero was shared by few other division commanders. *Library of Congress*

As a cavalry commander, Custer largely avoided the worst horrors of the infantry fighting. Grant's Overland Campaign of 1864 and the ensuing siege of Petersburg saw tens of thousands of infantrymen killed or wounded. The war disillusioned such intellectuals as Oliver Wendell Holmes, Jr., Ambrose Bierce, and Charles Francis Adams, Jr., but not Custer. Here African-American laborers bury Confederate dead en masse at the Cold Harbor battlefield. *Library of Congress*

In early 1865, Libbie's father and stepmother, Daniel and Rhoda Bacon, and her cousin Rebecca Richmond visited Custer's headquarters near Winchester, Virginia, where Libbie also resided over the winter. This photograph shows them and Custer's staff on the porch of the house he used for his quarters and office. Here Tom Custer sits at left, holding a dog, with Rebecca Richmond seated next to him. Standing directly above Tom is an unknown soldier; to the right, Libbie Custer, Daniel Bacon, George Armstrong Custer, and Rhoda Bacon. *Courtesy of the National Park Service, Little Bighorn Battlefield, Elizabeth B. Custer Collection*

Custer sat for numerous portrait photographs. This one captures his public image as a Civil War general, with his sailor shirt, red tie, and wide-brimmed hat over his long, curly hair. Here he wears the two stars of a major general. He received a promotion to major general of U.S. Volunteers and to brevet, or honorary, major general in the Regular Army at the end of the war. *Library of Congress*

Custer poses here with Libbie and his brother Tom at the end of the Civil War. He worked hard to bring Tom onto his staff, where Tom won two Medals of Honor. After the war he secured Tom's appointment as an officer in the Regular Army, in Custer's own 7th Cavalry Regiment. *Library of Congress*

Custer and his division played a prominent part in the final campaign that ended in Lee's surrender at Appomattox Court House on April 9, 1865. Alfred Waud's sketch shows a Confederate officer approaching Custer with a flag of truce, which led to the surrender negotiations that afternoon. *Library of Congress*

On May 23, 1865, the 3rd Cavalry Division led the Grand Review, the victory parade in Washington, D.C. Custer rode Don Juan, a famous race horse he had seized after Lee's surrender. The thoroughbred panicked, but Custer regained control amid applause from the crowd. He hoped to sell the horse for $10,000. *Library of Congress*

After the Grand Review, Custer took his wife, brother, and Eliza Brown to Louisiana. He led a cavalry division into Texas, where he grappled with the aftermath of emancipation. Here, on the steps of Custer's Austin headquarters, is Tom Custer, in front of the door at left, and to the right, Armstrong, Eliza Brown standing behind Libbie, Emmanuel Custer (father of Tom and Armstrong) seated with legs crossed, and next to him Custer's friend and aide Jacob Greene. *Courtesy of the National Park Service, Little Bighorn Battlefield, Elizabeth B. Custer Collection*

Custer returned to Washington, D.C., from Texas in March 1866 and plunged into a bitter political battle over Reconstruction between President Andrew Johnson, shown here, and the Republican Congress. Custer joined Johnson on a national speaking tour, supporting the president as he delivered shocking attacks on his enemies. A lifelong conservative Democrat, Johnson opposed all attempts to expand rights for freed slaves. *Library of Congress*

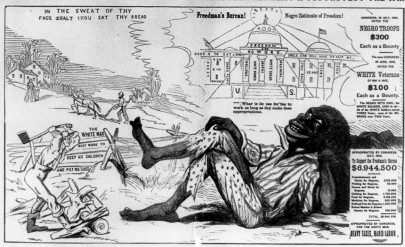

A partisan Democrat like his father, Custer supported the National Union Party in the critical midterm election of 1866, attending its national convention as a delegate for Michigan. It was the Democratic Party in all but name, which was intended to immunize against the Democrats' taint of wartime disloyalty. The gruesome racial tone of the campaign is illustrated by these two posters for Democrat Hiester Clymer in his race for governor of Pennsylvania. *Library of Congress*

line might be a mere picket or a massed column preparing to charge. He sometimes guessed wrong, but more often he judged right—far more than most. He had a talent for choosing the correct course amid chaos.[8]

After it was all over, though, he could not resist embellishing the story. In his official report, he inhabited the minds of his men, turning them into a grand unified supporting cast. "I informed them that we were surrounded, and all we had to do was to open a way with our sabers. They showed their determination and purpose by giving three hearty cheers." The band's music "made each individual member feel as if here was a host himself. . . . It required but a glance at the countenances of the men to enable me to read the settled determination with which they undertook the task before them."[9]

He told Nettie Humphrey (and, implicitly, Libbie Bacon) that just before his attack he pulled out a locket with Libbie's picture and opened it, in case it was his last chance to look at her. "Oh, could you but have seen some of the charges that were made!" he wrote. "While thinking of them I cannot but exclaim, 'Glorious War!' "[10]

Biographers would often quote the phrase, and one would use it as the title for a book about Custer's Civil War career.[11] Yet prosaic duties consumed most of his time as a brigade commander. In performing them, he created managerial friction. It is a phenomenon inherent in hierarchical organizations, with their tiers of authority and partitioned fields of responsibility. Officials at every level push up, push down, push sideways—demanding, defending, or simply disliking one another.

"It is an actual fact that there are men in my command who have been captured by the enemy, carried to Richmond, and rejoined my command in less time than it frequently requires for men to proceed to the Dismounted Camp and return mounted," he complained. The chief of the Cavalry Bureau, Maj. Gen. George Stoneman, blamed the riders. "I have understood that Custer's brigade are great horse-killers," he wrote.[12]

Some rattling of the chains of command was inevitable. Since the army pioneered the organizational society in America, it naturally pioneered bureaucratic infighting as well. And who is to say that Custer was wrong? He was responsible for his own unit; if kicking the machine delivered better horses faster, then he served his men well. Yet managerial friction exposed the self-important, self-destructive side of his personality.

What chafed him was the conduct of the Bristoe Station Campaign, the seesaw movements that included his narrow escape on October 11. Meade withdrew all the way to the Bull Run battlefield, escaping Lee's outflanking maneuver, and got the better of the battle that gave its name to the campaign. The Confederates retreated in turn to a position behind the Rapidan River, followed cautiously by the Army of the Potomac.[13]

"The movements of this army for the past three or four weeks have been a complete farce," Custer wrote to Judge Christiancy on October 29. "Could I see you I could make some developments [i.e., reveal information] which would astonish you, but I dare not trust it on paper. I do not refer to idle rumors, but to established facts," he wrote. Keep all this secret, he insisted. "I have never expressed an opinion in the presence of anyone and I should consider it wrong for me to do so were my opinion made public."[14]

Of course, Christiancy *was* the public, in that he was a very influential civilian. That was why Custer whispered to him. McClellan-like, he plunged again into insubordination, violating the chain of command to intrigue with his political sponsor.

To be fair, Meade's caution did spark controversy.[15] But Custer was a general, not a private soldier. If his letter reached the wrong desk, it might destroy him. He also exaggerated his place in the larger drama. As one of scores of brigadier generals in the Army of the Potomac, it is extremely unlikely that he possessed inside information about the highest levels of command. He rewrote his minor part into the lead. The true main characters remained offstage, unaware of Custer's wild claims. He never suffered the repercussions he feared. But this was not an isolated case. He possessed a self-destructive impulse that, in moments of indignation, drove him to assail the very highest authorities. And he would do it again, with consequences.

He was in a dark mood. He had learned that his friend Leroy Elbert had died of a fever on a steamboat on the Mississippi; the body was tossed onto the shore, where it was identified only by accident.[16] But the real provocation had come late in the Bristoe Station Campaign, as the Cavalry Corps pursued the retreating Confederates.

On the cold, wet morning of October 19, Kilpatrick pushed his division southwest from Gainesville, Virginia, with Custer's brigade in the advance. A strong enemy force stopped them near Buckland Mills, at a bridge over steep-banked Broad Run. Custer outflanked the Confederates, who retreated—a bit too easily.[17] Kilpatrick ordered Custer to give chase immediately. He refused. His men had not eaten since the day before, he said. He ordered his troops to unsaddle on the newly captured side of Broad Run. He was wary. He sent out scouts, and deployed the 6th Michigan under Maj. James H. Kidd to guard his vulnerable left flank, facing south. Impatient, Kilpatrick left Custer behind and took the 1st Brigade on a hunt to the southwest after the retreating foe, toward the town of Warrenton. Kidd's regiment advanced on foot to the edge of an open field. Confederate troops opened fire from the tree line beyond. They belonged to Fitzhugh Lee's division of cavalry, also on foot. The attack swelled quickly. A Union chaplain heard the famous rebel yell, "something between the shriek of a woman and the scream of a panther."

Kilpatrick had led the division into a trap. J. E. B. Stuart had lured the Union cavalry forward, ordering Lee to encircle and destroy the Union division by cutting off its retreat over Broad Run. Custer waged a hard, chaotic fight, one brigade against a division, to bring his men back across the stream. "Contrabands and camp followers were careering by in a state of panic," wrote the chaplain, who rode with the wagon train. "The pursuing enemy was now closing upon us from all sides. . . . It seems that they put to death at once all blacks taken while employed in any capacity in our service." Custer held off the Confederates long enough to escape. His long delay at the crossing had spoiled Stuart's trap. As Kidd wrote to his parents, "Dinner saved us."

Even so, the rebels smashed up the 3rd Division. Once Lee attacked, Stuart struck Kilpatrick and the 1st Brigade, which dissolved in a frantic gallop back to Buckland Mills. The rebels laughingly called the battle the Buckland Races.[18]

"Yesterday, October 19, was the most disastrous this division has ever passed through," Custer wrote to Nettie Humphrey. "All would have been well had General K. been content to leave well enough alone." He was about to follow Kilpatrick "when the enemy made a vigorous attack from the direction I had prophecied [sic] they would."[19]

Custer embellished. Kidd believed "that he was entirely unaware of the presence of a [sic] enemy in our immediate neighborhood." Ironically, he comes off better *because* he lacked perfect knowledge of the enemy's intentions. Acting on little more than a hunch, he halted at the crossing, despite the irritation of his commander, and took precautions against a surprise attack. It was the right hunch.[20]

Custer lost his headquarters wagon with all his papers. He blamed Kilpatrick, whose aide had redirected it. His brigade suffered 214 casualties in the campaign. Again he blamed Kilpatrick, who had detached a battalion from the 5th Michigan without Custer's knowledge. It was wiped out, reducing the regiment by a fifth or more.[21] "Yesterday was not a gala day for me," he wrote in his letter to Nettie. For a man so inclined to congratulate himself, this was a revealing admission. "My only consolation is that I am in no way responsible for the mishap, but on the contrary urged General K. not to take the step which brought it upon us, and the only success gained by us was gained by me."[22]

Tension with an immediate superior placed Custer in a dangerous position. Fortunately for him, Kilpatrick had the more controversial reputation, heard in his nickname "Kill-Cavalry." Even Pleasonton reprimanded him for "a very great want of discipline."[23]

Pleasonton's reliability as a friend was decisive in Custer's career calculations. After the Bristoe Station Campaign, he contemplated a transfer to the West, where he might command a division. He would have
to establish his reputation anew, he told Nettie, so he had to weigh the
strength of his existing support from Meade and Pleasonton against the
anticipated friendship of Gen. George Thomas, commander of the Army
of the Cumberland. Thomas "could scarcely do more for me, however,
than Genl. Meade and Genl. Pleasonton are willing to do," particularly
the latter. "I do not believe a father could love his son more than Genl.
Pleasonton loves me," he wrote. After a battle he often said to Custer,
"Well, boy, I am glad to see you back. I was *anxious about you.*"[24]

He chose the angel he knew. He remained in the Army of the Potomac.
He did his best to control his anger at Kilpatrick, but trusted Pleasonton
to watch over him.

"THE HAND OF THE LORD has been over you and around you. Nothing
els could have saved you," Emmanuel Custer wrote to his son on October
25. "We should look and trust in him and be vary thankful for his goodness and mercy shoan to wards us."

Later accounts would depict Emmanuel as a fun-loving prankster,
much like Armstrong, but his letters reveal a serious man living a hard
life, who cajoled, implored, and moralized. His method was to manipulate
his son with guilt. In this letter, he turned from gratitude to a sermon
aimed at his son's lack of piety. He never asked for money, but detailed
his financial distress. He implied that Armstrong should use his influence
to help his younger brother Tom, who served in the Western theater. "I
would be glad if this war was over doant forget to write to pore Tom give
him al the comfort that you can," he wrote. "I would be glad to here that
Thomas had been trasnfired to the Patomac Army."[25]

Emmanuel clearly loved his children, but his guilt-inducing moral
pressure heightened Armstrong's volatility. He responded to his parents'
poverty by indulging in luxuries he could not afford. He relished wartime
perks, boasting of the "elegant house" he had seized as his headquarters.
He simply ignored the calls to repent. Yet he loved his family as much
as they loved him, and began to work on transferring Tom into his own
brigade.[26]

Again and again, Custer adopted father figures.[27] He wanted guidance,
friendship, approval, and the prestige of proximity to important men. He
also wanted the benefits they might bestow. In this he was merely traditional. On one hand, the public celebrated the market economy, with its
values of competition and entrepreneurship. Competition—in business

or in war—focuses every effort on victory, which highlights the importance of real ability. Yet Americans still organized public life through personal connections, through networks of patrons and supplicants. The organizational society, with its impersonal standards and systematic assessments, had barely begun to sprout. So it was perfectly ordinary for Custer to seek patronage, but the obligations he owed in return could be complicated.

As a favor to Judge Christiancy, he brought his son James onto his staff. It embroiled him in a tormented relationship. The judge believed drink was destroying Jim. "Strict discipline & constant employment may sober him; if not, he is lost," Christiancy wrote. He urged Custer to fire him if he did not meet expectations. "He marches straight to the Devil. . . . Poor Jim! I have spent many a sleepless night in consequence of his errors. May God direct him. I have tried and failed."[28]

It may be impossible for a soldier in war to walk the path of righteousness. It may be impossible for a twenty-three-year-old commander to meet both the demands of combat leadership and the murky moral duties of a mentor and friend. Safely at home in Monroe, Emmanuel and Isaac did not know the dread, adrenaline, and kinetic chaos of the battlefield, or the tedium of camp life. The fathers of Monroe issued their judgments, and Custer did what he could.

He wanted one more father, of course, and his name was Daniel Bacon. The judge constantly mediated Libbie and Rhoda's conflicting emotions regarding Custer. "My more than friend—at last," Libbie wrote to Armstrong after her father approved their corresponding with each other. "I was surprised to hear how readily Father had consented to our correspondence. You have no idea how many dark hours your little girl has passed." She and her father had sat together in front of the fireplace one Sunday night and talked about Custer until the fire died. She saw him warming.

Her stepmother remained cold. Libbie wrote, "I love her dearly and respect her opinions, but not her prejudices." That word *prejudices* speaks to the importance of respectability to the Bacons, and to the social distance between themselves and the dirty-nailed Custers. Stories of Armstrong's promises to Fannie Fifield circulated in town—thanks to an angry Fifield. Judge Bacon asked his daughter how she would feel if Custer turned out to be false. Then she would be done with him, she said. That satisfied him. "When I say anything that would seem an impediment to my marrying Armstrong, Father is the one to explain it away," she wrote in her diary. He dismissed Custer's affairs, saying, "Why he was a boy then & never had been in society &c."[29]

She did not realize that her father had investigated the Boy General. Here Custer's pursuit of patrons proved its value. Bacon interviewed Col.

Frazy Winans and Col. Ira Grosevenor, discussed Custer with Chris-tiancy, and obtained letters about him from other officers in the Army of the Potomac. Nor did Libbie know that Custer sent a package to her father on December 7. It contained the large, hand-colored photograph taken in Washington. Custer asked Judge Bacon to hang it in her room as a surprise, a Christmas present. And he asked for permission to marry her.

"I can anticipate the strength of her lungs when [the portrait] shall meet her eye," Bacon replied on December 12. Then he turned to the great question. "I feel that I have kept you in suspense quite too long." She was his only child, he wrote, and his love and concern for her future delayed his reply. "I feel too that I have no right to impose terms over my daughter . . . or to make choices for her." Custer's "explanatory and excellent letter" had affected him. His inquiries, "as well as the wishes of my daughter, perfectly reconcile me to yield my hearty assent to the con-templated union." One thing nagged at him: Custer was not a Christian. But he could not refuse Libbie, and he took pride in Armstrong's "well earned military reputation." He warned that he was not a wealthy man.[30]

Armstrong replied immediately. Wordy, stilted, strenuously humble, his letter nevertheless rippled with his delight. A sample sentence: "I will endeavor throughout my future life to so shape my course, guided and activated by the principles of right, as will not only secure and promote the happiness of her who soon will become my wife, but I will also make it an aim of my life to make myself deserving of the high and sacred trust you have reposed in me, and I hope no act of mine will ever afford you the faintest foundation for supposing your confidence in my worth and integ-rity has been misplaced." That is to say, "I'll try to make her happy, do the right thing, and make you proud of me." Custer's sister, on the other hand, received a much chattier note. Armstrong asked if he and Libbie were the talk of the town yet, bragged that he got a $100 wedding coat as a present, and added, "Tell Pap I forgot to get his consent."[31]

"My dear 'Beloved Star,'" Libbie wrote to Armstrong. "If loveing [sic] with one's whole soul is insanity I am ripe for the asylum." Fannie Fifield appeared in new furs, Libbie wrote, wearing a diamond ring from a wealthy Boston merchant, only to learn Libbie was the talk of Monroe. Fannie interrogated one of her friends: Were Libbie and Custer to be married? Was the diamond on her ring bigger than Fannie's? It delighted Libbie, as everything did now. One day Emmanuel Custer rode up to her house on a fine horse that Armstrong had sent home. He told Judge Bacon that Libbie would have the "best of boys for a husband." Bacon dryly replied that he thought Armstrong would like Libbie after he got to know her better. Libbie laughed.

Now that her goal came within sight, she hesitated. "How I love my name Libbie BACON," she wrote to Armstrong. "Libbie B-A-C-O-N. Bacon. Libbie Bacon." Marriage challenged the identity she had forged in adversity and higher education; it threatened her sense of power over her own destiny. She wanted to delay the wedding for a year at least. "The very thought of marriage makes me tremble. Girls have so much fun. Marriage means trouble," she wrote to him.[32]

Her pause at becoming "his 'little wife'" is noteworthy given social expectations and the strength of her own passion, shaped by the sensibilities of her era and class. "I read him in all my books," she wrote that autumn. "When I take in the book heroes there comes dashing in with them my life hero my dear boy general." Another time she wrote, "Every other man seems so ordinary beside my own particular *star*." But the approaching reality sobered her. She criticized him, telling him that he had to stop swearing and gambling, and pressured him to profess faith in Christ.

He agreed to give up betting on cards and horses, but, as she would learn, he was often too quick to agree when it brought him closer to a goal. He never told Libbie how serious his affair with Fifield had been, and said nothing about Annie Jones, a young woman who had spent a week at his headquarters before he threw her out.[33]

Libbie herself still enjoyed being desired, and liked to remind Armstrong that other men wanted her. He remarked that Pleasonton had urged him to marry her quickly, noting how many other suitors pursued her. She wrote back, "Genl. Pleasonton has placed the number very small," and she listed them in detail. She told him of how a "handsome young man" stared at her in church, causing her to blush. "I am susceptible to admiration," she wrote.[34]

At a New Year's Eve party at the seminary, she wrote to Armstrong, she "made a conquest"—a young man from New York who insisted on kissing her cheek. He was "fearfully impertinent," she added. She liked it; as Nettie Humphrey noted, the New Yorker gave her "a 'slight turn' with his flatteries." She deliberately provoked Armstrong by telling him of it, inflating her sense of her own value by inflicting him with insecurity. Armstrong himself, of course, had tormented women in the past in precisely the same way. But the incident showed that Libbie was not all humor and charm. Those who knew her felt an edge behind her buoyant manner. Her stepmother criticized her sarcasm and accused her of saying "the most *withering* things," as she admitted.[35]

But Nettie knew Libbie would joyously marry Armstrong. After the party that New Year's Eve, the two friends went up to Libbie's room and followed their tradition, writing letters that looked back over the preceding year, to be read on the last night of 1864. "Here we are, on the floor, as usual, having just finished the perusal of last year's notes to each other," Nettie wrote. "Shall we ever spend another New Year's Eve together? You have just looked up from your writing to ask me the same question." A year before, Libbie had obsessed over other men, and wondered how she "*should* dispose of 'that Capt. Custer!'" And now, "*Genl* Custer's portrait looks down upon me from your chamber walls." Over the past twelve months, Libbie fell in love with Armstrong, and spent long days and nights believing "it utterly impossible that you could ever marry this dear man," Nettie observed. She tried and failed to love other men. She stole sweet moments at the Humphrey House with Armstrong. And she finally overcame all obstacles between them.[36]

ON NEW YEAR'S DAY, 1864, things went Custer's way. During the recent Mine Run Campaign, he had briefly led the 3rd Cavalry Division, quite capably. A crowd of Michigan foot soldiers begged to join his brigade. And he convinced the Bacons to agree to a wedding in February instead of months later. Libbie had resisted, not wanting to set a pattern of granting him all his demands. Her stepmother, Rhoda, of all people, took his side. She had agreed to an early wedding to her first husband, she said, yet "I always had my own way afterwards, in everything!" Libbie gave in.[37]

His mood changed on January 4. A friend in Washington warned him of a campaign to block Senate confirmation of his appointment as brigadier general. He said it was led by Brig. Gen. Joseph Copeland, the first commander of the Michigan Brigade.

Custer immediately wrote to Michigan's U.S. senators, Zachariah Chandler and Jacob Howard, as well as Representative Francis W. Kellogg. As he later remarked, he knew that if his home-state congressmen did not back him, his confirmation would certainly be defeated. Custer reminded Howard that they had met in Detroit in the fall, when the senator had offered help if he should ever need it. He asked Howard to use his place on the Military Affairs Committee to speed up his confirmation. He was just as direct with Chandler, asking "to favor me with your influence to secure my confirmation." He said he had heard of no other objection "than '*extreme youth*' and that '*older men wanted and should have had the place.*' This so far as I am informed is the extent of my crime. I am 'too young' consequently I am not *slow* enough."

Custer declared that his accomplishments should have rendered such lobbying unnecessary. This was disingenuous enough to be a joke. "Politics runs the thing," James Kidd wrote in early 1864. "Without political friends you are nowhere." No one knew this better than Custer, of course, who had cultivated patrons and political connections since before he left West Point.[38]

Just three days after this burst of letters, Custer heard that Howard opposed his confirmation because "I was *not* a *Michigan Man* but from Ohio and that my confirmation would interfere with aspirants from Michigan. This is not the first intimation that I have had of this kind, but I supposed that Senator H. was one of my surest advocates." He begged Christiancy to "bring influence to bear with both Howard & Chandler which would carry their votes in my favor."[39] Christiancy complied, inducing Howard to reply directly to Custer.

Custer later summarized Howard's letter. "It was reported to him that I was a 'Copperhead' and a strong opponent of the Administration and the present war policy." The charge was based on the fact that he had served on McClellan's staff. He suspected it came from Governor Austin Blair, an enemy of McClellan's.[40]

Custer contemplated Howard's letter at his desk on the first floor of an eighteenth-century house called Clover Hill that he had appropriated as his headquarters, a two-story, L-shaped building with a steep roof and white-painted porch near Stevensburg, Virginia. Outside, a hard winter rain pounded the earth into deep mud, like a layer of glue that sucked at wheels, hooves, and boots. With campaigning at an end for the season, wives and girlfriends came to visit officers in the brigade—some seventeen women, by one soldier's count. For Custer, this period of quiet and domesticity seemed as dangerous as any battle.

Howard asked for a statement of his political views. It was a difficult assignment, given the political gulf between Custer and the Radical Republican Howard, who called for a sweeping reconstruction of the South. "The people of the North are not such fools as to fight through such a war as this," Howard said, "and then turn around and say to the traitors, 'All you have to do is to come back into the councils of the nation and take an oath that henceforth you will be true to the Government.' "[41] He wanted Custer to renounce McClellan, which would mean an implicit rejection of Emmanuel as well. The price of advancement was personal betrayal.

Custer composed "a brief expression of my views regarding the war policy of the administration." It is worth quoting this letter at length, because it is one of the most shocking things he would ever write. "I have undertaken to be a soldier, and not a politician," he wrote. "So far has this sentiment controlled me that, at the last presidential election . . . I never expressed nor entertained a preference."

As a soldier, it was his duty to support the president's policies, and he did support them. "But I do not stop here," he wrote.

All his acts, proclamations, and decisions embraced in his war policy have received not only my support but my most hearty, earnest,
and cordial *approval*. . . . I seldom discuss political questions, but my
friends who have heard me can testify that I have insisted that so
long as a single slave was held in bondage, I for one was opposed to
peace on any terms. And to show that my acts agree with my words,
I can boast of having liberated more slaves from their masters than
any other general in this Army. . . . And rather than that we should
accept peace, except on our own terms, I would, and do, favor a war
of extermination. I would hang every human being who possesses
a drop of rebel blood in their veins whether they be men women
or children. Then, after having freed the country from the presence of every rebel, I would settle the whole southern country with
a population loyal and patriotic who would not soon forget their
obligations to the country. . . . I think the more rebels we kill the
fewer [there] will be to pardon and the better for us. Another question which has excited considerable discussion is that of military
arrests in states where the rebellion does not exist. If the President
has erred at all it has been in making too few arrests. . . .

I will now explain how and why the rumors arose which have
reached you, to the effect that I was an opponent of the administration. I was promoted and appointed on the staff of Gen. McClellan for an act of gallantry, and at a time when I was almost a total
stranger with McClellan, he having seen me but *twice* before and
never had spoken twenty words to me. During the time McClellan
was in command I, *as any soldier would*, supported him, but I have
never allowed my personal obligation to him for his kindness and
favor towards me to interfere with my duty. . . . There are those
who desire to see me defeated and no effort has been spared to bring
influence to bear with you and Hon. Z. Chandler to prejudice my
case. . . . To vouch for its [this letter's] correctness I can refer you to
Hon. I.P. Christiancy.[42]

It was all a lie. It was aggressively false, breathtakingly false, a great,
ramshackle house of lies. He was in fact a highly partisan Democrat, at
least formerly proslavery, who had passionately opposed Lincoln's election in 1860. Far from wanting "extermination," he maintained friendships in the enemy ranks, and, as we've seen, even stood as best man in a
Confederate wedding. Admittedly, war had hardened him, and he desired
victory with a ferocity alien to McClellan.[43] But he had never advocated
anything like the policies listed in this letter. It was as if he had written a
parody of Radical views.

He sacrificed his mentor. It was purely opportunistic. "Autie adored General McClellan," Libbie later wrote. "It was the hero worship of a boy and [even] when three years of responsibility had matured him . . . I think the worship of McClellan was still with him." As a general Custer was quite the opposite of McClellan, yet his admiration never dimmed, and they shared the same politics. He still blamed the Radicals for his hero's downfall. "General McClellan was a martyr in his eyes."[44]

Howard forced him to choose between his heart and his ambition, and Custer chose ambition. Judge for yourself, Custer wrote, if anything in his letter "can be considered as any endorsement of McClellan's policy." He distanced himself with such words as "stranger" and "any soldier," barely admitting his "personal obligation."[45]

His career was at risk, of course—and with it the romantic story he crafted for himself. To descend into sudden obscurity due to political intrigue would be shattering. Military success was the lever that had pried Judge Bacon out of resistance to his marrying Libbie—that had moved her to call him "my own particular *star*." A match with a fallen former general would be unacceptable; as Libbie once reminded him, "You are not marrying a girl *entirely* unknown in this State and elsewhere."[46]

Judge Bacon heard rumors about opposition in the Senate and wrote to Custer in alarm. Custer replied that "the subject . . . has caused me no little anxiety for the past few weeks." He assured Bacon that it was a misunderstanding, and he had cleared it all up. "But there are now no charges against me which have not been completely refuted and I have no anxiety about whatever in regard to my confirmation."[47]

He had, in fact, received reassurances from Kellogg, who said that both Howard and Chandler now stood behind him. Nothing was certain, of course; months would pass before the Senate voted. For the moment, though, Custer had done enough.[48]

"THE LABOR AND EXPENSE of passing through a wedding at this age of the world," Daniel Bacon wrote to his sister, "is no small thing. I never engaged in an enterprise with more cheerfulness, and yet a good deal was useless and largely extravagant."[49]

At six o'clock on the evening of Tuesday, February 9, 1864, the grim-faced and heavy-jawed Bacon had walked up the eastern aisle of the Presbyterian Church in Monroe, his only child's arm in his, she leaning on him as if she could not walk that final distance alone. In the western aisle, Armstrong supported Bacon's wife, Rhoda, still weak from a long illness, as they paced slowly forward. Between them, bodies crammed every available space, taking up the galleries above, the aisles, the vestibule—

"filled almost to suffocation," the *Monroe Commercial* noted. Amstrong had cut his hair short, to the disappointment of many, and Libbie wore a silk dress with a long veil suspended from the customary orange-blossom wreath atop her head. The service ended within an hour. Judge Bacon dryly noted, "There were no mistakes made."

The wedding party led some 300 guests to the Bacon home, where the reception went on for the next three hours. Everyone seemed to enjoy it, the judge noted, expressing dismay at the cost and pride in the result. The *Commercial* wrote, "We noticed among the wedding presents to the bride, a large and elegant silver tea set, from the 1st Vermont Cavalry, and a beautiful set of plain, solid silver, presented by the 7th Michigan Cavalry." The Bacons gave the sober gifts of a Bible and a watch.

"I yielded her cheerfuly [sic], not perhaps so much on my own judgment as a desire to gratify her ardent desire and wishes," Judge Bacon wrote his sister. "They both feel they have the highest possible treasure." He was both happy for Libbie and afraid for Libbie. She told him that day, "I have proved my admiration for your belief in self-made men by marrying one." It gratified him. But still he worried. He wrote, "What awaits Custer no one can say. Libbie may be a widow or have a maimed husband."[50]

WHAT WAS FORBIDDEN was now required. Knowledge denied to her now defined her. She had long known of it without knowing it; her husband, not she, had had the experience. Now, in the dark, he initiated her.

Not on the night of the wedding, though: there was no time for it then. After the reception ended, Libbie and Armstrong had changed into travel clothes—she in a brown dress of wool empress cloth with white buttons—and were driven to the railroad station, accompanied by friends, family (including Tom Custer, home on leave), and Custer's staff—many of them Monroe boys—most of whom had come home with him for the ceremony. The six bridesmaids and groomsmen boarded the midnight train to Cleveland with them. General and Mrs. Custer checked into the Waddell House hotel on arriving in the morning. Another reception ensued, and another party.[51]

Finally, more than twenty-four hours after the wedding, the couple were alone and in bed. A year later, Armstrong would tease Libbie about that night. "As that lady remarked in reference to piercing ears &c., There are a great many ways of *doing things*, some of which I believe are not generally known," he would write. "I know a certain young lady who had never worn ear rings, and when the piercing was about to be performed was quite reluctant as to both the time and manner of *doing* such *things*. How I smile sometimes when riding along as I think of the simplicity with which certain queries were proposed by an anxious searcher after information."[52]

It was their first truly private moment: the held breath of the first undressing, the sight of pale skin, the encounter of a confident, experienced lover and curious, hesitant virgin, stripped bare of her withering wit and sarcastic edge. But most of all, her questions reveal the truth of the instant. She was comfortable enough to ask, to speak of things she had never been allowed to speak of before. It was not an evening of mere resignation on her part—not of awkward silence, a forcible "piercing," and animal noises. Instead, they spoke. They asked and answered. Their physical intimacy began in emotional intimacy. It is no small thing that they began so well.

The next day, they continued east. In Buffalo, they went to the theater, where, figuratively and literally, they would live their lives. For Libbie, it had been forbidden; she had never seen a play. There (or perhaps in Rochester, immediately afterward, where they also went to the theater) Armstrong took her to a performance of *Uncle Tom's Cabin*. The various dramatic adaptations of the novel comprised the single most popular play in America at the time. With African Americans played by white actors in blackface and characters simplified to heroes, martyrs, and villains, it reduced the searing sins and political complexities of slavery to a melodrama. And so, ironically, Armstrong introduced Libbie to the worldly stage, so reviled by evangelists, through a schematic story of good and evil. She loved it.[53]

Physically, culturally, geographically, she journeyed out of her existence and into his—out of the fenced-in yard of the small-town seminary, out of the house of a nervous and protective father, and into the world. They clattered along the New York Central Railroad, stopping in Onondaga to visit her aunt's family. They transferred to the Hudson River Railroad and chuffed south. They crossed the frozen river on foot to West Point—a hired man pulling Libbie on a sled as Armstrong pushed. Faculty and senior officers honored the academy's prodigal son, and Libbie was delighted.

When they left, Libbie found Armstrong incensed. An old professor had kissed her. A group of cadets had walked her alone down a shaded path called Lover's Walk. She tried to explain, but he steeped in anger and said nothing. He knew that "school-boys," as she called the cadets, could be cunning and lecherous. They visited brothels. They joked about "wet dreams" and "jerking off." They lied to girls to sleep with them, then discarded them. (Did Custer see Mariah?) In the past she had flaunted the men who pursued her and reveled in her desirability; now his jealousy bubbled.

They crossed the river and boarded a train for New York in silence. Why wouldn't he talk? she asked. He claimed that he had formed the habit in his many hours of confinement and guard duty at West Point. Years later she wrote, "There were many silent seasons which I learned to understand and respect." The most telling word is "learned." It points to the awkwardness, the distance, that he could suddenly inject into their otherwise intimate relationship. She confronted an unreachable place within him; she agonized over it, but it defeated her. So she pretended it was a harmless quirk. On the page, at least, she would never reflect on what would have caused such dark withdrawals: the suspicion and jealousy that lurked behind his exuberance, the stress of his constant struggle to present an image of himself, his struggle to live up to the image, the constant biting of his insecurities. He was a mountain of explosive emotions. A volcano must sometimes collapse on itself.[54]

THE SIGHT OF LIBBIE surprised Ellen McClellan. She had read that Custer had married a widow. But that's impossible, she said. Libbie was too fresh, too young.

Libbie's recollection of their meeting suggests that it occurred shortly after the couple arrived in New York and checked into the Metropolitan Hotel, the five-story edifice that Custer knew well. It was easy to hire a horse-drawn cab on Broadway and Prince and ride to the McClellan town house at 22 East 31st Street. But it was also complicated. Less than a month had passed since the letter to Senator Howard. If McClellan learned of the letter, their relationship would be strained, if not broken; if word spread that Custer had visited him, any chance of confirmation might be ruined. Despite the risks, it is almost unthinkable that Custer would not bring his bride to meet his hero. "At that time General McClellan ran through our lives," Libbie later wrote. "We talked of him incessantly. . . . Autie adored General McClellan."[55]

But why, Libbie thought, did Mrs. McClellan think she was a widow? "I sometimes wonder if one of [Custer's] friends, who had often heard him announce that if he ever married . . . he did not care to have the 'left-over remains' of any man, had not inserted the hated word [into a press announcement] to play a joke on the 'widow' hater," she wrote. His disdain for widows infuriated her, she noted. "There was always warfare over the subject."

Their "warfare" opens a window on Libbie's attitude toward "the woman question," as it was discussed in politics. On the surface, she epitomized antebellum middle-class culture. She trained to be a good wife—to use her fine education to better herself and her family, not pursue a career. But she flared at that phrase, "left-over remains." It suggested that a woman had no life of her own. It reduced her to an item of consumption—like canned food, once the lid is removed what is left inside will rot. "I argued hotly for my sex and defended them by offering the fact that American women were illy prepared by their husbands to remain alone," she wrote. Living in a confined age, she did not lead the way to a future of freedom—but she felt it coming.[56]

But conflict did not define their journey from Monroe. "I was supremely happy," Armstrong later wrote to his father-in-law. Everyone who saw them remarked on their delight in each other, their intimacy. Libbie's cousin Rebecca Richmond wrote that she "was most agreeably disappointed after the reports I had heard [about Armstrong]. . . . He does not put on airs. He is a simple, frank, manly fellow. And he fairly idolizes Libbie. . . . She is the same gay, irrepressible spirit."[57]

Armstrong introduced Libbie to New York, the city he loved. There was so much to show her: Niblo's Theater, Barnum's museum, the bustle of oyster-cellar restaurants, the luxury of Delmonico's, the ship-crowded slips, the grim Five Points, the Battery, the brownstones. If they drove north out of the built-up city, there was the high-walled reservoir on 42nd Street and the most uncentral Central Park, crowded with carriages. "We saw all that was to be seen in the time we had allotted," Armstrong wrote.[58]

This first visit together began to mark out the geography of their lives as a couple. New York would be one pole of their new existence together. They had been born into the traditional society of farmers, artisans, and shopkeepers, in which the greatest cultural conflict was between Old Light and New Light Presbyterianism. New York was dense, sophisticated, and worldly; the extremes of life were packed between the Hudson and East rivers. It was the metropolitan center of the entire nation. More than that, it was the future—the laboratory of institutional innovation and financial abstraction, the conjuror's cauldron of capital, the training ground and garrison of writers and intellectuals who would celebrate, satirize, and critique what New York was making—the modern world.

They did not want to leave it. On February 13, Armstrong wired Cavalry Corps headquarters to ask for a ten-day extension to his leave. He received the reply at the Metropolitan Hotel: request granted. From New York they traveled on to Washington, a swamp village by comparison. In its dingy streets crowded with soldiers and inelegant hotels, they found only one interesting feature: powerful men.

These days of mutual intoxication and tossed-up sheets could not last long. On February 26, Pleasonton ordered Custer back immediately.[59]

WHEN ELIZA BROWN SAW four mules pull an ambulance up to the general's impounded farmhouse near Stevensburg, Virginia, and a petite, pretty, stylishly dressed woman step out, she knew enough to see a threat. By taking charge of the general's mess, Brown had established greater safety for herself than she had ever known. Slavery allowed no personal security, but Custer's invitation to cook for him meant consistent work, meals, and shelter—and much more. Through ingenuity and strength of personality, she had turned the tyranny of racial and gender roles to her advantage. White men were happy to leave the kitchen to her, so she made it her fortress, the seat of real authority. She used her position to trade information, food, and favors.[60]

But then Libbie Custer showed up. It was universally accepted in mid-nineteenth-century America that the wife controlled all things domestic—particularly the kitchen. Even in Southern homes filled with slaves or Northern ones staffed with Irish maids, the woman of the house supervised and scrutinized. If Mrs. Custer took command of the cookery, she would destroy Brown's security. She might fire Eliza in a moment of pique, or eradicate her authority by overruling or undercutting her. Brown faced the delicate task of keeping Mrs. Custer out of the kitchen without alienating her. Better yet, if she could turn her into an ally, Brown would be almost invulnerable.

She stood on the porch with Johnny Cisco as the general and his staff helped Mrs. Custer to the ground. Brown greeted her with a wide smile—what Libbie later called "motherliness and a beaming face." And that was her first defense against encroachment: smothering care.

Brown immediately recognized that Libbie was daunted by her new life in this sparsely furnished old house so close to the front, surrounded by soldiers. She played on Libbie's unease. "Day by day Eliza quietly and tactfully took us all in hand," Libbie later wrote. "She had taken care of her invalid master and elderly mistress and had that rock-a-bye tone and coddling way that I fell victim to very soon. It was protecting and enveloping and . . . she seemed to stand between me and care, or responsibility." Libbie soon learned that Brown was capable of "as delicate diplomacy as many a subtle, deep-thinking person could have exercised."[61]

Brown had Libbie at a disadvantage. For all of Libbie's education, intelligence, and outward advantages of race and marriage to the commanding general, she was a white woman in a white world. She had limited experience with servants, and had not given her interactions with them much thought. Eliza was a black woman in a white world. She had spent her life in radically unequal power relationships; adroitness with whites was her foremost survival skill. She understood just how hard to push back.

"She . . . was decidedly the King of the Kitchen Cabinet," Libbie recalled. "It was tacitly understood that I was [not] to know anything about the 'mess.'" Brown could flare in "wrath," but she calibrated it precisely. Libbie called it "some scolding that was not dangerous." Dangerous to the recipient, or to Brown? The truth is that anything that felt actually threatening to a white person was most dangerous to Eliza herself. She kept back intruders, including "Miss Libbie," without going too far.

In time, Libbie came to grasp how Brown outmaneuvered her. Years later she felt the need to explain why she did not assume the domestic authority expected of her. In her first memoir, she would promote the teenage Eliza to seniority, describing her as "the General's old colored servant." She would claim that her husband positively prohibited her from housekeeping. And she, too, would play on cultural expectations of femininity, by exaggerating her own weakness and inability. "I knew that I was not to be foisted upon anyone without perfect understanding of my ignorance of house lore," she would write. "I knew nothing about dishwater."[62]

But her education in Brown's diplomacy lay ahead of her. More immediately she learned the difference between a soldier at home, an attraction at parties in his dress uniform, and a soldier at war, surrounded by saluting subordinates, with a desk covered in maps and the army's ubiquitous forms. Almost immediately upon the Custers' arrival at Stevensburg, the brigade began to prepare for a raid. Bags of grain and crates of hardtack were stacked and loaded into wagons, carbines and cannons cleaned and inspected, horses saddled, companies and regiments formed into columns, flags and guidons raised overhead. Armstrong left.

Libbie went upstairs to the bedroom, lay down on the four-poster bed decorated with calico curtains by the wives of other officers, and wept. "I was completely overwhelmed with intense anxiety for my husband, bewilderment over the strange situation, and terror of the desolate place," she later wrote. Few soldiers remained in camp, and few women; a Southern family lived downstairs in the same house, which left her constantly uneasy. Brown followed her upstairs and "treated me alike an infant, coddling, crooning over me, 'He'll come back Miss Libbie. He always does you know. Didn't he tell you he'd come back?'" Before long, Brown erupted. "She could not resist, she could endure 'no longer' a secret she was bottling up: her wrath at what she termed 'onerous and outrageous' treatment of the General."

In the course of Brown's constant information gathering, she had learned about the operation that called Armstrong away. The idea for the raid, she told Libbie, originated with Kilpatrick. In November, he had gone home for the birth of a son. His wife and their child both had died during delivery. He had returned even more reckless than before. He had proposed a cavalry raid into Richmond to liberate Union prisoners, burn the Tredegar Iron Works, and distribute copies of the Emancipation Proclamation.

It was a preposterous plan, of course, but Brown heard that it had been approved through "political influence in Washington," as Libbie recalled. It was close enough to the truth. Kilpatrick had ignored the chain of command, taking his proposal directly to the White House. Lincoln authorized the raid, which was launched within days.

"General Custer was assigned the duty of attracting the whole Southern Army in another direction," Libbie gathered from Brown, "leaving this warrior [Kilpatrick] a clear field. It was for this reason the raid was delayed until General Custer's return." Even worse, Kilpatrick assigned Custer four regiments of unfamiliar troops and kept for himself much of the crack Michigan Brigade.[63]

And so Libbie tried not to cry, and Eliza tried to comfort her. Armstrong's sudden departure made them immediate allies. He was the foundation of both their lives, here on the right flank of the Army of the Potomac. Without him, each would be alone among strangers, with only the other for company.

"THE GREAT RAID ON RICHMOND has ended and U.S. is satisfied that Kilpatrick can't do everything. One thing at least he is unequal to, the capture of Richmond with cavalry," James H. Kidd of the 6th Michigan wrote to his parents. "Gen Custer you know distinguished himself as he always does."[64]

Armstrong returned—if not covered in glory, then "perfectly successful," General Meade concluded. Custer reported that he had burned a bridge and three flour mills, smashed six caissons and two forges, captured fifty prisoners and 500 horses, led more than 100 contrabands to freedom, and "on my return was cut off by a large force of cavalry and artillery." His friend Lt. George Yates, who came on the raid, wrote that Custer had ambushed his ambushers: "General Custer had massed his forces in a ravine out of sight of the enemy," and as his advance guard was driven back "ordered a charge of this entire force. Officers and men moved forward in magnificent style, charging desperately upon the enemy, driving them back in confusion."[65]

For Libbie, his return put everything right again. She wrote to her parents, "I am so charmed with the mountains." She considered many of the officers whom they socialized with daily to be "very superior men. . . . A great many are from Philadelphia and New York." It was a relief to be married, she wrote; she did not have to restrain herself so carefully as when she was single, and she liked the attention they gave her. One day, amid a cluster of officers, she praised "the pleasant gentlemanly air an officer in the regular army has." After they left, Armstrong warned her that the volunteers might resent it. It did not sink her buoyant mood. "Mother I haven't uttered a cross word since I was married. Now isn't that pretty well for me?"[66]

She and Armstrong visited his friends, dropped in on division and corps headquarters, inspected the troops. They went riding, and drove out in the fine carriage with silver harness that he had appropriated as the spoils of war, drawn by a beautiful matched pair of horses with four to six troopers riding behind as an escort. They were returning from a drive one day in the middle of March when the accident happened.

"Everybody seems to think it is a miracle I was not killed," Libbie wrote to her parents on March 20. Her written account is unclear, a fog speckled with specifics: the prize horses bolting down to the stable, toppling an ambulance and smacking into Eliza Brown's cow, and Armstrong lying on the ground as if dead. "He does not remember anything about the accident or subsequent delirium and I suppose he never will." He suffered a severe concussion. He needed rest, but Libbie could not convince him to remain in bed. About ten days after the accident, the brigade surgeon examined him and found him still suffering from traumatic brain injury.[67]

During this period, he received a troubling notice from Pleasonton. A young woman named Annie E. Jones had been arrested for spying. In a sworn statement, she claimed she had been "the friend and companion of Genl Custer" in the summer of 1863. She said Kilpatrick was jealous and falsely accusing her of being a spy. Pleasonton told Custer that he must respond to the charge.

Yes, he knew Annie Jones, he wrote. She had come to him asking for a position as a nurse. He had allowed her to stay at his "headquarters" (in her own tent? in his tent? in his bed?) as he made inquiries at army hospitals. No nurse was needed, so after a week he told her to leave. "I informed her that she must never visit my command again." Some weeks afterward she appeared late at night, driven in an army ambulance with a military escort, and demanded admittance. He reluctantly allowed her to spend the night but sent her away the next morning, and never saw her again. "It is simply untrue" that he and Kilpatrick quarreled over her. But he was curiously reluctant to condemn her. She was no spy, he argued, but was obsessed with the idea of performing some daring feat. "In this respect alone, she seemed to be insane."[68]

It is impossible to know if Custer's account was accurate, a fabrication, or significantly incomplete—or if his concussion affected his memory. Why was he so firm in sending her away the first time, after he spent a week trying to find her a position? Did she grow demanding? Did a brief sexual affair suddenly seem dangerous? And was he able to keep this exchange with Pleasonton secret from Libbie, who hovered over him as he recuperated? If he did keep it from her, she might have noticed that he was hiding something. If he did not, she might have been alarmed at the implications of the story, even if she believed him. It was not good.

On March 24, soon after Custer delivered his formal response, he applied for a medical leave of absence, supported by the surgeon's certificate. He needed to heal himself and, perhaps, his marriage. The request was granted.

Seven

THE HERO

"G EN. GRANT IS QUITE inferior looking," Libbie Custer wrote. Her husband introduced her to "the distinguished man" after they had boarded a special train from the Army of the Potomac to Washington. "So plain and not even a bright eye to light up his features. His hair and whiskers are sandy and his eyes are light greenish blue." She had to remind herself that everyone expected this "ordinary-looking" fellow to win the war.[1]

It had been two weeks since Ulysses S. Grant had first appeared at Meade's headquarters, freshly promoted to lieutenant general. He had won victory after victory in the West: the capture of Forts Henry and Donelson, the defeat of the Confederate attack at Shiloh, the capture of Vicksburg and its defending army, the victory at Missionary Ridge, breaking the siege of Chattanooga. He came east when President Lincoln named him general in chief.

The Army of the Potomac saw him as an outsider. "The feeling about Grant is peculiar—a little jealousy, a little dislike, a little envy, a little want of confidence," wrote Capt. Charles Francis Adams Jr., grandson of John Quincy Adams and brother of Henry. Grant left Meade in command, but planned to accompany him on the impending campaign, an unsettling arrangement. "All, however, are willing to give him a full chance," Adams added. "If he succeeds, the war is over."

"Grant is not a striking man," Meade wrote privately, "is very reticent, has never mixed with the world, and has but little manner, indeed is somewhat ill at ease in the presence of strangers; hence a first impression is never favorable." Not quite forty-two, Grant, like Custer, was the son of a struggling artisan in rural Ohio. Like Custer, he had graduated from West Point with a weak record. Like Custer, he had excelled at war, winning recognition as a young officer in Mexico. But rumors of alcoholism had plagued him afterward. He had left the army, failed in business, and ended up in Galena, Illinois, working in his father-in-law's tannery. When the Civil War began, he had volunteered, writing that he felt himself equal to the command of a regiment. Success followed success, promotion followed promotion, and this "stumpy, unmilitary, slouchy, and Western-looking" man (in the judgment of the genteel Col. Charles W. Wainwright) found himself in the nation's highest military position, surrounded by its loftiest people. It left him even more awkward and closemouthed.[2]

But not with Libbie. The pretty, charming young woman put him at ease, and he unfolded himself in a way that only his close friends usually saw. "No show-off but quite unassuming," Libbie described him, "talked all the while and was funny. Told the gentlemen that small army men invariably ride horses 17 hands high." That would make the horse very large—a joke about pretension, which he despised. But it was also self-deprecating; Grant himself was rather small and his horse, Cincinnati, was seventeen and a half hands high. He kept a cigar in his mouth constantly but went to the rear platform to smoke, "fearing that it might be disagreeable to me, till Autie begged him to return," Libbie wrote. "Tho disappointed in Grant's looks, I like him."

"Instead of speaking with men who could do so much for him, Autie sat by me and only spoke when necessary," she added.[3] For Custer, who so carefully cultivated patrons, such reticence is curious. Her explanation was modesty. But there was an unspoken dynamic between her husband and the hero in that rattling car, which swayed alarmingly over rebuilt track through fought-over country.

Grant's joke about pretensions in the army set the tone. He himself engaged in "no Napoleonic displays, no ostentation, no speech, no superfluous flummery," the *New York World* reported. The military historian John Keegan writes, "If Wellington eschewed ceremony, theater, and oratory, Grant actively disliked all three, with rigorous distaste." He wore a private's coat. He lived in a small tent with a cot, a pair of folding chairs, and a table. Libbie was right: he was "no show-off," but rather a man of quiet moral force. The contrasts with Custer went deeper. Grant *managed* his army—a hero who provided "unheroic leadership," in Keegan's words. Respectful of long-range firepower, he remained at a safe distance from the firing even when riding along the line. He directed battles largely through remarkably clear written orders and telegraph dispatches. He has been described as one of the first modern generals.

Did Custer become painfully aware of his black velvet jacket with gigantic coils of gold braid, the sailor shirt, and the giant star on his broad slouch hat? Was he embarrassed at the thought of his dramatic manner in front of his troops, his speeches, his band, his insistence on leading charges with his upraised straight saber? Did he grow ashamed of the comfortable farmhouse he took for his quarters, his personal cook, his private carriage with silver harness? Was he uncomfortable at seeing all the attention directed at someone else? Or was he merely polite? All that can be known is that, when confronted with the hero of the hour, Custer had nothing to say.[4]

THE REPRISE OF THEIR HONEYMOON began in Baltimore, which Libbie had never visited before. Armstrong took her to the theater to see a famous comic actor. In one skit, he played a servant who pretended to be the lord, dressed in his master's clothes. "He goes to see a young lady and the lord's pantaloons are so tight he cannot sit down without pain and has to keep his legs stretched out, and cannot bend his knees," she wrote. Armstrong "exhausted" himself laughing at someone trying to elevate himself beyond his place, in preposterous clothes that could not conceal the true man beneath. As Libbie wrote, "It was killing."[5]

When they were alone, they were playful and indulgent. "Do you remember how somebody's little girl used to amuse herself by tickling somebody's nose with his own mustache," he later asked her. He called her "my darling little durl" and "my Gipsie." Libbie no longer felt the hesitation of her wedding night. They invented intimate euphemisms. They asked each other for "just one." She would "sit Tomboy," straddling his lap in his chair. "Oh, I do want one so badly," he later wrote, when the war separated them. "I know *where* I would kiss somebody if I was with her tonight."[6]

"I am so sorry to hear . . . that your head is no better," adjutant and friend Jacob Greene wrote to Armstrong on March 30. Jim Christiancy accompanied the couple on their travels, but Greene worried. "You need perfect rest & quiet & that I know you are not getting." Greene knew Custer well, in some ways better than Custer knew himself. "You are only flesh & blood & can break down like any other man."[7]

Struggling with a brain injury, Custer still had to sway the Senate to confirm his appointment as a brigadier general. It fell to Libbie to cultivate the right men. It proved alarmingly easy. Senator Morton Wilkinson of Minnesota invited her to the "hop" held every Thursday night at the National Hotel. The Custers found Senator Chandler there, as always. "He is very fond of dancing," Libbie remarked. He begged her to dance, unsuccessfully, and insisted that she make up for it at the next hop.

"I have made so many friends in Washington it seems quite like home," Libbie wrote. In other words, she did her work well. On April 1, the Senate approved Custer's appointment, along with a long list of others. In the end, it was perfectly routine, but Armstrong was so relieved that he sent a telegram to the Bacons in Monroe.[8]

"I thought there would be so many generals in Washington he would be but little known," Libbie wrote to her parents from Washington. "If he were not naturally a modest man his head would be turned by the attention he has received this week." A sketch of him leading a charge appeared on the cover of the March 19 issue of *Harper's Weekly*. "It is very agreeable to be the wife of a man everyone knows and respects."[9]

CUSTER RETURNED TO CAMP as a man unmoored, because Grant removed his mooring. On March 25, Pleasonton was relieved of command of the Cavalry Corps and transferred to Missouri. Grant replaced him with Maj. Gen. Philip Sheridan, an infantry-division commander from the West. "We are blue as a whole whetstone factory," Jacob Greene wrote to Custer, who was still in Washington. "Pleasonton gone. You gone. Sheridan going to have the corps—& the Devil to pay generally. What are they sending a man for, that we don't know or care for."[10]

Kilpatrick fell on April 7, assigned to lead Maj. Gen. William T. Sherman's cavalry. Victor Comte wept at his farewell address. "If the Michigan Brigade has won a name in the Army of the Potomac, it is because of Kilpatrick and Custer; and if these two generals are famous, it is our brigade which has made them so." Comte's remarks show how closely Custer guarded his irritation with "Kill-Cavalry" from his men.[11]

Custer joined his brigade on April 14, and heard he would fall next. "Rumor says Gen. Custer may leave us," wrote Maj. James H. Kidd. "'Bad luck' to [us]. . . . We swear by him. His name is our battle-cry. He can get twice the fight out of this brigade than any other man can possibly do."[12] Custer believed the rumor. He often inflated his insecurity into a sense of persecution. "An attempt was made by some of Grant's favorites to have me relieved . . . the object being to give the brigade to one of Grant's friends," he wrote to Judge Bacon. He confronted Meade and Sheridan in person. They reassured him. But then Grant installed Brig. Gen. James H. Wilson as Kilpatrick's successor. Being passed over for command of the 3rd Division galled Custer, but seeing the post go to Wilson infuriated him. Recently chief of the Cavalry Bureau and formerly a member of Grant's staff, he had tormented Custer at West Point. Armstrong wrote to Judge Bacon that Wilson "is an engineer officer *of Grant's staff* and had never even commanded a company of men." He missed the irony that he, too, had been elevated directly from a staff post to an important command.[13]

"Had [Pleasonton] remained in command of the Cavalry Corps I would now be in command of a division," he fumed. He told Bacon that Grant fired Pleasonton "without apparent cause. . . . I know the reason but do not wish to state it on paper." Once again he spread rumors about a commanding general he disliked—now taking the side of Meade, who (he claimed) told him he was unhappy that Grant would accompany him during the coming campaign. Custer enclosed a letter from Congressman Kellogg that was critical of Grant, and asked Bacon to show it discreetly to Judge Christiancy.[14]

What saved Custer, ironically, was the man Grant put in Pleasonton's place. Custer's tone changed completely when he discussed him. "Gen. Sheridan is a very just man," he wrote to Judge Bacon. He told Libbie, "Sheridan has impressed me very favorably. . . . Everything is arranged quite satisfactorily now." Sheridan did not ask Custer to serve under Wilson, a less senior officer. He redesignated the Michigan Brigade the 1st Brigade of the 1st Cavalry Division, which had a new commander, Brig. Gen. Alfred Torbert, "an old and intimate friend of mine, and a very worthy gentleman," Custer wrote.[15]

Sheridan looked like a replacement patron, one who had much in common with Custer. "I was rather young in appearance," Sheridan later wrote. He was thirty-three years old, just nine years older than Custer, though a good deal smaller—"but five feet five inches in height, and thin almost to emaciation, weighing only one hundred and fifteen pounds." As an infantry division commander in the West, Sheridan had helped to salvage the battles of Stones River and Perryville through front-line leadership. At Chattanooga, he was ordered to launch a limited holding attack against Missionary Ridge; he and his division impulsively captured it, winning the battle. Dark-haired and broad-chested, with narrow, bullet eyes, prominent cheekbones, and a drooping handlebar mustache above a strong chin, he looked fierce. He *was* fierce. Like so many Irish throughout history (he was born to immigrant parents), he was a master of the English language—the profane part of it, at least. He wanted the Cavalry Corps to be a strike force that would whip J. E. B. Stuart. It was all that Custer wanted.[16]

Custer left Libbie in Washington while he prepared for the great offensive. "How completely my time has been occupied," he wrote to his father-in-law. Horses were rested and fed, and seven-shot Spencer carbines issued to men who did not yet have them. Contrabands piled sacks of grain, boxes of hardtack, and other supplies in wagons.[17]

The brigade moved forward. Custer inspected the new camps, then sat on a bench by a log fire to write to Libbie. One staff officer sat on the ground nearby, reading a novel; Jacob Greene was in his tent playing his flute. Libbie's absence freed Eliza Brown to tend to her own patronage network, using her control of the mess to distribute food and extend her influence with the brigade's labor force. Custer wrote, "Eliza is entertaining an interesting group of Contrabands who are posted near her cook fire."[18]

He kept his anger at Grant secret from his wife, but he missed her. If she were there, he wrote, "Somebody would have insisted upon 'Just one' or would have been seen pushed a la 'Tomboy' on somebody's lap."[19] Sheridan sent Custer to Washington on a final errand before the advance. He gave him forty-eight hours to complete it, knowing that Libbie was staying at a boardinghouse in the capital.

Libbie was in her room chatting with a female visitor when she heard someone running heavily up the stairs. The noise brought other residents rushing to the corridor, afraid it might be a fire. Armstrong threw her door open. "The lady left immediately," Libbie wrote to her parents. He had shaved off his mustache, which he had shaken into an envelope and mailed to her earlier. "He doesn't know how to act without it, his mouth seems so strange to him." His face was so smooth, she added, "it seemed like kissing a girl."

Outside, wagons rattled down the streets in long lines, carrying supplies to the vast depots of the Army of the Potomac. Veterans recalled from furlough and new recruits crowded the city on their way to their units—three regiments' worth a day, Libbie reckoned. The press suddenly stopped reporting about the Army of the Potomac—a sign "that a great battle is expected," she thought. The forty-eight hours ended, and Armstrong left to fight.[20]

ON MAY 3, CUSTER RETURNED to camp from Cavalry Corps headquarters with the order to move out the next day. "We ought to whip them," Jim Christiancy wrote to his father. "My piles are terrible but don't prevent me riding." He would not have to ride far. The next morning the Michigan Brigade remained in the rear of the army, guarding the supply trains. "'Pet' Wilson," as Christiancy called him, led the advance.[21]

Grant planned for his army to cross the Rapidan River east of the Confederate position, turning the Army of Northern Virginia's right flank in order to force it out of its fortifications and into the field. Sheridan assigned Wilson to screen the advance of the heavy infantry columns as they crossed two fords and marched south into the Wilderness, the dense forest where Lee had defeated Hooker a year earlier. Beyond it, the Union army would reach open ground where it could bring to bear its numerical superiority. It was essential that Wilson keep the rebels from detecting the movement.[22]

He failed. He briefly scouted the roads leading west out of the Wilderness toward the enemy army, and reported that he had the flank well covered when he did not. On May 5, a Confederate onslaught took the Army of the Potomac by complete and unnecessary surprise, while still deep in the Wilderness. Grant ordered his men to stand and fight. Confused battles raged on narrow roads as forest fires began to burn.[23]

Custer and his brigade joined the battle on May 6, fighting on the army's left flank. He drove off a Confederate cavalry brigade under the command of Brig. Gen. Thomas Rosser, his old friend from West Point. More than 100,000 Union soldiers fought some 60,000 Confederates in the Battle of the Wilderness on May 5 and 6. It cost the two armies almost 18,000 and more than 11,000 casualties, respectively, counting killed, wounded, and missing. That depleted the Army of the Potomac by a little less than 18 percent, and the Army of Northern Virginia by rather more. This level of lethality had been seen before, but the results were entirely new. Unlike every previous Union commander surprised by Lee, Grant did not retreat. On May 7, he ordered the army to continue to move south.[24]

The men cheered. They were right to do so on one hand, and crazy on the other. Right, because Grant chose the only path to victory. He understood clearly that he could not wage a Napoleonic campaign in which one decisive battle would break up the enemy army and convince the hostile government to surrender. The resilience of the armies on both sides over three years had proved that this was virtually impossible. This warfare had to demonstrate, day after day, the futility of rebellion. Grant believed that the key was to fight on, no matter what the result of any given day. He would bring to bear (on multiple fronts) the numerical and industrial superiority of the North. He asked his army to inflict pain and endure.

And that is why his men were also crazy to cheer his advance. This "Overland Campaign," as it would be dubbed, threw them into bloodshed of prolonged intensity unlike any campaign before. Each day the odds of any man surviving steadily dwindled. Hostile historians would deride Grant as a butcher, but his campaign was the logical conclusion of the seemingly inexorable trend of mass infantry warfare in an existential political conflict. The individual foot soldier was not the gallant hero of antebellum myth; he had become ammunition. More than just expendable, he *had* to be expended to secure victory.

In this war rode George Armstrong Custer, a living contradiction. He was a romantic and professional both. He had no sense of irony, no cynicism, no sardonic fatalism—the defining characteristics of the modern soldier. He used the word "gallant" with sincerity. He made himself a champion and a target with his costume and deliberately crafted persona. He fought on horseback with a sword in the age of long-range killing machines. Yet he was also a skillful commander who deployed that machinery mercilessly and well. He measured the means for each end accurately, and his ultimate end was total victory. He led charges on horseback because, under the right circumstances, they could still work, and he had a grasp of what made the circumstances right. The spectacle he made of himself was still useful in rallying and inspiring his men—for the material element in war had not yet eradicated the moral. But it had a way of eradicating spectacles.

THE PRISONER MARCHED SLOWLY, oppressed with the heavy Virginia summer heat. His name was Edwin. The Confederates had captured him in the Wilderness, where, in the noise and smoke of battle, he had not realized that his regiment had fallen back without him. The rebels had herded him together with nearly 380 others and looted their possessions, compensating them with Confederate currency, worthless even to Confederates. They slept in the open, shared what little food they had, and suffered in the heat, some collapsing along the road from exhaustion. Their guards told them that they were headed for Beaver Dam Station, where they would be fed.

At sunset on May 9, Edwin heard a train whistle. The station was close. Next he heard gunshots. "Gen. Custer, at the head of a brigade of cavalry, came thundering down upon us with sword drawn, hat off, and hair streaming in the wind," he wrote shortly afterward. The prisoners cheered as the column charged by in pursuit of the guards, most of whom escaped. The rescuers and rescued poured into the station. Edwin and the famished prisoners tore open boxes and barrels, and found 200,000 pounds of food for Lee's army.[25]

Less than an hour later Sheridan arrived with the rest of the Cavalry Corps. In the aftermath of the Battle of the Wilderness, Sheridan had fought with Meade over the proper role of the cavalry, demanding that he be allowed to take the Corps on a raid, with the particular goal of defeating his counterpart, J. E. B. Stuart. Meade had wanted the cavalry to guard the army's flanks, protect the trains, and screen and scout. Grant had backed Sheridan. And so the three divisions moved in a solid mass to strike the enemy. Sheridan named Custer's brigade the advance guard.[26]

At the station, Edwin wrote, "the heavens were brilliantly lighted nearly all night long by the burning buildings, cars, &c." Custer's men torched three long trains, mounds of supplies, and the station itself. Edwin snatched a blanket out of a captured wagon and slept soundly. Roused at dawn, he saw "the huge column of horsemen was again wending its way southward."[27]

Deep in the rear of the enemy army, marching slowly toward Richmond, Sheridan knew that Stuart would try to catch him. He counted on it. On May 11, he discovered that Stuart had taken a position near Yellow Tavern, a crossroads just north of Richmond, squarely across the Union line of march. The Confederate commander had only Fitzhugh Lee's division, less than half his total force, divided into two brigades. But Stuart was a cunning foe, never more so than when outnumbered.[28]

When Custer arrived from the west, he saw "the enemy was strongly posted on a bluff in rear of a thin skirt of woods, his battery being concealed from our view by the woods." Stuart assumed a concave line on two ridges; despite the Union preponderance in numbers, he felt confident enough to risk battle. The terrain favored him, and his deployment was clever. Generally speaking, long-range rifles and artillery gave the defense the tactical advantage in the Civil War. The Union cavalry shook out into a line. Custer's men cleared the woods, but the rebels remained firmly on the heights beyond. By late afternoon, Sheridan wanted decisive action. He sent orders for the 1st Division to capture the ridge on the right.[29]

Custer deployed his men just inside the far edge of the wood and made "a personal examination of the ground." The key was a well-handled artillery battery on the right of the rebel line, from Custer's perspective. "I discovered that a successful charge might be made upon the battery of the enemy by keeping well to the right," he wrote. Brig. Gen. Wesley Merritt, temporarily in command of the division, gave him permission to try. He ordered the 5th and 6th Michigan regiments to "occupy the attention of the enemy" and his own artillery to shell the enemy's front. In the woods, hidden from the enemy, he formed the 1st Michigan into a column; the 7th Michigan would follow as its reserve. When the men had formed up, Custer addressed them. "There is good ground over there," he said, meaning the right terrain for a charge, "and I think we can take their battery." He ordered the mounted band to play "Yankee Doodle" and led them out of the woods. Riding forward through enemy fire, the column broke down fences and crossed a narrow bridge, until they finally came close enough to the enemy to launch a charge.

Sheridan watched them pick up speed. "Custer's charge . . . was brilliantly executed," he reported; "first at a walk, then at a trot, then dashing at the enemy's line and battery." Riding up quickly on the Confederates' left flank, Custer ordered the men to spur into a full gallop. Sabers drawn, they screamed "with a yell which spread terror before them," he wrote. The horsemen hacked with their swords as they rode through a pair of cannons and dismounted Confederate troopers, who panicked and fled.[30]

The 5th and 6th Michigan moved up the slope as well. Colonel Russell Alger of the 5th reported that a subordinate pointed out an enemy

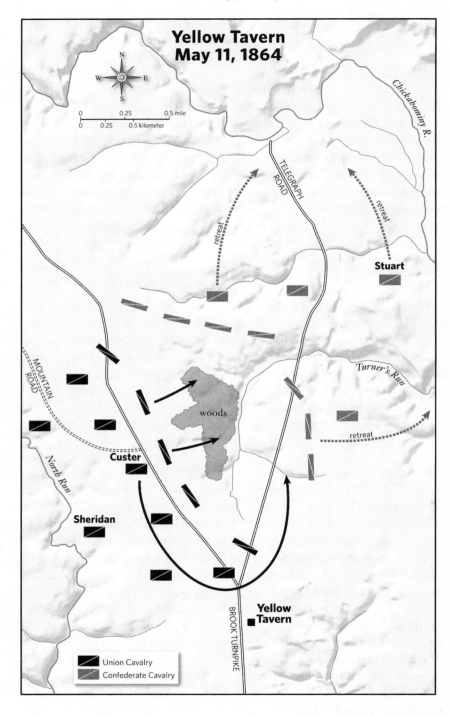

Yellow Tavern
May 11, 1864

N
W   E
S

0   0.25   0.5 mile
0   0.25   0.5 kilometer

Chickahominy R.

TELEGRAPH ROAD

retreat

retreat

Stuart

Turner's Run

MOUNTAIN ROAD

woods

retreat

Custer

North Run

Sheridan

BROOK TURNPIKE

Yellow Tavern

Union Cavalry
Confederate Cavalry

general and his staff on a hill beyond the ridge they had just captured. According to the *Chicago Tribune*, one of Alger's privates took a shot at the enemy general and missed. Another private remarked, "Too high and too far to the left." Someone asked the critic what he knew about shooting. He said he had served two years in the Berdan Sharpshooters, an elite unit of marksmen. He then laid his long-barreled Spencer rifle over a fence, aimed, and fired. The enemy general convulsively threw up his hands on the impact of the bullet. The marksman said to Alger, "Colonel, there is a spread eagle for you."

The private's name, Alger said, was John A. Huff. Thirty minutes later, Alger reported, the Michigan Brigade captured the hill where the enemy general fell. The federal troopers came to a house where a slave and a white woman told them that Huff had shot J. E. B. Stuart himself. His staff had carried him, mortally wounded, into the house.[31] He had insisted that the battle continue, telling his staff, "I had rather die than be whipped!" He would not have a choice between the two. The Union cavalry smashed his position and scattered the retreating rebels in different directions. As Custer reported, "His defeat was complete."

Stuart's death was, for the Union, a stunning accomplishment; for the Confederacy, a stunning loss—"a blow to Confederate leadership next only to the death of [Stonewall] Jackson a year and a day earlier," writes the historian James McPherson. Widely credited as a genius of mounted warfare, Stuart was close to Robert E. Lee, who relied on him heavily. And Custer's attack killed him.[32]

"The rebel General Stuart, who was wounded in the charge led by your Boy, is dead," Custer wrote to Libbie from Haxall's Landing on the Peninsula. To his mind, his pursuit of glory, victory, and fame was a gift to her, a sign of his love. "For you dearest and best of girls I am striving to make a name which will be a source of pride to you," he wrote. He said the risks he took made his love even more precious. "Even death staring me in the face only serves to render you more dear. Had I fallen in the late battles your dear name would have been the last spoken from my lips."[33]

Victory at Yellow Tavern and the killing of Stuart contrasted with the simultaneous struggle between the massed infantry of the Army of the Potomac and the Army of Northern Virginia. At Spotsylvania Court House, south of the Wilderness, Lee blocked Grant's outflanking maneuver. On May 12, Grant broke through Lee's line, only to be driven back. It was another indecisive battle with heavy casualties on both sides. George Templeton Strong, a well-placed New York lawyer, spoke for many when he wrote in his diary, "These are fearfully critical, anxious days."[34]

Custer, on the other hand, helped to win a clear victory, and he did it with flair. Flair mattered to the weary public. "I think it proper to say a few words about the personal appearance of Gen. Custer," wrote a *New York Herald* reporter; he found it important enough to interrupt a description of Custer's charge at Yellow Tavern. "The dashing young 'General of the golden locks' . . . dresses in somewhat of the old cavalier style—black velvet jacket, with a blue shirt collar turned over the same. . . . He wears a slouched hat with a star in the front, and a red scarf cravat around his neck." He embodied old-fashioned warrior virtues. "Whenever he orders a charge, he always leads it in person, and bursts upon the enemy with a yell equal to that of any Rocky Mountain aborigines." This persona— combined with success, of course—kept alive the public's faith in the heroic and romantic amid the disillusionment of war. As the rescued prisoner Edwin wrote, Custer was "the very personification of the gallant, dashing, daring, ideal soldier we read of in romances."

His men spoke of him in similar terms. Major James Kidd wrote home, "So brave a man I never saw, as competent as brave. Under him a man is ashamed to be cowardly. Under *him* our men can achieve wonders." Only Eliza Brown, who came on the march, resisted his charisma. When yet another trooper praised his courage in an awestruck tone, she remarked sardonically, "Why, Gin'ral, the men think you can do as much as the Almighty!"[35]

His most important admirer was Sheridan. He was a fighter who liked fighters, especially those who won victories. Yellow Tavern began Custer's rapid rise as Sheridan's favorite subordinate, the man he could always count on to press the attack home, to keep cool in a crisis. He told Alger, "Custer is the ablest man in the Cavalry Corps."[36]

"AFTER YOU WENT I watched you admiringly as you rode along," Libbie Custer wrote to her husband, "then I went up to my room to cry."[37]

She remained in Washington, in a boardinghouse shared by people who alarmed her, owned by a woman who complained about the Yankees who rented the rooms. She smelled the rosebuds in the garden. She played with her kitten. And she felt the void of Armstrong's absence.

She tried to like Washington by dwelling on Georgetown, if not in it. She enjoyed church, too, but it was a shallow puddle of piety in the city's filthy streets. "In this Sodom and Gomorrah everybody drinks," she wrote. When she went out, she draped herself in drab—nothing more colorful than gray, or else the soldiers who staggered down sidewalks would assume she was a prostitute. She could not even wear blue![38]

"Armstrong, like most nineteenth-century men, believed his wife his moral superior," writes Libbie's biographer, Shirley Leckie. In his letters, he described a marital division of labor, in which he would earn fame and she would keep him holy. He observed his old pledge to never drink, but gambled and cursed with enthusiasm. He assured her he swore less now. He belonged to no church, but described a private faith activated by his love for her. And he asked her to be "my treasurer." He wrote, "Only bear in mind we are just entering upon life's journey with all its cares, and, I hope, in a short time its *responsibilities*." It was an allusion to elusive parenthood. In the meantime, Libbie had plenty of responsibilities.[39]

The Republican ascendancy left Armstrong feeling vulnerable and anxious. But Libbie could now be his "friend at court." She could charm congressmen and senators with her beauty, style, and educated wit. Leckie writes, "They had formed a partnership, committed to moving the boy general up the ladder of success." But it would be complicated, in part, by Libbie herself.[40]

"Of course I am no abolitionist," she wrote. She declared this a year and a half after the Emancipation Proclamation, a year after the establishment of the federal Bureau of Colored Troops, and as tens of thousands of black men volunteered to fight in the Union army (ultimately reaching a total of 179,000). She wrote this after meeting and thinking well of Eliza Brown, the escaped slave who wanted to help win the war. She wrote this at a time when the sentiment in government favored abolition; even soldiers in the conservative Army of the Potomac now called for ending slavery to win the war. The nation was changing; Libbie was not.

It's revealing that she wrote, "Of course." It seems that anyone who knew Libbie knew her politics. Her tendency to express her opinions made men nervous. "You and Autie have cautioned me about holding my tongue on army and political matters," she wrote to her father— then expressed her outrage at a rumor that General Pleasonton had been sacked because the administration suspected he was a political enemy. Now she had to do more than keep her mouth closed. She had to cultivate her political foes.[41]

Representative Francis Kellogg, a stout fifty-three-year-old with a bulbous nose, took Libbie and his own wife to the White House. President Lincoln was holding a levee—a reception for the public. Carriages crammed wheel to horse nose on the curving drive to the front door. Libbie moved in a crush past soldiers standing with swords drawn. "The crowd was so dense I could not move my arms, but was fairly pushed in," she wrote. Finally the line brought her face-to-face with Lincoln, "his Highness" and "the prince of jokers," as she mocked him in a letter, "the gloomiest, most careworn looking man I ever saw." From his great height he briefly acknowledged her, then realized who her husband was.

He enclosed her small hand in his oversized grip "very cordially" and said, "So this is the young woman whose husband goes into a charge with a whoop and a shout. Well, I'm told he won't do so any more."

I hope he will, she replied. "Oh, then you want to be a widow, I see." He laughed and she laughed, but they both knew it was not really a joke. Lincoln carried the weight of the generation he had ordered toward death, and yet he had to push the thing to its end. He admired Custer, he needed Custer, but he understood the mathematics of modern firepower as well as anyone. Libbie generously accepted his remark simply as a kindness. "I never liked Mr. Lincoln particularly before I came here but I do now," she wrote to an aunt. "He is very genial and kind hearted and as he said some very pleasant things to me about my husband."

Her personal lobbying continued that very morning. Kellogg introduced her to Speaker of the House Schuyler Colfax. Colfax turned to Kellogg and said, "I have been wishing to be presented to this lady, but am disappointed she is a Mrs.!" It flattered her, but she appreciated the effect she had on men, especially men of power. She cultivated the righteous and the lecherous alike, as long as they possessed influence. She received a visit from the former congressman John A. Bingham, for example, the gentlemanly Republican who had appointed Custer to West Point. He was a judge advocate now, but still regarded Custer "as his protégé." And she went to the hops at the National, as Armstrong "urged" her, where senators slurred and stumbled over her. Senator Chandler, she wrote, "is an old goosey idiot. Now his wife is away he is drunk *all* the time. And O, so silly."[42]

She visited the Capitol, reminding congressmen of both her husband and her beauty. Colfax greeted her warmly "and oh he said lovely things about you," she wrote to Armstrong. "I like him best of all here, he is so polite and not a bit of a flirt," she added, in an implicit contrast with the rest of Congress. Stepping outside, she encountered Kellogg. "We are going to make him a major general, Mrs. Custer," he proclaimed.

"Scarcely anybody here likes Mr. K," she wrote, referring to Kellogg. "Some say he is dishonest and licentious. It makes no difference to me. I see nothing but a gentleman and a kind friend." Note that she did not dispute the characterization; she took a practical view, and indeed her husband urged her to stay close to the man. Kellogg shamelessly traded favors, webbing the Capitol with his influence. But he certainly was licentious. One evening he called on Libbie, alone, at her boardinghouse. He was "very cordial," she wrote. "Too much so." He moved in to kiss her, and she adroitly slipped aside, offering him her chair. She remained calm, and he pretended nothing had happened. "Any lady can get that man to do anything," she remarked.

His wife shocked Libbie more. "She is a flirt." She stopped by Libbie's boardinghouse with a friend, not to see Libbie, but a colonel who also lived there. "It was very bold. She is an *intense* woman." Libbie had never known prominent, purportedly respectable women to behave so freely.[43]

Grant's campaign progressed, impossible to forget. The wounded and dead rattled into the city by ambulance and wagon by the thousands. "We see so many crippled soldiers and bandaged up for wounds—men with one arm—one leg—walking about the streets." Funerals became constant; embalming establishments proliferated. Libbie visited the hospitals, crowded with men with infected wounds, the sick who vomited and fouled their beds with diarrhea, the piles of limbs cast off by surgeons. The stench was "horrible," she wrote. She went to see Custer's men, and they praised him, telling her they could not believe his luck at surviving. It did not reassure her.[44]

Libbie followed her husband's progress with rising anxiety. After Yellow Tavern, his brigade fell into the grinding combat that characterized the campaign. First came a hard battle through woods, on foot, against Hampton's cavalry at Haw's Shop, Virginia. It was followed by Cold Harbor, where Custer's dismounted troopers stormed defensive works and held off counterattacks. A far costlier infantry battle followed.[45]

Jim Christiancy arrived in Washington—carried there, for he could not walk. At Haw's Shop, he had ridden along the line with Custer and Jacob Greene as the troops ducked below enemy fire. A Confederate bullet killed Custer's horse. Another struck Greene in the head—painful, but the round's energy was "spent," in the language of the day, having lost its force by flying too far or passing through brush, and he suffered no serious injury. Christiancy, though, was hit in the thumb and, more seriously, the thigh.

Libbie refused to leave him in a hospital. She brought him back to her boardinghouse. She changed his bandages and cleaned his wound, which each day oozed pieces of his pants, driven into his thigh by the bullet. Already friends, they grew closer. When she cried over a letter, he did too. When she pricked her finger sewing, he fretted "as if it were a battle wound." She spoke frankly to him about his alcoholism; he needed a good wife, she said. She remarked that people treated her kindly because she was Mrs. General Custer; he said it was because she was Libbie Bacon. But no one saw anything suspicious in such close contact.

She feared for Armstrong, but she did not regret her choice. She wrote her aunt, "I believe if ever God sends men into the world for a special purpose Armstrong was born to be a soldier."[46]

———

ON MAY 30, BETWEEN the bitter battles of Haw's Shop and Cold Harbor, Custer rode up to a farmhouse northeast of Richmond and dismounted. He had been invited. A woman on the porch rose from her chair, handed a baby to an older child, and took both his hands. She told him he was nearly as welcome as if "the Confederate army [had come] to rescue us."

They were the family of an old West Point friend. He had intervened to protect them from foraging Union soldiers once before, probably during the Peninsula Campaign. It was easy to do so then, in McClellan's army; it was harder now. One group of Union soldiers after another dug up onions, beheaded chickens, collected meat hanging in the smokehouse, gathered strawberries and peas, and grazed their horses. To the family, the Yankees were "an army of devils." The woman who welcomed Custer wrote in her diary that she hoped every last Union soldier would die. When one set of Northern troops treated them kindly and returned some food, she wrote, "I felt so grateful, and thanked them warmly, though it made me feel humiliated to be under obligation for our own property to such a set of creatures."

"I tried to prevent this," Custer told her, but the guard he had sent had gotten lost. "The General came in and paid us quite a nice visit," she wrote in her diary. (Unfortunately her name has been lost.) "He seemed too honest and high toned, to mingle with the mass of that Abolition army of Lincoln's. Truly he is 'among them but not of them.'" After they had talked for some time, Custer said that she would turn him into a rebel if he listened any longer. "How I wish he was one, and then I could esteem and admire him as I do our own gallant leaders," she wrote. When he left, he sent a guard—as well as two photographs, one of himself and one of him with Libbie.[47]

There was nothing unusual about a Union general putting a halt to pillaging. Grant himself, ever the realist, tried to stop "marauding" because of "its impact on military efficiency," as the historian Mark Grimsley writes.[48] Custer, though, still faced rumors that he was a Copperhead, in part because of his close ties to Southerners. He had fought very hard to establish that he held Radical views about the prosecution of the war. Yet here was an outspoken rebel who identified him with her culture and her cause, an identification that flattered him. His conservatism lingered on.

Custer acted out of sincere kindness, but also an antebellum sense of gallantry. He wished to be seen as the embodiment of manly virtues— the noble soldier who confronts his foe and protects the weak. All around him, though, were the soldiers this war had created: pitiless veterans, eager to take whatever comforts they could find, by force if necessary, men who had thrown away their romantic notions about combat.

A few days after Custer's initial visit, the woman deigned to treat a Yankee badly wounded in the nightmare Battle of Cold Harbor. He told her that his regiment had lost all but fifteen men. "If they ever get us into those [enemy] entrenchments it will be worse still," he said, "but the men in power that have made the war don't care how many of us are killed." She did not realize it, but she had just met a modern man.[49]

BEFORE THE FIRST CONFEDERATE TROOPER appeared in front of the carriage, Eliza Brown knew disaster loomed. She had accompanied Custer on June 7 when the 1st and 2nd Cavalry Divisions had set out from the Army of the Potomac on a raid, under Sheridan's personal command. Grant wanted Sheridan to devastate the Virginia Central Railroad, one of Lee's primary supply lines, and then link up with the Union army under Maj. Gen. David Hunter in the strategic Shenandoah Valley. Grant may also have hoped that Sheridan would draw the Confederate cavalry after him.[50]

Brown had driven Custer's carriage-turned-rolling mess on the hot, dry march northwest. The column of perhaps 9,000 horsemen had kicked up clouds of gritty dust, mixed with horsehair, which plastered everyone's skin, clothing, and hair. The countryside offered little to eat or drink, having been scoured already. Horses broke down in large numbers, unable to carry their riders. On Sheridan's orders, the cavalrymen shot them and tossed their saddles and equipment into wagons.[51]

On the night of June 10, the raiders had bivouacked around a crossroads called Clayton's Store. One road branched out from there to the southwest, in the direction of Trevilian Station, and another to the south, toward Louisa Court House. Brown had cooked dinner for Custer in the southernmost of the Union camps, on the Louisa Court House road. Sometime near dawn, she had heard firing. After an hour, the Michigan Brigade had started south, then turned to the right off the road, entering a rough track through the woods, leading toward the vicinity of Trevilian Station. Brown had loaded her cookware into the carriage and followed.

She emerged into a clearing and encountered mayhem. Custer's brigade fought amid a sea of enemy soldiers—bullets cracking overhead, artillery shells exploding, mounted Confederates charging here and there with sabers swinging. The wagon master approached Custer and asked if he could lead the wagon train to the rear. Custer looked around and said, "Where in hell is the rear?"

The wagon master thought he knew. Eliza in her carriage followed the little train—several caissons, the artillery wagon, some captured vehicles, and Custer's headquarters wagon, which contained everything from his underwear to his letters from Libbie. The frightened wagon master led them all into a field that soon swarmed with enemy soldiers. Brown dismounted and ran to the headquarters wagon. She seized one of Custer's traveling bags and turned to flee. The rebels cut her off.[52]

The U.S. Army had no language for what she now endured. As a civilian, she would not be designated as "captured" or "missing." In any event, those words did not describe what she faced—what no white soldier faced. Under standing orders from General Lee, the Army of Northern Virginia enslaved any and all black persons it could seize—in Virginia, Maryland, even Pennsylvania during the Gettysburg Campaign. It made no distinctions between those who had escaped during the war, those born free, or those freed before the war under the laws of Southern states. If they were black, the men in gray took them as property.

Under official Confederate procedure, the captors were supposed to enter the names of the enslaved on a list and then send them to slave depots. There they might be claimed by their previous masters, sold to slave traders, or put to work for the Southern war effort. Not all went through such an orderly (if brutal) process. Sometimes the soldiers did with them as they liked. As one rebel wrote during the Gettysburg Campaign, "We took a lot of negroes yesterday. I was offered my choice." Eliza Brown could expect to be raped, repeatedly. All black captives could reasonably fear retaliation, including torture and murder.[53]

Brown knew all this. She lived in the world of contrabands as much as that of the Michigan Brigade, and collected information that passed quickly through their uprooted community. She had narrowly evaded capture a number of times. But she had continued to serve the general. She was undeniably attached to him, but she had her own reasons for serving. "I set in to see the war, beginning and end," she told Libbie at one point. "I was all ready to step to the front whenever I was called upon, even if I didn't shoulder the musket." She would do what she could to punish her enslavers.[54]

Now she stood surrounded by them. They snatched Custer's valise from her, but allowed her to retrieve her own small bag before they drove off with the carriage. With battle raging nearby, the rebels began to move the captured wagons and contrabands to safety. One of them ordered Brown to mount a horse he led behind him.

"I don't see it," she said.

"Ain't she damned impudent," the soldier remarked to his fellows. *Impudent* might apply if she accepted her place in their racial hierarchy. But she did not. *Defiant* would have been the correct word. They could

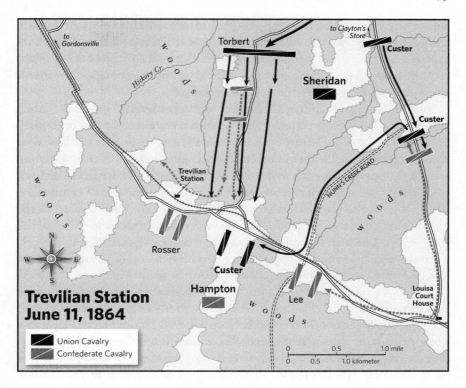

**Trevilian Station
June 11, 1864**

Union Cavalry
Confederate Cavalry

do anything they liked to her, without repercussions, and she knew it. Yet she defied them.[55]

CUSTER DID NOT LOSE his toothbrush. He kept that with him at all times, because he brushed after every meal. He washed his hands frequently as well. "I always laugh at him for this," his wife wrote. Of course, these habits may have kept him alive in an age in which microbes towered over humans in the food chain, in a war in which far more soldiers died of disease than of battle wounds.[56]

On June 11, 1864, battle wounds were the greater threat. Custer committed two of the gravest mistakes of his career that day, and followed with his greatest display of valor and ability. The first mistake was his failure to react to an unexpected appearance of the enemy before he broke camp. According to the historian who has studied these events most thoroughly, the Union command from Sheridan on down seemed unaware that a Confederate cavalry division under Gen. Wade Hampton held Trevilian Station, southwest of the federal camps, or that another division under Gen. Fitzhugh Lee camped at Louisa Court House, directly to the south. With some 9,300 men, Sheridan unwittingly faced most of the cavalry of the Army of Northern Virginia, about 6,500 men—less than a decisive advantage under the best circumstances.

Before dawn, Brigadier General Torbert ordered Custer to march down the Louisa Court House road, then turn southwest down the path through the woods. He was to "connect with [the rest of the 1st Division] at the station," as Custer reported. It was supposed to be an unopposed march. Instead, before 5 a.m. he was attacked from the direction of Louisa Court House by what he believed to be a full brigade of enemy cavalry.[57] They were the first enemy soldiers Custer's men had seen since the raid began, one trooper wrote. The assault "told us that the rebels had not only overtaken us, but had gotten around in our front." Yet apparently Custer never informed Torbert or Sheridan. He held his ground until the Confederates withdrew, then advanced to the southwest as ordered, leaving a large enemy force off to his left. In essence, he outflanked himself and told no one.

He made his second mistake when he emerged from the woods into a clearing east of Trevilian Station. He encountered General Hampton's wagon train and the horses being held for his men, who were fighting Torbert's two other brigades in the dense woods north of the station. Even if Custer did not hear the firing, these wagons and horses indicated a large enemy force nearby—and he knew that at least a brigade of Confederates lurked in his rear. It was a moment for discretion. He needed to get all his men out of the woods and into a compact formation, ready to fight. But he gave in to the temptation to take prizes. He sent the 5th Michigan to seize the wagon train before his other regiments arrived.[58]

The men of the 5th captured the wagons, but soon were engulfed in an enemy counterattack led by Custer's old friend Tom Rosser, commander of Hampton's reserve brigade. The twenty-seven-year-old son of a Texas cotton planter, the burly Rosser stood six feet two inches tall, with a full face, full beard, and thick black hair. He struck an aristocratic pose in his double-breasted gray general's uniform, and he fought well, winning praise from J. E. B. Stuart and Robert E. Lee.[59] Rosser captured nearly half of the 5th before the rest of Custer's brigade arrived. Col. James H. Kidd appeared with the 6th Michigan and found Custer and his aides blasting away at the advancing enemy with their revolvers. "Custer never lost his nerve under any circumstances," Kidd recalled. "He was, however, unmistakably excited." He had a simple order: "Charge them." Kidd added dryly, "It was repeated with emphasis." Kidd immediately charged, only to be cut off by the enemy, captured, and then rescued by a follow-up attack.[60]

The chaotic exchange of charges and countercharges turned into a desperate struggle to survive. Hampton sent more men to support Rosser's attack. Fitzhugh Lee advanced westward from Louisa Court House and attacked Custer in the rear. Custer dismounted most of his men and pulled them back into a position that he later described as a circle, though others have called it a triangle. He ordered them to pile up rails in order to improvise a fortification. The enemy pressed so close on every side that it worked to Custer's advantage, since the rebels sometimes had to hold their fire to avoid hitting their own men on the far side of the Michigan Brigade. Custer moved his guns again and again to meet the most dangerous threats. He gathered a hodgepodge of men to form a mounted reserve, and countercharged the enemy when they attempted to break his line.

"Custer was everywhere," Kidd later wrote. He rode back and forth constantly, giving orders, reconnoitering, fighting in person. Even the enemy thought him "gallant and manly," Rosser wrote. "Sitting on his horse in the midst of his advanced platoons, and near enough to be easily recognized by me, he encouraged and inspired his men by appeal as well as by example."[61]

A brief description of the battle cannot evoke the intensity of the experience, which lasted more than three hours. There was the unending noise of rifles and guns firing, shells exploding, bugles tooting, men screaming. There was the smell of burnt gunpowder, sweat, blood, urine, and feces. Smoke and dust clouded the air. Hunger and dehydration on this hot summer day drained the combatants, making mouths dry and gummy. Not least was the claustrophobia, the awareness of being surrounded in a constricted position. Custer kept them fighting.[62]

He seemed to be invulnerable. A spent bullet hit his shoulder and bounced off, merely bruising him. Another bullet hit his arm, but it too was spent. He spotted a trooper shot down in an exposed position, bullets kicking up dust around him. Custer ran out and picked him up, only to be hit again—a round that merely grazed his head, briefly stunning him.

Lt. Alexander Pennington, his gifted artillery commander, announced, "General, they have taken one of my guns!"

"No! I'll be damned if they have!" Custer replied. "Come on!" He drew his saber and led a scratch force in a charge. They were forced back, then charged again, driving the Confederates away from the cannon. They rode through revolver fire from Rosser's own staff. The rebels missed Custer but hit Sgt. Mitchell Beloir, his flag bearer. "General, they have killed me," the sergeant said. "Take the flag!" Custer ripped it from its staff and shoved it inside the front of his uniform.[63]

He lost the wagons he had captured plus his own little wagon train, including Eliza Brown and Johnny Cisco. He lost his Monroe friend and adjutant general, Capt. Jacob Greene, who wrote that he had gone in search of the wagons only to find himself "completely surrounded and facing more pistols and carbines at my head than were at all suggestive of long life." Greene met Confederate friends of Custer's, who promised to return Custer's commission as a brigadier general and his personal baggage, found in his headquarters wagon.[64]

Custer blamed Torbert, who he thought was tardy in getting to Trevilian Station. Kidd wrote that the Michigan Brigade "fought the entire force single-handed for three hours." In fact, Torbert pushed south all morning, fighting through thick woods toward Custer's position. Around midday, Brig. Gen. Wesley Merritt finally broke the siege. Custer said, "Merritt, they had me in a tight place that time." Sheridan arrived and asked Custer if the rebels had captured his headquarters flag. "Not by a damned sight!" Custer replied. He reached inside his uniform and pulled it out. "There it is!"[65]

The breakthrough turned looming disaster into a triumph. Sheridan's soldiers defeated and drove Hampton's men to the west—badly wounding Rosser in the leg—and Fitzhugh Lee's men to the east. But the fighting devastated the Michigan Brigade. As Lee's division pulled back, Custer did lead one last mounted charge aimed at its wagon train. "I recaptured two caissons, three ambulances, and several wagons," he reported. The caissons had no ammunition, and he did not recover his headquarters wagon, nor the carriage with Eliza Brown and Johnny Cisco.[66]

The fighting on June 11 cost the Union cavalry 699 casualties: 53 killed, 274 wounded, 372 captured. This was 7.5 percent of Sheridan's total force. The Confederates suffered nearly as many—530 casualties—which came to more than 8 percent of their entire force. Catastrophe had loomed for much of the day. But Custer had managed to hold on until relieved, and defeat turned into a rousing victory.[67]

As Custer sat at his campfire with Pennington, he heard cheers. They grew louder and closer. "What does that mean?" one asked the other. They got up and went toward the road, lined with happy men from Michigan, and saw for themselves.[68]

ELIZA BROWN COULD DO NOTHING for Johnny Cisco, because the rebels had separated them. Brown rode behind her enslavers on a horse led by a cavalry trooper, moving east toward Louisa Court House. A mile passed, and another, and another. The column turned off the road. A rail fence blocked their way. White men in the Confederate army never liked doing physical labor when slaves were at hand. They told Brown to dismount and take down the rails. She walked over, her bag strapped on her back or held in her hand or in the crook of her arm. She hefted the lowest rail loose and dropped it—then sprinted under and ran for the woods. Before her captors could get through the fence, she had disappeared.

It grew late. She did not know these woods. But she found her way back to the road and headed west. The cheer began when the first Michigan soldiers saw her. Others ran up and joined in. They had poked fun at her as the "Queen of Sheba," but had come to respect her. When the men went into battle, they trusted her with their money and personal items. When the fighting drew near, she always remained calm. And here she was, having engineered her own escape. She greeted Custer, found a tent for herself, and cooked him breakfast in the morning.[69]

Custer's heroic feat at Trevilian Station instantly became an iconic moment in his life. Coming close behind Yellow Tavern, it sealed his place as Sheridan's favorite. Historians and biographers would delight in calling it "Custer's First Stand" or his "First Last Stand." Like Custer himself, many would spend little time analyzing his mistakes that made his situation worse. And few would dwell on the next day, June 12, a day of clear defeat.

In the morning the Union cavalrymen fueled huge fires with the wooden railway ties, threw the rails on top, and heated them until they could be twisted and rendered unusable. Meanwhile the two widely separated Confederate divisions united west of the station. Sheridan decided to attack, hoping to break through and unite with the army in the Shenandoah, as ordered. The strongly posted rebels repelled assault after assault. The rebels counterattacked and outflanked the Union attackers, who withdrew.

Sheridan concluded that he could not complete his mission. He was burdened with hundreds of prisoners and casualties, slowed by men whose horses had given out or died, and followed by some 2,000 contrabands. He faced a large enemy force in his front, and had learned that the Union army he was supposed to join was not as close as planned. Rations and ammunition were dwindling. He turned east.[70]

Hampton too suffered heavy losses. The depleted Confederate force was unable to inhibit the slow Union retreat. And the raid still served Grant's strategy. It drew the rebel cavalry away, allowing him to cross the wide James River before Lee could react. He then besieged Petersburg, the vital rail center south of Richmond. More important, the raid led to a pitched battle that eroded enemy cavalry strength. This was consistent with Grant's general approach: to find as many opportunities as possible to land heavy blows. He liked Sheridan not because he was a gifted tactician or strategist, but because he was a fighter. At Trevilian Station, he fought. It was Grant's way.

"One witnesses in this Army as it moves along all the results of a victory, when in fact it has done only barren fighting," wrote Charles Francis Adams Jr., posted at the headquarters of the Army of the Potomac. "For it has done the one thing needful before the enemy—it has advanced."

A sophisticated, Harvard-educated observer, Adams was sardonic by nature, but the war fostered a grim realism in him, as in so many other soldiers. It made him an admirer of Grant's ability and manner. "It would require some study to find in his appearance material for hero worship," Adams told his father. "He sits a horse well, but in walking he leans forward and toddles." And yet, he wrote, "he is a remarkable man. He handles those around him so quietly and well, he so evidently has the faculty of disposing of work and managing men, he is cool and quiet. . . . He is a man of the most exquisite judgment and tact."[71]

Adams could not have conceived a description more precisely the opposite of Custer. Grant did not lead, but *managed*. He did not craft brilliant tactics, but *disposed of work*. He even looked funny—*no material for hero worship*. Was there room for Custer in the era of generalship as management, of industrialized slaughter as warfare? Just enough. But Trevilian Station brought him closer than ever to the nihilistic hell of the infantry battles of Spotsylvania or Cold Harbor, where fatalistic foot soldiers pinned their addresses to their uniforms so their families would learn of their deaths. His ordeal made him bitter. It threatened his illusions about glory and heroism.

If those illusions survived it was because he survived, and if he survived it was because of luck. Generals died in the Civil War, and those closest to the fighting—the brigade commanders—died at an extraordinary rate. "Custer luck," as he and his friends called it, kept him alive.[72] Bullets did not pierce his skin. Exploding shells sent shards of metal everywhere but into him. So he continued to fight, a living contradiction at the dawn of modern warfare.

"DARKEYS HAVE TAKEN POSSESSION of the city," Libbie Custer wrote to her parents. She marveled that the city's African Americans were so "orderly" in celebrating Independence Day. Having spent her life in whitest Michigan, she found them exotic, though condescension ran through everything she wrote about them. "There are processions of them, ranging in color from pale to sooty black, all dressed in the gaudiest colors," she wrote. And yet, she implied, it was the black population that was loyal "in this half-rebel city."[73]

Soon afterward she went to City Point, the James River landing that served as a supply depot for the Army of the Potomac. Congressman Kellogg had arranged the trip on a luxurious steamboat, bringing not only Libbie but Senators Chandler and Howard as well. "The Cavalry after two months . . . have a little rest given them now and I am *resting* too from the wearing anxiety I have endured," Libbie wrote to an aunt.[74]

Armstrong waited on the dock for her and the politicians on board. As soon as the Trevilian raid ended, he had written to Chandler "to invite you to pay us a visit. . . . I will be most happy to give you a review of the Michigan Cavalry Brigade." This was more than just a courtesy. "The Cavalry Corps is to be reorganized," he told Chandler. He wanted his men to be "recognized as they deserve"—and, by implication, that *he* should be recognized, and promoted.[75]

When the boat moored, Sheridan came aboard with him, as did a band, which played on deck in the evening. Sheridan was "short and so bright," Libbie wrote. He danced terribly, "but he enters into it with his whole soul." In the distance, the siege guns ringing Petersburg could be heard thundering. They distracted Libbie. But her husband and his fellow officers ignored them, immersed in something other than war.

When the boat steamed back to Washington, Custer remained aboard. The next day he said good-bye to Libbie and returned to his brigade. Three days later, as she sat in her room reading, "up the stairs came someone with such a bounding step as no one else has," she wrote. It was her husband.[76]

He was sick. On July 11, the surgeon for the Michigan Brigade submitted a report that explained his sudden return to Washington: "I hereby certify that I have carefully examined this officer and find him suffering from remittent fever and diarrhea."[77] One of the filthiest, most unpleasant ailments a soldier could suffer, diarrhea killed countless men. After so many narrow escapes in battle, Custer was struck down by his stool. Colonel Kidd, his friend and admirer, believed the situation to be grave. "Gen Custer is sick and has got a 20 days leave," he wrote to his parents. "I could not imagine a greater disaster to our brigade if he does not return before we take the field again."[78]

Eight

THE VICTOR

"I THINK OF THE DAYS of peace when little children's voices will call to us. I can hardly wait for my little boy or girl." Libbie Custer wrote these words to her husband amid their long separation during the Overland Campaign. But she saw no sign of pregnancy, despite their sexual intensity after their wedding.

Sex gave her pleasure. After her letters were captured along with Armstrong's headquarters wagon at Trevilian Station, he had warned her to "be more careful herafter in the use of the *double entendre*."[1] But sex did not give her children. During Armstrong's sick leave, they left sad and vulgar Washington for Monroe, a place suffused with children and grandparents, Thanksgiving and Christmas, all the things that had gone out of her life. They had twenty days to spend with each other, yet still no swelling, no quickening within her. She could only sketch a pair of imaginary children.

"I would not lose my individuality, but would be, as a wife should be, a part of her husband, a life within a life," she wrote later that year. "I was never an admirer of a submissive wife, but I wish to look to my husband as superior in judgment and experience and to be guided by him in all things." Without children, this tension—ambivalence, perhaps?—tended to strain. Why submerge herself within another, if not for offspring? How much individuality must she surrender? And yet, she loved and needed him, who left her alone in a strange city at the outset of their life together.

Armstrong recovered. In late July the couple boarded a train so that he could return to his brigade and Libbie could return to her lonely, barren life among drunken congressmen, unfaithful officers' wives, and the army of the wounded and the dead.[2]

VICTOR COMTE WAS DEAD. The funny, humane little Frenchman of the 5th Michigan Cavalry Regiment succumbed to wounds on July 11, 1864. "Do you think I'm foolish enough to get killed?" he had written to his wife. "I enlisted to kill Rebels and not to get killed. Besides, where's the danger? Out of 100 who go to battle maybe 10 are killed or wounded. Of those 10 wounded ones one dies. You must remember that I am small and the bullets find more room around me than on me." Such thoughts helped soldiers and their families endure. They were true for Comte until a bullet made them lies.[3]

There were almost more Victor Comtes than the nation could bear. "The people wildly laud Grant to the skies and call McClellan a traitor, for the one has been continually fighting—'being in earnest,' they call it—while the other would only fight when he saw some prospect of success," Col. Charles S. Wainwright complained in his diary. He was a conservative—a McClellan supporter—but he gave voice to a spreading disgust at the mounting casualties. "The army . . . do not appreciate the beauty of 3,000 or 4,000 of their number being stretched out on the ground, when there is merely a bare chance that something may come of it." By one estimate, the Union army suffered about 65,000 killed, wounded, and captured in the seven weeks following the first shots of the battle of the Wilderness; the Confederates lost some 35,000, proportionately about the same. After almost two months of this, the public began to pose difficult, despairing questions. "What is all this struggling and fighting for?" one Union general's wife asked. "This ruin and death to thousands of families?"[4]

There *was* a point to the constant bloodshed. If Grant had relinquished his grip on Lee, his gifted opponent would have regained the initiative and launched one of his famous counterstrokes. "We must destroy this army of Grant's before it gets to the James River," Lee had said in May. "If he gets there it will become a siege, and then it will be a mere question of time." After the Wilderness, though, Lee never again found an opportunity to strike at Grant, who kept him entirely on the defensive.

Grant bludgeoned, but not blindly. Again and again he sought a tactical advantage, attempting to outflank the Army of Northern Virginia or assaulting its lines with new tactics developed by young Emory Upton. The reason he failed was Lee himself, who skillfully blocked each maneuver—until Grant surprised him by crossing the James. By then, though, the Union troops were so afraid of another slaughter that they hesitated to charge into Petersburg, the key to Richmond. Lee gained just enough time to man its fortifications. Still, the campaign had ended in precisely the situation Lee feared: a siege. The two armies dug trenches and slowly bled as time ran out.[5]

But for whom? The North clearly had greater resources, but public resolve depended upon a sense of progress—evidence that the deaths brought the end of the war closer. There was little of it. Sherman's armies still had not captured Atlanta. Grant still had not captured Richmond. The main Confederate armies remained intact and dangerous. And the casualties kept rising. If the rebels could hold out until the U.S. presidential election in the fall—if the Democrats defeated Lincoln in his quest for a second term—Confederate independence seemed likely.

Lee made one last attempt to seize the initiative. In June, he detached the 2nd Corps and sent it under Lt. Gen. Jubal Early to the Shenandoah Valley, a rich source of food and supplies, to fight the Union army there under Maj. Gen. David Hunter. Lee also sent a cavalry division under his nephew Fitzhugh Lee. As Early advanced, Hunter withdrew west out of "the Valley," as the men who served there called it, leaving the road north wide open. Early took some 15,000 men across the Potomac on July 6, and descended on Washington on July 11. Grant sent VI Corps from the front to reinforce Washington's defenses, and Early withdrew. On July 24, though, Early defeated Hunter's Army of West Virginia and launched cavalry raids across the Potomac, burning Chambersburg, Pennsylvania, on July 30.

"Humiliation and disaster," wrote George Templeton Strong in his diary. A patrician Wall Street lawyer, he reflected the opinion of the most influential men in the country. After three years of war, the Confederacy could still penetrate the North.[6]

Grant had no choice. He had to occupy the Shenandoah, eliminate it as a supply source for Lee's army, and decisively crush the rebel army there, ending the threat of invasion. After consultations with the administration, he put Sheridan in command. His orders were simple: Destroy Early. Destroy the Valley. He gave Sheridan a large force, including the 1st and 3rd Cavalry Divisions. And so Custer went to the Valley. The Union *had* to win there, or possibly lose the entire war.[7]

THE BULLET DRILLED through the air toward Custer's head. In the turmoil of battle, the shooter may not have aimed at this particular skull, but that was where it went. During its flight, any number of forces acted upon it, from gusts of wind to gravity, altering its course. The target surely moved in and out of the bullet's path—a turn of his neck, a sneeze, his horse shifting its weight. With surgical precision, the spinning projectile severed several strands of hair on the right side of his head and flew on, leaving the skin untouched.

It was August 16, 1864. The field was on Crooked Run, near Front Royal in the Valley. Custer handled his men brilliantly that day, by all accounts. He threw back two Confederate brigades and captured scores of prisoners—hundreds, depending on the report. Yet the battle barely receives a mention in histories of the campaign.[8]

It was like that in the weeks following Custer's arrival at Harper's Ferry on August 9. Grant and especially the War Department warned Sheridan that Lee had reinforced Early's army—and made it clear that the Union cause could not afford another defeat in the Valley. So Sheridan marched his 35,000 infantry and artillerymen—three divisions of VI Corps, two divisions of XIX Corps, two divisions of the Army of West Virginia, and twelve batteries of artillery—forward and back, up and down the Valley, maneuvering for an advantage over Early's roughly 15,000 Confederates. The cavalry handled all of the combat. This was not the stuff of a war-winning campaign, though the men did not mind. "If [Sheridan's goals] can be accomplished without fighting I think all parties ought to be satisfied. We certainly shall be," wrote James Kidd to his parents.[9]

In any event, it was out of Custer's control. He seemed to have little say in any aspect of his life. For example, he had planned for Libbie to wait for him in Washington. But the capital alienated and bored her. She tried to compensate by spending. "Of the $500 you so generously gave me I have spent $300 for myself apart from board," she wrote to Armstrong on September 6. "It seems a great deal but as I had to have a whole new summer outfit it was not extravagant. Mrs. T. spent $600."[10]

When he sent for her in early September, she immediately boarded a train to Harper's Ferry. He met her and brought her to camp for a brief visit. She returned to Washington, then came back, lodging at a boarding-house. "I knew nothing of her coming until I heard she was at Harper's Ferry. It is all I can do to keep her from coming right out to camp," Armstrong wrote to his sister. She was lonely—for her husband *and* the children who refused to come.[11]

Everywhere she saw others bear children whether they wanted them or not. At her husband's camp she greeted Eliza Brown, for example. Libbie would later refer to Brown's "two nameless children whose parentage I would soon learn to ignore." Armstrong wrote to his sister that "I thought of sending Eliza's daughter to you." This cryptic, passing comment may refer to a different Eliza, but it suggests that even Brown managed to have or at least maintain children amid a struggle to survive, yet Libbie could not.[12]

During these busy early weeks in the Shenandoah, Custer balanced his marriage and incessant skirmishing with Early's army with career maneuvering. He had supported James Kidd's successful campaign to be named colonel of the 6th Michigan, and asked Kidd to return the favor by requesting that Governor Blair appoint Tom Custer to the 6th. That would allow Custer to select Tom for his staff. Kidd obliged, but so far Armstrong had had no success.[13]

His own advancement seemed more promising. In late August Torbert, now chief of cavalry in Sheridan's army, offered him command of Gen. Alfred Duffié's division. But Sheridan canceled the transfer, ostensibly because the division was in poor shape and might harm Custer's reputation. More likely the problem was that it belonged to the Army of West Virginia, meaning that Custer would not remain under Sheridan's command after this campaign.[14]

The press still loved him. "Future writers of fiction will find in Brig. Gen. Custer most of the qualities which go to make up a first-class hero," the *New York Tribune* wrote on August 22. "Gen. Custer is as gallant a cavalier as one would wish to see." The story captured his mix of traditional and modern, of romanticism and professionalism. "Always circumspect, never rash, and viewing the circumstances under which he is placed as coolly as a chess player observes his game, Gen. Custer always sees the 'vantage of the ground' at a glance. . . . Frank and independent in his demeanor, Gen. C. unites the qualities of the true gentleman with the accomplished and fearless soldier."[15]

Popular or not, Custer soon faced a threat to his career. On August 31, the delegates to the Democratic Party convention nominated George B. McClellan for president. In his acceptance letter, he implicitly rejected emancipation, writing, "The Union is the one condition of peace. We ask no more." He formally committed himself to continuing the war, though most believed he intended to halt the fighting. His chief political adviser, Samuel L. M. Barlow, said, "The General is for peace, not war." McClellan himself remarked, shortly before his nomination, "I will recommend an immediate armistice and a call for a convention of all the states and insist upon exhausting all and every means to secure peace without further bloodshed."[16]

McClellan's nomination placed Custer in a treacherous position. He had suffered before because of their well-known ties. He knew that neither the administration nor the military could tolerate support for McClellan. Libbie saw the danger clearly. When an officer asked her about Armstrong's politics, she told her husband, "I said if you had any I didn't know them, but I am for Abraham." Even in letters to him she was careful, as if fearful that someone else might read her words. She wrote, "People will think I am repeating your sentiments—and I don't even know them." He replied, "My doctrine has ever been that a soldier should not meddle in politics."[17]

Almost none of this was true. Her comments in unguarded moments showed that she and her husband had the same politics. And Custer still idolized his old chief. "I found the hottest discussions were going on regarding General McClellan and sometimes the vehemence of his admirers got them into trouble, for feeling ran so high it broke friendships and made an officer the target for persecution," Libbie later wrote.[18]

Back in Monroe, David Reed wrote to Armstrong, "There is a great inquiry how you are going to vote." One prominent Democrat "says you will make all your men vote for McClellan." Emmanuel campaigned loudly for the Democratic candidate. "I cant be quiet let me know my son what you think about the Army vote," he wrote. He even suggested that Armstrong could give McClellan political advice. "I am down on the present Administration from Abraham down to the last. . . . It has been nothing but ruin and distruction ever since they came into power."[19]

Armstrong decided that he had to act. On September 6, he wrote a letter to his political patron, Judge Christiancy, that he clearly intended for public release. "The Peace Commissioners I am in favor of are those sent from the cannon's mouth. The only armistice I would yield to would be that forced by the points of our bayonets." They could not stop now. Sherman had just captured Atlanta, he noted, and Rear Adml. David Farragut had won a major victory at Mobile Bay in August.[20]

He wrote the letter out of calculation, but events had indeed carried him away from his old hero. Custer very much wanted to win. His craving for victory had grown stronger in fourteen months of leading men on the battlefield. For all his sympathy for Southerners, he had abandoned McClellan's notion of a limited war. In the Valley, he found himself plagued by guerrillas (called "partisan rangers") under Col. John Singleton Mosby, who ambushed wagon trains and isolated soldiers with the support of the civilian population. On August 21, some thirty of Custer's men set out on a mission to burn crops and barns; the guerrillas ambushed them and executed the survivors. One wounded man pretended to be dead and lived to tell the story of what had happened. Custer ordered all homes in the immediate vicinity to be torched, along with the houses of ten "of the most prominent secessionists." When federal cavalry executed some of Mosby's men, Mosby blamed Custer (inaccurately) and vowed vengeance. Custer saw no alternative to a hard war.[21]

"Let the public sentiment be the echo of that which is found in the heart of every soldier in the army, that we are fighting for human rights and liberty, for the preservation of a free people, a free government and having secured these privileges to ourselves we desire and intend to transmit them unsullied and untarnished to those who come after us in all time to come," he wrote. *Human rights and liberty* resonated with the Radical program of abolition and greater racial equality. Yet these words could be read more in the context of "a free government," which was under attack by secessionists who refused to abide by the results of elections. The same words might refer exclusively to the rights of white men. The ambiguity was clever, allowing him to sound as radical or moderate as the reader might choose to believe.[22]

"The sentiments it breathes are worthy of a gallant soldier and a true patriot," Christiancy replied. He asked permission to publish the letter, and cautioned that it had given Custer's father "great anxiety. . . . But you know your father's politics." The judge warned that Emmanuel represented a threat to Armstrong. "Now it is not for me to say more than this, that the copperheads here will insist on claiming you to be one, and that this is a great injury to you."[23]

"My dear son with fealings of sorrow I pend these lines," Emmanuel wrote. His letter revealed how deeply Armstrong's declaration wounded him. "You are my darling son that I love you as I love my life. . . . Now what has caused my present truble of mind is the letter you wroat to Judg Christiancy." Emmanuel learned of it only because Christiancy read it to him, making it doubly painful. It was well written, he admitted, but the judge had shown it to his Republican friends, who delighted in it. How, Emmanuel asked, could you turn against McClellan? "I know you thought more of him than any other man," he wrote. "You doant know how I hate for a man to come up to me and ask me what I think of that letter." If Armstrong had remained a loyal Democrat, he wrote, he would have a chance of one day winning the presidency, but siding with Republicans doomed him.[24]

"You seem to disapprove of the sentiments I wrote in my letter to Judge Christiancy," Armstrong replied. He wrote to his father on October 16, almost a month after Emmanuel's agonized letter (which had been followed by at least one more on the same subject). The son took a cold tone with his father. "When I wrote that letter I endeavored to make my sentiments agree with my actions," he wrote. "We have passed the point at which conciliation and compromise might have secured peace." He would fight for the principles at stake for the rest of his life, if necessary. Defying his father, he gave Christiancy permission to publish the letter. It was excerpted by the *New York Times* and other newspapers before the election.[25]

Judge Christiancy and Emmanuel Custer represented deeper conflicts in Armstrong's life than politics alone. Christiancy was a man of learning, influence, and economic success; he was the more measured and sophisticated of the two. Armstrong's father was uneducated, provincial, poor, and volatile; he had once seen no better path for Armstrong than to apprentice him to a furniture maker. At some level, he embarrassed his son.[26]

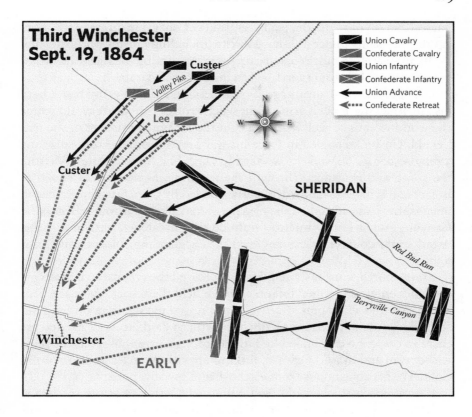

**Third Winchester
Sept. 19, 1864**

Union Cavalry
Confederate Cavalry
Union Infantry
Confederate Infantry
Union Advance
Confederate Retreat

Custer

Valley Pike

Lee

Custer

SHERIDAN

Red Bud Run

Berryville Canyon

Winchester

EARLY

But the battle for Custer's politics was not over, because his feelings were so closely tied to the war, and the war would end one day. For the moment, the question was when and how the end would come: through victory or appeasement?

When Custer wrote to Christiancy, the capture of Atlanta had finally brought some hope to the despairing North. But the Union had yet to win in Virginia. By the time he wrote back to his father, that had changed. He had learned what it meant to be truly victorious in battle. And there was nothing like victory in battle.

War gave Custer his greatest pleasure. It gave him purpose, praise, and the adoration of his men. Whatever would he do when peace returned?

ON THE MORNING OF SEPTEMBER 19, Custer ordered his brigade to march west to Locke's Ford on Opequon Creek. Sheridan had finally ordered an assault on the Confederate army, having learned that the enemy had transferred troops out of the Valley. He sent his infantry west through narrow Berryville Canyon, led by Wilson's cavalry. He directed his other cavalry divisions under Wesley Merritt (including Custer's brigade) and William Averell to move forward on his right, aiming for the Valley Pike, a strategic road that ran north-south in the Confederates' rear.[27]

Despite a marked advantage in numbers, the Union army had a hard task in attacking Early's army. One rebel wrote, "I thout we could whipe the world we was so well fortifide." On the far northern edge of the battlefield, Custer struggled to force his way across Locke's Ford, suffering a repulse before he won the western bank.[28] The din of battle rose from the south and continued through the morning. Sheridan had hoped to isolate and crush the Confederate division led by Gen. Stephen Ramseur, but a traffic jam had stalled the passage of his infantry through Berryville Canyon, giving Early time to reinforce the threatened part of his line. Attacks and counterattacks resolved into a grinding, inconclusive firefight.[29]

To the north, Custer waited. Having crossed the creek, the Union cavalry encountered fortified infantry, which held them back for nearly four hours. Around 12:30 p.m., Early—hard pressed by Sheridan's infantry—shifted his foot soldiers away from his northern flank, leaving the defense there to cavalry commanded by Fitzhugh Lee. Custer observed the rebel withdrawal and moved forward, linking up with Averell's division on his right. With a continuous front established, they advanced.[30]

Future generations would read omniscient histories of the battle and scan maps covered in neat lines, rectangles, and arrows. But Custer saw events horizontally, from one particular viewpoint. With his field glass he peered at flitting figures on hills, shadows in tree lines, and dim shapes hunched in ravines. He identified his own troops by their regimental flags and the fluttering red neckties they wore in honor of his own costume. Men milled about, bringing casualties back and ammunition forward. Dust rose from the hooves of countless horses saddled with soldiers or hauling wagons, ambulances, artillery pieces, and caissons. The gray smoke of erupting gunpowder drifted above the ground, along with the cacophony of guns, bugles, and bands. Fetid rivers of urine ran between piles of manure deposited by horses and men. Where the fighting was there was blood, and bodies, and pieces of bodies. That the commanders maintained any control at all was a tribute to army organization, the elaborately tiered pyramid of responsibility that made the military the model of corporate organization.

Surrounded by his staff, Custer listened to reports, dispatched aides with orders and messages, rode here and there to investigate, consult, and inspire. He was a professional and acted like one, maintaining his place in the great articulated whole. But if that was all, he would not have been Custer.

"The line of brigades as they advanced across the open country, the bands playing the national airs, presented in the sunlight one moving mass of glittering sabers," he wrote in his after-action report. "This, combined with the various and bright-colored banners and battle-flags, intermingled here and there with the plain blue uniforms of the troops, furnished one of the most inspiring as well as imposing scenes of martial grandeur ever witnessed upon a battlefield."[31]

On Custer's left, he saw the infantry lines engage in pitched combat. Sheridan had sent Brig. Gen. George Crook, commanding the reserve of two infantry divisions, toward his right; Crook had converted the movement into a flanking attack that bent back the left of the Confederate line. Fierce resistance stalled Crook's advance. Fitzhugh Lee attacked the Union cavalry. "The enemy relied wholly upon the carbine and pistol," Custer wrote. "My men preferred the saber. A short but closely contested struggle ensued, which resulted in the repulse of the enemy." The rebels in front of Custer's brigade rallied in a ditch; he ordered a general charge that broke their hastily formed line. Onward he galloped, until the retreating enemy reached the protection of their artillery and infantry.[32]

Hard pressed, Early contracted his lines. Custer carefully followed, and hid his men behind a "small crest within 500 yards of the enemy's position." He faced an enemy infantry division behind a stone wall—a formidable foe for mere cavalry.

An aide to Custer's division commander, Wesley Merritt, rode up with orders from Sheridan himself to attack. But Custer had examined the enemy line carefully. "Knowing that a heavy force of the enemy was lying down behind their works, facts of which I knew the division commander was ignorant, I respectfully requested that I might be allowed to select my own time for making the charge," he wrote. If Custer attacked immediately, he would be sending his men headlong against a fortified, well-prepared defensive line. It would be suicidal. But he expected the pressure of the Union infantry attacks to induce the Confederates to shift troops away from this sector, which was currently quiet. Merritt gave him permission. So he watched. As he hoped, the enemy troops stood up and began to move. Custer gave the order. His 500 men charged, followed by the Union brigades on his right and left.

The line of screaming horsemen galloped toward the Confederates, who turned and fired one volley before the cavalry crested their works and plunged in among them. One trooper saw Custer in the forefront, slashing with his saber. A rebel just a few feet away raised his rifle and aimed; Custer yanked hard on the reins, his horse reared on its hind legs, and the bullet missed. "Then a terrible sword stroke descends upon the infantryman's head, and he sinks to the ground a lifeless corpse," the witness recalled.[33]

"Boot to boot these brave horsemen rode in. The enemy's line broke into a thousand fragments under the shock," Merritt reported. A Confederate soldier wrote to his cousin, "That was one of the awfull times for us I ever saw and I hope to never see another such a time with our army. It was a perfect skidaddle every man fore him self."

The cavalry charge, timed and led by Custer, delivered the final blow that turned a drawn-out struggle into a crushing Union victory. It was almost unprecedented in the Civil War. As a rebel officer wrote in his diary, "It is the first time that I have ever seen cavalry very effective in a general engagement." Custer claimed his charge "stands unequaled, valued according to its daring and success, in the history of this war." He boasted, but he did not exaggerate. "Major," he said laughingly to Charles Deane of the 6th Michigan, "this is the bulliest day since Christ was born."

Men of both North and South agreed that only nightfall saved Early's army from complete destruction in the battle (called Third Winchester or, in the official federal designation, Opequon). Confederate casualties amounted to a quarter, perhaps as much as a third, of Early's army— more than twice the Union toll as a percentage. Many of the rebel losses were taken as prisoners, particularly by Custer's brigade. "My command, which entered the charge about 500 strong," he reported, "captured over 700 prisoners, including 52 officers, also 7 battle-flags, 2 caissons, and a large number of small-arms."[34]

On September 22, just three days after the battle, Sheridan smashed Early's army again at Fisher's Hill. He intended for the cavalry to cut off the rebels' escape; it failed to do so. Sheridan blamed Torbert and especially Averell; he removed the latter from command and turned his division over to Custer. But not for long: just a few days later, James Wilson gave up the 3rd Division to take over a new command in another theater, and Sheridan gave *it* to Custer. It gave him special pleasure; now he could outshine Wilson with his rival's own, and Custer's old, division. "He got his Division by merit, not by hinting and begging," Libbie wrote to her parents—a sign of how thoroughly and persistently her husband despised Wilson.[35]

But he had to abandon the Michigan Brigade. When he said farewell to his officers and men, he told them that Sheridan had promised that he could later swap one of his brigades for his old command. "Some of the officers said they would resign if the exchange was not made," Custer wrote to his wife. "Major Drew said some actually cried." Kidd later remarked that the Michigan Brigade without Custer was like *Hamlet* without Hamlet. In Custer's very first command, he had learned what it was like to be loved by his men. The memory of it would shape his expectations as an officer for the rest of his career.[36]

Yet the promotion delighted him. He told Libbie, "I have a tent almost as large as a circus tent." Soldiers typically view new commanders with skepticism, but not in the 3rd Division. Colonel William Wells wrote home, "Think you will hear better accounts of us now we have a gallant leader." One man said they "welcomed the change, though they knew it meant mounted charges, instead of dismounted skirmishing, and a foremost place in every fight." The word *though* suggests a hint of ambivalence. Under Custer, they expected to win, perhaps to become heroes—but they knew it would cost them.[37]

"THE HEAVENS ARE AGLOW with the flames from burning barns," a soldier wrote in his diary. With Early's army driven far to the south, Sheridan spread his men out and ordered them to turn the Valley into a "barren waste." They marched slowly north, driving in livestock and setting fires. They limited the burning to crops, barns full of the harvest, mills, factories, and railroad tracks, leaving residences alone—until partisans ambushed and shot Lt. John R. Miegs, Sheridan's chief engineer and the son of Gen. Montgomery Meigs, chief quartermaster for the U.S. Army. Sheridan took Miegs's death personally. He commanded that all buildings within five miles of the killing be torched. Seventeen houses were burned down.

Civilians in the Valley called the campaign of arson "the Burning." Both Union soldiers and Southerners exaggerated the completeness of the devastation. One study finds that the Valley's Rockingham County lost the equivalent of a quarter of the production reported in 1860. Nor did the atrocities of the guerrilla struggle, even when heightened by the Burning, approach the intensity of Missouri, the scene of death squads, summary executions, massacres, mutilations, and mass banishment of civilians. But it was still immensely destructive. Sheridan reported that he seized or eliminated 3,772 horses, 10,918 head of cattle, 12,000 sheep, 15,000 hogs, 20,397 tons of hay, 435,802 bushels of wheat, 77,176 bushels of corn, 71 flour mills, and 1,200 barns. The suffering fell on women, children, and the elderly. "Heart-sickening," a New Yorker wrote.

To the astonishment of white Virginians, countless African Americans seized this opportunity to escape. It had been a long time coming. Union armies had penetrated deep into the South, but for three years the Confederates had stood triumphant in the Valley, so close to the North. Now, at last, the enslaved could safely free themselves.[38]

Tom Rosser meant to stop it all—or at least to slow it down. The big, bearded twenty-eight-year-old called his 600-strong unit the Laurel Brigade, after the ancient symbol of victory. Laurel leaves adorned his troopers' uniforms and regimental flags. He came to reinforce Early's depleted army on October 5, and dubbed his men "the saviors of the valley." The crusty Early despised this "ridiculous vaporing." But Rosser and his brigade had an excellent record, and Early needed a good cavalry officer, since Fitzhugh Lee had been wounded at Winchester. So he attached the Laurel Brigade to Lee's old division and gave Rosser command of the whole. His orders were to harass the Union horsemen and interrupt their arson as best he could.[39]

Though a Texan himself, Rosser commanded Virginians, many from the Valley. As they followed "a smoky trail of desolation," one officer wrote, they wanted revenge. From October 6 through 8, they lashed out at Custer's rear guard amid blowing snow.

Sheridan lost his temper. The skirmishing made it appear that the federal cavalry was running from the enemy. He later wrote, "That night I told Torbert [now chief of cavalry] I expected him either to give Rosser a drubbing the next morning or get whipped himself." Sheridan would personally observe from Round Top Mountain.[40]

At six o'clock on the morning of October 9, Custer marched his division south, accompanied by Merritt on his left. Cresting a hill on the north bank of Tom's Brook, Custer saw that the Confederates had occupied "a high and abrupt ridge of hills running along the south bank," he later reported. Six enemy guns on a mound known as Spiker's Hill began to shell his men "with telling effect," he wrote.[41]

Putting his field glass to his eyes, Custer saw Rosser on Spiker's Hill. The wound inflicted by Custer's men at Trevilian Station, the last time the two generals fought, still seeped onto his pant leg, and it hurt. Rosser even wrote to his wife that he wished he were home. But he sat astride his horse, boasting "in a vaunting manner," according to a subordinate, "I'll drive them into Strasburg by 10 o'clock."

When Custer spotted Rosser, he galloped out in front of his line on his big black horse, recognizable to all. "Sweeping off his broad sombrero," wrote Frederick Whittaker of the 6th New York Cavalry, "he threw it down to his knee in a profound salute to his honorable foe."

"That's General Custer, the Yanks are so proud of," Rosser told his staff, "and I intend to give him the best whipping today that he ever got. See if I don't."[42]

Custer launched his attack, surprising Rosser with a flanking column.

A short time later, one rebel soldier "saw fully six hundred veteran Confederate troops flying madly along the back road," as Rosser's division caved in. "His retreat soon became a demoralized rout," Custer reported. "Never since the opening of this war has there been witnessed such a complete and decisive overthrow of the enemy's cavalry." On Custer's left, Merritt routed a smaller Confederate cavalry division commanded by Maj. Gen. Lunsford Lomax. The Union cavalryman called the battle the Woodstock Races, after the village they reached at the end of a twenty-mile pursuit. They found among the loot an ambrotype portrait of Libbie, captured by the rebels at Trevilian Station.

The next day Custer amused his men by walking through camp with Rosser's large coat draped preposterously on his wiry frame. He was happy. In a direct confrontation, on a battlefield of his opponent's choosing, he had crushed his old friend and rival. He had done it only days after taking command of the 3rd Division from Wilson. In the comically oversized uniform, Custer personified the great turnabout he and his comrades had achieved. They had deflated the rebel cavalry, once vastly superior, and rendered it hollow, a plaything for the Yankees.[43]

Just ten days later, disaster struck. Far from defeated, the Confederate commander engineered a stunning reversal. On the morning of October 19, Early launched a surprise attack on Sheridan's sprawling bivouac on the eastern side of Cedar Creek. His four divisions swept the Union infantry out of their tents and drove the survivors northeast in chaos. Sheridan himself was absent, having gone to Washington for a conference. Custer withdrew his division to a line improvised by the VI Corps commander, Maj. Gen. Horatio Wright. The Union army had time to rally because the famished Confederates stopped to loot its camp.[44]

Sheridan had spent the night in Winchester, eleven miles to the north, on his return from Washington. He rode south that morning with rising anger as he encountered fleeing soldiers. He cursed them to return and fight. Kidd wrote to his parents, "He came just at the time when we were all about to give up in despair. . . . You should have heard the cheers that went up when it was known that our glorious leader was again with us."

Dispatched to the right flank, Custer drove back Rosser's division and turned south. To his left he could see the start of the infantry counterattack ordered by Sheridan. He had a choice: he could chase Rosser's cavalry on his right, pursuing his private duel and gaining a certain victory, or he could assist the main assault by striking the enemy infantry. "For a moment I was undecided," he reported. He detailed three regiments to guard against Rosser, then led a charge for a bridge over Cedar Creek, the choke point on the Confederate line of retreat. The enemy already wavered under the infantry assault; Custer's thrust sparked a panic. "Prisoners were taken by hundreds, entire companies threw down their arms, and appeared glad when summoned to surrender," he wrote. They captured five battle flags, the badly wounded General Ramseur, and *forty-five* pieces of artillery (out of forty-eight taken by the entire army), all but unprecedented in the Civil War.

At about nine o'clock that evening, Custer rode to a stone house that served as Sheridan's headquarters. He charged up to the little army commander, wrapped his arms around him, hefted him into the air, and spun him around. "By God, we've cleaned them out and got the guns!" He dropped Sheridan, spotted Torbert, and seized him the same way. "There, there, old fellow," the chief of cavalry said. "Don't capture me!" Next the young general went to the bed where Ramseur, an old friend from West Point, lay wounded. Custer spoke to him warmly about their days together at the academy, but Ramseur was slipping away. He died the next day.[45]

Cedar Creek capped an extraordinary string of victories in which Custer played a central role. Already a Union hero, he emerged from the Valley a national icon.

ON OCTOBER 22, CUSTER rode in a special train to Washington, D.C. Ten captured Confederate battle flags flapped from the windows as it pulled into the station. For both sides in the Civil War, the regimental flag held enormous practical and symbolic significance. The regiment was the army's basic military unit; its flag oriented the men, signaled the advance or retreat, and provided a rallying point in moments of disorder. Soldiers came to see deeper meaning in it. They believed the flag was the soul of the regiment. No matter how badly defeated, the men would take extreme risks to keep it out of enemy hands. A captured flag was the ultimate trophy of victory. It showed that the enemy was not merely stymied, not merely pushed back, but crushed. Ten captured flags represented an epic victory.

A presentation ceremony was scheduled at the War Department, but Secretary Edwin Stanton postponed it for a day, giving Custer time to take a train to Newark to collect Libbie, who was visiting her stepmother's relatives. The couple returned and entered the War Department's reception hall with the enlisted men who had seized the flags. One by one they came forward—Sgt. David Scofield, 5th New York Cavalry, presenting the flag of the 13th Virginia Infantry, Chief Bugler T. M. Wells, 6th New York Cavalry, presenting the flag of the 14th Georgia Infantry, and so on. The seventeen-year-old James Sweeney told Stanton how he captured General Ramseur in his ambulance; Custer explained that Sweeney had been wearing a gray jacket, fooling the driver.

Stanton promised each a medal. "And, to show you how good Generals and good men work together, I have already appointed your command-ing general (Custer) a major-general. General Custer," he said, grasping his hand, "a gallant officer always makes gallant soldiers." The soldiers and audience broke into cheers. Custer, looking embarrassed, "bowed his thanks," a reporter wrote. It was a brevet promotion in the U.S. Vol-unteers, not an elevation in his service rank, but it was a much-desired honor.[46]

The ceremony over, Libbie went to her husband's side. Stanton re-mained for a moment and peered at Custer through his small round glasses, over his gray-shot fountain of a beard that sprayed down to his chest. He asked, Aren't you Emmanuel Custer's son? Custer said he was. "Well, he was once a client of mine." Stanton had practiced law in Cadiz, Ohio. "If he should come here I would do anything to make it pleasant for him. I have been trying to find his son. But learning you were from Michigan I thought it could not be you. Why have you never come to see me?"

"Because I never had any business to bring me to your office, sir." Lib-bie told her parents that Armstrong knew of Emmanuel's connection to Stanton, but did not wish to be seen to be seeking special favors. She may have been right. Custer adroitly used patronage to his advantage, and perhaps knew better than to overdo it. But Stanton, formerly a prominent Ohio Democrat and attorney general under President James Buchanan, also knew Emmanuel through politics. Custer may have thought that using his father's partisan connections to advance himself was too risky.[47]

In fact, he was safer than ever, politically speaking. Cedar Creek all but guaranteed Lincoln's reelection. The *New York Times* reprinted an excerpt of Custer's letter to Christiancy on the same page with the story of the flag-presentation ceremony. To his father's bitter disappointment, he had done as much as any brigadier general to secure a Republican victory.[48]

THE FAMILY CAME TOGETHER AT LAST. On October 23, Cpl. Thomas W. Custer received orders to muster out of his infantry regiment and report to the 6th Michigan Cavalry to receive his commission as a lieutenant. On November 8, Tom arrived in the Valley. Though Armstrong no lon-ger commanded the 6th Michigan, Sheridan approved Tom's assignment to his staff. Just nineteen years old, he had darker hair than Armstrong, with a broader, more conventionally handsome face but the same narrow mouth and soft chin. Armstrong formally received him, defined his duties, then threw his arms around his brother.[49]

Armstrong added Tom to a staff filled with Monroe friends, including Edwin Norvell and Fred Nims. Soon after his return from Washington he had sent for Libbie to join him, since the active campaign had come to an end. "You must make up your mind to [accept] fewer comforts than you now enjoy," he wrote. "You will not need any nice dresses this time."

"I love luxury, dress, comfort. But, oh, how gladly I will give them up," she replied. When she stepped off her train in Martinsburg, she saw that the conquered Valley remained dangerous. Mosby declared that he was hunting Custer, so 150 men escorted her to camp. Armstrong found rooms in "a fine old Virginia mansion about four miles south of Winchester," he wrote to her parents. It was limestone with a wing constructed of logs, all heated by fireplaces (Libbie marveled at the lack of stoves). Eliza Brown and the division staff commandeered various smaller buildings.[50]

"How much I wish that Mother and I could step in tomorrow morning while you are at breakfast," Custer's twelve-year-old sister, Maggie, wrote. "I think I hear Armstrong say, 'Well I'll declare,' and Libbie, 'Why bless me, how do you do dear?' and 'Old Tom from Ireland' would not say any thing until the confusion was over." Her letter showed how close the Custers were as a family. She asked Libbie if Armstrong and Tom pinched her, and if she was siding with Tom against the big brother.

But Monroe was far from Winchester. Margaret asked "Autie" to send "a good young colored girl for Mother." Their mother considered asking for Eliza Brown, but thought she could better control a young girl, that Brown "would not stay contented." That was as close as she came to grasping that Brown was a free woman who chose to be in this dangerous place.[51]

"I am still the only lady in the army. Gen. Sheridan has allowed no one but me to be in the army," Libbie wrote to her parents. Sheridan, a bachelor, cursed and shouted in battle, but Libbie found him to be quiet and pleasant. He politely called on her—indeed, her sitting room served as a social center for the officers of Armstrong's division. She found them high-spirited and jovial, "with apparently no thought of the future."[52]

On November 19, a Union cavalryman from another division glimpsed Custer and his wife. "She was a Splendid young Woman. Custur has a sallow complexion," he wrote in his diary, apparently referring to his tan. "Long curly hair. Tall And as Smart as a whip. It is said he has Some indian Blood in him."[53]

Victory and winter combined to slow army life in the Shenandoah. After weeks in the heroic role, Armstrong again attended to institutional duties. He trained Tom to be a staff officer, ordered target practice twice a week, inspected the men's sabers, conducted inventories of wagons and supplies, and served on a court-martial. He developed procedures for repairing weapons in the field, and the Ordnance Office of the War Department disseminated them to other units. The man who had graduated from West Point last in his class ordered his subordinates to conduct recitations of the cavalry tactics handbook and the articles of war.[54]

Whenever possible, Armstrong and Libbie went riding together. In the evening came card games with fellow officers and serenades from army bands. Libbie's friend Nettie Humphrey held their traditional New Year's Eve ceremony alone in Monroe. She wrote to Libbie that Jacob Greene had returned home after a prisoner exchange. On January 8, she wrote that "dear Jacob had become—dearer than ever before—and now I write to tell you that—God willing—I shall be married next Thursday."

Custer finally received twenty days' leave to visit Monroe in mid-January.[55] Back in Michigan, he participated in public receptions, visited families of his old Michigan Brigade troopers (though the unit never did join his division), delivered speeches, and enjoyed "a good deal of ceremony & display," as Daniel Bacon wrote impatiently.

On February 5, in the Presbyterian Church, Armstrong came to Jesus. Three days later Judge Bacon told him that he cherished his salvation more than anything else. He wrote with rare warmth. Libbie "is made so happy by marriage, I am made like happy. . . . You are all I could desire or wish and I am not without pride at your well earned and fully appreciated reputation."[56]

Custer's own father forgave his political heresy. "I will say that you have no superiors and I am proud that I am the father of such a noble boy," he wrote. Like a true Jacksonian, Emmanuel took special pride that his son was a self-made man. "You have clumb up the ladder of fame and honor your self what a great satisfaction it is to me." He, too, wrote that what made him happiest was Armstrong's turn to God. All he prayed for was that his son should "stick to and defend the . . . banner of King Jesus."[57] He did not even mind that Armstrong converted in the Bacons' church.

And yet, hanging over it all was the likelihood of Armstrong's early death. Judge Bacon wrote to his sister, "The war does not end and what awaits us no one can know. . . . It is a miracle how Custer has escaped, yet he may be the next victim."[58]

BACK IN VIRGINIA, CUSTER MADE elaborate plans for a party at his headquarters—now changed to another home near Winchester. He

invited Senators Zachariah Chandler, Benjamin Wade, and Jacob Howard, and Representative Kellogg, among others, and all their wives. "I
promise you a good time," Custer wrote to the hard-drinking Chandler.[59]

It never came off. Grant ordered Sheridan to march out of the Valley
and destroy the James River Canal and the Virginia Central Railroad,
prior to the start of the spring campaign. On February 27, 10,000 cavalrymen marched from Winchester. "It was a grand sight, requiring hours in
the passing," wrote a local woman. The *New York Herald* reported,

> The 3d division, Gen. Custar [sic] . . . was particularly remarked
> for their soldierly appearance. At its head was their gallant leader,
> who had won a proud name by his intrepid deeds. His appearance
> on this occasion was unusually striking. He looked more youthful
> than ever. His golden locks streamed over his shoulders, and his
> jaunty velvet suit of clothes, his sailor shirt, adjusted after the most
> approved man-of-war style, looked quite picturesque.

On March 2, Custer attacked and destroyed nearly the entire remnant
of Early's army at Waynesboro, capturing 1,600 men, eleven guns, and
the supply train. Early escaped almost alone. Reuniting his division with
Sheridan's column, Custer proceeded east, heading toward a rendezvous
with the Army of the Potomac. Sheridan intended to take part in final
battles against the Army of Northern Virginia.[60]

On reaching White House Landing on the Virginia shore, Custer
immediately wrote to Senator Chandler. He had written just prior to
departing the Valley, he noted, "but fear you never read my letter." Libbie
had attended Lincoln's second inauguration and had danced with Chandler at a ball, but he said nothing of the letter to her. "The object of writing you at that time was to ask you to interest yourself on my behalf at
the War Department and to try and secure promotion for me," he wrote.
"I believe that your powerful influence exerted at the Dept. in my favor
would obtain for me the full rank of Major General [of Volunteers], & I
am now only Brevet Major Genl. . . . I believe there are vacancies in that
grade now and I am confident your influence would easily secure one for
me." This direct request for patronage reveals the purpose of Custer's
party invitation. He listed the victories and trophies won by his units, and
said that Sheridan had recommended him for the higher rank. He added,
"I have been urged by my friends in the Army to make effort to obtain the
appointment of Brigadier in the regular army."

That would be an astonishing leap. Few generalships existed in the
Regular Army; it was a permanent institution and far smaller than the
U.S. Volunteers, which would be dissolved at the end of the war. Scores

of men had serious claims to be Regular Army generals, many with experience as corps or army commanders, and most with more years in the army than this twenty-five-year-old division commander. His elevation in the U.S. Volunteers under the emergency conditions of war was one thing; changing his captain's bars for a general's star in the Regular Army was another.

But this was precisely what impelled Custer to reach—perhaps to overreach—now. This moment was his only chance to slip through the usually locked gate of seniority that guarded access to higher rank in the Regular Army. His wartime achievements made it just barely possible, but the war approached its end. Once the Confederacy surrendered, his opportunity would disappear.

Not all ambition is alike. Americans admired men who sought to advance through achievement, and had mixed feelings at best about those who relied on favoritism. (Women could advance only through marriage, generally speaking.) Custer's moral contradiction is that he combined the two. He demonstrated his merit, yet he himself practiced nepotism and named old friends to his staff. He tirelessly worked the levers and pulleys of patronage to help himself. Was this routine at the time? Yes, but so was moralizing about it. Custer himself scorned Wilson for rising through Grant's favor.

Custer based his argument to Chandler less on his merit than his political strength. "I have friends in both houses who would aid you in this matter," he wrote. "I believe Secretary Stanton is well disposed towards me. Hon. John A. Bingham, an intimate friend of the Secretary, would do all in his power to effect my promotion." (Bingham did write to Stanton on April 3.) Less-deserving officers were "laboring" for promotion, he warned. He asked Chandler to act immediately.[61]

Did he act? Custer would not know until after he had fought the final battles of the war.

RAIN FELL ON CUSTER'S HEAD as the wagon train creaked and splashed toward him on the morning of March 30. Custer was relieved to see it. The wagons carried tents. His division had been marching through a constant downpour since the previous morning. He had spent the night in the open, lying next to the road, covered only in a rubber poncho. He awoke in a puddle of water two inches deep.

He watched alongside Eliza Brown. When he awoke in that puddle, he told her, the first thing he thought of was Libbie. "Oh of course. You would think of Miss Libbie the first thing," Brown said sarcastically. "And I expect you wanted her there with you. And Miss Libbie is just willing to come. If she had been there last night and found herself in the water she would have said, 'Eliza, can't you give me something just to keep my feet out of the water, *but I am very comfortable. This is nice.*'"[62]

Eliza Brown's brazen sarcasm with her brigadier boss gives a tiny glimpse into the way the war had empowered African Americans, and how they had transformed the war in turn. Historian Steven Hahn calls the Civil War the greatest slave rebellion in history. The Emancipation Proclamation by itself broke no shackles. The mere proximity of Union army campfires took no whips out of overseers' hands. The enslaved moved *themselves* off farms and plantations and into federal lines, asserting their autonomy in a positive act of resistance. Many carried it further by enlisting as soldiers, with profound implications for the status of African Americans. "Once let the black man get upon his person the brass letters, U. S. . . . there is no power on earth which can deny that he has earned the right to citizenship," Frederick Douglass declared. Brown's assertiveness reflected a revolution in race relations.

The slave rebellion threw the Confederacy into an existential crisis. The purpose of secession was to preserve a society based on black slavery. It was predicated upon the principle that all men are created unequal, that the African was uniquely suited to slavery and unsuited to freedom. The slaves themselves destroyed that premise.[63]

Meanwhile, the military situation had grown dire for the South. Union forces had seized the length of the Mississippi, isolated Texas, captured Tennessee, controlled most of the Confederate coastline, and occupied Atlanta. Sheridan had triumphed in that graveyard of Union generals' careers, the Shenandoah Valley. General William T. Sherman had marched his army through Georgia to the sea, cutting a swathe of devastation. Over the winter the trend had continued. On December 15 and 16, 1864, the rebel field army in the West was routed at Nashville. On January 15, 1865, Gen. Adelbert Ames—a class ahead of Custer at West Point—had led his division into Fort Fisher, shutting down ship traffic to Wilmington, North Carolina, the last operational Confederate port. In February Sherman marched north into South Carolina, destroying as he went, headed toward the Army of the Potomac.

Despite all this, Jefferson Davis refused to accept defeat. Much of the South remained unoccupied; Sherman's marches were raids, not true invasions or occupations. The Confederate army had some 100,000 troops—only a quarter of the military-age white males in the South, leaving a large reserve of manpower. Lee was outnumbered two to one in the siege of Petersburg, but he had worked miracles in the past with a similar numerical disadvantage. If he could break free and seize the initiative before Sherman arrived, who knew how the momentum might shift?[64]

To cut off and destroy Lee's army, the last truly formidable Confederate force, Grant ordered Sheridan to take the Cavalry Corps and capture Five Forks, a strategic crossroads beyond the siege lines. And so Custer led his division on a rain-soaked march west from Petersburg.

As fighting broke out on the 31st, Custer's wet and muddy division handled the inglorious task of protecting the wagon train for Sheridan's force. Yet Custer felt good. He had received a long letter from his "little durl," full of sexual double entendres, such as a reference to "a soft place upon Somebody's carpet." At midnight came a staff officer bearing a silk headquarters flag Libbie had sewn herself—a swallowtail guidon, red and blue with white crossed sabers. Even better, Governor Reuben Fenton of New York wrote to ask Custer to place a certain officer on his staff. Custer liked the officer, but what mattered most was putting a key Republican in his debt.[65]

A staff officer arrived with orders to come forward to stabilize the line. Custer's 3rd Cavalry Division consisted of three brigades under Cols. William Wells, Henry Capehart, and Alexander Pennington, who had brilliantly led the artillery previously attached to the Michigan Brigade. Custer dismounted his men and put them into a curved front defending Dinwiddie Court House.

They faced some 19,000 Confederates led by Maj. Gen. George Pickett, withdrawn from the trenches around Petersburg. Lee ordered him to hold Five Forks to block or if possible crush the Union flanking maneuver. After a day of seesaw fighting, Grant reinforced Sheridan with the V Corps of infantry. On April 1, after long delays, the Union foot soldiers stormed the rebels' left as Custer attacked their right—his band playing "Hail Columbia!" during his charge over and around the enemy fortifications. After a vicious struggle, Confederate resistance collapsed. Pickett lost perhaps half his men, most as prisoners, a fifth of the total strength of the Army of Northern Virginia.[66]

The next day, April 2, Grant sent the Army of the Potomac forward in a massive assault on Lee's lines. He broke through. Lee evacuated Petersburg and fled to the west. Jefferson Davis and the Confederate government escaped Richmond, setting fires that destroyed large parts of the city—extinguished by black Union soldiers who occupied the rebel capital.[67]

Custer kept moving as Sheridan drove on, hoping to cut off the Confederate retreat. Actually *two* Custers kept moving, for Tom rode with Armstrong.

What is it about brothers, that the same relationship can be so distinct in different families? The younger can see the older as a friend, hero, or villain. The difference lies in the deep snowfall of hours spent together at an age when they are too young to be anything other than authentic. As children, siblings see each other's true natures. Tom saw his brother as a hero, and that is to Armstrong's credit. Confident in his own ability, vibrating with energy and ambition, Armstrong towered over Tom in many ways, all of which the younger brother admired. He was now a national celebrity, indeed all the things the teenager Tom aspired to be. And yet, Tom's own opportunity for distinction slipped away with the escaping Confederate army. The hour of the hero ticked toward its end.

At Five Forks, he had joined Armstrong in the forefront of the fighting. On April 3, Tom accompanied Wells's brigade as it confronted three rebel cavalry regiments dug in at Namozine Church. Tom joined in the assault. Jumping his horse over enemy breastworks, he charged at a rebel color bearer and yanked the flag out of his hands. Tom leveled his revolver and ordered the nearby rebels to surrender. Three officers and eleven enlisted men threw up their hands. He later received a Medal of Honor for his valor that day.[68]

The chase continued. On April 6, at Sayler's Creek (called Sailor's Creek in Union reports), Custer threw his division into a battle between the Union VI Corps and the Confederate corps commanded by Lt. Gen. Richard S. Ewell. During the fighting, a prisoner hailed one of Custer's staff officers. He was Maj. Gen. Joseph B. Kershaw. "I look upon General Custer as one of the best cavalry officers that this or any other country has produced. I shall, indeed, consider it an honor to surrender my sword to him," Kershaw said. "All through today's battle I directed my men to concentrate their fire upon his headquarters flag. . . . I knew it was my only hope."

The battle raged on. Custer's horse was shot. His color bearer was killed by a bullet. The rising sound of gunfire indicated that VI Corps was attacking, and Custer ordered a final charge. Tom led the galloping line up and over the works. Again he spurred after a flag, but as he tried to wrestle it away the Confederate who held it fired his pistol, sending a bullet ripping through Tom's cheek. The muzzle pressed so close to his face that the blast burned him and threw him back. Tom righted himself in his saddle, grabbed the staff, shoved the revolver in his left hand into the rebel's chest, and fired. The enemy soldier fell dead. Tom reined around and rode for his brother, blood streaming down his face and neck. He had earned his second Medal of Honor.

The rebel line collapsed. Ewell and his corps surrendered en masse. That night Custer entertained Confederates Kershaw and Col. Frank Huger at his headquarters tent—and ostentatiously displayed the battle flags he had captured.[69]

On April 8, Custer's division captured three railroad trains carrying badly needed supplies for the Confederate army. During the dash into the railroad station, Custer's surgeon later wrote, two young women ran out from "a large and elegant mansion." They were frantic. They are robbing and trying to murder us, they yelled at Custer. He dismounted, ran up to the house, and encountered a Union soldier coming out the front door. Custer punched him in the face and knocked him down. Darting through the house, he saw a second man heading for the back door. "Catching up an axe, he threw it, hitting the brute in the back of the head. . . . In a moment he was in his saddle again, and after hurriedly directing Captain Lee, the provost marshal, to place a guard on the premises, he charged down the road at terrific speed." If the story is true, Custer's ferocity makes one wonder if the women said the men were *raping*, not *robbing*. (Other men in the cavalry had been executed for "insulting women.")[70]

Other divisions came forward, cornering the Army of Northern Virginia at nearby Appomattox Court House. On April 9, as the rest of the Army of the Potomac moved into position, Sheridan ordered a general assault. But first a Confederate officer rode forward under a white flag and asked for a truce. Custer sent his chief of staff back with him to discuss the Confederate proposal. He waited. Not long afterward he decided to ride ahead under his own flag of truce. A rebel guard brought him to Lt. Gen. James Longstreet, Lee's senior subordinate. "In the name of General Sheridan I demand the unconditional surrender of this army," Custer said, speaking in "a brusk [sic], excited manner," according to Longstreet.

Longstreet looked at the twenty-five-year-old brigadier general with "flaxen locks flowing over his shoulders," and told him that he, Longstreet, did not command the Army of Northern Virginia, nor would he ever surrender it to Sheridan. Custer, he noted, "was within the lines of the enemy without authority, addressing a superior officer, and in disrespect to General Grant as well as myself." Custer calmed down, Longstreet recalled, and was satisfied to learn that Lee would discuss surrender with Grant; another Confederate claimed that the rebuff left Custer "with his tail between his legs." Certainly he had overreached. Ending the war rather exceeded his authority.[71]

But it did end at Appomattox Court House—in the conventional sense. Grant and Lee met at the home of William McLean, who had previously lived on the battlefield of First Bull Run. "There in McLean's parlor the son of an Ohio tanner dictated surrender terms to the scion of a First Family of Virginia," writes the historian James McPherson. The meeting was brief, as were the terms that Grant drew up on an oval wooden table. He guaranteed that Lee's men would not be prosecuted for treason. He allowed them to go home, taking their own horses and side arms. Lee accepted. Afterward he noticed Ely Parker, Grant's military secretary, an American Indian of the Seneca nation. "I am glad to see one real American here," Lee said to him. Parker answered, "We are all Americans."[72]

"I never needed rest so much as I do now," Custer later wrote to his sister. "I have been working very hard for the past six weeks with but little cessation. However I feel more than repaid for all my risk and labor." A mood of relief or satisfaction rather than revelry prevailed when Lee surrendered, particularly as Grant prohibited celebrations. Custer's friend and West Point classmate John "Gimlet" Lea came to see him. It was a day of reunions.[73]

"Only time to write a word," Custer wrote to Libbie. "My heart is too full for utterance. Thank God peace is at hand and thank God the 3rd Div has performed the most important duty of the company and achieved almost all the glory that has been won." In a campaign of maximum effort by the Army of the Potomac, he went much too far to claim "almost all the glory" for his one division. And yet, who could say he had not distinguished himself? "I now have nearly 40 battle flags," he wrote to his wife. "Oh I have so much to tell you but no time. . . . Hurrah for peace and my little durl."[74]

He did take time to draft a congratulatory letter to his division. "The record established by your indomitable courage is unparalleled in the annals of war. Your prowess has won for you even the respect and admiration of your enemies," he wrote. He went on to enumerate their captures and victories. "And now, speaking for myself alone, when the war is ended and the task of the historian begins . . . I only ask that my name be written as that of the Commander of the Third Cavalry Division." The official copy was prepared by Jacob Greene, who had returned as Custer's adjutant in these final days.[75]

On April 10, Sheridan showed his feelings by sending a gift to Libbie: the writing table used by Grant to draft the surrender terms. Sheridan had purchased it from William McLean for $20. "Permit me to say Madam that there is scarcely an individual in our service who has contributed more to bring about this desirable result than your very gallant husband." At his urging, Custer finally won promotion to the full service rank of major general of U.S. Volunteers. He also received a promotion to brevet major general of the Regular Army, which would give him seniority of others of the same rank for the rest of his career.[76]

Custer ended the Civil War far from where he began. He had left West Point at the bottom of his class, court-martialed and convicted, the Regular Army's lowest ranking second lieutenant in its least-respected branch. Under the standard institutional processes, he had had the grimmest prospects. But the war disrupted everything standard and institutional. It consisted of successive crises that allowed Custer to distinguish himself. His energy, courage, and tactical skill propelled him upward.

But Custer never trusted to merit alone, and for good reason. The most important wartime development, in terms of his advancement, was the creation of the U.S. Volunteers. The Volunteers, with their state-raised regiments and politically appointed officers, made the military more like antebellum America's highly political, semi-corrupt society. Custer flattered, cultivated, and begged for favors from powerful sponsors within the army and government. Patronage gave him the chance to show his merit, and patronage sustained him.

But could he survive his success? Could he play the peacetime officer's role of technical expert, institutional professional, organizational man? Could he make his way in the nation he had helped to remake—one without slavery, overseen by a federal government expanded and empowered by war, increasingly dominated by the great corporations emerging in the triumphant North? How would his old-fashioned romanticism fare in a nation traumatized by at least three-quarters of a million dead?[77]

Custer was only twenty-five, and he held the second-highest rank in the army (disregarding seniority). He had killed men and won battles. He was a celebrity. His success taught him many lessons about himself and the world. And he would spend the rest of his life learning that they were all wrong.

Part Two

FALL
1865–1876

I have utterly lost all the little confidence I ever had in his ability as an officer—and all admiration for his character as a man, and to speak the plain truth I am thoroughly *disgusted* with him!

—Albert Barnitz, May 15, 1867

Gen. Custer is, to those who know him intimately, the very *beau ideal* of the American cavalry officer. He is a magnificent rider, fearlessly brave, a capital revolver shot, and without a single objectionable habit.

—*New York Times*, December 7, 1867

Custer is not belying his reputation—which is that of a man selfishly indifferent to others, and ruthlessly determined to make himself conspicuous at all hazards.

—Charles W. Larned, April 30, 1873

It was impossible for Custer to appear otherwise than himself.

—Lawrence Barrett, 1876

Nine

THE EXECUTIONER

O N APRIL 25, 1865, a black man named Junius Garland watched a group of Union cavalryman ride out of the woods and approach. Garland, a skilled groom, tended to a beautiful thoroughbred stallion: fifteen and a quarter hands high; solid bay with black legs, mane, and pert tail; and a proud, erect head. That's Don Juan, the soldiers said, referring to the horse. We've been looking for him for days.

Garland was illiterate, having spent his life in slavery, but he wasn't stupid. He had been Don Juan's groom for the past few years, and knew its value. In the days following Lee's surrender at Appomattox Court House, word had spread that Union troops were seizing good horses; Garland had received orders to hide Don Juan at a farm in the woods. But another freedman told the soldiers where to find it.

The troopers harnessed Don Juan to a sulky, a light two-wheeled cart with little more than a driver's seat. They demanded one more thing: Don Juan's pedigree, printed in a handbill. They took it and drove the horse away.[1]

Two weeks later, Dr. C. W. P. Brock visited the camp of the 3rd Cavalry Division, about five miles from Richmond. His own horse had been impounded by men from the unit, and he went to see Maj. Gen. George Armstrong Custer to ask for it. Custer received him, but he was distracted, excited. Have you heard of Don Juan? he asked Brock. Have you ever seen him? Brock said he only knew its reputation as "a thoroughbred race horse." Custer and an unnamed lieutenant took Brock to a stable to see the famous stallion, which was "being curried down," Brock recalled. "Gen. Custer said that that was the horse, that he had him, and that he also had his pedigree."[2]

Sixteen days after Lee's surrender, ten days after Lincoln's assassination, with all fighting at an end east of the Mississippi River, George Armstrong Custer stole a horse. He used his military authority to take what was not his, for no official purpose. Was it greed that corrupted him? A passion for fine horseflesh—common to most Americans in 1865, but particularly intense in this cavalryman? Was it power—the fact that he *could* take it? As John Keegan memorably wrote, "Generalship is bad for people."[3]

Custer was only twenty-five, an age more commonly associated with selfishness than self-reflection, and perhaps that explains it. But the theft was not impulsive. It had required investigation, planning, and henchmen. As peace began, all that was self-absorbed and self-destructive in Custer bubbled to the surface again.

"LIBBIE IS EVERY INCH a Genl's wife," wrote Rebecca Richmond, Libbie Custer's cousin. Richmond had come to Washington in the closing days of the war and witnessed Libbie's transformation into a public figure. E. A. Paul, war correspondent for the *New York Times*, hand-delivered mail to her. Senator Jacob Howard made a point of escorting her and Richmond to Secretary of War Stanton's office so they could witness the presentation of flags captured by the 3rd Division. And Libbie mastered the subtle and treacherous ways of Washington society, governed by (among others) the lovely Kate Sprague, twenty-four-year-old daughter of Chief Justice Salmon P. Chase and bride of wealthy Rhode Island governor William Sprague. Libbie took Richmond to parties attended by Chase and his daughter, Treasury Secretary Hugh McCulloch, and John Hay, Lincoln's private secretary.[4]

In April, after Lee surrendered, Libbie joined her husband outside of Richmond. She passed from the parlors and ballrooms of the nation's capital to the dirty white tents and sooty campfires of the 3rd Cavalry Division. She reunited not only with Armstrong but with old friends on his staff: Jacob Greene, Fred Nims, and Jim Christiancy, who had healed enough to resume his duties. (Tom Custer had gone to Washington to present captured flags and recuperate after being shot in the face.)

And she saw Eliza Brown again. How many contradictory emotions did she feel at the sight of this young woman, who had spent more days with her husband than Libbie had? She was the first black person Libbie had ever known as an individual, the first to confront her with the humanity of another race. "She was a marvel of courage," Libbie later wrote.[5] Yet Libbie was beginning to sense how skillfully Brown managed her with her comforting and attention, how she made the most of her position in the general's headquarters.

Brown presented an irony. The highly educated Mrs. Custer had complained of the restrictions placed on women, of the passive role expected of wives. In writing about her life in later years, she felt obliged to stress her own feminine frailty, her fearfulness and delicacy. In Eliza Brown she saw a woman born into slavery, denied education, judged by prevailing wisdom of the day to be servile and inferior by nature; yet Brown took charge of her fate, rebuked authority, and contrived to influence those who officially held all the power. Brown challenged the assumptions that Libbie had been taught not only about black people, but about herself as a woman. Here, in one person, Libbie faced the revolution of emancipation and glimpsed women's future of equal rights. She didn't know quite what to think of it.

In this moment of celebration, though, there was no resentment. If Libbie did not see the escaped slave as her equal, she did see her as a person. "Eliza and Libbie are in the room where I am writing," Armstrong wrote to his sister on April 21. "Libbie is listening to some of Eliza's stories. Eliza is wishing she could see all the folks back home." The old categories that separated the races were breaking down.[6]

When the division marched to Washington in mid-May, Libbie decided to ride on horseback at the head of the column, alongside her husband and the wife of brigade commander Col. Alexander Pennington. They marched "through the long sought city of Richmond in parade style," wrote one cavalryman. "How proud they all felt, few can realize but those who marched with them. Their toils were over and they were going home to be disbanded; that was in every one's heart. . . . Every where the landscape was full of memories, sad and joyful, glorious or disastrous."

They went into camp south of the Potomac, and Libbie's husband rode into the city to attend to his political support. He ordered Greene to loan a handsome cream horse to Senator Chandler and to send it in the care of "two or three well dressed orderlies," along with a horse for General Grant's daughter Nellie, to the National Hotel so the Custers could lead the distinguished guests on a pleasure ride. The great army of volunteers would soon be mustered out, and Custer did not intend to remain merely a captain in the Regular Army.[7]

THE GRAND REVIEW OF THE Armies began on May 23. Tens of thousands of spectators crowded toward Pennsylvania Avenue for the great victory parade. A reviewing stand had been constructed at the White House for the commanding generals, key senators and congressmen (including Chandler), foreign diplomats, and Lincoln's successor, President Andrew Johnson. Flags and bunting hung everywhere. The Capitol itself displayed a huge banner reading, "The only national debt we cannot pay is the debt we owe to the victorious Union soldiers."

The first day of the parade belonged to the Army of the Potomac. The legions of veterans formed up east of the Capitol, the men dressed as they had in the field, though now they were clean and tidy. Custer wore his wide-brimmed slouch hat over his long curly hair and the proper uniform of a major general. Sometime after nine o'clock in the morning the procession started. General Meade led the way, followed by the general staff and the leadership of the Cavalry Corps. The march of units began, led by the 3rd Cavalry Division, each man in a red necktie.

Bands marched ahead of each brigade, filling the air with brass notes. Battle flags, battered and tattered by bullets, embroidered with the names of victories, rose on wooden staffs, a moving grove of memory. As the procession wound around the north side of the Capitol, it passed by thousands of schoolchildren who burst into song—the girls in white dresses, the boys in blue jackets. Down the wide avenue the horsemen rode, shoulder to shoulder, curb to curb.

Custer led them. His sword rested loosely on his lap and over his left arm, with which he held the reins. His horse seemed "restive and, at times, ungovernable," thought a reporter for the *Chicago Tribune*. It was Don Juan, the powerful, beautiful, stolen stallion. Custer had had only a month with the horse, which had been raised solely to sprint down a track and to mate. Neither capacity particularly suited it to the cacophony and distractions of the Grand Review.

The crowd roared for Custer—the champion, the hero, gallantry incarnate. Women threw flowers to him. As he approached the reviewing stand, a young lady hurled a wreath of blossoms at him. He caught it with his free hand—and Don Juan panicked. "His charger took fright, reared, plunged and dashed away with his rider at an almost breakneck speed," a reporter wrote. Custer's hat flew off. His sword toppled to the street. "The whole affair was witnessed by thousands of spectators, who were enchained breathlessly by the thrilling event, and, for a time, the perilous position of the brave officer," the *Tribune* reported. He held the wreath in his right hand as he fought for control with the reins in his left. Finally he yanked Don Juan to a halt, "to the great relief of the excited audience, who gave the gallant general three cheers," wrote the *New York Tribune*. "As he rode back to the head of his column," the *Chicago Tribune* reported, "round upon round of hearty applause greeted him, the reviewing officers joining in."

To the *Harrisburg Weekly Patriot & Union*, the incident said something about the mismatch of the man and the times. His ride on the runaway horse was "like the charge of a Sioux chieftain," the newspaper stated. The cheers when he regained control were "the involuntary homage of the every-day heart to the man of romance. Gen. Custar [sic] should have lived in a less sordid age."

It was a splendid display of horsemanship, but also an embarrassing break in decorum. An orderly had to fetch his hat and sword off the street. He sat astride his sin, and it had nearly proved too much for him.[8]

THE SEAMS IN TIME appear obvious to us: a graduation, a wedding, a victory parade. Yet the seams are never stitched in time itself. Human beings are hurled from one day into the next, from circumstance to circumstance. We distinguish endings from beginnings, contrasting *now* and *then*, to find meaning in time. Yet we rarely alter our inner selves in pace with the clock.

The Grand Review offered as distinct a demarcation in time as one could imagine. It was a boundary, a living river of men separating the shores of war and peace, slavery and freedom, dying and living. But there is nothing like an ending to reveal the incompleteness of things.

Philip Sheridan was absent from the climactic parade, and Custer knew the reason. The state of Texas remained unconquered by Union forces. Isolated from the main body of the Confederacy after the fall of Vicksburg, the region was nicknamed Kirby Smithdom, after the rebel general Edmund Kirby Smith, who had not surrendered. The Union army might have to fight Smith's troops. Certainly it would have to occupy Texas, which posed special problems. Slavery continued in force there, never having been eroded by invading armies; and the population had no visceral sense of the South's defeat. Civilians might resist emancipation and federal authority.

Then there was the French occupation of Mexico. Emperor Napoleon III had taken advantage of the Civil War to invade and install the brother of Austrian Emperor Franz Joseph I as a puppet ruler, grandly titled Emperor Maximilian I. The U.S. administration—and especially General Grant—wanted to aid the Mexican rebels and intimidate the French into leaving.

As early as May 7 Sheridan knew that he would lead a mission to Texas. "Would you like to go with me should I go?" he asked Custer. The answer, apparently, was yes. On May 24, as the Western armies marched on the second and final day of the Grand Review, Custer said farewell to the 3rd Cavalry Division. Along with his wife, his staff, and Eliza Brown, he boarded a train, heading first to Baltimore.[9]

"The appointment of Gen. Custer to this Department has created great surprise," a special correspondent to the *New York Tribune* wrote from St. Louis. "The official order defining the appointment is looked for with anxiety by everybody." Some of this was ordinary bureaucratic scuffling and confusion. Where exactly would Custer be posted? Whom would he replace? But there was more to it than that.

"Certainly this Department offers no field for the peculiar talents of Gen. Custer, and it is hardly expected that he will assume an office purely executive while there is any fighting to be done under Phil. Sheridan down in Texas," the correspondent wrote. *Peculiar talents:* in two words, the writer swept up Custer's flamboyance and gallantry, his identity as a combat commander and leader of saber charges, and consigned them to another time and place, which might never come again.

Only days after Custer's apotheosis as the Union army's battlefield hero, it seemed natural to ask how the "fighting" man would fare when an "executive" was needed. These doubts came despite the fact that blood-shed plagued the West; as reported in the same article, Missouri's Con-federate guerrillas continued to kill, and warfare with American Indians had flared on the Great Plains. Yet the patient work of pacification seemed ill-suited to Custer's "peculiar talents." This anonymous writer saw Custer moving toward a frontier—a frontier in time—and wondered if he would remain stuck on one side.[10]

ELIZA BROWN LEFT THE SOUTH. She boarded a train along with the Custers (including Tom) and Armstrong's staff, breakfasted in Baltimore, then headed north to Michigan.[11]

In Monroe, Brown's employer and his wife enjoyed visits by leading citizens, a serenade by a band, and "a delightful little party at the Hum-phrey House" in their honor, the *Monroe Commercial* reported. But Brown herself faced awkwardness and embarrassment. In Virginia, she had been mistreated and oppressed, but she had a home in the large African Ameri-can population there, part of the continuum of black culture across the South. In Michigan she was seen as alien, exotic, not entirely human. During the war Custer's own mother had asked him to send an Afri-can American child home as a gift, as had his friend Marie Miller, who jokingly demanded "a *perfect negress.*" Even Libbie marveled at Brown's strangeness, as Libbie saw it—her "carefully braided wool," or hair, and her "charming" dialect. Eliza had survived slavery and war with courage and cunning, only to be regarded as a curiosity.[12]

Yet Libbie was her most sympathetic audience, and the closest thing she had to an ally in Custer's circle. The two women joined Custer and his "military family" of staff officers on a train to Louisville, Brown sit-ting apart by the door. Men had to accompany a female to enter the less crowded ladies' car, and so the soldiers pretended to offer assistance to the young black woman, laughing at the preposterous joke. When they stopped to eat in Ohio, Custer insisted that she join them in the restau-rant, since there was no assigned place for servants. The owner of the restaurant "told the General that no colored folks could be allowed at his table," Libbie later wrote. Custer insisted; his staff gathered threateningly behind him; the owner relented.

Custer did not intend to integrate the dining halls of Ohio. It was a lack of segregated facilities that provoked him. He did not stand up for African Americans in general, but for *his* cook. His staff declared, "The woman shall have food," not, "Blacks have the same rights as whites." He was a major general—how dare some civilian deny *his* servant a meal!

Libbie watched Eliza, who "uneasily and nervously tried to go," she wrote. "A position so unusual, and to her so totally out of place, made her appetite waver. . . . Eliza hung her embarrassed head, and her mistress [Libbie] idly twirled her useless fork—while the proprietor made $1.50 clear gain on two women that were too frightened to swallow a mouthful."[13]

Writing years later, she interpreted Brown's reaction through her own experience. It was the breach of decorum, she thought, that made the situation so difficult for this "best-bred of maids." She did not consider that, in Virginia, Custer's action might have ended in violence—and the black cook, not the white major general, would be the victim. But Libbie sympathized with Brown's powerlessness. Custer did not consult her when he defended her, even though *she* faced the repercussions.

From Louisville they all embarked on a steamboat that sailed down the Ohio and into the Mississippi. It was a new experience for all of them— the slow journey past snags, sandbars, and levees on the wedding-cake paddle wheeler, with its fine food, black waiters in white jackets, and lower deck low to the water. Excited to learn that Confederate General John B. Hood had come aboard, Custer spent hours talking to him, as if the two old enemies were old friends.

Custer relaxed as they steamed deeper into the warm, humid air of the South. "We have enjoyed our trip down the Mississippi very much," he wrote to his sister. On landing in New Orleans, he grew "enthusiastic over the city," Libbie wrote. They splurged in hat shops on Canal Street, dined in French restaurants, and paid a visit to the aged Gen. Winfield Scott, who lodged at their hotel. Custer "was so pleased with the picturesque costumes of the servants that Eliza was put into a turban at his entreaty," Libbie recalled. Again, powerlessness: Custer treated Brown like a prop so he could play the "creole grandee."[14]

Custer found orders from General Sheridan waiting for him in New Orleans. He was to go up the Red River to Alexandria, Louisiana, where he would organize five cavalry regiments into a division. He would march to Houston. He expected no fighting, but establishing order could prove challenging. Edmund Kirby Smith had now surrendered, but his troops had dispersed, and he himself had fled to Mexico. Grant told Sheridan, "The whole State should be scoured to pick up Kirby Smith's men and the arms carried home by them."[15]

Brown followed the Custers and staff onto the *Mittie Stephens*, which steamed into the Red River. "The river was ugliness itself," Libbie wrote. "The tree trunks, far up, were gray and slimy," strewn with hanging moss. The boat slowly wound up the crooked channel, past red-clay banks over-grown with underbrush. Custer spent hours at the rail, firing his rifle at alligators on the sandbars. Finally they arrived in Alexandria. The town was near the farthest Union advance during the war, and much of it had been burned, leaving isolated chimneys and scorched walls.[16]

The Custers took up residence in half of a fine old house on a sugar plantation. Brown sought out the slave quarters. She found only the elderly and infirm, the young and fit having "made a mighty scatter," as she told Libbie. They were in poor condition, possibly even starving. Brown insisted that Libbie see for herself.

Libbie went to the double row of shanties, and was so moved that she came back with Armstrong. One bedridden woman, whom they estimated at about 100 years old, asked Libbie, "And, missey, is it really true that I is free?" On being assured that it was so, she "blessed the Lord for letting her live to see the day," Libbie wrote. Her husband ceased to complain about Brown's custom of doling out food from the general's mess. "Our kitchen could be full of grizzly, tottering old wrecks, and he only smiled."

Eliza Brown won her point. Under her guidance, Armstrong came to see that "every plantation had its Simon Legree," as he wrote to his father-in-law. "In the mansion where I now write is a young negro woman whose back bears the scars of five hundred lashes." America would forever owe a debt to the Civil War, he added, for eliminating "this evil" of slavery.[17]

But Brown contended with her employers' deeply ingrained prejudice. The old woman surprised Libbie as being "intelligent for one of her race." At a black prayer meeting, Libbie found it "rather difficult to keep back a smile at the grotesqueness of the scene." The Custers laughed when Brown was tormented by "the soldiers, who loved to frighten her." The superstitious, comically frightened Negro was a familiar figure in popular entertainment, and they accepted it as truth.[18]

In Alexandria, the couple mingled with white planters, including, by chance, the only Southerner Libbie had ever met before the war. Amid this company they fell back into old racial assumptions. Libbie wrote, "The town and camp swarmed with the colored people, lazily lying around waiting for the Government to take care of them." She and Armstrong concluded that "the negroes of the Red River country were not an easy class to manage," that "the colored man [was] inflated with freedom and reveling in idleness." It did not occur to them that whites made the same complaint from Kentucky to South Carolina. When old slaveholders saw their former "property" assert themselves, they interpreted it as mere shiftlessness.

The Custers did not realize that freedom, if it were to have any meaning at all, must mean an escape from those who had whipped and raped and sold off children, who had shadowed every hour of the slave's life. They did not consider that African Americans did not wish to be *managed*. As a keen observer wrote, "The sole ambition of the freedman . . . appears to be to become the owner of a little piece of land, there to erect a humble home, and to dwell in peace and security at his own free will and pleasure . . . to be able to do *that* free from any outside control." This would be obvious if one considered blacks and whites equally human, but that lay beyond the imagination of Armstrong and Libbie. The freedom they envisioned involved freed slaves returning to (paid) gang labor under the direction of old masters.

Of course, such ideas were not unique to them. "Intense racism" suffused the Democratic worldview, writes the historian Jean Baker. It rested on the notion that sub-Saharan Africans comprised a distinct, inferior species. As one Democratic ideologue wrote of blacks, "The Creator has designed [that whites] should govern him," for his own benefit. The war and career ambition had suppressed Custer's politics; but here in the South it smoldered and flickered back to life.[19]

Libbie was correct in one thing: the army exerted a gravitational pull on the freed people. As throughout the war, able-bodied former slaves approached the Union camps, sometimes traveling long distances to get there. Custer responded with an order dated July 1. "Since the recent advent of the United States forces into this vicinity, many of the freedmen of the surrounding country seemed to have imbibed the idea that they will be no longer required to labor for their own support," he announced. "Such ideas cannot be tolerated. . . . Freedmen must not look upon military posts as places of idle resort, from which they can draw their means of support."

Having defined their search for work away from their old masters as "idleness," he sentenced the freed people to what they saw as a virtual return to slavery. "The proper course is to obtain employment if possible upon the same plantations which they were previously employed. . . . Hereafter no freedman will be permitted to remain in the vicinity of the camps of this command." The punishment would be arrest, imprisonment, and hard labor until civilian work was found for them. If a freed person violated the terms of his or her work contract—unreadable to most former slaves, who had been kept illiterate—the punishment was also imprisonment and hard labor. Then Custer delivered a final blow to any practical reality of freedom: "No freedman will be permitted to travel about the country unprovided with a pass from his employer. Those who do so will be punished as vagrants."[20]

So thoroughly had Custer absorbed the views of former slaveholders that he reproduced the infamous "black codes," laws at the heart of a brewing political struggle in Washington. In May 1865, President Johnson had issued a series of proclamations that pardoned all but the wealthiest secessionists, appointed provisional governors for the rebel states, and ordered elections for conventions to organize new governments. The balloting would follow the state laws prevailing in 1861—which excluded black participation. "White men alone must manage the South," Johnson said.

Given virtually a free hand, white Southerners enacted laws to control freed slaves, first in local ordinances and then state legislation. Regulating everything from their right to marry to their right to move, these "black codes" largely restricted African Americans to working for their old masters. New vagrancy laws subjected the freed people on the roads to an inspection and arrest regime almost as severe as the patrol system during slavery. Some states gave judges the power to assign black orphan minors to whites as unpaid "apprentices." Many adults were surprised to find themselves classified as orphans.[21]

Other Union generals in the Southwest issued orders regulating black "vagrancy." But many of them also established schools and medical care, reviewed labor contracts, and generally tried to protect the freed people from abuse and exploitation.[22] It's striking that Custer worked so hard to cultivate Radical Republicans, yet so disregarded their principles—even after living with an intelligent, independent black woman for nearly two years.

"A MAN WHO LIES to himself is often the first to take offense," Dostoevsky wrote in *The Brothers Karamazov*. Lying to oneself is a nearly universal human trait, to one degree or another. But some consciousness of the truth usually lurks; reminders make the liar brittle and defensive.

Richard Gaines pursued Custer's lie with the truth about a horse. He was the principal owner of Don Juan. The very day of the Grand Review, Gaines took affidavits from himself, the former slave Junius Garland, and Dr. C. W. P. Brock to the War Department, which was receptive. "The government stalls here were unsuccessfully searched," the *Washington Star* reported, "and the man finally ascertained that his horse had gone to

New Orleans with the General. The disconsolate owner follows immediately."[23]

Custer could track his pursuer's progress in the newspapers, which traced the hunt for the famous Don Juan. He had left the horse in Monroe, where it was safe for the time being. Technically it still belonged to the army, but Custer arranged for a board of officers to assess its value at $125, which he paid on July 1. He also claimed that the horse had been captured during one of Sheridan's raids. "I expected the former owner would make an effort to recover the horse, he being so valuable," Custer wrote to Judge Bacon. "He is the most valuable horse ever introduced into Mich. . . . I hope to get ($10,000) ten thousand for him." He asked Bacon not to mention the absurdly low purchase price, and added that he had "a complete history of the horse."[24]

He didn't explain how he would happen to have that history if he had captured Don Juan in the midst of a campaign. It was a conundrum. The pedigree was key to the sale price—Custer's one great chance at profiting from the war. But his possession of it undermined his alibi; it implicated him in precisely the theft the owner alleged.[25]

As June turned into July, Custer lingered in Alexandria, preparing his column for its march to Houston. All the while Gaines pressed his claim to Don Juan. The matter rose to the attention of Grant, who sent a direct order to Sheridan that Custer must deliver up the horse. But Sheridan put him off, repeating Custer's defense. "At the time the horse was taken I had given orders to take horses wherever found in the country through which I was then passing," Sheridan told Grant. "If this horse is returned so should every horse taken be returned." As the pressure continued to mount, Custer's protector was now implicated in his lie.[26]

"HE WAS A STRICT disciplinarian, and perhaps did not distinguish sufficiently between the volunteer who 'enlisted for the war' and the soldier who serves in time of peace," Grant wrote. "One embraced men who risked life for a principle, and often men of social standing, competence, or wealth and independence of character. The other includes, as a rule, only men who could not do as well in any other occupation."[27]

He wrote of Gen. Don Carlos Buell, but he could have been describing Custer, marshaling his force in western Louisiana. The observation points to a critical difference between the two men. Grant possessed an unusual "readiness to command by consent rather than diktat . . . that made him a master of people's war," John Keegan wrote in *The Mask of Command*.[28] Grant's approach reflected hard-won wisdom about himself as well as his fellow man—his knowledge, after a life of setbacks, that he could contend with the resistance of others and prevail. Custer had risen as suddenly as a volcanic eruption, and had no such understanding of himself or others. During the war he had taken his units immediately into battle upon assuming command; he had never needed to cultivate his men, to listen to them, to build a relationship upon anything other than shared danger and victory. He had never learned to win consent. Now, with no more battles, with all new troops, facing a vendetta over a horse and his own guilty conscience, Custer's mask of command grew hard and brittle.

"The cavalry here was very much scattered and the regiments were unknown to me," Sheridan wrote to Grant's chief of staff; but thanks to the "admirable system of inspection I was at once enabled to select the best regiments and to collect together two of the handsomest columns of cavalry that have been organized during the present war, one under General Merritt which moves from Shreveport, the other under Genl Custer." As mentioned, five of these highly praised regiments gathered under Custer's command for the march to Houston: the 1st Iowa, 7th Indiana, 5th and 12th Illinois, and 2nd Wisconsin cavalry. They included some 4,500 men, all proud veterans.[29]

The orders to join the expedition to Texas did not go over well with these men. Already the troops of the 2nd Wisconsin had petitioned to be mustered out of service as soon as possible. "There was growing discontent among the soldiers at being sent further south, when, as they supposed, the war was over," recalled a soldier of the 7th Indiana. A member of the 1st Iowa reported "outspoken dissatisfaction." Wives barraged the War Department with requests to release their soldier husbands so they could come home and support their families. Resignations of volunteer officers piled up in Custer's headquarters. An orderly summarized them in a large ledger book. "The war being closed thinks his services might be dispensed with," reads a typical entry. "Has for four years devoted his time to the service of his country to the great neglect of private business which now demands his immediate attention." Custer tersely replied, "The Government is the judge of the necessity of retaining this Officer's services."[30]

Still worse, they were short on supplies, from horses to horseshoes, and especially food. Plagued by diarrhea and fevers, the men had to pool their money to buy quinine. Rations consisted of wormy hard bread and hogs' jowls. "The jowls had about one-fifth of the hair still on them, and out of which tusks were taken measuring seven and one-half inches in length," one Iowan recalled. Some resorted to eating corn reserved for their horses. Despite all the fighting and suffering the men had endured, wrote another Iowa trooper, "until after the war had closed and we entered Custer's division, the real hardships of camp life had never stared us in our faces."[31]

"Had all the vegetables and fruit we wanted," Libbie wrote home. "I get so tired of meat that I sometimes get Eliza to make me a little cake." The Custers and their circle went on horseback through the country, Libbie wearing a special riding habit, the men hunting. Jacob Greene irritated even the Custers with his extravagance, as he threw away money on expensive hats and other frivolities; when an enlisted man entrusted him with $100, he spent it. Armstrong ordered his men to prepare a special ambulance so Libbie could accompany him to Houston. And they resented it.[32]

Custer knew of the supply problems. "It was almost impossible to procure good rations . . . hard bread and vegetables being entirely unfit for use," he explained to Sheridan several weeks later. Instead of tact, though, he offered the troops only discipline. "He was only twenty-five years of age, and had the usual egotism and self-importance of a young man," a soldier of the 7th Indiana thought. "He did not distinguish between a regular soldier and a volunteer. He did not stop to consider that the latter were citizens . . . men who had left their homes and families, to meet a crisis in the history of their country, and when the crisis was passed, they had the right to return to their homes. He had no sympathy in common with the private soldiers."[33]

"Numerous complaints [have] reached these headquarters of depredations having been committed [on civilians] by persons belonging to this command," Custer declared in General Orders No. 2, soon after arriving in Alexandria. Indeed, there may have been incidents of hungry soldiers shooting cattle and visiting farmhouses. Yet he did not consider that his men might not be to blame. "After Kirby-Smith's surrender, all authority inside Texas collapsed," notes one historian. "The state was swept by chaos and anarchy. . . . Dejected Texas troops roamed the countryside. The soldiers degenerated into disorganized mobs." This situation extended into western Louisiana; in Shreveport, civilians greeted Union troops "enthusiastically, glad to be rid of the looting Texans, who had fled westward."[34]

Instead, Custer implied that his own men were the cause of all problems. There was "no necessity for foraging," since they had a supply train, he wrote, without acknowledging the inedible food. He who stole from civilians "will have his head shaved, and in addition will receive twenty-five lashes upon his back, well laid on." It would be summary punishment. Trials were too inconvenient, he ruled, "owing to the delays of court martials, and their impracticability when the command is unsettled."[35] The edict stunned the volunteers—the assumption of guilt, the humiliating punishments, the abandonment of legal process. Some noted that Congress had banned flogging in 1861. "It is hard on a good soldier," one wrote, in the very mildest reaction.[36]

Custer did think court-martials worthwhile in the case of desertion. In late July, Pvt. William A. Wilson of the 5th Illinois Cavalry attempted to flee and was captured after a gunfight. A court-martial pronounced him guilty of theft of government property and desertion, and sentenced him "to be shot to death by musketry." At the time, Custer explained, "desertions became numerous and of daily occurrence. . . . As many as twelve have deserted from the same regiment in one night. Unless some action had been adopted which would check the system of desertion . . . the entire command would have in a short time dissapeared [sic]." Wilson was the first deserter they caught; he would serve as an example. Custer approved the execution.[37]

At 5 p.m. on July 28, Custer ordered the 4,500 men of his division to stand in a special formation, forming three sides of a hollow square, facing the interior. A firing squad stood within the open space, accompanied by Custer and his staff. They faced two open graves, fifteen feet apart. A cart entered the open side, carrying two condemned prisoners seated on their coffins, their hands tied behind them. It rattled slowly past the troops to allow each regiment a close look at the doomed men. A band played a funeral march; a muffled drum rolled. Finally the wagon halted at the center. The guard placed the coffins beside the graves, blindfolded the prisoners, and sat them on their coffins again, facing the firing squad.

One of the condemned was Wilson, and the other was Lt. L. L. Lancaster of the 2nd Wisconsin Cavalry. Lancaster's presence stemmed from the unpopularity of the 2nd Wisconsin's commander, Lt. Col. N. H. Dale. Lancaster had circulated a petition among the men, asking Dale to resign. "Instead of resigning, he took the matter to Custer, who issued an order placing all the commissioned officers who signed it under arrest," wrote a member of the regiment. Everyone retracted his signature except Lancaster. Custer had him tried for inciting mutiny. He was sentenced to death.

Lancaster was a popular man in the regiment, where his crime hardly seemed like mutiny. Petitions were a universal feature of American life, and were frequently circulated in the 2nd Wisconsin; indeed, Dale himself circulated a petition asking for leniency for Lancaster. Custer had promised to consider it, but here Lancaster rolled around the square on his coffin.

Now came the well-known sequence of orders for the firing squad. "Ready!"—carbines cocked. "Aim!"—barrels raised. Before the next order, the provost marshal put his hand on Lancaster's shoulder and pulled him aside. Custer had commuted his sentence to ten years at hard labor in the military prison in the Dry Tortugas, a desolate island over the horizon from Key West. "Fire!" The carbines cracked, and the deserter fell dead. The blindfolded Lancaster fainted.[38]

In the twenty-first century, the army bans mock executions as a form of torture.[39]

TWO WEEKS LATER THE LONG-PLANNED march to Houston began. Custer's column crossed 240 miles of impoverished pine forest in nineteen days. Drinkable water was scarce. Horses starved. "Nothing but the 'United States' can force . . . me to take another trip through Texas and especially under the guardian care of Gen. Custer," one Iowa trooper wrote to a friend. "It has been hotter weather, less forage, more timber, millions of 'ticks and chiggers,' thousands of 'centipedes and tarantulas,' scorpions common, and the most poorly equipped and supplied with rations of any expedition I ever saw." To prevent foraging, or even private purchase of food, Custer ordered the regiments to march end to end, without spacing, forcing the men to ride in choking dust in the August heat.[40]

Libbie Custer in her smart riding habit filled a saddle beside her husband or rested in a specially outfitted wagon pulled by four gray horses, one of only seventeen ambulances in the division. The sick—and there were many, many sick—filled ten of them. Seven were allotted to Custer's headquarters. One of those carried Libbie; another carried Custer's dogs.

After Custer had picked out the campsite for the day, he would change into local dress and go deer hunting. One day some passing troopers of the 7th Indiana Cavalry failed to recognize him with his new short haircut, broad-brimmed gray hat, linen duster, and double-barreled shotgun— "cow-boy style," one of them recalled. One asked, "Hello, stranger, will you trade hats?" The effrontery enraged him. Back in camp he sent for them to deal out their punishment, but when they arrived at his tent Libbie intervened, telling her husband he should wear "his *proper* uniform." He let the men go, but held on to his habit of dressing up in local costume.[41]

During the march Sheridan redirected their course to Hempstead, Texas, about fifty miles northwest of Houston. When they arrived, the men found themselves surrounded by some of the richest plantations in the state, yet still they ate hog jowls and hard bread crawling with vermin. Some of them stole and butchered cattle. When the lieutenant colonel of the 12th Illinois asked that his regiment be excused from drill for a week to put their new camp in order, Custer snapped, "If the comdg Officer of this Regt will keep his command in camp, instead of allowing them to be going about the country in violation of orders, stealing and committing [sic] depredations, there would be no need of an application of this sort." Custer ordered more whippings and head shavings on August 28 and September 11. He had a civilian horse thief whipped too, though no one complained, as Custer divided $55 found on him between the two soldiers who caught him. He also convened a board to investigate "the frauds perpetrated upon the enlisted men" by way of bad rations, with orders to inspect the food and find substitutes.[42]

It was too late. The chain of command had corroded. Officers bombarded Custer with more letters of resignation, which he indignantly denied. Desperate to go home, Capt. D. L. Riley of the 2nd Wisconsin appealed directly to Sheridan. Custer burst into a fit of pique at "so dishonorable and unmilitary a step. . . . It is evident that Capt. Riley needs to remain in the service long enough to learn the rules for the transaction of business and of courtesy."[43] The enlisted men, who could not even attempt resignation, pursued other options.

"It was a common occurrence to see soldiers at any time in the day draw up and shoot at Custer and staff," recalled George Stover of the 7th Indiana. "I was officer of the day one time and saw the whole transaction. General Custer asked, 'Who in the hell was doing that shooting?' I told him there would be more. . . . He was in the camp of the 7th Indiana, whose men he had whipped for killing a beef." Others also reported plots against Custer's life. Rumors even reached Libbie. She insisted that her husband keep a revolver under his pillow. She told Eliza Brown about her fears at night, when the two usually chatted. Nothing would happen to the general, Brown assured her. "Nothin' ever does, you know, Miss Libbie."[44]

Countless soldiers wrote letters home like one from an Iowan who called himself "a *slave* to the tyranny and petty caprices" of Custer. Families took up the crusade against him. Newspapers published the volunteers' accounts. Letters and petitions reached Secretary of War Stanton—as did the complaints of Governor William M. Stone of Iowa and Governor James T. Lewis of Wisconsin, who also wrote to Grant. The Iowa legislature passed a resolution calling for Custer's prosecution. "Custer knows and has seen the letters that our boys have sent to the papers," wrote Henry L. Morrill of the 1st Iowa. "Since Governor Stone's telegram to the War Dept. he [Custer] has watched us with a jealous eye. . . . We are almost the same as at open warfare though seemingly everything is cordial on the outside."

Representative Elihu Washburne of Illinois forwarded more complaints to Grant, his old protégé, adding, "I do not know but it is necessary for Custar [sic] to do all these inhuman and barbarous things to maintain discipline, but I have observed that it was not necessary for *you* to do such things in any Command *you* ever had."[45]

Finally Grant sent Sheridan a two-sentence telegram. It was classic Grant: clear, simple, trusting in his subordinate's judgment, and unsentimental, even ruthless. He wrote, "There is great complaint of cruelty against Gen. Custer. If there are grounds for these complaints relieve him from duty."

Not for the last time, Sheridan saved him. He had already defended Custer to Stanton, saying the shaving-and-whipping order "had been rescinded." He told Grant, "I have given my personal attention to the matter and know . . . Custar [sic] has not done anything that was not fully warranted by the insubordination of his command. If anything he has been too lenient."[46]

This reply proves Sheridan's loyalty, not his judgment. It's true that Custer faced difficulties with his column. Even the harshly critical regimental historians admitted freely that the men resented being kept in the army. But Washburne's criticism was fundamentally correct. The commanders of the other columns that Sheridan sent into Texas faced the same problems, yet they never resorted to such drastic measures. Custer's actions went beyond discipline to personal pique. He collected hostile letters printed in the newspapers, and lost his temper at reports of criticism. "He came near cowhiding a major in the 2nd Wis. Cav.," Morrill wrote in a letter home, "because he thought he had said that Gen. Custer's father who buys the forage here came to make money [off] the Gov't. . . . He denied it and thus saved himself, if he was guilty or not. He did not frighten . . . although a revolver lay on the table where their private interview took place and the Gen. was much excited."[47]

It was a test of command for which Custer was utterly unprepared by nature or experience. It was a test less of leadership than of *management*. He failed. Ironically, he created a furor that struck at his greatest insecurity: how others saw him. "The men of the 1st Iowa Cavalry remember this Custer," the *Des Moines State Register* would declare in 1868. "His memory will be a stench in their nostrils, and that of their 'children's children to the remotest generation.' "[48]

ON OR ABOUT OCTOBER 10, 1865, a nine-year-old girl came into the town of Hempstead from the broad, flat farmland that surrounded it, east of the winding Brazos River. How she traveled is unclear; perhaps she got a ride on a wagon, or hiked for several days. She came from a plantation twenty-three miles away, where she had been enslaved to Merritt Chambers. Slavery had separated her from her mother, who lived in Hempstead with a Mrs. Godey, and she wanted to be reunited with her.

Mrs. Chambers discovered the girl's absence. She told her teenage son Willis, "Bring her out or kill her." He rode his horse into town and found her at Mrs. Godey's house. She refused to go, holding tight to her mother. "He then tied her hands behind her and then tied a rope around her waist, pulled her out, and tied her to a ring in his saddle, mounted, and put spurs to the horse," reported M. P. Hanson, surgeon for the 2nd Wisconsin Cavalry. Long before young Chambers reached home she was dead. He cut her loose, "a mass of broken flesh and bones."

The mother complained to the army provost marshal in Hempstead. "He refused to meddle," Hanson wrote two days later. "She then went to Gen. Custer. He sent to arrest the boy."[49]

The case of Willis Chambers placed Custer in a dilemma. The crime itself was egregious—a nine-year-old girl brutally murdered because she wanted to be with her mother. The matter of punishment forced Custer to face the multilayered questions that defined this moment in history. How far could the military go to ensure justice? What was the role of the federal government, represented here by the army, in local affairs? Were Southern states ready to rule themselves at this basic level? What did emancipation mean?

As a soldier, Custer had been thrust into the role of an administrator of occupied territory, a role not yet fully defined in his orders. As an individual, he believed in the American tradition of separating the army from all civil matters. As a Democrat he particularly abhorred centralization and was deeply suspicious of federal power.

Race complicated the case and made it more significant. Race defined this moment in American history. The white body politic now confronted the self-assertion of other peoples in its midst and on its borders, from the hundreds of thousands who had risen up against slavery across the South to the Dakota Indians who had rebelled in Minnesota. The radicalism of the still-unfolding revolution can scarcely be exaggerated. In 1857, Chief Justice Roger B. Taney had declared, in *Dred Scott v. Sandford*, that blacks were "so far inferior, that they had no rights which the white man was bound to respect; and that the negro might justly and lawfully be reduced to slavery for his benefit." By 1865, so much had changed that Lincoln, in his last speech, called for the enfranchisement of literate and military veteran African Americans.[50]

Each day Eliza Brown reminded Custer that an African American could be just as resourceful, intelligent, and strong willed as any white person. On the march from Louisiana she haggled with white citizens for eggs, butter, and a feather pillow for Libbie, snapping at one offer of a barter that "we were not traveling peddlers." She gave orders to the headquarters escort when they made camp ("Now, you make a fire, and I'll go a-fishin"). She defied Custer's constant attempts to prevent her from distributing food out of his mess. "Yes," she told him, "I do take in some one *once* and a *while*, *off* and *on*." He replied, "Yes, more on than off, I should say." Once she hid a hungry child in the brush nearby, and came out of her cook tent to find Custer staring at the path through the weeds. "Well, what is it, Ginnel?" she asked innocently. "That's what *I* say," he countered. But he failed to stop her.

She rebuked Custer to his face. When he insisted on bringing along a mockingbird, she said it was "nonsense . . . toting around a bird, when 'twas all folks like us could do to get transportation for a cooking-kit." His growing collection of dogs necessarily made a mess, particularly since he brought them to bed with him, and even he feared Brown's reaction. Once one of his big hunting hounds actually kicked Libbie out of the bed. Brown exploded at Custer, "*Now* see what you've done. You keer more for that *pesky, sassy* old hound than you do for Miss Libbie. Ginnel, I'd be 'shamed if I was you. What would your mother Custer think of you now?" Libbie recalled that Brown "brought up that sainted woman in all our encounters," invoking the matriarchal authority of Custer's childhood to establish her own in his adulthood.

Once her cook tent caught fire. Flames roared up the canvas, nearly swallowing the structure. Brown remembered that Custer's can of gunpowder was inside. Knowing that it could explode, she darted into the fire, grabbed one of the can's handles, and dragged it outside. Custer marveled at "how cool and deliberate" she was during the crisis.[51]

Brown offered the only hope that the Custers might rise out of their racial stereotypes and condescension. She worked hard at it, guiding them into the world of slavery. She immediately connected with the black population in Hempstead. The Custers hired a teamster named Henry and a second cook, a preacher they called "Uncle Charley," who swore all week and sermonized on Sunday. "Our yard at that time was black with the colored race," Libbie recalled. "Each officer's servant had his circle of friends, and they hovered round us like a dark cloud."[52]

The crowds she described showed that they had penetrated the heartland of slavery in Texas. Here there were at least as many blacks as whites. That was due not only to the long history of the "peculiar institution" in the state, but because slaveholders elsewhere in the Confederacy had shipped their human "property" there for safekeeping as Union armies penetrated the South. In 1860, there had been 275,000 slaves in Texas, about a third of the state population; by 1865, the number had risen to

400,000. The rapid increase, followed by the chaotic demobilization of the Confederate army, followed by emancipation, led to rampant violence against African Americans.[53]

"Freedmen in every portion of the state not occupied with troops are being badly treated, in many instances, murdered," wrote Provisional Governor Alexander J. Hamilton on September 27. "There is scarcely a day that I am not informed of a homicide committed upon a Freedman." A white Texan himself, appointed by the deeply conservative President Johnson, Hamilton took up the plight of the freed people. He pleaded for help from Maj. Gen. Horatio G. Wright, the recently assigned military commander. "The manifestation of a settled purpose on the part of the Military Authorities of the Govt to promptly punish such offenses by a few examples, in proper cases would have a most happy effect," he wrote, almost as if he had Custer's case in mind. "It must be obvious to you, General, as it is to me, that we cannot depend upon the civil authorities of our state for some time yet to deal out justice to evil doers." He knew, he added, that the military at all levels did not want to "interfere with the civil authority," but until a state convention met and created a new government, the federal government was responsible. It had to act.[54]

Wright responded warily. As he understood it, "matters in which the freedmen were concerned were to be left to the action of the Freedmans Bureau," the federal body created to protect and assist emancipated slaves.[55] In Hempstead, though, there was no sub-assistant commissioner of the Freedmen's Bureau. Custer had to decide: Who would try Willis Chambers? Who would punish him? As a minor, would he be executed? Sent to military prison? "He finally concluded that he had nothing to do in the matter," wrote the surgeon of the 2nd Wisconsin, "and turned the prisoner over to a pretended civil officer who sent him home."[56]

The case marked a hardening of his policy. The freed people who crowded in to see Eliza Brown and Charley now found the provost guard waiting for them. "The freedmen in this section are in a very unsatisfactory condition, and the military authorities instead of aiding them are allowing the old masters to impose upon them," wrote Benjamin Brisbane, chaplain of the 2nd Wisconsin, from Hempstead. "Many have been shot [by their old masters] because they would not sign an agreement to work for little or nothing. They have been driven from our command & some for stealing, have been whipped by our [provost marshal] without due trial."[57]

Brown could not counter the racist influences that submerged the Custers. Emmanuel joined them in Hempstead, taking a sinecure as forage agent that Armstrong had secured in a brazen piece of nepotism. "You are well aware of how father Custer feels over the 'nigger' question," Libbie wrote home, referring to his "antipathy to the negro." Armstrong and Tom played endless racist jokes on their father. Armstrong promised to make him chaplain of a brigade of black soldiers. The brothers would drop small black boys ("nigs," as Libbie called them) over the transom into his room. On Christmas "everybody gathered round to see him [Emmanuel] open a box containing a nigger doll baby," she wrote in a letter. He took it all in good humor, but was no less outspoken in his political views or his bigotry.[58]

"The negroes in Texas and Louisiana were the worst in all the South," Libbie wrote in a memoir. She was taught this by her new social circle. For weeks, Eliza Brown had been Libbie's only female company; starting in Hempstead, her social life blossomed, and she left Brown behind. Libbie's dear friend Nettie Humphrey—now Nettie Humphrey Greene, wife of Jacob Greene—arrived, as did the wives of some colonels in Custer's division. The women formed "a reading society," she wrote in a letter, all reading Anthony Trollope's *The Small House at Allington*. She enjoyed parties again, she and her friends laughing at Emmanuel's expense as Tom pounded on the piano, cigarette in his mouth. Most significant, wealthy whites sought out the Custers.

"The planters about the country began to seek out the General, and invite him to go hunting," Libbie recalled. "Each planter brought his hounds, and I remember the General's delight at his first sight of the different packs." Soon their "house was always full of guests," who made no apologies for their racist views. "They could hardly say enough about the order . . . preventing the negroes from joining the column as it marched into Texas," Libbie recalled. After several weeks the command marched to Austin, and established headquarters in the Blind Asylum. "Refined, agreeable, and well-dressed women came to see us," Libbie wrote, and she tried to impress them.[59]

Amid her new society, Libbie distanced herself from her servant. At one point Brown received permission to throw a party in "the lower part of the house." Freed people from the area arrived, Libbie wrote, and "as the fiddle started the jigs, the General's feet began to keep time . . . and then, extracting, as usual, a promise from me not to laugh, he dragged me down the steps, and we hid where we saw it all." At one point she saw them form a dance line, clearing the floor so individuals could display their skill. But she laughed at their dancing, at "the fattest darkey," at clothes that "looked as if the property-room of a third-rate theatre had been rifled." She laughed at their hairstyles, and laughed at Eliza, as if to take revenge on her for manipulating the Custers so skillfully. Armstrong smirked, but kept silent. Libbie did not, and so Eliza found them laughing at her.[60]

Armstrong grew more conservative as he grew more comfortable. The long march from Louisiana had been stressful, personally as well as professionally. The worst moments came when he, Tom, and Libbie each suffered a severe bout of dengue fever, known as breakbone fever; even Emmanuel had "a slight attack," though they all recovered. In Texas they fell into a routine of horseback riding, racing, and hunting with the aid of a half-dozen dogs. Sheridan reassured Custer that he could keep Don Juan, which seemed to put him in an acquisitive frame of mind. "I hope to make some money before I quit Texas," he wrote to his sister. His letters frothed with ideas: buying horses, speculating in land and cotton, even importing apples. The only problem he saw was "the unsettled condition of labor."[61]

"Planters are everywhere losing extensive and valuable crops owing to the fact that the negros [sic] refuse to labor and there is no means by which they can be compelled to do so," he wrote to Libbie's parents from Hempstead. He adopted the planters' perspective, claiming, "A contract has no binding effect whatever upon the negro." They didn't care if they weren't paid as long as they were fed, he believed. "Negro troops are also being mustered out rapidly," he added.

> And I hope will continue until the last of the race has laid down the musket and taken up his more appropriate implement the shovel & hoe. There are white men, veterans, anxious and willing to fill up the army to any limit desired. To them the preference should be given. I am in favor of elevating the negro to the extent of his capability and intelligence . . . but in making this advancement I am opposed to doing it by correspondingly reducing or debasing any portion of the white race. And as to entrusting the negroes of the southern states with that most sacred and responsible privilege, the right of suffrage, I should as soon think of elevating an Indian chief to the popedom of Rome. All advocates of Negro suffrage should visit the Southern States and see the class of people upon whom they desire to confer the privilege.[62]

This was not merely prejudice, but an expression of the theory prevailing among Democrats that African Americans were inherently inferior. Elevate the Negro, he wrote, *to the extent of his capability*—positing an upper limit below that of whites.

Custer, as we've seen, had silenced himself on these questions after McClellan fell and Pleasonton lifted him to the rank of brigadier general. In order to cultivate Republican politicians, he had emphasized his desire for victory and detestation of treason, with utter sincerity. He also developed an honest degree of sympathy, even respect, when in personal contact with African Americans. He made fun of Eliza Brown, yet held her in high regard. Libbie had laughed at the "grotesqueness" of an emotional church service of freed people, but Armstrong had taken off his hat and showed reverence and respect. He proved capable of great decency toward others in an intimate, personal context. But in Texas the context changed. Surrounded by planters, he felt safe and justified in reverting to old opinions. Race was central to his worldview. "I regard the solution of the negro question as involving more difficulty and requiring the exercise of more real statesmanship than any political question which has been adjudicated for years."[63]

"I would like for those who say 'The Nigger won't work' to come here for a day or two, and I think that they would leave with the impression that Freedmen (in this neighborhood at least) were anything but lazy," reported a Freedmen's Bureau agent in Texas. "I say *they will work* and if they work well they shall be paid well or I don't approve the contract." What was required, he found, was a federal officer to enforce the agreements. He exhausted himself by constantly moving about to settle disputes, but he was proving that the freed people wanted safety and fairness, not free subsistence.

That officer reported from Hempstead, just two months after Custer departed.[64]

THE END WAS COMING. With it came fresh challenges to Custer's assumptions.

The final mustering-out had begun. The War Department started to dismiss from service the remaining volunteer regiments and volunteer officers. Custer would be among them, giving up his rank as major general of U.S. Volunteers. The army staggered the process in Texas, releasing seven regiments in September, twelve in October, twenty-four and a half in November, sixteen in December. Fifty thousand troops had marched into the state in June to crush any possible resistance; with the rebel surrender, they had fanned out to suppress disorder, garrison towns, and make a show of federal authority. Only 10,000 remained at the end of the year.

The regiments that stayed as others disbanded seethed with resentment. In San Antonio, where Jacob Greene governed the troops in Custer's name, a mutiny erupted in the 3rd Michigan Cavalry. Custer, now chief of cavalry for the Department of Texas, sent in the 4th U.S. Cavalry to suppress it. Greene narrowly survived the revolt. "To none of your friends is that announcement of your preservation more welcome than to me," Custer wrote. Keep the 3rd Michigan camped outside of town, he ordered. "The influence of citizens, grog shops, &c. cannot but be bad." Also he asked Greene "to procure me a full blooded chihuahua dog."[65]

Dog collecting aside, "the influence of citizens" pressed on Custer's mind, a counterweight to his warm relations with wealthy, refined planters. On January 11, 1866, Major General Wright wrote to him, "There are many complaints coming in from the northern part of the state of lawlessness, resistance to civil authority, and oppression and ill-treatment of freedmen. . . . Please give this matter careful attention." Custer deployed his dwindling manpower in sweeps of these northeastern counties, the scene of rampant, often organized violence against African Americans.[66]

In these chaotic closing days, Custer tried to secure the future for himself, his family, and his friends—which meant a renewed cultivation of Radical Republicans. He helped Tom prepare an application for an appointment as an officer in the Regular Army, and asked Senator Chandler to present it personally to the secretary of war. And he pushed once more for appointment as a brigadier general in the Regular Army. He told Chandler frankly, "I desire to solicit your influence in behalf of myself." He based his case not only on merit, but also on Michigan's representation in the officer corps.[67]

Two days after asking for patronage, Custer wrote again, in a tone entirely different from the one he used in private letters and conversations. "I dread the day when the states *not lately* but *still* in rebellion are permitted to send their representatives and occupy seats in the national Congress," he wrote. A week later he observed, "Justice to the freedman will not be granted voluntarily." He reported at least fifty murders of African Americans who refused to obey their old masters, and "several cases . . . in the northern portion of the state of Freedmen having been *bought and sold*. Comment is unnecessary. . . . A system of oppression is being inaugurated throughout this state upon the part of the former owners against the Freedman."[68]

He did not exaggerate. Reports of systematic terrorism fill the files of military commanders and the Freedmen's Bureau for Texas. At the same time, he told his sister and his brother-in-law "that Texas is a first rate state to make money," with no mention of violence.[69] For the moment, he lived in a convenient cloud of cognitive dissonance. His mind simultaneously contained his bigotry, ambition, political convictions, pleasure in the society of wealthy planters—and recognition of racist violence and resistance to federal authority. The battle for his soul, both political and moral, raged on.

Now, far more than at the end of the war, Custer faced the repercussions of his work. As a soldier, he had done as much as almost any other to destroy slavery, defeat separatism, and establish federal authority. But to what end? What kind of a world did he want? His ambivalence was, in a sense, the nation's ambivalence. A vast political struggle was beginning, a great conflict to seize control of the postwar future. Custer would struggle with contradictory impulses and convictions, resisting and riding the wave of change that he had helped make.

His career as a major general of U.S. Volunteers ended abruptly. On January 27, orders reached the headquarters of the Department of Texas mustering George Armstrong Custer out of the U.S. Volunteers effective February 1. Custer sent a flurry of final orders to Greene as Libbie and Eliza Brown packed. "Hurry up the close of business," he wrote. And it was over. They went to Galveston, where they boarded a crowded steamship and plunged into a sea that was, yes, stormy.[70]

Ten

THE POLITICIAN

G EORGE ARMSTRONG CUSTER WAS sick—terribly, violently sick. Caught in a storm on the short sea voyage between Galveston and New Orleans, helplessly tossed about in his cabin on an old blockade runner, he could not control the contents of his stomach.[1]

His life emptied out on the return from Texas. He had identified himself as a war fighter, a boy general—all stripped away now, leaving him only a boy. He was still a soldier—a Regular Army captain—but "boy captain" did not exactly ring out in glory.

Who was he? Who would he be? Like other men, he was defined by desire: for rank, money, adventure, control, attention, affection, and power. Along with desire came intelligence, curiosity, energy, love, loyalty, and a sense of decency; also prejudice, defensiveness, self-absorption, and a capacity for self-deception. There was something else as well. He wanted to live an extraordinary life and, more important, to *be seen* as extraordinary. "My every thought was ambitious," Custer wrote to Libbie a year later, as a youth looking back on his youth, "not to be wealthy, not to be learned, but to be great. I desired to link my name with acts and men, and in such a manner as to be a mark of honor, not only to the present, but to future generations." Born poor and provincial, he dreaded the mundane.[2]

Constant striving to be seen as exceptional placed a peculiar kind of stress on his personality, as ambition for achievement alone would not. His audience ultimately directed his actions. In 1866, this sensitivity to the watchers would send him on a wildly careening course as he sought to find a place for himself—and to define that self.

He began in Washington, where he went immediately after leaving Texas. On March 10, he was sworn in as a witness in a hearing room in the Capitol, before the Florida, Louisiana, and Texas subcommittee of Congress's Joint Committee on Reconstruction. He faced Senator George H. Williams of Oregon, Representative A. J. Rogers of New Jersey, and Representative Elihu B. Washburne of Illinois. As he answered the first question, he stepped into a burgeoning conflict between President Johnson and the Republican-controlled Congress.[3]

"When first announced, Andrew Johnson's Reconstruction policy enjoyed overwhelming Northern support," writes the historian Eric Foner. Johnson's fierce denunciations of secession as treason made him appear, at first, to be a natural ally of the Radical faction of Republicans. Custer had believed so, quoting the president's saying, "Treason is a crime," in a letter to Radical senator Chandler.[4]

The impression would not last long. Johnson shared the views of his closest advisers, the influential Blair family: the elderly Francis P. Blair, once close to Andrew Jackson, and sons Frank Jr., a major general in the Union Army, and Montgomery, once Lincoln's postmaster general. As Foner writes, "The key to postwar politics, they believed, lay in changing the focus of debate from slavery to race." The people of the North were happy to see slavery destroyed, but accepting blacks as equals was another matter entirely. "The soldiers are in great trouble to know *who* to vote for," Henry Morrill wrote from Texas in October 1865. "They don't want to vote for negro suffrage or for a nominee of the [Copperhead] party"— that is, a Democrat. Johnson would win such voters, the Blairs argued, with fierce Unionism and blatant racism.[5]

Radicals believed that Reconstruction would be meaningless without black suffrage. With prejudice prevalent even among Republicans, though, moderates took the lead in Congress. They hoped to cooperate with the president.

But the political dynamic was changing. Starting in May 1865, Johnson pardoned all but the wealthiest secessionists, and issued proclamations allowing white voters in the South to elect conventions to reorganize their own state governments. New legislatures convened and passed the punitive black codes, mentioned earlier. Civil authorities at all levels in the South condoned violence against both freed slaves and white Unionists. Former Confederates tried to "restore all of slavery but its name," one Yankee wrote. Rather than punish treason, the president's proclamations seemed to reward it. As the new Congress met in December 1865, more and more Northerners asked, What was the war for?[6]

At first neither congressional leaders nor President Johnson wished to fight. Johnson delivered a temperate annual message, acknowledging Congress's right to reject newly elected representatives and senators from the Southern states. In Congress, moderates John A. Bingham in the House and Lyman Trumbull in the Senate pushed a program of partial civil equality and personal safety for African Americans, not suffrage. They believed the president agreed with them.

In February 1866 Congress passed an extension of the life of the Freedmen's Bureau. To everyone's surprise, Johnson vetoed it on February 19. He did so in part on traditional Democratic principles, condemning the bureau as an "immense patronage" that the nation could not afford. And he attacked it for leading African Americans into a "life of indolence," saying the nation had never offered such benefits to "our own people." He also delivered a fierce Washington's Birthday speech that implied congressional Radicals were planning his assassination.

Alarmed by Johnson's unexpected opposition, Republicans prepared a piece of legislation that reached much further: the first federal civil rights bill in American history. As it moved toward passage in early March, anticipations rose of a much more serious confrontation with the White House.[7]

This was the moment when Custer testified before the subcommittee of the Joint Committee on Reconstruction. Judging by his recent letters to Senator Chandler, he did not grasp the extent of the conflict brewing on Capitol Hill. Cultivating Radicals had long been his strategy for advancement; he saw no reason to change it.

And so, as Senator Williams posed questions, Custer answered truthfully. Unrepentant rebels dominated Texas. "I have within my possession letters from prominent Union men in the state, saying that if the troops were to be withdrawn they wished to be informed of it, for the purpose of making arrangements to leave when the troops did," he said. "It would be unsafe and unwise for them to remain." The rebels had expected punishment. Leniency "has led the people of the South to forget the enormity of the crime they committed by engaging in the rebellion." They wanted to be allowed to elect their old secessionist leaders to public office.

"There is a very strong feeling of hostility towards the freedmen as a general thing," he declared, abandoning his own criticisms of former slaves. If old slaveholders had their way, "a system of laws regulating labor would be passed which would virtually place the freedmen under the entire control of their former owners."

"I have paid considerable attention to the action of the Freedmen's Bureau," he added. "I am firmly of the opinion that unless the present bureau or some substitute is maintained for an indefinite period, great wrongs and an immense amount of oppression would be entailed upon the freedmen." He said he had heard of secret terrorist organizations, and reported murders of blacks by whites "merely from this feeling of hostility to them as a class." African Americans, he declared, were universally loyal, eager to educate themselves, and willing to work. He even offered evidence in support of black suffrage, saying, "I believe the freedmen would consult their own interest in casting their votes, and, judging from their conduct during the past war, their votes would always be cast in favor of loyalty and union."

Historians agree that Custer spoke honestly and accurately about the state of affairs. But he contradicted his own private statements, as well as his long-held political convictions. To some degree he was pragmatic. When he talked about the acquiescence of former rebels to the Union victory, it sounded as if he were describing himself, seated in a Republican Congress: "To use their own words, they 'accept the situation,' but I think their motives are entirely selfish . . . it is from a desire to obtain the benefits of the government, rather than to give the government any support." He wanted to be a general, and he needed Republican backing for confirmation. One critic of his testimony wrote that it "goes to show that a Major General's is better than a Captain's pay." He also needed to shore up his reputation after the uproar over his treatment of his troops, and he wanted to counter a report that he had given a disloyal speech.

Yet his testimony was too expansive to be purely mercenary. When cornered he hedged with wordy obfuscation—but not this time. His answers were clear, direct, and true. Calculating or not, Custer did the right thing, and at some level he knew it.[8]

The evidence from Custer and other officers, Foner writes, "altered the mood in Congress by eroding the plausibility of Johnson's central assumption—that the Southern states could be trusted to manage their own affairs without federal oversight." The Radicals singled Custer out for praise, and their enemies attacked him in personal terms. A reporter for the conservative Republican *New York Times* criticized not only his testimony but "his glaring eccentricities," and added, "Officers upon Gen. Sheridan's staff, and others, asked me to say a kind word for the erratic General. . . . Notwithstanding this his brother officers had informed me that he had upon several occasions made some injudicious and offensive remarks, and abused his men."[9]

Soon after Custer's appearance, Congress sent the civil rights bill to the White House for Johnson's signature. It did not confer the vote on African Americans, but it did a great deal. It defined the "fundamental rights" of citizens, regardless of race: the right to make contracts, be paid for work, own property, enjoy personal security, and have equal access to the courts and equal penalties for crimes. It gave federal authorities the power to enforce these rights.

Congress hesitated at some of the implications of its own work. It adopted wording intended to exclude American Indians living in their own autonomous communities ("Indians not taxed") and Chinese residents ("persons . . . subject to any foreign power"), in large part out of bigotry.[10] But even in those cases it settled on grounds other than race or ethnicity. Almost in spite of itself, Congress moved toward a truly universal definition of individual rights. And it made the central government the protector of freedom, extending federal power to the local level as never before. (The exception was the Fugitive Slave Act, which had precisely the opposite purpose.)

Revolutionary or not, it was uncontroversial among Republicans. Protecting the freed people, a Republican newspaper declared, "follows from the suppression of the rebellion. . . . The nation is dishonored if it hesitates in this." If Johnson rejected it, he would reject the party that had elected him vice president. An Ohio politician wrote to Senator John Sherman, "If the President vetoes the Civil Rights bill, I believe we shall be obliged to draw our swords for a fight and throw away the scabbards."

On March 27, Johnson vetoed it. Again he objected in traditional Democratic terms, calling it a "stride toward centralization." But he went further. He opposed any attempt to legislate "a perfect equality of the white and colored race," and rejected African American citizenship. He tried to terrify the public with the possibility that blacks might vote, sit on juries, or marry whites. To use an anachronism, he argued that the bill would inflict reverse racism: "The distinction of race and color is, by the bill, made to operate in favor of the colored and against the white race."

The veto's political impact was immediate and overwhelming. As one newspaper declared, "The Separation Complete." A war between the president and congressional Republicans had begun.[11]

AS THIS NATIONAL CRISIS ERUPTED, Custer remained on Capitol Hill. He socialized with Senator Chandler and attended church with his wife. He went to Secretary of War Stanton's office, where Stanton—now emerging as a Radical stalwart—saw him waiting. "Custer, stand up. I want to see you all over once more. It does me good to look at you again!" Custer mentioned the reports that he had made treasonous comments in Texas, but Stanton said he never believed it. "He seemed so glad to see me," Custer wrote to Libbie, at home in Monroe. He learned that Tom's application for a Regular Army commission had been accepted. Stanton said, "I tell you, Custer, there is nothing in my power to grant I would not do, if you would ask me." Custer said he was offering quite a lot. "Well, I mean it," he replied.

Custer worked his connections to Chandler, Stanton, and other Radicals to help himself and his friends. "You would be surprised . . . for how many I have procured appointments" in the army, he wrote to Libbie.

The controversies in Texas, it seems, left his celebrity intact. Senators and representatives left their cards for him. Photographers and sculptors asked him to sit for them. Only Eliza Brown had seen enough of him for the moment. He wrote that she left to see her "old Missus," the wife of the couple that had held her in slavery; more likely she sought friends and family.[12]

As the separation between the president and Congress widened, though, Custer's conservative political convictions reemerged. He was troubled by the Copperhead taint of the Democratic Party, but his antebellum Jacksonian politics had changed little. He believed in a limited and economical federal government, and held that America was a white man's country. He considered the Republican bills to be unconstitutional and dangerous, and was cheered by President Johnson's firm stand.

"I think if I stay here much longer and Andy Johnson remains firm, the Constitution will be able to stand alone," he wrote to Libbie on March 12—a hint that he personally spoke against the civil rights bill. "A grand political meeting is to be held next Wednesday evening to endorse President Johnson. I should like to attend, but business will prevent." On March 18, he revealed the depth of his political engagement. "Am awaiting the acting of Congress on an important bill (not the Army Bill which passed the Senate last week) in which I am interested in as to my future," he wrote. "My confidence in the strength of the Constitution is increasing daily while Andy is as firm and upright as a tombstone. . . . He has grown. . . . He is a very strong Union man."[13]

Custer reinforced his conservatism with a visit to New York. He lodged at the Fifth Avenue Hotel, a vast edifice opposite Madison Square with a staff of 400—"a larger and handsomer building than Buckingham Palace," as the *London Times* called it in 1860. It pioneered such innovations as private bathrooms and the passenger elevator. He told Libbie that he socialized with the Chandlers, visited the actress Maggie Mitchell, looked at paintings, attended the theater, shopped at A. T. Stewart's famous department store, "and enjoyed a drive on the Harlem Lane and the famous Bloomingdale Road," the broad thoroughfares of rural upper Manhattan where Cornelius Vanderbilt and other wealthy men raced their expensive trotting horses.

The politically influential men of Wall Street cultivated Custer. They took him to eat at the Manhattan Club, for example. Located in a palatial building on Fifth Avenue at 15th Street, its rooms decorated with marble and hardwood paneling, the club was organized in 1865 by a group of Democratic financiers, including August Belmont and Samuel L. M. Barlow (both General McClellan's political mentors), Augustus Schell, and

Schell's partner Horace Clark—Vanderbilt's son-in-law and a former congressman who had opposed the expansion of slavery into Kansas before the war. The Manhattan Club served as headquarters for this faction of wealthy "silk-stocking" Democrats, who battled William Tweed for control of Tammany Hall, the organization that dominated the city. They provided national leadership for a party struggling with its reputation for disloyalty. And they strongly supported Andrew Johnson.[14]

"Oh, these New York people are so kind to me," Custer wrote to Libbie. The influential Barlow invited Custer to a reception at his house one Sunday evening, where he mingled with Paul Morphy, the great chess prodigy of the era, along with rich and famous men. "I would like to become wealthy in order to make a permanent home here. They say I must not leave the army until I am ready to settle here."

Custer's words contradict the image of him as a man of the frontier. He had that peculiar susceptibility of the rural, midwestern, ambitious boy for the cosmopolitan center, for the culture and intensity of New York— especially when it welcomed him. He saw himself depicted in a painting of Union war heroes. Escorted to Wall Street, he attended a session of the stock exchange. The brokers gave him six cheers, and he made a few remarks from the president's chair. His new friends hosted a breakfast for him that included the lawyer and Democratic leader Charles O'Conor, the poet William Cullen Bryant, and the historian and diplomat George Bancroft. He socialized with Pleasonton at the home of John Jacob Astor III, and he almost certainly visited McClellan.

Custer's friends invited him to take part in the new craze for masked balls at the Academy of Music, "New York's sanctum sanctorum of high culture," as two historians of the city write. "Nouveau riche Wall Street brokers in fancy dress rubbed elbows and much else with the city's assembled demimondaines, attired in costumes that exposed much, if not all, of their persons. As the champagne flowed, modesty was abandoned and the parties escalated to Mardi Gras levels." Custer attended one such "bal masqué" at the Academy of Music on April 14. He dressed as the devil, with red silk tights, black velvet cape trimmed with gold lace, and a black silk mask. Thomas Nast included Custer in a drawing of the ball for *Harper's Weekly*, surrounding it with political caricatures, including one of Johnson vetoing the Freedmen's Bureau bill.[15]

Amid this attention, Custer grew callously self-indulgent. He wrote to Libbie that he and old West Point friends visited "pretty-girl-waitress saloons. We also had considerable sport with females we met on the street—'Nymphes du Pavé' they are called." He added, "Sport alone was our object. At no time did I forget you." It was hardly reassuring; his descriptions of alluring women seemed a deliberate provocation, especially since Libbie remained at home to tend to her ailing father. At one party, he wrote, he sat on a sofa next to a baroness in a very low-cut satin dress. "I have not seen such sights since I was weaned." He said it did not make his "passions rise, nor *nuthin* else," but added, "What I saw went far to convince me that a Baroness is formed very much like all other persons of the *same sex*."[16]

One day he went to a clairvoyant with Wesley Merritt and some "girls" whom he did not name to Libbie. A fad for spiritualism had grown in America ever since two young girls claimed in 1848 to be able to communicate with a spirit through knocking sounds. With the great loss of life during the war, many survivors sought to contact the dead; even some intellectuals took clairvoyants and mediums seriously. "I was told many wonderful things, among others the year I was sick with typhoid fever, the year I was married, the year I was appointed to West Point, also the year I was promoted to Brig Genl. You were described accurately," Custer wrote to Libbie. The woman said he would have four children; the first would die young. He had had narrow escapes from death, but would live to old age and die of natural causes. She also said, Custer reported, "I was *always* fortunate since the hour of my birth and always would be." The group found her so spooky that the women refused to participate.

The clairvoyant also said "I was thinking of changing my business and thought of engaging in one of two things, *Railroading* or *Mining*." Custer added, "(*Strictly true.*)" Money filled his mind as he considered his future path. As he had said, he would have to make a great deal to live in the center of things, in New York. He labored over the new race history and pedigree for Don Juan, citing horse-racing publications, to replace the original, which implicated him in a theft. In Washington he had talked with Grant about taking a year's leave of absence to fight for Benito Juárez in his revolution against France's puppet emperor in Mexico, Maximilian I.

Grant wrote a letter of recommendation, though he interposed Sheridan between them. Custer "rendered such distinguished service as a cavalry officer during the war. There was no officer in that branch of service who had the confidence of Gen. Sheridan to a greater degree than Gen. C. and there is no officer in whose judgment I have greater faith than in Sheridan's." Then, as if he realized what he was doing, he added, "Please understand that I mean by this to endorse Gen. Custer to a high degree."[17]

This period is often described as an interregnum in Custer's life—a period of vacillation before he set out on his proper path. To the contrary, he revealed elements of his true self. It was a time when he pursued some of his deepest interests and indulged in some of his greatest pleasures. He loved New York, and always would. The things he chased there—money, culture, society, women, and politics—mattered to him. Soon he, too, would enter the political conflict. "I long to become wealthy," he wrote to Libbie from New York, "not for wealth alone but for the power it brings."[18]

DANIEL BACON WAS SICK. Over the winter of 1865–66, he wrote to his sister, "I have been quite unwell . . . have had dysentery & with something like the ague." After losing ten pounds, he recovered, and felt positively healthy. It proved a brief reprieve. Libbie tended to him, but he grew worse. Even Emmanuel Custer came to stay with the family, a sign that all believed the end was near. Bacon thought so. "He seemed triumphantly happy, so near Heaven, so contented with regard to me," Libbie wrote. He remarked, "Elizabeth has married entirely to her own satisfaction and to mine. No man could wish for a son-in-law more highly thought of!" To the very end, he viewed Custer through the lens of reputation and respectability. And he insisted that Libbie submerge her identity in her husband's, telling her, "Ignore self." Custer rushed home, but "when he returned it was too late," Libbie wrote. Bacon died on May 18, 1866.[19]

"Our house is not the same," she wrote. Armstrong now stood as her emotional pillar—supplying strength, but overshadowing her as well. "I should be far more miserable but for Armstrong's care. He keeps me out of doors as much as he can. I do not wear deep mourning. He is opposed to it." Yet she asserted herself. She told him not to go to Mexico, despite "handsome inducements" offered by the revolutionary Juaristas—reportedly $10,000 in gold. "I do not want him ever to go into battle again."

The devastating blow of Bacon's death did not stop Custer from moving forward with his plans—though Libbie's opposition made him cautious. He consulted with Sheridan, who had rushed to the Rio Grande from his headquarters in New Orleans to monitor the collapse of imperial power in Mexico. Sheridan thanked Custer for his commentary on politics in Washington, and sketched the French defeats at the hands of the Juaristas. "If you conclude to go you would have my warmest support. But I do not advise the introduction of Americans," he wrote. "If you do anything it will be necessary to do it soon."[20]

He did not go to Mexico. Secretary of State William Seward prevented it. Instead, Custer took Don Juan to the Michigan State Fair. After the last horse race on June 23, he rode Don Juan "at full speed past the stand, the horse displaying great speed and power," the *Chicago Tribune* reported. "His appearance was greeted with tremendous applause." Judges awarded Don Juan first prize over six thoroughbred rivals. With this rousing appearance, national press attention, and the re-created pedigree, Custer now felt certain that he could sell him for $10,000, an enormous sum. One month later Don Juan died of a stroke. Custer was left with nothing.[21]

He still had the army, of course. On July 28, Congress passed an act that authorized a maximum of 54,302 troops; the actual number settled out at 2,835 officers and 48,081 enlisted men. This was triple the size of the antebellum Regular Army, though smaller than Custer had expected. It wrecked his dream of becoming a general, especially given the flood of applicants for officer commissions and the equal allocation of ranks of captain and above to regulars and veterans of the U.S. Volunteers.

The act also created the Regular Army's first regiments of black soldiers, four of infantry and two of cavalry. During the Civil War the Union army had fielded some 179,000 U.S. Colored soldiers (as they were officially designated), who had served only for the duration of the conflict. The new regiments were permanent, with black troops and white officers. "I trust your influence may be used to secure [officers] . . . who always did and do yet believe that the negro could fight, and that he 'has some rights,' &c.," Senator Henry Wilson of Massachusetts wrote to Grant, listing Adelbert Ames as an example.[22]

During this period of reorganization, Grant felt the pressure of the demand for troops in the West. The Regular Army had largely withdrawn from the Great Plains during the Civil War, but the Sioux Uprising of 1862 in Minnesota had led to fighting in the Dakota Territory, and an atrocity carried out by volunteer troops at Sand Creek in the Colorado Territory in 1864 had sparked warfare with the Cheyennes. Grant suggested that the new black regiments be organized and deployed immediately. Therefore he had to place officers quickly. Each regiment would be led by a colonel, assisted by a lieutenant colonel. On August 2 Grant sent Stanton "my recommendations for the appointments of field officers for colored troops," including "Capt. & Bvt Maj. Gen. G.A. Custer to be lieutenant colonel." He would serve in the 9th U.S. Cavalry, Colored. Wesley Merritt received the lieutenant colonelcy of the 7th U.S. Cavalry.[23]

As Grant drew up his list, Custer went back to Washington. He wrote to the adjutant general of the army and asked for duty in Michigan, due to the death of his father-in-law—impossible if he were assigned to a black regiment on the Great Plains. Grant suggested Custer might swap his post with an officer in a white regiment.

That was precisely what Custer wanted. Ignoring the chain of command, he contacted Stanton, and even approached President Johnson for help. He asked Johnson that "I may be appointed Colonel of one of the new infantry regiments, provided I cannot be appointed Col. of Cavalry, but in what ever branch of the service I may be assigned I most respectfully request to be attached to an organization composed of *White* troops as I have served and wish to serve with no other class."[24]

Custer's appeal to the president changed the course of his career. While Grant and the War Department debated the propriety of transferring him to a white regiment, Custer won the attention of Johnson and his advisers. They could see that he shared their racial views, and they knew he could be very useful in the great political struggle.

An electoral campaign gripped the country, unlike any other in the nation's history. No midterm election came close to this one in its bitterness and intensity. It pitted contrary visions of Reconstruction against each other, the president's and that of congressional Republicans, in a battle for the future of the country. The central issues were race, justice, and a new role for the federal government in protecting individual lives and liberty. Rank-and-file Republican voters did not turn into racial egalitarians, but they were appalled that Confederates might return to power and shocked by the violence inflicted on the freed people—the only truly loyal population in the South.

White Southern hostility toward blacks was blatant. "If one had the power," the *Memphis Daily Appeal* wrote, "it would be a solemn duty for him to annihilate the race." On May 1, a three-day race riot erupted in that city, as policemen and firemen led white mobs on a rampage through black neighborhoods. Forty-six African Americans and two whites died; five black women were raped; ninety-one houses, twelve schools, and four churches were burned to the ground. On July 30, white police in New Orleans attacked delegates to a state constitutional convention called to enfranchise African Americans. They killed thirty-four blacks and three white Radicals, and wounded 119. Sheridan called the riot "an absolute massacre."[25]

The bloodshed outraged Republicans. Their solution outraged Democrats. It was a proposed Fourteenth Amendment to the Constitution, drafted to a great extent by Custer's old sponsor, Representative John A. Bingham. It would extend citizenship to all born in the United States, regardless of race; prohibit states from infringing on individual rights or denying equal protection of the law; and reduce any state's representation in Congress and the Electoral College proportionate to the percentage of the adult male population denied the right to vote, in order to coerce Southern states into enfranchising their large black populations. The amendment would be a profound and unprecedented step toward black equality and participation in government.

The repercussions would extend far beyond African Americans. Previously the Bill of Rights had been construed to limit only *federal* action, leaving states free to suppress freedom of speech, religion, and all the liberties in the first eight amendments. Bingham declared on the floor of the House of Representatives that the Fourteenth Amendment "was simply a proposition to arm the Congress of the United States, by the consent of the people, with power to enforce the Bill of Rights"—*against* state and local governments. It would leap toward the modern American conception of individual rights and the central government's role as their guarantor. "More than anything else," writes Eric Foner, "the election became a referendum on the Fourteenth Amendment."[26]

Custer opposed it. He understood the importance, he wrote, of "times like the present, when a new political era is being inaugurated—an era which is destined to remodel and develop the character of our political structure."[27] He saw America standing at a doorway between past and future, and he wanted to close that door.

AT THIS DELICATE MOMENT, the president asked him for help. Johnson and his advisers planned to build a Northern conservative coalition to retake Congress, through a National Union convention in Philadelphia. Lincoln had run for reelection under the same party name, but now it would essentially be the Democratic Party in disguise. After the convention Johnson planned to break with tradition and campaign personally on a national speaking tour, accompanied by Grant, Adm. David Farragut, Secretary of State Seward, and Navy Secretary Gideon Welles. The president asked Custer to attend the convention and join him on his journey.[28]

Libbie saw the risks more clearly than her husband. She had spent far more time on Capitol Hill, and understood the interplay of politics and personal relationships. She later cautioned, for example, that Senator Chandler "can be a very tenacious enemy," and must be cultivated, not provoked. So when Armstrong told her of the president's invitation, she advised against it. He insisted. "It is my wish to have Autie avoid politics but I can say nothing to prevent him because I know that he is so conscientious in what he is doing," she wrote to her cousin Rebecca Richmond. "If such a Congress is allowed to dictate laws to our country as it did last winter, he believes men, soldiers & all should work to prevent it, and so I did not oppose his present movements."

Libbie's words—not to mention her husband's actions—refute the idea that he was "a political innocent" who "allowed himself to be lured" into politics, as one of his best biographers writes. Even illiterate backwoodsmen understood and deeply felt the politics of this tumultuous year, and Custer was a well-educated man who had spent weeks on Capitol Hill, immersed in the struggle. But he did accede to his wife's wishes on one point, she wrote. "He has positively declined running for Congress and will do so on no consideration—much to my delight." Who asked him to run, we do not know. The president? Democratic leaders in New York? Michigan Democrats? Though Custer declined, it was a serious possibility.[29]

It's not as if he sought obscurity. At the state Union convention in Detroit on August 9, he was named a vice president of the Michigan delegation to the National Union convention. On August 14, he joined the throngs of conservatives from North and South who packed the Wigwam, a vast convention hall on Girard Avenue between 21st and 22nd streets in Philadelphia. Built specifically for this meeting, it was capable of holding 10,000 people in galleries and floor seating. Union General Darius Couch hooked his arm into that of Governor James L. Orr of South Carolina and led the delegates into the high-ceilinged amphitheater. The participants hailed the Boy General, whose presence helped them counter accusations that they were Copperheads. "There was Custer—how the nation loves and adores him!" wrote a *New York Times* reporter. "Custer!—the synonym of dashing gallantry and unfaltering fidelity!"

Behind the scenes, the *New York Times* editor and conservative Republican Henry J. Raymond tried to include protections for the freed people in the convention platform. He failed. Many conservative and moderate Republicans, writes the historian Albert Castel, "who were otherwise sympathetic to the president, felt uneasy about the predominance of Democratic and Southern delegates; this was not their idea of a 'national union' movement."[30]

Custer appeared in his native state of exuberance. As Couch and Orr proceeded up the aisle, the band played "Dixie." Custer stood on his seat, swung his hat in the air, and led three cheers for the Southern anthem. "Other men cheered and other men made fools of themselves, but the preeminence of this humiliating performance is freely conceded to Custer by everybody—to him alone belongs what honor comes from proposing a salute to the rebel flag," wrote the Radical *Chicago Tribune*.[31]

Republican newspapers ran editorials titled "Custer vs. Custer," contrasting his new faith in the South's loyalty and goodness with the evidence he gave to the Joint Committee on Reconstruction. The *Chicago Tribune* declared that Custer should decide which of his personas—the major general testifying under oath or the political delegate—"ought to feel the cheapest, and meanest, and let that one, which ever it may be, retire from the gaze of honorable men thereafter forever."[32]

Custer always grew brittle at challenges to his image. When John W. Forney made the same attack on him in the *Washington Chronicle*, he replied with a public letter, written in the ponderous, verbose manner he adopted whenever he felt vulnerable. He began, for example, with this endless, tortured sentence: "Departing from what I have ever considered a judicious custom, I deem it not only appropriate but incumbent upon me to correct the false impressions regarding my past and present position which at this time are being so assiduously disseminated throughout the country by a subsidized, unscrupulous, and fanatical press." He said his testimony to Congress merely described the outlaw class in Texas, whereas the best men were loyal now. This characterization was simply false, though he may have convinced himself of its truth.

He was more forthright in his defense of his decision to attend the convention. He declined to engage in the race baiting indulged in by Johnson, the Blairs, and many Democrats. "Duty, as well as interest, demands that this government shall be national; this cannot be as long as twenty-four States legislate for thirty-six States, and ten millions of our citizens are unrepresented," he wrote. He had fought earnestly as a soldier. "With that same earnestness I still desire peace, that peace for which our armies contended." Unfortunately he ignored the black citizens of the South, many of them Union army veterans, as the *New York Tribune* pointed out. They had fought as bravely as Custer, the paper noted, only to have their rights denied by Southern states and their lives taken in Memphis and New Orleans. "Is not the part you are playing toward these Black Union soldiers, your late compatriots in arms, intensely base and treacherous?"[33]

No mere spectator, Custer mixed with the leaders of the National Union movement, including the Blairs, Couch, and such former Confederate officers as Richard Taylor of Louisiana. Inspired, Custer met with a group of fellow generals and planned a follow-up convention of veterans of both the Union and Confederate forces, to be held in Cincinnati.[34]

On August 28, President Johnson departed Washington in a special train, embarking on his speaking tour of the North—soon dubbed the "Swing Around the Circle." Custer missed the first few stops in Baltimore, Philadelphia, and New York, where the Manhattan Club crowd of financiers hosted a luxurious dinner at Delmonico's, the city's most famous restaurant.[35]

When Custer and Libbie joined the president, they found an increasingly unhappy party. Secretary of State Seward, a small man with visible scars on his neck from the knife attack he suffered as part of the Lincoln assassination plot, grew ill with diarrhea. Secretary of the Navy Gideon Welles, with his enormous white beard, was rarely in a good mood, and he thought the tour a very bad idea. Grant smoked his cigars in silence, as always, but felt acutely uncomfortable. He knew Johnson wanted him along to give the impression that the great war hero supported the president politically. He came because Johnson had maneuvered him into a position where it would have seemed actively hostile to refuse.[36]

The president himself alternately simmered and boiled. Broad-faced and beardless, with narrow eyes and a perpetual frown as if he had just tasted sour milk, he was, in a word, combative. "He sought rather than avoided a fight," Congressman Shelby Cullom of Illinois observed. Originally a tailor from Tennessee, Johnson learned to read and write as an adult, and bitterly resented condescension. "Headstrong, domineering, having fought his way in a state filled with aristocratic Southerners from the class of so-called 'low whites' to the highest position in the United States, he did not readily yield to the dictates of the domineering forces in Congress," Cullom wrote. He had risen in politics as a rousing orator, and believed he could personally move Northern voters away from the Radicals. Welles said that when he suggested that Johnson might get himself into trouble on the Swing Around the Circle, the president "manifestly thought I did not know his power as a speaker."[37]

"It seemed to me we gained more enjoyment than the rest of the party," Libbie recalled. Welles and Seward supported Johnson more strongly than any other cabinet secretaries, but they "had their trials" on the trip. The staff officers in the group seemed at ease, as did Farragut and his wife. But the experience of the president, she believed, was "harrowing." That was because Johnson faced not only a hostile Congress, but a hostile public. And so did Armstrong.[38]

Falling back into the role of the Tennessee stump speaker, Johnson abandoned the high decorum that Americans demanded of their presidents. He viciously denounced Radical leaders Thad Stevens in the House of Representatives and Charles Sumner in the Senate, and suggested that they should be hung for treason. Hecklers filled many of the crowds he addressed from hotel balconies, and he replied in kind. "Is this dignified?" someone in the crowd in Cleveland demanded, after he had shouted back at a critic. "I care not for dignity," he said.[39]

"I have never been so tired of anything before as I have been with the political speeches of Mr. Johnson," Grant wrote to his wife, Julia. "I look upon them as a national disgrace." But Custer defended Johnson— fiercely, vocally, much the way that the president spoke. In Indianapolis, he interrupted Johnson's remarks to shout down the hecklers, yelling,

"Hush, you damned ignorant Hoosiers!" After the president retired to dinner, Custer watched as torch-wielding pro- and anti-Johnson mobs confronted each other outside the hotel; a burst of gunfire led to several casualties. Grant went to the balcony and restored calm with a few remarks.[40]

When the presidential train pulled into Newark, Ohio, Johnson began as he usually did, saying he was gratified "that he could present to them the flag of the country, not with twenty-five, but thirty-six stars." Onlookers interrupted him with calls for Grant to speak. Custer jumped forward. "You cannot insult the President through General Grant," he said, and led the crowd in three cheers "for the Union of the thirty-six States." In New Market, the citizens gave three cheers for Congress and three for Thad Stevens, and held up placards reading, "New Orleans." Custer shouted, "I was born two miles and a half from here, but I am ashamed of you." Arriving in Cadiz, Custer told a friendlier crowd that the people in New Market had been "the worst class of people he had seen since the beginning of the war." When someone interjected, "Except the rebels," Custer said, "No, I don't except them. The rebels have repented."

Johnson and Custer were synchronized in emotion and conviction. In Steubenville, they responded jointly to hecklers in a crowd of about 4,000. When the president began to speak, the crowd hooted and groaned. Custer shouted, "Wait till next October [Ohio held its elections in October], and worse groans than those will be heard." Johnson then quoted Christ, putting himself in the crucified savior's position: "Let them alone; they know not what they do." Not everyone was hostile, of course, in large part because many shared Johnson's views on race. When an aged black man approached the president at one stop, a bystander pointed at the elderly fellow and said, "There, boys, is the cause of all this trouble." Everyone laughed. Overall, though, the Swing Around the Circle alienated voters from Johnson—and Custer.[41]

Unlike the other officers, Custer openly aligned himself with Johnson. He sent a public letter to the *Detroit Free Press*, explaining why he declined invitations to run for Congress: "It is not from any lack of sympathy on my part for the principles and platform of the National Union Party. To that party and its supporters I look for . . . the return of peace, harmony, and prosperity."[42]

Amid heavy rain on September 17, Custer, dressed in his bright red necktie, helped to lead the Soldiers and Sailors Convention in a cold, muddy tent in Cleveland. A band played "Dixie." The delegates gave three cheers for Custer and other generals, including McClellan, who was absent. They voted Gordon Granger president of the meeting. "Custer felt hurt at this slight, and called it ingratitude," a hostile correspondent for the *New York Tribune* reported. "He felt that he was the chief spirit of the Convention, and the one who first originated the scheme. . . . The quarrel was compromised by putting Custer on the Committee to present the proceedings of the Convention to his Excellency [Johnson]."

The convention was an attempt to counter the Radical-leaning Grand Army of the Republic, a veterans' league formed by Gen. John Logan, an Illinois politician and Civil War hero. The speakers praised Johnson and the National Union Party. Privately one delegate remarked, "We are going to say this is a white man's government . . . and not a nigger's government. We are going to put ourselves on the President's side in this war against traitors."[43]

"The pet of the Cleveland convention was Custer," wrote a correspondent for the *Boston Advertiser*. A constant presence on the speaker's platform, "his manner is cold, but strangely impassioned," the correspondent thought. At one point the crowd cried out for him to give a speech. He slowly shook his head. The call grew louder. He walked to the back of the platform as Granger and another officer tried to quiet the audience. Custer stopped, leaped to the front, pushed the two men out of the way with either hand, and led three deafening cheers "for the old flag. How he did it I shall never know; but henceforth I can understand why the rebels feared his cavalry—can understand how he got such splendid service out of his horsemen."[44]

"It is a matter of painful regret to all who still hold to the views upon reconstruction which he expressed in his testimony, to see him now so fully espouse the cause of the very rebels whom he fought." That mournful assessment appeared on September 20 in the *Monroe Commercial*, Judge Christiancy's newspaper. It was the mildest criticism he received in the Republican press, but undoubtedly the most painful. He had hurt himself at home, among his old sponsors.[45]

This was true within the army to some extent. Custer received the transfer he had sought, from the black 9th Cavalry to the white 7th Cavalry, one of the new regiments, in which he would serve as lieutenant colonel, promoted from his Regular Army rank of captain. Whether the president pushed the transfer is unknown, but Custer clearly alienated Grant.

The general in chief's view of him had grown darker since the end of the war. Twice Sheridan had intervened to protect Custer from Grant's edicts, the first ordering the return of Don Juan, the second recommending dismissal after reports of Custer's cruelty in Louisiana and Texas. Now Grant watched Custer offer outspoken public support to a president whose behavior Grant found increasingly troubling. "I regret to say that since the unfortunate difference between the President and Congress the former becomes more violent with the opposition he meets," Grant wrote to Sheridan. "Indeed I much fear that we are fast approaching the point where he will want to declare the body itself [Congress] illegal, unconstitutional, and revolutionary."[46]

He lost patience with Custer and his role in, as Grant saw it, a national tragedy. The field officers of the 7th Cavalry "should be on duty with it [the regiment]," he wrote on September 24. "In view of the 7th Cavalry being at Fort Riley, [Kansas,] Gn. Custer's orders may be changed to 'joining his regiment without delay.'" The *Cleveland Herald* reported the summons and asked, "Did Colonel Custer, in that letter, get a hint as to General Grant's views in regard to army politicians?"[47]

Too late, Custer learned that Libbie had been right all along. She even hinted at her own disdain for Johnson, referring to him privately as "Mr. My Policy," a reference to a phrase he used that Americans found egotistical and belligerent. She moped as a friend read to her "some leading articles in half a dozen different papers denouncing Autie's course in the boldest manner," she wrote to her cousin. She took some small comfort in her ability to fight off "*settled* melancholy" (emphasis added).[48]

Custer abruptly reversed himself. Russell Alger, one of his regimental commanders in the Michigan Brigade, asked him publicly if he supported J. Logan Chipman, the pro-Johnson candidate in Michigan's First District. Custer replied with an open letter, claiming to have been "misrepresented." He disingenuously claimed that he would never advise his old soldiers on how to vote—then he denounced Chipman as a Copperhead. (Chipman complained to Johnson, "If I am to be slaughtered in the house of my friends, the fight better be abandoned.")

It was an obvious attempt to repair the damage he had inflicted on himself. A second public letter earned him further abuse from both Radicals and conservatives. The *Chicago Tribune* observed, "General Custer's rapid promotions are yet to be passed upon by the United States Senate. Is it possible that he had this trifling circumstance in mind when he wrote the letter denouncing Copperheads?"[49]

It was a valid question. Publicly and privately, Custer tried to convince senators that his actions had been the opposite of what they obviously were. He told Senator Jacob Howard, "I assure you I have been misjudged. . . . I have never been the supporter of Mr. Johnson's policy as represented, on the contrary I have always condemned his unlimited exercise of the pardoning power [of Confederates] as well as the conferring of political power upon leading rebels." This was false. The marvel is that he thought it might work. He even pretended to support limited black suffrage.[50]

By the time he wrote this letter, the election was over. The North returned a large Republican majority to both houses of Congress, which would take control of Reconstruction and, eventually, impeach Andrew Johnson. Publicly humiliated, Custer and his wife went west to Kansas. Perhaps there, on the remote frontier, he might set things right and restore his reputation.

Eleven

THE FALLEN

O N SEPTEMBER 16, 1867, ten officers of the United States Army
sat at a table in a wooden building in Fort Leavenworth, Kansas.
The unusual warmth made them rather uncomfortable in the uniforms of
their brevet ranks—or as close to such uniforms as they could get. Five of
them made do with borrowed generals' dress swords and sewn-on shoulder straps affixed with stars. Fort Leavenworth—or "11worth," to use the
customary shorthand—often surprised Civil War veterans, who expected
a piece of military engineering, a fortification. As a young soldier wrote
that year, "It is merely a military village." It was an administrative center,
headquarters of the military Department of the Missouri, which was why
they were there. They had convened as a court-martial to try Lt. Col. and
Brevet Maj. Gen. George Armstrong Custer.

All but one of the men had met briefly the day before. They had squabbled in the usual army fashion over seniority, determined by a complicated combination of their service and brevet ranks in the Regular Army.
Today, with the official reporter and the judge advocate, Capt. Robert
Chandler, 13th U.S. Infantry Regiment, they could proceed to the reading of the charges and specifications.[1]

Col. William Hoffman of the 3rd Infantry, a slender man of about
sixty with a mustache and chest-length, squared-off gray beard, presided.
Curiously, he had served on the court-martial that had tried and convicted
Custer in 1861. He was "dear old Genl H——" to another member of the
court, forty-one-year-old Col. Benjamin Grierson of the 10th Cavalry, a
regiment of black troops. Bearded and baggy-eyed, he had commanded
cavalry in the war as a major general of volunteers. He had denounced
Custer to his wife as one of Sheridan's "*toadies*" when Sheridan picked
him for the Texas command in 1865. "Sooner or later," he had written
privately of Sheridan, "I will get even with this man." Yet he also had a
reputation for judgment and integrity.[2]

Custer objected to the makeup of the court—not to the presence of
Hoffman or Grierson, but of Lt. Col. John W. Davidson. "First I objected

on the grounds of his being a material witness" as well as a judge, Custer wrote to a friend. Second, Davidson had publicly stated "that he did not see 'how General Custer expected to get out of these charges. He is a young man—a newcomer in the service—he only graduated in '61, and never commanded a company, and he must be taught that he cannot come out here and do as he pleases.'" Davidson rose, Custer reported, "and admitted that he had said all I charged him with and *much more.*" The court sustained the objection, "much . . . to my satisfaction," Custer wrote. The trial had not yet begun and already it was going well.[3]

At his court-martial in 1861, he had admitted his guilt. Now he acted like a man on trial for his life. He retained counsel, Capt. Charles C. Parsons, 4th Artillery. A West Point classmate with a distinguished record, Parsons had a good reputation as an army lawyer. And Custer devoted himself to the case, reviewing every detail.[4]

Custer's life *was* at stake—his professional life, not his mortal existence. That much was clear from the charges and specifications, which were read aloud to the court. *Charge:* "Absence without leave from his command." *Specification:* "That he, Brevet Major General G.A. Custer, Lieut. Col. 7th U.S. Cavalry, did at or near Fort Wallace, Kansas, on or about the 15th day of July 1867, absent himself from his command without proper authority, and proceed to Fort Harker, Kansas, a distance of about 275 miles, this at a time when his command was expected to be actively engaged against hostile Indians." *Charge:* "Conduct to the prejudice of good order and discipline." *Specification First:* That, on the first leg of his movement to Fort Harker, he marched without rest to Fort Hays, taking three officers and seventy-five men "upon private business," seriously harming the horses. *Specification Second:* During his march he procured two ambulances and four mules for his own use. *Specification Third:* After learning that some of his men had been ambushed by Indians, he did nothing to defend them; informed that two had been killed, he "did neglect to take any measures to pursue such party of Indians, or recover or bury the bodies of those of his command that had been killed."

The court heard an additional charge, preferred by one of Custer's subordinates, Capt. Robert M. West, 7th Cavalry, with four specifications. *Charge:* "Conduct prejudicial to good order and military discipline." *Specification First:* During operations between the Platte and Smoky Hill rivers, he sent a detachment in pursuit of deserters, and did "*also order* the said party to shoot the supposed deserters down dead, and to bring none in alive." *Specification Second:* That he ordered Bugler Barney Tolliver, Pvt. Charles Johnson, and a private named Allburger "*to be shot down* as supposed deserters, but without trial, and did thus cause three men to be severely wounded." *Specification Third:* That he ordered the three badly wounded men "to be placed in a government wagon, and to be hauled eighteen miles, and did . . . neglect and positively refuse to allow the said soldiers to receive treatment." *Specification Fourth:* That fifteen miles south of the Platte River he ordered "the summary shooting, as a supposed deserter, but without trial, of one Private Charles Johnson" on July 17, 1867, causing his death.

In sum, he was charged with placing himself above the law. The prosecution claimed that, in a time of active hostilities, he abandoned his regiment for personal reasons, drove government horses until they were virtually crippled, seized public property for his own use, and ordered the extrajudicial murder of his men.

He pleaded innocent on all counts. At 3:40 p.m., the court adjourned until the following morning. At ten o'clock on September 17, it would begin to hear witnesses.[5]

The purpose of the trial was simple: to establish the facts of Custer's actions between June 1, 1867—when he had marched out of Fort Hays, Kansas, on the hunt for hostile Indians—and about half past two in the morning of July 19, when he had arrived at Fort Harker. Only two questions mattered: What did Custer do? Did he have authority to do it?

The court would not ask *why*. Why had he plunged into such a crisis? Why had a national celebrity, one of the most accomplished generals of the Civil War, followed such a self-destructive course? Possible explanations abound. There were the difficulties created by the federal government's lack of a coherent policy toward the indigenous nations of the Great Plains. There was the failure of Custer's superiors to craft a successful military strategy, or even identify achievable goals. There were the new challenges Custer faced in taking a command position in a permanent regiment of the Regular Army.

And yet, other officers overcame the same difficulties without landing in a court-martial. To find the sources of Custer's downfall, it is necessary to delve into his personal life, going back at least as far as his departure for Kansas in the fall of 1866.

"WE CANNOT UNDERSTAND each other, except in a rough and ready way," E. M. Forster once said. We see just the surface of other human beings, and only glimpse the interior when thoughts and emotions emerge as actions. In that sense, he said, "fiction is truer than history, because it goes beyond the evidence, and each of us knows from his experience that there is something beyond the evidence."[6] So we do. But some translate their interior lives into action more directly than others.

"It was impossible for Custer to appear otherwise than himself," a close friend later wrote. At first glance, this seems like a bizarre thing to say. The Boy General of the Golden Locks comes across as nothing but affectation. Indeed, the same friend acknowledged his "fondness for theatrical presentations" and "love of military display." But he could not conceal his emotions. His interior state radiated through the surface, unfiltered, unmediated, uncalculated. It was one reason why his friends liked him so much. But it also posed a constant danger.[7]

Libbie Custer possessed a different temperament, and had been bred to a different role. She had been assigned by family and society to the emotional plane where restraint, persuasion, and even manipulation were essential tools. Her husband's raw displays forced her to use those tools regularly. In April 1866, for example, he had written confounding letters to her from New York, professing his intense sexual need for her yet glorying in the attention of the city's women. He was "nearly starved" for "a *ride*," he wrote. In Manhattan (with Libbie still in Monroe), "I cannot without great expense and *much danger* enjoy the luxury of such a ride as that I refer to. I never did enjoy riding strange horses." He was loyal, but tempted. "It is a great risk," he wrote. And he seemed to suggest that she should flirt with a politician who was coming to Monroe, making clear that the gentleman was quite lecherous.[8]

Did this behavior aggravate her? Or had these two flirtatious partners integrated it into their relationship? Libbie concealed the answer. Yet something about this period of her marriage clearly troubled her, as seen in her memoir *Tenting on the Plains*. There was, for example, the curious way in which she wrote about her friend Anna Darrah, who came with her and Armstrong to Kansas. She claimed to have staged an impersonal search for a companion, writing that she and Armstrong devoted "most of our attention . . . to the selection of a pretty girl." She gave a rather unsettling motivation: "A pretty girl . . . it was held by both of us, would do more toward furnishing and beautifying our army quarters than any amount of speechless bric-á-brac." In other words, they wanted to look at her.

Libbie implied that they chose a stranger, and disguised Anna as "Diana." Why? To protect her privacy? Perhaps the tale reflected her emotional memory of the uncomfortable proximity of her attention-loving husband and a pretty young friend who had confessed "jealousy & envy" at Libbie's marriage. After all, she described "Diana" as a remorseless flirt. And her discomfort would grow.[9]

If Libbie was accumulating wrath, she found a safe target for it in a new servant who worked alongside Eliza Brown, "a worthless colored boy, who had been trained as a jockey in Texas. . . . What intellect he had was employed in devising schemes to escape work," she would write. This "lazy servant" moved Armstrong's mother with stories of his suffering as a slave. Her "amazing credulity" disgusted Libbie.[10]

Armstrong, Libbie, Anna, Eliza, and the jockey began their journey to Kansas in Detroit, where they visited the recent mayor, Kirkland C. Barker. A friend of Armstrong's, Barker shared his enthusiasm for "dogs & horses & hunting," as Libbie put it. He insisted they take his private railroad car to St. Louis, in company with his daughter, niece, a young female friend, and two men. But the men disappeared from Libbie's account in her memoir, leaving only a "pretty galaxy of belles."[11]

In St. Louis, to Armstrong's delight, they traveled to the distant past. They attended a grand fair held by the Southern Relief Association, held to raise money for impoverished white families in the former Confederacy. It featured a medieval-style tournament, in which men dressed in feudal garb tilted with lances at tiny rings in an arena. "It was something so novel to us and reminded us of *Ivanhoe* and other descriptions of olden days," Libbie wrote to Rebecca Richmond.

The fair and the tournament formed part of a backward-looking cultural struggle against the Union victory. Missouri had officially remained in the Union, but as a slave state it had a militant corps of secessionists who waged a bitter guerrilla struggle during the Civil War. Now old Confederates asserted Missouri's Southern identity, using tournaments to celebrate the idealized chivalry of antebellum Dixie.

Custer loved it. "He longed to bound down into the arena, take a horse, and tilt with their long lances at the rings," Libbie wrote. The winner was to crown the Queen of Beauty at a "Calico Ball" at the Southern Hotel, where the Custers lodged.[12]

First the couple and their entourage went to the theater to see a romantic drama titled *Rosedale*. It starred Lawrence Barrett, a striking young actor only slightly older than Custer himself, who had begun to build a national reputation. During the war Barrett had moved to Union-occupied New Orleans, where he dominated the stage. He had first performed *Rosedale* there, winning acclaim by taking different roles on different evenings. Clearly a rising star, he brought the career-making play to St. Louis.

Barrett's performance mesmerized the Custers. After the final curtain, Libbie insisted that Armstrong go to his dressing room and bring him back to meet her.[13]

LAWRENCE BARRETT HEARD the rap at his dressing room door. "Entered a tall, fair-haired, blue eyed, smiling gentleman," he recalled. The stranger apologized for intruding and said he was General Custer. Barrett recognized the famous face and long hair. "He had been sent to bring me to the hotel where he was temporarily residing," Barrett recalled. "I was to go with him to meet Mrs. Custer and other members of his party. . . . He pleaded 'orders' which must be obeyed, and refusal was impossible."

He went. He met Libbie and the others, and went with them to the hotel. They chatted for an hour in the lounge. He impressed Libbie as "an elegant gentleman," and stunned her by revealing that he had started out as a bellboy in Detroit. Music floated out of the ballroom. Everyone rose to their feet, and Barrett prepared to say good-bye. Libbie placed her small hand on his arm—"and before he had realized it," she recalled, "he was being marched into the brilliantly lighted ballroom, and bowing from force of capture before the dais on which sat the Queen of Love and Beauty. . . . Mr. Barrett was not released until he pleaded the necessity for time to work."[14]

Libbie would later claim that her husband arranged it all, but Barrett recalled otherwise. After months of watching Armstrong revel in the attention of female admirers, after days of seeing him surrounded by beautiful young women—including the flirtatious Darrah—she maneuvered him into bringing *her* a handsome young star.

Barrett and Armstrong, though, found each other fascinating. The actor learned that the private Custer was quite different from the battlefield hero. "His voice was earnest, soft, tender, and appealing, with a quickness of utterance which became at times choked by the rapid flow of ideas, and a nervous hesitancy of speech, betraying intensity of thought," Barrett wrote. Custer had an infectious "chuckle of a laugh," but was also "peculiarly nervous." In conversation, he searched Barrett's face, "as if each word was being measured mercilessly by the listener."

Barrett glimpsed Custer's deepest fears. Among friends, Barrett noted, "he was all confidence, his eye would brighten, his face light up, and his whole heart seemed to expand. . . . He seemed in private to become as gentle as a woman." But he was "reticent among strangers. . . . He himself frequently complained that he could not be 'all things to all men.'" Custer had pushed onto the political stage in 1866, only to be judged on a national scale. As a celebrity, his image was beyond his control. So he retreated into tighter social circles. Soon after this evening, a large group of visitors came to his home and "there were incessant inquiries for the General," Libbie recalled. "It seems that he had begun that little trick of hiding from strangers, even then."[15]

In *The Sebastopol Sketches*, Tolstoy drew upon his army experience to explain the self-conscious officer. "The man who feels unable to inspire respect by virtue of his own intrinsic merits is instinctively afraid of contact with his subordinates and attempts to ward off criticism by means of superficial mannerisms," he wrote. Military veterans throughout history have seen this dynamic in martinets and missing commanders. In Joseph Heller's *Catch-22*, for example, Major Major receives his rank solely because his surname is *Major.* Knowing himself to be incompetent, he hides. He orders his clerk to tell callers that he's out whenever he's in, but to let them in whenever he's out.

In battle, Custer was no Major Major. Justifiably confident in his personal courage and skill with a horse and saber, he had put himself in front of the Michigan Brigade and 3rd Division. He assumed a rather different set of responsibilities after the war. He would not be called upon to lead so much as *manage.* In Texas, this mission had flummoxed him. He had indeed felt "unable to inspire respect by virtue of his own intrinsic merits," when those merits did not include combat prowess. An unexpected side effect of his rapid rise in rank turned out to be a lurking fear of inadequacy.

The situation in Kansas would be similar, but with a difference. The troops in Texas had been volunteers, anxious to return home; those in Kansas would be professionals. He now had to build lasting relationships in a permanent institution. The worst thing he could do would be to withdraw or put on airs. When a commander did that, Tolstoy observed, "his subordinates, who see only this superficial aspect of the man, one which they find offensive, are inclined, often unjustly, to suppose it conceals nothing good."[16]

THEY ARRIVED AT FORT RILEY, Kansas, roughly 120 miles west of Fort Leavenworth, in the middle of October 1866. The Union Pacific Railroad, Eastern Division—soon to be called the Kansas Pacific Railroad—already extended to within ten miles of Fort Riley amid its construction from Kansas City to Denver. The Custers, Anna Darrah, Eliza Brown, the jockey, and their various dogs rode the rest of the way in ambulances, accompanied by three horses.

"This is not a *fort*, tho' called so," Libbie wrote to Rebecca Richmond. "For there are no walls enclosing it." It was one of the older posts on the Great Plains, established in 1853 near the junction of the Republican and Smoky Hill rivers, forming the Kansas River. Libbie described Riley as "a little city" of limestone buildings. Three two-story barracks faced three others across a large square parade ground, framed on the remaining sides by matched sets of three two-story officers' quarters, each consisting of two attached houses. The fort also included stables, the store run by the sutler (the civilian merchant permitted to operate at a military post), express company office, post office, civilian housing, mess halls, chapel, ordnance building, and more. After shifting about, the Custer

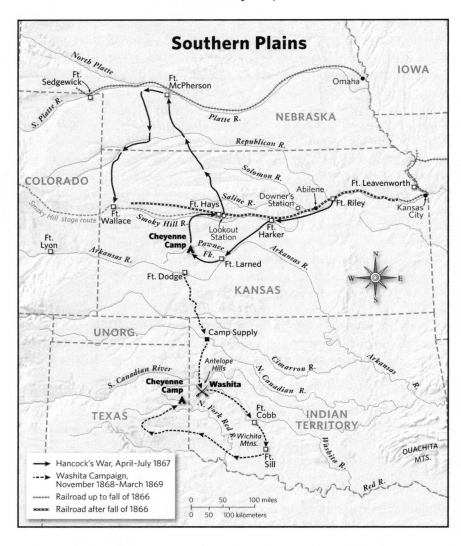

Southern Plains

IOWA

North Platte

Ft. Sedgewick

Ft. McPherson

Omaha

S. Platte R.

Platte R.

NEBRASKA

Republican R.

Solomon R.

COLORADO

Ft. Leavenworth

Abilene

Saline R.

Downer's Station

Ft. Hays

Ft. Riley

Kansas City

Smoky Hill stage route

Ft. Wallace

Smoky Hill R.

Lookout Station

Cheyenne Camp

Ft. Harker

Ft. Lyon

Pawnee Fk.

Arkansas R.

Arkansas R.

Ft. Larned

N

W   E

S

Ft. Dodge

KANSAS

UNORG.

Camp Supply

S. Canadian River

Antelope Hills

Cimarron R.

N. Canadian R.

Arkansas R.

Cheyenne Camp

Washita

N. Fork Red R.

Ft. Cobb

INDIAN TERRITORY

Washita R.

OUACHITA MTS.

TEXAS

Wichita Mtns.

Ft. Sill

Red R.

→ Hancock's War, April–July 1867

---▶ Washita Campaign, November 1868–March 1869

╟┼┼┼ Railroad up to fall of 1866

╳╳╳╳ Railroad after fall of 1866

0   50   100 miles

0   50   100 kilometers

household settled into a permanent home. It had a large porch, a room
in the back for Brown, and a sizable kitchen. Beyond the fort they could
shop for supplies at nearby Junction City.[17]

As a new regiment, the 7th Cavalry was still undergoing organization, and not all of the personnel had arrived. In 1866, cavalry regiments
consisted of twelve companies, each with no more than 100 enlisted men,
and usually far fewer. By the start of 1867, the 7th Cavalry would count
fifteen officers and 963 troopers. For many privates, joining the army was
a last resort; as one wrote, peacetime society considered the word *soldier*

"a synonym for all that is degrading and low." About half of them were immigrants, particularly Irish or German. Poorly paid, badly fed, subject to harsh discipline, they could still make fine troops if well led. "Each company rated a captain, a first lieutenant, and a second lieutenant, nearly always reduced to two or even one [officer] by details to detached service," the historian Robert Utley explains. "The field grades were a colonel, lieutenant colonel, and three majors. In theory each major commanded a battalion of four companies, although this rarely happened in practice." Rarely, because the overstretched peacetime army split up regiments to man small posts in the West and the Reconstruction South. The 7th Cavalry would serve as a complete unit only once in Custer's lifetime, with disastrous results. On the other hand, the roster of officers in a peacetime regiment remained extraordinarily stable, year after year.[18]

Custer found that some of his fellow officers had already arrived. Others (including Tom, now a first lieutenant transferred to the 7th Cavalry) trickled in over the next few months. Custer's senior subordinate was Maj. Alfred Gibbs, a jowly man with a mustache and goatee turning to gray. An 1846 graduate of West Point, he had served with Custer in the Cavalry Corps of the Army of the Potomac. Gibbs drilled and organized the men, and he and his wife provided the Custers with pleasant company.

When Capt. Albert Barnitz learned in January 1867 that he had been assigned to the 7th Cavalry, he wrote to his future wife, Jennie Platt, "Custer is Lieutenant Colonel of the Reg't . . . and in command! Then of course his amiable little wife, whom you would love, I think, will be there! Isn't that pleasant! I hope it will prove true." Barnitz, like all the other officers, was a Civil War veteran, and had proudly served in Custer's 3rd Division. Lt. Thomas B. Weir had been Custer's subordinate in Texas, along with Maj. Joel Elliott. Other key officers included Maj. Wyckliffe Cooper, Capt. Louis Hamilton, Capt. Robert M. West, Capt. Frederick W. Benteen, and Irish-born Capt. Myles Keogh, who had fought in the Papal army against Italian unification.[19]

Many of them were quite young. Elliott turned twenty-six in October 1866, the same age as Keogh. Hamilton was only twenty-two and Lt. William W. Cooke just twenty. They belonged to a generation that would dominate the officer corps for the next three decades; fully 42 percent of commissions in that period were issued within two years of Appomattox. Most had served in the U.S. Volunteers, and tended to resent what they saw as West Pointers' clubby, superior attitude. Worst of all, they were stuck. "The army moved into the long interwar period [ending with the Spanish-American War] with a large number of officers in the same age range, regardless of their new rank," writes the historian William Coffman. "Since the army did not increase in strength and because so many officers were in the same age group, there was little hope for advancement. Year in and year out they went about their company-level routines. . . . It is surprising that this situation did not cause more disharmony than it did."[20]

If disharmony in the 7th Cavalry began with anyone, it was with Captain Benteen, a soft-faced but bitter man.* He had performed well in the Civil War, and would prove himself a cool-headed combat officer in the years to come. He used political connections to get an appointment in the Regular Army, as many officers did, and made a hobby of lobbying for retroactive brevet promotions for his valor in the Civil War. Benteen's hostility toward Custer colored all of his later writings, making him the most untrustworthy of narrators. He would claim that his resentment began in his first interview with Custer at Fort Riley. He took offense at Custer's reading of his congratulatory order to the 3rd Division and at comments about Gen. James Wilson, Custer's old rival and Benteen's former commander. True or not, he hated Custer immediately.[21]

In the beginning, though, an outside observer detected little dissension at Fort Riley. "Came here Thursday evening," Jennie Barnitz wrote to her mother on February 26, 1867. "We were at once invited to Gen. Custer's." Jennie had just married Barnitz and traveled with him to Fort Riley. "Mrs. Custer is a charming woman, and very gay. We were constantly receiving calls from officers, some times a half dozen at a time. They are splendid—I should think all of them from the best class of society."[22]

On the day she wrote this letter, Custer assumed command of the 7th Cavalry, though the regiment's senior officer remained Col. Andrew Jackson Smith. An avuncular, bearded old horseman, Smith had graduated from West Point in 1838 and served throughout the West. He had fought well in the Civil War against the feared Nathan Bedford Forrest. Smith relied heavily on Custer from the outset, and handed the regiment off to him when he assumed command of the military District of the Upper Arkansas, taking Lt. Weir as adjutant. Custer would remain a *lieutenant* colonel—if he passed a test.[23]

ON NOVEMBER 9, 1866, CUSTER left Fort Riley for Washington. Having jumped to the Regular Army rank of lieutenant colonel, he had to

---

* Benteen remains a divisive figure for biographers and historians. Given Benteen's investment in his hatred of Custer, his reliability as a source is dubious. In these pages he will only be quoted or cited regarding matters of which he had firsthand knowledge, and where other sources substantiate his claims.

appear before an examining board that tested newly appointed officers. He passed easily, but the examination had a larger significance. It spoke to an ongoing change in the United States: the rise of professionalization.[24] West Point educated *and* a flagrant nepotist, Custer himself epitomized the transitional nature of this moment, as America transformed into an organizational society. These first proficiency tests pointed in the new direction.

Libbie did not accompany him. He spent more than a month away from her, returning on December 16.[25] The prolonged separation is striking. Perhaps they could not afford for Libbie to go, or felt that she could not abandon Darrah at Fort Riley. Or she may have wished to keep Darrah away from Armstrong. Curiously, none of his letters to Libbie during this trip survive in the public record. He made a habit of writing to her daily when they were apart, but she chose not to excerpt his correspondence in her memoirs or preserve it in the collections that she deposited in archives.

When he returned, she left. In Washington Armstrong had seen Adelaide Ristori, a world-renowned Italian actress on her first tour of the United States. Crowds filled theaters to see her even though she spoke no English. (According to her obituary, she would not perform a full play in English until 1882.) When Ristori appeared in St. Louis, Libbie went, leaving him for almost a week, despite their long separation.[26]

Winter ended. Spring began. Something was wrong between the Custers.

AT 8:30 IN THE MORNING on March 27, 1867, the "Hancock Expedition" marched out of Fort Riley. The long, slow-moving column consisted of 1,400 men, including seven companies of the 37th Infantry; Battery B of the 4th Artillery; eight companies of the 7th Cavalry; dozens of six-mule wagons; a canvas pontoon bridge; nine engineers; two federal agents for native nations of the Great Plains; a half-Cheyenne, half-French Canadian interpreter named Edmund Guerrier; and fifteen Delaware Indian scouts.

White civilian scouts rode as well. One was Deputy U.S. Marshal James Butler Hickok, better known as "Wild Bill." A blue-eyed man with a long, narrow nose, mustache, long hair, and wide-brimmed hat, he had signed on to work for the 7th Cavalry in January. He spent the next few months gambling in Junction City and enjoying the attention from a feature story in the February 1867 issue of *Harper's New Monthly Magazine*. It celebrated his 1865 gunfight with Dave Tutt in the town square of Springfield, Missouri. In the archetype of the mythical main-street walkdown, both men drew their revolvers and fired. Tutt missed. Hickok didn't.[27]

Custer commanded the cavalry. Colonel Smith, as head of the District of the Upper Arkansas, technically commanded the expedition, and Maj. Gen. Winfield S. Hancock commanded Smith. Custer had first met Hancock as a temporary aide at Williamsburg, the battle that established Hancock's reputation as a combat commander. That reputation had grown over the Civil War. Named to command of the Department of the Missouri, including Missouri, Kansas, Colorado, and New Mexico, Hancock was ordered to pacify the central Great Plains.[28]

This force was less than half the size of a full-strength brigade in the Civil War, but it "made a formidable appearance in the Indian Country," wrote Dr. Isaac Coates, a civilian from Pennsylvania who signed on for an adventure. He was an agreeable man with dark hair parted in the middle and brushed back, and a full beard. He first met Custer at Fort Riley and immediately liked him. "The first thing I noted about the General was his laugh," he wrote, "which, soon after I had entered the room, burst forth volcano-like until the very windows shook. There was an intellectual vigor, a whole-souled manliness, and an indomitable energy represented in that laugh." Libbie impressed him as well. "I was surprised to find with what fluency the ladies discussed the Indian Question."[29]

Custer rode his wife's horse, Custis Lee, past foot soldiers trudging in bitter cold, "a strong prairie wind blowing right in our faces, strong enough to blow a man over," an infantry officer wrote. In camp each night, Custer erected his conical Sibley tent apart from the others. He brought a barrel of his beloved apples and an efficient stove, which drew visitors, including Colonel Smith. But Custer visited no one in camp. He mostly kept to his own canvas quarters. He even had to apologize to Hancock for avoiding him.[30]

It was in the saddle, he told Libbie, that his blood moved again. "Contemplating these vast and apparently boundless prairies seems to give me new life." In Custer, though, introspection was not a natural and happy state. When confident, he boasted and mailed off his press clippings. His moody reflections on the expedition spoke to unease, even guilt. "Where I was once eager to acquire worldly honors and distinctions," he wrote, "my desire now is to make myself a man worthy of the blessings heaped upon me." By implication, he was not worthy yet.[31]

Major Gibbs teased him for shutting himself in each night to write to Libbie. One evening they crowded against each other at Custer's camp table. "It's a pretty thing that a man cannot write to his wife without being disturbed," Custer snapped. Gibbs replied, "Any man who writes to his wife once a day deserves to be disturbed."[32]

They marched south from the Smoky Hill River over the treeless, waterless plain to Fort Larned, "a green oasis in the Sahara of bleached grass," according to the reporter Henry M. Stanley (who would later presume that he had found Dr. Livingstone). A blizzard struck, piling up snow as thick as two feet deep. Dr. Coates wrote, "The thermometer of my romantic ideas of travel on the Plains was, indeed, now at zero."[33]

"You have been dreading an unsettled future, and perhaps separation," Custer wrote to Libbie on April 8; "but General Hancock said to me today, 'After you reach your [new] post . . . I will give you a chance to become settled.'" Hancock promised him command of Fort Garland in southern Colorado, he claimed. They would be together soon, he promised in letter after letter. War was unlikely, he thought. "Particularly do I desire peace, when I know that war means separation."

"I saw many strange and interesting sights today," he wrote, just before the snowstorm hit. The skeleton of a buffalo. An owl emerging from a prairie-dog village. "Today I also saw that peculiar natural phenomenon called 'mirage.'"[34]

AT 8 P.M. ON APRIL 12, Custer stood in front of a bright fire in full dress uniform, along with Smith, Hancock, Gibbs, and the other officers of the expedition. Fifteen tall men of the Cheyenne nation filed past them, solemnly shaking hands. "The Indians were dressed in various styles, many of them with the orthodox army overcoat, some with gorgeous red blankets, while their faces were painted and their bodies bedizened in all the glory of the Indian toilet," Stanley wrote. "Their ears were hanging large rings of brass; they wore armlets of silver, wrist rings of copper, necklaces of beads . . . breast ornaments of silver shields . . . and their scalp locks were adorned with a long string of thin silver disks."

Edward W. Wynkoop, the federal agent for the tribe, introduced Tall Bull and White Horse, their spokesmen, and they all sat on logs around the fire. Hancock stood, removed his coat, and spoke. The half-Cheyenne Edmund Guerrier translated as he went, a sentence at a time. Hancock soon reached his point.

"Now, I have a great many soldiers, more than all the tribes put together," he said. "I have heard that a great many Indians want to fight. Very well, we are here, and we come prepared for war. If you are for peace, you know the conditions; if you are for war, look out for its consequences." He demanded the return of captives, "white or black," and promised to punish both Indian and white violators of the peace. "We are building railroads, and building roads through the country. You must not let your young men stop them. . . . These roads will benefit the Indian as well as the white man, in bringing their goods to them cheaply and promptly. The steam car and the wagon train must run."

Hancock sat. Tall Bull silently lit a pipe, took a few puffs, then passed it to his colleagues. "With much dignity in his bearing," Stanley wrote, he stood in his red-and-black robe and shook Hancock's hand. "You sent for us. We came here. . . . You can go on any road. When we come on the road your young men must not shoot us." As Guerrier translated, he tapped his foot impatiently, "in a very defiant manner," according to Barnitz. Tall Bull briefly discussed a captured Indian boy whom Hancock had brought to return to his family, then returned to the main thrust of his remarks. "The buffalo are diminishing fast. The antelope that were plenty a few years ago are now few. When they will all die away we shall be hungry. We shall want something to eat, and we shall be compelled to come into the fort. Your young men must not fire on us. Whenever they see us they fire, and we fire on them."

Hancock interrupted him at one point to say that he was coming to their village with all his men. When Tall Bull finished, Hancock stood again. "We know the buffalo are going away. We cannot help it," he said. "The white men are becoming a great nation. You must keep your young men off the roads. Don't stop the trains and travelers on the roads, and you will not be harmed." He finished by saying, "I have spoken," and went back to his tent. The meeting ended.[35]

Hancock believed that he had been disrespected. The next morning, he marched his men west, along the river called Pawnee Fork, toward a large winter encampment of Southern Cheyennes and Oglala Lakotas. He wanted to intimidate them. The weather grew sunny and warm. Pawnee Killer, an Oglala leader, rode up with some warriors, followed by White Horse of the Cheyennes. All the leaders in the village would come in to talk the next morning, they said, indicating how high the sun would be in the sky. They agreed to spend the night in the camp.

Custer took *Harper's* artist Theodore Davis and went into the visiting Indians' tent uninvited. "My entrance and presence did not seem to disturb their stoicism or equanimity in the least," he wrote to Libbie. "All were seated upon the circumference of the tent upon buffalo robes. I made my way through the smoke to a vacant robe, and joined the circle, but did not 'swing round' it." They ignored him as they cooked meat over an open fire. When Custer left, they remained as opaque to him as ever.[36]

Early the next day, April 14, Pawnee Killer left, promising to get the other leaders. They never came. Furious, Hancock broke camp and advanced on the village. "We had gone but a few miles," Dr. Coates wrote, "when reaching the summit of a little hill, we beheld in the valley, a mile distant, several hundred Indian warriors approaching us. They were in a line. . . . Everything now looked like war."[37]

THE WAR THAT CUSTER would fight against "these dusky and certainly savage-looking chiefs," as he called them, had roots dating back to 1492.[38] Christopher Columbus called the natives of this hemisphere "Indians" to promote the idea that he had found a route to India. But any common name would have been foreign, imposed from the outside. In their multiplicity of languages and cultures, they had no shared identity except in relation to the newcomers from Europe.

Their various societies specialized to meet regional environmental demands, adapting to changing climate, new opportunities, and conflicts with neighbors. Custer confronted the nomadic peoples of the high plains—the elevated western half of the Great Plains. To Custer, these nations were exotic, alien, and isolated from the United States. This impression was false. From the moment they refounded their societies upon the horse—first introduced to North America by Spanish colonizers—they locked themselves into relationships with their European-derived neighbors. They depended upon transactions with them as much as on hunting bison (commonly called buffalo). Indeed, there was no separating the two.[39]

The Comanches of the Southern Plains pioneered their material culture. In the late 1600s, they first acquired horses and iron tools from the northern reaches of the Spanish empire. "The Spanish horses they pilfered in New Mexico and then rode onto the plains found a nearly perfect ecological niche on the southern grasslands," writes the historian Pekka Hämäläinen. These tough little horses descended from North African ancestors, bred to subsist on grazing and infrequent access to water. The Comanches built vast herds, transforming themselves into nomads to hunt the bison. "But," Hämäläinen adds, "there was another enticement: commerce."

Aggressively battling other nations, the Comanches seized a strategic position on the grasslands between the Spanish, French, and English empires. Comanches traded slaves seized in raids and bison meat and hides in return for iron tools, firearms, and corn. They controlled trade through their realm, warred against native neighbors to maintain their advantages, pillaged Mexico, and halted the expansion of American settlement in Texas. They amassed a "commercial empire" from the Arkansas River to the Rio Grande, writes Hämäläinen, reaching their peak of power in the 1840s.[40]

Other indigenous nations adopted their nomadic ways in the eighteenth and early nineteenth centuries. The Kiowas emerged as their closest allies. Arapahoes and Plains Apaches embraced the horse as well. In the north, the Lakotas, or Teton Sioux, moved onto the Great Plains grasslands from the wooded Great Lakes region.

So did the Cheyennes. Their tradition holds that a prophet, Sweet Medicine, held a four-year conclave with Maheo, the All Being, inside Naohavose, a Black Hills peak later called Bear Butte. "You may have horses," Maheo told Sweet Medicine. "You may even go with the Comanches to take them. But remember this: If you have horses everything will be changed for you forever. . . . You will have to have fights with other tribes, who will want your pasture land or the places where you hunt. You will have to have real soldiers, who can protect the people. Think, before you decide."[41]

Converting to a mounted culture dominated by the hunter and warrior, the Cheyennes migrated to the Central Plains between the Platte River to the north and the Arkansas to the south. They allied with the Arapahoes and fought the other high-plains tribes, the Comanches, Kiowas, and Lakotas. In 1840, these nations made peace at a grand meeting on the Arkansas River. As allies they warred against the low-plains tribes to the east, who practiced horticulture in permanent settlements and forayed onto the high plains seasonally to hunt—the Pawnees, Potawatomis, Omahas, Osages, and various nations removed from their eastern homes by the U.S. government and forced west, including Delawares, Creeks, Cherokees, and others. They fought to control trade and critical natural resources.[42]

White merchants came. Access to trading posts became so important that the Cheyennes split into Northern and Southern branches in the 1830s, largely according to whether they dealt with merchants on the Platte or the Arkansas. Traders provided ironware, gunpowder, and firearms, and demanded hides. After the beaver population collapsed around 1840, they wanted bison skins—hundreds of thousands each year.

The Indians' commercial slaughter of bison exacerbated the inherent environmental instability of nomadism. Drought and predators, particularly wolves, frequently caused dramatic declines in the bison population. The famously gigantic herds of buffalo that astonished newcomers, and made convenient targets for hunters, only gathered during the rutting period in the summer, when the short grass of the high plains was dense enough to sustain vast numbers of grazing animals. At other times they dispersed into smaller, more elusive herds. And the huge numbers of Indian ponies competed directly against the nomads' main prey for resources, Hämäläinen notes, since horse and bison ate the same grasses and had similar water needs.

The demands of bison hunting and horse herding forced each nation to disperse into small bands. The Cheyennes created a governing institution, the Council of Forty-Four, to maintain unity. They also created six warrior societies: Kit Foxes, Crazy Dogs, Elk Scrapers, Red Shields, Wolf Soldiers, and, most famous of all, the Dog Soldiers. Their members came from across the various bands. When a cholera epidemic killed half of the Flexed Leg band, the survivors joined the Dog Soldiers, giving it a mixed character as both a voluntary military society and the community of a band. These societies—the Dog Soldiers in particular—emerged as centers of militancy, pressing for an armed response to encroachments on the plains.[43]

Just as the indigenous nations were misleadingly grouped together as "Indians," so too have the people of the United States in this period been oversimplified as "whites." Of course whites predominated, but black faces appeared almost everywhere in the West, particularly after the deployment of the new regiments of black regulars, who came to be known as the "buffalo soldiers." All groups in the nineteenth century commonly used "Americans" as a national term for U.S. citizens and soldiers. None of these labels is entirely satisfactory, yet they cannot be entirely avoided.

These Americans, white and black, began to settle the eastern fringe of the Great Plains with the passage of the Kansas-Nebraska Act in 1854. As of 1867, they had seized large sections of the lands of the low-plains nations, but their zone of occupation had not yet reached the high plains.[44] The immediate threats they posed to the Cheyennes and their allies were more invasive. One was disease, including smallpox, whooping cough, and cholera. The other was migration—not into but through their country. Starting in 1843 with the "Great Migration" on the Oregon Trail, surging with the California gold rush in 1849, and picking up again in 1859 with the discovery of gold in the Colorado mountains, tens of thousands of people burst across the plains.

The migrants followed the rivers that ran west to east—the Platte, Republican, Smoky Hill, and Arkansas, in particular. These and other narrow river valleys comprised only 7 percent of the high plains, but they were crucial for the survival of both bison and Indian horses. These ribbons of precious resources striped the dry grasslands, providing water, stands of trees, grazing (including cottonwood bark), and shelter from the weather in the depths of winter. But they were vulnerable. The nomads' winter encampments shunted bison herds to marginal places, putting pressure on their population. The American travelers tipped the precarious balance, if it can be called a balance. They cut down trees for fuel, polluted the water, killed or drove off game, and brought their own livestock that ate up grass and other forage.

Even worse, the army established permanent posts at the most desirable points on the rivers—"protective islands," as the historian Elliott West calls them. Fifteen forts went up in the half-dozen years after the start of the Colorado gold rush in 1859. The garrisons consumed resources all year round, turning the richest locations into dead zones. They attracted passing migrants and freighters, further devastating their surroundings. The Butterfield Overland Despatch stagecoach and freight-wagon line began service along the Smoky Hill in 1865, with regularly spaced stations that duplicated the process.[45]

Then there were railroads. Fixed pieces of infrastructure, the symbiosis of the federal government and business corporations, they crept west from Omaha and Kansas City, bound for San Francisco and Denver, respectively. General Sherman, head of the Military Division of the Missouri, described their significance on October 1, 1867.

> They aid us in our military operations by transporting troops and stores rapidly across a belt of land hitherto only passed in the summer by slow trains drawn by oxen, dependent on the grass for food; and all the States and Territories west have a direct dependence on these roads for their material supplies. When these two great thoroughfares reach the base of the Rocky mountains, and when the Indian title to roam at will over the country lying between them is extinguished, then the solution to the most complicated question of Indian hostilities will be comparatively easy, for this belt of country will naturally fill up with our own people.[46]

It was an astute if brutal analysis. In private, though, Sherman worried. On June 11 he wrote to Grant about the difficulty of protecting the railroads and transit corridors. "The claims for guards at every stage station, every telegraphic hut . . . will leave us with little or nothing to carry war into the enemy's country." He wanted to go on the offensive. As Robert Utley writes, no army officer thought forts alone offered "a long-term solution of the Indian problem. . . . Most [were] so weakly manned as to accomplish little except to show the flag."[47]

The Cheyennes and their allies knew better. Those undermanned forts, wagon trains, stagecoach lines, and railways were making life on the high plains untenable. Nor were the Indians ignorant of the size and power of the United States. In 1863 a delegation of high-plains leaders traveled to New York and Washington, D.C., where they met President Lincoln. They saw the armed might of the fully mobilized republic.

They found themselves in a terrible dilemma. If they did nothing, in the long run they were doomed. If they fought back, in the short run they might be doomed. Their leaders debated their options endlessly. Some signed the successive treaties that restricted residence and hunting to defined zones, in return for food and supplies. Others, especially the Dog Soldiers, committed themselves to nomadism and armed resistance. The militants were bolstered by a massacre at Sand Creek of the Southern Cheyenne band led by Black Kettle. In 1864, he and his people had reported as requested to Fort Lyon in southeastern Colorado. On November 29, two volunteer Colorado cavalry regiments, led by Col. John M. Chivington, attacked. The soldiers murdered 150 men, women, and children, mutilating many of the dead.[48]

Young men from virtually every Cheyenne band took part in retaliatory raids. The fighting quieted before the Hancock expedition set out in March 1867, but the Indians' existential dilemma remained. Satanta, a militant leader among the Kiowas, explained it to General Hancock later that spring. "All tribes are my brothers," he said, speaking of the allied nations of the high plains. "This country here is old, and it all belongs to them. But you are cutting off the timber, and now the country is of no account at all." He complained of migrants' water consumption and the loss of wild game. But he admitted that he didn't know how to respond. "Other tribes are very foolish. They make war and are unfortunate, and then call upon the Kiowas to aid them and I don't know what to think about it."[49]

Sherman had ordered Hancock "to go among the Cheyennes, Arapahos, and Kiowas . . . and notify them that if they want war they can have it now; but if they decline the offer, then impress on them that they must stop their insolence and threats." In other words, the point of the expedition was to crush their pride.[50]

"THEY WERE FORMED IN A LINE, with intervals, extending about a mile," Custer wrote to Libbie. It was the afternoon of April 14, 1867, near a winter encampment of Southern Cheyennes, including Dog Soldiers, and some Oglala Lakotas. The troops under Hancock confronted some 300 warriors. "The sun was shining brightly, and as we arrived the scene was the most picturesque and novel I have ever witnessed," Custer added. "What rendered the scene so striking and so magnificent were the gaudy colors of the dress and trappings of the chiefs and warriors."[51]

A parley interrupted the seemingly inevitable fight. Hancock insisted on camping near the Indians. The Cheyennes who met with him returned to their line, which immediately turned about and withdrew. Custer and his men pursued. "Notwithstanding that the cavalry marched at its most rapid pace, there was not an Indian to be seen after marching five miles," he wrote.[52]

A dozen miles away they found the village—an impressive collection of nearly 300 tepees, or lodges, in a curve of the Pawnee Fork, sheltered amid cottonwoods. A group of Cheyenne men approached and told Hancock that the women and children had fled. Roman Nose, a prominent Dog Soldier, asked him if he had not heard of the Sand Creek Massacre. Hancock insisted that they return, so he could properly intimidate them. He sent Guerrier, the translator, to be sure that the men did not sneak away as well.[53]

That night an orderly appeared at the flap of Custer's Sibley tent and said Hancock wanted him. In the headquarters tent, Hancock told him that Guerrier had found that "the Indians . . . were saddling up to leave about sunset," Custer wrote to Libbie. Hancock wanted the 7th Cavalry to detain them.[54]

Barnitz heard Custer ride up to his tent and ask for him. "I knew very well, from the tone of his voice, that something was to be done, which required haste and secrecy, and so I got up at once, drew on my boots, and reported for orders." Custer told him to wake his men quietly but quickly. "In fifteen minutes our four squadrons of cavalry were all in line," William W. Cooke wrote to his mother. "Not a word was spoken over a whisper. We moved slowly and without noise towards the Indian camp."

By midnight Custer had deployed the troops in a cordon around the village. He led a small party, including Guerrier and Dr. Coates, in to investigate. He could see in the moonlight that the lodges still stood among the trees and fires still burned. He told Guerrier to announce that they had come in peace. Still the village was silent. One of the group dismounted and entered a lodge. He called out, "Gone, by Jupiter." Going from lodge to lodge, they found the entire camp had been abandoned.[55]

Barnitz and his men remained to hold the village as the rest of the regiment returned. "On entering the [Indian] camp I was astonished at its magnitude and magnificence!" he wrote to his wife. "Each tent would contain 20 or 30 persons." An inventory ordered by Hancock found 272 lodges, 814 buffalo robes, 283 saddles, 243 whetstones, 165 frying pans, 49 coffee mills, as well as brass kettles, spades, bridles, ropes, hatchets, crowbars, horn spoons, tin cups and plates, and much more.[56]

Jesse H. Leavenworth, federal agent for the Comanches and Kiowas, was astounded that Hancock "marched his column right up to the Indian village." Even Custer grasped that they feared another Sand Creek. Leavenworth added, "I am fearful that the result of all this will be a general war."

Hancock had no legal or treaty grounds for detaining the Cheyennes or Lakotas. He admitted to Sherman that they committed "no hostilities." But he saw their flight as a "provocation," an act of "bad faith." He ordered Custer to pursue at daylight.[57]

At 5 a.m. on April 15, Custer led the eight companies of cavalry out of camp, followed by a train of supply wagons. Guerrier rode along, as did six Delaware and three white scouts, including Wild Bill Hickok. The Delawares found the fleeing Indians' trail, leading to the northwest. Custer's column passed still-smouldering fires and worn-out ponies. The Delawares spotted Cheyenne or Lakota scouts watching them from hilltops. "We continued to gain on them and were so close that, although the heat of the sun was quite high, the earth disturbed by the feet of their ponies and by dragging their lodge poles was still damp and fresh," Custer wrote the next day.

They noticed smaller trails diverging off the main track, which "gradually grew less, and more faint," he reported. They lost it entirely thirty-five miles from the village. On the horizon he saw puffs of smoke rise into the sky—"signal smokes"—yet none was closer than ten miles away.[58] After a few hours of rest, he ordered a march to the Smoky Hill River, twenty-one miles to the north. On the way they mistook an elk herd for Indians, then did the same with a bison herd. The prospect of a buffalo hunt thrilled him. "General Custer was wild with excitement, and yelled as if he was going into a desperate cavalry charge," wrote Coates. They killed two and pushed on.[59]

Custer rode ahead of the column with his chief bugler and his dogs. Spotting some antelope, he spurred Custis Lee into a gallop. Four miles later he gave up. The column and his bugler were now far behind him and one dog was missing—gone forever. Then he saw a large, solitary bison. He chased it for three miles, then came up on its left. At full gallop, he drew his revolver, cocked the hammer, and aimed it at the animal's side. It turned on him. Startled, Custis Lee veered sharply left. Custer grabbed the reins with both hands. The cocked pistol went off, sending a bullet into the horse's brain, killing the animal instantly. "I was thrown heels over head, clean over Lee, but, strange to say, I received not a scratch or bruise," he wrote to Libbie. "This is the second dangerous fall I have had within ten days." Regaining his feet, he was relieved to see the huge buffalo merely glare at him for a moment, then amble off.

With his men somewhere over the horizon, he trudged over the treeless plain, hoping to intersect the column's course. Finally he saw the white tops of the wagons cresting a rise of ground a couple of miles off.

He sat and waited. When they reached him he borrowed a mount as a detail retrieved his saddle. Killing his horse embarrassed him—deserting his men to indulge himself did not. He tried *again* the next time he saw a bison. This time he succeeded. The men, on the other hand, were exhausted. "As soon as we halted every man threw himself on the ground & fell asleep," William Cooke wrote.[60]

At Downer's Station on the Overland Mail route along the Smoky Hill River, two men told Custer of rumors that Indians—Sioux, they thought—had attacked Lookout Station to the east. With this uncertain information, Custer reported, "There is no doubt that the depredations committed at Lookout were by some of the same Indians who deserted their lodges on Pawnee Fork."[61]

On April 18 Custer advanced thirty-five miles east to Lookout Station. Riding in the lead, he reached it ahead of his men. He "found the station house, stable, & haystack a pile of ashes, a few pieces of timber being still burning. The bodies of the three men were lying near the ruins," he reported. "The hair was singed from their heads, the skin & flesh burned from their breasts and arms and their intestines torn out."[62]

The next day they reached Fort Hays. The column's horses were debilitated. Unlike Indian ponies, they could not subsist on grazing alone. The cavalry had to carry forage with them, grain and hay hauled in wagons. Custer expected a large supply at Fort Hays. He found almost nothing. He asked Wild Bill to ride overnight on a fresh mule to request forage from Fort Harker. "He was armed with two revolvers (and a carbine I loaned him for the trip)," Albert Barnitz wrote of Wild Bill, "and [he] thought he was good for a dozen Indians at all events"—meaning, of course, that if he were attacked he could kill a dozen hostile Cheyennes or Lakotas before he died. He made it through, but Harker had little to send.

"It is with regret that I turn from the pursuit of the Indians, who have just gone north and who are the perpetrators of the massacre at Lookout Station and of other depredations," Custer reported to Hancock. He had hoped for peace and a rapid reunion with Libbie. Ironically, Custer's report on the attack at Lookout Station convinced Hancock to destroy the abandoned village. Smith, Wynkoop, and Leavenworth argued against it, but Hancock insisted. He wiped out the homes and possessions of thousands on the flimsiest evidence. The inevitable outbreak of war that followed put Custer in an impossible situation. Unable to see Libbie because of the fighting, unable to fight for lack of forage, he was stuck.[63]

"WAVES OF FLAME" SWEPT ACROSS the plain toward Fort Riley. They terrified Libbie Custer. "In an incredibly short time we were overshadowed with a dark pall of smoke," she wrote. The soldiers deployed in a line, beating out the fire before it could reach the buildings. Yet those same men frightened Libbie far more than the conflagration.[64]

"I had seen with dismay that the cavalry were replaced by negro infantry, and found that they were to garrison the post for the summer," she later wrote. They were from the 38th Infantry, one of six Regular Army regiments staffed by black enlisted men. "The early days of their soldiering were a reign of terror to us women, in our lonely, unprotected homes," Libbie wrote. "I was very much afraid of a negro soldier."[65]

Libbie hinted at the nature of her "terror" with the phrase, "*in our lonely, unprotected homes.*" She assumed they would rape her. Anna Darrah, she wrote to Armstrong, "has loaded her pistol to protect us" from "a negro." Libbie believed in the racial stereotype of the black man as sexual predator of white women. Indeed, the racism in her letters and memoirs grew increasingly frantic.

She invariably called these men "darkies." She compared them to "apes" and "monkey acrobats." The "black-faced and shiney-eyed," she wrote, were, "as usual, slack and careless." She took offense when some off-duty men danced as another patted out a beat, complaining, "[W]e seemed transformed into a disconnected minstrel show." As she sat in church, depressed over her husband, "two darkies who sat behind me began to sing some of the service," one humming as the other "shouted in regular camp-meeting style." She scornfully assumed they were ignorant of the lyrics. "If I had not been so forlorn, I would have thought it too funny to refrain from laughing at."[66]

Many were indeed fresh recruits, in a new regiment still establishing its identity. As with all raw troops, some broke protocol on occasion, or consumed their pay or rations too soon; to this day officers struggle to keep young soldiers away from payday lenders who flourish on the outskirts of bases. At that very moment white troops in the field committed misdeeds worse than any at Fort Riley. But Libbie interpreted everything in terms of race.

"I had known enough of their life, while in Texas and Louisiana, to realize what an irresponsible, child's existence it was," she wrote. "Entirely dependent on someone's care, and without a sense of obligation of any kind, they were exempt from the necessity of thinking about the future." This was how she defined the killing stress of being enslaved: the threat of random whipping, the struggle to care for one's own family in the moments away from serving the master, the realistic fear that a spouse or child might be taken away and sold, the constant deprivation, the fear of being caught communicating between plantations, the slave-catching patrols, and the frantic few hours, if one was lucky, spent earning a little money by selling one's labor on Sundays. They had worked, planned, schemed, struggled, and seized the chance at freedom when they could. They had taken care of themselves as Libbie never had.[67]

Most white Americans shared Libbie's views—yet this was also the moment when African Americans began to challenge them. After decades of slave owners' propaganda that blacks could not manage their own affairs, they were organizing politically, starting schools, demanding to be heard. Many white Northerners who went to the South saw this, and learned that the freed people were as fully human as themselves.

The black regiments brought this revolution to Kansas. African American men saw military service as an assertion of citizenship. The chaplain of the black 10th Cavalry said the troops "are possessed of the notion that the colored people of the whole country are more or less affected by their conduct in the Army." They wished to be full participants in the society they had helped to build as slaves. Black recruits were more likely than whites to see the military as a career; their units' desertion rates were far lower and reenlistment rates higher than those in white regiments. Barred by the Johnson administration from deployment in the South on Reconstruction duty, they served year after year in the West, becoming some of the most effective troops in the Indian wars. But all this was lost on Libbie, even though she had her own tutor living and working along-side her, outspoken and righteous.[68]

"Eliza kept my sympathies constantly aroused," Libbie recalled. "Her whole soul was in the wrongs, real or fancied, of her race." In 1867, Libbie could not see those wrongs. She felt vulnerable and isolated. The sheer irrationality of her attitude flummoxed Eliza Brown. One day, as black troops protested the withholding of part of their rations, she saw that Libbie was terrified. "Lord, Miss Libbie," she said, tapering *Lord* so that it sounded like *law*, "they won't tech you." There was no persuading Libbie that African American men were not congenital rapists, but Brown reasoned with her. "You done wrote too many letters for 'em, and they's got too many good vittles in your kitchen ever to 'sturb you."

"To me she was worth a corporal's guard," Libbie wrote of Brown, "and could not be equaled as a defender, solacer, and general manager of our dangerous situations—indeed, of all our affairs." This statement put Libbie in the role society expected of a respectable white woman: one of vulnerability, frailty, dependency—femininity, as they saw it. Yet it was also a frank admission that this diminutive young black woman, ostensibly Libbie's inferior, dominated their relationship. Brown had more fortitude and control over her place in the world than Libbie ever had. It's startling to realize that Libbie wrote this even though Tom Custer remained in the same house as he recovered from rheumatism. He did not reassure her as Brown did.

Part of Libbie's problem was that she had been dropped into Brown's world when Fort Riley suddenly became a black community. Brown "profited by the presence of the negro troops," Libbie admitted. As usual, Brown exploited her control of the Custers' larder for her own social advantage. Men from the regiment "waited on her assiduously, and I suspect they dined daily in our kitchen, as long as their brief season of favor lasted," Libbie added. Some tried to cultivate Brown by giving gifts to Libbie; one planted a garden for her. The illiterate asked her to write letters for them to family and girlfriends (though black regiments organized well-attended literacy classes). Libbie did the same for Brown, who would learn to read and write in time.

As the post transformed into a black town, Brown gained a rich social life. She would change out of her work clothes and call on the fort's African American women, many employed as laundresses. Here, too, she asserted her independence. One night she came back "boiling with rage," Libbie wrote to Armstrong. Brown had heard a husband tell his wife to light his pipe. "Eliza says managing men like that is too great drudgery to please her."[69]

Libbie would later blame her discomposure on Armstrong's absence. She missed him, she would write. No doubt she did. Yet the core problem posed by their separation was how it prevented them from resolving the crisis in their marriage.

Shirley Leckie observes that Armstrong's letters to his wife reveal ongoing trouble. Even those that Libbie later chose to publish hint at his emotional distress. On April 25, he wrote that he had been uncharacteristically praying to God "that I may be made worthy, and be led to pursue such a moral life" so as to be an example to others. He included a poem on sin and redemption. It read, in part, *"Blest, indeed, is he who never fell . . . / Strong is temptation, willing are the feet / That follow pleasure; manifold her snares / . . . Pardon, not wrath, is God's best attribute."* When he did not hear from her, he wrote, "Something wrong seemed a-brewing."[70]

Leckie examined letters then held by the Custer family (now apparently in the hands of private collectors), and found even clearer evidence of persistent "dissension." He was afraid of losing her because of his sins. "You know that I promised never to give you *fresh* cause for regret by attentions paid to other girls," he wrote (emphasis added). He wished that she could "read my innermost heart and see the disgust" he felt at the memory of other women. Curiously, he referred not to a single affair or flirtation, but to at least two. His love for Libbie, he wrote, drove "all

thoughts even of *them* from my mind. . . . I never thought of a single girl
to whom I ever paid the slightest attention with any feeling but that of
supreme indifference, and without wishing to see them, have cared nothing if I never met either of them again."[71]

Guilt explains Armstrong's agitation to unite with Libbie as separation alone does not. After all, he had voluntarily spent much of 1866 apart
from her, and she had left him to spend a week in St. Louis. Nor did he
express any particular fears for her as Indian attacks spread across the
plains; indeed, he urged her again and again to cross an active war zone
to join him at Fort Hays, and later at Fort Wallace. Guilt can be a shattering emotion for anyone. How much more so for a man who assiduously
cultivated an image of gallantry?

Something even worse than guilt may have goaded him: the fear of
discovery. In the same family papers, Leckie discovered a later letter to
Armstrong written by "Anna." She told him that she had just heard a love
song. "I am so forcibly reminded of you that I cannot resist the temptation of telling you how I wish you were here," she wrote. If he did have
an affair with Anna Darrah, even if they merely flirted with infidelity, his
anxiety to unite with Libbie makes sense. Every day he remained in the
field—every day that Libbie and Darrah spent together in his absence—he
was powerless to prevent his wife from discovering his sins against her.
Once he rejoined her, he would regain a sense of control, and might begin
to repair the damage.[72]

For there was already damage. The problem went deeper than any particular flirtation or even infidelity. It was in his nature to seek the attention of women. Libbie's alienation forced him to look hard at himself, and
the possible cost of how he behaved. Under orders to march back into the
wilderness, he could do nothing to save their marriage.

"The inaction to which I am subjected now, in our present halt, is
almost unendurable," he wrote on April 22. He said he was reading
Anatomy of Melancholy by Robert Burton. He demanded she come to Fort
Hays—otherwise he would "try to kill time by killing Indians," as if the
campaign were a sidelight to his marriage.[73]

Sherman intervened. He appeared at Fort Riley in May and personally escorted Libbie, Darrah, Brown, and Tom Custer to Fort Harker.
Colonel Smith took them to Fort Hays on May 17. But things only grew
worse.[74]

TO CAPT. ALBERT BARNITZ, the wait at Fort Hays began well. Thirty-
two years old, with a broad mustache and curling, bristling hair brushed
back from his forehead, Barnitz was an enthusiastic man, prone to ending

his sentences with exclamation points. He was inclined to think well of Custer.[75] The cavalry camped outside the fort, a cluster of "rude log and adobe huts," as General Hancock described it, on the banks of Big Creek. Custer organized footraces, horse races, and a bison-hunting contest. He told Barnitz they would be there for three weeks, and he had sent for Libbie; Barnitz's new bride, Jennie, could come as well.

Barnitz informed his wife of all this on May 4. On May 6, his tone changed. Custer required a dress parade every evening. He demanded perfection in cleaning the camp. He banned swearing—an order he "rigidly enforced," Barnitz wrote. "General Custer has become 'billious' notwithstanding! He appears to be mad about something, and is very much on his dignity!" Custer took offense at Petroleum V. Nasby's columns in recently delivered newspapers. Nasby, pseudonym of the political satirist David Locke, mocked Custer's role in the Swing Around the Circle in a trademark exaggerated vernacular. And Barnitz heard that Hancock was irritated with Custer as well.

Theodore Davis, the artist for *Harper's*, wrote years later that Custer was "sombre." Writing at the time, Barnitz used the word "obstreperous." Most of the officers pretended to be sick to avoid serving as officer of the day so they would not have to make the arrests he continually demanded for petty or nonexistent crimes. Custer ordered a rapid march to Lookout Station, hoping to catch hostile Indians reported there, but he found nothing. Frustrated, he arrested Barnitz for an imaginary offense.[76] By May 15, Barnitz seemed on the verge of mutiny. He wrote,

> General Custer is very injudicious in his administration, and spares no effort to render himself generally obnoxious. I have utterly lost all the little confidence I ever had in his ability as an officer—and all admiration for his character, as a man, and to speak the plain truth I am thoroughly *disgusted* with him! He is the most complete example of a petty tyrant I have ever seen. You would be filled with utter amazement, if I were to give you a few instances of his cruelty to the men, and discourtesy to the officers.

Two days later he wrote that six enlisted men were caught buying canned fruit in the fort, hoping to stave off the scurvy now sweeping the camp. They were away for less than an hour, and missed no roll call or duty. Yet Custer ordered their heads shaved on one side and had them carted through the camp. "Tyrannical," Barnitz wrote. By contrast, Gibbs enforced discipline without being "a martinet, like Custer."[77]

In Texas, Custer had also punished with humiliation. This approach to discipline came from deep within his character. He was complex. He could be emotionally sensitive. He had taken pity on enemy civilians, dead and wounded comrades, and former slaves whose backs told the history of whipping in keloid Braille. He loved the theater, which is the mimetic experience of others' lives. Yet he was a practical joker, finding amusement in causing embarrassment or pain. He had a faculty for sympathy, but it had a faulty switch. When it malfunctioned, he saw no farther than himself. It may be why he was so good at killing. But it served him poorly at Fort Hays.

Libbie arrived on May 17. Custer set up the new arrivals in a canvas complex some 200 or 300 yards away from the main camp. Barnitz stayed away, wanting to be "independent entirely!" But when his wife, Jennie, arrived, they too tented together beside Big Creek.

In her memoir, Libbie gave few details about this long-awaited reunion, though she insisted she was happy. On June 1 Custer finally ordered the men to move out. He himself lingered until midnight, when he rode off with four Delaware scouts and "Medicine Bill" Comstock. Eliza approached him as he mounted and shook his hand. "Ginnel, I don't like to see you goin' off in this wild country, at this hour of night," she told him. He had to go, he said. "Take care of Libbie, Eliza."[78]

LIBBIE, ANNA, AND ELIZA REMAINED in camp on Big Creek. It nearly killed them. On June 5, Libbie and Darrah went on a walk outside Fort Hays with Lieutenant Weir. A sentinel mistook them for Indians and opened fire. They dove for cover in a dip in the ground. Weir crawled to the fort to stop the firing, and the women returned safely.

Two days later a thunderstorm erupted. "The whole air was filled with electricity," Jennie Barnitz wrote. "The thunder I cannot describe. Much heavier than cannonading, & so very near us." Rain pounded the tents of the wives and married couples, now clustered together on a rise above the nearly dry Big Creek. At three o'clock in the morning, "Smith came to our tent & screamed, 'For God's sake Barnitz get up, we are under water,'" she wrote. The shallow creek had become "a mighty rushing river, & I think I never saw so strong a current."

The knoll where they camped became an island. They could hear the screams of men swept away in the current close by. Libbie desperately tried to untie a rope from a tent stake to save them. Eliza ran to her and shouted over the storm. "Miss Libbie, there's a chance for us with one man. He's caught in the branches of a tree; but I've seen his face and he's alive. He's most all of him under water, and the current is a-switchin' him about so he can't hold out long." She offered her clothesline. They made a loop and showed it to the man in a flash of lightning, then threw it to him, missed, threw it again, and again. He finally caught it and they pulled. Brown got into the water up to her waist, and they finally pulled him free. Brown recalled that they saved two more that night. As many as nine others drowned, by Jennie Barnitz's count.

The water dropped rapidly the next day. Gibbs believed the danger had passed, so they remained in their camp. Another storm burst over them that night. As the creek rose once again, the Barnitzes dressed and went to Libbie's tent. They found her calm. "Well we will all go down together. I am glad the General doesn't know of it," she told them. But they survived this night too.

The flooding caused them to exit the camp. The fort itself was abandoned, and a new Fort Hays was later positioned a dozen miles farther up Big Creek. On June 16, Smith took all the women in ambulances to Fort Harker. Shortly afterward Libbie, Darrah, and Brown returned to Fort Riley, farther from Armstrong than ever.[79]

CUSTER'S DOWNFALL BEGAN on June 1, 1867. For all of his personal difficulties, for all his petty cruelty within his regiment, his superiors did not fault his conduct. That changed after he set out on the march that ended seven weeks later in his arrest.[80]

On May 3 and again on the 21st, Smith had ordered Custer to march north to Fort McPherson on the Platte River, then west to Fort Sedgwick, then south to Fort Wallace. "The object of the expedition is to hunt out and chastise the Cheyennes and that portion of the Sioux who are their allies between the Smoky Hill and the Platte," Smith wrote.[81] It was clear language—and Custer ignored it.

Custer reached Fort McPherson on June 10, after a hard 229-mile march. As the men made camp, six Lakotas rode up. They included Pawnee Killer, the Oglala leader who had previously tricked Hancock. A tall man with narrow eyes, a long nose, and a wide mouth, he wore a high-crowned hat with a feather tucked in the band. He claimed to be peaceful, blamed the Cheyennes for recent attacks, and offered to bring his band in and remain under army protection. The Oglalas were amused by the wild animals kept as pets by the cavalrymen, including a tame antelope named Little Bill. Custer agreed to Pawnee Killer's proposal. He provided sugar, coffee, and hard bread, and let them go.[82]

Custer did not want to fight. He wanted to see Libbie again, but he also had professional reasons, which he had enumerated a month earlier in a letter to his wife.

Wo be unto these Indians, if I ever overtake them! The chances are, however, that I shall not see any of them, it being next to impossible to overtake them when they are forewarned and expecting us, as they now are. . . . I regard the outrages that have been committed lately as not the work of a tribe, but of small and irresponsible parties of young men, who are eager for war. The stampede of the Indians from the village I attributed entirely to fear. . . . My opinion is, that we are not yet justified in declaring war.[83]

"If you have faith in Pawnee Killer, which I have not, hold him and three of his men as hostages, then send the others out with two of your companies to bring in the other Sioux at once," Sherman wrote to Custer from Fort Sedgwick. The general had waited impatiently for Custer's arrival on the Platte, and was irritated at his parley. He rushed to McPherson, but Pawnee Killer had already disappeared, and did not return.

Sherman blamed Pawnee Killer's band for numerous attacks. But personal guilt mattered little to him—the problem, he thought, was the Indians' very existence. On June 11 he wrote to Grant,

It is an inevitable conflict of races, one that must occur where a stronger is gradually displacing a weaker. The Indians are poor and proud. They are tempted beyond the power of resistance to steal of the herds and flocks they see grazing so peacefully in the valley. To steal they sometimes must kill. We in our time cannot discriminate—all look alike, talk alike, and under the same passions act alike, and to get the rascals, we are forced to include all. . . . Hostilities between the races will continue till the Indians are all killed or taken to a country where they can be watched.

Those hostilities frustrated him—even worse than fighting Nathan Bedford Forrest, he wrote. He told Stanton, "Fifty hostile Indians will checkmate three thousand soldiers." It was best to "get them out as soon as possible," whether "coaxed out . . . or killed."[84]

Custer and Sherman were both wrong, though they each had insights. They were correct in their military assessments. The Cheyennes and Lakotas possessed superior mobility and knowledge of the terrain, and benefited from a very low force-to-space ratio. These advantages allowed them to conduct asymmetrical warfare, striking the army where it was weak with surprise raids and escaping safely. Custer was correct that Hancock had needlessly provoked the current fighting. But Sherman was wrong to think the attacks could go on forever, or resulted from "temptation." And Custer was wrong to blame merely "irresponsible . . . young men."

Instead of the irrational savages these officers imagined, the Cheyennes, Lakotas, and their allies clearly understood the threats they faced. Armed resistance was a rational policy option, quite apart from the spontaneous actions of individual warriors. Their existence was based on war. They had won their lands in fierce aggression against other peoples (as Pawnee Killer's very name testified). Signing treaties had only brought more pressure on the critical river valleys. It was natural to think that force—a familiar tool—might work where diplomacy had failed. To the north, the Oglala leaders Red Cloud and Crazy Horse orchestrated attacks along the Bozeman Trail; these would help convince the U.S. government to abandon the trail and its forts.[85]

Sherman saw Pawnee Killer as treacherous. From Pawnee Killer's point of view, his deception of Custer was a ruse, entirely appropriate in an unequal war for survival. More than a mere trick, his maneuver was strikingly courageous; to execute it, he had had to place himself in Custer's power. It revealed Pawnee Killer's sense of humor, too. He rode right into the enemy camp, thoroughly hoodwinked his opponent, and even convinced Custer to issue him supplies. Then he left Custer to wait around uselessly as the Oglalas trotted away. It was funny.

When Custer realized that Pawnee Killer had fooled him, as Sherman predicted, it added to his accumulating frustrations. Nothing was quite right. His brother Tom finally joined him in the field, but something about Tom's "conduct"—most likely his drinking—aggravated him. Always drawn to theatrics, to the exotic, Custer dressed in full frontier style: buckskin suit, twin revolvers belted at his waist (butts forward, as Wild Bill wore them), knee-high moccasins fringed along the calves, along with his usual long hair and low-crowned, wide-brimmed hat. The outfit highlighted his failures as a plainsman. He repeatedly lost Indian trails, shot his own horse twice again that year, and mistook an elk herd for the enemy. He had yet to fight a single skirmish.[86]

"Killing Indians" eluded him. Death did not. Before reaching Fort McPherson, someone burst in as Custer ate with Tom, and told them that Wyckliffe Cooper had gotten drunk and shot himself. The Custers ran to his tent and found him on his knees and face, blood pooling on the ground. Increasingly distressed, Custer anxiously insisted that Libbie meet him at Fort Wallace.

Marching west, he arrived at the headwaters of the Republican River on June 21, entering the heartland of the Cheyennes and Oglalas. On June 24, an Indian war party shot a sentinel at his camp and tried to stampede his horses. The troopers turned out to fight. It was Custer's first chance to wage a battle with his elusive foe. Instead, he sent his interpreter to signal for a talk. The man rode forward in a zigzag, the sign for a truce, then he rode in a circle, trotted forward, and circled again—the sign for a parley. Custer and a half-dozen officers met a like number of Oglala men.

Their leader was Pawnee Killer. The sight of him should have made Custer wary. Pawnee Killer had fooled him once before, and Hancock before that. But Custer still hoped to avoid fighting, which gave the Lakota leader a chance to play his funniest joke yet. Of course he wanted peace, he assured Custer, and he invited the troopers to follow him back to his camp. The men of the 7th Cavalry saddled up and rode behind the Oglalas, who picked up their pace and soon outdistanced the soldiers. Custer lost the trail. He gave up the chase and turned back, only to discover Pawnee Killer's punch line: as one man wrote, they "found Indians had been in our camp while we were away." The Oglalas had circled back to pillage their tents.

Alarmed, Custer sent reinforcements to escort a supply train expected from Fort Wallace. Then he sent more. It was a wise decision, for Pawnee Killer could be as lethal as he was humorous. The troops arrived in time to save the wagons from a siege. Custer turned north toward Fort Sedgwick and marched through searing heat and fierce fields of prickly pear cactus, which caused the dogs to howl in pain when they leaped from the wagons. Custer and three others rode ahead to find a campsite on the Platte. They collapsed in exhaustion when they arrived, leaving the troops to find their own way to water. At a stage station he wired a message to Fort Sedgwick, and learned that Sherman had already sent new orders in the care of Lt. Lyman Kidder and an eleven-man escort. Custer had not seen Kidder. Ordered south to Fort Wallace, where he expected to see Libbie, he led his men back into cactus country with hardly a rest.[87]

"You cannot imagine my anxiety regarding your whereabouts, for the reason that, if you are now at Wallace, you can join me in about six days, and we can be together all summer," he wrote to her. He did not know that Libbie was now at Fort Riley, nor that the *New York Times* and other newspapers had reported rumors that the Indians had overwhelmed his column and killed him. "I have never been in a more uncertain frame of mind about you, than since I returned here," Libbie wrote on June 27. "The road between Hays and Harker grows more and more unsafe, and the officers say we came away just in time." Sherman, she said, had advised her to wait out the summer quietly. "Quietly! He may talk about living quietly, but I cannot."[88]

As Custer marched toward Fort Wallace, he knew—or should have known—that he had failed. He had irritated his superiors, put his wife in danger, and still had not settled her anger or discontent. His own men abandoned him. White regiments in the West after the Civil War suffered staggering rates of desertion; in 1871, the overall rate would peak at 32.6 percent. Custer's troopers faced forced marches, cholera, scurvy, arrest for buying food to prevent scurvy, head shaving, and ferocious discipline that extended even to swearing. "The soldiers are frequently heard canvassing the best method of leaving the command," wrote one reporter with the 7th Cavalry. Between July 6 and 8, thirty-four men deserted Custer's column.[89]

On July 7, in full daylight, a dozen men broke from camp with all their arms and equipment. Custer ordered Maj. Joel Elliott to take a force and stop them. As Elliott mounted his horse, Custer came up and said, "I want you to shoot them." Elliott overtook four of the men and ordered them to halt and lay down their arms. He believed that one of them, Pvt. Charles Johnson, was starting to "present" his carbine—raising it to shoot. Elliott and his men opened fire. Bullets struck three of the deserters, including Johnson, who was wounded in the head. They loaded the casualties into a wagon and herded their unharmed prisoners back to camp. The troopers crowded around the wagon when it rolled in. Custer loudly forbade Dr. Coates to treat the deserters. Private Johnson died from his wounds.

At least one observer never forgave Custer. Capt. Robert West, a hard-drinking veteran of the plains, decided to find justice for the men Custer had ordered shot.[90]

Custer pushed his dwindling column over the plains. He found the trail of the missing Kidder and his escort. A day later they caught up to them: a dozen bodies splayed on the ground, including Kidder, ten soldiers, and Red Bead, a Lakota scout. "Every individual of the party had been scalped and his skull broken," Custer later wrote. Only Red Bead kept his hair. Medicine Bill Comstock, Custer's guide, said Indians would not take away the scalps of men of their own tribe—suggesting to him that Pawnee Killer's Oglalas had ambushed Kidder's force. "Even the clothes of all the party had been carried away; some of the bodies were lying in ashes," Custer wrote. "The sinews of the arms and legs had been cut away, the nose of every man hacked off, and the features otherwise defaced." He observed dozens of arrows sticking out of each naked corpse. Custer ordered a trench dug, and the dead were buried in silence.[91]

The next evening, July 13, Custer and his men finally emerged from this nightmare landscape to the haven of Fort Wallace. But Libbie was not there.

Soon after, Barnitz came to Wallace from an assignment in Colorado. "Found Genl. Custer's command encamped near the post," he wrote to his wife, "the General himself having gone post haste, with an escort of

75 picked men, to Harker, to see 'Libby!' They do say that he just squandered the cavalry along the road!" On August 5 he added, "Genl. Custer is not very popular here! The officers of the regiment do not speak of him in amiable terms!" According to rumor, Custer had been arrested. In army slang, he explained, an officer under arrest had *the measles*. "If he *has* the measles," he wrote, "I hope he has them powerful bad!!"[92]

AT TEN O'CLOCK in the morning on September 17, 1867, in Fort Leavenworth, Kansas, the first witness took the stand in Custer's court-martial. He was a twenty-three-year-old New Yorker with a neat little handlebar mustache barely wider than his mouth, heavy dark eyebrows, and an oval face. Asked to state his name, rank, and regiment, he replied, "L. M. Hamilton, Captain, 7th U.S. Cavalry."

He said he recognized the accused and had served under his command during the summer. The judge advocate, Capt. Robert Chandler, asked primarily about what happened after Custer's column reached Fort Wallace on July 13. Hamilton explained that Custer ordered six privates and a noncommissioned officer to be drawn from each company for a detail, totaling seventy-two men and three officers, commanded by Hamilton. The force left Fort Wallace on July 16, escorting Custer on the 150-mile march along the Smoky Hill River to Big Creek, near Fort Hays. They arrived on July 18. Hamilton briefly described an Indian attack at Downer's Station during the march, but mostly answered questions about how fast they marched and wore out the horses. Custer, he said, left the men at Big Creek and drove an ambulance to Fort Harker.

Those who testify at trials tell stories, but in fragments selected by their questioners. Their tales are largely out of chronological order; they repeat some incidents again and again, and leave out others entirely. The transcripts do not reveal the emotional strain on the witnesses and the accused. Hamilton was a very young man. He admired Custer. He tried to minimize the impact of his words.[93]

On September 22, Lieutenant Cooke testified to many of the same points. He said that he rode in an ambulance with Custer and his brother Tom from Fort Hays to Fort Harker, driving sixty-seven miles in thirteen hours.[94]

That same day, Thomas B. Weir, recently promoted to captain, took the stand. A wide-faced man with narrow eyes, Weir authenticated Smith's various orders to Custer, which he had helped to prepare as Smith's adjutant. The last, dated July 13, 1867, directed Custer to use Fort Wallace as a base. It read, "The cavalry should be kept constantly employed."

Captain Parsons, Custer's counsel, cross-examined Weir. He asked,

"At what hour on the night of the 18th and 19th did the accused arrive at Fort Harker?"

"About half past two. . . . Some person woke me up—it was my impression it was Gen. Smith, and said Gen. Custer is here. I got up and went over to Gen. Smith's room and saw him there."

"Was that the only place you saw him?"

"I saw him from that time till he left on the train." Since the fall, the railroad had been constructed far beyond Fort Riley, reaching Fort Harker.

"On what train and where for?"

"Fort Riley."

"Did you go with him to the train?"

"Yes sir."

"For what purpose?"

"Simply socially."[95]

A rumor would later circulate that Custer had left Fort Wallace for Riley because he had heard that Libbie was having an affair with Weir, and attacked him physically when he arrived at Fort Harker. Parsons asked Weir about their friendly interaction simply to establish that Custer believed that he had permission to go to Fort Riley—yet the testimony undermines the tale of jealousy as well.[96]

Having carried Custer through from Fort Wallace to Fort Riley, the judge advocate now began to look at key incidents on his grueling march. First came the question of orders. Did Custer know that he was supposed to remain at Fort Wallace?

Capt. Charles C. Cox of the 10th Cavalry testified that he encountered Custer about thirty miles west of Fort Harker. "I gave him a dispatch that was sent to me from Gen. Smith's headquarters," he said. This was the order that instructed Custer to operate from Fort Wallace.

The judge advocate turned to the attack at Downer's Station. Cox said he asked if Custer had seen any Indians; Custer replied that two men had "loitered behind the column and were taken by the Indians." It was an unfortunate choice of words.[97]

Capt. Arthur B. Carpenter testified that he commanded a company of the 37th Infantry, posted at Downer's Station. Custer and his escort arrived a little after eleven in the morning on July 17, he said. "Some time after the command arrived a detachment came in . . . and reported that the Indians were near and that they had lost two men. After the command went away I sent out to pick up the bodies of those killed and they brought in one dead man and one wounded man."

"Do you know whether any action was taken by the accused to recover the dead or wounded man?" asked Chandler, the judge advocate.

"I do not."

"Did the whole command leave Downer's Station before the dead and wounded men were brought in?"

"Yes sir, except one man who remained there at the Station."

Carpenter discussed the incident more bluntly in a letter to his mother. "You have probably heard of that conceited upstart called Gen. Custar [sic]," he wrote on August 15. "He came through here about the middle of last month. . . . While at dinner his rear guard was attacked about 3 miles west of here, and those who came in reported two killed. Custar remained unconcerned—finished his dinner, and moved on without saying a word to me about the bodies, or thinking of hunting the Indians." In prior testimony, Cooke had said Custer considered it "inexpedient" to go after the attackers, who could not be caught. Carpenter was outraged that Custer assumed that both his men were dead and abandoned them. The wounded man, Carpenter wrote, "says that he would have died before morning if I had not sent out and brought him in. That is Gen. Custer out and out. . . . I hope for the good of the service he will be dismissed."[98]

Sgt. James Connelly took the stand. He commanded the detail attacked near Downer's Station on July 17. He made it clear that the casualties had *not* been stragglers. "Gen. Custer told me to take six men and go back after a man named Young, who had his [personal] mare," Connelly testified. "I did so, and found him." Young's worn-out horse was unfit to ride, so Connelly remounted him. A body of fifty to sixty Indians suddenly attacked. "They kept it up for three or four miles. One man got killed and one was wounded," Connelly said. "That was about the hottest of the fight and we were forced to leave him on the field." The frightened troopers fired only two shots; two galloped off to save themselves.[99]

Connelly's testimony could hardly have been more damning, in the moral as well as legal sense. Custer sent Connelly and six men into danger to retrieve his personal property. Young had fallen behind because his own horse had given out due to the relentless pace of the march. The sergeant's demoralized men had panicked when attacked. When they caught up to Custer, he chose to abandon his casualties.

The trial's fragmented narrative now jumped to the end. On September 25, Col. Andrew J. Smith took the stand. A largely bald man with a gray mustache and beard that divided at the chin into two tufts, he answered the judge advocate's questions without equivocation. Did Custer have permission to march from Fort Wallace to Fort Hays? "He had no orders or authority from me." Was there important public business that might explain his movement? "None that I know of."

The court—the judging officers—asked a question that led him to describe Custer's arrival at Fort Harker more fully. "Gen. Custer came to my quarters between two and three o'clock at night and I don't know that I asked the question how he came down. It was my impression he came by stage," Smith said. The next morning Weir told him that Custer had come with a large escort, and drove an ambulance from Fort Hays. "I ordered him back the next morning [by telegraph] after I learned how he came down." It appears that Smith, groggy at two o'clock, assumed that Custer had come on a quick visit while his men carried out their mission at Fort Wallace. Clearheaded in daylight, he was angry to learn that Custer had halted operations and diverted troops for personal reasons. Custer returned from Fort Riley on July 21 and was arrested.[100]

The trial now took one more jump backward in time. The judge advocate took the court back to July 7, to the lethal pursuit of the deserters from Custer's column. To tell the story, Chandler called 1st Lt. Thomas W. Custer.

Tom answered a rapid succession of quick, pointed questions with terse sentence fragments. Bit by bit, he acknowledged that he rode under Elliott to help bring the deserters back. Tom said his brother spoke to him personally, and gave a verbal order. Chandler asked for the precise language.

"The accused spoke to me and said, 'I want you to get on your horse and go after those deserters and shoot them down.' That is near as I can recollect it," Tom testified. "Maj. Elliott and Lt. Cook caught up with them before I did. . . . I saw the men laying down their arms and Maj. Elliott and Lt. Cooke rode toward them. One of the men, I think it was a man named Johnson, ran to get his carbine and a man named Atkins, a scout who was along with the party . . . [rode] up to the man and said he would blow his brains out if he attempted to touch his carbine. In the meantime I saw Maj. Elliott and Lt. Cooke firing on them." Tom opened fire as well. He acknowledged that Johnson probably did not have his carbine when he was hit.

On cross-examination, Parsons guided Tom into providing more context. The night before, Tom had lost ten men from his own company; he was not alone. The deserters took arms, equipment, rations, and ammunition. The pursuers brought some back unhurt.

Chandler returned to ask some final questions, two of them devastating. "You mentioned that as you approached you saw them laying down their arms; had they laid down their arms at the time you saw Maj. Elliott and Lt. Cook firing on them?"

"I believe they had," Tom answered.

"Were those three men wounded by reason of carrying out the order of the accused to shoot them?"

The question cornered Tom. It forced him to affirm or deny his brother's guilt on the most serious charge. The transcript gives no hint of his emotions. It merely records his final two words: "Yes sir."[101]

Dr. Coates testified on the 26th about Custer's denial of medical attention for the wounded deserters. "I had at that time an idea the objection was made for effect. There had been a great many desertions—some 30 or 40 the night previous—and the men were crowding around the wagon and I had an idea the General wished to make an impression on the men that they would be dealt with in the severest and harshest manner." But Custer took him aside and said, "You can attend to them after a while."[102]

The court went into recess.

FOR ALL THAT HAD HAPPENED during Custer's own desertion—his flight from Fort Wallace—the only thing that mattered to him was how it ended.

Libbie was at home in Fort Riley when she heard "the clank of a sabre on our gallery, and with it the quick, springing steps of feet," and Armstrong burst in. Eliza Brown, she wrote, began "half crying, scolding as she did when overjoyed, vibrated between kitchen and parlor, and finally fell to cooking, as a safety-valve." What Libbie did not record was whether she forgave her husband.[103]

She did. "He took a leave himself, knowing none would be granted him," she wrote to Rebecca Richmond. "When he ran the risk of a court-martial in leaving Wallace he did it expecting the consequences . . . and we are determined to not live apart again, even if he leaves the army otherwise so delightful to us."

The precise sins that drove the couple apart that spring and summer remain uncertain. Her letter to Richmond—and Armstrong's actions—suggest that she required more from him than mere words. She wanted atonement—a sacrifice. So he defied orders and deserted his men, proving that he would do anything to get her back. She accepted his gift. "There was in that summer of 1867 one long, perfect day," she wrote in a memoir. "It was mine, and . . . it is still mine, for time and for eternity."[104]

Now he paid for it. He was indignant, unable to believe that he was being tried. All of his life, exceptions had been made for him. This trial was not Custer luck at all—but he tried to convince himself that it was.

"Everything is working charmingly," Custer wrote to a friend after the court recessed on September 26. Captain West, who had preferred the charges for shooting the deserters, "is drinking himself to death, has the delirium tremens to such an extent that although summoned as a witness by the prosecution they have determined not to allow him to appear on witness stand." General Sheridan had written privately to offer advice, and to tell him that everyone in Washington "regarded my trial as an attempt by Hancock to cover up his failures."[105]

As the trial approached, Custer drafted an article about the Hancock Expedition for *Turf, Field and Farm*, an outdoor sporting magazine, and mailed it to them on September 9. Under the pseudonym Nomad, he wrote self-deprecatingly about killing his wife's horse. He wrote nothing about his trial, dwelling instead on the exotic—eating broiled rattlesnake and beaver tail, hunting buffalo. He finished another piece on September 29.

With these articles, he began to craft new identities for himself: those of writer and plainsman. He layered them onto his old persona; for example, he referred to himself as a frequent visitor to Niblo's Garden, the Manhattan theater, which signaled that he was a cosmopolitan sophisticate as well as rugged outdoorsman. And though he described himself as a newcomer to the Great Plains, he wrote in a voice of hard-won authority, as if determined to erase the humiliations of 1867. The editor liked his work, declaring, "General Custer wields the pen almost as skillfully as he does the sword."[106]

During the trial, Libbie wrote that they had had "a delightful time" at Fort Leavenworth. "The court called some of our warmest friends here from the regiment and we had company incessantly." Davis of *Harper's*, on the other hand, was "an insufferable *bore*. His conceit confuses me." She spent days copying documents for the trial. The whole thing was "nothing but a plan of persecution toward Autie, but I have no alarming fears of the result."[107]

ON OCTOBER 5 THE TESTIMONY resumed with two final prosecution witnesses, Maj. Joel Elliott and 2nd Lt. Henry Jackson.[108] On October 7 the defense began. Tom took the stand again and spoke of a dinner meeting between Custer and Sherman at Fort McPherson. Sherman had told Custer "that if he wished, he could go to Denver City, or he could go to hell if he wanted to. That he could go to any post he wanted to." Other witnesses testified about the plague of desertions. Parsons introduced telegrams showing that Hancock had previously given orders to "kill or capture the deserters."

The last defense witness was Weir. He described how he had gone to Smith's quarters and shook hands with Custer after his arrival at Fort Harker. Custer said he had to hurry or he would miss the 3 a.m. train to Fort Riley. Smith, then, clearly knew where Custer was going. As Weir accompanied Custer outside, Smith remarked, "Give my respects to the ladies."[109]

For the second time in his life, Custer prepared a closing statement for a court-martial. He, not Parsons, wrote it, and it was enormous—more than 8,000 words, composed in overstretched, artificially hifalutin sentences. For example, he tried to say, "Reasonable men can disagree," with this sentence: "The mind of man is so diversely constituted that individuals governed by the same honorable motives, and laboring for the same generous ends"—and so on for thirty-five more words. His defense was plausible on some points, laughable on others, and turgid throughout. He was lucky that the court did not press fresh charges after Parsons read this enormity aloud on October 11.[110]

When Parsons finished, Chandler stood and delivered his summary. It was less than half the length of Custer's statement. It was direct in style, concisely reviewing the evidence, "applying it distinctly to the facts of the charge."

The court cleared the chamber for deliberations. They did not take long. Custer and Parsons were called back into the room in the wooden building in Fort Leavenworth to hear the verdict.[111]

Twelve

THE INDIAN KILLER

W HEN CUSTER'S CASE REACHED the desk of Ulysses S. Grant, one of the greatest political crises in American history enveloped the commander of the army. He steered between two contending forces, each wanting him as an ally, even as he pursued his own agenda. Yet Grant still found time to review Custer's court-martial—appropriately so, since the crisis and the case intertwined.

In 1867, the Republican-controlled Congress battled President Andrew Johnson for control of the Reconstruction of the South. The struggle now centered on Congress's determination to give all black men the vote, a fringe idea just two years before, at war's end. "The astonishingly rapid evolution of Congressional attitudes that culminated in black suffrage," explains Eric Foner, "arose both from the crisis created by the obstinacy of Johnson and the white South, and the determination of Radicals, blacks, and eventually Southern Unionists not to accept a Reconstruction program that stopped short of this demand." It was a historic issue on the grandest scale. The daily political struggle, though, still came down to tactics. There Grant was the necessary man.[1]

In March 1867, Congress passed the Tenure of Office Act, requiring the president to obtain Senate approval before removing any previously confirmed cabinet secretary. Republicans wanted to prevent Johnson from sabotaging the first Reconstruction Act, passed that same month, by firing Secretary of War Stanton and replacing him with a conservative. The Reconstruction Act put ten former Confederate states under military jurisdiction until they ratified new constitutions with universal manhood suffrage and ratified the Fourteenth Amendment. Congress put the army in charge because it was the only federal body capable of this huge task, and also because Republicans trusted both Stanton and Grant to execute the act as they intended.

Johnson hated the Reconstruction Act, and believed the Tenure of Office Act was unconstitutional. In August 1867, between sessions of Congress, he suspended Stanton and named Grant as interim war secretary, believing him to be more pliable. It was not a direct confrontation with the Tenure of Office Act, as Congress could restore Stanton when it reconvened, but Johnson cunningly placed it in an awkward position by forcing it to remove Grant, a national hero and favorite among Republicans.[2]

Grant tried to preserve the appearance of neutrality. He had agreed to go on the Swing Around the Circle, for example, yet had said nothing to endorse the president and left the tour before it was complete. He accepted the appointment to replace Stanton only on an interim basis, since that much was legal, but he refused to participate in a violation of the law.

But Grant increasingly disagreed with the president over Reconstruction. He made that clear when Johnson decided to remove Sheridan from command of Louisiana and Texas. As noted previously, Sheridan condemned the New Orleans riot of July 30, 1866, as "an absolute massacre by the police." After the Reconstruction Act passed, he fired the mayor, Louisiana's attorney general, and a district judge. He denounced racial violence in Texas, too. He wrote in his annual report, "Over a white man killed by Indians on an extensive frontier the greatest excitement will take place, but over the killing of many freedmen in the settlements, nothing is done." Johnson wanted him out of the South.

Grant told the president it was "unmistakably the wish of the country" to keep Sheridan in place. Johnson ignored his advice and swapped Sheridan with the conservative Hancock. On September 12 Sheridan formally took charge of the Department of the Missouri.[3]

Despite the intrigue, Grant's work went on. Clerks and messengers continued to deliver reports, letters, and telegrams from departments, districts, and posts around the country, informing him of the molecular life of the military. Piece by piece, they revealed the army's institutional opinion of Lt. Col. George Armstrong Custer.

On August 22, 1867, Judge Advocate General Joseph Holt brought up Custer in a letter to Grant. The sixty-year-old Holt knew the Regular Army and its culture. He had served as President James Buchanan's secretary of war, and was named to his current post by Lincoln. He wrote to Grant that 2nd Lt. Levant W. Barnhart had been convicted of forging Custer's name on a claim for a horse, lost while on duty in Texas. Holt wanted leniency for Barnhart, who had thought that as a staff officer he was entitled to sign Custer's name on the form. "It is thought that his education while with Gen. Custer may have easily blinded him to the gravity of the offence of which he is convicted, serious as it is."

Sherman wrote to Grant about Custer that same month. Hancock, he said, "is not satisfied with Custar [sic] who has not fulfilled our wishes."

Leading the best cavalry available, Custer "simply moved . . . from place to place" as the Indians evaded him. "On his arrival at Wallace instead of starting at once after the Cheyennes he came into Fort Riley to see his wife. Gen. Hancock reports to me that he has arrested him."[4]

These few daubs of paint portrayed a self-indulgent man, unserious about duty, convinced the rules did not apply to him. On November 8, the picture grew fuller and darker when Holt reported the verdict in Custer's court-martial.

On the first charge, absence without leave, the court found Custer guilty. On the second charge and its specifications—that he rendered his horses and men unfit for service, took two wagons for his own use, and neglected to look after the men shot at Downer's Station or pursue their attackers—the court found Custer guilty, with no criminality attached to the matter of the wagons. On the additional charge and specifications— that he ordered a detachment to shoot dead a group of deserters, caused three men to be severely wounded, hauled these casualties in a wagon, refused them medical treatment, and caused the death of Pvt. Charles Johnson—the court found Custer guilty. It saw no criminality in the medical treatment question.

The court sentenced Custer "to be suspended from rank and command for one year, and forfeit his pay proper for the same time," Holt reported. The conviction was correct, he wrote. The sentence was an open question. Grant would have to settle it. Custer was guilty of "the crime of murder," unless he was justified by "imperative necessity." Murder lay outside of military law, Holt observed; it required a civil trial.

Should Gen. Custer's act be considered as an unwarrantable exercise of lawless power, the result of the habits of thought acquired while controlling in time of open war a large command, and when accustomed to the doing of those deeds of arbitrary energy that war sometimes necessitates, and not as justified by the peculiar and difficult circumstances under which this deed was committed, the sentence pronounced by the Court in this case is utterly inadequate, and measures should be at once taken for Gen. Custer's trial before a court of competent jurisdiction. If on the other hand, it is believed to have been ordered to be done, in the exercise of a wise and conscientious discretion . . . the sentence as now recorded should be regarded as sufficiently rigorous.[5]

Holt put Custer's life in Grant's hands. If Grant referred a murder case to a civilian court, Custer would face the death penalty. But the commanding general had more to consider than justice alone. There were the wishes of Custer's new department commander, Sheridan. Grant trusted him more than any subordinate except Sherman. In a time of national crisis, a man feels the need to stand by his friends.

PARADES AT FORT LEAVENWORTH could be tense. Once in 1867, Col. William Hoffman derided the soldiers of the 10th Cavalry as "nigger troops" and told them to march farther away from his own 3rd Infantry. Col. Benjamin Grierson, commander of the 10th, angrily confronted Hoffman, and the two argued in front of the men.[6]

When the troops assembled for dress parade on the evening of November 25, the tension was all Custer's. It was announced to the gathering that General Grant had completed his review of the court-martial. He confirmed the conviction and sentence. He elected not to refer Custer to a civilian court to face murder charges, but did release his personal opinion in the matter. As the *Leavenworth Bulletin* reported, "Gen. Grant, in reviewing the case, declared that the decision of the Court Martial was altogether too lenient." Morally if not legally, he implied, Custer was guilty of murder.[7]

"There is considerable astonishment expressed at the result of the trial," wrote the *New York Times* correspondent on the scene. He declared Custer content with the sentence. "Gen. Custer is anxious to have it stand, as it gives him a respite he has desired for a long time, not perhaps in this precise way. . . . It may be, too, that some of this wished-for leisure time will be devoted to the preparation of a work that will be decidedly interesting to those who have followed the fortunes of the General through his many campaigns." If the writer's prejudice were not obvious enough, he concluded,

> Gen. Custer is, to those who know him intimately, the very *beau ideal* of an American cavalry officer. He is a magnificent rider, fearlessly brave, a capital revolver shot, and without a single objectionable habit. He neither drinks, swears, nor uses tobacco in any form. His weakness, if he has one, is a fast horse, to get all the speed out of which there is no better man than the long-haired hero of the Shenandoah.[8]

After two years of Custer's racing from controversy to controversy—after his failure, trial, and conviction—there were still Americans who saw him as a romantic hero. It's telling that the conservative *New York Times* published this tribute. Custer was its man.

The Custers made a great show of equanimity. Armstrong wrote to a friend that he had asked Sheridan to refrain from lobbying for clemency "as I would not accept it." He and Libbie would remain in Leavenworth until spring, he said, then go to Monroe to have fun. He looked forward to the presidential election in the fall of 1868. Living in Kansas had kept them out of society, forcing them to decline an invitation to the fashionable wedding of two members of New York's patrician circle, Eva Lorillard, daughter of Pierre Lorillard III, and Lawrence Kip, formerly of Sheridan's staff. No longer.[9]

Inwardly the Custers seethed. Armstrong wrote privately that the evidence did not support the verdict; everyone told him his punishment was "unjustly severe." Libbie called the trial "nothing but a plan of persecution toward Autie." General Hancock, they believed, needed a scapegoat for his own failure. Custer also blamed Capt. Robert West, who had filed the most serious charge. He took great satisfaction in believing that West was "drinking himself to death," and retaliated by filing his own charge against him for inebriation. But West was not done.[10]

On January 3, 1868, Custer drove a buggy with Libbie and some guests from the fort into town, singing as they went, until they were stopped by two civilian officers. They arrested him for murder. Faced with the army's inaction, West had filed his own charges.

Despite everything, many in the regiment still liked and admired Custer. A dozen friends, including Weir, accompanied him to the judge's office. He paid his bail, and they enjoyed an oyster supper before returning to the post. Custer hired an attorney, as did his codefendant, Lt. William W. Cooke. The judge heard now-familiar testimony about the desertions and shooting. On January 18 he dismissed the case.[11]

Custer still fumed. He could never conceal his emotions, but seemed compelled to publicly perform his private flaws, driven to shout down the judgment of others. He had done so in private before; now he published his indignation to the world.

On October 26, 1867, he mailed his third article for *Turf, Field and Farm* under the pseudonym Nomad. It appeared in the November 9, 1867, issue. However good Hancock was at battling "a civilized foe, his experience the past year on the Plains has shown him that in order to outwit or circumvent the wily red man he has much to learn," he wrote. The same could be said of Custer; indeed, the article provided a perfect example of psychological projection. "Indian warfare is a distinct and separate species of hostilities," he explained, "requiring different talent, different *materiel*, as well as *personnel*, and different rules of conduct." He depicted Hancock's strategic error in burning the village on Pawnee Fork as a personal moral failing. When the Cheyennes and Lakotas fled, "the commander of Uncle Sam's forces was enraged," he wrote. "Was his favorite plan to be thus thwarted? Were the laurels he was to reap from his Indian policy to prove a crown of thorns?"[12]

He finished two more pieces for the magazine on November 11 and December 15, published on November 23, 1867, and January 4, 1868, respectively. He defended his failure but also described his education as a plainsman, tutored by Indian and civilian scouts. "No cavalry in the world, marching even in the lightest manner possible . . . can overtake or outmarch the Western Indian, when the latter is disposed to prevent it," he wrote. The Indian pony was an "insignificant specimen of the equine species," but it could subsist on grazing alone, whereas "the white man's horse" needed grain. There was truth in these observations, which would influence his thinking in years to come.[13]

If he had left it there, all might have been well. But as he wrote the last piece there came the public reading of his sentence. It put him in a dark frame of mind. Then he heard from Alvred B. Nettleton, a Civil War subordinate and editor of the *Sandusky* (Ohio) *Register*, asking about another newspaper's report on his court-martial.

Nettleton published Custer's reply on December 26, 1867. In legalistic detail, Custer defended himself against the charges. "Most officers," he claimed, believed that the evidence would "wholly exculpate me." The problem was "the composition of the Court." He presumed that Hancock had personally selected his judges. He complained that four of them were his inferior in rank, three had never commanded troops in the field, and three came from Hancock's staff. He suggested that some on the court were "jealous" because he had been promoted over older men. And he called West "a confirmed inebriate, a victim of *delirium tremens*, and one who is now resting under infamous charges" (preferred by Custer himself, of course). There was much more.

The *New York Tribune* announced the letter's publication. The *New York Times* excerpted it at length, along with Nettleton's editorial comment that Custer's "temporary political error could not blind us to his great qualities as a soldier, or dim his well-earned fame," a hint of how his public conduct in 1866 had set him against the large majority of Union veterans. The army officially took offense.[14]

JUDGE ADVOCATE GENERAL HOLT SENT the *Sandusky Register* clipping to Grant on February 14, 1868. He included "the joint protest against said publication of all the members of the court which sentenced Gen. Custer, forwarded by Bvt. Major General Hoffman." Holt wrote that he agreed with them.

Genl. Custer, in the manner of his thus appealing from his sentence to the public, in his misrepresentations in regard to the evidence in his case, in his attacks upon the impartiality and justice of the members of the court, in his criticisms of the course pursued by Genl. Hancock, and in the language with which he assails one of the officers who preferred charges against him, must be deemed to have been at least guilty of *conduct to the prejudice of good order and military discipline.*

Custer had challenged the legitimacy of the institutional processes of the Regular Army. To the military profession it was an unforgivable crime. Holt drew up specifications carefully, as some of Custer's language had been "cautious and indirect," and submitted them for review. If Grant approved, Custer would face another court-martial, potentially more destructive to his career than the first two.[15]

Grant had other matters on his mind. The political crisis had grown still more treacherous—in part because of his own ambitions. In 1867 his chief of staff and close friend John Rawlins had told John Forney, editor of the *Washington Chronicle*, that Grant "thinks the Republican party may need him, and he believes, as their candidate [for president], he can be elected and re-elected." Forney wrote up a long story about how Grant would make a fine Republican president; he gave it to Rawlins, who told him the general in chief approved. Grant all but declared himself to be Johnson's rival.[16]

On January 13, 1868, the Senate reinstated Stanton as secretary of war. The next day Grant moved out of the War Department and back to his old office. He refused to be Johnson's tool for confronting the Republican Congress. At a cabinet meeting that same day, the president looked at Grant and demanded a report from the secretary of war. Grant said he no longer held that office. "Johnson, after two and a half years of wooing Ulysses Grant, tore into him not with a wild tirade, but much more tellingly, with an icy dressing-down," writes William McFeely. Johnson leaked word that Grant had lied to him; two days later the *National Intelligencer* published the accusation.[17]

Humiliated—though undiminished in public opinion—Grant stood by as Johnson dismissed Stanton again on February 21, defying the Tenure of Office Act. On February 24, the House of Representatives impeached the president for the first time in American history. It had been coming for more than a year, as Johnson challenged Congress on every point of Reconstruction. On March 4, the trial began in the Senate.

Amid these great events, Holt's charge and specifications against Custer

sat on Grant's desk, neither approved nor denied. One reason might have
been Custer's past support of Johnson. If Grant allowed another court-
martial to proceed so soon after the latest one, it might seem as if he
were purging the army of the president's loyalists.[18] Or he may have been
preoccupied, or wanted to wait for further provocations by Custer before
prosecuting him again. Besides, Custer was now Sheridan's problem.

Sheridan had visited Fort Leavenworth to relieve Hancock of command. As an icon of Union victory, he was familiar to all, with his narrow
eyes, mustache, stubby figure, and emphatic manner. He and his staff
departed after only a few days for New York and Washington, not to
return for months. But he sent signals of his support for Custer. When
the Custers were forced to vacate military quarters for the duration of the
suspension, he loaned them the large house at Fort Leavenworth assigned
for his use. Sheridan was loyal to the man who had served him so well in
the war, and liked him.[19]

But he was not blind. Regular Army in gristle and bone, Sheridan knew
that Custer had violated both military law and culture. On March 2, 1868,
he returned to Fort Leavenworth. Soon after, he brought up Custer's case
with Grant. "I feel a great sympathy for General G. A. Custer," he wrote
on April 15. "Custer has done many things which I do not approve of—
especially the letter he wrote and had published, reflecting on the court
which tried him—but I would be exceedingly gratified if the General
could have him pardoned." He pleaded on the grounds of Custer's past,
his potential for improvement, and pity.

> He feels very sensibly [i.e., deeply] his punishment, and I think
> would, if he were re-instated, make a better officer than if the sen-
> tence were carried out to its full extent. He held high command
> during the Rebellion and had difficulty in adapting himself to his
> altered position. There was no one with me whom I more highly
> appreciated than General Custer. He never failed me, and if his late
> misdeeds could be forgotten, or overlooked on account of his gal-
> lantry and faithfulness in the past, it would be gratifying to him and
> to myself, and a benefit to the service.[20]

Difficulty in adapting himself to his altered position. Sheridan stated the obvious: Custer was a man of the past, unable to find a place in the world he
had helped make.

But was it a valid reason for mercy? Custer himself had been an unfor-
giving commander, shaving heads and shooting deserters, even whipping volunteers in Texas, as Grant knew. And Grant soon learned that
Custer had been no more merciful during the Civil War. On May 8, Holt

reported that Lt. A. V. Burnham had applied for "the revocation of orders dishonorably dismissing [him] from the service." During the war, Burnham, a soldier under Custer's command, had left his reserve post, far from the enemy, for five minutes to purchase a canteen of milk. "It appears that charges were preferred against him, and that for the purpose of making an example Gen. Custer recommended his summary dismissal." Holt supported Burnham's appeal.[21]

The irony could not be more obvious. Custer believed he had done nothing wrong by riding hundreds of miles away from his command, in the face of hostile forces, to see his wife—but he had dishonorably discharged a man for leaving a quiet post for five minutes to obtain food. Grant never missed such evidence of a man's character. He let Sheridan's petition sit as the trial of the president played out.

CUSTER DID NOT understand his peril. On May 2, 1868, he wrote from Fort Leavenworth to a friend that he had learned of the court's petition to Grant to order his prosecution over his letter to the *Sandusky Register*. "I . . . hope most earnestly he will," Custer wrote; he could "substantiate and make good" everything in it. As his West Point roommate once said, he was too clever for his own good.

"As it is now I am like Micawber waiting for something to turn up," he added. That was not quite true. He had made an agreement with Harper and Bros. for his wartime memoirs, which he hoped to finish by the beginning of August. It was another sign of his ambition to become a literary figure. What he was really waiting for was the next set of charges, which he suspected would come after his suspension ended.[22]

Libbie, at least, seemed content. Armstrong was with her and behaving as well as a husband should. Anna Darrah remained with them at Fort Leavenworth. Libbie's beloved cousin, Rebecca Richmond, visited, along with her sister Mary Richmond Kendall and her new husband, Charles Kendall. All of them gathered in the front parlor to receive callers on New Year's Day, 1868, in keeping with the genteel American custom. Some forty men paid their respects and browsed at the refreshment table, from Tom Custer to Colonel Smith, from Barnitz to Capt. George Yates, an old Monroe friend for whom Armstrong had long served as patron and had maneuvered into the 7th Cavalry. One of the officers brought some sheet music and led an impromptu chorus. The Custers endured Armstrong's trial for murder, attended parties, and threw their own through the winter and spring.[23]

During the interregnum at Fort Leavenworth, Emmanuel Custer wrote to Armstrong that he had received a mysterious package, purporting to come from a group of Confederate sympathizers. "I doant correspond with Rebels, and I do not appreciate his Package vary highly," Emmanuel wrote. He suspected it was a trap, an attempt to expose himself as a Copperhead, though perhaps it was just a taunt. He denounced the Radicals, wrote that Grant would be "a Beat man" if he ran for president on a Radical platform, and praised Johnson's "back bone and nerve."[24]

The mailing may have been a response to his son's support of the president. Now that Armstrong was a public figure, his actions affected his family. His little sister Maggie sent him the bill for her next quarter at Boyd's Seminary in Monroe. "Autie I do not know how I shall ever be able to repay you for your kindness to me," she wrote. Now that he had lost his salary for a year, how could he continue to support her, his parents, and his own domestic establishment?[25]

Tom Custer, of course, remained on duty with the 7th Cavalry. After years of pressuring Armstrong to help his brother, Emmanuel was happy for once.[26]

May passed. The impeachment trial in the Senate ended with Johnson's acquittal by one vote. June arrived. The Custers made the long train trip back to Monroe. No word came from Washington of another court-martial.

The presidential campaign began. The New York leaders of the Democratic Party ignored Johnson and secured the nomination of New York governor Horatio Seymour for president and Missouri's Frank Blair Jr. for vice president. The Republicans nominated Grant. Blair in particular was just the man for Emmanuel Custer: a Union general, son of one of Andrew Jackson's closest allies, and a vicious racist. He denounced African Americans as "a semi-barbarous race of blacks who are worshippers of fetishes, and poligamists." He would have the White House "allow the white people to reorganize their own governments."[27]

Custer went to New York for Independence Day. He attended a "grand ratification meeting" at Tammany Hall to endorse Seymour and Blair, and he gave a speech. As in the past, the Democrats used his standing as a Union hero to refute Republican charges of disloyalty. The *Des Moines State Register* saw him differently. "It is announced with a grand flourish that Custer supports Seymour. We are glad of it," it wrote. "No officer that ever treated soldiers as Custer did, should be anything else except a Johnson man and a Seymour man. The men of the 1st Iowa Cavalry remember this Custer. His memory will be a stench in their nostrils, and that of their 'children's children to the remotest generation.'"[28]

His inability to adapt to life after the war had converted at least some of his celebrity into notoriety. Notoriety was a weight, and Libbie carried it too. Kansas, she would write a year later, "is entirely unfitting me for the restraints of Monroe society, as I found the everlasting 'they say' troubled me somewhat" during her return home in 1868. She would blame it on her new disregard of "style," but hometown gossips had much more to chatter about, with Armstrong's controversies and conviction. After his appearance at Tammany Hall, they put down the burden and lived quietly in Monroe.[29]

The 1st of August came and went. Custer did not complete his Civil War memoirs, as he had anticipated. For whatever reason, his work on the book stalled.[30]

Then something turned up. On September 24, Sheridan wired him from Fort Hays. "Gen Sherman and myself and nearly all of the officers of your regiment have asked for you and hope the application will be successful," he wrote. "Can you come at once. Eleven (11) companies of your regiment will move about the first of October against the hostile Indians from Medicine Lodge Creek towards the Wichita Mountains."[31]

For months Grant had let the appeal for a new court-martial sit alongside Sheridan's request for commutation, acting on neither. As the presidential campaign accelerated, he gave in to Sheridan's wishes. Sherman urged him to, writing that he had asked the army's adjutant general for "the remission of the balance of his sentence but have no answer. Cannot you expedate [sic] that also as Sheridan wants Custar [sic] now [and] I want to give him everything he asks for."[32] Returning Custer to duty also conveniently removed him from politics. Grant gave Custer what he wanted most—a chance at redemption.

DURING CUSTER'S ARREST AND TRIAL, federal relations with the high-plains nations underwent a legal transformation. Congress voted on July 20, 1867, to establish a peace commission. Nathaniel G. Taylor, commissioner of Indian affairs, led the group, which included Generals Sherman, Alfred H. Terry, and William S. Harney (retired), the humanitarians Samuel F. Tappan and John B. Sanborn, and Senator John B. Henderson of Missouri. On October 19, the group held a grand conference with representatives of the Southern Cheyenne, Arapaho, Kiowa, and Comanche tribes, at a traditional council site on Medicine Lodge Creek in southern Kansas. (General Christopher C. Augur temporarily replaced Sherman.)

Thousands of native people camped nearby. The band associated with Black Kettle—an advocate of accommodation even after surviving the Sand Creek Massacre—put up some sixty lodges near the council grounds. The militant Dog Soldiers and others gathered a few miles away. The separation reflected a philosophical split. At one point Tall Bull demanded that Black Kettle come to the Dog Soldier camp to make the case for peace, threatening to kill all his horses if he refused. He came.[33]

Divisions existed on the government side as well. Robert Utley writes, in a mixed metaphor, that Indian Commissioner Taylor "made the peace pipe the keystone of his administration." Sherman spoke for most army officers when he told Grant, "I am convinced that somehow we must whip these Indians terribly to make them fear & respect us." And yet, as Utley also notes, the white advocates of peace and war merely debated the means toward the same sequential goals: clearing the main rail, stage-coach, and wagon routes across Nebraska and Kansas, opening the rest of those two states to settlement, and coercing the Indians into abandoning nomadic culture. The Comanche leader Ten Bears told the commission, "I love the open prairie, and I wish you would not insist on putting us on a reservation." Senator Henderson said the buffalo were doomed. "The Indian must change the road his father trod."[34]

To the nations represented at Medicine Lodge Creek, the commission offered a reservation in the Indian Territory (modern-day Oklahoma), with broad hunting rights south of the Arkansas River so long as bison herds still existed. The Southern Cheyennes and Arapahoes would have to give up their hard-won territory between the Arkansas and the Platte. "The terms pushed hard toward the 'civilized' life of farmers and stock-raisers," writes the historian Elliott West. "Children would be educated in traditional schoolhouses; women would be issued flannel skirts and men given pantaloons, hats, and homemade socks." The commission stacked up immediate gifts for the bands that signed, with the promise of annuities for the next three decades. On October 28, leaders of the assembled peoples signed the treaty.[35]

"The Cheyennes were with great difficulty persuaded to sign the treaty," Barnitz wrote in his journal. "*They have no idea that* they are giving up, or that they have ever given up the country which they claim as their own, the country north of the Arkansas." The latter sentence has often been quoted by historians, yet it contradicts Barnitz's first observation, and was far too condescending to be true. They faced an impossible situation, and they knew it. They could not reverse demographic and environmental reality. They were vastly outnumbered. The passage of migrants slowly rendered their lands uninhabitable. The Southern Cheyennes and their allies signed in anger, not ignorance. When Bull Bear took the pen, he stabbed clear through the sheet.[36]

This resentment exacerbated internal divisions. Young men from across the Southern Cheyenne nation called for resistance. Despite the treaty, the Dog Soldiers largely returned to "their beloved middle country" of central Kansas, as West calls it. But the Kansas Pacific Railroad continued to snake west and homesteaders began to plow up the grass-lands along the lower Saline, Solomon, and Republican rivers—edging right into the "middle country."[37]

Even worse, Congress failed to fund the promised annuities until July 1868. A large body of Kiowas, Arapahoes, and Southern Cheyennes gathered on Pawnee Fork near Fort Larned "to make complaint of their condition," Sherman wrote to his wife on July 15, 1868. He blamed Congress. "We kill them if they attempt to hunt, and if they keep within the Reservations they starve." Their anger overflowed when Sheridan visited Fort Larned and held a council with them. The Cheyenne leader Stone Calf said to him, "Let your soldiers grow long hair, so that we can have some honor in killing them." Sheridan issued them rations but prepared for hostilities.[38]

The chain of events that pulled Custer back from suspension began slightly earlier, in June 1868. Southern Cheyenne warriors raided a Kaw village near Council Grove, Kansas, and stole some livestock. It was merely another skirmish in their decades-old war on the low-plains tribes. The Indian Bureau, though, saw it as a breach of the peace, and refused to issue arms and ammunition stipulated in the treaty.

"The Cheyennes were furious at this," writes the historian Paul Hutton. They saw their wars with other Indian nations as their own business, and "they had carefully avoided clashes with white men." Their federal agent, Edward W. Wynkoop, agreed with Lt. Col. Alfred Sully, the new commander of the District of the Upper Arkansas, to distribute 160 revolvers and eighty old-style muzzle-loading rifles for hunting.[39]

It didn't help. The next day a raiding party of some 200 Cheyenne men rode to attack the Pawnees. They changed their minds. They descended on the settlers in the Saline and Solomon valleys. They raped five women and murdered fifteen men. Little Rock, a Cheyenne leader, later told Wynkoop that two men in the group started the attacks without approval, but finally all "gave way, and all went in together." Two army scouts, including Custer's friend Medicine Bill Comstock, went to a Dog Soldiers camp to investigate the raids. The Cheyennes killed both of them.[40]

Cheyennes ambushed and slaughtered a group of soldiers in the vicinity of Fort Dodge, stole sixty-five head of livestock near Fort Wallace, and attacked ranches and stagecoaches. In September Sully led nine companies of the 7th Cavalry south into the Indian Territory. Their opponents dragged lodge poles to create false trails that lured the cavalry into sand hills, where the terrain bogged them down amid heavy fighting. It broke Sully's nerve, and he ordered a retreat to Fort Dodge.[41]

Sully's failure disheartened the 7th Cavalry, but it encouraged the fighters of the high-plains tribes. After a month of bloodshed, Sheridan counted "110 citizens killed, thirteen women raped, and more than one thousand head of livestock stolen," writes the historian Jerome Greene. "Buildings, farmhouses, stagecoaches, wagon trains, and rolling stock had been lost to raiding Indians." The raiders took captives, including Clara Blinn and her two-year-old son, Willie. They attacked fifty civilian scouts under Maj. George A. "Sandy" Forsyth who were searching the headwaters of the Republican River, and besieged them on a sandbar that Forsyth dubbed Beecher's Island. The scouts suffered five dead and fifteen wounded before the 10th Cavalry rescued them. As Elliott West writes, "The Dog Soldiers still held the initiative in their homeland."[42]

In theory, Sheridan might negotiate for the surrender of the perpetrators of the initial attacks, and let the inexorable process of railroad construction, settlement, and environmental degradation continue to constrict nomadic culture and the attendant raids.[43] But it is hard to imagine any army officer reacting to raids on civilians with restraint—particularly to rape and the abduction of women and children, which struck squarely at nineteenth-century masculine honor. But the best response was not obvious.

Were the raids of the Cheyennes and their allies crimes or warfare? The loose governing structure of the high-plains nations muddled the question of responsibility. Little Rock said, "I think the only men who ought to suffer and be responsible for these outrages are the men . . . who ravished the women, and when I return to the Cheyenne camps and assemble the chiefs and headmen, I think these two men will be delivered up to you." But Edmund Guerrier swore in an affidavit, "I was with the Cheyenne Indians at the time of the massacre. . . . As near as I can remember nearly all the different bands of Cheyennes had some of their young men in this war party, which committed the rapes and murders on the Solomon and Saline."[44]

There *was* something collective, something communal, about the attacks, even if they were not initiated by the Cheyenne Council of Forty-Four. As they multiplied after the initial bloodshed, more and more men took part. Ironically, treating them as a crime would import an alien view of this conflict. The Southern Cheyennes had won their lands through costly wars against neighbors that featured such raids. Now they rebelled against an intrinsically unfair relationship with the United States, which was stripping them of those conquests.

Sheridan was not about to question that relationship. As far as he was concerned, he was at war. He would inflict collective punishment, as Sherman wrote, "to make them fear and respect us."[45]

Sheridan summoned two officers he trusted to carry out an offensive. One was Maj. Eugene A. Carr, commander of the 5th Cavalry. An 1850 graduate of West Point, Carr served on the frontier from 1852 to 1860, and won the Medal of Honor in the Civil War. Carr would serve Sheridan well in the months ahead.

The other officer was Custer. He arrived at Fort Hays on October 4. Sheridan ate breakfast with him and briefed him on his plan for a winter campaign. On October 10 Custer rode into the camp of the 7th Cavalry, thirty miles from Fort Dodge. He had "his hair cut short, and a perfect managarie [sic] of Scotch fox hounds!" Barnitz wrote to his wife. "We will march on the long contemplated expedition toward the Wichitaw [sic] Mountains and sand hills, and will in all probability see a great many Indians before we return. Some of us may never return."[46]

CUSTER NAMED IT CAMP SANDY FORSYTH, after his friend Maj. George A. Forsyth. It provided a temporary home for eleven companies of the 7th Cavalry in south-central Kansas (the twelfth company was on detached duty at Fort Lyon). Colonel Smith had gone on leave, leaving Custer in command of the regiment. The arrival of recruits brought his force to twenty-nine officers and about 844 enlisted men.

Custer ordered mounted drills and target practice, and selected the forty best marksmen for an elite unit of sharpshooters under Lieutenant Cooke. He received a shipment of manuals from Washington, and ordered the officers to take classes on long-distance signaling. Fresh horses and mules arrived, as well as hundreds of wagons. Custer requested pistols, a sign that he expected close-range combat. He received 550 .44 caliber army revolvers. Blacksmiths shoed horses and the quartermaster distributed flannel underwear, greatcoats, and other winter clothes.[47]

"He was impatient to proceed," recalled Benjamin Clark, a civilian scout, "and harassed the men and his subordinates by his arbitrary conduct. He was a hard master, but his dash and cavalier bearing held the admiration of his troopers." Clark offered his memories thirty years later, but his evenhandedness gives weight to his observations. At the time he was twenty-six, a former Union cavalryman and veteran of the plains.[48]

The most controversial step Custer took was to "color the horses." On November 3—the day the nation elected Ulysses S. Grant as its next president—he required the various companies to exchange horses so that each had a single color. Captain Benteen hated the horse exchange, though he hated everything Custer did. Barnitz had softened toward Custer since his return, but even he called it a "*foolish, unwarranted, unjus-*

tifiable order." The officers wanted to keep mounts they had trained and trusted. It has often been condemned as an example of Custer's obsession with appearances.[49]

In fact, "coloring the horses" sent a clear message to the 7th Cavalry. Custer later wrote that it was an old cavalry tradition, "bordering on the ornamental perhaps, although in itself useful." It was a command-and-control device—needless for isolated patrols or garrison duty, but valuable in massed combat. A nineteenth-century field commander relied on sight to identify his own troops as well as the enemy. Cavalrymen charged, scattered, and swirled across the landscape. Uniform horse colors helped a commander make sense out of the chaos and give direction to his units. Custer's order told the 7th Cavalry that they were going into battle.[50]

Of course, Custer indulged himself. He ordered one of his men, a tailor in civilian life, to make him a buckskin suit with fringes, which he wore instead of his uniform. He hunted daily. "I brought my shotgun and twenty-five pounds of shot with me and expect to have my table loaded with game every day," he wrote to Kirkland Barker, president of Detroit's Audubon Society. Custer's two greyhounds and three staghounds, Maida, Blucher, and Flirt, were "my inseparable companions."[51]

"We are going where white men have never been," Custer exaggerated to Nettie Humphrey Greene on November 8. He described the arrival of his twelve Osage guides. Led by men named Little Beaver and Hard Rope, they impressed Custer, who enjoyed the exoticism of their painted faces and native clothes. He watched them mount "green untrained horses," throw a stick on the ground, and fire at it as they galloped past at full speed. *"Every shot struck the target."* He also complained that he had written two prior letters to Nettie without a reply. He did not know that this friend who had helped him court Libbie and married his best man had herself died.[52]

"We are going on what is likely to prove a pretty hard campaign, both on men and horses," Custer wrote to J. Schuyler Crosby, Sheridan's assistant adjutant general. "I do not ask to shorten the campaign. On the contrary I am in favor of pounding away as long as we can stand it or as long as we can find Indians." It was, he knew, his only chance to prove himself after his humiliation. But he remained the same man. As he closed his letter, he added, "Be virtuous and you'll never be happy."[53]

CUSTER DID NOT LIKE Alfred Sully. Though Sully held the same service rank, he had graduated from West Point two decades earlier and now commanded the Department of the Upper Arkansas. With a weak chin hidden behind a scraggly gray goatee, he dabbled in painting, which he had learned from his father, Thomas, a well-known artist. Sully was a veteran of the Mexican War, had fought on the Peninsula, then led an incursion into the Dakota Territory in response to the Sioux Uprising in Minnesota in 1862. Well regarded within the army, Sully married a Sioux wife. "Now, unaccountably, he turned into a cautious, slow-moving general who set the pace in an ambulance rather than on horseback," writes Robert Utley.[54]

The command marched south from Camp Sandy Forsyth on November 12, along with five companies of infantry and an extensive wagon train. Six days later, they encountered a trail. Custer ordered his Osage scouts to examine it. They concluded that it was recently made by a large war party headed north. Custer wanted to follow it backward to strike the unprotected villages. To his consternation, Sully refused.

Soon afterward they camped between Wolf Creek and Beaver River in the Indian Territory. Following Sheridan's instructions, Sully ordered the men to construct a permanent post that came to be known as Camp Supply. They erected palisade walls around a rectangular enclosure, with log blockhouses on two opposing corners. Here they were outside of the District of the Upper Arkansas. Custer demanded command by virtue of his brevet rank of major general (Sully held a brigadier brevet). Again Sully refused.

On November 21, word came that Sheridan was approaching. Custer galloped out to meet his patron. The stout little general immediately ordered Sully back to Kansas and put Custer in charge of the strike force.[55]

Jubilant, Custer invited his subordinate officers to go after nightfall to serenade Sheridan. "He received us in his good, genial way, shaking hands with all," Barnitz wrote of the general. "He received us in the open air, around a big camp fire. Like Grant, Sheridan is a man of few words, but he always *looks* very animated." Barnitz thought he was disappointed that Sully had not allowed them to follow the war-party trail. "It has commenced to snow since I returned from General Sheridan's camp," Barnitz added, "and if it continues I suppose it will greatly facilitate the tracking up of our 'Indian Friends.'"[56]

Sheridan planned for the 7th Cavalry to serve as the most important of three columns that would converge on the tribes believed to be wintering on the Washita River in the Indian Territory. This was outside the reservation established by the Medicine Lodge Treaty, but they were entitled to hunt anywhere south of the Arkansas. The ongoing hostilities, not the Indians' location, gave Sheridan his justification for an offensive. He ordered Major Carr to lead a column out of Fort Lyon on a southeasterly course, and Maj. Andrew J. Evans to move east with another force from Fort Bascom, New Mexico Territory. The 7th Cavalry would march south under Custer. Sheridan said he intended "to strike the Indians a hard blow and force them on to the reservations set apart for them, and if this could not be accomplished to show to the Indian that the winter season would not give him rest." He wished to ensure that "these Indians, the enemies of our race and of our civilization, shall not again be able to begin and carry on their barbarous warfare." They must surrender unconditionally or face "utter annihilation."[57]

Sheridan wanted to deny hostile Indians any shelter near Fort Cobb in the Indian Territory. Wynkoop resigned as agent for the Cheyennes, refusing to be a party to another massacre. General Sherman sent a special agent, William B. Hazen, the man who had arrested Custer at West Point in 1861. He welcomed the Comanches and Kiowas, but told the Cheyennes and Arapahoes that they must make peace with Sheridan.[58]

Some historians have argued that Sheridan based his strategy in 1868 on his use of "total war" in the Shenandoah Valley. There, Utley writes, Sheridan and Custer "had deliberately set out to spread such poverty and despair as to destroy both the ability and will to fight. Now they planned the same treatment for the Indians." Certainly past experience influenced Sheridan, but its impact should not be exaggerated. The "total war" in Virginia was not so total after all. The federal army took care to spare civilian lives—far more than in the Indian wars. Military necessity dictated the army's focus on American Indian populations. The high-plains nations could never be defeated purely through combat against their fighting men. The entire people had to be controlled. And it was obvious that the best time for an offensive was winter, when their ponies were weak from poor grazing. The army had frequently conducted winter attacks against villages full of noncombatants. The true novelty of Sheridan's campaign was the scale of his operation, with its logistics, multiple columns, and new bases.[59]

At Camp Supply, Sheridan had expected to find the 19th Kansas Cavalry, a volunteer regiment organized after the raids on the Saline and Solomon rivers. Led by former governor Samuel J. Crawford, it was supposed to support the 7th Cavalry, but no one knew where it had gone. With the trail of the hostile war party growing colder by the hour, Sheridan decided not to wait. On November 22, he called Custer into his tent and ordered him to move out at dawn.[60]

"The stars were still shining when Custer arose, swearing and charging around," recalled Ben Clark. Custer ordered reveille at four o'clock, two hours before daylight. His brother Tom drew out his breakfast as Custer berated and damned the teamsters, surgeons, civilian scouts, Osage scouts, and eleven companies of cavalrymen until they aligned into marching formation before six o'clock. Tom's delay "brought on an explosion of wrath from Custer, who charged into the tent, kicked over the mess table, and sent dishes and victuals flying in all directions," Clark said.[61]

Clark served as Custer's chief of scouts. The thin twenty-six-year-old "has long light hair, falling below his shoulders," one observer noted. Quiet and unpretentious, "he is a man of excellent judgment and superior intelligence," steeped in the lore of the plains. Yet he was not Custer's first choice. He initially picked Moses Milner, a heavy-bearded, corncob-pipe-smoking, hard-drinking Westerner known to all as California Joe. A decade older than Custer and far more colorful than Clark, he went west during the Mexican War and spent twenty years wandering from Montana to New Mexico. Custer enjoyed his stories, as he rode along on an undersized mule. But he was a drunk, so Custer replaced him with Clark, who led a detachment of several civilian scouts, including Jack Corbin and Raphael Romero.

Roughly twenty-five, Romero was said to be a Mexican who had been taken by Indians as a boy—or else of mixed Mexican and Arapaho ancestry. He certainly knew the languages and ways of the Cheyennes and Arapahoes. "His hair never made the acquaintance of a comb, and his hair is almost equally unacquainted with water," Custer wrote to Libbie. The men mocked him as "Romeo," which amused Custer. "We have a great deal of sport with him. I threaten to put kerosene oil on his hair and set it on fire." He added, "Yet he is a very good and deserving person, in his way."[62]

At the last moment, Custer rode over to Sheridan's tent. "His first greeting was to ask what I thought about the snow," Custer later wrote. "To which I replied that nothing could be more to our purpose. We could move and the Indian villages could not. If the snow only remained on the ground one week, I promised to bring the General satisfactory evidences that my command had met the Indians." Custer led the column out of camp—on schedule—as the band played, "The Girl I Left Behind Me."[63]

Snow fell, heavier, denser. The horses trudged through a white mire that reached twelve inches. "A *very* disagreeable day," wrote Barnitz, who rode with "buffalo overshoes and lodge-skin leggings" to protect his legs as they poked out from under his greatcoat. The great horizontal of the plains disappeared behind a vertical, opaque wall. "It became unsafe for a person to wander from the column a distance equal to twice the width of Broadway," Custer wrote, making a cosmopolitan reference to New York's most famous street. He pulled out a compass and guided the regiment himself. Twelve hours after departure, they camped in the snow. The troops caught rabbits to roast over their campfires, and the Osages beat drums until long after dark.[64]

The next day the storm relented. Custer did not. When some teamsters took too long to harness their mules in the morning, he made them walk as punishment. The column moved out through the snow, hooves and wagon wheels cracking through the ice when crossing streams. The Osages directed the regiment toward the South Canadian River, into sight of an impressive set of buttes called the Antelope Hills.[65]

On November 26, on the bank of the South Canadian River, Custer decided to search for the trail of the war party detected near Camp Supply. He sent three companies to march eastward along the river, under Maj. Joel Elliott. At twenty-eight, Elliott was a year younger than Custer, and had commanded the regiment during his suspension. Born to Quaker parents in Indiana, the Burnside-whiskered Elliott saw heavy combat during the Civil War, rising from an enlisted man to the rank of captain in the 7th Indiana Cavalry. In 1865 he had served as Custer's judge advocate in Texas. Impressed, Custer had added his support to a lobbying effort by Elliott's political friends to secure him his post as major in the 7th Cavalry.[66]

Elliott took his three companies along the north bank as Custer crossed the river with the rest of the regiment. Custer marched south into the Antelope Hills, which he ascended to survey the country below. He was about to order the column to move out when a rider appeared in the distance. Putting his field glass to his eyes, he saw Jack Corbin, a scout who had gone with Elliott. He brought word that Elliott had discovered a fresh trail twelve miles away, made by the Indian war party as it returned south, 150 strong. It crossed the river and angled to the southeast.

Custer sent Corbin back on a fresh horse with orders for Elliott to follow the trail. Custer would head southeast, aiming to intercept him near nightfall. He had the bugler blow a signal to call the officers together. For greater speed, he said, they would leave their tents and extra blankets with the wagons, which would follow behind with an eighty-man escort. Each trooper would carry rations and forage in his saddlebags, along with 100 rounds of carbine ammunition. Four ambulances would follow more closely, along with two wagons carrying extra ammunition and forage.

Just as Custer was setting out, Captain Hamilton came up. He had been assigned command of the main wagon train. He begged to be allowed to join the strike force. Custer allowed him to switch places with Lt. Edward Mathey, who suffered from snowblindness. The command rode out. They remained in the saddle until 9 p.m., when they found Elliott's camp some thirty miles from where they started.[67]

Custer allowed only an hour for rest and dinner. They were now in the enemy's country. There were no more bugle calls and no smoking.

Anything that clanged or jangled was tied tight. The band did not play, the men did not sing, nor did they talk.

Hard Rope and Little Beaver led the pursuit on foot, examining the ground to keep on the war party's trail. The temperature dropped again, and the snow developed a hard crust. The sound of several hundred horses crunching through the surface seemed thunderous. Custer followed, several hundred yards back, and the reunited regiment remained another half mile behind as it marched through freezing darkness.[68]

Hard Rope and Little Beaver stopped. Custer quietly sent an order to halt the column and went forward. "What is the matter?" he asked.

"Me smell fire," Little Beaver answered. (If the broken English sounds suspiciously stereotypical, other witnesses described the same speech pattern.) Custer smelled nothing, and ordered the march to continue. Less than a mile later the Osages halted again. Little Beaver pointed to a dying campfire about seventy-five yards away.[69]

They were very close to their target. The regiment waited as Custer, Hard Rope, and Little Beaver crept up one hill after another, peered over, then moved ahead to the next. Around midnight, Custer met Little Beaver on another ridge as the scout returned from a search of the valley beyond. "Heaps Injuns down there," he said.

Custer stretched out in the snow on the crest next to his guide. He peered at the valley in the moonlight. Given the trees clustered along the Washita, it was hard to make out anything. He heard a tinkling bell, indicating a pony herd. He was convinced. Then he heard something else: "the distant cry of an infant."[70]

He ordered Clark to take Corbin and Romero to reconnoiter the village, hidden in a wooded bend in the river, and its surroundings. When they returned, Clark guessed it contained perhaps 150 warriors. Custer ordered the regiment to double back to reduce the chance of discovery. He told the officers to remove their noisy sabers and ascend the ridge to familiarize themselves with the landscape below.

Custer quietly explained his improvised plan. The roughly 800 men would divide into four columns. Elliott would take three companies to the left and swing around to the far side—the eastern side—of the village. Capt. William Thompson would lead two companies to the right and place them south of the village. Capt. Edward Myers would take two companies to the right as well, though not so far. Each of these three detachments would use hills and ridges for cover. Custer would remain in place with one squadron (two companies) under Captain Hamilton and another under Capt. Robert West. He would also have the sharpshooters and the band. There would be no fires, and he insisted on absolute silence.

They would attack from all sides at dawn, when the band struck up the jaunty drinking song "Garry Owen." Ben Clark recalled, "Custer said that this air more nearly suggested the trampling and roar of a cavalry charge than any other he knew of."[71]

This was what Custer did best: plan and fight battles. Few if any of his officers had spent more time in combat, and none had so much command experience. He took every precaution in his approach. He assessed the terrain and improvised accordingly. He plotted the converging attack and explained it with professionalism and clarity. His plan was not an innovation, though. "The tactic was a mainstay during the Indian wars—both before and after" the coming battle, writes the historian Jerome Greene.

As the officers listened to Custer, a star flared in the sky, catching everyone's attention. It was so unusual that someone speculated that the Indians had gotten ahold of pyrotechnics and had fired off a signal. Clark recalled, "Custer, who was impressed by such incidents, called it 'the Star of the Washita,' saying that it presaged victory for him." The meeting broke up, and the various columns moved out.[72]

Frozen, exhausted, unable even to stamp around to keep themselves warm, the men of the 7th Cavalry took their positions and waited for daylight. One of Custer's hounds, left with the wagon train, suddenly appeared. It heard dogs bark in the village, and barked in return. Fearing discovery, Custer muzzled it. It was not enough. He and Tom strangled it with a lariat. Finally the sky brightened in the east. Smoke could be seen drifting up from lodges among the trees. Custer's detachment mounted, except for the sharpshooters. Custer turned to order the band to play. A gunshot rang out in the valley. He signaled. "Garry Owen" blared from the ridge. Custer spurred his black horse, revolver in hand, as the men cheered and galloped forward.[73]

ON NOVEMBER 20, 1868, as Custer feuded with Sully at Camp Supply, a sixty-seven-year-old man with long black hair hanging in braids on either side of his face spoke to Col. William B. Hazen, special military agent at Fort Cobb, Indian Territory. The man had lived out the history of the Southern Cheyennes. Born near the Black Hills, he had experienced his people's final adaptation to a fully nomadic culture, their migration south, and the wars that established them as the dominant force on the Central Plains. He won fame as a warrior against the Kiowas, Comanches, and Plains Apaches, and lived through the great peace that made these nations allies. He married into the Wotapio band, and emerged as one of its senior leaders around 1850. Despite the reputation he had earned in combat, he was a realist when it came to the whites who began to appear in large numbers in the 1840s. He wanted peace with the Americans. His reward was the Sand Creek Massacre. His name was Black Kettle.[74]

He came to Fort Cobb to keep his band out of the war. The reason they had camped on the Washita River, he told Hazen, was to distance themselves from the fighting. "The Cheyennes do not fight at all this side of the Arkansas, they do not trouble Texas, but north of the Arkansas they are almost always at war."

Black Kettle knew there was little he could do. High-plains culture was shaped more by consent and consensus than authority. His past disaster and his opposition to militancy drained his influence, even in his own band. "I have always done my best to keep my young men quiet, but some will not listen, and since the fighting began I have not been able to keep them all at home." He asked to camp at Fort Cobb. Hazen refused. Sheridan was sending soldiers to fight, he said, "and with him you must make peace."[75]

In the midst of the same blizzard that enveloped Custer's column, Black Kettle and his handful of companions rode back to their camp. They arrived late on November 26. Black Kettle called a council of his band's senior men, and told them soldiers were on the march, searching for them. The group discussed the situation late into the night, as Custer peered down on them from a ridge to the northwest. They decided that they must improve their defenses by moving to camp with the other Cheyenne bands nearby.

The evening before Black Kettle came back from Fort Cobb, the war party tracked by Elliott had appeared. The 150 or so men had split into two groups at the South Canadian, one heading directly for the main Cheyenne village, the other for Black Kettle's. Some of the warriors lived in the latter camp; others likely had friends and relatives there. According to Edmund Guerrier's sworn statement, a number of warriors from Black Kettle's band took part in the August atrocities on the Saline and Solomon. One of them, Man Who Breaks the Marrow Bones, led the attacks and carried out the rapes, along with Red Nose of the Dog Soldiers.

Black Kettle and the others who had stayed up late for the council slept through the predawn hours of November 27. Fifty-one lodges comprised the village, containing perhaps 250 people, including a handful of Arapahoes, a visiting Kiowa warrior, and perhaps more men from other Cheyenne bands, back from the raid.[76]

Black Kettle awoke to a woman's voice. She ran through the camp, warning of soldiers. He grabbed his rifle, darted outside, and fired in the air to alert his people.[77]

THE OPENING NOTES of "Garry Owen" echoed in the valley, followed by the cheers of the 7th Cavalry. For the first time in three and a half years, Custer enjoyed the thrill of a cavalry charge. Ben Clark said he "rode stirrup to stirrup" alongside him. He watched Custer leap his horse clear over the Washita, nine to twelve feet wide, landing on the south bank where the village was located. A warrior emerged from a lodge and raised his rifle. Clark saw Custer aim his revolver and shoot him down, then ride straight through the camp to a rise of ground beyond, where he could better observe the fight.[78]

Captain Hamilton rode next to Custer. As they plunged into the village, Custer heard him say to his squadron, "Now men, keep cool, fire low, and not too rapidly." Almost immediately a bullet struck and killed him. The young aristocrat—grandson of Alexander Hamilton—had begged to join the attack, and was the regiment's first casualty.[79]

Soldiers galloped through the camp, firing revolvers into lodges. Women and children ran screaming from the tepees as men fired back. Many of the Cheyennes took refuge in the freezing Washita, where they found a kind of natural trench behind its high banks. Black Kettle rode his iron-gray horse into its waters with his wife, Medicine Woman Later (or Woman Here After), behind him. They were both shot dead. The soldiers gained control of the village in a few minutes. They began to root out the people who had fortified themselves in the river, firing whenever a head appeared. Some of the warriors took to the trees or ravines outside the village. Steady, slow sniping, led by the sharpshooters, brought them down, one by one.

The cordon Custer had thrown around the village proved incomplete. Some escaped the camp, followed by detachments of cavalrymen. Clark told Custer that one squadron was gunning down women and children, and he ordered it stopped at once. He told Romero to gather all the women and children he could find in a central location, and assure them that they would be spared. In the chaos of the initial attack, though, the troops shot down dozens. And all Cheyenne men, writes Jerome Greene, were executed "as a matter of policy."[80]

Lt. Edward Godfrey received orders to gather up the pony herds around the camp. As he finished up, he later wrote, "I observed a group of dismounted Indians escaping down the opposite side of the valley." He took part of his company and followed them downstream, riding farther and farther until two of his sergeants began to grow nervous. He ascended a ridge for a better view. "I was amazed to find that as far as I could see down the well wooded, tortuous valley there were tepees—tepees. Not only could I see tepees, but mounted warriors scurrying in our direction."

Godfrey and his men made a fighting retreat, one squad firing to cover the withdrawal of the other. He sought out Custer and told him of the big village. "He exclaimed, 'What's that?' and put me through a lot of rapid fire questions." Godfrey said he had found Barnitz's horse. Custer told him Barnitz had been shot.[81]

Custer ordered the camp destroyed. The troops piled the lodges and their contents together and set an enormous fire—though not until after Custer had selected, as his personal trophy, an exceptionally large, fine tepee. He also ordered the slaughter of the horse herd. One by one, 875 ponies were shot dead over an hour and a half.[82]

By then scores of warriors swarmed on the heights around the valley. Some of them found the pile of greatcoats left by Custer's detachment; they waved them in the air and dared the soldiers to come get them. Skirmishing erupted around the perimeter as the cavalry drove back the enveloping Indians. Ammunition ran low. Just in time, the two wagons carrying additional rounds and forage for the horses burst onto the scene, driven at top speed by Lt. James Bell.

Custer interrogated Godfrey further about the huge village he had seen—clearly the source of the fighters who surrounded them. (It was, in fact, a mass encampment a few miles downstream of about 6,000 Arapahoes and Southern Cheyennes.) And Elliott could not be found. Custer asked Clark if he knew where Elliott was, without success.

The men of the 7th Cavalry faced growing danger. They were surrounded, perhaps outnumbered. They were cut off from their supply train, which was vulnerable to capture. They could not risk remaining overnight, despite their exhaustion. Custer believed that fighting his way back would simply lead the enemy to his own wagons.

Instead, he thought up a ruse. He ordered the regiment into a consolidated formation, with the captive women and children in the center. He put out flanking riders, Clark recalled, to look for Elliott and snipe at their besiegers. With the band playing, "Ain't I Glad to Get Out of the Wilderness," they marched slowly *toward* the main village. The warriors immediately rode back to defend their own. The heights above the valley emptied. As darkness fell, the column abruptly changed face and rode quickly in the other direction. And still they had found no sign of Elliott.[83]

TWO WEEKS LATER, Sheridan and Custer looked down at Elliott's body. It was one of eighteen naked corpses, mutilated, perforated with bullets and arrows, and "frozen as solidly as stone," an observer reported. They were inside a perimeter fifteen yards wide, surrounded by spent cartridges.

Custer had returned to Camp Supply immediately after the Battle of the Washita, as the fight was called. Sheridan delighted in his success. It was precisely what he had demanded of his protégé. But Elliott's disappearance haunted the victory celebrations. The 7th Cavalry rested and refitted for several days. On December 4, Sheridan and all the officers of the regiment buried Hamilton. (Barnitz survived his wound, to everyone's surprise.) On December 7, they had set out again for the Washita along with Sheridan and the 19th Kansas Volunteer Cavalry, which had finally arrived.[84]

They had come on December 10. The next day they went to the killing field. Dense black clouds of flapping crows and ravens, startled by their approach, lifted off the corpses of horses and men, women, and children. A number of the dead had been tended to by survivors and placed in branches of trees, in the custom of the high-plains peoples. Soon afterward they found Elliott and his party. Early in the battle he had seen some Cheyennes escaping, and had called for volunteers to go after them. They were surrounded by warriors riding up from the main village and wiped out.[85]

The discovery of Elliott and his men completed the list of casualties the 7th Cavalry suffered on November 27. Two officers and eighteen enlisted men died, and two officers and twelve enlisted men were wounded. Tom Custer suffered a minor wound to his hand. The losses inflicted on the Southern Cheyennes and their allies remain uncertain. Custer tallied up reports from his subordinates and gave a total of 103 warriors killed (with fifty-three women and children held as prisoners). He did not tally the dead noncombatants. After returning to the Washita, he claimed that his report undercounted the Indian fatalities. Ben Clark later guessed that the 7th Cavalry killed seventy-five warriors and roughly the same number of women and children. Custer's prisoners and Cheyennes who spoke to federal agents identified their dead as thirteen Cheyenne men, three more from other nations, sixteen women, and nine children.

The true number of Indian dead must lie between these figures. Custer's total of 103 may be taken as an upper limit of lost fighting men. But, as Robert Utley writes, the "Indian calculations . . . are as improbably low as Custer's are high." At least two, Cranky Man and Double Wolf, were killed as they emerged from their lodges; Barnitz alone killed at least two, and likely a third, elsewhere; Elliott's doomed party killed at least a few; and Black Kettle himself died on his horse. It is highly improbable that in the many hours of fighting, including clashes with the warriors from the main village, the entire regiment killed only four or five more men. More women and children may have died as well. The Cheyenne count was subject to human error just as Custer's was. Witnesses agreed that it had been an extremely bloody affair. It essentially wiped out Black Kettle's band, and cost the Cheyennes dearly in destroyed goods and horses.[86]

On December 12, Sheridan and the two regiments passed through the abandoned site of the main village. There they found Clara Blinn and her son, Willie. They had been murdered while eating corn bread. Custer blamed the Kiowas. But Hazen sent word that the Kiowas were peaceful, and their leaders Satanta and Lone Wolf rode to meet Sheridan's force. Sheridan arrested the two men and held them as hostages until all the Kiowas reported at Fort Cobb. To bring in the remaining Cheyennes and Arapahoes, Custer selected one of his prisoners, a woman named Mahwissa, as an envoy. She was Black Kettle's sister. She said she could convince them to surrender, since Custer held so many prisoners from the Washita. Some came in, but she herself never returned.[87]

Large numbers of members of various nations poured in to Fort Cobb before the end of 1868, all fearing that Sheridan would attack them if they remained at large. On New Year's Day, Custer held his own council with the Kiowas, Comanches, Arapahoes, Plains Apaches, and Southern Cheyennes. "The arrogance and pride is whipped out of the Indians," he wrote to Libbie. "They have surrendered themselves into our keeping." Recognizing that humble Fort Cobb was overwhelmed, Sheridan established a new post thirty miles away on the edge of the Wichita Mountains. He called it Fort Sill.[88]

Custer took a detachment to search the Wichita Mountains for the other Southern Cheyennes. After returning to Fort Sill in February he wrote to Libbie, "None of us feel that we could or aught to leave here until we see the end of the Indian matter."

As he prepared the regiment for another foray, he remained as demanding as ever. He made a point of arresting his own brother for a minor offense, along with Capt. Robert West, the man who had charged him with murder. He hectored Tom to write home, and complained that "he is becoming more profane & a little vulgar." But he displayed none of the brittleness that marked his nadir in 1867. He felt wonderful, as exuberant as during the war. He joyfully promised Eliza Brown a buffalo robe. "Custer luck" would prevail, he wrote. "It is better to be born lucky than rich."[89]

Spring approached. Soon the grass would spring up, the Cheyennes' ponies would regain their strength, and the army would lose its advantage in mobility. The army estimated that the Cheyennes still at large comprised 1,400 individuals in 200 lodges—a group four times larger than the band Custer had crushed at the Washita. Increasing the pressure on Custer were two white women held by the Cheyennes as captives, twenty-four-year-old Anna Brewster Morgan and eighteen-year-old Sarah White. Morgan's brother, Daniel Brewster, was a civilian teamster, driving a wagon with the troops.[90]

Custer moved out from Fort Sill on March 2 with the 7th Cavalry and ten companies of the 19th Kansas, which lacked horses for many of its men. He led them southwest toward the Texas Panhandle. Custer divided the force in half. Captain Myers took the dismounted men to a supply depot near the Washita battlefield. Custer led troops who still had horses, from both regiments, into the emptiness of Texas.

"We had marched but one day when we struck the trail of a single lodge, which we followed through a country almost impassable, and utterly destitute of wood or pure water, for several days," wrote a noncommissioned officer in the column. "We were now on the edge of a desert, with no wood or water west of us for two days' journey," he added. "We were nearly all dismounted, one-fourth of our wagons had been burned [for fuel], and we were subsisting entirely on mule meat."

Custer pressed on. They found an old trail. He asked the Osage scouts about it. "Very old, two months old at least," they told him. He decided to follow it anyway. It led to a fresh trail. He prohibited bugle calls, shooting, anything that might alert the Cheyennes to their approach. On March 15, they surprised a large camp, some 260 lodges, on Sweetwater Creek, a tributary of the Red River. One of its leaders was Medicine Arrows, keeper of the sacred arrows, some of the holiest Cheyenne artifacts.[91]

Custer could have attacked. The Kansas troops demanded it. With his force of more than 1,000 men—and no women and children to protect—he almost certainly would have prevailed. But he considered the consequences. Hundreds would likely escape and continue the war indefinitely. He also remembered the captives Anna Morgan and Sarah White—and the fate of Clara and Willie Blinn after he attacked at the Washita. "I knew that the first shot fired on either side would be the signal for the murder of the two white girls," he wrote. So he signaled for a parley. Medicine Arrows himself rode out to meet him, and Custer agreed to come to a council in the village, accompanied only by Lieutenant Cooke. On the ride in, he spotted Mahwissa.

Fifteen senior men sat with Custer in Medicine Arrows's lodge in the center of the camp, in a circle around a large fire. Cooke was kept out. A ritual pipe was prepared, given to Custer to smoke, then passed around; a Cheyenne report claims that the ashes were dumped out on Custer's boots to curse him. The Cheyennes acknowledged that the captives were in the camp, promised to return them, and agreed to let his troops bivouac nearby. They would surrender and come in with him.

"I felt confident that as soon as it was dark the entire village would probably steal away," Custer later wrote. Indeed, he initially deployed his men to cut off any flight. Over the next four days, complicated negotiations unfolded. The Cheyennes did not release the captives immediately. At one point the women and children fled, only to be coaxed back with the promise of being allowed to collect their possessions—a sign he had learned from Hancock's mistake at Pawnee Fork in 1867. Finally Custer seized three leaders, Dull Knife (also called Lean Face), Big Head (also called Curly Head), and Fat Bear. If the two white women were not released by sundown on March 19, he warned, he would kill the three men. He showed them the tree where he would hang them, so there would be no misunderstanding. After he executed them, he planned to assault the village.

Late in the afternoon of the designated day, the Cheyennes released the captives. When Daniel Brewster saw Anna Morgan and Sarah White, they were starving, dressed in rags sewn together from flour sacks and bits of old tents and blankets. One scout said, "I never saw such heartbroken, hopeless expressions on the face of another human being." One Kansas volunteer thought Morgan looked fifty—twice her actual age. "She was stooped, pale, and haggard."[92]

Custer trusted that his three hostages would induce the Cheyennes to come in to army custody. He set out on a miserable march to Camp Supply, his men suffering from a shortage of water and rations, the horses dying of starvation and exhaustion. He was often self-indulgent as a commander, lacking any sympathy for the enlisted men—but not on this expedition. The officers split up the food "equally with the men," wrote David Spotts of the 19th Kansas, "even to Gen. Custer, who turned his private wagon over to the men and told them to divide what it contained among themselves, for he could live without eating as long as any of them."[93]

Months would pass before the last of the Cheyennes and their allies came in to the forts. But the Dog Soldiers returned to the middle country when the grass came up. On July 11, 1869, Maj. Eugene Carr led the 5th Cavalry and a detachment of Pawnee scouts in a surprise attack on their camp near Summit Springs in the Colorado Territory. They killed the famous Tall Bull along with scores of men, women, and children. It was "the effective end of the Dog Soldiers as a force of resistance," writes Elliott West, definitively terminating the Southern Plains War of 1868–69.[94]

Custer congratulated Carr on his extraordinary summer victory. It was a sign of his satisfaction with himself. "I have been successful in my campaign against the Cheyennes," he wrote to Libbie on March 24. "I outmarched them, outwitted them at their own game, [and] proved to them they were in my power." He had accomplished everything Sheridan asked of him and more. His redemption was complete.[95]

"THE CHARACTER OF THE BAND of Indians, almost annihilated in the late attack by Gen. Custer, has been the subject of much discussion, some maintaining that they were friendly Indians," wrote the *New York Observer and Chronicle* on December 24, 1868.[96]

As soon as Sheridan announced the Battle of the Washita, a controversy erupted over whether Custer had committed an atrocity. Black Kettle was well known as an advocate of peace. The slaughter of his people at Sand Creek still resonated as a symbol of the brutal excesses of the Indian wars. In striking him again—with a surprise attack that completely destroyed his band—Custer appeared to have repeated it. Edward Wynkoop denounced the attack as "simply a massacre." Other public figures said the same thing. The *New York Times* fiercely defended Custer against "the charge that [he] had attacked and massacred a band of peaceful Indians," but even it observed that the Washita fight was "a pretty murderous affair. . . . Nothing is said of a single [male Cheyenne] being captured—from which we may guess that all were dispatched."[97]

It was an inescapable fact that Custer killed the leading Southern Cheyenne peace advocate. But he did not show unusual carelessness in launching his assault, within the context of the Indian wars. He attacked Black Kettle because that was where the trail of a war party led. He and Sheridan pointed to mules, mail, and other loot in the village which had been stolen in recent raids. Even disregarding this evidence, the testimony of Edmund Guerrier, Little Rock, and Black Kettle himself identified members of the latter's band as participants—one as a leader—in the atrocities on the Saline and Solomon and subsequent attacks. Custer has been criticized for not knowing who he was attacking; but no army officer with similar orders would have surrendered the advantage of surprise to sound out the band's leaders. In any event, Custer only struck Black Kettle's band because Sheridan refused to allow any Cheyennes a refuge at Fort Cobb. This order led directly to Black Kettle's death, and Sheridan issued it long before Custer first set out from Camp Supply.

Was it a massacre? He did charge a population center and kill women and children. The historian Jerome Greene notes that he did not order their murder, but rather intervened to save them. The surprise attack on a sleeping village was a standard tactic because it was effective. "The presence of women and children immobilized the warriors and forced them to defend their ground," writes Richard Slotkin. It inevitably killed noncombatants, though not as intentionally as the gruesome bombings of cities in World War II, for example. The point is not to justify this tactic, but to place Custer in context. At the less controversial Summit Springs, Major Carr produced a similar tally.[98]

And yet, Custer clearly carried out an atrocity, at Sheridan's command. His orders were stark: "To destroy their villages and ponies; *to kill or hang all warriors*, and bring back all women and children" (emphasis added). The 7th Cavalry took no adult male prisoners—though not because of any special villainy on Custer's part. Few field officers objected to such orders. They saw themselves at war with "the enemies of our race," as Sheridan called them, and were outraged by Indian attacks on civilians. Sully, no friend to Custer, wrote privately that the Washita was entirely justified, and he hoped that there would be no "peace before these red devils are properly punished." Custer's bitterest enemy, Benteen, described the foe at the Washita as "the murderous redskin." Of course, posterity need not excuse this murder of all men, no matter how ordinary at the time. Ever since the Nuremberg trials, orders have not been considered justification for crimes against humanity. In subsequent campaigning Custer himself refrained from slaughter even though it was expected of him. It could be avoided.[99]

The most telling criticism of Custer, then and now, is not that he personally was unusually bloodthirsty, but that the wars themselves were unjustifiable. The relationship between the United States and the high-plains nations was one of an industrializing, rapidly growing, and aggressive society overwhelming far smaller and less powerful peoples who relied on hunting, gathering, and trade. It was not fair. One may question whether "war" is the proper term; the United States might have withheld its military power and still prevailed. The very existence of the United States was predicated on the dispossession of the indigenous. If Custer was wrong, ultimately it was because the nation was wrong. Many believe it was. But he was no outlier.[100]

When given a second chance to score a military victory, Custer held back. He was motivated by his hope of saving the two white women. It was a humane decision, but also a romantic one. With the desperate brother of one prisoner at his side, he recast his military mission as a rescue. Would Sheridan, Sherman, or Grant have held back? Masters of modernity's grim realism, they may well have accepted the captives' deaths as the price of the state's assertion of its authority. What we know is that Custer, despite his reputation for impetuosity, exercised discretion.

A second controversy over the Washita exploded while Custer was still in the field. On February 9, 1869, the *St. Louis Democrat* published a letter written by an officer of the 7th Cavalry (reprinted within days by the *New York Times* and *Chicago Tribune*). It gave a vivid account of the Battle of the Washita, simultaneously florid and sarcastic. For example, it described the killing of the ponies this way: "Our Chief exhibits his close sharp-shooting and terrifies the crowd of frighted, captured squaws and papooses by dropping the straggling ponies in death near them. Ah! he is a clever marksman." The main thrust of the letter was to condemn Custer for failing to look for Elliott. "But surely some search will be made for our missing comrades. No, they are forgotten. Over them and the poor ponies the wolves will hold high carnival, and their howlings will be their only requiem."[101]

Benteen wrote it. He blamed the lieutenant colonel for Elliott's disaster. He asked Ben Clark to swear that Custer had ordered Elliott to his death. Clark refused, knowing that Custer had had no idea where he went. On the feint toward the main village, Clark said, flankers were told to look for Elliott. He noted that they were in serious danger after capturing the village, and Custer's priority had to be extricating his force.[102]

Sheridan believed that he should have tried harder. Indeed, Custer's departure from the Washita without Elliott echoed his abandonment of two casualties in 1867. But the Washita was not such a clear case. Elliott rode off on his own, and sent no word of his intentions. By the time his absence was noted any rescue would have been too late. Historians would later debate whether Elliott's death can be blamed on Custer's failure to carry out a thorough reconnaissance before the attack, which might have detected the downstream villages. Perhaps, though Custer did dispatch his scouts to search around Black Kettle's village; after marching all night, he feared any more maneuvering would eliminate the crucial advantage of surprise. But emotion, not logic, ruled Benteen.[103]

Ten years later, a friend of Benteen's named Robert Newton Price, still a cadet at West Point during these events, published a secondhand account of the consequences of Benteen's anonymous letter. Custer called his officers together, "and they assembled to find him walking up and down, switching his legs with a riding whip. He referred to the letter, saying it could only have been written by some officer of that regiment, and directed the author to step up to the front. Colonel Benteen did so at once." According to Price, Custer folded, saying only, "Colonel, I'll see you again on this matter."

This hearsay account would be embellished over the years, with Benteen placing his hand on his revolver in a threatening manner and urging Custer to commence whipping. The latter version is preposterous on its face. Cowardice was not one of Custer's faults; he had likely killed more men in close combat than Benteen ever had. Nor did Benteen display such physical bravado with his commanding officer on any other occasion. Rather he would defend his insubordination with petty excuses.[104]

It's difficult to know what to make of even Price's more straightforward account. This scene repeats one that occurred in Texas, where Custer threatened to whip a major in the 2nd Wisconsin for slandering him.[105] That could lend credibility to Price's account, as Custer might have repeated himself. Alternatively Price or Benteen might have heard the earlier story and inserted Benteen into it; Benteen could have developed a sincere but false memory after retelling the tale. Or perhaps some kind of confrontation took place, though not so flattering to Benteen. If it occurred as Price described it, it would have been dramatic, yet contemporary accounts from other witnesses have yet to surface. Indeed, Custer would have had grounds to arrest Benteen for the letter alone; we know he had the will, as he arrested officers for far less. If Benteen confessed—if he threatened his superior officer—why no charges? Why no official complaint? Whether it occurred or not, Custer now knew he had an enemy in the regiment.

BENTEEN TOLD ANOTHER STORY about Custer that is more likely true. In the weeks and months that followed the Washita, he said, Romero acted as a pimp with the female captives, bringing them to officers' tents for sex. Custer selected the daughter of Little Rock, Young Grass That Shoots in Spring, or Monahsetah (also referred to as Meotzi).

Ben Clark described the same thing years later to the researcher Walter Camp, insisting that he not be quoted. He claimed that Custer disguised Monahsetah's role as his mistress by making her the helper to the white woman who was his cook. Indeed, Custer himself praised her beauty in his published writings, and he brought her along on his last march. Cheyenne tradition agrees, and states that they had a child. The story has been closely scrutinized. Historians agree that he did not father a baby born to her in January 1869, though reportedly she became pregnant again soon after the birth. Jeffry Wert theorizes that he was sterile from treatment for gonorrhea at West Point—a plausible if unprovable conjecture. But Clark's account gives weight to the tale of a liaison, particularly since he did not share Benteen's spite. It would not be surprising if Custer took Monahsetah. He was enthusiastic about sex, considered American Indians exotic, and thought she was attractive. He lived in a frontier culture in which white men saw "squaws" as not fully human and "Indian wives" as acceptable regardless of legal marital status.[106]

Custer may have been willing to take the risk because of his restored confidence in his relationship with Libbie. His letters from the field lacked the agonized quality of his 1867 correspondence. Now he addressed her as "my little bunkey," but in a tone of authority, even moral superiority. On February 8, 1869, he observed that she placed herself "upon guard" when he mentioned "a certain mutual friend against whom I warned you." He said that he hoped to go to Washington but that she might not want to go, "as you so longed for 11worth last summer when away and have opposed my obtaining a leave heretofore." He had told her before that "I *must go* for twenty days. This is on my own account. I will go for a longer period if *you* deserve it and intend accompanying me."[107]

Did he suspect her of having an affair in Leavenworth? Of flirting with someone rather too blatantly? Or did he merely resent her not wanting to go with him? If nothing else, he clearly felt that he had the upper hand.

His victory at the Washita restored some of his fame. Friendly accounts in the *New York Times* and elsewhere more than balanced the controversy, recasting the Boy General as a "cavalier in buckskin," to quote the title of Utley's biography. But he would discover that the nation no longer needed cavaliers.

In St. Louis in 1866, the Custers met actor Lawrence Barrett, one of the stars of the stage after the Civil War. Enormous fans of the theater, the Custers developed a close friendship with Barrett over the years. *Courtesy of Dr. David S. Shields, Broadway Photographs, http://broadway.cas.sc.edu*

Fort Leavenworth, Kansas, headquarters for the military Department of the Missouri, 1867. Custer spent many months there during his years in the state. Like most forts on the Great Plains, it was built on an open, rectangular pattern. *Library of Congress*

Motion, not settlement, caused much of the conflict with the American Indian nations of the high plains in Kansas, Colorado, and Nebraska. As illustrated here, railroad construction crews and migrant wagon trains crossing to Denver and points farther west consumed and degraded resources in river valleys that were critical to the survival of nomadic culture. *Library of Congress*

Gen. Winfield Scott Hancock first met Custer in the Peninsula Campaign. He took command of the Department of the Missouri after the Civil War and led an expedition onto the Great Plains to intimidate the Southern Cheyennes and their allies, sparking a war that led to Custer's court-martial in 1867. Faced with marital difficulties and a frustrating campaign, Custer abandoned his troops to reconcile with his wife. For that and other offenses he was tried, convicted, and suspended from pay and duty for a year. *Library of Congress*

Gen. William T. Sherman commanded the vast Division of the Missouri, and attended personally to the war that Hancock ignited in 1867. Grimly unsentimental, he advocated harsh measures to crush indigenous resistance, but despaired at the difficulties in policing the vast West. *Library of Congress*

The Oglala Lakota leader Pawnee Killer (center) made a fool of Custer in the summer of 1867. Sherman ordered his detention as a hostage, but Custer allowed him to go after Pawnee Killer inspected the 7th Cavalry's camp and talked Custer into giving him supplies. *Library of Congress*

After Custer allowed Pawnee Killer to escape, he searched the headwaters of the Republican River. Sherman sent him new orders in the care of Lt. Lyman Kidder, a scout, and a ten-man escort. Custer (standing at left) found them all dead, likely at Pawnee Killer's hands. They were stripped naked, mutilated, and riddled with arrows. Artist Theodore Davis of *Harper's Weekly*, a witness to this scene, rendered the dead as skeletons since the gruesome reality was unpublishable. *Library of Congress*

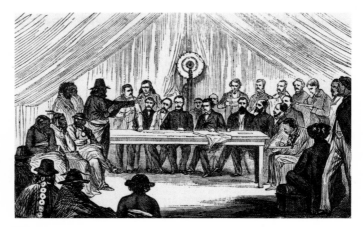

ABOVE: On October 19, 1867, a federal peace commission negotiated with the native nations of the Central and Southern Plains at Medicine Lodge, Kansas. Here the Kiowa leader Satanta addresses the council. The result was a treaty that created a new reservation for them in the Indian Territory (modern-day Oklahoma). Southern Cheyenne anger at the loss of their homeland, along with federal missteps, led to an outbreak of fighting in 1868. *Library of Congress* LEFT: Custer received a reprieve and returned to duty in late 1868. Sheridan, now in command of the Department of the Missouri, assigned him to strike the Southern Cheyennes in winter, when snow limited their mobility. Custer wore this buckskin outfit, which was typical of his costume in the West. *Courtesy of the National Park Service, Little Bighorn Battlefield, Elizabeth B. Custer Collection*

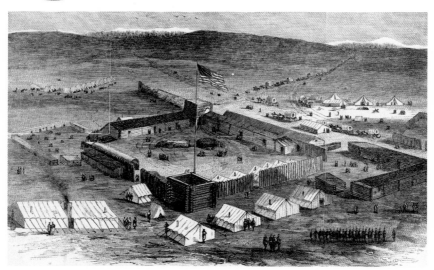

At the start of the 1868 campaign, a new base in the Indian Territory was established for Custer's column, called Camp Supply. Custer brought his prisoners back here. Unlike most Western forts, it featured enclosing walls. *Library of Congress*

GENERAL CUSTER'S COMMAND MARCHING TO ATTACK THE CHEYENNE VILLAGE.

BURNING OF FORT LAFAYETTE.

ABOUT noon, on the 1st inst., Fort Lafayette took fire from the chimney of a fire-place in which a fire had been kindled by one of the workmen engaged in repairs upon the work. The roof was soon ablaze, and the fire continued through the afternoon and night, fed by the pine shingles and lumber crowded inside of the fort for the use of the workmen. The alarm was immediately given, and, as it was known that the fort inclosed a magazine containing ten tons of powder, the inhabitants of Fort Hamilton were filled with consternation, and fled in panic to a safer neighborhood.

Fortunately the flames did not reach the magazine, which was protected by two doors several feet apart and by a thick wall of brick.

Fort Lafayette was built after the close of our Revolutionary contest with Great Britain, to guard the entrance of New York harbor. It stood on the Long Island side of the bay, about six miles below the city, and almost directly opposite Fort Wadsworth on Staten Island. It was built on a reef about 300 yards from the shore, and at low tide was surrounded by about six feet of water. The structure was quaint in appearance from the outside as well as within. The inner wall was diamond-shaped, and rose five or six feet higher than the wall surrounding it. The top surface of the inner wall sloped toward the centre, and it was upon this strong rampart that the heavy guns were mounted.

The original name of the work was Fort Diamond, but about forty-four years ago it received its present name in honor of General LAFAYETTE, the French Revolutionary hero.

The progress made in the construction of ordnance long ago rendered this fortification almost useless for defensive purposes. It is chiefly noted as "the American Bastile," in which political prisoners were confined during the late war. In its cells were placed men who, like BENJAMIN WOOD, abused the liberty of the press; commercial speculators who were implicated in blockade-running; the lake pirate COLES; MARTIN, the hotel burner, and other lawless men. Cases there were, doubtless, in regard to which a great deal might be said on both sides, but the Government was obliged to act promptly. It

CAPTAIN LOUIS M. HAMILTON.—[PHOT. BY SLEE BROTHERS, POUGHKEEPSIE.]

was a time when patriotism must be like the virtue of Cæsar's wife, beyond suspicion.

The loss by the fire at Fort Lafayette is estimated at $100,000, upon which there is no insurance. Of the armament there were destroyed twenty-two 10-inch Rodman guns, with their carriages, together with one dismounted gun; ten 100-pound Parrott guns and carriages, and twelve 32-pounders with wooden carriages. The new lumber destroyed, which was used in repairing the fort, was valued at $1330.

ELECTION RIOTS IN ENGLAND.

OUR engraving on page 813 illustrates the character of the riots which formed a prominent feature in the late election. It was the first election for members of Parliament under the operation of the new Reform Bill.

We in this country can well understand how that which calls itself conservatism most readily allies itself with the elements of disturbance. DISRAELI, in appealing to the "No Popery" sentiment in England, did exactly what HORATIO SEYMOUR did in his address at the New York Academy of Music July 4, 1863. But never has it occurred in the history of this country that a popular election has been accompanied by riotous manifestations so violent and so extensive as those which attended the recent elections in England. Even the isolated instances in the Southern States during the late November election are scarcely noteworthy in the comparison. The riots in England were due to two causes: first, to the fact that a large number of the voters were unaccustomed to the exercise of the suffrage; but, secondly, and mainly, to the religious element which was allowed to enter so prominently into the contest.

Our illustration relates particularly to the disturbances at Blackburn, in the county of Lancaster. Blackburn is a manufacturing town containing 28,000 inhabitants. The mayor and other civic authorities found it impossible to quell the riot without resorting to force; and with the most energetic efforts of the police order was not restored before a great deal of mischief had been accomplished. A large number of Liberal voters in all the manufacturing districts of England were intimidated by these disturbances, and thus kept from the polls.

THE SEVENTH U. S. CAVALRY CHARGING INTO BLACK KETTLE'S VILLAGE AT DAYLIGHT, NOVEMBER 27, 1868.—[SEE PAGE 811.]

Custer's column moved out in a blizzard on November 23, 1868. He followed the trail of a Cheyenne war party to the Washita River, as depicted at the top. At dawn on November 27, the 7th Cavalry stormed a village led by Black Kettle, a spokesman for peace among the Southern Cheyennes. The cavalry suffered significant casualties, including the death of Capt. Louis Hamilton, shown here. *Library of Congress*

At the Washita the 7th Cavalry took no male prisoners. They killed all the horses of Black Kettle's band, destroyed all the lodges and other possessions, and fought off warriors from a much larger camp down the river. They returned to Camp Supply with all the surviving women and children as prisoners, shown here. *Library of Congress*

Custer closed his campaign after surprising a large Cheyenne village on March 15, 1869, on Sweetwater Creek in the Texas panhandle. Rather than attack, he negotiated for the release of two captive white women and for the Cheyennes' surrender. To secure both he seized three hostages: Big Head (also called Curly Head), Fat Bear, and Dull Knife. Big Head and Dull Knife later died in a fight with guards at Fort Hays, Kansas. *Kansas State Historical Society*

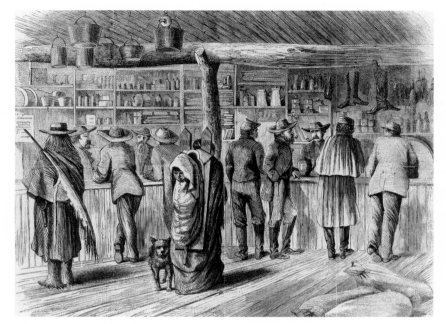

Theodore Davis drew the interior of a store operated by a sutler—a military post merchant—at Fort Dodge, Kansas. It shows the typical sutler's operation on the frontier, a combination of a crude bar and a general store. *Library of Congress*

This rare photograph captures a buffalo hunt led by Custer on the Kansas plains. He remained on duty in the state for two years, alternating between Leavenworth and Big Creek outside Fort Hays. He engaged in no more warfare there, but frequently led lengthy buffalo hunts for visiting dignitaries. *Kansas State Historical Society*

Impeached by the House of Representatives, Andrew Johnson endured a trial in the Senate in the spring of 1868, shown here, and escaped conviction by one vote. Regardless, the Republicans reigned supreme in the federal government for several years. After they lost the House in the 1874 election, Custer appeared in the Capitol, visibly associating himself with the Democratic leadership. *Library of Congress*

LEFT: Inaugurated as president in 1869, Ulysses S. Grant tried with mixed success to guide the nation in a more humane direction. He inaugurated a "peace policy" toward American Indians and enforced civil rights laws and black suffrage in the South. But the office isolated him as political foes and the white South resisted his initiatives, Indians declined to abandon their cultures and independence, and close friends proved corrupt. *Library of Congress* RIGHT: Taken in Omaha on January 11, 1872, this portrait shows Custer in both cosmopolitan finery and a sealskin cap that he wore on a grand hunting expedition with the Russian grand duke Alexis. The combination captures Custer's many roles at the time: frontiersman, public intellectual, popular magazine writer, mine promoter, gambler, stock speculator. He spent most of 1871 on leave, attempting to capitalize on his fame in the West to find a fortune on Wall Street. *Kansas State Historical Society*

Thomas Nast's 1874 engraving captures the outrage in the North at the wave of violence unleashed on African Americans in the South. State and local organizations of white supremacists adopted the common name, costumes, rituals, and brutality of the Ku Klux Klan. They helped to restore the Democratic party to power in several states by suppressing black votes. *Library of Congress*

President Grant signed a law popularly known as the Ku Klux Klan Act on April 20, 1871. It armed federal authorities with new powers to investigate and prosecute individuals for civil rights violations. Custer was assigned to enforce the act in Kentucky, a former slave state wracked by racial political violence. Custer complained about his troops' being used in this manner. *Library of Congress*

In March 1873 Custer and the 7th Cavalry were redeployed to the Dakota Territory in preparation for a march west to the Yellowstone River basin to escort a surveying party for the Northern Pacific Railway. The expedition commander was Col. David S. Stanley, who bristled against Custer and his terrible reputation within the army. "He is universally despised," Stanley wrote to his wife. *Library of Congress*

On the 1873 Yellowstone Expedition, Custer forged a good working relationship with Bloody Knife, a half-Arikara, half-Hunkpapa Lakota scout. Bloody Knife grew up with the Hunkpapas, and felt a deeply personal as well as national enmity toward them. He was a highly effective guide. *National Archives*

Sitting Bull emerged as a galvanizing religious and political figure among the Lakotas, or Teton Sioux, in the 1860s and '70s. Committed to the nomadic culture of hunting, trade, and warfare against neighboring peoples, he rejected the treaties with the United States. He helped organize two attacks on Custer's 7th Cavalry during the Yellowstone Expedition of 1873. He is shown here at left with his nephew, One Bull. *Library of Congress*

This photograph from 1891 shows the interior and exterior of Oglala Lakota lodges. The buffalo hides that comprised the lodge's skin represented countless hours of labor, and the right trees for good support poles could be difficult to find. *Library of Congress*

On September 18, 1873, word went out on Wall Street that the great banking house of Jay Cooke had fallen. Cooke could no longer market the securities of the Northern Pacific, the railway that Custer defended both under arms and in print. A financial panic ensued, shown here outside Cooke's Wall Street offices, sparking a great depression. Yet Custer himself returned to these streets two years later to speculate on the stock exchange. *Library of Congress*

In 1874, Custer led an expedition to explore the Black Hills, on the southwest border of the Dakota Territory and the Great Sioux Reservation, and select a site for a fort. His discovery of gold led to an influx of illegal immigrants amid the depression. During the expedition he shot a large bear, which he believed to be a grizzly, shown here. (Bloody Knife is at left.) *National Archives*

Custer commanded Fort Abraham Lincoln on the Missouri River, opposite Bismarck, from 1873 to 1876. This scene in his house there offers a glimpse of his social circle, including many family members. Left to right: Custer's brother Boston, his sister Maggie Custer Calhoun, who married one of his officers, Lt. Winfield S. Edgerly, Libbie, Leonard "Bert" Swett, Richard E. Thompson, Nellie Wadsworth, Tom Custer, George Armstrong Custer, Emma Watson, and Emily Watson. *Courtesy of the National Park Service, Little Bighorn Battlefield, Elizabeth B. Custer Collection*

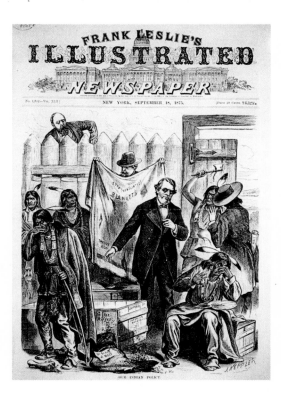

A wave of corruption scandals swept over the Grant administration late in the president's second term—some a continuation of longstanding graft, some the work of Grant's dishonest friends and relatives, but all pressed home by Democratic politicians. Custer began to leak accounts to the *New York Herald* of corruption in the Indian agencies, depicted here. *Library of Congress*

Representative Hiester Clymer took the chairmanship of the House Committee on Expenditures in the Department of War after the Democrats swept the midterm election of 1874. In early 1876 he prepared impeachment charges against his old college roommate, Secretary of War William W. Belknap. He brought Custer to Washington to testify against Belknap, delaying a planned offensive against Sitting Bull. *Library of Congress*

Rumors had long circulated that Secretary Belknap took kickbacks or bribes from merchants or political fixers in return for lucrative sutler contracts for army posts. His first and second wives (sisters, curiously) were implicated in the scandal when it broke in 1876, as shown here. *Library of Congress*

Custer's ill-considered participation in the Democrats' investigations led President Grant to remove Custer from field command of the 7th Cavalry in the offensive against Sitting Bull. Custer had by now angered Sheridan as well, but Custer's department commander, Gen. Alfred Terry (shown here), intervened on his behalf. His tactful lobbying helped persuade Grant to relent. *Library of Congress*

Capt. Frederick Benteen was one of Custer's two most senior subordinates in the 1876 campaign. A capable combat officer, Benteen was a petty, arrogant man steeped in resentments. He hated Custer to the point of vendetta, which raises serious questions about his decisions on the first day of the Battle of the Little Bighorn, June 25, 1876. *Courtesy of the National Park Service, Little Bighorn Battlefield, Seventh Cavalry Military Records Collection*

Custer's senior subordinate in 1876 was Maj. Marcus Reno. A deeply troubled widower, afflicted with a drinking problem, he performed weakly at best at Little Bighorn, and was accused of drunkenness and cowardice. Reno demanded a court of inquiry to clear his name. It was the closest thing to a formal investigation of the battle ever conducted by the army. *Courtesy of the National Park Service, Little Bighorn Battlefield, Seventh Cavalry Military Records Collection*

Custer in his dress uniform as lieutenant colonel of the 7th Cavalry Regiment. (His service rank as a general during the Civil War was only in the U.S. Volunteers, an organization created strictly for the duration of the conflict.) This 1876 portrait shows him near the end of his life. He cut his hair short before riding out on his last campaign. *National Archives*

Custer ended his military career as he began it: conducted up from the Hudson River landing to the Plain of West Point, where his remains were interred at the U.S. Military Academy. *Library of Congress*

Thirteen

THE FINANCIER

"HE WAS BORN INTO a time when all young men of his age caught the fever of speculation, and expected to get on in the world by the omission of some of the regular processes which have been appointed from of old."

Mark Twain and Charles Dudley Warner wrote those words in 1873 in their novel *The Gilded Age*. They could have been writing about Custer as he entered the Age of Grant.[1] When Ulysses S. Grant took the presidential oath of office on March 4, 1869, the nation that emerged out of the Civil War approached maturity—or what we might call its first maturity. All that was "appointed from of old" seemed to disappear.

For both good and ill, the federal government challenged traditional, inherited distinctions and communities, as policy makers sought to turn all into individual agents, transacting business under uniform rules in a national market. For African Americans, this meant liberation; for American Indians, cultural destruction. Railroads, the telegraph, and the increasingly national media integrated the republic, connecting local markets to the whole, unifying literary tastes and culture.

Great institutions rose over this nation of individuals. Both the federal government and business corporations attained size and reach never seen before—again, for both good and ill. Antebellum companies merged to form giants. They constructed vast factories, refineries, warehouses, port facilities, rail yards, and depots. The largest firms each employed tens of thousands, from unskilled laborers to lawyers and engineers. During Grant's presidency, John D. Rockefeller, Andrew Carnegie, and J. P. Morgan would outdistance the mass of men in building industries and fortunes, and the venerable Cornelius Vanderbilt, lord of a railroad empire, would be hailed by the *Chicago Tribune* as "probably the most powerful individuality in America."[2]

The same machinery that cemented empires spun "rings" as well. In the new corporate economy, all roads ended on Wall Street, where the modernizing stock exchange and other financial markets concentrated and multiplied capital. If legitimate enterprises received funds, so did well-positioned speculators, for this was also the age of conspirators and inside traders, including Jim Fisk, Daniel Drew, and such political buccaneers as William "Boss" Tweed and Orville Babcock.[3]

Custer caught the fever. After an interregnum in Kansas in the Washita's wake, he would leave the edge of American civilization and go to its center. He would go to New York, the capital of business, media, and (in some ways) politics, where the future of each was being made. He largely rejected the changes to the country, yet he would try to profit from them. He would seek the secret of his times.

"He saw people, all around him, poor yesterday, rich today, who had come into sudden opulence by some means which they could not have classified among any of the regular occupations of life," Twain and Warner wrote. It takes no imagination to see Custer making the same observation, and concluding that he "will find somehow, and by some sudden turn of good luck, the golden road to fortune."[4]

ELIZA BROWN WENT to see the Indians. The women and children seized at the Washita remained prisoners after the Custer household reunited in April 1869 and settled into a tent camp on Big Creek near Fort Hays, which had been rebuilt after the floods that Brown and Libbie had endured two years earlier. The three hostages Armstrong took at the end of the campaign were held there as well, as the Cheyennes slowly surrendered.[5]

They were a curiosity to Brown as well as the whites all around her. With emancipation, African Americans belonged to the same economic and political system as every white from Custer to Cornelius Vanderbilt— though with vast disadvantages and cultural and social distinctions, to be sure. Black citizens handled the same currency, spoke the same language, argued about the same political questions as whites. As Custer's cook, Brown came to the West as a small part of the federal government's presence in the region, which had a tremendous impact on this sparsely populated landscape. That was true of many Western black men and women, who often found employment with the military or enterprises that served the military. The Cheyennes did not belong to this society and economy. They had a separate history, culture, language, and economy, even a separate system for relations with other nations.

They had been treated as external clients of the American economy— though that would soon end. Already the U.S. government attempted to break down the Indians' distinctiveness in order to digest them. The Medicine Lodge Treaty defined a fixed location for the residence of the Southern Plains nations—giving three million acres in exchange for the ninety million they had roamed across—and promised them farm implements, schools, teachers, skilled artisans. Grant called for their integration into U.S. society; in his inaugural address, he supported "any course toward them which tends to their civilization and ultimate citizenship." He inaugurated a "Peace Policy," relying heavily on Quaker missionaries as agents to the Indians; he meant well, but the policy constituted an attack on their religions, cultures, and languages. He named as commissioner of Indian affairs Ely S. Parker, his former military secretary. Parker was a Seneca with an extensive English-language education and engineering expertise, integrated into American society—the symbol of what Grant wanted for all Indians.[6]

This was a great contradiction, or conundrum, produced by the civil rights revolution of Reconstruction. With the Civil Rights Act of 1866 and the Thirteenth, Fourteenth, and later the Fifteenth amendments to the Constitution, Americans brought to fruition the vision of universal, individual rights expressed by the Declaration of Independence. As noted earlier, the triumph was flawed. The framers of the Civil Rights Act meant to exclude resident Chinese and "Indians not taxed," and the latter phrase reappeared in the Fourteenth Amendment. With black men, the intended beneficiaries, equality long remained merely theoretical; and women did not receive the right to vote until the twentieth century. Still, for the first time, the nation's basic law guaranteed the same freedoms to every person regardless of race. It was a profound break with the European past. Before the modern era, *liberty* generally referred to the protected status of a given location or population, not universal, personal rights. The Edict of Nantes, for example, issued by France's King Henry IV in 1598, exempted the Protestant Huguenots from religious laws and granted them armed sanctuaries in designated towns; it did not establish a general principle of freedom of conscience. And the British colonies in America were long exempt from taxation.[7] Something of this traditional concept of liberty persisted in relations between the United States and the Indian nations. As Chief Justice John Marshall wrote in *Worcester v. State of Georgia* in 1832, the federal government acknowledged "the Indians as a separate and distinct people, and as being vested with rights which constitute them a state, or separate community—not foreign, but a domestic community . . . existing within [the United States.]" American Indian rights were *community* rights, in the eyes of U.S. law—the exemptions and privileges of people who stood apart, yet lived within the domain claimed by the federal government. Grant wished to extend to the indigenous the revolution of individual rights—but their autonomy stood in the way. They would have to move out of the category of "Indians *not taxed*," or the category itself would have to be abolished, if they were to be citizens. The Peace Policy's irony is that it could only work *after* the Indians' functional independence had been crushed.[8]

The Washita captives showed that the crushing continued in the summer of 1869, when it came to the Southern Cheyennes. "The whole camp seemed like an animated zoo," Libbie later wrote. She referred to the wild animals kept as pets by the soldiers—antelopes, wolves, and wildcats—but she could have been speaking of the women and children, penned in the stockade, examined by curiosity seekers.

Brown went too. Custer, always passionate for the exotic, had studied the sign language commonly used on the plains; he took Brown in and introduced her through signs. The Cheyennes gathered around the young black woman, felt her skin, patted her on the shoulder, "rolled up my sleeve to see if I was brown under my dress," Brown recalled. "They had never seen a colored person." Brown herself was now the curiosity.

Custer slipped out, leaving her alone with them as a practical joke. The older women were "making ready to give me a pipe to have me smoke their tobacco," she said, when "I looked around and found the ginnel gone." She darted out of the stockade as Custer watched and laughed at her. "Well, I *was* scared." But she overcame her fear. Her experience allowed her to perceive them as others did not. She saw their anxiety at their imprisonment. She remarked on how they often asked Custer when he would release them, and their joy when the time finally came. Brown recognized women who had suffered. "I never did see such hard old women. They looked like they had been lashed with trouble."[9]

Libbie came and looked as well. She wanted to see one captive in particular, the young woman who was daughter to Little Rock, the member of the Cheyenne Council of Forty-Four killed at the Washita. "Monahsetah had in many . . . ways made herself of service to the command," Libbie wrote. "She was young and attractive, perfectly contented, and trustful of the white man's promises, and the acknowledged belle among all other Indian maidens." It is unclear what "service" Libbie meant. Had she heard the stories of how Romero had provided the prisoners for sex—how Armstrong had taken Monahsetah as his concubine? As the biographer Louise Barnett observes, he wrote publicly of her as a woman with "sex appeal."

Monahsetah presented Libbie with a conundrum. On one hand, she embodied Armstrong's sins. Libbie had remarked even before she married him that he "fibs" with regard to other women. No one had to tell her the rumors for her to see that he might have slept with this young Cheyenne woman. On the other hand, Monahsetah represented the romance and excitement of life with Armstrong. As Barnett observes, Libbie called her "the Princess," imposing on her a literary archetype that dated back to Capt. John Smith's account of Pocahontas at the beginning of the seventeenth century. Monahsetah personified the pain and pleasures of her marriage to Custer. The one thing she was not, in Libbie's eyes, was a full, complex human being.[10]

Nor in Custer's eyes. On May 26, 1869, he mailed a special shipment to his friend Kirkland Barker for presentation to the Detroit Audubon Club. It included a variety of artifacts captured at the Washita: a large shield, a bow and a quiver of arrows, a beaded buckskin dress. He also sent a scalp, cut from the head of a man killed in the battle. It belonged to Little Rock, father of Monahsetah.[11]

"WE TOOK TURNS IN GIVING our cook an order, if it was absolutely necessary to give her any," Libbie recalled. "It was very odd to hear a grown person, the head of a house, perhaps, say, 'You tackle Eliza this time. I did it last time.'"[12]

On Big Creek, Eliza Brown steeped in frustration. Having experienced a rich social life in a post with a black garrison, she now found herself in a remote tent camp, surrounded by white soldiers, officers' wives, tourists, and wild animals. "I ain't got nobody," she said. Libbie claimed that Brown had an on-and-off relationship with the Custers' private teamster, Henry, and quoted him as saying, "We kissed and we fought and we loved and we fought." If so, it did not make up for her isolation.

The Custers lived in a very pleasant canvas structure with a gallery overlooking the creek, but the kitchen consisted of little more than a cookstove and the grass, under the constant bombardment of high winds. "In the kitchen tent we found it well to leave the field completely to Eliza," Libbie wrote. She battled floods, the lack of "anything cookable," and the taunting of Armstrong and Tom Custer, who kept a pet wolf named Dixie, a raccoon, and a chest full of live rattlesnakes. "Under these various circumstances it was a marvel how she kept her temper at all," Libbie added.[13]

Years later, Libbie would emphasize the social pleasures that she, Armstrong, and Tom Custer enjoyed on Big Creek. Col. Nelson Miles, commander of Fort Hays, showed them great hospitality. Numerous hunting parties arrived on the Kansas Pacific Railroad, eager to be taken out to look for buffalo. Some were random, tiresome visitors. Some were welcome strangers, such as two English aristocrats, Lord Berkeley Paget and Lord Waterpark, whom Armstrong and Libbie both liked very much. Some were close friends, including Kirkland Barker, who was so fat, at 230 pounds, that he had difficulty mounting a horse. On his expedition, a soldier accidentally killed Maida, Custer's favorite dog. Sheridan—

promoted after Grant's inauguration to commander of the vast Military Division of the Missouri, with headquarters in Chicago—sent some of these visiting hunters, hoping to impress his friends with an escort by his favorite subordinate, newly famous as a frontiersman.[14]

There were tensions, too. Monahsetah embodied Armstrong's dalliances, flirtations, or infidelities—whatever Libbie believed them to be. And his gambling continued, worse than ever. Lacking a mission, with no hope of seeing combat, he found his excitement in risking money over cards and horse races, to Libbie's rising frustration.[15]

The bloodshed sputtered on. On May 9, Big Head and Dull Knife—two of the three hostages Custer seized at the Sweetwater camp in Texas—died in a fight with their guards. Cheyennes—the Dog Soldiers in particular—launched a dozen raids in May, June, and July in the Solomon, Saline, and Republican valleys of central Kansas. The 7th Cavalry chased them fruitlessly; Custer himself took part only once. He left it to Carr to strike a decisive blow against the Dog Soldiers at Summit Springs on July 11.[16]

On the banks of Big Creek in the fall of 1869, the long-building conflict between Libbie and Eliza Brown finally erupted. For five years they had been allies in the most masculine of environments; yet they also had made each other suffer. At her worst, Libbie had afflicted Brown with blatant racism and open mockery. For her part, Brown had subtly defied Libbie, manipulating her and siphoning the Custers' resources to maintain her social position. At times she openly scorned her employers. Now she became short-tempered, and Libbie grew more determined to assert her dominance. Her rising irritation is reflected in her words, "You tackle Eliza this time."

"Have you heard that Eliza has left us? We had to send her away as she got on a spree & was insolent," Libbie wrote to a friend on September 18. "I thought the whole establishment would fall through on her departure as she had so long been supreme as general superintendent." A *spree*? It implies drunkenness—but the rest of the sentence reveals the truth. *Insolent*. It is a nasty word, spoken only out of a belief in one's own superiority over others. It says that Libbie found Brown guilty not of disrespect, but of a refusal to show deference, a refusal to accept her inferior status. Pressed by Libbie's condescension, Brown had finally lashed out. The only evidence of what she said, of her open anger, is that word. Perhaps it is all we need.

Libbie, too, had changed. Brown's authority over the kitchen had long perplexed her, and increasingly troubled her. "She had so long been supreme," she wrote of Brown; she wrote disapprovingly, appalled at the inversion of mistress and servant, white and black. In firing her, Libbie restored the old order upended by the war. "I am now attending to the superintending myself," she added, "& with my very economical cook [a black woman named Mary Adams], I think we shall manage to 'eat up' considerably less of the pay than we did while Eliza cooked for us & entertained her visitors."

Libbie enjoyed deference at last. "Mary's temper has never failed her," she later wrote to Rebecca Richmond. "She is so much better than Eliza."[17] It was a foreboding change. For eight years, Custer—later Custer and his wife—had lived "on the picket line of freedom," to quote another Union soldier.[18] In the Civil War, he had effectively destroyed slavery everywhere he had marched. In his private life, he had given Eliza Brown responsibility and respect, and proved more tolerant of her cultural distinctiveness than Libbie ever had. But Brown's assertiveness and authority had come at the cost of Libbie's own. In the wider world, the fight for civil rights raged on. Within the tents' white walls on Big Creek, Libbie decided that she did not want an equal.

Brown eventually reached Ohio, where she began a new life, made possible by the revolution of civil rights, incomplete as it was. She would meet Libbie again one day.

ON MARCH 3, 1869, Andrew Johnson's last full day as president, he signed an act that decimated the army. Twenty out of forty-five regiments disbanded, including two of the four black infantry regiments. The number of brigadier generals fell from ten to eight. The authorized strength of the service went from 54,000 to 37,313.

The reduction pushed the transformation of the army from a warfighting organization to a constabulary service—sufficient to provide garrisons, concentrate on one or two major outbreaks of fighting with the Indians, and enforce Reconstruction in the most troubled parts of the South. It further restricted the room for the patronage and nepotism that flowered during the Civil War; retirement committees and "Benzine Boards" (named after the petroleum refining process) sought to eliminate low-quality officers to maintain professional standards. Nepotism still existed, of course. Custer continued to practice it, as did Sheridan and many others. But the reduced size of the force put a premium on institutional processes, and tended to squeeze out personal exceptions.[19]

Colonel Samuel D. Sturgis, the new commander of the 7th Cavalry, respected Custer. But Sturgis represented the obstacles facing the younger man if he were to advance up the ranks of the shrinking army. An 1846 graduate of West Point, Sturgis had served in the Mexican War, and in California, the Great Plains, and New Mexico in the succeeding years. He had fought in Missouri and elsewhere in the West during the Civil War. He accumulated a respectable record, but attained none of the spectacular achievements that made Custer a national celebrity. He rose to command one of only twenty-five regiments simply because it was his turn. There were many, many officers whose turns came before that of the twenty-nine-year-old Custer.[20]

The autumn of 1869 brought the Custers back to Leavenworth, and winter separated them. They visited the Southern Hotel in St. Louis, then in November Armstrong headed east alone. He enjoyed himself with his friends on Sheridan's staff in Chicago. He journeyed to New York and returned to Michigan for the holidays, where he tended to the affairs of Judge Bacon's estate—a source of trouble rather than a bounty—and visited Kirkland Barker in Detroit. He spent his thirtieth birthday and another Christmas apart from Libbie. It was becoming a pattern, contrary to her later claim that they had pledged never to be apart again. Armstrong had repeated many patterns lately, and finally provoked a crisis in his marriage.[21]

He spoke to it in an extraordinary letter. Libbie's literary executor, Marguerite Merington, edited it by clipping, preserving three fragments in two different archives. She did not retain any portion with a date, but Armstrong's mention of his visit to Chicago, their time at the Southern Hotel, and his discussion of *returning* to the plains, with other references, make December 1869 the most likely date, though he might have written it in late 1870. The letter is a tissue of guilt, creased with characteristic efforts to minimize his misdeeds. Perhaps *misdeeds* is the wrong word—*addiction* serves better.[22]

He earnestly declared that he would give up gambling. "You may laugh at me, perhaps taunt me with the remark that I am unable to carry out the resolution," he wrote. "I have often heard you express the idea that I was incapable of doing it." This was a revealing passage, showing the depth of his gambling problem, but also Libbie's sarcastic cutting edge, something she acknowledged but that rarely appears in her curated archives. They had fought at the Southern Hotel. He wrote that she had "seen me in anger" and that he had used a "profane word."

"I know that however badly I may have acted at times there have been periods when you were satisfied with me. I can scarcely write my eyes are blinded with tears but I will try." He feared that any warmth she showed him before he left concealed contempt. "I am not judging merely from the distressing words you spoke at the Southern. They were merely the culmination of thoughts which have long filled your mind against me. . . . In your manner you have been more or less mechanical." He longed for her to show real love for him again. He hoped to persuade her that she was wrong, that "however errattic [sic] wild or unseemly my conduct with others may have been, you were still to me as you always have been, the one great all absorbing object of my love."

Here the letter seems to veer away from gambling to other women. "I will not pretend to justify my conduct with others," he wrote. "Measured by the strict laws of propriety or public opinion I was wrong. I knew it then as plainly as I know it now." Their difficulties refined his love, he claimed. He had felt that way in the spring—the time when Libbie faced Monahsetah, though he never mentioned her. "I labored to free your mind from all doubt," he wrote, "but this dream was dispelled at St. Louis."

Custer confronted the consequences of his nature. Again and again they had fought over his gambling; again and again he had promised to reform, only to fall back into his addiction. Again and again he had indulged in flirtations, perhaps even infidelities, then promised Libbie his heart was true, only to do it again.

The irony of this letter is that it reveals emotional strengths. He suffered addictions; he tried to minimize them, yet he confronted them. He possessed emotional sensitivity, seen in his alertness to her merely "mechanical" behavior, her lack of real warmth. And Libbie forgave him. She accepted his contrition as sincere. But she was a smart woman, and she must have suspected that he would always be true to his nature.[23]

CUSTER RETURNED TO KANSAS, where the spring and summer of 1870 brought visitors, merriment, and professional stagnation. Libbie's cousin Rebecca Richmond and Armstrong's little sister Maggie visited them at Fort Leavenworth. They helped to throw a "grand masquerade," which featured dancing until five o'clock in the morning, and joined them at a dinner at Colonel Sturgis's house, eating multiple courses of turkey, oysters, veal, and other dishes, followed by dancing at the Custers'.[24]

On April 30, Maj. Gen. John M. Schofield, the Department of the Missouri's new commander, sent Armstrong back to Big Creek. He ordered him to calm the "uneasiness of the settlers" along the Saline and Solomon rivers. It was dull work. "Indian Kansas," write two historians, ended rapidly as the dispossessed were shunted out of the state. "Where over ten thousand Native Americans had, at the beginning of the Civil War, made their homes, by 1875 fewer than one thousand . . . remained."[25]

The Custers remained very much on the frontier—not a meeting zone between cultures but the ragged margin of American civilization. "It was Wild Bill who said there was 'No Sunday west of Junction City, no law west of Hays City, and no God west of Carson City,'" a newspaper reported, quoting Custer's former scout, Wild Bill Hickok. "At Hays [City] a burial-place was pointed out which seemed well filled for so small and new a place," the *Chicago Tribune* wrote on September 22, 1870. Only two had died in bed. "The other twenty-seven died 'with their boots on'—that is, were shot in brawls or were hanged by their fellow citizens to the trellis-work of a railway bridge over a ravine nearby, which is considered in that neighborhood one of the most important facilities which the opening of the railroad afforded them."[26]

Hays City, located near the fort and the Big Creek encampment, seemed to consist entirely of saloons, brothels, and billiard halls, tethered to civilization with a railroad depot. For contemporary observers and mythologizers—Libbie Custer counts as both—it embodied the anarchy of life on the frontier. In fact, it represented the leading edge of incorporation into America's economy and society. Founded as a business venture, it attracted Texas cattle drovers who rode north to exploit the rail access to Chicago, center of the meat packing industry that fed northeastern and foreign markets. The Texas Longhorn, like the Indian pony, represented a remarkable biological adaptation to the environment of the Great Plains. The result of cross-breeding between Spanish Criollos and English cattle, they needed only grass, not grain; could endure the extremes of plains weather; and resisted Texas fever, carried by ticks. Starting in 1867, a vast new livestock business emerged as Texas cattlemen drove herds to Kansas railheads. Farmers fought the passage of the tick-carrying, grass-devouring Longhorns, so the drives gradually shifted west, ahead of the line of settlement, to one "cowtown" after another: Abilene, Hays, Dodge. On June 21, 1870, the *Leavenworth Bulletin* called Abilene "the great Texas cattle mart . . . a town entirely built by this cattle trade. Cattle drovers, buyers and shippers, monopolize everything. There are now in the neighborhood waiting for transportation something like 50,000 head of stock and beef cattle."

Hays City embodied entrepreneurship poured into a civic void, where a robust marketplace established itself before civil institutions and rule of law. It was suffused with a culture of violence bred in Indian conflicts and the Civil War. Here old Confederates from Texas collided with their former foes from abolitionist Kansas, in streets awash with alcohol and firearms. The businessmen of Hays City turned to a paragon of that culture to keep it under control.[27]

In August 1869, the people of Ellis County, Kansas, elected Wild Bill Hickok as their sheriff. His job was to stabilize Hays City. "His buckskin suits were discarded in favor of a Prince Albert coat and all the trimmings," writes his biographer Joseph Rosa. His nickname associated him with bloody, untamed nature, yet he now represented the establishment.

He developed a "passion for taking a bath, at first frowned upon by the wild men of Hays," Rosa adds. He put up signs around town announcing that firearms were forbidden.

He was still the killer his electors wished him to be. Within two months of taking office, he shot two suspects dead. Perhaps the only reason he killed no more was that he left town, and his office, in January 1870. He returned as a private citizen. On July 17, 1870, he got into a brawl with several troopers from the 7th Cavalry. He ended the fight by shooting two privates, Jerry Lonergan and John Kyle. Lonergan recovered; Kyle did not. But Custer did not mind. "I have personal knowledge of at least half a dozen men whom he has at various times killed, one of these being at the time a member of my command," Custer wrote. "There is not a single instance in which the verdict of twelve fair-minded men would not have pronounced in his favor."[28]

Annie Gibson Roberts described Custer much as Custer described Wild Bill. The daughter of a noted civil engineer working on a revolutionary iron and steel bridge across the Mississippi at St. Louis, designed by the famous James B. Eads, she went out to Fort Hays in the summer of 1870. "I should think [him] about 165 pounds—no spare flesh, well-knit—strong muscles lean & lithe," she later recalled. "Eyes—A piercing blue; keen, thoughtful, observant & very quick in glancing at any object & sizing it up. . . . Voice—Pleasant in tone but quick & energetic with sometimes a slight hesitation if words rolled out rapidly. . . . A nervous forceful manner in speaking." He filled her with confidence and impressed her with his generous nature. "He was slightly moody at times & sometimes silent for hours—but usually possessed high animal spirits and was very humorous, and very appreciative of that quality in those around him." She observed him to be an excellent horseman and a remarkable shot with a rifle.[29]

Roberts's warm impression of Custer stands out because she also befriended Benteen. She spent a great deal of time with the officers of the 7th Cavalry at Big Creek and on hunting expeditions on the plains; she shot and killed buffalo herself, breaking with expectations of femininity. She grew close to the stocky, blond-haired Capt. George Yates. Before many months passed the two were engaged to be married.

The summer of 1870 also revealed to her the crueler side of Custer. July 6 found Roberts on a bison hunt with Libbie and Armstrong, Mary Reno (wife of Maj. Marcus Reno, a relatively new officer in the 7th Cavalry) and her young son Robert, Col. Wesley Merritt, Tom Custer, Lt. Edward Mathey, and other officers. Strange riders appeared on the horizon. Custer quickly saddled, as did Tom and a few others, and left Mathey and Merritt with the women. They rode out toward the approaching figures, who turned out to be Indians. Shots rang out. Someone toppled from a saddle. Mary Reno clutched her boy as Libbie fell to her knees and screamed, "Autie will be killed!"

Mary Reno guessed from the behavior of Mathey that the attack was staged. "Mr. Mathey, if they are Indians, tell us so and don't make a fool of yourself." Merritt, "now thoroughly irate," broke in. "Yes, quit this damned nonsense—don't you see they are frightening the ladies?" Mathey sheepishly admitted that it was a practical joke; the Indians were army scouts. Roberts recalled that they laughed when it was all over. But it took a peculiar sense of humor for Custer to derive amusement from convincing his wife that he was about to die in front of her eyes. If, that is, one can call it humor at all.[30]

CUSTER CAME HOME—or to the place closest to home other than Monroe itself.[31] After visiting St. Louis with Libbie in December 1870, staying at the Southern Hotel, he went to New York, alone. He took a room in the Metropolitan Hotel on Broadway and Prince, the five-story mono-lith next to Niblo's Garden where he had stayed in 1863 while assisting McClellan. Indeed, he saw much of his old hero in the coming days.

Soon he journeyed to Washington, appearing as a material witness before one of the "Benzine Boards" that culled out inferior officers. He had other business with the army bureaucracy that year, too: he applied to be superintendent at West Point (he failed), and asked for Lt. James Cal-houn's transfer to the 7th Cavalry (he succeeded). He returned to spend several days with Libbie at Leavenworth. As soon as he could obtain a leave—on January 11, 1871—he hurried back to New York alone.[32]

On his return he lodged at his new favorite, the Fifth Avenue Hotel, situated far uptown on Madison Square. "Within an hour I had received more invitations than I can accept," he wrote to Libbie. He attended a dinner thrown in his honor by stockbrokers; he called it "elegant," held in a house filled with fine art. Custer knew the wife of the host and won-dered at her absence, but he was told she was "indisposed." The host said quietly, "To tell the truth, General, there is nothing the matter with her, and she is disappointed, but I thought we would have a better time with-out her, so bade her remain upstairs." Custer commented in his letter, "I thought of a little girl without money whose Bo would not want anyone at this table without his Bunkey." The fact that he went to New York with-out her tended to lessen the romantic impact.

The "without money" part clawed at him. He dined out on his celeb-rity with relish, but it only reminded him of his relative poverty. This brownstone and private-art-gallery world was far from his nearly illiterate father's anvil, fire, and water barrel in little New Rumley—far even from Monroe, where his mother had once feared to ask him for $5 to fix a shed. As an army officer, he always felt short of money. He breathed it in and out without ever accumulating any. Now, as a guest of the men of finance, he dined well, had an admirer's fine carriage at his disposal, and attended performances at the patricians' theater, the Academy of Music. Prolonged exposure to luxury when financially shackled is a goading experience, especially for one prone to self-indulgence.

Custer felt it, too, because it touched the reason why he came to New York. He faced a hard choice about his future. The Washita gave him a new reputation as an Indian fighter, but to what end? The army treated him no differently. He remained an interchangeable component in a regiment that was posted according to the army's bureaucratic procedures, not any particular merits or capacities. Was this all there was? To waste years without hope of promotion, in primitive stations, attending to petty regulations? He had finally regained some public admiration, but derived nothing from it. Others acquired power or fortunes on the credit fame gave them. He would too.

He came on a mission. He hinted at it in his letter to Libbie. He mentioned that he had been invited to go on a two-week press excursion on the Northern Pacific Railroad, one of the new transcontinental lines being built after the completion of the Union Pacific–Central Pacific axis. "But business will prevent," he wrote.[33]

This "business" was an enterprise of his own. He hoped it would allow him to raft the whitewater currents on Wall Street. His exposure to financiers revealed the scale and power of financial markets, which created millions seemingly instantly. Capital was changing the world. He could see it in the very landscape of New York.

He needed only to step outside his hotel door, board a horse-drawn railcar, and ride twenty blocks up Fourth Avenue, through the Murray Hill Tunnel and onto 42nd Street. There a vast new railroad depot rose. Started in 1869, it would be completed in late 1871. It stretched 692 feet long, 240 feet wide, and 160 feet high at the top of its central tower. Teams of workers scurried over scaffolding and milled between the skeletal walls; they assembled ten million bricks and eight million pounds of iron, and placed 80,000 feet of glass in the vast train shed roof alone. It would be the largest railroad station in the hemisphere, second largest in the world. They called it Grand Central.[34]

Grand Central would be the capitol for a new kind of empire: the New York Central & Hudson River Railroad, one of the first truly giant corporations in American history. It was formed in January 1870 by the merger of two of the nation's largest and most important railroads. It carried more than seven million passengers and four million tons of freight in 1870, running nearly 10,000 locomotives and cars. The *New York Times* called its first semi-annual dividend, $3.6 million issued on April 15, "the very largest single dividend ever paid in this country by any one corporation."[35]

Its creation told the story of the changing corporation and the rise of finance. Its mastermind was Cornelius Vanderbilt. Born in 1794, this tall, tough former sailor won the nickname "Commodore" (the highest rank in the U.S. Navy before the Civil War) with shipping lines from New York to California and Europe. He spent his early career condemning corporations as monopolies. In the early republic, they were tools of mercantilism, used to create privately funded public works. But Vanderbilt and others came to see their potential and changed them from within. When he first seized a ferry corporation in 1838, he was promptly sued for operating it "with the sole view of profit." That complaint reveals a silent revolution that helped to make modernity.[36]

Railroads began as community enterprises, chartered to serve the public in specific locations. Vanderbilt and his peers changed that. In 1863 he took over the New York & Harlem Railroad, followed in 1864 by the Hudson River Railroad, followed in 1867 by the New York Central. His merger of the latter two lines created a single corporation that spanned the entire width of New York State. In 1869 he won the Lake Shore & Michigan Southern, connecting the Central to Chicago. The mercantilist public-works corporation of the past was dead; the modern business corporation was born.[37]

The titanic scale of these behemoths startled the public. As early as November 10, 1866, the *Times* blasted "The Tyranny of Corporations," arguing, "The tendency of power—of the modern aristocracy of capital—is toward disregard of individuals and individual convenience and comfort. . . . Every public means of transit is in the hands of the tyrants of modern society—the capitalists." *Harper's Weekly* and other major publications joined in the outcry. In January 1867, during Vanderbilt's battle with the New York Central, he refused to accept its trains onto his own Hudson River or Harlem railroads—during a winter storm that prevented most ferry or ship traffic from reaching Manhattan. One man was able to blockade America's largest city. Charles Francis Adams Jr. wrote in July 1869, "Vanderbilt is but the precursor of a class of men who will wield within the state a power created by the state, but too great for its control. He is the founder of a dynasty."[38]

The corporation had created a layer of economic reality that existed purely in the imagination. A secondary market arose, where shares of corporate ownership could be traded. The New York Stock Exchange emerged as the most important of many. In a formal trading room and in a mob on the curb outside, brokers bought and sold stocks and bonds at prices that varied from minute to minute. As in a mirror facing a mirror, there appeared a limitless vista of derivatives—tradable rights based on the share.

The stock exchange became a major source of revenue in the 1850s and especially the '60s, quite apart from actual business operations. Financiers manipulated the market, driving stock prices up and down, sometimes for short-term profit, sometimes for strategic reasons as well. In 1869, Vanderbilt seized the Lake Shore Railway in a fierce battle with LeGrand Lockwood, who owned his stock in the company on margin—on credit, with the stock as its own collateral. Vanderbilt seized a moment when money was tight in New York, then dumped all his Lake Shore stock at once, sparking a collapse in price and contributing to a panic. Lockwood was forced to sell off all his stock, and went bankrupt. Vanderbilt used the transatlantic telegraph to borrow money from Baring Brothers in London. He bought back all his and Lockwood's stock at reduced prices and ended the panic. His profits were immense, his control complete. This vast operation revealed how finance now overshadowed the American economy.[39]

Corruption abounded. An early credit bureau reported that Daniel Drew, as treasurer of the Erie Railway, habitually engaged in insider trading, but it merely noted that this made him a good credit risk. J. Edgar Thomson and Thomas A. Scott, managers of the Pennsylvania Railroad, skimmed money by channeling the company's business through dummy corporations. They demanded kickbacks from contractors—which gave their assistant and protégé, Andrew Carnegie, his start as an investor.[40]

In the twilight world of Wall Street, perceptions mattered almost as much as business reality—more, in fact, in a short-term campaign to manipulate a stock price or win initial investors. Augustus Melmotte, the master financier in Anthony Trollope's 1875 novel *The Way We Live Now*, describes "the nature of credit, how strong it is,—as the air,—to buoy you up; how slight it is,—as a mere vapour,—when roughly touched." The underlying truth of business profits or losses could not be escaped forever, but a fortune could be made in the dark space between anticipation and realization.[41]

Into the shadows between the flat-faced buildings that shouldered together on Wall Street came George Armstrong Custer.

HE WENT TO SEE a man about a mine. George B. McClellan, it appears, recommended that he start with August Belmont. Belmont, fifty-six at the time, had come to America as the representative of the Rothschilds, but his German accent had faded after thirty-three years in the United States, and he had succeeded to a remarkable extent in overcoming the social taint of his Jewish ancestry. An eminent financier in his own right, he had crowded in among New York's patricians and politicians. He was a prominent member of the "silk-stocking" Democrats who belonged to the Manhattan Club, the center of Democratic opposition to the corrupt ring led by William M. Tweed.

Custer should have known all this. Belmont, William H. Aspinwall, and Samuel L. M. Barlow—all wealthy and influential New York Democrats—had advised McClellan back when Custer served on his staff. With money, political influence, and connections, Belmont was the ideal man to help Custer with his business.[42]

His enterprise was the Stevens Lode Silver Mine, located near Georgetown in the Rocky Mountains west of Denver. The origin of his connection to the mine remains obscure. He had traveled to Denver in mid-1870, a trip that may indicate the start of his involvement. The property included the eastern half of a large vein of silver, as yet undeveloped; the Crescent Silver Mining Company owned the western half and had started to dig. His partner was Jairus W. Hall, colonel of the 4th Michigan Infantry during the war, who frequently corresponded with him about the mine.

What Custer and Hall needed from Belmont and others was money—they had little of their own—and the credit that would flow from their goodwill. They needed it simply to begin operations—to dig for silver, crush and refine the ore, and sell it—and to try to create and ride a great updraft on Wall Street. If they convinced Belmont and his peers to invest, their support would generate confidence on the Street, automatically increasing the value of the property. Then they could sell out, if that's what they wished to do. "In no other theater of speculation [than mining stocks] did promoters reap more success with the airy products of their fancy," wrote an early Wall Street chronicler. "The public bore enthusiastic testimony to the maxim that it delights to be humbugged."[43]

Belmont initially proved cautious. So did Levi P. Morton of Morton, Bliss & Co., a forty-six-year-old New Englander who had risen from a lowly job as clerk to become the principal of a prestigious banking and brokerage firm in New York. Unlike Belmont, or Custer, for that matter, he was a Republican, and would in later years serve a term as vice president of the United States. Regardless, he admired the Boy General and wished to help him.

Two problems stood in the way. The first was the uncertainty of the unopened mine. The second was its size. "It is a small thing," Commodore Vanderbilt said of the Harlem Railroad in 1869, "with a little capital of only about $6,000,000." By contrast, Custer planned a par capitalization of $200,000, divided into 2,000 shares. (The par value of a corporation was supposed to equal the expenditure it made on land, buildings, equipment, and other real property.) Compared to the Harlem, the Stevens Lode Mine was microscopic.

Morton sent a letter of introduction to yet another Wall Street man, Joseph Seligman. Custer, he wrote, "has a good thing in that way, he thinks, & will be glad to have you look into it. You are 'up' mining enterprises & can judge." Seligman, though, offered no help.[44]

The search for investors proved frustrating. Custer wrote to Libbie that he "often . . . approached a capitalist and he threw cold water over my scheme." Hall grew discouraged. So did McClellan, whom Custer had made a partner as well, indicating how close he remained to his old hero.[45]

As the hunt dragged on, Custer took care to preserve his place in the army. He had spent his entire adult life within this institution, and, even as he bucked against it, he found security and structure within it. His current experience in New York underscored the uncertainty of the marketplace. He applied to army headquarters to extend his leave another thirty days beyond its expiration on January 11, then applied for another extension, and another, and another. "My reasons . . . are wholly of a business character. A large amount of property is involved," he wrote from New York. On another application he stated his calculations explicitly. "My reason for requesting the delay is that . . . my presence in this city . . . will probably secure to me the sum of about thirty thousand dollars which I am liable to lose if called away at the expiration of my present leave."[46]

Custer did not write of putting his business on a sound footing and deriving steady dividends. He saw his mine purely in terms of speculation. "Can it be," he wrote his wife, "that my little standby and I who have long wished to possess a small fortune, are about to have our hopes and wishes realized?" It was, he wrote, "the stepping stone to larger and more profitable undertakings." Having recast himself as a frontiersman, he ironically gained credibility in New York. Morton wrote to Seligman, "As you are aware [Custer] has been in command on the plains for several years & is personally familiar with the mining districts." His buckskins gave him the authority to transform wilderness into greenbacks and literally capitalize on his image.[47]

To sway the men with money, Custer circulated in society—what a later generation would call networking. He dined at Delmonico's. He went to parties. He stayed out all night. He had a horse shipped from Leavenworth as a gift to Jim Fisk. Vice president of the giant Erie Railway, the brash, corpulent, mustachioed Fisk was the partner of Jay Gould, the line's president. Reporters loved to hear Fisk joke and declaim about the pair's latest thrust and parry with Commodore Vanderbilt, their perennial enemy. Fisk stashed his mistress, Josephine Mansfield, in an apartment near the Erie's offices, and kept a national guard regiment as a pet. Custer wrote, "Fisk's regiment is going on an excursion to Boston next month and a fine looking horse accustomed to the band of soldiers was in demand."[48]

With months to spend in his favorite city, Custer indulged himself. He saw his friend Lawrence Barrett and watched performances by Barrett's colleague Edwin Booth, one of the great actors of the age and brother of Lincoln's assassin. Armstrong tormented Libbie with detailed accounts of his encounters with women. He went often to the Academy of Music to see the young Clara Louise Kellogg, an acclaimed young soprano. "Miss Kellogg also expects me behind the scenes," he wrote to Libbie. He began to call on her. They went for strolls together on Broadway, and he joined her in her private box at the opera house when she was not performing. He told Libbie that he waited for her in her changing room or at her house as she dressed. "I could hear her moving about overhead, and it reminded me of you in Monroe days when I sat in the parlor below, waiting."[49]

Was that supposed to be reassuring? He bragged about a young woman who told him, "Oh, why are you married?" He mentioned a blond teenager who lived across the street from Belmont and tried to get his attention on the street. "Twice for sport I followed her," he wrote. He described a married friend who took him to see his married mistress, confiding to him that she had had an abortion after he had impregnated her.[50]

Custer's agonized letter to Libbie, admitting his "wild or unseemly . . . conduct," preceded these events—yet his letters from this period show no remorse. To the contrary, he returned to the flaunting manner of his earliest correspondence to her from the city. There was an element of cruelty in it. And his letters spoke to his never-ending insecurity. Even if he remained faithful, he craved female attention; it affirmed a self-image that he was never quite sure was real.[51]

There was good reason for Libbie to be suspicious. Recently Custer had received the romantic letter from "Anna," very likely Anna Darrah. A Hattie Mitchell wrote to him from Virginia; he had asked her to mask her identity with the pseudonym "Gloria." These or other letters may have been delivered to Libbie during Armstrong's absence in New York. Morton wrote a note to Custer in which he offered to do "anything to make your visit to New York agreeable to Mrs. Custer as well as yourself." Perhaps Custer had introduced a mistress as his wife, as he claimed Wesley Merritt had done.

Libbie wrote to Armstrong in New York and demanded to know if he had mentioned his wife to one of the young women he bragged about. "I told her I love you and you alone," he responded. "She frankly said she would only ask me to love her next to you, which I did not consent to do." Then he mentioned *another* woman "who so far forgot herself as to make the advances."[52]

Married, respectable men carried on affairs all around Libbie, and she knew it. She grasped how much her husband liked—even needed—the admiration of women. She also knew that he did indeed love her. He followed every boast of flirtation with an avowal of his dedication to her. There's no reason to think he was insincere. His history with Fannie Fifield proved that he could believe two irreconcilable ideas simultaneously—he could pursue a flirtation or a mistress and still convince himself that he remained true to Libbie in his heart.

The question Libbie faced was not so much factual—was he cheating?—but emotional: Could she endure his behavior? Was she willing to push their marriage to a crisis to stop him? Or would she be happy with what he gave her, knowing that he felt more passion for her than most husbands for their wives, even if he were unfaithful?

She herself glowed when men admired her. She was lively and social, and immensely charming. In the summer of 1870, Annie Roberts observed that Libbie was "incessantly funny" and enjoyed the company of many of the 7th Cavalry's officers. Armstrong grew jealous when she corresponded with them; as Leckie writes, he enforced a double standard in their marriage. He wrote from New York that he might think she was unfaithful, "were I of a suspicious disposition"—thereby demonstrating a suspicious disposition. "The fewer notes or letters of yours, no matter how ordinary, that get into gentlemen's hands the better for your reputation." Yet he remained in New York, month after month, looking for money at all the best parties.[53]

HE FOUND HIS GUIDE. Custer needed a native scout to lead him through this cutthroat wilderness, like the Osages who worked for the army on the plains. To his good fortune, the man who chose to help him was William R. Travers. He had long been a partner of Leonard W. Jerome, one of a pair of brothers renowned as brokers, bankers, and men of leisure. "Both Jerome and his partner, the shrewd, witty, and admired William R. Travers, were men of wide social prominence and possessed of a fondness for manly sports," wrote a contemporary observer of Wall Street. "They were leaders in club life and pleasure-loving society." Travers particularly liked horses, and took a leading role in building the racetrack at Saratoga Springs, alongside John Morrissey and Commodore Vanderbilt.

A clean-shaven man with a ruddy face, Travers stood tall and thin, and never smiled. And yet the brokers of Wall Street celebrated his cutting wit, delivered through a pronounced stutter. "You seem to stutter more in New York than you did here, Mr. Travers," a friend remarked during a visit to Baltimore, his old home. Travers replied, "Have to— *it's a bigger place.*" After an endless monologue by an insufferable British guest at a dinner on his yacht, Travers loudly declared, "It is now a debatable point among scientists as to whether or not the oyster has brains. I think the oyster must have b-b-brains because it knows when to sh-sh-shut up." Once, in the mob on the curb outside the stock exchange, he bought shares from a dealer known to be Jewish, then humiliated him by demanding that he give his "C-C-C-Christian" name, "whereat the crowd was convulsed," reported William W. Fowler, a contemporary. Anti-semitism aside, Fowler wrote, "he bears the reputation of an honorable business man, a kind friend. His judgment is called in to decide bets." A highly social man with Southern connections and thought to be worth $3 million, he was Custer's ideal mentor.[54]

With Travers to advise him, Custer prepared a prospectus and personally subscribed for 700 of the 2,000 shares at $50 each. This was 50 percent of the par or face value. Custer hoped to create confidence with his announced $35,000 investment, showing that he risked his own money. He possessed no such sum.[55]

Custer met the appropriately named James H. Banker, one of the most important figures on Wall Street. Vice president of the venerable Bank of New York, founded by Alexander Hamilton, Banker belonged to Vanderbilt's inner circle. He had often served as the Commodore's personal representative ("He is true & will not deceive us this is certain," Vanderbilt once wrote to a colleague), and hosted him in the Bank of New York offices during his successful campaign to stifle the panic of 1869. Together with Augustus Schell, a financier and leading Democrat, and Horace F. Clark, Vanderbilt's son-in-law, Banker ran the Lake Shore railway on Vanderbilt's behalf. The trio speculated on their own; they bought control of Western Union, for example, and set about reforming the telegraph monopoly's finances. The press called Banker "the prime mover in all the current cliques and contrivances that move the Street, and the biggest man known around brokers' offices." He built a mansion on Fifth Avenue, bought $1.5 million in real estate, and ordered a custom-made yacht.[56]

The "prime mover" agreed to buy 200 shares at $50 each—a critical success in Custer's campaign, sure to influence others. And yet, despite the minuscule scale of the mine compared to Banker's other investments, he demanded extremely favorable terms. He received a 50 percent discount on the par value, but he did not pay even that much. In the nineteenth century, initial investors often paid a small percentage of the share price, providing more as needed. Further payments might be contingent upon progress in business operations. It appears that Banker delivered barely $1,000.

John Jacob Astor Jr., prestigious heir to the fortune his father had accumulated in fur trading and real estate, asked for the same treatment. On April 7 he sent a note to Custer at his room at the Fifth Avenue Hotel: "My Dear General, You can put my name down on your list for $10,000.00 on the same terms & conditions as Mr. J. H. Banker." Belmont, too, signed up for $15,000, or 300 shares, and Travers subscribed for $10,000. Like Banker, none paid anything close to the amounts written next to their names.

Custer took Astor's note to Delmonico's, where he had lunch with broker Charles J. Osborn, one of his social companions in the city. Osborn and his partner Addison Cammack belonged to the influential "Twenty-third Street Party," a clique of bearish stock operators that included Russell Sage, Frank Work, and Travers, too. He knew oil and mining stocks, which were traded on their own exchange, the Petroleum and Mining Board, organized in 1866. Another partner who attended this lunch said to Custer, "Oh General, you are bound to succeed now that you have gotten the names of those gentlemen, some of the best in New York." Osborn, though, was more cautious; mining stocks had collapsed dramatically in the recent past, and he was a bear by nature, inclined to see the downward potential of any investment. He asked some questions and concluded, "Well, Custer, I want to see you further about this."[57]

The financiers overshadowed Custer in New York, and that was precisely the appeal of his Wall Street adventure. "Is it not strange to think of me meeting to confer with such men as Belmont, Astor, Banker, Morton and Bliss?" he wrote to Libbie. A mutual friend told him that "Mr. and Mrs. Belmont speak very highly of me, Mr. B. most encouragingly of my business prospects." He found himself at a higher altitude of wealth and power than he had ever experienced, and he felt a certain light-headedness at it all. A small-town boy at the center of everything, he was impressed with *himself* for dining with the mighty, socializing with famous actors, discussing Albert Bierstadt's paintings with a legendary singer. In his idiosyncratic mix of enthusiasm, vanity, and insecurity, he could not consider himself a peer, or else he could not be so pleased with himself. His thrill came from his sense that he had risen above his proper standing.[58]

As Custer's campaign advanced at last, Libbie left Kansas and returned to Monroe. Custer's leave extensions were now approved by the Department of the South. On March 20, 1871, most of the 7th Cavalry was shifted to Southern states. For now Custer remained in New York. He told Libbie that he had asked Travers to take over the stock sales so that he could see her, visit the mine in Colorado, or both. "He thought I should remain," particularly with the first stockholders' meeting imminent. So he did. He socialized with the McClellans, and at the Fifth Avenue Hotel he saw P. M. B. Young, his fellow West Point cadet and wartime foe. The two "greeted each other as old friends," the *New York World* reported. He enjoyed more dinner parties, trips to gambling saloons (where, he swore, he spent hours not playing faro or baccarat), evenings at the theater, days and nights with Miss Kellogg. "Oh, the magnificence and the luxury!" he wrote.[59]

In May he left New York for an Army of the Potomac reunion in Boston, apparently on a steamship provided by Jim Fisk. The writer Bret Harte submitted a grimly whimsical poem for the meeting, titled "The Old Major Explains." Its narrator tells his "Colonel" that farmwork will prevent him from attending the reunion, *And my leg is getting troublesome; it laid me up last fall, / And the doctors—they have cut and hacked—and never found the ball.* The veterans thought it hilarious. Custer joined Generals Kilpatrick, Meade, Pleasonton—and Sheridan, back from observing the Franco-Prussian War. Custer finally returned to Monroe in June, saw Libbie, then left.[60]

On July 15, the *New York Times* reported that he had arrived at Saratoga Springs, the summer resort of the nation's elite, north of Albany, New York. Newport, Rhode Island, had begun its climb as the premiere "watering place," where the wealthy built mansion-sized summer "cottages," but Saratoga still thrived. It reflected the less lavish lifestyle of an older generation of the wealthy, who stayed in hotels rather than private houses. The *New York Tribune* described it as a place of "huge dining halls with walls of staring white . . . ball-rooms with the same shadowless surfaces, with blinding glare of gas [lights], and stifling atmosphere of odors." The hotel dining rooms witnessed "a constant procession of overdressed women, of flippant and loud-tongued men," who scorned each other as they competed for social status.

How could Custer *not* like Saratoga, with its racetrack, John Morrissey's gambling saloon, the fashionable social scene on the Congress Hall veranda, its balls and hops, its worldly sophistication? But he went there for practical reasons. "At other watering places, they *talked* stocks; at Saratoga they *bought* and *sold* them," William Fowler wrote. "Little knots of dealers stood in the piazzas of the United States Hotel, the Union, and the Congress, and traded in Erie and Harlem. The great pulsations of the heart-financial, 180 miles away, throbbed here through the telegraphic wires."[61]

Custer returned to New York, still hunting for money. He made other important contacts as well. He attended a dinner for the city's leading journalists, taking a seat next to Horace Greeley, founder and editor of the *New York Tribune*, Whitelaw Reid, Richard Henry Dana, and Edmund C. Stedman, who was both a banker and a literary man, and would author a history of the New York Stock Exchange. Stedman compared Custer to the fifteenth-century French warrior Pierre Terrail, the Chevalier de Bayard, famous as "the knight without fear and beyond reproach." He derived a more immediate benefit from Francis P. Church, a prominent Democrat, editor, and founder (with his brother William) of the *Galaxy*, a literary monthly. Custer had reached an agreement with Church on March 8 to provide articles on his adventures on the plains for $100 each, granting Church the option to publish them as a book.[62]

Jairus Hall took little joy in Custer's progress. He learned that Custer, in chasing the vapor of Wall Street, had neglected the rock of the Stevens Lode Mine itself.

"IN REGARD TO TAKING CHARGE of the mining in Colorado, of course we will have to do that, and then there will be no doubt about the success of the company," Hall wrote to Custer on April 21, 1871. The remark implies that Custer had hoped to avoid any actual business management. The idea flummoxed Hall. "I will work with you in regard to further operations on the mine &c &c.," he added.[63] He filled his letters with details that Custer never mentioned: a man sent to assess the lode, the manager who directed the work, the Crescent Company's progress on the western half.[64]

In the fall of 1871 Custer finally left New York and reported for duty in Kentucky. After all those months of escorting a famous singer, attending all-night parties, dining at Delmonico's, and visiting Saratoga, his fortune had still not materialized. The great financiers, who put their names down for ostensibly hundreds of thousands of dollars' worth of stock, contributed a total of $12,000.

Custer purchased his stake in the mine on credit, but Hall invested a good deal of his own money. Hall, too, hoped to sell out in the near term. He assigned a banker in Georgetown, Colorado, to serve as his proxy in "all matters pertaining to the sale of the Stevens." He went to London in early 1872, hoping to find buyers there. Unlike Custer, he inquired into the actual business, and pressed their man on the spot to finally begin digging. He heard nothing from anyone, including Custer. In London he wrote on June 6, "I am in utter ignorance in regard to the state of affairs in Colorado *at the Stevens mine.*" In Paris on June 14 he begged Custer, "Write me fully." On July 15 he wrote, "I arrived in New York last week, but found no letters from *anyone* in regard to the Stevens mine, nor did I find Travers at home."[65]

Finally, on July 26, 1872, Hall received a letter from Custer. "Your dispatch is as unsatisfactory as the silence of the past," Hall wrote. Relations with the stockholders verged on disastrous. The friendship of Custer's backers turned out to be as thin as a balance sheet. (Custer wasted a horse trying to get the support of Jim Fisk. On July 6, 1872, a rival for his mistress shot Fisk twice in the Grand Central Hotel, and he died the next day.) Hall asked Custer "if there is any chance you could go back to New York to fix things up." The business demanded Custer's attention to both finance and actual mining. "I think you had better go out yourself and look at the mine." Once they straightened it out, "we can then look into a speculation for next winter in London."[66]

Hall, not Custer, went to the mine. Almost nothing had been done. The Crescent Company produced tons of ore, but Frank Dibben, the man who managed operations for Hall and Custer, "is *totally unfit* for business." He was so ill that he could barely speak. "He is liable to die any day. I don't think he will live through another winter. . . . Things are in bad shape, and we must look the matter square in the face."[67]

Hall saw the hollowness of Custer's financial engineering. The investments collected on Wall Street pumped some air into the balloon, but could not make it fly. "I am very sorry that we ever accepted the 12000 dollar proposition at all," Hall wrote. It was barely enough to begin digging, whereas now they needed to buy out the sick Dibben, who was not a hired hand but a partner—the original owner of the Stevens Lode. Ask the stockholders to advance enough to pay him off, Hall pleaded. "Get rid of him. We can then go on, work the mine and make some money, and have it understood & agreed that as soon as we can pay back the money advanced we shall have the balance of 100,000 either in cash or stock of said mine." He sent a report by a mining engineer on the Stevens Lode, noting that the Crescent Company netted a profit of $1,000 per month. Despite their sick partner and Custer's inattention, they might still get rich.

Custer wrote to Travers, but it did no good. The Wall Street men had made their token contributions to the famous soldier's pet project, and would put up no more. On September 23, 1872, Hall wrote, "I have delayed writing three or four days that I might possibly tell you of a favorable report—but . . . I must ask you to wait." Then—silence.[68]

In falling into the fever of the era, Custer failed to understand it. Only the massively wealthy could move the market at will—Vanderbilt, Drew, Gould, Fisk, and a few others. The lesser species tried to ride currents, not make them. The murkiness of this environment taught them to be wary. They did not exactly trust Custer, but risked only a tiny percentage of their subscribed amounts until the mine began to pay. His grand plan for snatching an easy fortune on Wall Street stalled.[69]

Custer did not see that the financial ether still rested upon the real economy. He did not grasp that Vanderbilt's stock market power derived from his ability to create large enterprises and run them profitably. Even the notorious Gould tried to make the Erie Railroad a success, and later achieved that goal with other companies. Custer thought appearances alone would do, because appearances had deceived him—the mistresses, mansions, and theater boxes. He failed to attend to the real work of management. He never fixed the mine's problems or pushed the work forward, never even sought much information. The financiers cut him off. And so the fortune he had imagined vanished in the dark space between anticipation and realization.

Fourteen

THE WRITER

C USTER TURNED TO HIS mission at last. It was a mission he hated.
In September 1871, his long leave ended. He departed New York
and reported to his new post in Elizabethtown, Kentucky, some three
dozen miles south of Louisville. He lodged at the Hill House, an "old-
fashioned hotel" with "humble accommodations" and a "quaint landlady"
assisted by "a small darkey," as he described it to Libbie. She came and
looked over the town with a lacerating eye. "Everything is old, particularly the women," she wrote to Maggie Custer. The landlady was old, a
long-standing boarder was old, the grandfather clock was old, the dog
was old and could barely walk. "The most active inhabitant of the place
is a pig."[1]

Custer commanded two companies in Elizabethtown, one of the 7th
Cavalry and another of the 4th Infantry. "The [7th Cavalry] regiment
was stationed in various parts of the South, on the very disagreeable duty
of breaking up illicit distilleries and suppressing the Ku-Klux [Klan],"
Libbie later explained. That much was true. "Fortunately for us, being in
Kentucky, we knew very little of this service," she added. That was false.
She was wrong, too, to blame her husband's disdain for the post on his
preference for "the free open plain."[2]

The reality of life in Kentucky could be seen in Elizabethtown itself, the
village Libbie found so boring. On November 1, 1871, with Custer away,
command fell to Capt. A. B. Cain of the 4th Infantry. He reported, "The
town authorities are very dilatory in dealing out justice to the offenders of
their laws, which I attribute . . . to the terror in which they hold the lawless offenders." A few days earlier a man had been arrested and brought
before the town judge. "He arose from his seat in the court house and
addressed the judge in the most foul and abusive language, branding him
a coward and a man of the vilest character &c." The judge fined him for
contempt of court, and "the accused drew a pistol . . . threatening to kill
the first man that laid hands upon him. In this case I had the man arrested

and disarmed and returned to the civil authorities, when the judge . . . from sheer fear discharged the offender from custody."[3]

On the day that Cain tried to restore the rule of law in Elizabethtown, Custer was in Louisville with his wife. They attended a performance by a former star of the minstrel shows. "We have laughed until our sides ache," he wrote to his sister Maggie. Lawrence Barrett came through town and sent a custom-made ring up to the Custers' hotel room. Libbie came back first and opened the case. When Armstrong walked in, she said, "Oh, see here what a handsome present Mr. Barrett has sent you. I'm afraid you can't get it on." She was "hoping all the time I could not," he noted. "Imagine her disappointment when I slipped it on my finger." It was a curious incident, one that illuminates the famous actor's sublimated love triangle with the Custers.[4]

It also shows Armstrong's disregard for Kentucky's turmoil. As Cain reported, simple lawlessness was an enormous problem. The James-Younger gang often operated in the state, where the James brothers enjoyed the protection of friends and relatives. They robbed a bank in Columbia, sixty miles southeast of Custer's post, on April 27, 1872. Just a few days before Custer reported to Elizabethtown, the troops there provided an escort for a train carrying a payroll, for fear that outlaws might rob it.

Overwhelmingly, though, it was racial violence that plagued Kentucky—precisely the kind that Libbie dismissed as a far-off problem of the Deep South. "About the year 1870 bands of armed men, disguised and masked, began committing depredations," a resident of Owen County reported to the U.S. district attorney. "They were known as Kuklux, and were in the habit of visiting the houses of citizens . . . in the nighttime. . . . Sometimes they would kill the parties whom they visited. Sometimes they would whip their victims severely, and occasionally burn the houses in which they lived." They targeted black Union army veterans, teachers, and organizers. Sometimes they ordered the entire black population of an area to leave. They struck in every region of the state. "The violence perpetrated by the [Ku Klux] Klan in the bluegrass state would equal in ferocity and frequency the attacks on Afro-Americans anywhere in the old Confederacy," writes the historian George Wright.[5]

African Americans comprised 16.8 percent of the Kentucky population in 1870. Among states that had remained in the Union during the Civil War, only Maryland had a larger proportion of black residents. Ironically, they suffered *because* this was a Union state. The most rapid advance in civil rights came from the Reconstruction Acts; they applied only to ten states of the former Confederacy, requiring new constitutions that guaranteed civil liberties and gave black men the right to vote. Mississippi elected its first black officials long before 1871, whereas black Kentuckians could not even testify against whites in state courts. They did not take it quietly. African Americans mobilized, holding political conventions and organizing schools.

Then the Fifteenth Amendment was ratified in 1870, prohibiting racial discrimination with regard to suffrage. A shift in power was imminent. Though a minority statewide, African Americans had concentrated in towns after emancipation. Lexington's black population increased 300 percent between 1860 and 1870, compared to 10 percent for the white population. In key places black votes could decide elections. They organized.[6]

Their political activity met an intensified terror campaign. In 1871, the Klan—which was not a nationally unified organization, but more of a model followed by local groups—"virtually usurped the local governments in several counties," according to Wright, who counted fifteen so affected. "Kentucky was the only non-seceding state that had any significant Ku Klux Klan presence," notes the historian Patrick Lewis. "Kentucky's Klan members, in great contrast to their fellows in Republican-governed states elsewhere in the South, rode secure in the knowledge that their Democratic state government was hardly concerned with punishing them." The official state militia, the Kentucky National Legion, behaved as the Klan's partner. In Frankfort on August 7, 1871, a militia force assassinated a black political organizer, along with another man—merely two of scores of murders during this period. The Democratic legislature refused to pass legislation to suppress the violence.[7]

African Americans mounted successful defenses in several instances. The man who reported to the U.S. district attorney also wrote of attacks in and around Stamping Ground in Scott County. "The negroes in one place returned the fire, killing one of their party, who was left by them on the road." Yet they could never resolve the problem themselves. Outnumbered and outgunned, they faced the hostility of the entire machinery of state and local government. As early as 1866, black Kentuckians appealed for federal troops—as did victims across the South.[8]

Congress hesitated. Despite a Republican majority (and president), it shrank from further intervention in state and local affairs. White Democrats denounced "occupation" and demanded "home rule," even though Southern states ran their own affairs under the new constitutions mandated by the Reconstruction Acts. Amos T. Akerman, a white Republican from Georgia, went to Washington after Grant's inauguration; the changing sentiment troubled him. "Even among Republicans," he reported, there was "a hesitation to exercise the powers to redress wrongs in the states." If Washington did not act now, "while the national spirit is still warm with the glow of the late war . . . the 'state rights' spirit may grow troublesome again."[9]

The mass violence by the Klan and similar organizations across the South halted this political drift. The moderate Republican senator John Sherman called the bloodshed an "organized civil war," and said the only option was to once more "appeal to the power of the nation to crush [it]." In 1870 and 1871, Congress passed the Enforcement Acts to punish individuals for interfering with the protections in the Fourteenth and Fifteenth amendments. The first two acts codified violations of the right to vote and provided federal oversight of elections. The most dramatic law went into effect on April 20, 1871. Known as the Ku Klux Klan Act, it made federal crimes of conspiracies and violence to deprive citizens of their rights, and authorized the use of the military and even suspension of habeas corpus.

"The Ku Klux Klan Act pushed Republicans to the outer limits of constitutional change," writes Eric Foner. Previously, only state and local governments punished "private criminal acts." Now Washington would directly prosecute individuals. Asserting national power to protect national rights at the personal level, Congress "moved tentatively into modern times."[10]

The violence moved President Grant as well. In 1870 he replaced his distinctly prejudiced attorney general, Ebenezer Rockwood Hoar, with the astonishingly egalitarian Amos Akerman. Born in the North but long resident in the South, Akerman had served as U.S. district attorney in Georgia during the first year of Grant's administration. "For a man with young children to combat the Klan took courage, which Akerman did not lack," William McFeely writes. As attorney general, equipped with new federal legislation, he intended to strike hard.[11]

He struck in Kentucky, among other places. Kentuckian Benjamin H. Bristow, the solicitor general, piped messages and requests from the state directly to Akerman's desk. In August 1871, Akerman authorized the district attorney G. C. Wharton to organize "a secret service force" to investigate attacks in Kentucky. By the end of September Wharton reported that he "had several persons engaged in this work." The army joined in, deploying more troops in Kentucky than in Mississippi. Some of them assisted the Internal Revenue Bureau in raids on illicit distillers. But many aided deputy U.S. marshals as they hunted and arrested Klansmen.[12]

The troops stationed at Elizabethtown went on mission after mission with deputy marshals in late 1871 and 1872. They had an effect. During 1871 Wharton concluded seven civil rights prosecutions, winning six convictions; by December 31 he had twenty-six cases pending, plus three under the Ku Klux Klan Act (in addition to numerous tax prosecutions).

On March 27, 1872, Wharton reported that the Ku Klux Klan "is now being broken up in every part of the state." But he couched his optimism in caveats; the situation was not yet "as is to be desired." Klansmen had deep roots in Kentucky; they continued the old system of slave-hunting patrollers, he wrote, and "are or have been equally endorsed by public sentiment." He recommended that the federal courts in the state be tripled from three to nine "if these outrages continue."[13]

But Kentucky's public officials thwarted him. The state legislature extended the terms of local white officeholders where black voters were concentrated. Towns such as Lexington enacted poll taxes that suppressed the black vote. Hostile judges and juries believed civil rights laws to be unconstitutional. Wharton won no convictions under the Ku Klux Klan Act in all of 1872, and only one under the Civil Rights Act.

Letters complaining of terror continued to arrive in Washington. White Unionist Thomas Webb wrote to President Grant that he had been threatened with a revolver because he wasn't a "reb." W. D. Linkins complained to Grant that "the grand wizzard" had forced him to take the Klan oath, or else "it is deth with mee."[14]

On September 24, 1873, Hiram C. Whitley, chief of the Secret Service, submitted a "Special Report to the Department of Justice on Outrages in Kentucky." As head of the only federal detective force (the Federal Bureau of Investigation was decades in the future), he had conducted an extensive undercover investigation of the Klan in Owen, Henry, and Franklin counties. He submitted evidence for "upwards of fifty cases." A year after promising a quick death for the Klan, Wharton concluded, "The citizens in the infested regions are entirely subjugated or are in sympathy with the Ku-Klux."[15]

By then the crusading Akerman had been pushed out of office. The conservative secretary of state Hamilton Fish had intrigued against him, seeing his campaign against the Klan as undignified and contrary to American political traditions. Jay Gould and Collis Huntington wanted him out as well, as he had resisted the lobbying of their railroad corporations. "Even such atrocities as Ku-Kluxery do not hold their attention," Akerman wrote of the cabinet. "The Northern mind being active and full of what is called progress runs away from the past." He had it reversed. It was Akerman who had the active, progressive mind, and his opponents who wished to delay the future.[16]

DURING THIS WAR against racist terror, Custer enjoyed the company of the very people who led or cooperated with the Klan, as he circulated among genteel horse farms and attended meetings of the equine Kentucky Association. In *Turf, Field and Farm*, he depicted "the true Kentuckian" as a white man or woman who raised horses in "the Blue Grass Region." He wrote, "The women are as charmingly beautiful as the men are proverbially chivalrous, which is saying not a little." By contrast, he described Louisville women as phonies who hid under "pencil, paint, and hair-dye." He sided with the rural "chivalrous" South against the crass urban South. Louisville, incidentally, was home to the Klan's most outspoken critics in the state.[17]

Custer did buy and inspect horses for the army, but he mostly wandered the turf for his own pleasure and profit, at times speculating with his own purchases. At one point Tom wrote to Libbie to warn his brother to get back to his post because Gen. Alfred Terry, commander of the Department of the South, "intends to inspect all the Kentucky Posts, so you may look out." With their characteristic ribbing of each other, Tom wondered if "Armstrong is too confounded mean to write. . . . Tell him to write and let me know when that sale of horses is to come off. And he must be sure and get a fine horse for me." Armstrong often took Libbie to the elegant Galt House in Louisville, whose society she "enjoyed so much," he wrote. He had to talk her into returning to Elizabethtown.[18]

In January 1872 came his highest-profile departure from his duties, when he joined a hunting party organized for the Russian grand duke Alexis. It was a kind of bison-killing diplomacy. As historian Paul Hutton notes, President Grant wanted to steer the visiting royalty away from Washington, where he was embarassed by a "bitter feud" between the Russian minister and Secretary of State Fish. Unlike the English or the French, the Russians had unequivocally supported the Union during the Civil War, and Grant wanted to maintain close relations despite Fish's spat. He asked Sheridan to take the visitors on a high-plains adventure among the buffalo. Sheridan called upon two of his most trusted frontiersmen: "Buffalo Bill" Cody and Custer.[19]

Custer arrived late at the hunting camp on the Nebraska plains, his wagon having broken down five miles away, forcing him to walk. He joined a party of about twenty men, including the grand duke, eight other Russians, Sheridan, Cody, and a *New York Herald* correspondent; they were guarded by a large escort of troops.

"General Custer appeared in his well-known frontier buckskin hunting costume, and if instead of the comical sealskin hat he wore he had only had feathers fastened in his flowing hair, he would have passed at a distance for a great Indian Chief," the reporter wrote. "Buffalo Bill's dress was something similar to Custer's." When they found a bison herd, "the Duke and Custer charged together. . . . Custer charged through an open space and scattered them. He kept his eye close on a big bull that was waiting 'to go for' the Grand Duke." Alexis scored the first kill, as planned; many more followed. He and Custer enjoyed each other's company; the camp fostered camaraderie. The reporter wrote, "After dinner some songs were sung and yarns spun over the blazing camp fire, and one by one the members of the party retired to their tents."[20]

The hunt proved a great diplomatic success, though it was not perfect. On the second day of the hunt, Custer rode his horse so hard it died of exhaustion. At one point he and the grand duke chased some wounded buffalo, firing away, only to meet an enraged Sheridan. They had nearly hit him with stray bullets. He cursed at both of them and "all their kinsfolk, direct and collateral," according to a witness. "It was a liberal education in profanity." Alexis took it well. He and Custer posed together for a portrait with rifles in hand, Alexis with his wide, full-lipped mouth and twin fins of cheek whiskers, wearing a double-breasted jacket, a beardless Custer with a walrus mustache, short hair and receding hairline covered with his brimless sealskin cap.[21]

The expedition lasted only a few days. Custer returned to Elizabethtown. The grand duke stopped there in a special train as he traveled to see Mammoth Cave. Custer met him at the station with his horses and dogs, which Alexis found much more interesting than the crowd of townspeople who came to see him. Libbie joined the royal party at Memphis, where they boarded a steamboat for a trip through the South.[22]

Custer also took time out for politics. President Grant stood for reelection in 1872; this time he faced the Liberal Republican Party, a splinter faction that opposed his continuing intervention in the South. It nominated the newspaper editor Horace Greeley, long considered a Radical. The Democrats saw an opportunity. They backed the Liberal Republicans, declining to run their own man. Custer supported the decision. He did not take part in the political campaign, as he had in 1866 and 1868, but he did win national attention in one incident. At the Galt House in Louisville, he encountered Blanton Duncan, who had organized a convention of "Straight-Out Democrats" who refused to support Greeley. Custer accused him of taking a Republican bribe to split the common front against Grant. They argued, and a friend of Custer's hit Duncan in the face.[23]

Despite these distractions, Custer did in fact command Post 198, as the army officially designated the garrison in Elizabethtown. He displayed his characteristic tendency to ignore regulations. At one point he ordered a private's horse removed from the stable to make room for his personal horse, leading to a formal protest to the Department of the South from Lt. Algernon Smith. Smith complained that Custer violated War Department orders, and had ignored him as company commander. Smith belonged to the circle of subordinates who admired their lieutenant colonel; he and his wife even shared a house with Armstrong and Libbie in 1872. Yet Custer failed to respect his place in the chain of command, to recognize the authority that matters so much to a junior officer.[24]

Lt. James Calhoun joined the Custers in Elizabethtown as post adjutant. Custer's sister Maggie came as well, because she had married Calhoun in Monroe on March 7, 1872. He was twenty-six and she was twenty. She called him Jimmie. Initially they lodged at the Hill House as well, where she learned that their landlady, a "queer old soul," was called "Aunt Beck" by all, and called the Calhouns "children" in return. She would say *Calhoun* quickly, through her nose, "so that it sounds like 'Culloon.'" Maggie liked Elizabethtown, Mrs. Hill, and the hotel. "Our parlor is just the dearest, prettiest little place," she wrote to Ann Reed.[25]

Her husband was less happy. In June he and Custer formally complained about the cost of lodging. Mrs. Hill told Custer he had to move out of his room at the hotel in July. He then rented the house that the Custers shared with the Smiths. Libbie tried, for once, to do the cooking herself. "The men courageously partook of the results," she wrote. "Being in perfect health, they survived the experiments." Custer went to a church festival and bought so much food that the church women "postponed [their next fair] until General Custer returned from duty out of town."[26]

He responded to requests from U.S. deputy marshals for assistance, dispatching two men to make an arrest here, two men to make an arrest there, again and again. "They have no original authority and no right to use force," he ordered, "unless specially directed by [the deputy marshal] or in the last extremity of self preservation." His troops even went to Alabama to assist the Department of Justice.[27]

"Before long I hope your duties may be changed to such as are more to your taste," wrote a friend from England. "What you told me of the state of things in the South was very interesting," he added, particularly since it contradicted the reporting of American newspapers, which "is, as you say, liable to be coloured by party feeling." This echo of Custer's views suggests that he sharply disagreed with Grant's policies toward the South and endorsed the Democrats' opposition to federal enforcement of civil rights laws. It appears he even sympathized with the Klan. Another British friend, Member of Parliament Samuel R. Graves, wrote, "Your explanations about the Ku Klux give a good insight into the creation and objects of this curious band and clears up what [was reported] in England."[28]

The clearest evidence of how Custer viewed Reconstruction duties came on the second to last day of 1872, when he responded to a list of questions submitted by the army's inspector general. He reported that the Elizabethtown garrison held drills twice a day, a parade and inspection of arms once a day. The infantry had 7,600 rounds on hand, the cavalry 2,000. The new recruits spoke English. Noncommissioned officers held recitations; the articles of war were read monthly. "Officers do not wear prescribed uniform," he wrote. Apparently he went about Kentucky in civilian clothes.

Asked to "report upon the associations of the officers," he wrote, "Cap. A. B. Cain is unfit for active service owing to his intemperate habits." Unlike Custer, Cain believed the army had a duty to intervene in civil affairs to maintain order and the rule of law. It may be no coincidence that Custer singled him out for reprimand.

Custer turned defensive, even sarcastic, when it came to his own habits. "Exactly what meaning is intended to apply to the word gambling, which is construed differently by different persons?" he asked. "I am at a loss to understand." As always when challenged, he grew wordy and argumentative.

> If by gambling the act of betting money or risking it on games of chance or contests of speed between horses and if among games of chance are included that usually known as poker and similar games my answer is that so far as my knowledge and belief extend none of the officers of this command [have an] addiction to gambling except the Cmdg [i.e., commanding] Officer and he is addicted to it only so far as neither to interfere with his duties, violate any rule of propriety, nor meddle with other people's business.

This brittle reply, remarkable in an official document, speaks to the guilt he felt at his "addiction," to use his word. It must have been pronounced if he felt compelled to admit it to his superiors. It helps explain Libbie's dislike of the post and travels without him. Underneath his sarcasm can be heard her biting criticism, her refusal to believe he could give up gambling. He could not.

The report seethes with discontent—at his post, his duties, and himself. He concluded with as close to a denunciation of the Ku Klux Klan Act as he could get in an official communication: "The only means and facilities for physical exercise by enlisted men are those enjoyed at drill and on fatigue duty, and in escorting Dep. U.S. Marshalls through the country, of which methods I regard the first two as highly preferable."[29]

In part through the unexpected twists of political battles, the Republicans had stumbled into a broad new vision of America. This new nation brought to fulfillment their free-labor philosophy, in which each person would work or contract for himself, regardless of race—a nation of autonomous economic agents in a free market of labor and capital. They had expanded that concept into one in which all men (and they did mean *men*) participated in balloting and civic responsibilities, in which all were equal before the law, with national civil rights, regardless of local prejudice. Custer rejected that vision. He refused to let go of the past.

TWO TRUTHS MUST BE REMEMBERED, when it comes to Custer's hostility to Reconstruction. First, he was hardly alone in his views. The Northern public rapidly shifted back in his direction. Horace Greeley's turn against intervention in the South showed how great a change was under way; though always erratic, Greeley had been an icon of abolitionism. Second, Custer always had a choice. He did not simply believe what everyone believed. To the contrary, he put his career at risk by opposing the views of Sheridan and campaigning against the election of Grant.

We know the alternative. The path he rejected was the one chosen by Adelbert Ames, who graduated from West Point the same year as Custer (though one class ahead). Son of a Maine sea captain who later took up wheat milling in Minnesota, he came to the military academy as an abolitionist. Like Custer, Ames was a highly social cadet, organizing hops and parties; unlike Custer, he graduated near the top of his class. Like Custer, he fought at First Bull Run; unlike Custer, he came under fire, and refused to leave his artillery battery when badly wounded (he later received the Medal of Honor for his valor that day). Like Custer, he sought a regiment of his own; unlike Custer, he received one: the 20th Maine. Soon after he stepped down from command, the unit played a critical role in saving the Union line at Gettysburg. Afterward the men honored him with their tattered battle flag.[30]

Like Custer, Ames received his general's stars extraordinarily young, took command of a brigade, then got a division—both of infantry, though he fought with Custer at the great cavalry battle of Brandy Station. Where Custer played the gallant, dashing cavalier, Ames won respect for calm professionalism, courage without flamboyance. His division led the successful attack on Fort Fisher; he entered the bastion with the second wave, walking forward with equanimity as sharpshooters gunned down his staff all around him.

Like Custer, he served in the South after the war, then went on an extended leave in 1866. "I . . . have accomplished much—but to what end?" he wrote on a tour of Europe. "Instead of having that which gives peace and contentment, I am adrift, seeking for what God only knows. I do not. Thus far my life has been with me one severe struggle and now that a time of rest is upon me, I am lost to find my position."

Then their lives diverged profoundly. Ames returned to duty, and on June 15, 1868, he took office as Mississippi's provisional governor. "I found, when I was military governor there, that the negroes had no rights whatever," he later told Congress. He acted immediately to change that, appointing the first black officeholders in state history. "General Ames's knife cut deep," wrote a white Republican in Mississippi, "but . . . Ames's surgery was courageous and skilled." Both white and black delegates rewrote the state constitution, opening the way to rule by the black majority. Mississippi's Republican Party asked him to serve as a U.S. senator. (At the time the state legislature elected senators, and the party controlled both chambers in Mississippi.) He agreed. As he told the Senate, "I believed that I could render them [African Americans] great service. I felt that I had a mission to perform in their interest, and I hesitatingly consented to represent them, and unite my fortune with theirs."

Custer considered black suffrage an absurdity; Ames saw it as justice. He embodied everything Custer hated about the new nation. In the Senate, Ames pushed (unsuccessfully) to end the segregation of the army and force every regiment to accept black as well as white recruits. He helped lead the fight for the Ku Klux Klan Act that Custer so despised. In 1873, he won election as Mississippi's governor. Defying "carpetbagger" stereotypes, he led an administration that was frugal, honest, and fair. He did not condescend to his African American allies and constituents, but worked closely with black leaders, such as Representative John R. Lynch and the state senator Charles Caldwell. Ames's governorship marked the farthest advance of Reconstruction.

In 1875, an election year in Mississippi, the Democratic Party organized as an armed force. While Democratic representative L. Q. C. Lamar made soothing speeches about peace and reunion in Congress, his party dispatched armed gangs to attack Republican rallies, assassinate black leaders, and seize entire counties. Scores died. Caldwell defied them, leading a militia company through the countryside. It was not enough.

Ames called for federal troops. Attorney General Edwards Pierrepont stunned him with his response: "The whole public are tired out with these annual autumnal outbreaks in the South, and the great majority are ready to condemn any further interference on the part of the government." It had become too tedious to preserve the equal rights of every American.

The swing in Northern opinion, seen in the mere fact of Greeley's 1872 candidacy, halted the great historical movement that produced the first civil rights acts and remade the Constitution. A Democratic legislature took power and filed trumped-up impeachment charges as snipers fired at the governor's mansion. Ames's friend and ally Caldwell was assassinated; one white Republican said, "He was as brave a man as I ever knew."

Ames agreed to resign. He went to Northfield, Minnesota, to mind the family mill. On September 7, 1876, the James-Younger outlaws—most of them former Confederate guerrillas—rode in to rob a bank he had invested in *because* he had invested in it. Ames witnessed the gunfight on the street. The townspeople drove off the bandits; eventually all but Jesse and Frank James were killed or captured.

Custer took risks in opposing Reconstruction, but the political momentum decisively turned in his direction within a year of his departure from Kentucky. Ames's fate shows that Custer chose the safer side, in terms of his career and personal safety. And yet, on the September day when Ames faced Jesse James, Custer was already dead.

"THE JANUARY MAGAZINES are beginning to make their appearance, freighted with rich promise for the coming year," the *Chicago Tribune* commented on December 20, 1871. Like many newspapers, the *Tribune* previewed the monthly offerings in the exploding medium of magazines. "Foremost among them all is the *Atlantic*—fresher, more brilliant, more entertaining than ever before." It featured a Longfellow poem, a posthumous work by Hawthorne, and contributions from Dr. Oliver Wendell Holmes and Henry James. The paper surveyed others, too, including a fairly new magazine called the *Galaxy*. It serialized Anthony Trollope's novel *The Eustace Diamonds*, but the *Tribune* found little to like. It "makes no very striking announcements for the new year, except of a serial by General Custer, under the title, 'My Life on the Plains.'"[31]

Writing filled Custer's time in Kentucky, when he wasn't gambling, attending races, or sullenly assigning his men to assist the deputy marshals. He wrote five articles on horses for *Turf, Field and Farm*, published between December 1, 1871 and January 10, 1873. He reached a wider audience with his *Galaxy* pieces. They comprised a monthly memoir of the Indian wars in Kansas, starting with the Hancock Expedition of 1867. Apart from his silver mine, it was his most serious attempt to ride the changing times, and appeared to be the most successful by far. But appearances often do not equal reality.[32]

Print culture in the United States began with newspapers. Like the passenger pigeon, they appeared everywhere in mind-boggling numbers.

Whenever Americans paused in the same spot long enough to set up a printing press, a newspaper began—more than one, usually, each with its own political stance. Magazines lagged behind. Technical improvements to printing in 1825 made production cheaper, multiplying the number of publications, but most focused on narrow topics. The commercial general-interest magazine originated as a phenomenon only in the 1850s. *Harper's New Monthly* started in 1850, for example, followed by *Putnam's Monthly* in 1853 and the *Atlantic* and *Harper's Weekly* in 1857.

A truly national, and nationwide, periodical literary culture emerged much more slowly than magazines themselves. The United States did not recognize foreign copyright, and so the vast output of British publications could be pirated without penalty. Writers have never been paid well, but when editors saw that they could pay nothing instead of a little, they chose to pay nothing. George Palmer Putnam recalled in his memoirs that "magazines were either very local in their character, or, like *Harper's* [*New*] *Monthly* . . . were dependent for their contents chiefly on material which had been selected, that is to say appropriated, from British periodicals." *Putnam's Monthly Magazine* made a choice to pay American writers for original content, a culturally profound but financially difficult policy.[33]

A new generation of magazines erupted onto the cultural landscape after the Civil War. By 1870, 1,200 titles circulated in America, up from 700 in 1855. The tally rose to 2,400 by 1880 and 3,300 by 1885. Many were specialized—such as *Turf, Field and Farm*—but others fostered a national discussion of literature, science, and politics, much as *Putnam's*, the *Atlantic*, and the venerable *North American Review* had before the war. Now the *Nation*, *Lippincott's*, *Scribner's*, and the *Galaxy* joined those older titles. As the United States modernized, "the magazine industry became an enormous mirror, reflecting these changes, from the grandiose to the minute," write two historians.[34]

Simply by writing for the *Galaxy*, Custer joined in this transformation. But he had larger ambitions, as revealed in his first two contributions. He knew that he embodied the spirit of adventure in American culture—the daring soldier, the intrepid frontiersman. He wanted to be a public intellectual as well. When his first pages arrived at the *Galaxy* offices at 40 Park Row in New York, across from City Hall Park, the editor Francis Church found not a ripping adventure tale but a geographical, environmental, and anthropological exposition on the Great Plains.

Custer's first essay attacked the "geographical myth" that the Great Plains were the Great American Desert. "Instead of what had been regarded as a sterile and unfruitful tract of land . . . there existed the fairest and richest portion of the national domain." He described the elevation, the topography, soil and water, grass cover, and environmental impact of fires lit by American Indians. He used the Latin names of the tree species, explored bison ("buffalo") behavior, surveyed insects, birds, game, and the mirage.[35]

It was an intelligent discussion, reflecting Custer's sincere scientific interests. He developed a fascination with natural history, and collected fossils in the West. He paid attention to new thinking about the geological origins of the earth and the theory of evolution, as presented by Charles Darwin in *The Origin of Species* in 1859.[36] But his essays were also the work of an amateur, a gentleman hobbyist of the old school. He wrote enthusiastically about the colors of the plains, comparing the scenery to the landscape paintings of Albert Bierstadt and Frederic Edwin Church. He declared his sophistication with this reference, but also revealed the romanticism that mingled with the scientific in his view of the world.

Toward the end of his first contribution he introduced the subject of his second: the American Indian. He criticized "well-meaning but mistaken philanthropists" for accepting James Fenimore Cooper's depiction, which was "more romance than reality." He used the words "real" or "reality" again and again, with unintentional irony. Yet his own views were divided. The Indian "is, and, so far as all knowledge goes, as he ever has been, a *savage* in every sense of the word; not worse, perhaps, than his white brother would be similarly born and bred, but one whose cruel and ferocious nature far exceeds that of any wild beast of the desert."

Did he believe that native peoples were inherently "savage," or that circumstances made them so? Custer went back and forth on the question, as if trying to discover his own mind on the page. He wrote that it was equally wrong to cast them as either "simple-minded 'sons of nature,'" or as a "a creature possessing the human form but divested of all other attributes of humanity, and whose traits . . . and savage customs disqualify him from the exercise of all rights and privileges." But neither did he believe that they were the same as white people. He called them "a race incapable of being judged by the rules or laws applicable to any other known race of men."[37]

Custer's apparent confusion had roots in the so-called science of race developed decades earlier in the United States. Its pioneer was Samuel George Morton, "the most famous anthropologist of his day," writes Louis Menand. Morton devoted his life to confirming his racial prejudices with superficially scientific methods. He published his first study of skull measurements in 1839; ten years later he produced a comprehensive study of the skulls of various races, ranking them by the size of their brain pans. Morton tweaked his unrepresentative data—or rather wrenched them with both hands—to fit his preconceptions. Not surprisingly, he found the Caucasian race had the biggest brains, then Mongolian, Malay, American Indian, and Negro. Among whites, Anglo-Americans stood supreme; among everyone else, American blacks had among the smallest. Morton attributed various characteristics to each race, depicting Native Americans as inherently hostile to farming and prone to war and revenge.

Morton theorized that the different races emerged separately, a theory known as polygenism. His follower Louis Agassiz announced that Negroes were an entirely different (and inferior) species from whites. In 1854, Josiah Nott and George Gliddon published the influential *Types of Mankind*, which expanded on Morton and Agassiz's work. "The leading theme of the volume was the supremacy of the white race," Menand observes; "the servitude of Negroes and the extinction of Native Americans were explained as natural outcomes, scientifically confirmed, of human history."[38]

Directly or indirectly, these theories influenced Custer. He agreed completely when it came to African Americans. But he struggled with the purported inferiority of American Indians. He had, after all, engaged with their leaders as equals. In his serialized memoir, he would tell the story of how they had outsmarted and outmaneuvered him again and again. How could he account for that if their brains were so small and disposition so irrational? On the other hand, he had witnessed the ferocity of warfare on the plains—the victims who were burned to death and mutilated. On the question of "savagery," he had no doubts. "Stripped of the beautiful romances with which we have been so long willing to envelop him," he wrote, "the Indian forfeits his claim to the appellation of the '*noble* red man.'"

In his second article, he expressed frank admiration for the Indian as "the fearless hunter, matchless horseman, and warrior of the Plains." He presented a long list of qualities: "his remarkable taciturnity, his deep dissimulation, the perseverance with which he follows his plans of revenge or conquest, his concealment and apparent lack of curiosity, his stoical courage when in the power of his enemies, his cunning, his caution, and last, but not least, the wonderful power and subtlety of his senses." He praised the "eloquence and able arguments" of Red Cloud, Red Jacket, Osceola, and Tecumseh, along with a Kiowa leader Custer himself had encountered. "Sa-tant-ta is a remarkable man—remarkable for his powers of oratory, his determined warfare against the advances of civilization," he wrote. Custer then arrived at the most quoted passage in his serialized memoir: "If I were an Indian, I often think that I would greatly prefer to cast my lot among those of my people who adhered to the free open plains, rather than submit to the confined limits of a reservation."

Quoted less often is the next sentence: "The Indians can never be permitted to view the question in this deliberate way." The Indian may consider civilization an "insatiable monster," he added, but when it demanded his lands he must submit, or "it will roll mercilessly over him, destroying as it advances. Destiny seems to have so willed it, and the world looks on and nods its approval."

Having posited in his first essay that the white man might be just as savage under similar conditions, Custer now turned in a different direction, asserting an inherent distinction between the races. With the Indian, he claimed,

> Civilization may and should do much for him, but it can never civilize him. . . . Nature intended him for a savage state; every instinct, every impulse of his soul inclines him to it. The white race might fall into a barbarous state, and afterward, subjected to the influence of civilization, be reclaimed and prosper. Not so the Indian. He cannot be himself and be civilized; he fades away and dies.

The Indian's noble attributes were inseparable from his savagery, Custer argued. The plow "deprives him of his identity." An education destroys his spontaneous, untutored eloquence. The arrival of civilization inevitably destroys him, whether it kills him in warfare or drains away his vitality by taking him out of his natural habitat.

And so Custer resolved his dilemma. By binding Indians' positive attributes to their savage, hostile state, he preserved his racial scheme—and superiority—without denying the truth of his experiences. He justified their destruction without scorning their prowess, much as hunters esteemed the mountain lions even as they drove them nearly into extinction. "Study him, fight him, civilize him if you can, he remains the subject of your curiosity," he wrote, "a type of man peculiar and undefined, subjecting himself to no known law of civilization, contending determinedly against all efforts to win him from his chosen mode of life."[39]

"General G.A. Custer . . . administers a well-deserved rebuke to Fenimore Cooper," the *Independent* wrote. The *San Francisco Chronicle* excerpted Custer's second article at length. "The subject is narrowed down to the simple proposition, either the progress of civilization must be stayed or the red man must be driven away or exterminated," it remarked. By justifying the public's demand to strip Indian title to large tracts of land, Custer won general applause.[40]

CUSTER'S ANALYSIS OF THE LAND and people of the plains bridged romanticism with a scientific—and pseudoscientific—outlook. He presented a seemingly modern study, yet it reaffirmed the traditional racial hierarchy. So did the *Galaxy* itself. In the March 1872 issue, this thoroughly modern magazine released the third installment of Custer's memoir, along with "The Colored Member," a "scathing satire" of black lawmakers in Southern legislatures, as the *Literary World* characterized it.

The *Literary World* also wrote that Custer told his story "not very interestingly." After the first two months, his articles turned from analysis and argument to narrative, but the criticism continued. The *New York Tribune* observed, "Gen. Custer's 'My Life on the Plains' has apparently no end." Not every critic took such a dim view. *Turf, Field and Farm* predictably called it "stirring." The *Massachusetts Ploughman* wrote that Custer "tells a story of adventure with great spirit, and in a way to command readers." The *Chicago Tribune* excerpted Custer's "pen-sketch" of Wild Bill Hickok.[41]

The mixed response reflected the changing style of American periodical literature. The editor E. L. Godkin of the *Nation* helped lead the way in the 1860s and '70s, along with *Putnam's*, the *Atlantic*, and, yes, the *Galaxy*. "The kind of eighteenth-century prose that had characterized periodicals before the war could still be seen in some magazines," write two historians of the medium, "but a brighter, more journalistic kind of writing was infiltrating many of the others." Crisp, sharp, and clear, the new prose took a paring knife to its subject, compared to the older style of smothering it with endless coils of sentences. "Strike out all superfluous words, and especially all needless adjectives," Henry Adams advised his subordinates on taking command of the *North American Review*. Nothing could be more modern.[42]

By contrast, Custer could have written his articles in the antebellum era, so outdated and orotund was his style. His first sentence of his first article was so long that it seemed he *must* have started it before the Civil War in order to have finished by 1872: "As fitting introduction to some of the personal incidents and sketches which I shall hereafter present to the readers of 'The Galaxy,' a brief description of the country in which these events transpired may not be deemed inappropriate." An antiquated sensibility echoes in this expanse of words. So too does Custer's memory of being an obscure blacksmith's son scraped off the underside of Ohio, afraid that he will not be taken seriously. The *Galaxy* editors realized he was trying too hard; Custer himself referred to their request to "boil down" his narrative.[43]

It's not that he was a consistently bad writer. He knew how to build suspense and highlight the drama of events. He was not afraid of mocking himself, as in the notorious incident in which he killed his horse, Custis Lee. And his sketch of Wild Bill Hickok was indeed a deft portrait. His heart was in it, as shown by his far shorter sentences, each hitting its target as directly as a striking cobra.

Yet the passage also shows the distance between himself and the leading intellectuals of his generation. He mythologized Hickok, depicting him as an idealized frontiersman: "One of the most perfect types of physical manhood I ever saw. Of his courage there could be no question. . . . His skill in the use of the rifle and pistol was unerring. . . . [He] was entirely free from all bluster and bravado."[44] Critics would fault him for distorting events—Benteen sneered at his memoir as "My Lie on the Plains"—but he generally warped the facts in pursuit of just this kind of sentimentality.

He cast the captive Monahsetah in the role of the Indian princess, shy in civilization yet wise in the ways of the savage nomad. She agreed to go on a dangerous mission, he wrote, and he led her to her starting point, "she clinging to my hand with the natural timidity of a girl." He romanticized the return of the two captives at Sweetwater Creek. The brother of one of the two girls dashed out and embraced her, and Custer "bade them a hearty welcome to liberty. In a moment officers and men were struggling about them upon all sides, eager to take them by the hand, and testify the great joy felt at their deliverance from a life of captivity," he wrote. "Men whom I have seen face death without quailing found their eyes filled with tears, unable to restrain the deep emotion produced by this joyful event." He barely alluded to the women's harrowed appearance or deeply traumatized demeanor, described by other witnesses.[45]

How different was the work of Mark Twain, Ambrose Bierce, Oliver Wendell Holmes Jr., or Charles Francis Adams Jr. Irony was their mode, "a posture of distance and doubt in relation to experience," as Drew Gilpin Faust writes. Twain, for example, was disgusted by Elizabeth Stuart Phelps's bestselling *The Gates Ajar*, published in 1868. Phelps's novel describes a war widow who develops a new understanding of heaven; she sees her dead husband as "not lost, nor asleep, nor annihilated," but merely invisible and close at hand, sending his love. Twain said she "had imagined a mean little ten-cent heaven about the size of Rhode Island." He wrote a parody in which the vast majority of American angels in heaven turn out to be Indians, making his dead protagonist "less than entirely comfortable in paradise," as Faust writes.[46]

Twain witnessed only the tiniest fraction of the Civil War, yet his writing showed the impact of the war as Custer's did not. The disillusioning hammer of mass killing shattered sentimentality. After Ambrose Bierce fought for four years in the infantry, he resolved, "Cultivate a taste for distasteful truths. . . . Most important of all, endeavor to see things as they are, not as they ought to be."

Edmund Wilson wrote that "death itself is Bierce's favorite character,"

indeed, "his only real character." Death ruled Bierce's universe, proving
its power daily as the "man-made God" of the Bible never did. It did
not wait for man to offer sacrifices, but took them arbitrarily, for death
was whimsically homicidal (to paraphrase Wilson). The randomness of
killing and maiming in the war haunted Bierce. Human dreams, beliefs,
and intentions became instantly meaningless when a shell exploded over
a group of soldiers, killing the noble-hearted lad, slashing a leg off the
regiment's fastest runner, and leaving a cowardly scoundrel unharmed.
In an essay about his first skirmish, he wrote of how his regiment was
marched to within enemy artillery range and ordered to lie down. Solid
shot ripped through their ranks. One cannonball lodged in the corpse of
a fellow soldier; when removed from his torso they found it was stamped
with a name, which happened to be the name of the soldier it struck.
Death was a practical joker.[47]

   "I am not the same man (may not have quite the same ideas)," Oliver
Wendell Holmes Jr. wrote to his father during the Overland Campaign
in 1864. On the back of the envelope he wrote, just before the Battle of
Cold Harbor, "It is still kill—kill—all the time." He joined the Union
army filled with high ideals. At some point the idealism bled out of him,
perhaps out of the bullet hole through his neck at Antietam or in the mental and physical exhaustion that wrecked him after the Wilderness. He
had no use for sentimentality or moral righteousness. As Louis Menand
observes, Holmes learned one clear lesson in the kill—kill of the Civil
War: "Certitude leads to violence." He resolved to be a realist. As a judge,
he saw his duty as allowing contending forces in society to fight without
imposing his own understanding or wisdom. He believed in progress, but
without any of the romantic or heroic notions of the antebellum era. "To
many of the men who had been through the war, the values of professionalism and expertise were attractive," Menand writes; "they implied
impersonality, respect for institutions as effective organizers of enterprise, and a modern and scientific attitude—the opposites of the individualism, humanitarianism, and moralism that characterized Northern
intellectual life before the war."[48]

   Charles Francis Adams Jr. took this realism to the level of cynicism.
Unlike his brother Henry, he served in the Union army. As a cavalry
officer he had mocked the lyrical language so often sprinkled on military
operations (by Custer, among others). The truth, he wrote, "would knock
the romance out of you." It knocked it out of Adams himself. Promoted
to command black troops, he scorned them as "nigs" but harbored even
grimmer views of whites, writing, "I have little hope for them in their
eternal contact with a race like ours." The stupidity of superiors and the
filthy brutality of the army dismayed him. His early enthusiasm turned

into "a Dead Sea apple," he wrote. By the end, "We were so sick of the whole thing! . . . The life had become hateful."[49]

With peace he devoted himself to the study of the defining feature of modernity: the railroad. It brought industrial technology into daily life, drove the rise of finance, connected communities, disrupted local economies, and pioneered the institutionalization of society. He emerged as perhaps the foremost writer on the subject. He wrote influential articles for the Boston-based *North American Review*, paying particular attention to the stock market. In July 1869, he published his masterpiece, "A Chapter of Erie." It vividly told the story of the bribery-driven battle for control of the Erie Railway, expressing deep disgust with financiers, the courts, and elected government. "Individuals and corporations of late not unfrequently have found [legislators to be] commodities for sale in the market. So with judicial venality." Market-manipulating capitalists ruled finance, and corrupt officeholders ruled politics.

Adams's cynicism turned him against democracy itself. The Erie Ring, he wrote, united Tammany Hall and stock speculators Jay Gould and Jim Fisk; it "represents the combination of the corporation and the hired proletariat of a great city." Like other liberal reformers, he favored a professional, nonpartisan civil service to replace the system of politically appointed government workers. In part this reflected his respect for professionalism, in part his distrust of the mob. Adams wrote, "Universal suffrage can only mean in plain English the government of ignorance and vice."[50]

To be sure, these early modernists did not typify national culture. Drew Gilpin Faust vividly describes the "era's romanticization of death." She shows how the public clung to sentimentality amid war's horrors. Americans held to a moral order, a divine order, that made sense of suffering and promised a final reward in death. Bierce and the others, she writes, were "dissenting" against their generation.[51]

But Custer cannot be dismissed as merely a typical American. He aspired to be a public intellectual; he placed himself in the company of thinkers. He can only be understood in the context of the leading edge of change as well as the inert mass. Clearly he was not an antisentimentalist like Holmes, nor a cynic like Adams, nor an apostle of professionalism, as both men were. He possessed none of Twain's sardonic distaste for nonsense, let alone Bierce's obsession with realism and death. Custer could not have written "An Occurrence at Owl Creek Bridge" if someone had put a gun to Libbie's head and ordered him to write the darkest story imaginable.

Why did the war affect him so differently? Custer had endured just as much combat as these other men; indeed, he may have spent more days fighting than any of them. It cannot be explained by lack of education, lack of interest in intellectual pursuits, or a religious disposition. A few possibilities do suggest themselves. His war had been very different from that of Holmes or Bierce. As a staff officer, he had flitted in and out of combat; he was not mired in a rifle pit or firing line. As a cavalryman, he had primarily fought other cavalrymen. The numbers of troops involved tended to be much smaller. Firepower mattered less. Cavalrymen fought with sabers, or pistols and carbines that had far shorter effective ranges than infantry rifles. Foot soldiers tended to face more artillery as well, suffering the unpredictable slaughter of shell fire and solid shot.

In cavalry clashes, Custer had swirled around the field on horseback instead of standing in a file of men who were gunned down in blasts of flying metal. He had led charges, galloping at the enemy and fighting with a sword like a medieval knight. Combat with saber and pistol required personal skill. Instead of facing random death, Custer had survived and won in part because of his personal prowess.

That sense of control meant everything. Having power over one's fate vaccinates against cynicism, even if the power is illusory. His early promotion to brigadier general cemented his belief that he mastered his own destiny. As a brigade and then division commander, he had directed events. His decisions had shaped his fate.

He had often witnessed the random brutality and brutal ironies of war, but the lesson did not take before he was elevated to McClellan's staff. And so the lad who went to war never died. He ended the conflict as any boy at the outset would have imagined, having led charges over enemy works, having dueled with a sword and dispatched the foe, having shattered the enemy line and seized his guns and flags. And he was never seriously wounded, never struck dead by the diseases that killed hundreds of thousands. His illusions remained intact—more than intact, reinforced.

And that is one reason why so much of the public found him so admirable and endearing. They had struggled to maintain their own sentimentality amid so much death. They tried very hard to keep their illusions about heroism and gallantry, as soldiers returned home with missing limbs and abundant irony, as so many soldiers remained on battlefields, shoveled anonymously into trenches. These Americans needed Custer, the amateur, the enthusiast, the romantic. He was what they feared they could never be again.

CUSTER LUCK BARRED HIM FROM joining the ranks of the most modern American intellectuals—his good fortune in having a happy experience in the nation's saddest event. His intelligence won respect, his storytelling won an audience, but his pen could not win a living. His serialized memoir came out monthly, earning him $1,200 by the end of 1872. It was helpful but not enough for him to abandon the army.

He bided his time in Elizabethtown. *Turf, Field and Farm* announced his horse purchases. Lawrence Barrett corresponded with him: "Custer, still be my friend and the same good fellow I have always found you." In January 1873 Custer wrote to Senator Chandler to ask for tickets for Libbie and himself to Grant's second inauguration in March. But they would not be able to attend. In February Custer learned that the 7th Cavalry would be shifted to the Dakota Territory, starting March 1.[52]

Now began the routine so familiar to a military family in peacetime: his unanswered requests for information, the rapid packing, the movement of troops, horses, and supplies to railroad depots and steamboat landings. On April 1 the transports began to steam from Memphis and Louisville, paddling up the Mississippi and Missouri to the last home George Armstrong Custer would ever know.[53]

Fifteen

THE ENEMY

"I DON'T KNOW WHETHER I am glad or sorry that you are going so far away again," Lawrence Barrett wrote to Custer on March 23, 1873. "My sorrow arises from the fear that we may not soon meet again, now that you are so far away. . . . I am glad again, my dear comrade, to know that you are on the service you like best." Barrett wished he could join him—not for an outdoor life, which Barrett abhorred, but to "get free from the thralldom of dress coats and drawing room behavior. . . . To sit for hours thinking of *nothing*—no night of performance hanging over me—no costume—no Hamlet—no Cassius."[1]

The Custers reached the faraway place on April 10, "with bags, dogs, and cages of canaries and mockingbirds," writes Shirley Leckie. Much of the 7th Cavalry camped in the southeastern corner of the Dakota Territory, on the prairie outside Yankton, the capital. The census had counted barely 2,000 people in Yankton County in 1870, and just 11,319 white and 70 black residents in the entire Territory. This was Indian country. There were many indigenous peoples living here, but the army concerned itself with two in particular: the Northern Cheyennes and their allies, the Sioux. Custer would face them on an expedition to the Yellowstone River over the summer of 1873, and as the commander of a new post on the Missouri River, Fort Abraham Lincoln.[2]

Barrett imagined that the frontier assignment excited Custer, who "delights in riding to the death the startled game." Libbie, too, wrote that "life in the saddle on the free open plain is his legitimate existence." It was the truth. But it was not the entire truth. Custer also longed for the civilization that wearied Barrett. Later in 1873 he would write to Libbie, "What a delightful two years we have spent in the States." He predicted a great future—looking east, not west. "I think it will not be long before my business and horse matters will be so arranged so as to require less looking after and instead of being a drain upon our resources . . . will be yielding us something. That is my plan." Stock, livestock, and letters would make them rich—including, he hoped, the Stevens Mine, which lingered on, neither sold nor developed.[3]

He loved the West, but he was not *of* the West. He projected a new image of himself through the lens of the frontier, but he cast himself as the cosmopolitan sophisticate who mastered the wilderness, inserting knowing references to New York in essays about rattlesnake broiling, buffalo hunting, and Indian fighting. Buffalo Bill Cody was dramatizing his own frontier image, which would lead to his famous Wild West show. Underneath the spectacle, though, Cody *was* an authentic child of Kansas. He went east as Custer went west and mastered the world that Barnum made.

The only real master Custer recognized was his own ambition. "It is such a comfort to me to feel independent, much as I dote on my profession and earnestly as I am devoted to it," he wrote to Libbie later in 1873. "Yet should accident cast me adrift and I be thrown upon my resources I have not a fear but that energy and willingness to put my shoulder to the wheel would carry me through triumphantly." He gloried "in this country," where a "modest education" opened up "many and varied . . . avenues to honorable employment."[4] The rising corporate economy slowly made that classic antebellum vision obsolete, as it narrowed the space for an independent, self-made life. Ironically Custer never found a way to sustain himself outside a large institution. He bristled against the army's regimentation, yet he did as it demanded.

And so Armstrong and Libbie found themselves on the plain outside of Yankton. She later recalled that he fell sick on April 13, when snow began to fall. Soon "the air was so thick with whirling, tiny particles that it was almost impossible to see one's hand held out before one." The air was comparatively warm, hovering near freezing, making the snow heavy and wet. Fierce winds piled up drifts and blew down tents. Custer called the blizzard "the worst I remember. . . . Mrs. Custer and myself took shelter in an unoccupied and unfurnished house near camp where we have remained . . . without a particle of fire and with but little food." The townsfolk helped the fugitive soldiers, lodging many in the hall of the Territorial legislature. Forty laundresses and their children remained in the wrecked camp as snow fell for forty-eight hours.[5]

"The first morning after the storm was bright, but cold and windy," wrote 2nd Lt. Charles W. Larned. He had graduated from West Point in 1870, and had spent most of the time since in Louisville or on leave. Just twenty-three, this long-faced, sophisticated New Yorker had a talent for drawing and a sneer for almost everything.[6]

With ten of the regiments' twelve companies collected at Yankton,

Larned had his first opportunity to look down on the 7th Cavalry en masse. He disdained the food on a Missouri River steamer as "the most atrocious boat fare." Most of the officers' wives lodged in "the slovenly outrage they call a hotel." After a few weeks together, the women "have succeeded in discovering each other's failings with astonishing distinctness, and . . . made the atmosphere pretty warm." He scorned a ball thrown by the town of Yankton for the officers as "a homespun affair." The locals were proud of their well-organized fete, but he found it briefly amusing "to have seen the bumpkins and their sweethearts" dance. He mocked his fellow officers and their wives as "the fair bluebloods of our own patrician circle."[7]

When he turned to the Custers, he put down his razor and picked up an ax. He started by chipping at Libbie. "She and the general seem to keep pretty close," he wrote home on April 25. "She rather took me to task for lack of attention, the prerogative of her royal rank which she never forgets. There is an odor of much ineffable condescension about her stereotyped sweetness that I am bored by it and stay away from court."[8]

He chopped Custer with full force. He "wears the men out by ceaseless and unnecessary labor," Larned wrote. "He keeps himself aloof and spends his time in excogitating annoying, vexatious, and useless orders which visit us like the swarm of evils from Pandora's box." Later that spring, "Custer undertook to bully and insult" a court-martial on which Larned served. "He is making himself utterly detested by every line officer of the command, with the exception of one or two toadies, by his selfish, capricious, arbitrary, and unjust conduct."[9]

"The army is a great school for grumblers," Samuel Barrows wrote later that year. A correspondent for the *New York Tribune*, he spent months with the 7th Cavalry in 1873. (Larned liked him, "notwithstanding that he wears checked trousers.") He continued, "There are more chronic grumblers in the army than anywhere else I know of. The officers are frequently as bad as the men." Barrows's observation puts Larned's complaints in context, correcting some of the distortion resulting from Custer's great notoriety. The 7th Cavalry is by far the most-studied unit in the nineteenth-century Regular Army; this narrow focus exaggerates the significance of spats and grievances, making routine friction appear as extraordinary dissension. In 1873 Custer aroused no public outcry, as in Texas in 1865, nor did the army move to punish him, as in Kansas in 1867. He remained within the limits of tolerable behavior. Larned's remarks draw attention because he mastered the art of complaining.[10]

But he cannot be dismissed. At the very least, he revealed that Custer still took no interest in management, though it was now his primary duty. He was capable of tact, sympathy, and empathy, but he turned to them last in his official capacity. The verbs Larned chose to describe Custer's treatment of his subordinates were specific and damning: "bully . . . insult . . . hector . . . annoy." He also wrote something more significant, that spoke to Custer's relationship to the army as an organization: "Custer is not belying his reputation—which is that of a man selfishly indifferent to others, and ruthlessly determined to make himself conspicuous at all hazards."[11]

The word *reputation* encapsulates the lasting consequences of past misbehavior. Larned spoke the institutional consensus about Custer, passed from man to man, from Fort Riley to San Francisco's Presidio and New York's Governors Island. Subordinates and superiors now approached him with a set of expectations, and not in Custer's favor.

The antagonism was deeply rooted. Regular Army culture disdained pretension and self-promotion. Libbie later recalled that the wives of officers who had served before the Civil War were "a trifle condescending. . . . These women with experiences of a life with the Old Army (the latter phrase was emphasized) . . . called their husbands 'Mister' even when they were a Major General, and instantly held myself to account for having spoken of my husband, such a boy, as General."[12] In this atmosphere Armstrong earned widespread disapproval with his flamboyance, self-indulgence, misdeeds, and public letters.

His reputation afflicted him after he took command of the ten companies at Yankton. His orders required him to march some 400 miles north along the Missouri River to Fort Rice, the staging point for the foray to the Yellowstone River basin. The 7th Cavalry would form only one component of the expedition, which would be led by Col. David S. Stanley, who also commanded the 22nd Infantry, Fort Rice, and the Middle District of the Department of Dakota. Their mission was to escort surveyors for the Northern Pacific Railway, protecting them from Sioux attacks.

As Custer exchanged telegrams on preparations for his march with Stanley and Department of Dakota headquarters in St. Paul, he squabbled with virtually the entire chain of command. Asst. Adj. Gen. O. D. Greene forwarded Custer's messages to the department commander, General Terry, who was temporarily in New Jersey; the two commiserated about his barrage of demands and complaints. "Custer's request for wagons is absurd," Terry wired to Greene, after learning he wanted scores more than he was allowed. "He can have made no calculations." Remind him a steamboat will accompany the march to carry baggage and the laundresses, he added. Custer complained to Greene about Colonel Stanley's orders, saying Stanley was too far away and didn't understand the problems in Yankton. He requested a new superior—"someone . . . familiar with the questions which should determine this movement."

Greene wired Terry that Custer had sent "a telegram of ten pages . . .
principally fault finding and making unnecessary difficulties in regard to
the march. . . . I report it extremely difficult to get along with the present
Commander."

Terry authorized Col. Samuel Sturgis, still senior officer of the 7th
Cavalry but now on duty in St. Paul, to go to Yankton and straighten
out the mess. Once on the scene, Sturgis largely supported Custer (the
regiment did lack sufficient wagons for the march, for example). This
controversy, insignificant in itself, shows that the army saw Custer as a
problem officer. Department headquarters viewed everything he wrote
with skepticism, taking umbrage at his requests. And Custer was not
the man to alleviate the problem. His pestering and indignant tone only
made it worse.[13]

Sturgis disentangled affairs at Yankton and returned to St. Paul. On
May 7 the regiment set out for Fort Rice. A month and a half later the
column finally arrived. But the post had no lodging for the officers'
wives, and housing at Custer's permanent station, Fort Abraham Lincoln, had not been completed. Libbie and Armstrong said good-bye, and
she returned to Monroe with her sister-in-law, Maggie Custer Calhoun.
Armstrong prepared for a summer in the wilderness with Stanley and the
Sioux.[14]

"THE GREAT, HEAVY COLUMN WOUND slowly along like an immense black
serpent," an infantry officer wrote to the *Chicago Tribune*. It set out from
Fort Rice on June 20, aiming to unite on the march with the railroad
engineers and their military escort, who moved west from the Northern
Pacific's terminus on the Missouri River, farther north. Even disassem-
bled, it was an impressive body for the Northern Plains: 79 officers and
1,451 men, 4 three-inch rifled artillery pieces (known as Rodman guns),
353 civilian employees, 27 Indian scouts, hundreds of head of cattle, more
than 2,000 horses and mules, and 275 wagons, each overburdened with
4,000- to 5,280-pound loads, including a total of sixty days' worth of
rations and forty-two days' forage.

"It is indeed a strange sight to see the hundreds of great army-wagons
lumbering along," wrote the *Tribune*'s correspondent, "laden with every
conceivable implement of war and all kinds of food, picks, shovels, hoes,
shells, thousands of cartridges, tons of hard bread, bacon, coffee, sugar,
rice, flour, grain, and an endless number of ropes, chains, spare wagon-
tongues, wheels, and tents. The mules tug and pull, and the monster
machines roll slowly on to the westward." The column struggled and

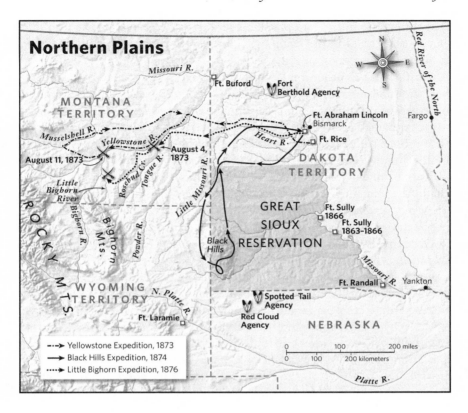

straggled slowly onward in suffocating heat, beset by thunderstorms. It rained fourteen of the first seventeen days, Stanley reported; "the usually hard prairie . . . usually as good as a macadamized road . . . became a swamp." It took six days to go forty-five miles.[15]

The pace aggravated Stanley, a true officer of the Old Army. "Dignified," Larned thought, on meeting him in June. "Impressed me very favorably." An 1852 graduate of West Point, he had served on a reconnaissance for the first transcontinental railroad from 1853 to 1854, among other assignments in the West. He rose to the rank of major general of volunteers in the Civil War, and would later receive a Medal of Honor for his heroism in the defense of Franklin, Tennessee, on November 30, 1864. Promoted from captain to full colonel in the reorganized Regular Army, he had commanded the escort of the Northern Pacific surveyors in 1872, completing an impressive résumé of service on the Great Plains. Ostensibly he was the ideal leader for the 1873 survey—but he drank. His alcoholism had marred the 1872 expedition, pockmarking it with binges that threw him into a dark place. He looked as if he were much more than eleven years older than Custer, with lines around light-colored eyes and a full beard threaded with gray.[16]

Custer, on the other hand, enjoyed himself. He commanded less than half the total force—his ten companies of cavalry were outnumbered by nineteen of infantry, not counting the artillery and civilians—and wore his responsibilities lightly. He brought his band, of course, which played throughout the march. He trotted beside the trudging foot soldiers and lumbering wagons, his pack of hunting dogs trailing behind him. Other officers brought dogs as well. Custer led hunters into herds of antelope that often swarmed around the column on the soggy grasslands. He took great pleasure not only in hunting but in the praise of others. He boasted in a letter to Kirkland Barker, as he often did to Libbie, "My fine shots have been discussed not a little." His perennial look-at-me hunger for attention seems juvenile because it was; yet the hunters' marksmanship, the racing dogs, and the band delighted the bored soldiers. Even the cynical Larned wrote, "The dogs . . . afford many an exciting chase."[17]

As Stanley steeped in the frustration of command, Custer emerged as the star of the expedition. One infantry officer exclaimed, "What an admirable cavalry-soldier Custer is! Not only his dash and bravery, which are [famous] world-wide, but his good sense, makes him just what a successful leader of cavalry should be." A newspaper correspondent wrote, "In buckskin hunting jacket and familiar broad-brimmed slouched hat, from beneath which streams his long flowing locks, mounted on a blooded horse, with rifle in hands, . . . he dashes with a free rein over hill and through valley. . . . The general is a crack shot." Professor William Phelps of the scientific corps that accompanied the expedition drafted a more careful and revealing portrait. "Gen. Custer is of medium stature, with body slightly inclined forward in walking, face spare, nose rather large and pointed, and hair hanging in slight curls to the shoulders," he wrote. "In talking he is intensely earnest and lively, and during [an] interview he sat leaning forward with his arms crossed and resting on his knees, which were also crossed—not a very soldierly attitude, to be sure. His manner is quick and nervous and somewhat eccentric." Phelps admired Custer's energy. They all found him fascinating.[18]

"I have had no trouble with Custer, and will try to avoid having any; but I have seen enough of him to convince me that he is a cold blooded, untruthful, and unprincipled man," Stanley wrote to his wife on June 28. "He is universally despised by all the officers of his regiment excepting his relatives and one or two sycophants. He brought a trader in the field without permission, carries an old negro woman and cast iron cooking stove, and delays the march often by his extensive packing up in the morning. As I said I will try, but am not sure I can avoid trouble with him." He saw Custer's popularity and independence, and concluded, "He was just gradually assuming command."[19]

"General Stanley is acting very badly, drinking, and I anticipate official trouble with him," Custer wrote to Libbie (using Stanley's brevet rank, as was the custom). Custer often asserted moral superiority by accusing a rival of drinking. He compensated for his character flaws by giving special emphasis to one clear strength, his freedom from alcoholism. In this case, of course, Stanley *was* an alcoholic, which filled Custer with towering self-righteousness.[20]

Stanley ordered Custer to take the cavalry and move ahead of the main column to rendezvous with the railroad engineers, whose wagons had been smashed in a fierce hailstorm on the far side of the Heart River. Relieved to be released, he soon reached their camp, where he met his old academy friend and wartime foe, Thomas Rosser.

Rosser had spent five hard years trying to recover from the defeat of the Confederacy. He studied law to no end, failed with enterprises in New Orleans and Baltimore, and delivered lectures to empty halls. In St. Paul, with "three cents to my name," he found a job as an engineer with Northern Pacific. He had participated in the 1872 surveying expedition, and led the 1873 contingent.

Professor Phelps described Rosser as "about six feet two inches in height, broad and erect . . . weighing about two hundred and twenty pounds. His face is round and full, his hair black, his complexion fair, and with a ruddy tinge." Phelps listened as Rosser and Custer discussed their battles, clearing up mysteries and misconceptions. One such conversation, he wrote, "was well worth the trip to Dakota to enjoy."[21]

Rosser and Custer's friendship further aggravated Stanley. For his part, Custer unfairly blamed a delay in the arrival of the main column on Stanley's drinking. Then came successive incidents that provoked an open break. First Custer took off without orders and escorted Rosser several miles ahead to continue the survey during the delay. Next, on July 7, Stanley sent Custer an order prohibiting him from using the cookstove that Stanley hated so, and demanded to know why Custer had loaned an army horse to Fred Calhoun, a civilian and brother of Lt. James Calhoun. Stanley called Custer to his tent. Custer, visibly angry, approached in his shirtsleeves and refused to salute. Stanley placed him under arrest and forced him to ride behind the column the next day.

"The sympathy for him was deep and universal outside of Stanley's headquarters as far as I had any opportunity to observe," a reporter wrote. "But there was no disguising the fact that Custer had used language that was disrespectful toward his superior officer. . . . The provocation, however, was great, as it was felt that Stanley's conduct was unnecessarily irritating in his interference with the domestic concerns of the cavalryman's headquarters." On July 8 Rosser intervened, and Custer went free.[22]

Rosser called it "a reconciliation" in his diary, but the meeting left each man convinced that he was right. "I was placed in arrest for . . . the strict conscientious discharge of what I knew was my duty," Custer wrote to Libbie, "feeling self justified in my course." He claimed, unbelievably, that Stanley apologized and admitted being wrong. Stanley wrote to his wife, "I had a little flurry with Custer as I told you I probably would. . . . I knew from the start it had to be done, and I am glad to have had so good a chance, when there could be no doubt who was right. . . . Now he knows he has a commanding officer who will not tolerate his arrogance."[23]

The "reconciliation," then, resolved nothing. Custer compensated by escaping. He frequently volunteered to ride ahead and find a campsite for the evening, essentially abandoning his command duties, and Stanley let him go. He led Rosser and an escort on a search for the steamboat that waited for the expedition on the Yellowstone River; he took terrible risks guiding them up and down impossibly steep bluffs and hillsides as they hunted for a way down into the valley. At one point, he wrote to Libbie, "It was impossible for us to retrace our steps as the sides of the peak were so steep our horses could not turn about without great danger of tumbling hundreds of feet." They escaped when Custer found an alternate path, first dislodging a boulder that blocked the way, sending it bounding down the slope.[24]

He also enjoyed the company of the scientific corps. He enthusiastically hunted for fossils in cliffs and river bottoms, boxing up specimens that included "reptiles" and "sea fish." He studied taxidermy with an expert in the column. The coral-like rock formations of the desolate badlands they encountered fascinated him. He spent hours with Fred Grant, the president's son and a recent West Point graduate now on Sheridan's staff, who accompanied the expedition for the first month or so.

And he socialized with his "royal family," as Larned called his loyalists and family members. "I have told Satan to get behind me so far as poker goes," he wrote to Libbie, acknowledging "the excitement and pleasure I used to take in it." But Tom played (well) as did Calhoun (badly). Tom won $300 and Calhoun borrowed from any who would lend. "How do they tease and devil Mr. Calhoun," who had no sense of humor, Custer wrote. When Buffalo Bill's success onstage came up in conversation, Tom exclaimed that they should go on tour; they could call Calhoun "Antelope Jim" and make him the star. "I think that's a little thin," Calhoun said, and they laughed. Custer said that "all [were] jolly and good humored, full of their jokes, all disgusted with the infantry and prouder than ever of the modest 7th."[25]

On July 20, Stanley went on a three-day drinking binge. "Stanley is very drunk, and I fear Custer will arrest him and assume command," Rosser wrote in his diary on July 21. Despite Stanley's state, the army might treat his arrest as mutiny, unless Custer could prove the column faced imminent danger. The fact that Custer openly contemplated it reveals the depth and danger of their hostility.[26]

At the end of Stanley's bout, soldiers destroyed whiskey belonging to Augustus Baliran, the civilian sutler who came with Custer. When Custer complained, Stanley claimed that he gave no orders on the subject. Custer believed Stanley's subordinates acted independently to save him from himself. Baliran filed an official protest, claiming $4,000 in losses, and Custer supported him. It had been perhaps the best thing for Stanley, yet it only aggravated his feud with Custer.[27]

THREE PROTAGONISTS COLLIDED on the Northern Plains in 1873—if large groups or organizations may be described as protagonists. And a single sentence describes them all: They came from the East, determined to take lands in the West regardless of the peoples who already lived there.

The force that precipitated the Yellowstone expedition was the Northern Pacific Railway, part of the second wave of transcontinental railroads that followed the Union Pacific/Central Pacific trunk from Omaha to San Francisco. Outwardly it embodied the future of the United States: organization, industrialization, and capital, combined to tame the wilderness and exploit its resources. This giant business corporation operated on a scale unknown just a generation earlier. It made use of the latest technology, engineering methods, and scientific knowledge. Its fixed infrastructure and motorized trains would eliminate the immensity of distance in the West, bringing it into immediate contact with the rest of the country, integrating markets and society. Northern Pacific would centralize, modernize, and dominate the lives of thousands of individuals who would work for it or depend on its services.

Ironically, it also embodied the past. As mentioned earlier, corporations began in America as mercantilist tools of government policy. Legislatures chartered corporations to persuade private investors to finance projects believed to serve the public good. By the 1870s, businessmen had turned the corporation into a vehicle for private profit. But the old concept lingered in transcontinental transportation. In 1847, for example, Congress subsidized steamship corporations to connect to California. During the

1850s, Congress debated a transcontinental railway, and the army scouted the routes. Under President Lincoln, the Union Pacific railroad received its federal charter. Its executives, together with those of its connecting line, Central Pacific, secured extensive government backing because federal policy makers saw them as a means of enhancing national unity.

From a business point of view, the first transcontinentals were highly speculative. Relatively few white Americans lived on the Pacific coast, and very few in the interior of the West; railroad management could only hope that, if they laid the tracks, the people would come. Leaders of successful eastern railroads tended to stay away from the early transcontinentals, except for short-term stock speculations. As the *Railroad Gazette* observed, "A connection a hundred miles long in a State east of Chicago might easily give a more profitable traffic [to the Vanderbilt railroads] than the entire thousand miles of the Union Pacific."[28]

To encourage private investment, the federal government offered the first transcontinentals such support as vast land grants (which the lines could sell to settlers) and federal bonds. But this aid also invited profiteering. The transcontinentals helped inspire the 1873 novel *The Gilded Age* by Mark Twain and Charles Dudley Warner, a satire of government corruption, not the lavish lifestyles of the rich. For example, Congress insisted that Union Pacific's government-backed shares and bonds could only be sold at par, or face value; but investors demanded a discount, making them unmarketable. Union Pacific's managers, acting as private individuals, bought a dummy corporation to use as an intermediary; named Crédit Mobilier, it took UP securities at par and resold them at market prices or issued them to its own stockholders. The scheme gave Union Pacific access to credit markets, but invited self-dealing. Union Pacific pretended Crédit Mobilier was a construction company and overpaid it for work that it passed off to real contractors. Insiders collected huge profits, as much as 610 percent of their investment in just five years. The controlling ring kept congressional investigations at bay with bribes until a major scandal broke in 1872.[29]

Congress chartered Northern Pacific in 1864 as another tool of federal policy, and, like Union Pacific, the corportion faced skepticism from experienced railroad men and possessed great potential for corruption. As Cornelius Vanderbilt said of the line in 1873, "Building railroads from nowhere to nowhere at public expense is not a legitimate undertaking." And yet, one of the greatest American bankers, Jay Cooke, began to back the railroad in 1870, serving as its financial agent and guarantor. Famous for successfully marketing huge volumes of federal bonds during the Civil War, Cooke kept the line going as it laid track west from Duluth to a point opposite Fort Abraham Lincoln on the Missouri River, where the town of Bismarck sprouted. Immediate market conditions lured him, but he saw Northern Pacific's immense long-term potential. As historian Richard White writes, its federal land grant equaled all of New England rolled out in a strip from Duluth to Puget Sound.[30]

If Northern Pacific's origins were rooted in the past, Cooke's involvement pointed to the future—and its problems. He represented the centrality of finance in the new economy. (Cooke himself was a Philadelphian; Northern Pacific kept its headquarters in Manhattan.) Large corporations raised funds through bonds and stocks sold on formal exchanges to (or through) banks and investment firms. Investors and institutions traded these securities or used them as collateral for further borrowing, often from New York banks that held the reserve deposits of banks located across the country. The result was a web of equity and debt that sustained *and endangered* the entire economy. Each component was necessary to prevent the entire structure from collapsing. Should a major player—such as the house of Jay Cooke—fail to pay its debts, those it owed could not pay their own obligations; even firms unaffected directly might panic and curtail their operations or call in loans. The resulting shut-off of capital and revenue could force corporations, now the dominant economic force, into bankruptcy. That could lead to a depression.[31]

As the Yellowstone expedition moved across the plains, Cooke's worries multiplied. The all-important European market for American securities had softened over the last year; ironically, cheap American exports had hurt the continent's economies. In May, a financial crash in Vienna prompted many European investors to dump the riskier securities of American railroads. Northern Pacific overspent, forcing Cooke to step in and personally make up the difference, even as his own finances tightened. And corruption afflicted the line. With the vast enterprise trembling, the last thing Cooke needed was war with the Sioux.[32]

To the army, though, the entire point of Northern Pacific was to defeat the Sioux. Just before the 1873 survey mission began, Sherman explained to Congress, "This railroad is a national enterprise, and we are forced to protect the men during its survey and construction through, probably, the most warlike nation of Indians on this continent, who will fight for every foot of the line."[33]

"THE WINNING OF THE WEST": That was the title Richard White gave a seminal 1978 article on the Sioux. Ethnologists and Western historians, he observed, had long described the fighting among American Indians not as true warfare, but as "individualistic. . . . A series of raids and counter-raids; an almost irrelevant prelude to the real story: Indian resistance to white invasion." In reality, he writes, the Sioux fought for national objectives. Starting in the early eighteenth century, they expanded westward from the Minnesota woodlands onto the Northern Plains, seizing valuable territory. Black Hawk, a Sioux leader, told American officials in the mid-nineteenth century, "These lands once belonged to the Kiowas and the Crows, but we whipped those nations out of them, and in this we did what the white men do when they want the lands of the Indians."[34]

The Sioux, like the Comanches far to the south, maintained national identity despite the absence of an overarching governing structure and an abundance of internal fissures. They divided into three groups, with a broad spectrum of territory, dialect, and material culture. The eastern group was known as the Santee: four tribes (sometimes called subtribes) who lived along the Minnesota River in comparatively permanent communities, hunting, harvesting wild rice, engaging in horticulture. Many had fled west during the 1862 war known as the Sioux Uprising. The result of corruption and mistreatment by government officials, it saw the killing of hundreds of white settlers and Indians, including the largest mass execution in U.S. history, when thirty-eight Sioux were hanged in Mankato, Minnesota.

Sioux was a name imposed from the outside—reportedly a French corruption of the Ojibwe word for "enemy." It's convenient because of the range of Sioux dialects. The Santee called themselves Dakota. So did the Yankton (or Yanktonai), the middle group, who by the 1870s occupied the plains east of the Missouri River. Farther west were the seven tribes of the Teton Sioux—or, to use their own word, Lakota. As Robert Utley enumerates them, with translations of their common French or Lakota names, they included "the Oglala ('Scatters Their Own'), Brulé ('Burned Thighs'), Miniconjou ('Planters by Water'), Two Kettle ('Two Boilings'), Sans Arc ('Without Bows'), Hunkpapa ('Campers at the Opening of the Circle'), and Sihasapa ('Blackfeet')," the last tribe being distinct from the Blackfeet nation to the west.[35]

In the late eighteenth and early nineteenth centuries, the Lakotas advanced from the eastern edge of the Northern Plains to conquer the middle Missouri River country, the stretch of river that extended north through the center of what became the Dakota Territory. In the first half of the nineteenth century, they expanded south and west, to the Platte and Yellowstone river basins. Like the Comanches and the other high-plains nations, the Lakotas were attracted by natural resources, trade, and the need for space as they acquired horse herds and abandoned horticulture and beaver trapping for bison hunting. Ironically, the arrival of smallpox gave them an advantage over sedentary neighbors such as the Arikaras, Hidatsas, Mandans, and the Omahas and Poncas to the south.

Three epidemics between 1779 and 1802 afflicted those peoples' fixed, fortified communities far more heavily than the dispersed Lakota bands. The Lakotas then hit them hard, wiping out entire villages at times. They turned the Arikaras and others into vassals, controlling their trade and punishing them for resistance.

Meanwhile the Teton Sioux grew in strength, thanks in part to high birth rates, smallpox inoculations administered by American emissaries, and an inflow from Santee and Yanktonai tribes. Drawing on admittedly inaccurate counts, White estimates that the Lakotas rose from as few as 5,000 in 1804 to perhaps 25,000 in the 1850s. They climbed out of comparative poverty in horses (which lasted as late as the first quarter of the nineteenth century) to ownership of large herds, often acquired through attacks on their neighbors. They developed a reputation as fine riders, which they previously had lacked. Yet they suffered heavy casualties in these wars for land and horses, as did their enemies. In the early nineteenth century, men died in such large numbers that women constituted 65 to 75 percent of the population of the various Northern Plains nations.

In fierce competition for bison with white hunters and other Indian nations, they continued fighting even after they seized the terrain they would occupy in 1873. To the south they struck at the Pawnees, who mixed a low-plains horticultural economy with seasonal bison hunting on the high plains. To the west they fought Crows, Shoshones, Blackfeet, and others. As White observes, the bloodshed created unoccupied terrain between the hostile nations where the buffalo flourished—which in turn became an incentive for further aggression. The summer of 1873 saw the climax of the long war against the Pawnees, when an Oglala offensive slaughtered perhaps the last major Pawnee hunting party, on the Republican River. But the Lakotas formed alliances as well. With the great peace forged on the Arkansas River in 1840, they formed close bonds with the Cheyennes and Arapahoes.[36]

American observers mostly noticed the military virtues of Lakota society: stoicism, courage in battle, shrewd tactics, brilliant riding, and the formal displays of war paint, feathers and headdresses, decorated lances and shields. What they generally knew of the rich Lakota spiritual life was limited to the dramatic sun dance ritual. Few whites knew much about their military and religious societies, the office of the Shirt Wearers, the police who helped coordinate the people under their leaders' guidance, their highly social culture, or their robust humor. At times young Hunkpapa men cracked jokes about their most dignified and public-spirited leader, Sitting Bull. They even did so when he was present. He didn't mind.[37]

Sitting Bull gained influence across Lakota society, far beyond the

Hunkpapas, thanks to the impact of two leaders of the Oglala tribe. From 1866 to 1868, Red Cloud rallied opposition to the opening of the Bozeman Trail from the North Platte River to Montana, running along the eastern side of the Big Horn Mountains. The army constructed new forts to protect migrants on the Bozeman. As with the trails and posts on the Central Plains, these represented points of continual consumption and destruction of water, forage, and game, desolating resource-rich areas. They also represented an intrusion into hard-won Lakota territory, which had suffered far less from such incursions than the lands of the Southern Cheyennes and Arapahoes between the Platte and Arkansas rivers. Red Cloud helped to convince Miniconjous, Sans Arcs, Brulés, and others to join the Oglalas in harassing the posts and traffic on the trail.

As Red Cloud led politically, Crazy Horse inspired militarily. On December 21, 1866, he led a small party in an attack on men cutting wood for Fort Phil Kearny. Captain William Fetterman and seventy-eight soldiers, plus two civilians, marched out of the post in pursuit. But Crazy Horse's group was a decoy—an old Lakota tactic, though difficult to execute. This day they executed it perfectly. The Lakotas ambushed Fetterman's column, killing everyone. They even put an arrow into a soldier's dog as it tried to run away. It was the greatest defeat the army suffered in its wars against the Plains Indians, until another not quite ten years later.[38]

The Fetterman Massacre, as Americans called the battle, produced profound results. First, it began Crazy Horse's rise as a legendary foe in the American mind, and boosted his status among his own people as well. Second, it elevated the Teton Sioux in the eyes of the army and the U.S. public as the most powerful and intransigent native enemy. Third, it helped convince the 1867 Peace Commission to close the Bozeman Trail and its guardian forts, an unheard-of admission of defeat by the federal government in an Indian war. Perhaps it was an embrace of expediency, since impending completion of the first transcontinental railroad would soon make the trail unnecessary, but it was remarkable nonetheless. In April 1868, federal officials and Indian leaders signed the Fort Laramie Treaty. It created the Great Sioux Reservation, including all of modern-day South Dakota west of the Missouri River. It granted hunting rights as far south as the North Platte and Republican rivers, as long as the buffalo were abundant enough "to justify the chase." It also designated the region west of the reservation to the highest points in the Big Horn Mountains and south to the North Platte as unceded Sioux territory. The army could carry out official business on the reservation, but needed permission to enter the unceded land, whose northern border remained undefined.[39]

This rousing triumph led to a fourth consequence of the Fetterman Massacre. The treaty established agencies for the Sioux and Northern Cheyennes, granting annuities in food and goods. It offered incentives for the Indians to settle permanently on the reservation and take up farming. Contemporary white observers, and many writers since, have characterized the Lakota response as a binary division between "treaty" and "nontreaty" Indians—those who settled and accepted rations, even wearing American clothes and adopting agriculture, and those who rejected it all. But the real response appears to have been a spectrum, with the vast majority of the people adapting to new conditions with a great deal of historical continuity.

Viewed from the perspective of the United States, the only meaningful conflict was between "Indians" and "whites." Therefore the Sioux appeared to be either accepting or rejecting white civilization. Viewed from the Lakota perspective, however, the Americans were only one enemy in a matrix of hostilities, as Richard White points out. They continued to battle Crows, Pawnees, and other nations over territory, resources, and access to trade. If the U.S. government recognized their territory, so much the better; if the U.S. government issued them rations, it gave them another advantage. Red Cloud and Spotted Tail of the Brulés were considered leaders of the "treaty Indians," but into the 1870s they hunted buffalo, fought, and traded between visits to the agencies to collect the offerings of the Americans. In many respects, the Lakotas stood at the height of their power at the time when Custer first entered their domain. That sense of strength invigorated them. They even forced the removal of two agencies from the Missouri River, on the reservation, to northern Nebraska, the homeland of the Oglalas and Brulés. At times Lakotas intimidated agents, assumed control of distribution of treaty rations and goods, even killed officials and soldiers, thus establishing their authority. Indian cooperation with the army must be seen in the same light. Osage, Pawnee, Arikara, or Crow scouts were not race traitors or mercenaries. They simply made a rational alliance against a dangerous enemy.[40]

Yet a faction of Lakotas did reject any relationship with white culture, apart from the traditional, transactional one of trade. The Hunkpapas provided the core of this core, and their leader was Sitting Bull. Born perhaps in 1831, he won fame as a warrior and a holy man. As his biographer Robert Utley notes, Lakota accounts of him may be exaggerated, given how supremely admiring they were, yet they were notable for the complete lack of dissension. Generous, brave, skilled, mystical, he possessed profound moral clarity that drew followers to him. He saw their entire culture at stake, their independence and survival as a people. "Look at

me—see if I am poor, or my people either," he said to those who settled
at the agencies. "You are fools to make yourselves slaves to a piece of fat
bacon, some hard-tack, and a little sugar and coffee."[41]

Sitting Bull raided forts on the Upper Missouri only days after his
people signed the 1868 treaty. He emerged as a galvanizing force for
independence, often allied in the field with the Oglala Crazy Horse.
He directed his followers, in part, against Northern Pacific. As Richard
White observes, "The government did not actually own much of this
land" given to the railroad in its land grant; "it belonged to the Indians." The treaty failed to define the northern boundary of the unceded
territory, but legalisms mattered little to either side. The Lakotas saw
their ownership of the Yellowstone basin as a living fact. For its part, the
government was happy to transfer land "directly from the Indians to the
railroads," White writes, free of "competing claims from settlers."[42]

In 1872, Sitting Bull personally took part in fighting against the
Northern Pacific survey party. At the beginning of August 1873, his people spotted another expedition after it crossed over to the north bank of
the Yellowstone—known as the Elk River to the Lakotas—and marched
toward a point opposite the mouth of the Tongue River, a tributary.
"Some four hundred lodges of Hunkpapas and Miniconjous, with Sitting
Bull in residence, were camped in the very path of the military column,"
writes Utley.[43]

And so the Lakotas—Sitting Bull himself—directly confronted the
third force shaping events in 1873: the United States Army.

"I PRESUME YOU HAVE SEEN the July *Galaxy* by this time and read the
Washita account," Custer wrote to Libbie. "But oh no I forgot—you do
not read those articles I believe except when the author is present and you
are forced from politeness to glance at them." Whatever the quality of
his writing, he certainly had a writer's mind-set. His life reached a climax
in print, but his current expedition proved undramatic. "I do not believe
we are going to have any serious difficulty with the Indians at least that
is Gen Rosser's opinion." More than forty days passed without a single
incident.[44]

"No day since the expedition started opened more monotonously"
than August 4, wrote Samuel Barrows, the correspondent for the *New
York Tribune*. Roughly speaking, the Yellowstone River ran from west to
east, curving in a northeasterly direction toward its junction with the
Missouri River. On July 26, the column had crossed to the northern side
with the aid of a steamboat, and headed west toward Pompey's Pillar, a
natural stone monolith marked with petroglyphs that Lewis and Clark

encountered in 1806. The troops marched over the bluffs and on "arid, barren" plains above the river. Thermometers went up to 120 degrees in the sun. "It is too warm to write, read, or think," a scientist told Barrows. A soldier snapped, "Curse the Jay Cookery that got up this expedition." Custer rode ahead with a cavalry squadron—two companies—to select a nightly bivouac close to the water for the expedition.[45]

Some days before this monotonous August 4, they had found evidence that they were being shadowed. A scout named Bloody Knife had pointed it out to Custer. The cavalryman would write of Bloody Knife as his "favorite" native auxiliary, and most accounts repeat the word. It did not yet apply. They first met on this expedition; Custer still knew so little about him that he misidentified him as a Crow in his official report. But Bloody Knife rapidly earned his regard. About the same age as Custer, he had a Hunkpapa father and an Arikara mother. (The soldiers commonly called the latter nation "Arickaree," or simply "Ree.") He grew up with the Hunkpapas, enduring bullying from the other children because of his mixed ancestry. He received his worst treatment from Gall, who grew to become a powerful young man and disciple of Sitting Bull. As a teenager, Bloody Knife left to join the Arikaras, and fought the Lakotas in the years that followed with deepening bitterness. In 1862, two of his brothers fell to a war party led by Gall, who killed and scalped them. Bloody Knife found it logical, both on a personal and a tribal level, to ally himself with the U.S. Army against his enemies.

Custer always enjoyed associating himself with what he saw as exotic, but he began to admire Bloody Knife's personal merits. He described him as perceptive, shrewd, and dignified, "his Henry rifle poised gracefully in his hands." He even wrote that he had a "handsome face" under shoulder-length black hair, parted in the middle. And everyone recognized the scout's mastery of tracking the Lakotas. "Bloody Knife," wrote Barrows, "reads dates and numbers, histories and prophecies, in the travois tracks, the pony foot-prints, and the whole alphabet of Indian signs and evidences as easily almost as your readers will read this letter." (A travois was a frame and platform for carrying baggage, made from poles and dragged behind a horse.)[46]

At about 9:30 a.m. on August 4, about ten miles in advance of the main column, Custer's squadron descended from the bluffs on a buffalo trail to the Yellowstone, and stopped at a fine campsite in a stand of cottonwoods. Up the river, a mile or two to the west, they saw another, larger grove. It was quiet. They did not expect the infantry and wagon train to arrive until the afternoon. Custer ordered the men to unsaddle their horses and put them out to graze in the tall grass in the trees. He posted a picket to stand guard in a spot with views up and down the valley. He told his bugler to stay close at hand, then lay down on the ground and went to sleep in the heat.

A scattering of shots startled him awake. Custer got to his feet and bellowed, "Bring in your horses, bring in your horses." A half-dozen Lakotas had galloped up to the camp in an attempt to stampede the horses, and the pickets drove them back. He ordered Capt. Myles Moylan to have the men saddle up. Custer's orderly, Pvt. John H. Tuttle, brought his horse and he mounted. Together with Tuttle, Lieutenant Calhoun, and twenty men under his brother Tom, Custer chased the six raiders up the river.[47]

As they approached the woods to the west, Custer grew suspicious. "When almost within rifle range of this timber, I directed the squadron to halt," he reported. He and Tuttle continued forward. "Tuttle," he said, "keep your eyes on those woods." He noticed that the six warriors matched his movements, stopping when he stopped, riding off when he advanced. He sent Tuttle back to tell Moylan to dismount in the trees where the horses had been grazing.

Custer concluded it was a trap. Watching the Indians' strange behavior, he remembered what he had read of the Fetterman Massacre, and guessed that he was chasing a decoy force. He was right. When he halted his pursuit, about 250 warriors rode out of the trees "in a perfect line," he wrote, adorned for battle in paint and coup feathers, "with their characteristic howls and yells." Custer reined around and galloped back toward Tom, shouting orders for him to dismount his men and form a skirmish line. The hostile force, composed of Lakotas and some Northern Cheyennes, chased at full speed. As soon as Custer cleared the line, Tom gave the order to fire. The volley broke the charge. Custer and his detachment retreated toward the main force.

Custer had about ninety men. By the most conservative estimate, he faced three times as many enemies. Back in the woods, he deployed his men in a semicircle, with each flank anchored on the river. To improve his odds, he ordered the horse holders to hold eight instead of the usual four horses. He retained no reserve, but put every available carbine on the line. The Lakotas and Cheyennes swarmed around them and "displayed unusual boldness, frequently charging up to our line," he reported.

One hostile warrior showed his courage by riding along the firing line at top speed. Custer spoke through his interpreter to Bloody Knife. Pointing out a landmark, he suggested that when the rider reached that point, Bloody Knife should shoot the rider and Custer would shoot his pony. Bloody Knife liked the idea, Custer recalled, and aimed his Henry repeater as Custer aimed his Remington rolling-block breech-loading rifle. When the rider reached the designated point, both rifles barked. The man threw up his hands and fell as his horse tumbled. He had hardly hit the ground before other warriors galloped up and picked him up without stopping.

Neither side suffered many casualties. Riding quickly, the attackers could not fire accurately, but neither could they be hit easily. At one point, Custer saw men crawling through the high grass toward them. Bloody Knife explained that they would try to fire the grass to burn them out, but not to worry. Sure enough smoke rose along the line, but the grass refused to burn. They spotted an enemy sneaking along the riverbank, and chased him off. Later they learned that a large party had been following him, and that they narrowly escaped a surprise attack from behind.

Hours rolled by. The troopers grew short of ammunition. Custer ordered the horse holders to deliver up their cartridges, but the supply soon dwindled again. In the afternoon, Custer noticed that something startled the Lakotas and Cheyennes. From beyond the bluffs rose the dust cloud of the approaching column. "Now," Custer said to Moylan, "let us mount and drive them off." The troops saddled and advanced out of the woods. The trumpeter sounded a charge. The men cheered and spurred into a gallop. The Lakota withdrew.[48]

Surprised, outnumbered, isolated in the enemy's country, Custer handled his force with discretion and skill. He did not smash his enemy, to be sure, but he survived where Fetterman had not. He benefited from his studies and mustered all his old tactical instincts. He correctly read an ambush, kept his troops well in hand, maximized his firepower, and seized just the right moment to break the stalemate.

But the battle was not without cost. Some Hunkpapas cut off a small group that had separated from the approaching column. They killed the veterinarian John Honsinger, the sutler, Augustus Baliran, and Pvt. John H. Ball. "I shall issue no further orders about straggling," Stanley told the reporter Barrows, "for none will be necessary."[49]

BETWEEN 400 AND 500 LODGES, Bloody Knife said, as he and Custer examined the remains of a recently occupied Indian campsite on August 7. The scout said the Lakotas and Cheyennes had moved the village off to a new location about the same time as the battle, three days or so earlier. On August 8 Custer found a second camp, about the same size, broken up at about the same time. "The discovery of these villages created a material change in our plans," Barrows wrote to the *Tribune*. "There is only one way in which a hostile Indian tribe can be thoroughly crippled and intimidated, and that is by attacking and destroying one of their villages. . . . Custer was confident that, if he could overtake the Indians, he could make short work of their village and repeat the victory of the

Washita." Stanley authorized him to take all the cavalry still with the expedition, about 450 men, and pursue Sitting Bull and his people.

"The scene that evening at the cavalry camp was active indeed. By 10 o'clock everything is ready. The trumpet sounds to horse," Barrows wrote. "We march from the glowing woods into the silver moonlight in the beautiful valley below." They followed the trail through the night and into the next day, covering forty miles. Late on August 9, the tracks veered down from the hills to the bank of the deep, fast-moving Yellowstone. They crossed here, Bloody Knife said; by now they've sent runners to nearby camps of their allies to recruit reinforcements. Custer spent the next day trying to get his men and heavy cavalry horses to the south side of the Yellowstone. (The river meandered to the northeast here; the "south" bank was actually almost due east of Custer's position.) Sitting Bull's entire village of men, women, and children had crossed with their lodges, horses, and other possessions, but Custer failed. He finally quit and let his men sleep.[50]

As the pursuer, Custer never imagined that the prey would turn and strike back. But Bloody Knife guessed correctly: Sitting Bull had called in help, and prepared an attack on the cavalry stuck on the north (or west) bank of the Yellowstone. At four o'clock in the morning on August 11, he struck. A few shots echoed in the valley, then a ripping crackle of fire burst from the far bank of the river, sending bullets zipping through the cavalry camp. "The Indians! The Indians! They are firing on us from the other side!" a soldier shouted. The men rushed to the water's edge with their rifles and shot back. Custer ordered them to cease fire until more hostiles came and provided "a better target," Barrows wrote. They came. A large force descended the far hills and redoubled the fire. The two sides exchanged shots across the river, each finding cover in the trees that lined either bank.[51]

Custer again ordered most of his men to cease fire. The range was 400 to 500 yards, and few of his troopers could shoot with any accuracy at that distance. Rather than waste ammunition, he allowed only "the best marksmen among the men" and some of the officers to return fire, Barrows reported. Custer also stationed troops on the bluffs behind his position "to guard against the Indians crossing and attacking us in the rear." When the firing slacked off for a time, the Lakotas taunted the cavalry's native scouts, daring them to cross the river. "Come, man, why don't you? We'll give you all you want," the interpreter translated. "We are bound to have those horses of yours anyhow. We are going to cross and take them in spite of you."

One of the best sharpshooters was Custer's orderly, Tuttle, who used a long-range Springfield sporting rifle. "I want to drop a few more of them fellows before I leave here," he said. He pointed out a warrior across the river, aimed, and fired. The man fell from his saddle. He rapidly hit two more. He poked his head out from behind his tree to shoot again, and a Lakota bullet struck his forehead, killing him.

Custer fired with the others, taking cover between shots, when he saw the guard on the bluffs signal that the enemy were swimming their ponies over the river on either flank. Custer sent reinforcements to the heights and rode to see for himself.

Lt. Charles Braden and perhaps twenty men held the upstream flank. His platoon occupied a deep ravine, a natural trench, and a knoll that offered passage through it. Some 100 enemy warriors approached, dressed and painted for battle, driving the scouts before them. Gall, Bloody Knife's special enemy, led them on. Braden received a message from Custer that he must hold his position "at all hazards." Then Gall led a charge. Braden waited until they were only thirty yards away before he ordered his men to fire. The close-range volley halted the attack. Gall and his allies charged again and again, but the troopers held. Braden stood to inspect the field; a bullet ripped into his thigh, shattering the bone and tumbling him into the ravine. Before his men could panic, three additional companies rode up to bolster their defense.

Unknown to Custer, Sitting Bull observed the fighting from the hills across the river. He was "in reserve," as his comrade White Bull later said; as a senior eminence, he was no longer expected to lead the fighting personally. Whether he *commanded* in the tactical sense is an open question. Certainly he orchestrated the concentration of warriors and the assault. Whether he gave directions on the field or not, it was his fight.

Again Custer found himself in something of a stalemate. His ammunition dwindled and he did not expect Stanley's column for another day or so. The main threat seemed to be from upstream, where Gall pressed Braden. The Lakotas and Cheyennes there grew in strength, and now numbered as many as 300. Many of them worked their way into another ravine and strafed the cavalry with accurate fire, killing Custer's own horse. Custer left one company to guard the northern (downstream) flank, one company to protect against a direct crossing of the river, and concentrated his remaining six companies on his upstream, uphill flank, against the men with Gall.

Unexpectedly, Stanley approached from downstream. (Due to the bend of the river, he was northeast of Custer.) He was almost an entire day ahead of schedule. As many as 100 Lakotas who were caught between his column and the 7th Cavalry turned and attacked him. He consolidated his men and continued his advance. Stanley unlimbered his artillery and began to shell the old warriors (including Sitting Bull) and crowd of noncombatants on the hills across the river. The cavalry cheered as they scattered.

With his downtream flank secure, Custer formed his six companies into a line, with the band immediately behind them. He stood out as always, astride a white horse, wearing a red shirt, his long hair flying. "Strike up Garry Owen," he told the band leader. "The familiar notes of that stirring Irish air acted like magic," Barrows wrote; the brisk brass horns galvanized the men. Custer ordered a charge. "Away they went 'pell-mell,'" Barrows continued. "Every man keeps in his place. On they go like a whirlwind." Tom Custer led his company into the ravine occupied by the enemy and cleared it out. The men of the 7th Cavalry killed few, if any, though they shot Gall's horse, among others. The Lakotas and their allies fled upriver before the massed cavalry attack. Custer pursued for eight miles before he relented, and the Indians crossed back to the far bank of the river.[52]

"As we rode back to the infantry after the charge, with the band playing in front of us, our pennants flying and the éclat of so complete a victory to back us, our sensations were pleasurable enough to repay for all the hardships of the campaign," Larned wrote to his mother. "The second battle at the mouth of the Big Horn was the coup de guerre and as thoroughly demoralized the Indians as it enhanced the prestige of the cavalry."

The battle reversed Larned's bitter tone. He looked at Custer in a new light—not hero worship, of course, but with willingness to acknowledge his generosity and ability. He noted that Custer selected him to make a topographical survey, recognizing the skill that would later make Larned a professor of drawing at West Point. "This action on Custer's part was so spontaneous and unsolicited as quite to astonish me. From that time to this, nothing I have asked for has been refused." Custer allowed him to suspend his work and join the pursuit and second battle, and kept him close during the return to Fort Rice. "Accordingly I lived on Mount Olympus with the Gods, and have an orderly at my behest." Despite the sardonic tone, he did not insist on distancing himself from Custer, as he had before. Larned did retain some of his suspicions. For example, he attributed "a great deal of consideration" on Custer's part to Larned's status as a correspondent for the *Chicago Inter-Ocean*, "and between you and I [that] is quite a power with Custer whose appetite for notoriety you know." (Typically, Custer believed it was his own example that inspired "our young fellows to take to the press.") But the battles clearly changed Larned's attitude.[53]

In the formative days of the 7th Cavalry, Libbie later wrote, her husband told her it would take a major fight to bind the regiment together, "that it was on the battlefield, when all faced death together, where the truest affection was formed among soldiers." This romantic view was hardly a practical philosophy of personnel management—the 7th Cavalry waged very few pitched battles—yet it reflected an important truth. After all the petty squabbling, nitpicking orders, and dull misery of daily duty, the burst of Lakota gunfire across the Yellowstone reminded the troops that their regiment existed to fight. The sight of the fleeing enemy taught them that Custer knew his business, that he could lead them to victory. Afterward, Custer wrote to Libbie, he enjoyed warm relations with all the officers, barring only one—who could only have been Benteen. As for Larned, he was still sarcastic, still cynical, but nonetheless felt pride in these battles, and an almost begrudging respect for his commanding officer.[54]

"We have had two fights with the Indians," Stanley wrote to his wife on August 15. "This all fell to the share of the cavalry, which did very well, all men could do." His regard for Custer rose just as Larned's did. He no longer wrote of Custer as an arrogant upstart, but praised his conduct. Stanley said he was glad to have left the fighting to him. He added that Custer "has behaved very well since he agreed to do so." He, too, was proud, and let Custer and his regiment ride home ahead of the wagon train.[55]

The battles on the Yellowstone did not change the strategic balance on the Northern Plains. The Lakotas and their allies remained unmoved and almost unhurt. Custer inflicted no more than three dozen casualties on them on August 11, and he failed to find, let alone destroy, one of their villages. Yet these clashes enhanced Custer's professional standing, providing a counterweight to his terrible reputation within the military. His deft performance against the Indian nation that the army feared most reminded his critics that, whatever his institutional failings, he could still fight. It gratified Sheridan, who had assigned him to this region precisely because he anticipated a Lakota war. When Custer reached Fort Abraham Lincoln, he wrote to Libbie on September 21, he found a telegram from Sheridan: "Welcome home."[56]

BACK IN MONROE, LIBBIE OPENED a letter about Armstrong's erection. "Good morning my Rosebud," he wrote. "John has been making constant and earnest inquiries for his bunkey for a long time, and this morning he seems more persistent than ever, probably due to the fact that he knows he is homeward bound."

He devoted most of his letter to other matters than his anthropomorphized penis, but the passage marked a return to his early passion.

After all their trouble, he still longed for her. He felt happy in general, pleased with himself and proud of his praise, particularly from Northern Pacific's engineers. "My little durl never saw people more enthusiastic. . . . The expedition would've turned back long ago and abandoned the enterprise . . . had not your Boy stepped generally to the front," he wrote. His ambition rose with his self-assurance. He told Libbie, "A letter from the *Galaxy* people is stirring me up for more articles and states that they intend to try and make arrangements for [Theodore] Davis of Harper's to illustrate my book. Once on the march we halted for two days. . . . Your bo sat down and almost completed a *Galaxy* article."[57]

"It's no use for me to try to see anything but a world of anxiety and the glory cannot cover the risks you have run," Libbie wrote back. After the Civil War she had hoped that he would never go into battle again, yet here she was. In quiet Monroe, ten years after he had first courted her, she found herself still immersed in dread. When he left her for the field, he left her alone—without even children. As Shirley Leckie reflects, childlessness haunted Libbie; it may be why she doted on their dogs as much as Armstrong did.[58]

And yet, her return to Monroe illustrated the alternative. She encountered a lawyer who had pursued her so many years ago. "What a humdrum life I escaped by not marrying him," she wrote. She often reflected that summer on the "drudgery" of the typical woman's existence in Monroe. "So monotonous so commonplace and besides I see every day that great ambition I have for you and how I bask daily in the sunshine of your glory."[59]

Ambition! That power that drives so much of what human beings do was wired with entanglements and traps for middle-class women in 1873. They felt its force as much as men did, of course, but knew the dangers if they pursued it freely. Some did. They ran businesses, wrote books, and embarked on careers, but only to the extent that they were willing to accept limits or flout the culture of respectability. Elizabeth Cady Stanton and Susan B. Anthony had long campaigned for voting rights for women, and founded the National Woman Suffrage Association in 1869. But they suffered. That very summer of 1873, a court convicted Anthony of illegally voting in the 1872 presidential election. Victoria Woodhull and her sister Tennessee Claflin worked as spiritualist mediums and magnetic healers, paths considered appropriate for women, who were seen as passive vessels for larger forces. They became notorious when they went further, starting a brokerage house on Wall Street (though they had to make their trades through men) and a radical newspaper. In 1872, Woodhull offered herself as a candidate for president. Society treated them as outrageous curiosities at best, and more often as outcasts.

Libbie Custer embodied the emerging modern woman: intelligent, highly educated, critical of the restrictions placed on her by society. Since her school years, the percentage of college-educated Americans had doubled—to 2 percent—and 21 percent of them were women, who also comprised a majority of high school graduates. Yet Libbie was no Anthony and certainly no Woodhull; she had too much respect for custom, too high a regard for society, to adopt an independent position outside marriage, let alone risk arrest. Her natural profession would have been writing, but that would have forced her to compete against her husband. She shared her dilemma with the middle-class women of her era. The historian Heather Cox Richardson notes that the protagonists of Louisa May Alcott's *Little Women*, first published in 1868, sought public careers as a writer, actor, and painter, yet ultimately married and had children, "changing the world as mothers rather than independent professional women." With no children, Libbie channeled all of her ambition into Armstrong. She believed women in the West were "making history, *with our men*" (emphasis added). She thought of herself as a participant, even a partner, but respectability demanded that her husband should act publicly for them both. The thought of all that he—that is, *they*—could achieve shrank her anxiety and swelled her enthusiasm.[60]

"Autie, your career is something wonderful," she wrote. "Can you realize what wonders come constantly to you while other men lead such tame lives?" Enthusiasm turned into calculation. Nearly five years after the Washita, his victories on the Yellowstone were "well-timed," she wrote. She had ideas on how to exploit them—and how *not* to exploit them. She knew her husband. She understood his partisanship, his desire to fight the Republicans. The possibility that he might enter politics gave her "a shudder of fear." Life in Washington had taught her that elections were best left to political professionals. "Oh how thankful I am they did not entrap you. . . . I tell you, Autie, I have never felt more ambitious for you nor more confident of your success than this summer. I am only a little afraid I can't keep up."

"I read him in all my books. When I take in the book heroes there comes dashing in with them my life hero my dear boy general," she had written a decade before. Her pairing of Armstrong and literature spoke to the importance of writing in her life. Now her goal for him was to triumph as both author and hero of her books. "You must write up with many an embellishment the stories of this Summer's campaign," she instructed. "My ambition for you in the world of letters almost takes the heart out of my body. . . . You are going on to more honors & greatness than we dreamed of a few years ago."[61]

Her husband agreed. Leckie observes that their relationship matured by 1873. If he wrote less priapic letters than he once did, he ceased to afflict her with boastful, jealousy-inducing tales of other women. Ironically, though, his renewed fame also gave new discomforts. In mid-October he attended the annual reunion of the Army of the Tennessee in Toledo. He had not served in that army, but was invited because he was a celebrity. During a public reception, a crowd besieged Grant, Sherman, Sheridan, and Custer. Hectored into kissing babies, they found young girls asking for pecks on the cheek; then Grant kissed a young woman on the lips. "Immediately there commenced a friendly rivalry between Generals Phil Sheridan and Custer to see who could get the most kisses," reported *Leslie's Illustrated Newspaper.* The *Chicago Tribune* noted, "Custer took to the kissing as naturally as if accustomed to it from his earliest youth." The tally of "ladies" kissed was Grant: 38, Sherman: 28, Sheridan: 63, and Custer: 67.[62]

Libbie seems to have coped with it well. She took the train from Monroe to Toledo, as she had not seen him since she left Fort Rice back in June. "As I walked along the street, looking into shop-windows," she wrote, "I felt, rather than saw, a sudden rush from a door and I was taken off my feet and set dancing in the air." She looked into the "sunburnt and mottled" face of her husband, and was happy.[63]

After a visit to Monroe, Libbie and Armstrong embarked on the long journey to Fort Abraham Lincoln, accompanied by her friend Agnes Bates. Their new home placed Libbie farther beyond American civilization than ever before. But she possessed greater internal strength than she would allow in her memoirs.

She needed all her resilience soon after arriving. On February 6, 1874, their new house—the commander's house, largest in the fort—caught fire in the middle of the night. She demonstrated courage as the blaze consumed the building, as she waited inside until Armstrong escaped into the bitter cold of the Dakota winter. But she lost her most valuable dresses and many sentimental items, including a wig made from her husband's famous long hair, cut when they married a decade ago. Soon she moved back into the reconstructed house, and endured.[64]

"THE PANIC," READ THE *New York Times* headline on September 19, 1873. "The first intimation which came into the Stock Exchange [on September 18] . . . was contained in a brief notice, which said authoritatively that Jay Cooke & Co. had suspended payment. To say that the street became excited would only give a feeble view of the expressions of feeling. The brokers stood perfectly thunderstruck for a moment . . . [then] surged out of the Exchange, stumbling pell-mell over each other in the general confusion, and reached their respective offices in race-horse time." Rumors spread that the "strongest banks" stood to fail, due to losses on loans to Jay Cooke, who could no longer sustain the weight of Northern Pacific. "In an hour or two after the announcement hundreds of people gathered about the concern [i.e., Cooke's New York office], on the sidewalks, and peered curiously into the windows, as if some wonderful transformation was about to be witnessed."[65]

It was—though it would not be so wonderful. Nor would it be inside Cooke's firm, but rather on the streets, even within the crowd itself. The sell-off of stocks that immediately ensued led the New York Stock Exchange to close for ten days, starting on September 20. It did not stop the crisis. Fifty-five railroads defaulted on payments on their securities within the first month. Over the next thirty-six months, half of all the railroads in the United States would go bankrupt. Iron and steel production, closely tied to the demands of railway companies for new and replacement rails, plummeted by nearly half in the year following the panic. A quarter of all New Yorkers lost their jobs within a few months. In January 1874, 7,000 unemployed workers rioted in the city's Tompkins Square. Wages fell and fell, eventually descending to the level of 1860. Cooke's failure led to sixty-five months of economic contraction. As one historian notes, before 1929 the term "Great Depression" referred to the one that began in 1873.[66]

Perversely, Custer benefited from the catastrophe. His status as a federal employee immunized him from firing or pay cuts. His real income rose as deflation gripped the economy, cutting the cost of living as his salary remained constant.

Yet the panic complicated his public image. He had close ties to Northern Pacific, the railroad that sparked the conflagration. His involvement with the line went beyond the Yellowstone expedition to personal relationships with key figures in the company. Rosser, of course, was his friend. Alvred B. Nettleton, a wartime subordinate who published Custer's attack on his court-martial in the *Sandusky Register,* served as agent for the trustees. The line's chief engineer, William Milnor Roberts, was the father of Annie Yates, wife of Capt. George Yates, Custer's friend and subordinate. The railroad hired Custer's old Monroe chum, Fred Nims, as well. It rewarded Custer himself with passes and the use of private cars. And it asked for help.[67]

"Inclosed I send you an effusion of the gallant Col. of the '6th foot,'" Rosser wrote to Custer on February 16, 1874. The article in question appeared in the *New York Tribune,* written by Col. William B. Hazen of the 6th Infantry, commander of Fort Buford on the upper Missouri. It condemned the railroad in the strongest terms.

"I am as certain as can be that Jay Cooke is perpetrating a grand swindle," Hazen wrote privately to Representative James A. Garfield. After reading the railroad's advertising, he had felt compelled to respond publicly. "For two years I have been an observer of the effort upon the part of the Northern Pacific Railroad Company to make the world believe this section to be a valuable agricultural one," Hazen wrote in his piece. He called these claims "shameless falsehoods" and "wicked deceptions." The lands in question would not sell for more than "one penny an acre" except through "fraud or ignorance."

Given the ferocity of Hazen's assault—and the precarious position of the railroad—Rosser understandably wanted a rebuttal from a third party, one who could speak authoritatively, like Custer. "A line or two from your pen would render us great service at this time and I hope you will now come to our aid. You are in better condition to discuss this question than any officer in the army," Rosser wrote.[68]

Fortunately for Custer, in this case it was Hazen who bridled against the Army's conventional wisdom. Hazen proved to be a contentious officer over the years; he had feuded with Stanley, for example, since the Battle of Shiloh in 1862. Hazen had arrested Custer in 1861, leading to his first court-martial, and clashed with him and Sheridan during the campaign of 1868–69. Even as Hazen published his attack on Northern Pacific, he accused Sheridan of assigning the 7th Cavalry to Fort Abraham Lincoln as part of a corrupt scheme to enrich the sutler there. More important, Hazen flouted army policy of supporting Northern Pacific, regardless of the veracity of its claims. Sherman wrote to Sheridan, "I think our interest is to favor the undertaking of the Road, as it will help bring the Indian problem to a final solution." Sheridan agreed.[69]

Custer went to work on a reply, producing more than 4,000 words, many of them taken directly from railroad promotional materials. His voice did ring through. He mocked Hazen, for example, as following the advice of an unnamed humorist: "Never kick a man who is down—unless you are sure he cannot get up again." Oddly, the joke implied that Northern Pacific would never recover. Custer made another unintentional jest by presenting himself as objective, "one who is engaged in the public service, and . . . is entirely free from personal feeling in the matter." He praised the agricultural potential of the Yellowstone basin, and stated that "rich mines of gold, silver, lead, copper, iron and coal" were waiting for "the coming of that most enterprising and persevering member of our western population—the miner." He finished it on April 9 and the *Minneapolis Tribune* published it on April 17. It thrilled the managers of Northern Pacific, who sent him their thanks and printed his letter as a pamphlet.[70]

Custer entered Hazen's list of enemies. After the 1874 publication of Custer's *Galaxy* articles as a book, *My Life on the Plains*, Hazen took offense at his claims that the Kiowas killed two captives and escaped punishment with Hazen's connivance. In 1875 he published a rebuttal in a pamphlet, *Some Corrections to "My Life on the Plains."*[71]

Custer hated public criticism, but it followed him everywhere. The very fame he sought as an Indian fighter made him a symbol of the use of force against native peoples, and a target for those who opposed it. The *Independent* noted that his only previous success in the West came when, "in midwinter, at the break of day, he surprised a camp of sleeping Indians, greatly inferior in number, and after killing indiscriminately men, women, and children, beat a hasty retreat, refusing an open battle on equal terms with pursuing Indians." On the Yellowstone, instead of punishing hostile Indians, "the punishment was all the other way." It was a polemic, inherently unfair, yet held just enough truth to feed Custer's resentment.[72]

As the defender of Northern Pacific, he appeared to be a modernizer, a champion of the transformative railroad. Under the surface, it was more complicated. As mentioned earlier, the transcontinentals were a mercantilist atavism, an almost obsolete kind of corporation. And this one had brought down the economy and was headed for bankruptcy in June 1875. It laid no new tracks in Custer's lifetime. His advocacy of it is understandable, but it did not reflect sound economic judgment.[73]

Isolated in the remote upper reaches of Dakota Territory, he had little contact with the depression that shadowed the rest of the country. He passed the months with Libbie and his inner circle, hosting dances, throwing dinners and parties, playing cards, and presenting plays. Libbie saw her husband frequently retreat from social events to his office. "None of Custer's West Point classmates would have recognized the studious individual Libbie described, a man who shunned company," writes Louise Barnett. True—but at West Point he had performed for an audience of fellow cadets. Now he addressed the entire nation. He reached the public through his writing. The company of relatives and subordinates mattered less than the acclaim of anonymous readers.[74]

In this insular post, Custer awoke once more to the Stevens Mine. On April 14, 1874, he wrote to Jairus W. Hall to tell him that the New York investors had demanded to know its status. "Of course I am unable to give them any information," he wrote. Custer's letter went awry and did not reach Hall until mid-August—or so Hall claimed. He replied optimistically, but revealed that little work had been done apart from some digging. Necessary buildings had not been constructed nor equipment acquired. The Crescent Company had mined so deeply that it had dug into their segment. Hall promised imminent profits, but they seemed more remote than ever. He never even mentioned their biggest threat: the Coinage Act of 1873, which demonetized silver. Previously anyone could take refined silver to a mint and have it stamped into coin. The 1873 act abruptly ended silver's status as a legal-tender precious metal, throwing the value of their mine in doubt. Undercapitalized, undermanaged, and oversold, its very purpose in question, Custer's mine staggered on, just barely alive.[75]

An individualist in an increasingly organizational society, Custer struck the denizens of institutions as a problem, even an enemy. He did not rotate smoothly as a cog in the Army's bureaucratic machine; he misled investors on Wall Street, wittingly or not; he promoted a necrotic railroad. He flourished only in the most solitary work, as a writer, but could not sustain himself that way. An offender against Old Army culture, an infuriating kink in the chain of command, he rescued himself from yet another crisis with his fine performance on the Yellowstone. But for how long? Custer himself foresaw a time when he could no longer survive in the Army—unless, of course, he could save himself once more with a well-timed victory.

Sixteen

THE ACCUSER

"THE FINAL SOLUTION": After Adolf Hitler, the phrase became synonymous with systematic, industrialized genocide. In an unfortunate coincidence, William T. Sherman used it in the 1870s in reference to the "Indian problem," as noted earlier. Though unrelated, it draws attention to other unfortunate coincidences, such as naming an entire minority population as a "problem." The words "extermination" and "extinction" often appeared in discussions of American Indians. The white public in the West, Sherman wrote to Grant in 1867, "are clamorous for extermination, which is easier said than done, and they have an idea that we are moved by mere human sentiments."

Sentiment played no part in his or Sheridan's thinking, but neither did genocide. Sherman often spoke outrageously (as when he seemed to reject extermination for mere practical reasons, "easier said than done"), but his ruthlessness did not extend to indiscriminate massacres—just discriminating ones. "I would not hesitate to approve the extermination of a camp" that sent out "thieving, murdering parties," he specified, "but I would not sanction the extermination" of a band that remained quiet.[1]

The quote shows that his rejection of genocide hardly equaled humanitarianism. Sherman and Sheridan, like most Americans of the 1870s, believed in an aggressive ideology of civilization—defined, of course, as the European-derived society, free labor market economy, and elective government of the United States. In this view, civilization marched onward by force of arms. In the South, Sherman held that civil rights could only be established through social conflict, not rule of law or federal enforcement of civil rights. "Until the Union whites, and negroes too, *fight* for their own rights they will be trodden down," he wrote approvingly.[2] In the West, as the historian Richard Slotkin and others have observed, Americans believed that civilization must be staked out in the wilderness through violence. Indeed, civilization must *supplant* nature. It was the Indian who was natural—savage, to use their word—and savagery must be conquered.[3]

In particular, Sherman and Sheridan wished to destroy the natural basis of the power of the high-plains nations: the buffalo. The Medicine Lodge and Fort Laramie treaties granted hunting rights well beyond the reservations as long as bison herds "justify the chase." That perpetuated their nomadism, wars with other Indians, and clashes with migrants and settlers. As the historian Paul Hutton writes, "Sheridan wanted quickly to reduce the buffalo population so as to terminate the hunting right." He desired one kind of extinction to promote another—for many believed that the American Indian would wither and disappear upon the destruction of his "savage" existence. Sheridan approved of the rapid increase in commercial buffalo hunting, which harvested millions on the Southern Plains. The Indians themselves conducted a large portion of this market-driven slaughter. As the historian Andrew Isenberg notes, "Although the nomads knew how to utilize nearly every part of the bison . . . when they hunted bison for the fur trade they sought only the animal's marketable parts: its skin and, less often, its tongue. In pursuit of robes and tongues, Indian hunters were exceptionally destructive." Yet the numbers of white hunters multiplied in the 1870s, dramatically reducing the once-massive herds. The Comanches responded with an attack on a party of hunters at Adobe Walls in the Texas Panhandle on June 27, 1874, igniting the Red River War of 1874–75, the final conflict in that region.[4]

Having cleared the Central Plains of the Southern Cheyennes and Arapahoes, the generals contemplated the Lakotas. The halt of Northern Pacific's westward expansion removed an immediate cause for hostilities, but it also denied the army a decisive means of destroying nomadic culture. Neither Sherman nor Sheridan wished to rush into war with such a powerful enemy, and they did not want to be blamed if one did erupt. They feuded with Secretary of the Interior Columbus Delano, who ordered the arrest of the Lakota leaders who fought Custer in 1873. Sheridan stopped it, calling it so provocative that the army would "have to fight all the Sioux, guilty or not."[5]

"I suppose we had better let things take their natural course until the mass of Indians commit some act that will warrant a final war," Sherman remarked. The military, greatly reduced by Congress across successive appropriations, lacked enough men to wage an extensive campaign on the Northern Plains in 1873–75, with troops tied down by first the Modoc War and then the Red River War. Yet Lakota militancy grew toward a crisis, particularly at Red Cloud's Oglala agency and Spotted Tail's Brulé agency south of the Great Sioux Reservation. There Lakotas murdered a federal agent and rigged the ration system to acquire funds for scarce ammunition for their repeating rifles (the same men took issues of cattle at multiple agencies then sold the hides back to the agencies for cash). Sheridan sent troops, but tensions remained high. Sitting Bull continued to refuse rations and ignored treaty boundaries, roaming freely, warring on Indian enemies, and attracting followers outside his own Hunkpapa tribe. Sherman, stripped of real power by Secretary of War William Belknap, could do no more than state his opinions, stark as ever: "Sooner or later these Sioux have to be wiped out or made to stay just where they are put."[6]

"Meantime, the raids of Sioux Indians on the settlers and friendly Pawnee Indians continued south of the North Platte, and a constant apprehension was entertained that there would be what is called a general Indian War," Sheridan explained to a critic. Sheridan liked clarity: clear boundaries, clear rules, clear consequences. But the unceded land west and south of the Great Sioux Reservation was a very large, very fuzzy edge. He developed an interim plan to contain the Lakotas by restricting access to this area. "I . . . thought it would be the best policy for the Government to surround this Reservation by large military posts to ultimately keep the Indians within its bounds and white people from encroaching on its limits," he wrote. The latter point is noteworthy. Though Sheridan supposedly said, "The only good Indians I ever saw were dead," he held his own race in only slightly higher regard after witnessing racist atrocities in the South. Far more than Sherman, he believed in federal authority and the use of force to maintain it.

Sheridan presented his plan at a meeting with President Grant, Sherman, Secretary Belknap, Secretary Delano, and Commissioner of Indian Affairs Edward Smith. He noted that several posts already hemmed in the reservation, except to the west. With a fort on the southwest boundary, next to the unceded territory, "I would be able to make it a little hot for the villages and stock of these Indians [if] they attempted to raid the settlements south." Until he had enough troops for the "final war" that Sherman envisioned, he could retaliate from that point, creating a deterrent.

Grant and the assembled officials approved. Sheridan decided to build his fort in the mysterious Black Hills, a large expanse of wooded, rocky heights and valleys. He would have to send a large force to scout this unknown region and select a location. He thought of launching it from the south, but that would carry the troops through the restive Nebraska agencies, inviting trouble. Fortunately for Sheridan, his favorite subordinate commanded a fort north of the reservation. He decided to give Custer command of the expedition.[7]

———

"ON THE 15TH OF JUNE we bid adieu to civilization and civilized beings . . .
and plunge into regions hitherto unvisited by white men," Custer wrote
to Lawrence Barrett on May 19, 1874. He begged his actor friend to join
his expedition to the Black Hills. After a summer in the wild, "you will
return a new man and feel as if you had really been drinking the true
elixir of life." Maj. George "Sandy" Forsyth and Lt. Fred Grant would
join him; Custer's younger brother Boston would come, too, though he
did not mention the latter to Barrett. Custer would have ten companies
of the 7th Cavalry, Gatling guns, Indian scouts, and scientists to examine
the geology and hunt for fossils. "It is the freest easiest sort of life one can
imagine. I generally wear buckskin coat & pants winter & summer. . . .
You will never regret it I am sure, and I know [you] would enjoy your visit
more than language can express. But give me at once your decision. I am
in the midst of busy preparations for the march."[8]

Barrett cheerfully declined. "I am compelled to forego the happiness,"
he wrote. "My policy of life insurance could become invalid in case of
death on the trip." As he had implied in an earlier letter, he preferred
wearing a wig onstage over losing his scalp to the Indians.[9]

Reporters, on the other hand, clamored to go. "Who has not heard of
the Black Hills and the rich treasures of gold and other precious metals
supposed to exist there," asked the *Bismarck Tribune* on May 27. "Year
after year expeditions have been formed or talked of to explore this
region . . . [only to be] checked by Government interference or driven
off by the Indians. Only a month ago, the Bozeman expedition returned
disorganized . . . after a month's continuous fighting with the Indians."
Everyone thought Custer could push through. Recently a Lakota raiding
party stole a mule herd at Fort Lincoln; within twenty minutes, the *Sioux
City Journal* reported, Custer led the garrison in pursuit. He recovered
most of the herd. "He is a 'screamer,' in the language of this country, and
the reds are beginning to find it out."[10]

Perhaps the most influential newspaperman to appear at Fort Lincoln
was young William E. Curtis of the *Chicago Inter-Ocean* and *New York
World*. "I came here expecting to find a big-whiskered, swearing, rant-
ing, drinking trooper, and I found instead a slender, quiet gentleman,"
his blond hair cut short, his complexion clear, his eyes bright blue, a man
who did not drink, swear, or smoke, he wrote of Custer. At twenty-four,
Curtis had been a teenager during the Civil War; only now did he awake
to Custer's potential for exciting copy.

"He is a great man—a noble man is General Custer," he wrote. "Since
I have been here I have heard anecdotes of his goodness and manliness
from his soldiers and others that would fill columns." He claimed to have

entered Custer's study and found him with two little girls—one black and one white—teaching them to read. "His wife, a charming lady, who has shared his marches and victories since early in the war, is as gentle and cultivated, and yet as soldierly as a woman can be," he added.[11]

If the presence of reporters and scientists on the Black Hills foray fit Custer's tastes, it was entirely coincidental. The press always accompanied major military expeditions in the West. Sheridan encouraged scientific discovery, inviting a professor from Yale University to join the Black Hills column. With Sheridan's support, Minnesota's state geologist, Prof. Newton Winchell, and other scientists went as well.[12]

Custer also bore no responsibility for the public impression of the expedition. He set out to explore a little-known region and find a site for a fort. But the typical newspaper headline resembled one that ran in the *Baltimore Sun* on July 25: "Looking for Gold—Custer's Exploring Expedition." As just noted, the public expected Custer to find the precious metal. The *Chicago Tribune* and a few others editorialized against the mission because it would lead to a white influx and provoke a war; and some insisted that the Fort Laramie Treaty prohibited the survey. The *Boston Advertiser* claimed it was "but a continuation of the long course of bad faith which the United States has consistently pursued in its dealings with the red men." But most newspapers cheered for gold, knowing it would give hope to the public during the terrible depression.[13]

What they sought, they found. "GOLD!" declared the headline of the *Chicago Inter-Ocean* on August 27, 1874. "From the grass roots down it was 'pay dirt,'" Curtis wrote. The two prospectors who first found the "color," he added, "will be the pioneers of a new golden State." Newspapers closer to the scene scooped Curtis's story. "STRUCK IT AT LAST!" shouted the *Yankton Press & Dakotaian*, neatly summarizing the expectations surrounding the expedition. "PREPARE FOR LIVELY TIMES!"

Custer took care not to overstate the find in his official reports, but he supported the gold claims amid lavish praise for every aspect of the Black Hills, from average rainfall to the taste of the wild berries to the region's sheer beauty. The expedition left him in good spirits. It had operated smoothly, without any conflicts with the Lakotas. He wrote to Libbie, "At last I have reached the highest rung in the hunter's ladder of fame. I have killed my grizzly after a most exciting hunt & combat."[14]

After his return he told the *Bismarck Tribune* that reports of gold "are not exaggerated in the least," and claimed (without evidence) that the Indians "seldom visited" the Black Hills. But, he added, "the Government has entered into a solemn treaty with the Indians whereby they agree to keep off all trespassers. This is a law of the land and should be respected, and General Sheridan has already issued instructions to the military to prevent expeditions entering upon the reservation. . . . Until Congress authorizes the settlement of the country the military will do its duty."[15]

Talk of law and duty mattered less than his emphasis on the gold's *accessibility.* "On some of the water-courses almost every panful of earth produced gold in small, yet paying, quantities," his report stated. "It has not required an expert to find gold in the Black Hills, as men without former experience in mining have discovered it at an expense of but little time or labor." As the historian Patricia Nelson Limerick notes in her seminal *The Legacy of Conquest,* classic gold rushes began with an egalitarian phase, when the metal could be found through low-skill panning or placer mining. Such gold finds drew both poor and well-capitalized migrants.

And why not? In the 1870s, gold was not simply *worth* money, it *was* money. The gold dollar continued in existence alongside the greenback; anyone could take refined gold (and gold was easy to refine) to the mint and have it stamped into gold coin. In mining regions, gold dust and nuggets circulated as currency. Later—and often not much later—gold became harder to find, requiring investment in heavy equipment and tunnels to extract and isolate the ore. But Custer promised everyone a chance at riches.[16]

He told the *Bismarck Tribune* that he would recommend the acquisition of the Black Hills. He was not alone. "Well, I don't know about the minerals," Sherman told a reporter, when asked about the region. "But there is evidently an immense and valuable region to be opened to civilization, and the army alone can do it." For now, the Black Hills remained Sioux property, and the army remained committed to stopping the prospectors who loaded wagons and set out to find gold.[17]

"GEN. CUSTER IS A BRILLIANT and brave soldier, a fact of which, we may remark, he is perfectly aware," the *Independent* observed on November 5, 1874; "but his egotism does not prevent him from writing sketches which are both interesting and useful." The newspaper almost liked Custer's newly published book, *My Life on the Plains,* despite often criticizing the man and his prose. His fame, refreshed on the Yellowstone and in the Black Hills, helped. It gained him invitations to reunions of the Army of the Cumberland in September and the Army of the Tennessee in October of that year.

He and Libbie also attended the wedding of President Ulysses S. Grant's son Fred in Chicago on October 20. But the Grants kept Custer at a distance. At a grand lunch at the Palmer House hotel, Charles Larned sat with the groom but Armstrong and Libbie were exiled to another table.[18]

Grant and Custer had encountered each other many times in the decade since they first met on a special train to Washington. During the Civil War Grant had appreciated Custer's willingness to fight and ability to win. After Appomattox he found Custer troublesome, even dangerous, in case after case: the affair of Don Juan, his mistreatment of troops in Texas, the Swing Around the Circle, his sins of 1867, his public attack on his court-martial, his opposition to Grant's election in 1868, his hostility to Reconstruction in Kentucky, his rankling the chain of command in 1873. But nothing indicates that Grant, as president, gave Custer much thought. The cavalryman had wisely stepped back from overt politics in recent years, and other matters demanded Grant's attention. That would soon change. A gale blew through their lives; it would catch hold of their personal flaws and propel them into a very public collision.

The White House seems to attract individuals who combine ambition and tragic failings, and Grant was one. The popular memory of Grant's presidency dwells on those failings, but his strengths dominated his first term. This unpretentious man had spent much of his life immersed in adversity. It polished his sense of justice, his simplicity and decency. In a classic example of Grant's humor, he mocked the vanity and self-importance of Charles Sumner. Told that Sumner didn't believe in the Bible, Grant said, "No, I suppose not; he didn't write it." And yet his personal distaste did not prevent him from taking action on Sumner's central issue, civil rights. When white supremacist violence ravaged the African American South, he picked the principled Amos Akerman as his attorney general and supported efforts to crush the Ku Klux Klan. The sincerity of his Peace Policy may be gauged by his appointment of Ely Parker, a member of the Seneca nation, as his first commissioner of Indian affairs. It was an unprecedented act of racial diversification in an administration, showing personal sensitivity. At the beginning of his presidency, Jay Gould and Jim Fisk pressed him to support their attempt to corner the gold market, corrupting his brother-in-law Abel Corbin and setting up a gold account for First Lady Julia Dent Grant. Grant refused, and ordered a sale of gold that broke their corner in September 1869.[19]

Yet Grant's years of failure had deepened other traits as well. He only felt comfortable with a cluster of friends who had stood by him during his worst years in peace and war. He made his old chief of staff John A. Rawlins—"the honest voice of humanitarian conscience," according to William McFeely—his first secretary of war, named his ally Sherman commander of the army, and put the trusted Sheridan in charge of the West. All proved their ability. Other friends exploited their proximity to the president for personal gain. They included Grant's private secretary, Orville Babcock, who had served on his wartime staff, the quartermaster Rufus Ingalls, an old West Point roommate and longtime intimate, as well as such opportunistic relatives as Corbin and younger brother Orvil Grant.

Obscurity also gave Grant and his wife, Julia, a dread of poverty and a longing for respectability. He named Hamilton Fish his secretary of state, and sometimes heeded his advice even when it contradicted his instincts—particularly after the death of Rawlins, his moral rudder, in September 1869. Fish personified patrician New York. Born to a prosperous and socially eminent family, he served as governor and U.S. senator, moving from the Whig to the Republican party. He frowned on egalitarian measures such as black suffrage, which Grant supported. Grant did not change his opinions, yet he held tight to this paragon of high society. Fish managed their relationship with great tact, as seen in the attempted annexation of Santo Domingo (known today as the Dominican Republic). Fish disdained the idea, but it mattered a great deal to Grant. The president believed that, as a bastion of mixed-race American citizens, it "would make slave labor unprofitable" in such nearby places as Cuba, where slavery still existed, and give African Americans from the mainland a refuge, which would somehow undermine racial hatred in the South. To negotiate the treaty, Grant dispatched his private secretary, Babcock, who along with Ingalls sought personal profit by speculating in land. Sumner opposed the treaty, and the Senate refused to ratify it. The defeat embittered Grant against Sumner (who died on March 11, 1874) and divided the Republican Party. The president relied even more heavily on Fish, who adroitly preserved his status in Grant's eyes as the indispensable adviser.[20]

Fish also voiced Wall Street's orthodox opinions on financial matters. Conventional wisdom can prevent overreaching, but it also inhibits innovation. If there was ever a time to try something new, it was after the panic of 1873. In April 1874, Congress passed a bill to put more money into circulation. From a twenty-first-century perspective, the legislation embodied a modest and conventional monetarist response to contraction. Called "quantitative easing" in recent times, the idea was to counter hoarding by frightened lenders and battle the curse of deflation. The Treasury had already conducted one such operation after the panic, so the bill could hardly be considered revolutionary. But at least it would do *something* to alleviate suffering. Grant personally knew the reality of hard times, and seemed to lean toward signing it.[21]

The men of finance blasted it as the "Inflation Bill." It outraged them, and it outraged Fish. The passion surrounding currency questions can seem bewildering to later generations. Americans in the 1860s and '70s saw the nature of money as a deeply moral, even theological question. To "hard money" advocates, the gold dollar had intrinsic value, free from human manipulation. They wanted to *reduce* the volume of greenbacks until the Treasury could freely exchange them on demand for gold dollars, one for one. Then the supply of gold alone would determine the dollar's value.[22]

Financial stakes also drove the debate. Bankers, bondholders, and shareholders hated inflation, which ate away the real value of interest and dividends. But shrinking the volume of dollars made borrowing more costly, angering farmers, country merchants, and other soft-money types (i.e., opponents of the gold standard).[23]

Both sides projected larger political philosophies through the narrow aperture of currency. Gold stood for limited government; in deriding paper currency as dishonest, hard-money men expressed a fear of Washington's corruption and extravagance. Greenbacks stood for active government; its supporters believed government *should* intervene in the economy by, at the very least, controlling the medium of exchange. Indeed, a populist third party emerged during the depression, winning seats in Congress, and it was called the Greenback Party.

The Civil War created a new debate over government's role, fostering a political ferment as well as ambivalence. Wartime measures revealed just how much Washington could do when necessary: levy income taxes; create a national paper currency; create a federal banking system; charter and subsidize the transcontinental railroads; destroy slavery; and define and defend nationwide individual rights. With peace, some Americans wished to move back to antebellum norms of limited government, and others wanted to press further. In 1868, Congress had contemplated the distinctly modern idea of government oversight of business corporations. The House Committee on Roads and Canals reported that the largest railroads had "the power to crush out all competition" and concluded that Congress possessed the constitutional power to regulate them. It balked at actually doing so—it was too radical. But the demand for regulation grew in the West, led by the rural Granger movement (formally called the Patrons of Husbandry). Some state legislatures passed laws to control railroad rates, but federal regulation remained out of reach.

In Congress, this new struggle over active government came down to the more modest question of currency. Should Washington act against the depression by slightly increasing the paper-money supply—or do the opposite? The "inflation bill" was so limited that the hard-hit public could reasonably ask, if not this, then what? But it was too much for Fish, and Fish was too much for Grant. He vetoed it.[24]

"The President's veto of the inflation bill is the most important event of his administration," *Harper's Weekly* declared. The historian Nicolas Barreyre argues that it provoked a political realignment. The veto alienated voters outside the major financial centers, giving the Democratic Party an opportunity to win over Republicans in the trans-Appalachian West. These voter-rich states "will scatter the dry bones of the Shylocks and sophists like chaff," a Cincinnati newspaper wrote. In the midterm election of November 1874, the Democrats essentially doubled their seats in the House of Representatives, winning a two-thirds majority.[25]

The new Congress would not sit until December 1875, but Grant entered the year newly vulnerable. Support for protecting African Americans in the South fell off even within his own administration. He dispatched Sheridan to black-majority Louisiana to battle a white-supremacist attempt to control the 1874 election by force; but he was urged to step back by Fish and others. The Justice Department denied Governor Ames's request for troops in Mississippi. The outgoing Congress passed a Civil Rights Act in 1875, but watered it down first. Grant and his party were weak, and felt it.[26]

"My blood boils within me with indignation when I think of the unjust course now being pursued towards our brethren of the South," Custer wrote to Lawrence Barrett in early 1875. "But for the glorious results of the last election I would feel that men had good cause to have their faith shaken in the permanency of free popular government."[27] His comments show how opposition to Reconstruction united Democrats, who were split by the very currency issues that gave them victory in 1874.

His outburst also reveals that the "glorious results of the last election" emboldened him. He expressed partisanship more ferociously than at any time since 1866. In fact, he wrote to Andrew Johnson on February 2, 1875, after the Tennessee legislature chose him as a United States senator. "My dear friend," Custer wrote, "[w]ith all lovers of constitutional government I congratulate you." He had watched events closely, he added, and was thrilled that Johnson would again speak for "a pure government by the people," words with racial overtones. (Johnson died on July 31.) But Custer's enthusiasm would turn into overconfidence, and overconfidence into overreaching.[28]

CUSTER NEUTRALIZED ONE PERSONAL ENEMY, only to gain another. On March 1, 1874, Colonel Stanley had telegraphed General Terry's headquarters about a Hunkpapa warrior at the Standing Rock agency who boasted of having killed Dr. Honsinger and the sutler Baliran during the 1873 Yellowstone expedition. "The arrest of the Indian will be a matter requiring address, and force, as it may lead to a collision with all of the Uncpapas camped at Standing Rock. I respectfully advise that the arrest be entrusted to Lieutenant Colonel G. A. Custer, and not less than three hundred men."[29]

Custer's performance against the Lakotas had converted Stanley into something of an admirer. But Custer received no information on the suspect until December 7, when he requested permission "to arrest the Indian referred to and test the proposition as to whether a white man has any rights which a reservation Indian is bound to respect." His words were ripe with sarcasm. They echoed the U.S. Supreme Court's notorious *Dred Scott* decision of 1857, in which Chief Justice Roger B. Taney declared that African Americans were "beings of an inferior order . . . so far inferior, that they had no rights which the white man was bound to respect." Custer likely agreed with Taney; by reversing the formulation, he expressed profound outrage at the Lakotas.

It was a legally ambiguous step, arresting an individual for actions during a battle. Custer wrote, "It may be claimed that this [murder of Baliran and Honsinger] was an act of war, but the claim is unfounded." There was no war at the time, he said. And, typically, he accused the Indian bureau of supplying hostile Indians with rifles.[30]

Terry approved the mission. Custer dispatched his brother Tom, Captain Yates, and 100 men through the shocking cold of the Dakota winter. Yates feared the federal agent would give their mission away to the Hunkpapas, so he pretended to be looking for three other fugitives. He learned that the suspect was at the trader's store and went with Tom Custer and "five picked men."

Their target was Rain in the Face, a renowned warrior. Tom tackled him and subdued him. Within minutes scores of angry Lakotas surrounded the store. Yates reported that an unnamed "chief" gave a speech, "saying, 'Now was the right time to rescue the prisoner. Those who did not attempt it were cowards.' Whilst speaking he loaded his rifle and commanded the young men to 'close up around the troops,' at the same time remarking that he was 'willing to die first in attempting a rescue.'" Yates extricated his force and his prisoner quietly, crediting his troops' "determined stand."[31]

Back at Fort Abraham Lincoln, Custer locked Rain in the Face in the stockade. He interrogated him personally, though he continued to misidentify him as "Ring Face." On December 18 he reported to Terry that the warrior "admitted to me yesterday that he shot Dr. Honsinger once and Mr. Baliran twice with arrows," an accurate description. Custer wished to have Rain in the Face tried in a civilian court for murder, but as Robert Utley notes, that "raised practical as well as legal questions."

The Hunkpapa lingered in captivity for four months, eventually sharing his cell with two white thieves. On April 18, 1875, friends of the outlaws broke open the wall from the outside, and Rain in the Face escaped along with his cell mates.

The affair did not spark an open war, but it left a legacy of anger. As Custer himself wired Terry after the arrest, "The Uncapapas . . . vow vengeance."[32]

CUSTER REMEMBERED HIS FRIENDS. Isaac Christiancy was elected to the United States Senate at the same time as Andrew Johnson, and Custer wrote to congratulate him as well, even though Christiancy was a Republican. He mentioned his outrage at the army's interference in Louisiana, where, as Eric Foner writes, "Democrats attempted to seize control of the state assembly by forcibly installing party members in five disputed seats." One of Sheridan's officers had removed the five Democrats from office. "I do not think my views differ materially from your own," Christiancy replied, declining to fight with his old protégé. His letter was another sign of the Republican retreat from Reconstruction—and Custer's willingness to risk controversy by stating his political views.[33]

In early 1875, he seemed ready to fight with everyone. He bitterly attacked the commissioner of Indian affairs in an open letter for seeming to criticize the Black Hills expedition. When Professor Winchell, the geologist, contested Custer's report of gold, he accused Winchell of "professional pique" because amateurs had found the metal, and said Winchell had declined to walk the short distance to see for himself. [34]

Custer often became combative when he felt vulnerable or guilty. Tantalizing hints in the archives suggest that 1875 left him financially crippled and morally compromised. Early in the year, an exasperated William Travers demanded that Jairus Hall explain the Stevens Mine's inertia. Hall told a tangled tale of disputed deeds and lawsuits, of the Crescent Company encroaching on their property. Hall tried to prod Custer. "If we can clear off the indebtedness on the mine, raise a few dollars for our pocket and raise a working capital," perhaps by borrowing in New York, "we have a bright future before us," he wrote. But even Hall's salesmanship wilted. He had borrowed a huge sum in England against the mine. On June 3 he wrote, "The debt against the property cripples it." He said he would do his best to get rid of it without a loss. Custer's dream of gold from selling the dream of silver finally evaporated.[35]

As a man with a gambling problem, Custer felt the seduction of the big score—the deal of the cards that would reverse his luck and erase all debts and worries. It is characteristic that the investment into which he poured his own money was racehorses. He had spent heavily on the champion thoroughbred Frogtown, only to see the horse fall ill in the great epizo-otic of late 1872, a wave of disease that killed thousands of horses. Frog-town survived, but fat purses from racing victories failed to materialize.[36]

Custer had written to Libbie in 1873, "It is such a comfort to me to feel independent," with "many and varied . . . avenues to honorable employ-ment."[37] In 1875 he found avenue after avenue barricaded. The mine proved barren. Congressional cuts to the army eliminated any hope of promotion. But the army *did* give him a name. His name allowed him to start writing, and his writing added to his name. A scientist from Bos-ton asked for help with a study of bison, given Custer's "taste for natural history." Robert Roosevelt, a patrician New Yorker and an anti-Tweed Democrat, wrote to praise *My Life on the Plains*. "I suppose you never come East but if you do you must not fail to call on me as it seems I am never to get west & kill a buffalo under your auspices."[38]

The most significant admiring letter came from James Gordon Ben-nett Jr. A year and a half younger than Custer, he was the worldly editor of the *New York Herald*, which his late father had delivered into his hands several years earlier. For most of the nineteenth century, newspapers played an explicitly political role; editors led parties and factions, articu-lating political philosophy. The *New York Times* editor Henry J. Raymond served as a congressman; the *New York Tribune*'s Horace Greeley ran for president. The *Herald*, on the other hand, pursued profits before politics, though it was Democratic in tone. Bennett might devote its columns to a political scandal or a wilderness explorer, depending on how the story might boost circulation. A flamboyant playboy, Bennett had a flair for creating news. In 1869, for example, he had famously sent Henry Morton Stanley to Africa to find David Livingstone.[39]

"I write to ask a *favor* of you." Bennett gathered that Custer would lead another expedition to the Black Hills in 1875, but he had no reporter to send with him. He admired Custer's articles and reports, which "are so well written that I should like you to use the columns of the *Herald*. If you wish you can write over your own name, or, on the other hand, employ a *nom de plume*." He gave him code words to use in his telegraphed reply. Bennett added, "Of course I shall be willing to pay you." The talk of money, the conspiratorial tone, the appeal to his reputation—Custer liked it.[40]

Bennett wrote on April 1, 1875. Soon after Custer went to New York. On May 22, after he had been there for some weeks, the *New York Tribune* reported that he was in the city, "consumed in the completion of the necessary arrangements for his Summer expedition to the Black Hills." He told the reporter that he would start around July 1.[41]

It was not true. Lt. Col. Richard Dodge led that year's expedition to the hills.[42] Custer wandered the humid streets of Manhattan as a private citizen—both a gambler, looking for the big score, and a partisan opponent of the Grant administration. Instead of supplying the *Herald* with colorful letters from the field, Custer would leak tales of corruption at Western posts and Indian agencies. He began to work closely with the *Herald* reporter Ralph Meeker and others. Custer also stopped by the offices of the *New York World* on Park Row, wedged between the warehouses and wharves of Lower Manhattan, the shipyards of Corlears Hook, and such narrow, twisting lanes as Wall Street, Pearl Street, and Exchange Place. The *World* represented the wealthy Democrats who had helped drive Boss Tweed from Tammany Hall—the Belmont, Barlow, Schell, and Tilden group, well known to Custer. (Another key figure, William H. Aspinwall, had died in January.) Custer called to see editor Montgomery Schuyler, who wrote that he regretted missing Custer's visit but would like to publish his letters.[43]

On May 17, Custer returned to lower Manhattan. He went to the office of the broker Emil Justh. For a member of the New York Stock Exchange, Justh had led an adventurous life. Born in Hungary around 1825, he had joined the revolution against the Austrian Empire led by Lajos Kossuth in 1848, a year when revolts swept across Europe. It failed, though Justh remained proud of his participation for the rest of his life. Along with thousands of other Hungarians, he fled, finding refuge in San Francisco at the height of the California Gold Rush, where he worked as an assayer. He moved to New York and opened a brokerage house in 1862. In 1867, hearing noise outside his house on 34th Street, he opened the door and was shot in the chest. The *New York Times* later called him "a straightforward and sagacious man of business."[44]

"I trusted him, you know, naturally," Justh said of Custer. The dashing, famous soldier appealed to the former revolutionary. Custer certainly looked respectable, with his hair cut short, mustache neatly trimmed, his buckskins and uniform set aside for a dark civilian suit.[45]

That day's *New York Times* reported, "The depressed and unsettled tone which has characterized the Stock Market for the past week was more marked today than heretofore." Prices of the volatile "fancy stocks"—including Western Union, Pacific Mail Steamship Company, and the Erie, Lake Shore, and Northwestern railroads—were falling. Yet Custer plunged in, speculating on 100 shares of Lake Shore, one of the weakest of the Vanderbilt railways, which traded at far below its par value of $100 per share. That day it tumbled from 68 ¼ to 67 ⅜. When Custer returned to Justh's office two days later, Lake Shore had slipped to 67 ¼. Yet his transactions earned him a profit of $183, less $50 in brokers' fees.[46]

Though the records do not specify, he could only have been short selling. He ordered Justh to sell 100 shares of Lake Shore, even though he did not own them. Justh borrowed the shares for delivery from another broker or customer, charging Custer interest. When the price fell, Justh bought the stock to return to the lender. Instead of the conventional formula of buy-low-sell-high, the short strategy was sell-high-buy-low. Again, the records are unclear, but Custer seems to have turned around his short sales on the same day, on both May 17 and 19, though possibly he bought one day and closed the next.

The fact of his short selling was significant. For a small investor like Custer, it was a purely speculative technique, used almost exclusively for gambling on short-term changes in prices. In the more respectable approach, one purchased a stock for the long term, looking for a steady, gradual return in the form of dividends. Custer relied on credit from Justh, which ordinarily would have required him to put up a margin, an amount sufficient to protect the broker from a loss if the market went the wrong way. But, Justh said, "I trusted him." Whatever he saw in Custer—a celebrity, a fellow adventurous spirit, or "Custer luck"—he told him he merely had to cover any potential losses.

That first small profit sent electricity sparkling through the gambling-wired synapses in Custer's brain. He began a long-term relationship with Justh, following a "bear" strategy that counted on the depression to drive down prices. He also traded in a class of derivatives known as the "put"—the right to sell a given stock to someone at a set price within a specific time frame. All this required a sophisticated understanding of the financial markets, the strengths and weaknesses of specific corporations, and the larger picture of the national economy. More than that, it demanded deep financial resources, because some reverses were inevitable. Custer had none of those things.[47]

Years later, a judge would analyze a pair of letters from Custer to Justh about these trades and draw broad conclusions. "It seems to us impossible to read these papers without being impressed with the idea that they refer to an illicit business, with which Custer was rather ashamed to be connected," the judge would write. He would explain this discomfiture by claiming that the transactions were unusual and illegal. Illegal, perhaps—but not unusual. They were well within the bounds of ordinary behavior on nineteenth-century Wall Street.[48]

Custer *was* ashamed, not because he broke the law but because he broke faith with Libbie. He had often pledged to give up cards, only to return to the table, losing money amid financial stress. She had scolded him, mocked him, driven him to admit that his addiction was the equivalent of "Satan." In Justh's office, he may have assured himself that he was keeping his promise. But he knew she would see his trades as bets.

Intelligent people tend to be complicated. Certainly Libbie was. She loved her husband, struggled with his failings, and thrilled to his fame. She, too, deliberately presented an idealized version of herself; it was one of the ways she negotiated the gap between her aspirations and reality. She wanted her existence to be like her books. When the 1874 expedition returned from the Black Hills, one soldier recorded in his diary, officers left the column to "embrace and kiss" their waiting wives. "Mrs. General Custer came to meet her husband, but just as she came in 'catching' distance she 'fainted?' A very pretty piece of byplay for the men of the command."[49]

Friends and enemies alike described her as the queen of the court that surrounded Armstrong. She played the social leader grandly. It suited her, and she knew the importance of the role at such a remote post as Fort Abraham Lincoln, a place with few women and virtually no entertainment.

"I like Mrs. Custer very much. She is quite young and rather pretty," wrote Leonard Herbert Swett—known as Bert or Bertie. He was the son of Lincoln's old law partner Leonard Swett and his wife, Laura. Now residents of Chicago, the couple had befriended Libbie in Washington during the war; recently the senior Swett had renewed their acquaintance on a visit to Dakota. Their son was just sixteen. He had dropped out of Phillips Exeter Academy because of anxiety. The Custers offered to take him for the summer; outdoor exercise might help his condition. Armstrong picked him up in Chicago on his return from New York at the end of May. After a stop in Minnesota to see Minnehaha Falls, they arrived at Fort Abraham Lincoln on June 2.[50]

"The Gen. has got a beautifull [sic] house with five servants and they live in high style," Bert wrote. He often played billiards with Armstrong, Libbie, Tom Custer, and Boston Custer, all of whom lived together. He went horseback riding every morning, played cards, read, watched the cavalry drill, "and loaf the rest of the time," he told his parents. "In the evenings the house is crowded with company and they have dancing in the parlor." He noticed that Libbie often hosted social affairs—costume parties, dances, and plays—but her husband isolated himself. "The Gen. does not care very much about company," Bert wrote to his mother, "and he keeps himself locked in his private room when there is much company here (outsiders I mean)."[51]

"My son . . . is delighted with his trip and I can tell you how thankful I am to you for the kindness which you have extended to him. His head is full of going on an expedition with you," Leonard Swett wrote to Custer. Bert felt all the thrill of frontier life but faced little of the danger. He carried a revolver he had purchased for $13.50, went hunting, rode out with the Custer clan for a grand camping trip to the Little Heart River, and witnessed a council that Armstrong hosted to prevent fighting between the Sioux on one side and the Arikaras and Mandans on the other.

For Custer, the summer proved less satisfying. Bert wrote that he had said they might yet go to the Black Hills, but "by the way he talks he does not expect us to go, I think." They never did go.[52]

AS CUSTER STEEPED IN HIS POST, hundreds of prospectors set out for the Black Hills in illegal mining expeditions. Captain Benteen reported that he caught forty-five prospectors. More slipped past the patrols. On August 16 the *New York Tribune* reported that a group on French Creek voted to create the town of Custer, electing Ellis Albert Swearengen as chairman. Soon thousands staked out claims.[53]

The frenzy caught the attention of the Western transportation entrepreneur Ben Holladay and his close friend Rufus Ingalls, Grant's old West Point roommate. Custer knew them both. He may have first met Ingalls as early as the Peninsula Campaign, but the origin of his ties to Holladay are unclear. A fifty-seven-year-old Kentuckian, Holladay had started the largest stagecoach line in the country in San Francisco, sold it to Wells Fargo for $1.5 million, and emerged as the leading shipping and railroad man in Oregon—the "steamship king of the Pacific," as the *New York Times* called him. As a mail contractor, he had learned how to lobby Congress; the secret was to forgo all scruples. But the Panic of 1873 hit him hard. In 1874 he was forced to go to Europe to explain his railroad's troubles to German bondholders, and he slid inexorably toward losing control. He was eager to find new opportunities.[54]

Holladay foresaw the opening of the Black Hills to white settlement, and he wanted to profit from it. On August 22, 1875, Ingalls sent Custer a cryptic letter on the subject. "How long I have waited to be able to write *positively*, but even now I cannot!" He referred to Holladay as "Ben," a sign that Custer knew him well. "We want to do a big thing in the Black Hills," he wrote. "Ben wants to put in stages and be sutler in new forts. He has promise of [the Department of the] Interior of an Indian trade[rship]." (The secretary of the interior named Indian agency traders.) "Now, what think you? Ben counts much on you. . . . What should he do to be in right *place*, right *time*?"

Historians have argued over whether the letter shows that Custer took part in a corrupt ring run by Ingalls and Holladay. It suggests prior business discussions, but also shows that Ingalls and Holladay had spoken of nothing specific. Left unexplained is precisely what Holladay counted on him to do. Custer had no influence over the appointment of sutlers, a power concentrated in the hands of the secretary of war since 1870. Ingalls knew this, for he was the army's acting quartermaster general while Montgomery Meigs was in Europe for several months. Ingalls also had a personal connection to President Grant. By contrast, Custer found himself rather isolated in 1875. When Libbie later examined her husband's estate, she would see neither profits from Holladay nor debts in connection with this matter. Ingalls also mentioned he might get "control over the whole subject of horse shoes," and asked Custer to serve as head of a board that would choose a supplier; but no such board came to be. Weaknesses in the case for Custer's role in any ring, though, do not prove his moral rectitude. He *had* talked of some kind of business deal with them, knowing Ingalls's taste for graft.[55]

In September, Secretary of War William W. Belknap stopped briefly at Fort Abraham Lincoln. A broad-faced man, six feet tall and some 200 pounds, he filled a room whether standing or sitting. Born ten years before Custer, educated at Princeton and Georgetown, he had risen as a volunteer in the Civil War from major to brigadier general, fighting at Shiloh and marching to the sea with Sherman, who had recommended him for his cabinet post. Once in office, though, Belknap had maneuvered Sherman out of any real power.

Custer, sick with dysentery, rose from his bed to greet the secretary of war. He had heard the rumors about Belknap—stories that centered on the last two of his three wives. The first had died during the Civil War. The second, Carrie Tomlinson Belknap, had been a lovely woman, fond of luxury. Tuberculosis killed her in late 1870, and her sister Amanda— undeterred by precedent—married Belknap next. Even more beautiful than her sister, she possessed "charming grace and manner," according to an acquaintance. Amanda Belknap and First Lady Julia Dent Grant were "friendly rivals" in throwing the most elegant New Year's Day reception in Washington, according to William McFeely. The rumors explained that elegance as the fruits of graft, saying Belknap took payoffs from post traders for their lucrative concessions.[56]

Custer tended to believe rumors that reinforced his prejudices, and he was emphatically prejudiced against Belknap. Effective July 1, 1874, Belknap had replaced the Fort Lincoln sutler with Robert C. Seip, who immediately raised already high prices. Custer had told his officers to go across the river to Bismarck to buy goods for themselves and the men. Seip had insisted that he possessed a legal monopoly on the troops' business. Custer recalled, "I have known the post-trader at Fort Lincoln to go out and stop an officer's wagon, driven by his servant, and inspect the wagon . . . and threaten to use his influence with the Secretary of War because we trade with a town five miles distant, where we got things at about half his prices." Custer had wired a protest to the War Department. Belknap had backed Seip.

Custer curtly returned to Seip the wine and cigars that the trader had provided for the secretary's entertainment. "I was just as suspicious of the Secretary as I was of the sutler," he later explained, but he treated Belknap correctly. He mentioned that Seip "was trying to hold a whip over the officers' heads by asserting that he would bring his influence to bear upon the Secretary of War," implying that it was "improper" in some way. Belknap waved it off, saying, "You must not believe all you hear."

Custer later asked Seip about his affairs. The sutler said he paid a tax to two political brokers, John Hedrick and Elliott Rice, who had arranged his appointment. That was why he raised his prices and insisted on a monopoly. He cleared a profit of $15,000 a year, he said, but after paying off the fixers he kept less than $3,000.[57]

Did Custer press Holladay's case with Belknap? He never mentioned any such discussion, which would have been premature. Most likely he said nothing about it, or Belknap would have revealed it when he and Custer met in open battle in March 1876.

BELKNAP LEFT, AND SO DID the Custers. Armstrong, Libbie, and Tom all boarded an eastbound train. Libbie went to Michigan; Armstrong went to New York. He arrived at the end of September and rented an apartment at 222 Fifth Avenue between 26th and 27th streets, across from the Hotel Brunswick, where he took his meals and mail.

A *Herald* reporter found him and posed a few questions. "What do you think, General, of this morning's news about the Black Hills negotiations?" he asked. A conference between a federal commission and Sioux leaders for the purchase of the Black Hills had broken down. The Sioux were divided, but the only terms they proposed were seen as outrageous by the commissioners. Just what he had expected, Custer said. "It is the result of holding the council right in the heart of the Indian country, where the chiefs had the squaw men (the whites married to squaws) to advise them."

The interviewer brought up corruption at the Indian agencies. "Breaking up the monopoly" of assigned traders would solve much of the economic mistreatment of the Indians, he said. The reporter asked about recent articles in the *Herald* on graft at the Fort Berthold agency. "They are just what is wanted, and the correspondent who wrote them deserves credit, as he took his life in his hands, venturing to expose the frauds of the Indian ring when right in their midst. He must have worked hard." It seems Custer kept a straight face, though the *Herald* reporter Ralph Meeker had just written to him about a $50 payment for information that Custer had provided for those very stories.[58]

Money, politics, and pleasure: he chased all three in New York. He saw Bennett. He saw Belmont. And he returned to the office of Emil Justh, where he pursued his short-selling speculations in the stock market. The volume of transactions, as officially measured, mounted rapidly: thousands of dollars, then tens of thousands, a hundred thousand, two hundred thousand, three hundred thousand. With Justh financing his gambling, Custer pressed on. Some bets paid off; others failed. Then more failed.[59]

He faced the consequences of old sins, and new virtues could not compensate. The Atlantic Publishing Company sued him in Marine Court—a kind of small-claims court in New York. The dispute was probably over the war memoir he had contracted to write in 1867 but never delivered. The process server found him in the office of the Hotel Brunswick. Custer refused to accept any papers. Finally he told the court that he had a "good & substantial defence on the merits," but refused to make it as he didn't live in New York and the suit was improper. Pressed for cash on several fronts, he asked Sheldon & Company on November 10 to pay him for *My Life on the Plains*. They had promised him a flat fee in return for the copyright instead of paying royalties. Isaac Sheldon, son of the company's founder, replied that they owed him $171.22 minus various charges, leaving $131.94, "for which we will send you a check." It was not enough to save him from his Wall Street reverses or pay a lawyer.[60]

Libbie joined him in the city. She felt the restraints on their finances. "The holidays have been rainy, gloomy," she wrote to Tom in late December. "I did not have half the fun I had anticipated, looking in at the shop windows. On Christmas morning I went to church, but came back, weary, disgruntled." And yet her husband's name gave them access to a world they could not refuse. They saw Lawrence Barrett star in *Julius Caesar* at Booth's Theatre, a block away from their rooms, free of charge. They often dined with Barrett and his wife. They attended a dinner at the Lotos Club, a social hub for writers and artists; had lunch with the artist Albert Bierstadt in his studio; saw exhibitions; and ate at Delmonico's.[61]

Bert Swett came to Manhattan and went to the Hotel Brunswick to find Custer. He happened upon him as he picked up his mail. Custer told him he had agreed to write his war memoirs for the *Galaxy*, and lodged across the street so he would not be annoyed by constant visitors. They went to get Libbie, and the three traveled to Union Square to see a performance of trained fleas. Afterward they went down Broadway to a phrenologist to have Bert's head examined. "Mrs. Custer played the part of mother for me very well," he wrote. The phrenologist pored over Bert's skull, feeling the bumps and swells, and described various aspects of Bert's character—pausing each time to ask Libbie "if she did not think it was so." When the day was done, she invited Bert to Fort Lincoln in the summer of 1876, and he promised he would come. He said good-bye.

Young Swett was only a few years too old to be the Custers' own child. For a brief spell in 1875, he gave them the gift of a glimpse into the lives they would never have. Libbie played the part of mother for him not only in the phrenologist's office, but in all their time together, from their tents on the Little Heart River to their rooms on Fifth Avenue. Bert's own mother sensed something of their relationship and grew jealous. "You say 'I am afraid I should lose my boy [to] Mrs. Custer,'" Bert wrote to her. "Mrs. Custer . . . has my highest respect and admiration as a truely [sic] lovely woman." As a teenage boy, he may have felt a furtive, half-sublimated attraction to Libbie. But what he allowed *her* to feel was something rare indeed.[62]

For all the pleasures of New York, money and politics clouded Armstrong's months in Manhattan more than Libbie realized. Meeker sent a note urging him to go to Washington in 1876 to watch the new Congress in action. "The Democrats will make things lively, and we expect to have lots of fun before the season is over," he wrote. He observed with satisfaction that the Indian agent they had exposed at Berthold was gone, and he alluded to Custer's tales of corruption in the appointment of sutlers—that is, Belknap's corruption. "If this thing is investigated during the coming session there will be weeping and wailing around the White House."[63]

Custer wanted to see the Democrats punish Grant's administration, but money consumed him. He wrote to the Redpath Lyceum Bureau in Boston. The leading lecture agency in the country, it represented the famous biographer James Parton, P. T. Barnum, Charles Francis Adams Jr., and Frederick Douglass, among others. The manager wrote back with good news. "I have been considerably interested in your lecture prospects. I *believe* we can do something for you." Custer chattered happily about the possibilities, noting that Thomas Nast earned $20,000 in a single season, and he was told that he could keep going for a decade "or as long as I could stand it." The problem was that the bureau wanted him to start in the spring, "but I declined as I desired longer time to make any preparations," Custer wrote.[64]

This income lay in the uncertain future, but his finances demanded immediate action. By now he had carried out $398,983 in stock trades through Emil Justh. He had lost $8,578. It's rather remarkable that he lost such a small percentage of the total, but in absolute terms it represented an immense amount of money for Custer. It was larger than the annual salaries of major railroad presidents. It was far more than he could pay. And he wanted to keep the debt secret from Libbie.

On February 10, 1876, three days after he heard from the lecture bureau, he wrote a promissory note—an IOU—for $8,500, made out to himself to disguise the debt and endorsed to Justh. He dated it six months in the future, and agreed to a heavy 7 percent interest. By that time, he hoped, he would have started his speaking tour, bringing in enough money to pay off or renew the note. But Justh no longer trusted him; he demanded a cosigner to guarantee the debt. Custer went to Ben Holladay, the steamship king, the mail contractor, the manipulator who wanted inside help with his Black Hills scheme—this, at the same time that Custer fed information of graft to the *Herald*. Holladay endorsed the note.[65] Financially, even morally, Custer had brought disaster down upon himself over the past year. Things would get worse.

PITY THE PRESIDENTS, FOR THEY enter the White House imagining that they have attained the height of power, only to discover a special kind of powerlessness. Lincoln famously said that events controlled him, not the other way around, but the public never believes it, which makes it even worse. Political considerations dilute each dose of policy; the need to balance priorities inhibits strong measures. The president finds himself trapped within the cabinet, his ability to act mediated by his secretaries. He loses touch with the world through the layers of bureaucracy surrounding him.

Even in the 1870s, when those layers were far fewer and thinner, Grant felt the difference between his office as general in chief, where he *commanded*, and the mummy-wrapped presidency, entombed in reasons to do nothing. Someone was sure to mock him whether he failed, as with the annexation of Santo Domingo, or succeeded, as with the Treaty of Washington, settling Civil War claims with Britain. When he intervened in the South, he found himself blamed for half measures by one side and tyrannical overreach by the other. In this era before the Secret Service erected ramparts around the president, supplicants ambushed him daily, asking for favors.

Such was the presidency. But Grant cut the ribbon on a new kind of White House hell, which has become a defining feature of modern political battles: the congressional investigation. There had been many in the past, the evidence and reports printed in the fat volumes of the Congressional Serial Set. But now it was different. After the 44th Congress began its first session in December 1875, the Democratic House of Representatives opened investigations of every department.[66] They honed scandal into a lethal partisan weapon, flaying the administration in an attempt to show that it was gangrenous with corruption. The Democrats believed it, but they also knew stories of graft supported their arguments about the dangers of an overlarge central government.

The House investigations created a false sense that Grant's administration suffered "exceptional rascality," as the historian Mark Wahlgren Summers writes. He studied malfeasance before and after the Civil War, and concludes that the *issue* of corruption, not corruption itself, was the real novelty. The problem went back to Andrew Jackson's emphasis on a political spoils system. Each president swept out postmasters, tax collectors, steamboat inspectors, and every other federal employee, and installed loyalists. The richest prize, customs collector for New York, controlled a thousand lesser jobs and derived an enormous income. All these officials, high and low, supported the president politically, building patronage networks and funneling money into elections. Private enterprise's not-so-invisible hands passed money to Congress as well, long before Grant's inauguration. Lobbyists flourished in the 1850s, accused (convincingly) of bribing congressmen to influence awards of steamship subsidies. Crédit Mobilier's corruption of Capitol Hill started under Andrew Johnson.

Instead of numbing the public to graft, this history made it more sensitive. The 44th Congress launched its attack amid near paranoia. Railroad corporations were thought to be bribing state governments; at times they did, most notoriously in the Erie War of 1868, in which New York legislators lined up outside Jay Gould's hotel room in order to be bought. When not accepting gifts, officials proposed damaging bills and demanded ransoms to table them. Then there was New York's Boss Tweed and his ring, destroyed by the joint efforts of the *New York Times* and the most respectable citizens of New York. The press kettle-drummed these stories, editorializing on the disastrous state of public morals. Summers writes, "Exaggeration, misapprehension, and well-grounded allegations mingled together, and created a sense of crisis."[67]

Note, though, that he includes "well-grounded allegations" in his list. Corruption did exist within Grant's administration. And it differed from past graft in key ways. First was the increased size of the take, skimmed from a bigger economy. Next was the proximity to the president. The scandals would implicate department heads as well as Grant's closest friend, a man who dipped his beak in many mud puddles. Then there were the investigators. The House Democrats' attacks followed where a member of Grant's own cabinet led.

That betrayal began, fittingly, with a scandal. In the spring of 1874, the revelation of fraud in the Internal Revenue Bureau forced Treasury Secretary William Richardson to resign. At the urging of the most respectable men around him, particularly Fish, Grant replaced Richardson with the former solicitor general Benjamin Bristow. This portly Kentuckian could not have had a cleaner reputation. Like Fish, he believed in the gold standard—or "honest money," as gold ideologues called it. He also had dreams of higher office. No one is more untrustworthy than an honest man with ambition.[68]

Bristow learned that whiskey tax revenues fell far below legitimate expectations. His undercover agents discovered the Whiskey Ring, a huge conspiracy of distillers and Internal Revenue agents who undercollected taxes in return for kickbacks. Part of the money maintained Grant's political support. Much of it flowed into the hands of Orville Babcock. In his post as the president's private secretary, this handsome West Pointer showed that he possessed great ability, almost no scruples, and Grant's unshakable friendship. With Rawlins dead and the administration beset by enemies, Grant leaned heavily on Babcock.

Bristow launched a wave of raids on May 13, 1875, arresting 350 distillers and government officials. When Grant learned that the evidence implicated Babcock, he burst into tears—but refused to admit its truth. He came to believe that Bristow's real target was Grant himself, which made him more protective of Babcock. He saw the investigation as a betrayal by an ambitious cabinet secretary.[69]

Bristow had not yet finished with Babcock before he targeted a fellow cabinet secretary and a member of Grant's family. He found evidence that Secretary of the Interior Columbus Delano's department was a tangled nest of corruption. There were payoffs for Indian agency traderships (the stuff of Custer's leaks to the *New York Herald*) and surveying contracts issued to Delano's own non-surveyor son. The president's younger brother, Orvil Grant, received a contract as well, though he did no work. "Grant was not close to his younger brother . . . and had more than once remonstrated with him for capitalizing on their relationship," writes William McFeely. But he hated it when someone undermined him or his family. Even more aggravating, Bristow won. Grant replaced Delano in October 1875 with a loyal Republican, Senator Zachariah Chandler.[70]

Despite all this intrigue and scandal, serious decision making could not wait. On November 3, Secretary Chandler came to the White House to meet with Grant, Belknap, Commissioner of Indian Affairs Edward Smith, Sheridan, and Gen. George Crook, commander of the Department of the Platte. The group discussed the Black Hills. Miners eluded military patrols, but no one particularly wanted to keep them out. It was a distasteful duty for Sheridan, and it forestalled the economic development of the region. But the Sioux had refused to sell.

They did not discuss the significance of the Black Hills to the Lakotas. The region constituted a vitally important resource bank—a "food pack," in Sitting Bull's words. The hills' wooded valleys, rich with game, functioned much as the river bottoms did on the open plains, providing year-round forage, food, and shelter from winter storms. Even worse, by demanding the Black Hills Washington insisted on a reversal of Lakota history. From a Lakota viewpoint, the Fort Laramie Treaty had recognized Sioux conquests; giving up the hills would do the opposite. It would cost them land they had captured decades before and seriously undermine their hunting and trading culture. They refused not because they were victims, but out of a sense of their hard-earned power. A conquering people could not be expected to surrender without a fight.

Grant and his advisers agreed to stop enforcing the order to keep trespassers out of the Black Hills, though the order remained on the books. They believed that the sale of the land had been vetoed by the influence of Sitting Bull and his non-reservation allies and followers; therefore they would have to break his power. Sheridan's goal of exterminating the bison remained too distant. They decided to order the hunting bands to report to the agencies; if they failed to do so Sheridan would launch a winter campaign to defeat them. As Robert Utley notes, they technically justified a war by citing Lakota attacks on the Crows, Arikaras, and others. But the purpose was clear: to seize title to the Black Hills and destroy Lakota nomadism.[71]

Within a week of the meeting, Inspector E. C. Watkins of the Office of Indian Affairs submitted a report on Sitting Bull's and allied bands. It made the White House group's plan seem relatively easy, but absolutely necessary. "They are still as wild and untamable, as uncivilized and savage, as when Lewis and Clark first passed through their country," he wrote. Worst of all, they "scorn the idea of white civilization." He cast them as insolent inferiors who must be put in their place. "They openly set at defiance all law and authority," held the U.S. Army "in contempt," were "lofty and independent in their attitude to Govt. officials as well as the whites generally and claim to be the Sovereign Rulers of the land." But Watkins thought them weak and divided, "all told, but a few hundred warriors," easily crushed by a thousand troops.

Watkins's report did not shape the White House plan, but it articulated the thinking behind it and eliminated any hesitations. Preparations began for a winter offensive. Interior Secretary Chandler instructed the

Sioux agents to send word to Sitting Bull and others that they must report in by January 31, 1876.[72]

Grant's Peace Policy, a hallmark of his administration and one of his most deeply felt initiatives, finally dissolved. He did not protest, but agreed that it was for the best. So much of what mattered to him had slipped away, like his daughter, married to an English cad with a distinguished name; his friend Rawlins, taken by disease; his intention to give justice to African Americans, nearly terminated. He felt isolated, besieged. Democrats took control of the House. Cabinet members fell away, crippled by scandals, struck down by Bristow. Then, on December 9, Babcock was indicted.

For him, Grant fought. He assigned an agent to Chandler's department with orders to prove him innocent. It turned out to be impossible. He ordered a halt to plea bargains with prosecution witnesses. The trial proceeded just the same. On February 12, 1876, Grant gave a deposition that exonerated Babcock, who was acquitted on the 28th.[73]

Yet the siege did not lift, the isolation did not end. The Democrats battered the administration with their tsunami of investigations. In hearing after hearing, the House aired tales of corruption. Most dramatically, they attacked Secretary of War Belknap. As an isolated case Grant might not have taken it personally, but he had lost too many friends, suffered too many blows. He believed that it, too, was an attack on himself.

Ralph Meeker opened the battle with a story in the *New York Herald* on February 9, 1876, followed by Bennett's editorial, "Extravagance and Corruption in the War Department." The main assault began at 2 p.m. on February 28, when Caleb Marsh testified at a hearing of the House Committee on Expenditures in the War Department. In 1870, he said, Belknap's wife, Carrie, urged him to apply to be the sutler for Fort Sill, Indian Territory, suggesting that he could sublet the store to an actual merchant. Using a front, Marsh received the appointment and collected large profits. He sent half directly to Belknap. When Carrie died and her sister Amanda married the secretary, she told Marsh to carry on. Marsh said he paid a total of $20,000 to Belknap, often in person.[74]

The chairman of the committee, Representative Hiester Clymer of Pennsylvania, had shared a room with Belknap at Princeton University. Clymer fairly represented the postwar Democratic Party, in that he stood for racism. (One poster from his 1866 campaign for governor against John W. Geary featured a grotesque Sambo-style caricature of a black man; it declared, "CLYMER'S platform is for the White Man. GEARY's Platform is for the Negro.") Now he had clear evidence against a Republican cabinet secretary—head of the very department used to enforce civil rights laws in the South. Clymer wanted to impeach his old roommate as soon as possible.[75]

On March 1, Belknap appeared before the committee with Montgomery Blair as his counsel. He wept as Blair read his statement aloud. He offered to make a full confession if his wife, Amanda, were left out of the affair. Clymer refused. The next day the committee drew up articles of impeachment. Belknap went to the White House to offer his resignation. To the outrage of Bristow and Fish, Grant accepted it.

When Clymer learned of the resignation he rushed to the House floor. He read aloud Marsh's testimony, concluding, "The late Secretary of War is but the proper outgrowth, the true exponent of the corruption, the extravagance, the misgovernment which has cursed this land for years past." The House debated the legality of impeaching Belknap, who no longer held public office, then voted to do so.[76]

Clymer's statement confirmed Grant's belief that the attack on Belknap was intended to destroy his presidency. As if to prove it, Clymer continued his hearings on Belknap. On March 29, he reached into Grant's beloved army to find another betrayer to denounce the administration. He presented George Armstrong Custer. [77]

CUSTER REMAINED IN MOTION from the moment he and Libbie left New York in February, crossing and recrossing the country. In St. Paul, General Terry explained to him his plan for their offensive against the Lakotas. They would move out from Fort Abraham Lincoln on April 6. Terry would establish a base on the Yellowstone River and simply unleash Custer and the 7th Cavalry. Armstrong and Libbie barely made it to Fort Lincoln alive. A blizzard snowed in their train between Fargo and Bismarck. Someone on board the train tapped a telegraph line and sent word of their plight. Tom Custer—now a captain—drove a sleigh out to rescue them, bringing them to the fort on March 13.

On March 15, Armstrong received a telegram ordering him to return east to testify before Congress. He went back alone, stopping in Monroe on the way. The morning after he arrived in Washington, he appeared before Clymer's committee.[78]

The summons to Washington forestalled his advance against Sitting Bull, but he had already voiced ambivalence about his return to the field. "I was fully expecting to remain [in New York] until May," he had told a reporter. "I had doffed the military guise for the sober civilian suit, and had begun to feel as if I were actually settled down to solid comfort." The order to go west had been a surprise. "It was too bad, wasn't it?" The reporter wrote, "The General heaved a melancholy sigh." He might face as many as 8,000 to 10,000 warriors, Custer had added, "enough to do a vast amount of damage."[79]

He found himself in Washington only because *he wanted to go*. By choosing to work with the *Herald*, he willingly, if furtively, entered into politics. More than that, he must have been in contact with Clymer at some point. As a committee chairman, Clymer functioned as a prosecutor—and prosecutors never call witnesses unless they know what they will say. Somehow Clymer knew to summon him. Robert Utley writes that he found Custer on a list of recommended witnesses submitted by Col. William Hazen. But Clymer swore in Custer immediately after the latter reached Washington. If they did not communicate beforehand through one of the many available channels, then Clymer was guilty of gross negligence as a political inquisitor.[80]

In Clymer's committee room, Custer described the change of sutlers at Fort Abraham Lincoln, the rapid rise in prices, his confrontations with Robert Seip, his meeting with Belknap, and Seip's admission that he paid off insiders, including "an intimate friend of the Secretary of War here in Washington." Many observers remarked upon the hearsay quality of his testimony. "It was a matter of common report and common information among the officers and men that the trader had to pay a tax to outside people," he declared, in a typical statement. The president's brother Orvil had been implicated in questionable dealings with the Department of the Interior; Custer confirmed them, describing an encounter with him on his way back to Fort Abraham Lincoln. Custer even implied that the boundary of the Sioux reservation had been altered by the president to benefit the rings run by Delano and Belknap.[81]

Custer's relationship with the *Herald* did not stay secret. Robert Seip testified that he had cashed the newspaper's drafts (i.e., checks) for Custer. On March 31 the *Herald* published an article with the headline, "Belknap's Anaconda," depicting a vast conspiracy of graft; many accused Custer of writing it. Clymer called Ralph Meeker to testify, at Custer's request. The reporter claimed authorship of the *Herald* pieces and said that the drafts were to repay Custer for loans. This testimony was at least partially false. Some drafts must have been for Custer, given all the talk of payment in his communications with Bennett and Meeker. The *Herald*'s managing editor had promised to keep his identity as a writer secret. Even now he worked on a piece for the newspaper. He assured Libbie, "Its authorship cannot be traced."[82]

Political partisanship overcame him. Excited to be so close to power, thrilled to participate in "the glorious results of the last election," he literally took a seat at the Democrats' table. He wrote to Libbie at Clymer's committee room desk and in his chair on the floor of the House, on official House of Representatives stationery. He ate with Clymer in the House restaurant, strolled across Capitol Hill with him, and called the proudly racist congressman "an exceedingly cultivated gentleman." Democratic senator Thomas F. Bayard of Delaware held a dinner in Custer's honor, attended by Clymer and a clutch of Confederate generals. Custer also dined with Representative Henry B. Banning, who consulted him on the army appropriations bill and called him to testify before the Committee on Military Affairs.

Custer used his time before that committee to attack a senior officer in his own regiment, Maj. Lewis Merrill. Popular memory recalls Frederick Benteen as his greatest foe in the 7th Cavalry; Custer himself saw Merrill as a more insidious threat, having feuded with him since 1871. Richard Slotkin notes Custer's political motives, since Merrill actively pursued the Ku Klux Klan in South Carolina. Custer said Merrill had taken a bribe from the state legislature there. He had no direct evidence, but fed the story to the *Herald*, "calling attention to his disgraceful proceedings." Custer happily implicated South Carolina's Republican government, whose black legislators and officials were scorned by Democrats as incompetent and corrupt.[83]

President Grant could not have been surprised by Custer's participation in the congressional offensive. It was typical of his self-dramatizing self-righteousness, partisanship, and recklessness in insulting the chain of command. For the first time, though, Custer attacked Grant himself—or so it seemed from Grant's perspective. The president had long disdained Custer; now he saw him as an enemy.

An undemonstrative man, the president showed no emotion at Custer's public betrayal of his administration and his family. But he was not inclined to reward an enemy, particularly not the enemy within. He knew that war sustained Custer—and the war against the Lakotas and their allies had already begun. On March 17, Gen. George Crook had dispatched Col. Joseph Reynolds to attack a Northern Cheyenne and Oglala camp on the Powder River, but Reynolds had retreated in the face of a counterattack. Sheridan planned for Custer to lead the next thrust, under Terry's command. Custer had built his fame on battles, sustained his credibility upon Western adventures. And it was within Grant's power to take them away.[84]

IN THE HALLS OF CONGRESS, Custer felt powerful. He was politically ascendant. Others saw him that way too. "The men who in Army circles had influence a few days ago now hide away," he wrote. "You would be surprised if you knew the high rank of some of the Army people" who asked him to intercede for them. Then he wrote, in two curiously juxtaposed sentences, "I care not to use or abuse whatever influence I have. The House Committee is heavily opposed to Sheridan." The client cut the patron loose.

His corrupt friend Rufus Ingalls, on the other hand, "is in great trouble and anxiety in regard to these investigations," Custer wrote to Libbie. "I told him I could ascertain in five minutes all there was in the hands of the committee. I did so today and will see Rufus this PM and relieve his mind of a load that has troubled him greatly." Confident in his strength, he left his fire-damaged hotel to stay with Ben Holladay.

He cultivated Sherman, and described him as particularly warm. He may have seen the conservative commanding general as a new patron, a replacement for the unfashionably Radical Sheridan as the Democrats took power. He could see that Sherman had regained his authority under the new secretary of war, Alphonso Taft. Sherman introduced him to Taft with compliments. George Corkhill, editor of the *Washington Chronicle*, hosted a breakfast for Custer, Sherman, and Supreme Court justice Samuel Miller. And Custer received an invitation to a dinner at the Manhattan Club ("*the* Democratic club of N.Y.," he stressed to Libbie), though he declined.[85]

After a couple of weeks in the capital, a creeping sense that he had exposed himself overtook Custer. In mid-April he began to write about his eagerness to leave. He complained that he had too many supplicants, asking him to do too much. Each choice to help or not help exposed him further, making a potential enemy of someone. Finally he departed Washington. He stopped in Philadelphia to see the Centennial Exhibition, a grand fair given to celebrate the nation's 100th birthday, then went on to New York, where he dined with August Belmont. There, on April 24, he was called back to Washington to testify in Belknap's impeachment.[86]

By now he realized his danger. Despite the election, the army chain of command remained in place—and he had aggravated it. Sheridan wrote to army headquarters to dispute a claim he made about a corrupt transaction involving corn at Fort Abraham Lincoln. He did not intend "to do any harm to Col. Custer," Sheridan wrote, but he resented how Custer had impugned "army administration in this command." Lt. Col. James "Tony" Forsyth, brother of Custer's friend Sandy Forsyth, wrote Belknap a letter, part of which appeared in print. He said Custer repeated mere gossip. "I have yet to meet a single officer of the army who approves" of his testimony. "The fact of the matter is, both Hazen, and Custer, are now working to make capital with the Democratic party—*they want stars.*" The Republican press attacked him on a daily basis; it worried Custer, who mentioned it often in his letters, affecting not to care.[87]

Now almost frantic to escape Washington, Custer asked Sherman for help in being released from testifying in the Belknap case. Sherman agreed. He asked Secretary of War Taft to write to Congress. Taft told Grant about it at the next cabinet meeting. No, Grant said, Taft would write no such letter. He was "not pleased with General Custer." Sherman telegraphed Sheridan in Chicago on April 28: "The President has just sent me instructions through the Secretary of War, to send someone else than General Custer in command of that force from Fort Abe Lincoln. Detail and instruct someone else." Sheridan replied that General Terry would go in Custer's place.[88]

Custer went to see Sherman, who saw that he was "much troubled." Go talk to the president, Sherman advised. On May 1, Custer went to the White House. He had gone before, only to be turned away. In an ambiguous way, his letters suggest that Grant did see him previously, allowing him time to praise Bloody Knife, as he had promised the scout he would. If so, they had had no substantive conversation. From Custer's point of view, they now had a great deal to discuss. Grant made him wait, hour after hour. Ingalls saw him in the anteroom, and promised to speak for him to the president. Grant sent out a note that he would not see Custer that day.[89]

"I desired this opportunity simply as a matter of justice," Custer wrote to the president, adding that he regretted that he would not be allowed to see him. With the start of the expedition now past due, he decided to simply leave. Sherman was out, but he believed the general had approved his departure. The House impeachment managers in the Belknap case said they did not need him. He took a train to Chicago.

On arriving, Custer checked in with Sheridan, then boarded a train to St. Paul. Immediately after he left, Sheridan received a telegram about him from Sherman: "He was not justified in starting without seeing the President or myself. Please intercept him at Chicago or Saint Paul and order him to halt and await further orders. Meantime let the expedition from Fort Lincoln proceed without him." Sheridan sent a man to pull Custer off the train before it left the station.

That same day in Washington, Grant sent Sherman and Taft a clipping from the *New York World*. It read, "President Grant has to-day performed an act which appears to be the most high-handed abuse of his official power which he has perpetrated yet." The article claimed that Grant removed Custer from command in retaliation for his testimony, and that Sherman and Taft protested, saying "that Custer was not only the best man, but the only man fit to lead the expedition now fitting out against the Indians. To all their entreaties Grant turned a deaf ear." It said Custer believed he had merely done his duty by testifying, and that he had gone to see Grant only to be sent away.

It infuriated Sherman and Taft, who could only conclude that Custer planted the story. Taft told the president, "These statements are entirely untrue." Sherman stated "most emphatically that General Custer though relieved as a witness by the Committee was not justified in leaving Washington." He observed that he had *not* protested Custer's removal from command, that in fact "the Army possesses hundreds who are competent for such an expedition," including General Terry. He added, "General Custer is now subject to any measure of discipline which the President may require." He did not know if Custer was responsible for the *New York World* article, adding, "I surely cannot believe that he could so misrepresent the case." But who else knew the details it related, let alone Custer's private thoughts?[90]

Custer wired Sherman twice on May 4, protesting that he had waited all day to see the president. Sherman replied to Sheridan, saying that Grant would allow Custer to return to Fort Abraham Lincoln but not to go on the expedition. Custer took the train to St. Paul. There, on May 6, he made a final appeal to President Grant, which Terry sent up the chain of command. "I respectfully but most earnestly request that while not allowed to go in command of the expedition I may be permitted to serve with my regiment in the field. I appeal to you as a soldier to spare me the humiliation of seeing my regiment march to meet the enemy & I not share in its dangers."

The circle closed. In the final trial of his life, Custer made the same appeal for clemency that he had made at his court-martial in 1861. After so many years, he again faced the consequences of his self-indulgence, his blindness to his obligations. His peril drained away his sense of power, his belief in his ascendance. Again he asked for pity—to be saved from the mortification of being held back as others went into battle.

Terry endorsed Custer's note, telling Sheridan that he did not intend to question the president's orders but "Custer's services would be very valuable with his regiment." Sheridan forwarded Custer's message to Washington with his own comments, making it clear that he had had quite enough of Custer's misbehavior. "I am sorry Lieutenant Colonel Custer did not manifest as much interest by staying at his post to organize & get ready his regiment & the expedition as he does now to accompany it." Sheridan pointed out that he had asked for clemency for Custer in 1868, also so he could join his regiment in a foray against the Indians; "& I sincerely hope if granted this time it will have sufficient effect to prevent him from again attempting to throw discredit on his profession and his brother officers." Custer had alienated his last patron.[91]

Sherman sent a final telegram in this flurry, directed to Terry. He said that Grant had seen his message and "Custer's urgent request to go under your command with his regiment." The president relented. Custer could go. Sherman added fatherly advice to pass along to the lieutenant colonel, showing that he had not given up on Custer yet.

> Advise Custer to be prudent, not to take along any newspaper men, who always work mischief, and to abstain from any personalities in the future. Tell him I want him to confine his whole mind to his legitimate office, and trust to time. That newspaper paragraph in the *New York World* of May 2nd compromised his best friends here, and almost deprived us of the ability to serve him.[92]

The Democratic press and many historians find Grant guilty of "harsh, politically motivated treatment of Custer," as Utley writes. His anger at the siege of his administration clearly affected him. He felt betrayed, first by Bristow and then Custer. But that should not distract from the sheer recklessness of Custer's actions. He planted political stories in the press, apparently writing some himself. He testified to corruption in the administration and Grant's own family, though he had no personal knowledge of it. He publicly impugned an officer of his own regiment on mere hearsay evidence. Worst of all, he compromised the core principle of the American military—not incidentally the first professional institution in the country—by openly intriguing with the political opposition to the civilian commander in chief. And he did it to help a party dedicated to restoring white supremacy (even as he imperiled his family's fortunes with a secret, unsecured debt from reckless gambling on stocks). Whatever Grant's motives, Custer deserved serious discipline, dismissal, or a court-martial.

He should have known better. Libbie warned him not to alienate politicians. She feared that he put himself at risk by praising McClellan in his war memoirs now appearing in the *Galaxy*, that he might have lost the friendship of Chandler. Her comments were more apt than she perhaps realized. For fifteen years, Custer had worshipped McClellan; now he had duplicated his flaws, nearly ending his career by politically assailing the president of the United States.[93]

At Fort Abraham Lincoln he jumped into the preparations for the expedition. For the first time, all twelve companies of the regiment would ride out under his command. The officers gathered—Marcus Reno, whom Custer had hardly seen in their years in the 7th Cavalry, Benteen, Yates, Moylan, Keogh, Calhoun, Tom Custer, and the rest. He hired his little brother Boston as a civilian forage master, and his nephew Autie—Harry Armstrong Reed, his sister's son—as a herder. "You must rely on the ability of your own column for your best success," Sheridan wired Terry on May 16. "I believe it to be fully equal to all the Sioux which can be brought against it, and only hope they will hold fast to meet it. . . . You know the impossibility of any large number of Indians keeping together as a hostile body for even one week."[94]

The next day Custer led the 7th Cavalry on a parade through the fort's grid of wooden buildings, the band playing "Garry Owen." Libbie and his sister Maggie rode with him. The band struck up "The Girl I Left Behind Me." With Bloody Knife, 21 Arikara scouts, 3 Gatling guns, and 150 wagons, the column marched up from the river bottom to the plateau above. Libbie and Maggie camped with them that night. On May 18 the women said good-bye and watched the men march out of sight.[95]

EPILOGUE

A<small>T ELEVEN O'CLOCK IN</small> the morning on January 13, 1879, a collection of military officers took seats in a room on the mezzanine of the Palmer House hotel in Chicago. They wore full-dress uniforms— double-breasted tunics, now standard for all officer ranks, and white gloves. They began by reading the order for these proceedings.

> By direction of the President and on the application of Major Marcus A. Reno, 7th Cavalry, a Court of Inquiry is hereby appointed . . . for the purpose of inquiring into Major Reno's conduct at the Battle of the Little Big Horn River* on the 25th and 26th days of June, 1876.

The directive assigned Col. John H. King, 9th Infantry, Col. Wesley Merritt, 5th Cavalry, and Lt. Col. William B. Royall, 3rd Cavalry, as judges. The recorder (in essence the prosecutor), 1st Lt. Jesse M. Lee, noted, "There is a man by the name of Whittaker whom I understand has made certain accusations against Major Reno." Indeed, Reno had asked for this inquiry because the writer Frederick Whittaker publicly blamed him for the disaster that struck the 7th Cavalry at the Little Bighorn.[1]

The court reconvened the next day. A half-dozen reporters and some twenty civilian observers attended, interested less in Reno than in his former commander. This would be the closest thing to an official investigation of the mysterious fate of Lt. Col. George Armstrong Custer. Even Lieutenant Lee seemed to feel the public's anticipation; he denied that he was Reno's prosecutor, saying, "The course seems to be to get at the whole truth of the matter." Regardless, Reno brought counsel: Lyman D. Gilbert, deputy attorney general of Pennsylvania.

The *Chicago Times* described King, the presiding officer, as wearing a

---

* Current spelling collapses the last two words in the name into one, "Little Bighorn." It will appear this way except in quotations of primary sources.

"perpetual smile." A rather soft-looking officer of medium height, he had silver hair and a giant English-style mustache—a contrast with Merritt on his right, still boyish, with "a dark-brown, coarse mustache, with a comfortable Jeff Davis beard." The bald Royall sat silently on the panel's left. Reno and his lawyer took their seats. Speaking in "clarion tones," the newspaper wrote, King ordered the proceedings to begin.[2]

Lee called 1st Lt. Edward Maguire to the stand. The *Chicago Times* thought him "a trifle nervous," observing that his hand shook as he took the oath "to testify to the truth, the whole truth, and nothing but the truth." Maguire explained that he served on Gen. Alfred Terry's staff in St. Paul. At the time of the battle, "I accompanied Gen. Terry as engineer officer . . . to within about eight miles of Gen. Custer's battlefield on the Little Bighorn." He added that Col. John Gibbon commanded the troops that he and Terry accompanied, and they were "moving to form a junction with Gen. Custer."[3]

Maguire did not explain the preliminaries. Weeks earlier, Gibbon had marched east from Fort Ellis, Montana, with almost 500 men of the 7th Infantry and 2nd Cavalry. He had met Terry and Custer on the steamboat *Far West* on the Yellowstone on June 21. Terry outlined a classic hammer-and-anvil operation, often used by the U.S. Army against guerrillas and raiders. Custer was to march south with the 7th Cavalry, up the Rosebud valley, find the Lakota and Northern Cheyenne trail and follow it west, toward the Little Bighorn, then drive north, attacking any villages he found from the south. Terry wanted Custer to drive the surviving Lakotas toward Gibbon, who would march up the Little Bighorn (i.e., south from the Yellowstone) with his slower-moving foot soldiers. On June 22 Custer had set out with a stripped-down column of all twelve companies of his regiment, taking no sabers, Gatling guns, or wagons, packing all supplies on mules. Terry and Gibbon proceeded south at an easy pace.[4]

"When did you arrive there?" Lee asked, referring to the battlefield.

"At about 10 o'clock on the morning of the 27th of June, 1876," Maguire responded. He described the valley of the Little Bighorn: "There was a river bottom proper, which is timbered and is very narrow. . . . Then comes the first bench, which is treeless, an open grassy plain." (This dry "bench" was described by most of the troops as the river "bottom.") Beyond that, Maguire added, came slopes and bluffs, and then the broad prairie. "When we arrived the ground was strewn with saddles, camp kettles, and things the Indians had left. . . . The ground was covered with tracks."

Lee's questions broke Maguire's account of Terry's arrival into disordered fragments. Restored to chronological sequence, they narrate Terry's discovery of the Little Bighorn battlefield on June 27. "The first two officers I saw were lieutenants [George] Wallace and [Luther] Hare. They were riding rapidly towards us." They guided Maguire to "the position which Major Reno occupied . . . on the bluff across the river on the opposite side. They were, I should say, from 80 to 90 feet high. . . . Gen. Terry and the rest of them rode up. There were shouts and there were enlisted men and also officers crying. That is, some had tears rolling down their cheeks, and others showed it in their voices. They were talking rapidly and excitedly about the affair."

Four and a half miles down the river, "we found dead bodies in a circle around the crest of a little hill and quite a number of empty shells. . . . There were empty shells lying all around and the marks of ponies or horses having been ridden all around." There were corpses scattered and clustered in this general area. Maguire found a ford nearby. "My theory was that Gen. Custer went to the ford and was met there and driven back, and they separated into two bodies." He provided a rough map.

Maguire's words evoked powerful images: the ghost of a vast Indian village; Reno's demoralized, exhausted cluster of soldiers atop a high bluff; and down the river the horror of bodies and shell casings—"government shells, and Winchester shells, and one peculiar brass shell . . . which was supposed to belong to Gen. Custer's pistol," one of his two English Webley revolvers. What Maguire could not describe was the battle.[5]

WHEN THE COURT finished with Maguire, it accommodated rising public interest by moving to room 229 in the Palmer House, which could hold 100 people. On January 15, Reno and his counsel sat with their backs to a window as tables were arranged into a T. The witness and recorder sat facing each other at the bottom, the stenographer sat next to them, and the judges were aligned in a row across the top.

Lee called 1st Lt. George D. Wallace, one of the two officers who rode out to meet Terry and Gibbon's column. The *Chicago Times* observed that Wallace was "the second lieutenant of Company G of the 7th Cavalry at the time of the battle on the Little Big Horn. . . . He is a tall young fellow, with considerable of the military dash about him." He would be the first to speak of how the disaster unfolded.[6]

Lee began by asking his role at the time. "I was acting engineer officer with Gen. Custer's column," Wallace replied.[7]

Having elicited a description of the battlefield and aftermath from Maguire, Lee asked Wallace to begin with Custer's approach to the Lakota and Cheyenne village, the morning before the fighting began. "On the 25th day of June, 1876, what were the indications, if any, of the proximity of hostile Indians?"

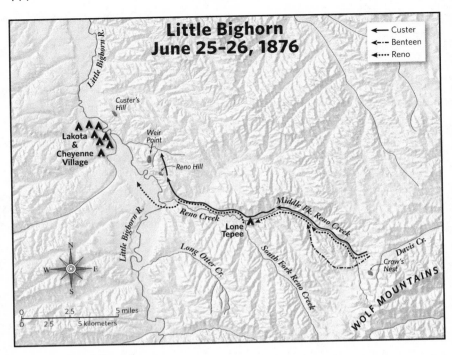

"All signs, and the reports of our Indian scouts, indicated that they were within 20 or 25 miles of us."

"Please state to the court what disposition or separation, if any, Gen. Custer made of his command preparatory to his proposed advance on the hostile Indian village."

"About a quarter after 12 o'clock, the command was halted. Three companies were given to Major Reno, three companies were given to Capt. Benteen, and one company to Capt. [Thomas] McDougall, who was placed in charge of the pack train, and General Custer took the other five companies with him." Wallace estimated that Reno had 110 men, Benteen had a slightly larger force, and Custer had 225 men. "Capt. Benteen with his battalion moved to the left. Gen. Custer moved down the right bank of a little stream with his command and Major Reno down the left bank." The stream, a tributary of the Little Bighorn, would be dubbed Reno's Creek after these events; the Lakotas called it Sundance Creek.

"After going ten or twelve miles, Major Reno was called across to the same side of the stream on which Gen. Custer was moving. The two battalions then moved along parallel to each other for some distance further. We passed [an isolated] tepee which had some dead bodies," Wallace explained, "and soon after passing that the adjutant came to Major Reno and said that the Indians were about two and a half miles ahead, and Major Reno was ordered forward as fast as he could go and to charge them and the others would support him."

A flurry of questions interrupted the narrative. Wallace said he didn't know where Benteen's column went, or what his orders were. Asked for the wording of Custer's order to Reno, he quoted from memory: "The Indians are about two miles and a half ahead, on the jump. Follow them as fast as you can and charge them wherever you find them and we will support you." Asked to describe Reno's force, he said, "There were 22 Indian scouts and three companies of cavalry averaging from 35 to 40 men. They had been marching for three or four days, making long marches. . . . The men were tired and the horses worn out."

"You have testified that Major Reno received on the 25th of June an order to charge the Indians. Please begin at that point," Lee directed.

"We moved at a gallop. After going some distance the trail led to the left [away from Custer's battalion and down to the river]. . . . We came to a ford on the Little Bighorn that had been used by the Indians," Wallace said. "After passing the ford . . . the command was halted and reformed. . . . The command [i.e., Reno's battalion] moved forward, first in a trot and then in a gallop." At this point they rode across the broad, open land of the river bottom—what Maguire called the first bench. "The Indians when the order was given were apparently running from us. There was a big dust, but as we moved on the dust cleared away, and the Indians were seen coming back." The troops approached a bend or hook in the river that extended partially in front of them. "There the command was halted, the men dismounted and prepared to fight on foot, the horses going in the timber and the three companies then deployed as skirmishers [in a line across the river bottom]. . . . The Indians instead of pressing our front passed around to our left and opened a flank fire."

The winding river was on their right, lined with timber. The Indians rode around their open left flank and into their rear. The exposed troops on the left retreated into the timber, swinging the line back like a door. Wallace claimed that they ran low on ammunition. "After waiting there some time, word was passed down that we would have to charge them. We were being surrounded, no assistance had come, and we would have to get on higher ground. . . . The companies were mounted and commenced getting out."

Wallace hinted that Reno's "charge" was more like a panicked rout, every man racing for his life as the Lakotas and Cheyennes swirled around them. "At the creek [the enemy] halted and fired at the men as they crossed. They came over with the rear of the column, and one or two men were killed there." The troops forded the river and spurred their horses up to a bluff above. "After getting on top of the hill the command was halted and preparations were made to give them a stand-off," Wallace said. "Soon after it was reported that Capt. Benteen was coming up and we were joined by him. What passed between him and Major Reno I don't know. We were out of ammunition, one company had several wounded, and I could find but seven men of my company."

After a time the pack train arrived and the men replenished their ammunition. "We attempted to move on, but Capt. Moylan could not move his wounded. It took six men to carry one, and the Indians were coming up thicker, and we were compelled to fall back and took the position we occupied on the 25th and 26th." The men spent the night of the 25th digging in as best they could with tin cups and only three spades. Early on the 26th the Lakotas and Cheyennes opened fire, and kept up the siege throughout the second day. "Sometime near sunset we saw the Indian village moving off."

Wallace's account established the basic narrative of the battle, as experienced by Reno's battalion. Of course, Custer's movements remained unclear. Lee asked how many Indians they faced at the outset. "When we halted and went on the skirmish line, there were some two or three hundred Indians there, and they increased from that time till we got out of the bottom."

"What movements, if any, did the Indians make?"

"They were fighting in regular Indian style, riding up and down; some few on foot, and some few in the hills to the left passing around and coming in on our rear, filling the whole space in our rear. . . . Not a solid mass, but riding around, yelling and hooting and those within range were shooting." During the escape from the trees, he thought the enemy were "as thick as trees in an apple orchard or thicker. The men were moving in column of fours, and as they would come up to the Indians the Indians would give way and let them pass through and then fire on them. After the men passed through, if they saw a man was not using his pistol they would ride close to him and fire. . . . They would ride along with the men and shoot at them."

"State when you last saw Gen. Custer or his column," Lee directed.

"Soon after the order was given to move forward. He was moving to our right as we moved off at a gallop. He was moving at a slow trot. I did not see him again. I supposed he was following." Gilbert objected to the question, knowing Reno might be doomed by any evidence that his battalion was aware of Custer's movements, but he was overruled. Yet Wallace's testimony helped Reno. In fact, he probably lied. When Terry arrived on June 27, Wallace had said that he last saw Custer on a bluff across the river, headed toward the village, while Reno was still fighting in the river bottom.

Lee asked if anyone who retreated to the hill expressed "any solicitude or uneasiness" over the fate of Custer's force. "There was no uneasiness whatever. I heard a great deal of swearing about Gen. Custer running off and leaving us." Lee asked about the movement forward from the hill, "in the direction which proved to be toward Gen. Custer's battlefield." Wallace admitted that it had been initiated by Capt. Thomas Weir, not by Reno or Benteen. He could not explain why the advance was made if no one suspected Custer's location or knew that he had launched an attack.[8]

The next day, Wallace answered more questions. He approved of Reno's decision to retreat from the river-bottom timber to the hilltop refuge. Gilbert scarcely needed to cross-examine him, though he did induce Wallace to describe Terry's arrival on the morning of June 27, after the battle. They spotted a dust cloud in the distance, Wallace said, and scouts reported the approach of Terry and Gibbon. "I mounted my horse and rode down . . . and met Gen. Terry beyond the point where our skirmish line had fallen back." He told Terry that Reno, Benteen, and seven companies occupied a nearby hill, and described the battle. "When I got time I then asked him where Gen. Custer was, and received a reply that gave me to understand that they all had been killed."[9]

LEE CALLED HIS THIRD WITNESS, who presented a different view of these events. He was a drab-looking middle-aged man in a civilian suit with "short-cut hair and stiff beard," according to the press. His name was Frederic F. Gerard, translator for the Arikara scouts. "Mr. Girard [sic] has spent thirty-one years among the North American savages and has been the hero of many strange adventures," the *Chicago Times* wrote. Heading west at the age of sixteen, he had worked as an Indian trader and interpreter. In 1857, he told a reporter, he had stumbled into a Hunkpapa camp and faced certain death. Running Antelope, a friend he had cultivated over the years, rescued him. "He mounted our wagon and cried out in a loud tone, 'This is a fine day to die'—an Indian idiom meaning he was ready to lay down his life for his friends."[10]

On the stand, Gerard took the court even farther back than Wallace's account. At eleven o'clock in the evening on June 24th, he said, Custer told him to ride with him at the head of the column, along with the Arikara scouts Half-Yellow Face and Bloody Knife. Half an hour later they set out on an overnight march. Custer told Gerard "to be sure to have the

Indians follow the left-hand trail, no matter how small it might be—he didn't want any of the camps of the Sioux to escape him. He wanted to get them all together and drive them down to the Yellowstone."

Gerard relayed the instructions. Bloody Knife replied, "He needn't be so particular about the small camps; we'll get enough when we strike the big camp." Gerard recalled how Custer "asked me what number of Indians I thought we would have to fight. I told him it wouldn't be less than twenty-five hundred."

Custer worried that the Lakotas would learn of their approach. The scouts told him they could not cross the divide into the watershed of the Little Bighorn before daylight, and were certain to be discovered. So he pushed hard. They marched twelve miles that night, Gerard estimated, made coffee, advanced another five miles to the divide, then marched another dozen or so miles to the river. When Custer ordered Reno to launch his attack, he gave him the Arikara scouts, so Gerard went with Reno.

Gerard remembered passing the lodge with corpses inside. (He referred to "lodges," plural; there appear to have been two, one of which had collapsed.) What no one realized at the time was that the bodies were casualties of a fierce fight on June 17, 1876, on the Rosebud. The Lakotas and Cheyennes had attacked a column led by General Crook. Casualties were light compared to a clash in the Civil War, but it had been a pitched battle, a rarity in Indian warfare. Though tactically indecisive, it was a resounding strategic victory for the Lakotas, and they knew it. They halted Crook's advance and induced him to retreat in search of ammunition and supplies. The funerary tepees sent a message that even Custer's Indian scouts could not understand, that the Lakotas and Cheyennes were more confident and belligerent than ever before.[11]

Near the lodges of the dead, Gerard recalled riding up a hill and spotting the Lakotas and their allies in the river bottom in a flurry of movement. He waved his hat at Custer and shouted, "Here are your Indians, running like devils!" The phrasing suggested that he saw them fleeing, which is precisely what Custer feared most. The high-plains nations always ran rather than expose their women and children to an attack like that at the Washita. But Gerard's impression changed as he descended to the river with Reno's command. "The scouts . . . called my attention to the fact that all the Indians were coming up the valley. I called Maj. Reno's attention to the fact," he testified. "I thought it was of importance enough that Gen. Custer should know of it, and I rode back toward Custer's command." Under cross-examination, Gerard later specified, "I knew that Gen. Custer was laboring under the impression that the Indians were running away, and if he knew they were coming to meet us I thought he would do something. I did not know what." He encountered Lt. William Cooke, Custer's adjutant, and said the Indians were riding to attack Reno's force. He replied, "All right, Gerard. I will go and report. You go on." He wheeled his horse around. Both Reno and Custer followed Indian trails, he recalled; Custer tracked the larger one, veering to the right.[12]

Gerard crossed the river and followed Reno's battalion to the timber where the horses of the dismounted skirmishers were being held. Just short of the trees, he encountered Bloody Knife, a legendary white scout named Charley Reynolds, and some others. Gerard counted Reynolds as perhaps his closest friend, and he had never seen him like this. Twice on the march, Gerard later explained under cross-examination, Reynolds had "told me he had a presentiment of his death—that he would never return from that expedition." He had asked Terry to be excused, but "Gen. Terry shamed him out of it." Here, Gerard continued, near the largest Lakota village the army had ever encountered, "he asked me if I had any whisky. He said he never felt so in all the days of his life, and he felt depressed and discouraged, and he thought it would be well to have something to stimulate him, and I gave him some. . . . I took a little myself."

Gerard and Reynolds joined Reno's skirmish line and opened fire. Then the two men decided to tie up their horses in the timber. As they did so, the skirmish line suddenly collapsed, rotating and falling back into the trees. Bullets began to strike home. Though Gerard did not see it, Bloody Knife—Custer's most trusted scout—took a round to the skull directly in front of Reno, spattering the major with his brains. Gerard heard, "Men! To our horses! The Indians are in our rear!"

"Charley Reynolds looked at me and I said, 'What damn-fool move is this?'"

"I don't know," Reynolds replied. "We will have to go. We will have to get out of here." Reynolds mounted his horse and whipped it ahead as Gerard led his own animal on foot. "As I saw Mr. Reynolds just then, I saw several Indians cut him off and shoot him down, and he fell. . . . I knew I was discovered and I turned my horse . . . and hunted a place where I could defend myself." He returned to the trees to hide or fight.[13]

The court adjourned and reassembled the next day, January 18. Gerard took his seat once again in that elegant hotel room in Chicago, and tried to describe to the officers in their dress uniforms and the decorous civilians the chaotic escape of Reno's battalion from the river-bottom trees, the panicked race through the swirling current of Lakota horsemen, who shouted in triumph as they rode alongside the troops and gunned them down like so many stampeding buffalo. "The troops I saw in the timber were in a great hurry to get off. There seemed to be no order at all. Every man was for himself." Rather than risk death in the open, Gerard hid in the trees until dark.

As he waited for nightfall, he heard another fight erupt. "I could see Indians going up these ravines on the right-hand [far] side of the stream"—that is, on Custer's side of the Little Bighorn. "I could hear the firing as though they were firing at troops going up there. I knew there was some troops going by, because I had seen them. . . . There was a continuous firing all the time." He could hear the fighting across the river move downstream, toward the village, "scattering shots, sometimes three or four, . . . and when it got down below there, where Custer's battlefield was, it became heavy."

"How long did that general firing last?"

"I should judge it to be about two hours." It died down to scattered shots, one or two at a time. "It is customary with Indians, even if they find an enemy that has been killed two or three days, in riding by they will be pretty apt to put a shot into him as he lies there."

Lee asked if Reno could have held the timber, from which point his battalion might have threatened the village and directly supported Custer's attack. "Yes, sir, I think they could have held out against the whole number of Indians as long as their ammunition and provisions would have lasted—that is, resolute, determined men." Gerard had already established that Reno's men were the opposite of resolute. Despite a fierce cross-examination on January 20, Gerard stood by his testimony.[14]

IN AN INSIGHTFUL account of the hearing, James Donovan notes that the officers of the 7th Cavalry were reluctant to impugn Reno, as demonstrated by Wallace's apparent perjury. Yet points against him added up. Gerard and Lt. Charles Varnum both testified to seeing Custer across the river riding to the attack, contradicting Reno's claim that he had no idea where Custer went. The major clearly had not executed his orders to charge the village; his only "charge" had been a panicked retreat. The civilian packers John Frett and B. F. Churchill described Reno as drunk. More than likely he was.

Reno can only be described as troubled. His wife had died in 1874, deepening the isolation of a man who did not make friends easily. After the Little Bighorn disaster he got drunk and engaged in a fistfight at Fort Abraham Lincoln, and nearly faced charges. He was assigned to remote Fort Abercrombie, where he sexually assaulted the wife of an officer while the husband was away. Her resistance prompted him to take revenge by slandering her. In 1877, Reno was court-martialed and convicted of conduct unbecoming an officer, and was sentenced to dismissal. President Rutherford B. Hayes commuted his punishment to a two-year suspension. But then came Frederick Whittaker's campaign against him. Whittaker had published an admiring biography of Custer with the support of Libbie, who gave him access to private correspondence. He blamed Reno for Custer's death. Reno's fragile career could not survive this hammering. He saw little choice but to ask for an investigation to clear his name.[15]

Leaving aside Reno's guilt, the testimony so far established the basic outline of the battle, and some of the key officers' motives. Custer feared the Lakotas would escape. Anticipating an archipelago of encampments, he wanted to catch them all and drive their inhabitants down the Little Bighorn toward Gibbon. He sent Reno with a smaller battalion to follow a smaller trail into the upper valley, and he followed the larger trail with a larger detachment toward the lower valley. Reno halted his attack to dismount his men; outflanked and outnumbered, he and his troops broke for the rear. They found refuge on a hilltop, where Benteen and the pack train joined them.

The court never learned precisely what maneuvers Custer made, but Gerard's auditory observations revealed them in general terms. He advanced on the opposite side of the river from Reno in the face of increasing resistance. He came under an immense attack as Lakota and Cheyenne warriors returned from fighting Reno. The assault eventually overran his column, killing Custer and all of the men with him.

When General Terry arrived, he found the dead in clusters—different groups that were shot down as they rode or ran or made their separate last stands. He found George Armstrong Custer's body atop a hill, grouped with his brother Tom, his old friend George Yates, Cooke, and two other officers, amid the corpses of thirty-nine horses they had shot to improvise fortifications. Forty-nine troops were killed just down the slope. They located Custer's brother Boston and nephew Autie Reed together, about 100 yards away. The bodies were almost all mutilated, especially that of Tom Custer, which was missing its eyes, tongue, genitals, and scalp; Tom's skull had been thoroughly crushed, almost everything else lacerated. But Armstrong's corpse survived almost intact. One bullet had struck him in the chest, another in the left temple. He was found stripped naked, reclining against two corpses, his thigh cut (a Lakota tradition), his penis stabbed with an arrow, but his scalp intact. Spent cartridges surrounded him.[16]

Two other divisions of the 7th Cavalry remain to be accounted for: Capt. Frederick Benteen's battalion and the pack train. Grave historical questions hover over them: Did Benteen do all he could to support Custer? Could he have saved him? Did he follow his orders? Or did his personal hatred affect his actions?

Benteen did not answer directly, but he did take the stand in the court of inquiry. His testimony established one thing for certain: it is possible to sneer continuously for days at a time. He appeared in the full flower of his petty arrogance, steeped in an embittered subordinate's nitpicking resentfulness and a pervasive disdain for Custer.

On the eighteenth day of the inquiry, February 1, 1879, Lee asked Benteen to describe the orders to break the regiment into battalions. Oddly, this deceptively soft-faced man began at a point in the events just after Custer returned from the Crow's Nest, an observation point on a peak used by the Crows in their war with the Lakotas. "General Custer told us that he had just come down from the mountain, that he had been told by the scouts that they could see a village, ponies, tepees, and smoke. He gave it to us as his belief that they were mistaken, that there were no Indians there, that he had looked through his glass and could not see any and did not see any there."

Benteen's recollection was wrong. Custer had difficulty spotting the Lakotas, but he believed that Indians had sharper senses and did not doubt them. Benteen's version made no sense. Everything Custer did thereafter proved that he believed the Lakotas were in the Little Bighorn valley; nothing indicated any doubts. Eager to cast Custer as a fool, Benteen twisted his words to make him solely responsible for his own death.

This recollection set a pattern. He derided Custer's every order, coloring each one as foolhardy, as picayune, wrongheaded interference with Benteen's affairs. Custer reasonably asked his company commanders to be sure each had detailed seven men to escort the pack train and that each trooper carried 100 rounds of carbine ammunition; Benteen depicted it as an absurdity that he executed for "formality's sake."

"Describe where it was that you separated from General Custer's column," Lee directed Benteen. "What orders did you receive . . . ?"

"My orders were to proceed out into a line of bluffs about 4 or 5 miles away, to pitch into anything I came across, and to send back word to General Custer at once if I came across anything." He said further messages directed him to search beyond the first and second lines of bluffs. "I forgot to give some instructions of General Custer's which were that I was to send an officer and about six men in advance of my battalion and to ride rapidly." In other words, Custer wanted Benteen to send out scouts so the captain could remain in communication with him. Typically, Benteen ignored the intent of the orders and rode *ahead* of his own scouts.

On cross-examination, he told Gilbert his orders amounted to "valley hunting ad infinitum." Lee followed up, asking about the phrase. "That is the way I understood it," Benteen said. "I understood it as a rather senseless order. We were on the main trail of the Indians. There were plenty of them on that trail. . . . It was scarcely worth hunting up any more. . . . Why I was sent to the left I don't know."

But this elaboration came after Benteen's original narrative, which continued. "As there were no Indians there and no valleys I thought my duty was to go back to the trail and join the command." He reached the tepees with the corpses; the erect lodge now stood aflame. "A mile or so from that tepee I met a sergeant coming back with instructions to the commanding officer of the pack trains to bring up the packs. I told him the pack train I thought was about 7 miles back and he could take the order back as I had nothing to do with that." Resentful of any imposition, he declined to take any responsibility beyond his official sphere, despite the importance of the order. "About a mile after that I met trumpeter [John] Martin who brought a written order. . . . It says: 'Benteen. Come on. Big Village. Be Quick. Bring Packs. W. W. Cooke P. bring pacs.'"[17]

It was an unequivocal, positive command to join Custer, and an insistent demand for ammunition and supplies. The order was in keeping with Custer's tactics that day; he divided his regiment for a reconnaissance in force, apparently intending to consolidate upon contact with the enemy. But Benteen moved without urgency, and declined to hurry along the pack train. He did not go in search of Custer, though his commander's battalion left a clear trail toward the right bank of the river, along with the main Lakota trail that Benteen himself stressed was so critically important.

In the witness chair, he made contradictory excuses for his refusal to follow Custer's clear instructions. First he said that Martin (an Italian immigrant with imperfect English) told him the Indians were "skedaddling" and there was "less necessity" to bring up the pack train—implying that the trumpeter's personal impression outweighed an emphatic written order. Then he excused himself by saying that he saw Reno's retreat from the river bottom. "I thought the whole command was thrashed and that was not a good place to come. I saw the men who were up on the bluff and I immediately went there and was met by Maj. Reno." He said he showed Reno the order. "I asked him if he knew where General Custer was. He said he did not."

Lee asked Benteen if he had asked Reno for permission to go in search of Custer, or to his aid. He replied with his third excuse. "Not at all. I supposed General Custer was able to take care of himself." Then came a fourth excuse, contradicting the third. "I think now there were between 8 and 9 thousand" hostile warriors, he claimed, a number wildly beyond all other estimates. "I wish to say before that order"—the one delivered by Martin—"that I believe that General Custer and his whole command were dead." Putting all four excuses together, Benteen claimed that he believed that Custer was perfectly safe and that he was dead; that the Lakotas were running away and that they had smashed the regiment. He never suggested the most likely explanation: that in his petty, self-absorbed spite against his commanding officer, he seized the first available pretense to avoid helping him or the hundreds of men with him. He even derided the movement from the bluff in search of Custer, initiated by Captain Weir, as "a fit of bravado without orders."[18]

After his testimony, Benteen wrote to a friend, "I was close mouthed as I could be, or my testimony might possibly looked like a too high flying of my own kite. . . . I almost regretted I was not allowed to turn loose on Custer, tho' Qui Bono [sic]?" It is true that Benteen effectively took command from Reno of the troops cornered on the bluff, where he displayed true bravery and a sure hand. This portrait of a cool leader in a desperate siege colored the public's impression of his testimony. Yet it is striking that Benteen, who loathed Custer for purportedly abandoning Maj. Joel Elliott and seventeen men at the Washita, should so lightly excuse his own abandonment of ten times as many troops. Could his and Reno's combined battalions have reached Custer, let alone rescued him? No one can ever know. What is certain is that they never tried.[19]

AFTER TWENTY-SIX DAYS, the court of inquiry exonerated Reno. Judge Advocate General William M. Dunn agreed. In his official review of the inquiry, he wrote, "The object of Gen. Custer in detaching Maj. Reno is shown to have been to attack the Indians simultaneously on opposite sides of their encampment or village. Their number appears to have been far greater than Gen. Custer imagined, and very far in excess of the force under his command."[20]

It is difficult to improve upon that conclusion. Reno may have been drunk; he may have been cowardly; Benteen may have been insubordinate; yet the most important facts were the superior numbers of Lakotas and Cheyennes and their unprecedented willingness to stand and fight. Believing that his primary problem would be preventing the escape of satellite camps from his net, Custer made a grave tactical error in dividing his force, exposing it to destruction in detail. It was fatal, but understandable. No one in the army expected him to encounter such a huge and determined hostile force. When Sherman learned of the disaster, he said, "I can't believe that Custer and his whole command would be swept away. I don't think there were enough Indians there to do it like this."[21]

To be sure, this brief, fragmented sketch provides nothing close to a complete portrait of the battle. It was a complex event that hundreds of experts have examined in minute detail. But the obvious answer is often the right one, and in this case it is the moral and numerical superiority of the Cheyennes and Lakotas, who fought with great skill as well as courage. If Reno had proved braver and more capable, Benteen more trustworthy, or Custer less imaginative—launching a straight-on attack with the entire regiment—probably the most that could have been accomplished would have been a tactical standoff like Crook's battle on the Rosebud, or a different kind of defeat. But Custer might have survived.[22]

Immediately after the battle, the military and much of the public concluded that it was Custer's fault. Colonel Samuel Sturgis, who lost his son, an officer in the 7th Cavalry, railed against him. An unnamed "officer of distinction" at a Civil War reunion in Philadelphia told a reporter, "Custer threw his command away by an act of bravado."

Fittingly, the press split over Custer along partisan and regional lines, according to the scholar James E. Mueller. Republican newspapers echoed the *Chicago Daily News,* which claimed that he defied Terry's instructions, running such headlines as, "DISOBEDIENCE OF ORDERS—A FATAL BLUNDER." To the champions of progress, this romantic, archaic individualist brought doom down on himself and his men. The *New York World* and other Democratic journals praised him as a noble hero and blamed Grant's policies for his death. "Custer's most passionate defenders were the Southern newspapers, especially those in Kentucky and Texas, where Custer had served on Reconstruction duty," Mueller writes. Custer had done his best to obstruct Reconstruction there; he would have been pleased at the local white support.

But Custer as glory-obsessed, arrogant fool emerged as the persistent narrative. It prevailed just after his death, receded for many years, then rose again, predominating in the present day. Emmanuel Custer protested in vain. "They should not have said so," he said. "He fought to whip and not for praise. He was not reckless. He had much to live for, and he would not throw his life away. No, no. They wrong my dead boy. They shouldn't say so."[23]

The popular narrative contains some truth about every aspect of Custer's life *except* his performance in battle—the one field in which he displayed consistent good judgment and self-possession. From the Civil War through his two battles on the Yellowstone, he proved decisive, not reckless; shrewd, not foolish. In every other regard, he danced along the emerging modern world, unable to adapt to it. He failed in the new sphere of finance, rejected new thinking about equality, and wrote antiquated prose. He offended his military superiors, mismanaged subordinates, alienated civilian authorities, meddled inappropriately in politics, endangered his marriage, and gambled away his estate. Again and again he saved himself through his ability to fight. And yet, ironically, we now remember him as a bad commander.

The last word about the Little Bighorn belongs to perhaps Custer's most insightful chronicler, Robert Utley. "The simplest answer, usually overlooked, is that the army lost largely because the Indians won," he writes. "To ascribe defeat entirely to military failings is to devalue Indian strength and leadership." The invasion of the Black Hills and the order to abandon the unceded lands galvanized the Lakotas and Northern Cheyennes. Inspired by Sitting Bull and Crazy Horse, they gathered in a huge village on the Little Bighorn. They could not remain together long: their vast pony herds consumed the nearby grazing, campsites became polluted, and demand for food forced them to spread out and hunt in smaller bands. Sheridan feared that the Lakotas would disperse before Custer reached them; it was Custer's bad luck that they did not.[24]

Soon after the victory, they did break into smaller bands. For them, the Little Bighorn turned out to be a turning point for the worst. Crook attacked them again, and over the winter they faced the dogged pursuit of Custer's old friend, Col. Nelson Miles. Continual military pressure wore them down and prevented them from hunting and sustaining themselves. Over the next year most of the nomadic bands gave themselves up. Crazy Horse was killed on the reservation in 1877. Sitting Bull fled to Canada; he returned in 1881 and surrendered to the federal authorities. He was killed by reservation police in 1890, shortly before the massacre at Wounded Knee.[25]

Contrary to white expectations, the indigenous nations did not go extinct. The Cheyennes, Lakotas, Arapahoes, Kiowas, Comanches, and others still survive, as do such former foes as the Crows, Arikaras, Pawnees, and Osages, and the many peoples whose histories did not intersect Custer's life. They now endure incessant cultural appropriation by a majority society in the United States that celebrates an idealized American Indian but ignores reservation life—the economic blight and marginalization of what are, in effect, national internment zones, exacerbated by federal inattention and mismanagement. In Indian country there are also thriving cultural traditions and creative genius, but these often receive little more recognition than the problems.

ON OCTOBER 24, 1885, IN Athens, Ohio, a roughly forty-year-old black woman composed a letter to Elizabeth Bacon Custer. She could write, after a fashion, but appears to have dictated the note to someone capable of better spelling and penmanship. "I receive your kind and welcom card and my heart leaps for joy to think that I have heard from you once more," she said. "The card has brought back to me memery of many places we have been together and its make me feel as if I must see you. and have a talk with you. I have often pray to the Lord to spar me till I could see you once more. I have change very much since I saw you." Her hair was turning gray, her health declined, but she had a good home and a "very good husband." Her son John sent his love as well, she wrote.[26]

Her name was Eliza Brown Davison. She had thoroughly reconstructed her existence since the day she stormed out of the Custers' lives—or was thrown out, accused by Libbie of being "insolent." She had a good life, one that spoke to the future of American society. Her husband was Andrew J. Davison, a prominent black attorney in Ohio and a sought-after public speaker—a level of professional attainment scarcely imaginable for an African American before the Civil War. The revolution in race relations had been slowed, even reversed in the South, but had not been erased.

The card from Libbie reminded her that she carried her extraordinary history within her still. Eliza wrote again to Libbie in her own hand, in March 1886 and on June 6. "My Dear friend, i rite you a few Lines to Let you [know] i am Well and reSived the Book all rite an i am very proud to get the the Book i could not help Shedding teers When i reSived the Book thinking of the Times that has past and gone."[27]

Libbie's decade between the Little Bighorn and her correspondence with Eliza had been hard. The loss of a spouse can be shattering, but Libbie's pain had been compounded again and again. There was the violence of Armstrong's death; the newspaper stories and comments by army officers that blamed her husband for the disaster (even President Grant faulted him); the annihilation of two of Custer's brothers and his nephew and namesake; and the death of the husbands of Maggie Custer Calhoun, Annie Roberts Yates, and other women in her circle.

And then there were the debts. The first inventory of Armstrong's estate assessed the total value at $2,140. Adding in 116.4 acres on the Raisin River that Armstrong had shared with his sole surviving brother, Nevin, the tally came to $2,790.15. The liabilities, including a $2,000 mortgage on the real estate, came to $4,372.28. She received a federal pension of only $30 per month; an attempt to increase her benefit failed in Congress. The *Army and Navy Journal* raised $13,800 for the widows of the 7th Cavalry, out of which $900 went to Libbie. She also received a claim of $4,750 from New York Life—only after a struggle, since Armstrong missed his final premium payment.

Now, at the worst possible moment, Libbie learned of Armstrong's financial betrayal—his gambling on the stock market. Emil Justh presented his $8,500 promissory note for payment. With interest, the debt came to $9,260. She finally settled her debts, paying Justh ten cents on the dollar. (Victimized by a fraud, the hard-pressed Justh filed a revealing lawsuit against note cosigner Ben Holladay, to biographers' delight.)[28]

She struggled. She refused a federal post, angry at Grant's treatment of her husband. She took a job as secretary for the Society of Decorative Arts in New York, and moved to Manhattan. She publicly criticized a statue of Armstrong at West Point; it was taken down. Eventually her finances improved. She received an inheritance when her mother-in-law passed away in 1882, and Congress raised her monthly pension to $50. She left her secretarial job to write the first volume of her memoirs. Even then trouble followed her. Fire ravaged the apartment she shared with Maggie Custer Calhoun; her husband's letters survived, locked inside an iron safe.

In 1885 Harper and Brothers published her book, *"Boots and Saddles," or Life in Dakota with General Custer.* Written with the self-deprecating, feminine charm she had practiced over the years, it narrated her last years with Armstrong. She wrote with skill, evoking the drama of a blizzard or a fire, paying particular attention to their domestic existence. The press liked it, and so did readers. Ironies mushroomed around her germinating career: Her husband's death freed her to become a public figure in her own right—freed her to be an author—yet her husband remained her main subject. She started to write for newspapers, and planned another autobiographical volume. Her return to her past led her to seek out Eliza Brown (now Davison) and mail her a copy of her book.[29]

In the fall of 1886, Eliza came to see Libbie in New York. Together the two women peered into history, and into the future that was emerging in Manhattan. At Eliza's insistence, they went to see the Fifth Avenue Hotel. She recalled how Armstrong had taken them all there. Libbie wrote, "We went through the halls and drawing-rooms, narrowly watched by the major-domo, who stands guard over tramps"—and, she might have added, over well-dressed black visitors. They visited the Brooklyn Bridge, the newly erected Statue of Liberty, the elevated railroad. Eliza attended Buffalo Bill's Wild West Show—without Libbie—and called on the star himself with Libbie's card to introduce herself. "They had twenty subjects in common; for Eliza, in her way, was as deserving of praise as was the courageous Cody," Libbie wrote.

The two women, white and black, walked together like equals through the streets of New York. "Miss Libbie, you don't take notice . . . how the folks does stare at us," Eliza commented, as Libbie recalled. "But I see 'em a-gazin', and I can see 'em a-ponderin' and sayin' to theirsels', 'Well, I do declare! That's a lady, there ain't no manner of doubt. She's one of the bong tong. But whatever she's a-doin' with that old scrub nigger, I can't make out.'"

In Libbie's next memoir, *Tenting on the Plains*, she wrote of Eliza's visit to New York, how they reminisced about their dramatic history and the long-lost Armstrong. Libbie described her "delight" at going out with Eliza, at "her unique criticisms" and "manner in which she brought back our past." But she did not reflect on how different it all looked to Eliza. Her former servant did not characterize *herself* as an "old scrub nigger," but rather described how white people saw her, even though she dressed as the wife of a prominent lawyer. Libbie heard it as praise for herself for indulging a social inferior, but Eliza actually commented on the shock of white Manhattanites at a black woman asserting her equality with a white woman.

Graying, ailing, and overweight, Eliza understood better than Libbie how the world had changed. In many ways, she better understood the past as well. Eliza's memories helped make *Tenting on the Plains* Libbie's most vivid and compelling book (published in 1887, followed by *Following the Guidon* in 1890). The young black woman emerges as a central character in that volume, vivid, resourceful, and admirable; yet Libbie's racial condescension starkly colors the account. At times she veers from respect for Eliza to undermining or even scorning her, as if she were still struggling with her for domestic power, retroactively extracting a small degree of literary revenge for how Eliza outmaneuvered her in life. The book offers a glimpse of the America Brown knew, but no more. Most of it remained invisible to Libbie. Eliza gave her a subtle reminder in New York, saying, "I done took the colored part of town fo' I come; the white folks ain't seen what I has." She spoke a universal truth. The white folks never knew what they were missing.

And yet, in strolls down Broadway and Fifth Avenue, a decade after Armstrong's death, the joy of reunion dominated their time together. They had been through so much; they had lost so much. Eliza remembered little Johnny Cisco, the homeless white boy adopted by Custer as his informal valet during the Civil War; he had resurfaced in Kansas and obtained a job in the express business with Custer's help, only to die in the wilderness. His loss devastated Eliza, who carried his battered suitcase long afterward. But if their reunion called up their ghosts, it dispelled them as well. Eliza exclaimed, "Oh, *what* a good time me and you is having, Miss Libbie, and *how* I will 'stonish them people at home!"[30]

Eliza Brown Davison returned to Ohio, and Elizabeth Bacon Custer remained in New York. She became the archetype of the professional widow, never remarrying, fighting to the end to maintain an idealized public image of her late husband. He had put her through so much conflict and hardship, yet he had loved her fiercely. He had lifted her out of the ordinary, and she never returned. But she sustained herself with her own intelligence and effort. She prospered with her writings and lectures about military families on the Western frontier. She invested wisely in real estate in the developing Westchester suburb of Bronxville. Her biographer Shirley Leckie observes that she managed her money far better than her father or husband ever had. She died on April 4, 1933, on Park Avenue.[31]

It's fitting that she lived out her life in New York. When given a choice, Custer had always picked the footlights over a campfire, Broadway over the open plains, much as he sincerely loved the latter. Young men might go West, but Manhattan forged the corporate, technological future. Its vitality and promise drew Custer to it, yet he never mastered it. His sudden, offstage ending left him suspended forever between East and West, past and future, to be misremembered as needed by each new generation.

Acknowledgments

IN MY LAST BOOK, I wrote that I believed in researching in terror, writing with confidence, and publishing with humility. That was in a work about a subject who left behind no collection of papers and had not received a serious biography in nearly seventy years. Custer, on the other hand, is one of the best-documented and most-discussed individuals of the nineteenth century. In addition to the mountain ranges of papers in the public archives, unknown masses lurk in private hands, inaccessible to researchers. That makes for a lot of terror, for I did not see every source. I've done my best to write a strong, confident narrative, but Custer makes humility imperative. How many gifted writers and scholars have told his story, in pieces or in full? How many researchers know the most minute details and obscure documents? Authors inevitably make mistakes; with this subject, an unusually large number of readers will notice them. I have found some sources and stories that should be new to *most* people familiar with this subject, but I would not dare say *all*. Trying to say something truly original about Custer is rather like trying to cross the main floor of Grand Central Terminal by walking only where no one has stepped before. The freshness of this work ultimately must be found in the cumulative effect—the change in emphasis and perspective—rather than undiscovered facts or sources.

First I must thank the John Simon Guggenheim Memorial Foundation for the generous support of a fellowship that contributed greatly to my ability to complete this book. My thanks to Ethan Nosowsky of Graywolf Press for his encouragement to apply one more time. I offer my gratitude to the Pulitzer Prize Board and the National Book Foundation for the generous awards that came with the recognition given to my last book, which helped to sustain me while working on this one.

I have benefited from the advice and friendship of some of the finest authorities not only on George Armstrong Custer, but on American history. I must thank the historian Shirley Leckie first. As I worked on my book, poring over primary sources, my admiration for her biography of Elizabeth Bacon Custer only grew. She graciously—and I do mean *graciously*—read and commented on my unedited, overlarge chapters as I wrote them. With similar generosity, Heather Cox Richardson read chapters that I lobbed at her, even though she was finishing a book of her own, and offered detailed feedback that improved the manuscript tremendously. The great Robert Utley walked me through some of the issues of Custeriana, shared notes and sources with me, and reviewed the manuscript, offering very helpful suggestions. Mr. Utley has created a profoundly important body of work on the nineteenth-century West, and deserves his status as the most sensible and best-informed scholar of Custer and the history surrounding his frontier career. I find it very difficult to improve upon his characterization of Custer's personality and actions. Paul Hutton, Andrew Graybill, and Robert Bonner also generously read the manuscript and offered suggestions. In addition, Maury Klein and Christopher Phillips offered advice on specific chapters. In correspondence or conversation, Nancy Isenberg and Drew Gilpin Faust suggested reading and avenues to explore. I am grateful to them all.

I believe in conducting research myself, but for a few missions that just weren't cost-effective for me to execute personally, I received some very professional assistance from Carrie Millington and Marie Killmond. Thanks to all the archivists and librarians who supported my research, including those at the Library of Congress, National Archives, the United States Military Academy, the New York Public Library, Brigham Young University, the Virginia Historical Society, the State Historical Society of Iowa, the State Historical Society of Kansas, the Minnesota Historical Society, the Newberry Library, the Monroe County Historical Museum and Archives, the Monroe County Library System, the Denver Public Library, the San Francisco Public Library, the Berkeley Public Library, the Bancroft Library of the University of California, Berkeley, the Old Records Division of the New York County Clerk's Office, and the U.S. Army Military History Institute in Carlisle, Pennsylvania.

Of the many archivists and librarians who helped me, a few deserve mention by name. David Ferriero, Archivist of the United States, has been a friend since his days at the New York Public Library; he pointed me to a few key professionals in his organization who were tremendously helpful, including Trevor Plante. Richard L. Baker, senior technical information specialist at the U.S. Army Military History Institute, went far out of his way to help me obtain copies of the Jacob Greene papers, still undergoing processing. Christine Bradley of Clear Creek County, Colorado, helped me find that there was nothing to find in her county's legal records—a critical if unsung part of the research process. Chris Kull at the Monroe County Historical Museum and Archives and Charmaine Wawrzyniec of the Monroe County Library System in Monroe, Michigan, both provided tremendous assistance, as did Cindy Hagen of the National Park Service. And William Stingone, the Charles J. Liebman Curator of Manuscripts at the New York Public Library, once again proved enormously helpful in my research.

Thanks also to the members of the San Francisco Writers Grotto, a marvelous community where I maintained an office for part of the time I spent writing this book, and where I have found friendship, advice, and support. Thanks also to Jane Ganahl and Jack Boulware and the volunteers of Litquake.

I am extremely fortunate to have a long-standing relationship with one of the best editors in the business, at a publishing house committed to literary values. The brilliant Jonathan Segal took a chance on my first book, *Jesse James: Last Rebel of the Civil War*, some fifteen years ago, and we have worked together ever since. The faults of this book are my own, but its strengths owe a great deal to his literary guidance, as well as his support during the long process of research and writing. I owe him a great debt. My thanks to the staff of Alfred A. Knopf and Vintage, who have developed and supported my work so effectively. There is a lot of blather about how publishers are unnecessary these days; obviously the people making these arguments were never published by Knopf and Vintage. Few know how much these unrecognized professionals add to the value of a finished book. I also thank my agent, Jill Grinberg, a friend and effective advocate who has worked to advance my writing career from its beginning.

I have been very fortunate to serve on the board of the Authors Guild, and I wish to thank my fellow board members, President Roxana Robinson, former president Scott Turow, general counsel Jan Constantine, former executive director Paul Aiken, the new executive director Mary Rasenberger, and most of all my fellow rank-and-file members of the guild for their advocacy on behalf of authors and books.

My heartfelt gratitude goes to my family, particularly my wife, Jessica, my son, Dillon, and my daughter, Sasha, all three smart as hell, funny, and loving. They put up with my crazy schedule and extensive travel, and I am grateful. Thanks too to my parents, Dr. Cliff and Carol Stiles, who have always encouraged me to follow my dreams but not to slack off while I was at it. My mother-in-law, Susan McKenna, provided love and care for my children when Jessica and I had to be away. So did my father-in-law, Laurence Frank, who has been tremendously supportive. Thanks to them and all my extended family.

As I started to write this final paragraph, I learned that one of my mentors had just passed away. Richard Maxwell Brown died on September 22,

2014, at the age of eighty-seven. I read his work as a young employee of Oxford University Press, where I had landed, directionless, after abandoning an academic career amid personal turmoil. His systematic approach to violence in American history, particularly in the nineteenth-century West, restored my intellectual curiosity and eagerness to write history. He showed me that celebrated people and events can be taken seriously without merely debunking them—that new meaning and importance can be found in them, without falling into the condescension that scholars too often feel for all that is popular. That approach has driven all of my work. Professor Brown's enthusiastic support for the publication of my first book proved crucial to my getting my start as a biographer. His generosity never flagged in the years since; it kept me going through some difficult times. As important as he was to me as an intellectual and professional mentor, it was his decency and humanity that had the most profound impact on me. It was an honor simply to know him.

Notes

ABBREVIATIONS

B&L 1, 2, 3, 4   Robert Underwood Johnson and Clarence Clough Buel, eds., *Battles and Leaders of the Civil War*, vols. 1–4 (New York: Century Company, 1884–88).

Barnett   Louise Barnett, *Touched by Fire: The Life, Death, and Mythic Afterlife of George Armstrong Custer* (Lincoln: University of Nebraska Press, 2006 [orig. pub. 1996]).

Coffman   Edward M. Coffman, *The Old Army: A Portrait of the American Army in Peacetime, 1784–1898* (New York: Oxford University Press, 1986).

CRM   George Armstrong Custer Reference Microfilm, National Archives, Washington, D.C.

Cullum 1, 2, 3   George W. Cullum, *Biographical Register of the Officers and Graduates of the United States Military Academy at West Point, N.Y.*, vols. 1–3 (New York: D. Van Nostrand, 1868–1891).

DSB   Daniel S. Bacon

EBC   Elizabeth Bacon Custer

EBC, *Boots and Saddles*   Elizabeth B. Custer, *"Boots and Saddles," or Life in Dakota with General Custer* (New York: Harper and Brothers, 1885).

EBC, *Following the Guidon*   Elizabeth B. Custer, *Following the Guidon* (New York: Harper and Brothers, 1890).

EBC, *Tenting on the Plains*   Elizabeth B. Custer, *Tenting on the Plains, or General Custer in Kansas and Texas* (New York: Harper and Brothers, 1887).

Foner   Eric Foner, *Reconstruction: America's Unfinished Revolution, 1863–1877* (New York: Harper and Row, 1988).

Frost, *General Custer's Libbie*   Lawrence A. Frost, *General Custer's Libbie* (Seattle: Superior Publishing, 1976).

GAC   George Armstrong Custer

GBM   George Brinton McClellan

HED   House of Representatives Executive Document

HR   House of Representatives Report

LAFCC   Dr. Lawrence A. Frost Collection of Custeriana, Monroe County Historical Museum Archives, Monroe, Mich.

LAR   Lydia Ann Kirkpatrick Reed

LBH   Elizabeth Bacon Custer Collection, Little Bighorn National Battlefield, Microfilm: Roll 1, Elizabeth B. Custer Correspondence, George A. Custer Correspondence; Roll 2, Other Sources: Correspondence, Orders, Miscellaneous Documents; Roll 4, Elizabeth B. Custer Miscellaneous Manuscripts and Notes; Roll 5, Elizabeth B. Custer Literary Manuscripts and Notes; Roll 6, Broadsides, Clippings, and Memorabilia

LOC   Manuscripts Division, Library of Congress, Washington, D.C.

Leckie   Shirley A. Leckie, *Elizabeth Bacon Custer and the Making of a Myth* (Norman: University of Oklahoma Press, 1993).

McPherson   James M. McPherson, *Battle Cry of Freedom: The Civil War Era*

(New York: Oxford University Press, 1988).

MCHMA   Monroe County Historical Museum and Archives, Monroe, Mich.

MCLS   Monroe County Library System, Monroe, Mich.

Merington   Marguerite Merington, *The Custer Story: The Life and Intimate Letters of General George A. Custer and His Wife Elizabeth* (Lincoln: University of Nebraska Press, 1987 [orig. pub. 1950]).

MMP   Marguerite Merington Papers, Manuscripts and Archives Division, New York Public Library, Astor, Lenox, and Tilden Foundations

Monaghan   Jay Monaghan, *Custer: The Life of General George Armstrong Custer* (Lincoln: University of Nebraska Press, 1971 [orig. pub. 1959]).

NA   National Archives, Washington, D.C.

NA II   National Archives, College Park, Md.

OR   *The War of the Rebellion: A Compilation of the Official Records of the Union and Confederate Armies* (Washington, D.C.: Government Printing Office, 1880–1901).

PHS   Philip H. Sheridan

Reynolds   Arlene Reynolds, ed., *The Civil War Memories of Elizabeth Bacon Custer: Reconstructed from Her Diaries and Notes*

(Austin: University of Texas Press, 1994).

SED   Senate Executive Document

SR   Senate Report

Stiles, *First Tycoon*   T. J. Stiles, *The First Tycoon: The Epic Life of Cornelius Vanderbilt* (New York: Alfred A. Knopf, 2009).

Stiles, *Jesse James*   T. J. Stiles, *Jesse James: Last Rebel of the Civil War* (New York: Alfred A. Knopf, 2002).

Starr 1, 2   Stephen Z. Starr, *The Union Cavalry in the Civil War*, vols. 1 and 2 (Baton Rouge: Louisiana State University Press, 1979, 1981).

USMA   Special Collections and Archives, United States Military Academy, West Point, N.Y.

Utley, *Cavalier in Buckskin*   Robert M. Utley, *Cavalier in Buckskin: George Armstrong Custer and the Western Military Frontier* (Norman: University of Oklahoma Press, 1988).

Wert   Jeffry D. Wert, *Custer: The Controversial Life of George Armstrong Custer* (New York: Simon and Schuster, 1996).

Whittaker   Frederick Whittaker, *A Complete Life of Gen. George A. Custer: Major-General of Volunteers Brevet Major-General U.S. Army, and Lieutenant-Colonel Seventh U.S. Cavalry* (New York: Sheldon and Co., 1876).

Preface

1. Heather Cox Richardson, *West from Appomattox: The Reconstruction of America After the Civil War* (New Haven, Conn.: Yale University Press, 2007), 78–79, 92–93.

2. Modernization theory includes a vast literature. I am influenced by some of it without adopting or advocating any particular theoretical construction. See, for example, the work of Max Weber and Eugen Weber's landmark *Peasants into Frenchmen: The Modernization of Rural France, 1870–1914* (Palo Alto, Calif.: Stanford University Press, 1976). In the American context, I draw upon Alan Trachtenberg, *The Incorporation of America: Culture and Society in the Gilded Age* (New York: Hill and Wang, 1982), and, in the Western context, Richard Maxwell Brown's adaption of Trachtenberg's incorporation thesis to the armed conflicts in the mid- to late-nineteenth-century West, in *No Duty to Retreat: Violence and Values in American History and Society* (New York: Oxford Univer-

sity Press, 1991), and "Violence," in Clyde A. Milner II, Carol A. O'Connor, and Martha A. Sandweiss, eds., *The Oxford History of the American West* (New York: Oxford University Press, 1994), 393–425.

3. The themes presented here have not been completely ignored in the vast literature about GAC. Richard Slotkin pays the most attention to the broader transformation of the country, but he too approaches GAC in terms of his cultural role as frontier hero. In an extended discussion in *The Fatal Environment: The Myth of the Frontier in the Age of Industrialization, 1800–1890* (Norman: University of Oklahoma Press, 1994 [orig. pub. 1985]), 375–76, 386–87, 397, he calls GAC a member of the "professional class of soldierly gentlemen . . . an early type of organization man, hiding in the costumes of the cavalier trooper and the Frontier buckskin." I admire this book and Slotkin's other work immensely, but I find that GAC was the antiorganization man, unable to thrive in an institutional or corporate environment. The only role in which he flourished was that of the cavalier trooper.

PART I

One: The Accused

1. Proceedings of the 1861 Court-Martial Trial of George Armstrong Custer (II-385) (to be referred to hereafter as "1861 Proceedings"), Records of the Office of Judge Advocate General, RG 153, CRM; Edward C. Boynton, *History of West Point, and Its Military Importance During the American Revolution and the Origins and Progress of the United States Military Academy* (London: Sampson Low, Son, and Marston, 1864), 258. For an excellent discussion of the trial, and the underlying incident that precipitated GAC's offense, see Minnie Dubbs Millbrook, "Cadet Custer's Court-Martial," in Paul A. Hutton, ed., *Custer and His Times* (El Paso: Little Big Horn Associates, 1981), 59–83.
2. 1861 Proceedings; John A. Bingham to Jefferson Davis, November 18, 1856, George A. Custer Application Papers to the U.S. Military Academy, Records of the Adjutant General's Office, 1783–1917, RG 94, CRM.
3. Entry 333, Cullum 1: 243–44. In 1861 Proceedings, the list of court members runs from highest rank to lowest, and Nauman at the top.
4. Entry 558, Cullum 1: 347–48.
5. Coffman, 45; Cullum 1: 347–8; 1861 Proceedings.
6. 1861 Proceedings.
7. 1861 Proceedings; Millbrook, "Cadet Custer's Court-Martial." Millbrook shows that Ludlow was court-martialed as well for striking Ryerson, suggesting that GAC was actually intervening on behalf of Ryerson.
8. 1861 Proceedings.
9. Wert, 26. GAC's arrival in June is verified in a letter, GAC to Brother and Sister, January 27 [likely 1858], Box 1, GAC Papers, USMA.
10. Stiles, *First Tycoon*, 102–09, 253–54; Edward Harold Mott, *Between the Ocean and the Lakes: The Story of Erie* (New York: Ticker Publishing, 1908), frontis, 109–13.
11. Morris Schaff, *The Spirit of Old West Point* (Boston: Houghton Mifflin, 1912), 13–14; Stiles, *First Tycoon*, 102.
12. GAC to Minnie St. John, August 7, 1856, Box 1, GAC Papers, USMA.
13. Schaff, 14–16; George C. Strong, *Cadet Life at West Point* (Boston: T. O. H. P.

Burnham, 1862), 46 (to be referred to as "Strong" hereafter); James L. Morrison Jr., *"The Best School in the World": West Point, the Pre-Civil War Years, 1833–1866* (Kent, Ohio: Kent State University Press, 1986), 64, 70. Tourists regularly took the steamer to West Point; see, for example, George Templeton Strong's diary entry for August 4, 1851, in Allan Nevins and Milton Halsey Thomas, eds., *The Diary of George Templeton Strong*, vol. 2: *Turbulent Fifties, 1850–1859* (New York: Macmillan, 1952), 60. (George Templeton Strong should not be confused with the West Point cadet George C. Strong, whose memoir is referenced as "Strong" below.) For an example of visiting royalty, see Catherine S. Crary, ed., *Dear Belle: Letters from a Cadet and Officer to His Sweetheart, 1858–1865* (Middletown, Conn.: Wesleyan University Press, 1965), 53–56.

14. Strong, 46–47.
15. Morrison, 64–65.
16. Schaff, 23–25; Morrison, 64–68.
17. Boynton, 260–61; Morrison, 64–65, 71.
18. Morrison, 63.
19. Morrison, 66, 72, 122; Schaff, 28; Whittaker, 33.
20. GAC to Minnie St. John, August 7, 1856, Box 1, GAC Papers, USMA.
21. GAC to Minnie St. John, August 7, 1856, Box 1, GAC Papers, USMA; Morrison, 69, 118–19; Strong, 325.
22. Schaff, 23–25; Morrison, 64–68, 72, 115, 119. Morrison, 83, notes the great extent to which the academy relied on cadets to police themselves.
23. Schaff, 24; Crary, 40.
24. Herman Melville, *Billy Budd, Sailor, and Other Stories* (New York: Bantam Books, 1984), 3–4; Peter Michie, "Reminiscences of Cadet and Army Service," in A. Noel Blakeman, ed., *Personal Recollections of the War of the Rebellion: Second Series* (New York: G. P. Putnam's Sons, 1897), 186.
25. Crary, 39; Michie, 194.
26. GAC to Minnie St. John, August 7, 1856, Box 1, GAC Papers, USMA.
27. GAC to Sister, December 12, 1856, GAC Correspondence, LBH.
28. Roger L. Geiger notes that "boys of about twelve assumed an economic role and semi-independence from their families," in "The Era of Multipurpose Colleges in American Higher Education, 1850–1890," in Robert Geiger, ed., *The American College in the Nineteenth Century* (Nashville, Tenn.: Vanderbilt University Press, 2000), 127–52. See also, in the same volume, Roger L. Geiger, "The Rise and Fall of Useful Knowledge: Higher Education for Science, Agriculture, and the Mechanic Arts, 1850–1875," 153–68.
29. Wert, 15–18. In a letter, GAC wrote of his parents, "If they were only in better circumstances and were able to get along without working as hard as they have had to, I would have nothing whatever to trouble me. And if there is any one reason more than another which makes me wish I was through at West Point it is that I might be some aid to them." See GAC to Brother and Sister, May 29, 1860, GAC Correspondence, LBH.
30. Wert, 15–18; Charles B. Wallace, *Custer's Ohio Boyhood: Third Edition* (Cadiz, Ohio: Harrison County Historical Society, 1993), 5–7.
31. Wert, 20–22; Utley, 13; Reynolds, 11–12; Gerard N. Magliocca, *American Founding Son: John Bingham and the Invention of the Fourteenth Amendment* (New York: New York University Press, 2013), 49–50. Jurgen Herbst writes in *And Sadly Teach: Teacher Education and Professionalization in American Culture*

(Madison: University of Wisconsin Press, 1991), 112, that even those educators who attended teacher-training normal schools "were not necessarily interested in diplomas, but they were eager to get back to work and support themselves through their teaching," and were attempting "to brush up on their skills and knowledge for as long as they could afford it." See also Carl Kaestle, *Pillars of the Republic: Common Schools and American Society, 1780–1860* (New York: Hill and Wang, 1983).

32. Ralph Kirshner, *The Class of 1861: Custer, Ames, and Their Classmates After West Point* (Carbondale, Ill.: Southern Illinois University Press, 1999), 3; Stiles, *First Tycoon*, 227–36.

33. GAC to Brother and Sister, Jan 27, n.d. [apparently 1858], Box 1, GAC Papers, USMA; Morrison, 62, 158–59. The Charles Francis Adams family (offspring of Presidents John and John Quincy Adams) was aghast when Charles Francis Adams Jr. enlisted in the Union army during the Civil War; Edward Charles Kirkland, *Charles Francis Adams, Jr., 1835–1915: The Patrician at Bay* (Cambridge, Mass.: Harvard University Press, 1965).

34. James S. Robbins, *Last in Their Class: Custer, Pickett, and the Goats of West Point* (New York: Encounter Books, 2006), 193: Stiles, *Jesse James*, 308; Millard Kessler Bushong and Dean McKoin Bushong, *Fightin' Tom Rosser, C.S.A.* (Shippensburg, Pa.: Beidel Printing House, 1983), 1–2.

35. GAC to John, April 7, 1860, GAC Collection, L. Tom Perry Special Collections, Harold B. Lee Library, Brigham Young University, Provo, Utah. As Geiger notes, "In an age when boys of about twelve assumed an economic role and semi-independence from their families, attending college most likely meant the prolongation of dependence and control. . . . Collegians were expected to undertake thorough preparatory study, followed by a continuous four-year course. And while most young people enjoyed considerable personal freedom, collegians were constrained by myriad rules, enforced in the spirit of petty but inefficient despotism." See Roger L. Geiger, "The Era of Multipurpose Colleges in American Higher Education, 1850–1890," 140, and Geiger, ed., *The American College in the Nineteenth Century*, 127–52.

36. Morrison, 73.

37. Robert L. Geiger, "Introduction: New Themes in the History of Nineteenth-Century Colleges," 1–36; Roger L. Geiger with Julie Ann Bubolz, "College As It Was in the Mid-Nineteenth Century," 80–90; Roger L. Geiger, "The Era of Multipurpose Colleges in American Higher Education, 1850–1890," 127–52; Roger L. Geiger, "The Rise and Fall of Useful Knowledge: Higher Education for Science, Agriculture, and the Mechanic Arts, 1850–1875," 153–68; all in Geiger, ed., *The American College in the Nineteenth Century*; Morrison, 110–11, 115–19.

38. GAC to Brother and Sister, January 27 [no year named, but the contents show it must be 1858], Box 1, GAC Papers, USMA.

39. Michie, 194. For other such assessments, see Wert, 31.

40. On daily recitations and general examinations, and the impact of graduation standing on future promotion, see Morrison, 87–88.

41. Morrison, 73–74, 120–21.

42. Register of Delinquencies, 1856–1861, 192–93, 342–43, 448–49, USMA. Note, by contrast, that Adelbert Ames, one class ahead of GAC, did not even fill one page with demerits over the same period of time (Register of Delinquencies, 4).

43. Register of Delinquencies, 341; Wert, 32.
44. EBC, *Tenting on the Plains*, 320; Morrison, 116. The Spanish class incident appears in virtually every account of GAC's life. See, for example, Reynolds, 22.
45. Schaff, 25–28, 66–67.
46. Schaff, 116, 193–94.
47. Crary, 42–43, 214–15.
48. Schaff, 193–94.
49. GAC to John, April 7, 1860, GAC Collection, L. Tom Perry Special Collections, Harold B. Lee Library, Brigham Young University, Provo, Utah; GAC to Brother and Sister, October 2, 1859, GAC Correspondence, LBH.
50. GAC to Brother and Sister, October 2, 1859, GAC Correspondence, LBH. On his illness, see also GAC to Cousin, December 13, 1859, Letters: Copies and Transcripts, GAC Papers, USMA.
51. GAC to Brother and Sister, June 30, 1858, GAC Correspondence, LBH.
52. GAC to Brother and Sister, October 2, 1859, May 29, 1860, GAC Correspondence, LBH.
53. Morrison, 119, 121–22; GAC, "War Memoirs: From West Point to the Battlefield," *Galaxy* (April 1876) (to be called War Memoirs I hereafter).
54. Whittaker, 31; Morrison, 78; War Memoirs I; Gary W. Gallagher, *Stephen Dodson Ramseur: Lee's Gallant General* (Chapel Hill: University of North Carolina Press, 1985), 26–27.
55. GAC to Cousin, December 13, 1859, Letters: Copies and Transcripts, GAC Papers, USMA.
56. Tully McCrea to GAC, August 13, 1861, GAC Correspondence, LBH.
57. Crary, 215.
58. Monaghan, 10–11; Wert, 22–23. The quotations are from Monaghan, who was not above fictionalizing (placing GAC in a scene from the memoirs of a fellow cadet, for example), but he explicitly stated that he saw this correspondence, and judging from GAC's letters to Mollie preserved at Yale University's Beinecke Library, he is credible on this point.
59. GAC to Mollie, November 13, 1858, GAC to Mollie, January 1, 1859, GAC Letters to Dear Mollie, Beinecke Library, Yale University, New Haven, Conn.; Monaghan, 10–11; Wert, 22–23; Magliocca, 49–51; Erving E. Beauregard, *Bingham of the Hills: Politician and Diplomat Extraordinary* (New York: Peter Lang, 1989), 32–33; Wallace, 21–22.
60. GAC to Mollie, November 13, 1858, GAC to Mollie, January 1, 1859, GAC Letters to Dear Mollie, Beinecke Library, Yale University, New Haven, Conn.
61. GAC to Mollie, January 1, 1859, GAC Letters to Dear Mollie, Beinecke Library, Yale University, New Haven, Conn.
62. Wert, 34–35. For a thinly veiled account of how cadets discussed brothels in New York, see Tully McCrea to GAC, August 13, 1861, GAC Correspondence, LBH.
63. EBC, *Tenting on the Plains*, 245–46, 284.
64. Richard L. Aynes, "The Continuing Importance of Congressman John A. Bingham and the Fourteenth Amendment," *Akron Law Review* 36: 589–615; War Memoirs I; Schaff, 145.
65. Stiles, *First Tycoon*, 93–99.
66. The struggle over the expansion of slavery has given rise to a vast historical literature. For summaries, see McPherson, 47–249; Stiles, *Jesse James*, 46–55.

67. Stiles, *Jesse James*, 46–55; Heather Cox Richardson, *To Make Men Free: A History of the Republican Party* (New York: Basic Books, 2014), 6–24.
68. Wert, 28–29; War Memoirs I; Schaff, 159; Morrison, 129–30.
69. Schaff, 29; Morrison, 129–30; Thomas Rowland, "Letters of a Virginia Cadet at West Point, 1859–1861," *South Atlantic Quarterly* 15, no. 4 (October 1915): 330–47. GAC wrote in 1876 that the sectional division among cadets was "at first barely distinguishable, but in later years immediately preceding the war as clearly defined and strongly drawn as were the lines separating the extremes of the various sections in the national Congress"; War Memoirs I.
70. McPherson, 152–53, 202–13.
71. Schaff, 142–49; Crary, 64; Morrison, 129–30.
72. GAC to John, April 7, 1860, GAC Collection, L. Tom Perry Special Collections, Harold B. Lee Library, Brigham Young University, Provo, Utah. Kirshner, 6, observes that GAC checked Cooper's novels out of the West Point library, while Tom Rosser took out a biography of Philip II and Adelbert Ames borrowed Aristotle's *Rhetoric*.
73. GAC to Friend John, May 5, 1860, GAC Collection, L. Tom Perry Special Collections, Harold B. Lee Library, Brigham Young University, Provo, Utah.
74. Curiously, GAC voiced the same sentiments in his War Memoirs I, but put them in the mouth of the secessionist cadet P. M. B. Young.
75. Crary, 70–71.
76. McPherson, 213–35; Morrison, 126.
77. War Memoirs I.
78. Schaff, 84, 207–08; Crary, 78.
79. Crary, 42–44. McCrea stated that GAC did not know why he was reinstated. Utley, *Cavalier in Buckskin*, 15–16, writes that the attempted theft of the questions took place after GAC failed the main examination, while he was preparing for the second round. This may be so, though I find no evidence to indicate whether it was for the initial test or the reexamination. Judging from the mid-month date of McCrea's letter, I believe it was more likely a theft before the initial test. Utley stresses how this incident illustrates GAC's extraordinary luck.
80. War Memoirs I. Henry A. du Pont, a class ahead of GAC, described "cutting heads" to his mother on February 26, 1860, which means that GAC would have been practicing the same drill in early 1861. See Kirshner, 4.
81. Tully McCrea to GAC, August 13, 1861, GAC Correspondence, LBH.
82. War Memoirs I.
83. GAC to Sister, May 31, 1861, Letters: Copies and Transcripts, GAC Papers, Special Collections and Archives, USMA.
84. McPherson, 273–74.
85. McCrea quoted in Schaff, 220.
86. GAC to Mrs. David Reed, April 26, 1861, typescript copy, GAC Collection, L. Tom Perry Special Collections, Harold B. Lee Library, Brigham Young University, Provo, Utah.
87. GAC to Sister, May 31, 1861, Letters: Copies and Transcripts, GAC Papers, Special Collections and Archives, USMA.
88. Wert, 38–39.
89. War Memoirs I.
90. 1861 Proceedings.
91. Mark R. Wilson makes this important point about the army in *The Business of*

Civil War: Military Mobilization and the State, 1861–1865 (Baltimore, Md.: Johns Hopkins University Press, 2006). Though the Regular Army had fewer than 16,000 men before the Civil War, it was still enormous compared to almost any private enterprise in 1860, and its wide dispersal across the West required a high degree of organization for supply. As Wilson notes, 35–36, "Well before 1861, the U.S. military supply bureaus were among the most stable, most bureaucratic, and most important governmental institutions in America. . . . During the years before the Civil War, most army quartermasters were stationed at far-flung posts in the great West, where they handled small-scale procurement and long-distance logistics. . . . During the decades before the Civil War, the military regularly accounted for well over half of the total national government expenditures."

92. War Memoirs I.

Two: The Observer

1. Mark R. Wilson, *The Business of Civil War: Military Mobilization and the State, 1861–1865* (Baltimore, Md.: Johns Hopkins University Press, 2006), 5–7.
2. GAC, "War Memoirs: From West Point to the Battlefield," *Galaxy* (April 1876) (to be called War Memoirs I); Ernest A. McKay, *The Civil War and New York City* (Syracuse, N.Y.: Syracuse University Press, 1990), 59–65, 87; Stiles, *First Tycoon*, 336–44. See also Frederick S. Lightfoot, ed., *Nineteenth-Century New York in Rare Photographic Views* (New York: Dover, 1981).
3. War Memoirs I; William Howard Russell, *My Diary: North and South*, vol. 1 (London: Bradbury and Evans, 1863), 44–45; Oliver Wendell Holmes, "My Hunt After 'The Captain,'" in *Pages from an Old Volume of Life: A Collection of Essays, 1857–1881* (Boston: Houghton, Mifflin and Company, 1891), 22. Note that GAC, in War Memoirs I, misdated his arrival in Washington as "soon after daylight, Saturday morning, the 20th of July." Even in 1861 it only took twelve hours to travel from New York to Washington, not thirty-six. See Edward K. Spann, *Gotham at War: New York City, 1860–1865* (New York: Rowman and Littlefield), 69. By GAC's own account he spent a sleepless night in Washington and spent the following night riding to McDowell's army, which means he could not have arrived on the 20th and reached the army by the early hours of the 21st.
4. War Memoirs I; Russell, 46–47.
5. Ibid. Adam Goodheart is especially good on the pervasive role of slavery in Washington in *1861: The Civil War Awakening* (New York: Alfred A. Knopf, 2011), 61–64.
6. War Memoirs I. On Ebbitt House, see, for example, *NYT*, November 30, 1865.
7. The story presented here of GAC's trip to Washington through his journey to McDowell's army relies on his own account from fifteen years later, in War Memoirs I. The quotes are from his memory, and should be viewed in that light.
8. See, for example, Russell's fine account of a dinner with Scott in the spring of 1861, 105–10.
9. War Memoirs I. See also Catherine S. Crary, ed., *Dear Belle: Letters from a Cadet and Officer to His Sweetheart, 1858–1865* (Middletown, Conn.: Wesleyan University Press, 1965), 103–06. On August 8, 1861, GAC wrote a twenty-four-page letter to his old roommate, Tully McCrea, about his adventures—though he clearly exaggerated in some places.

10. GAC, "War Memoirs: Was the Battle of Bull Run a National Disaster?," *Galaxy* (May 1876) (to be called War Memoirs II); William C. Davis, *Battle at Bull Run: A History of the First Major Campaign of the Civil War* (New York: Doubleday, 1977), 157.

11. Davis, 203–10; War Memoirs II. On the din of battle, see Earl J. Hess, *The Union Soldier in Battle: Enduring the Ordeal of Combat* (Lawrence: University Press of Kansas, 1997), 15–19.

12. Davis, 204–12; War Memoirs II.

13. Crary, 103–06.

14. War Memoirs II.

15. Crary, 105; GAC, "War Memoirs," *Galaxy* (June 1876) (to be called War Memoirs III hereafter).

16. Wert, 45; Crary, 106.

17. Tully McCrea to GAC, August 13, 1861, GAC Correspondence, LBH; Davis, 112.

18. GAC to Mrs. David Reed, April 26, 1861, typescript copy, GAC Collection, L. Tom Perry Special Collections, Harold B. Lee Library, Brigham Young University, Provo, Utah.

19. Wert, 45–46; W. J. Rorabaugh, *The Alcoholic Republic: An American Tradition* (New York: Oxford University Press, 1979), 187, 191–218. See also James L. Morrison Jr., *"The Best School in the World": West Point, the Pre-Civil War Years, 1833–1866* (Kent, Ohio: Kent State University Press, 1986).

20. GAC to Sister, February 21, 1862, GAC Correspondence, LBH.

21. GAC to Sister, February 21, 1862, GAC Correspondence, LBH. Nellie Van Wormer emerges as increasingly significant in his correspondence. Her full name is identified in GAC to Brother and Sister, July 13, 1862, GAC Correspondence, LBH.

22. GAC to Parents, March 17, 1862, GAC Correspondence, LBH; Crary, 106–07.

23. Stephen W. Sears, *George B. McClellan: The Young Napoleon* (New York: Da Capo Press, 1999 [orig. pub. 1988]), 10–12, 35, 43–49, 51–67; Richard Slotkin, *The Long Road to Antietam: How the Civil War Became a Revolution* (New York: W. W. Norton, 2012), 15–16.

24. Stephen W. Sears, *To the Gates of Richmond: The Peninsula Campaign* (Boston: Houghton Mifflin, 2001 [orig. pub. 1992]), 22.

25. EHC to GAC, February 2, 1862, Folder 20, Box 1, LAFCC.

26. GAC to Parents, March 17, 1862, GAC Correspondence, LBH.

27. GAC to Parents, March 17, 1862, GAC Correspondence, LBH; Stephen W. Sears, ed., *The Civil War Papers of George B. McClellan: Selected Correspondence, 1860–1865* (New York: Da Capo Press, 1992), 211. Sears notes in *To the Gates*, 21, that GBM kept a portable printing press with him even in the field, and "the Yankee camps were flooded with copies" of the address to the troops quoted here.

28. GAC to Parents, March 26, 1862, GAC Correspondence, LBH; Sears, *To the Gates*, 23; Sears, *Civil War Papers*, 220; Stiles, *First Tycoon*, 159.

29. GAC to Sister March 28, 1862, GAC Correspondence, LBH. See also Allan Nevins, ed., *A Diary of Battle: The Personal Journals of Colonel Charles S. Wainwright, 1861–1865* (New York: Da Capo Press, 1998), 28.

30. Crary, 107; GAC to Parents, March 26, 1862, GAC Correspondence, LBH.

31. Prince François de Joinville, *The Army of the Potomac: Its Organization, Its Com-*

mander, and Its Campaign, trans. William Henry Hurlburt (New York: Anson D. F. Randolph, 1862), 30–37; Sears, *To the Gates*, 24.

32. Richard Slotkin offers a fine summary of army units in *The Long Road to Antietam*, xxix–xxxi. A note on terminology: "rifle" refers specifically to a long firearm with rifling, or a spiral groove, inside the barrel, to spin the bullet and add greatly to accuracy. Most rifles carried by infantry in the Civil War were rifled muskets, loaded through the barrel like the smoothbore muskets used by armies for centuries past.

33. Wainwright, 35.

34. Joinville, 38, 53; *OR*, Series 1, Vol. 5: 38.

35. Joinville, 60. Brig. General Andrew A. Humphreys, commander of the topographical corps, noted that another part of his men's work was to map the Army of the Potomac's own position, so GBM and his subordinates knew where their various units were. See Humphrey's report, *OR*, Series 1, Vol. 11, Part 1: 152–53.

36. GAC to Sister, [April] 11, 1862, GAC Correspondence, LBH. Note that this letter is actually dated March 11, which is impossible; in such misdating of months or years in correspondence, the most common error is the use of the preceding month or year. Again, a useful summary of artillery munitions appears in Slotkin, *Long Road to Antietam*, xxxi.

37. GAC to Sister, April 19, 1862, GAC Correspondence, LBH. On the skirmish that produced these casualties, see Sears, *To the Gates*, 55–56.

38. Drew Gilpin Faust, *This Republic of Suffering: Death and the American Civil War* (New York: Alfred A. Knopf, 2008), 3–31. See also her discussion of burial rituals, 61–101.

39. GAC to Sister, April 19, 1862, GAC Correspondence, LBH.

40. GAC, "War Memoirs: Yorktown and Williamsburg," *Galaxy* (November 1876) (to be referred to as War Memoirs IV). This is the primary source for the account given here of GAC's balloon ascensions, but at least one contemporary letter confirms some specific details; see GAC to Sister, May 15, 1862, GAC Correspondence, LBH. Robert Utley confirmed by e-mail that he had examined a map drawn by GAC in a balloon, at the time in the private collection of Brice C. W. Custer, since alienated to an unknown private collector.

41. Sears, *To the Gates*, 41, 54–55; War Memoirs IV.

42. War Memoirs IV.

43. War Memoirs IV; *OR*, Series 1, Vol. 11, Part 1: 526, 533–34. On the slow counter-fortification of the Union line opposite the Confederate Yorktown line, see Sears, *To the Gates*, esp. 57–59. GAC remained a topographical engineer, but performed his duties specifically for Smith after his assignment.

44. *OR*, Series 1, Vol. 11, Part 1: 526, 533–36 and Vol. 11, Part 3: 140; Sears, *To the Gates*, 70–71.

45. *OR*, Series 1, Vol. 11, Part 1: 526, 533–36 and Vol. 11, Part 3: 140; Sears, *To the Gates*, 76, 78; William A. Blair, "The Seven Days and the Radical Persuasion: Convincing Moderates in the North for the Need for a Hard War," in Gary W. Gallagher, ed., *The Richmond Campaign of 1862: The Peninsula and the Seven Days* (Chapel Hill: University of North Carolina Press, 2000), 153–80.

46. *OR*, Series 1, Vol. 11, Part 1: 526, 533–36; Sears, *To the Gates*, 76, 78–80; War Memoirs IV; Glenn David Brasher, *The Peninsula Campaign & the Necessity of Emancipation: African Americans and the Fight for Freedom* (Chapel Hill: University of North Carolina Press, 2012), 126–29.

47. *OR*, Series 1, Vol. 11, Part 1: 537–40; Sears, *To the Gates*, 79–83; GAC to Sister, May 15, 1862, GAC Correspondence, LBH; Brasher, 129–30.

48. GAC to Sister, May 15, 1862, GAC Correspondence, LBH; Wert, 52.

49. Wainwright, 71, 70. I am combining quotes from Wainwright's diary from May 26 ("most tropically") and May 24 ("sea of mud"). See also Sears, *To the Gates*, 108–09.

50. Entry 1850, Cullum 2: 496–97; *OR*, Series 1, Vol. 11, Part 1: 111, 652–54; *Monroe Commercial*, June 12, 1862. Previously GAC had sounded the Chickahominy under the supervision of Brig. Gen. John Gross Barnard, chief engineer for the Army of the Potomac. See *OR*, Series 1, Vol. 11, Part 1: 639; William J. Miller, "I Only Wait for the River: McClellan and His Engineers on the Chickahominy," in Gary W. Gallagher, ed., *The Richmond Campaign of 1862: The Peninsula and the Seven Days* (Chapel Hill: University of North Carolina Press, 2000), 44–65.

51. *OR*, Series 1, Vol. 11, Part 1: 111, 651–54; *Monroe Commercial*, June 12, 1862.

52. GBM, *McClellan's Own Story* (New York: Charles L. Webster and Co., 1887), 364; Sears, *Civil War Papers*, 275–76; *OR*, Series 1, Vol. 11, Part 3: 198–99. GAC later wrote that, before being taken on staff by GBM, the general had only seen him face-to-face twice and had not said twenty words to him; GAC to Jacob Howard, January 19, 1864, reproduced in Hamilton Gay Howard, *Civil War Echoes: Character Sketches and State Secrets* (Washington, D.C.: Howard Publishing, 1907), 306–13. On GAC's state of mind, see Reynolds, 74. Reynolds collated EBC's unpublished notes on the Civil War (all of which may be found in the LBH collection, though I am citing Reynolds for the convenience of researchers). Though this insight into his mind was related by EBC years after his death, it rings true, given GAC's own frequent commentary in his letters on how he was unable to change his uniform for days on end. GAC's promotion is commonly attributed to his fording the river to sound its depth, under the command of Brig. Gen. John G. Barnard, chief engineer of the Army of the Potomac; according to this version, the armed reconnaissance was conducted *after* GAC's promotion. This version seems to be based on a misleading account of GAC's promotion that was circulated by the headquarters staff not long after the event; see next chapter for a full discussion. In fact, GBM specifically named the armed reconnaissance in his memoirs as the reason he called GAC to his tent; even Barnard's report on the fording of the river attributed its importance to its facilitating the subsequent raid described here. See *OR*, Series 1, Vol. 11, Part 1: 111.

Three: The Protégé

1. James H. Wilson, *Under the Old Flag*, vol. 1 (New York: D. Appleton, 1912), 100–01; Letter of August 12, 1863, quoted in Catherine S. Crary, ed., *Dear Belle: Letters from a Cadet and Officer to His Sweetheart, 1858–1865* (Middletown, Conn.: Wesleyan University Press, 1965), 214.

2. Stephen W. Sears, *George B. McClellan: The Young Napoleon* (New York: Da Capo Press, 1999 [orig. pub. 1988]), 10–12, 35, 43–49, 51–67; Richard Slotkin, *The Long Road to Antietam: How the Civil War Became a Revolution* (New York: W. W. Norton, 2012), 15–16. For my ideas of how economic dynamism created a competitive social arena and rendered social status unstable, see Stiles, *First Tycoon*, 37–43, 49, 148–50.

3. *OR*, Series 1, Vol. 5: 23; Edwin C. Fishel, *The Secret War for the Union: The Untold Story of Military Intelligence in the Civil War* (Boston: Houghton Mifflin, 1996), 123; Sears, *George B. McClellan*, 135.

4. *Hartford Courant*, July 3, 1862; Wilson, 101–02. GAC did test the river, but not spontaneously and not under GBM's eye. He was ordered into the river by Brig. Gen. John G. Barnard, chief engineer of the Army of the Potomac; *OR*, Series 1, Vol. 11, Part 1: 111. GAC's staff promotion to captain was effective June 5, 1862, and his Regular Army promotion to first lieutenant was dated July 17, 1862; HR 3328, CRM.

5. *Hartford Courant*, July 3, 1862. Barnard's reconnaissance of the river with GAC clearly was the basis for this muddled account, which has often been repeated in biographies of GAC with many embellishments of the great dangers involved. In fact, Barnard's report makes no mention of the enemy at all, though he notes, "The attack and capture of the enemy's pickets by him [GAC] and Lieutenant Bowen was founded upon these reconnaissances." See *OR*, Series 1, Vol. 11, Part 1: 111. See also GBM's proud reference in a letter to "some youngsters I have caught," Sears, *George B. McClellan*, 237.

6. Slotkin, *Long Road to Antietam*, 45–46; see also Stephen W. Sears, *To the Gates of Richmond: The Peninsula Campaign* (Boston: Houghton Mifflin, 2001 [orig. pub. 1992]), 21.

7. Sears, *George B. McClellan*, 105–06, 110–11, 137, 189; Sears, *To the Gates*, 21. The chief engineer of the Army of the Potomac, Brig. Gen. John G. Barnard, later expressed a disillusionment that reveals how great the illusions about GBM had once been, complaining of "the erroneous ideas disseminated concerning *his* capacity, merits, and agency." See William J. Miller, "I Only Wait for the River: McClellan and His Engineers on the Chickahominy," in Gary W. Gallagher, ed., *The Richmond Campaign of 1862: The Peninsula and the Seven Days* (Chapel Hill: University of North Carolina Press, 2000), 44–65, and Barnard's own *The Peninsular Campaign and Its Antecedents* (New York: D. Van Nostrand, 1864).

8. Sears, *To the Gates*, 163–65; Miller, "I Only Wait for the River," 44–65. Sears, *George B. McClellan*, uses the term "fatalism" and develops this argument at length, demonstrating convincingly that GBM's messianic belief in himself and his fear that God would crush his hopes were intertwined. Curiously, GBM's need to control every variable blinded him to the danger that delay would give the enemy time, creating new contingencies, or that exhaustive safeguards for battle led to rising losses from sickness as his men remained in the field.

9. GBM quoted in Ethan S. Rafuse, *McClellan's War: The Failure of Moderation in the Struggle for the Union* (Bloomington: Indiana University Press, 2005), 179. Sears, *To the Gates*, 159, notes that GBM was conducting an "active defense" as taught at West Point, which the general said would protect "against the consequences of unforeseen disaster." As Sears writes in *George B. McClellan*, 175, GBM "was invariably brought up short by the unexpected." Slotkin, *Long Road to Antietam*, 51–52, similarly observes that GBM played the role of "the fighter for the press when his real purpose was to escape the chaos of a battle he could not control."

10. Prince François de Joinville, *The Army of the Potomac: Its Organization, Its Commander, and Its Campaign*, trans. William Henry Hurlburt (New York: Anson D. F. Randolph, 1862), 52–53; Mark R. Wilson, *The Business of Civil War: Mili-*

tary Mobilization and the State, 1861–1865 (Baltimore, Md.: Johns Hopkins University Press, 2006), 35–36.

11. Sears, *George B. McClellan*, 50–51, 107–09, 179–80, 187–88; Fishel, 102–29; Sears, *To the Gates*, 98–99; Stephen W. Sears, ed., *The Civil War Papers of George B. McClellan: Selected Correspondence, 1860–1865* (New York: Da Capo Press, 1992), 271, 274; see also Stiles, *Jesse James*, 251–52. Fishel, 102 and 238, argues that most of the blame was not Pinkerton's: "As for McClellan, he could not have been *deceived* by Pinkerton's overestimates, for he was a party to them—the dominant party, in fact. . . . It is now clear that George McClellan was his own intelligence officer; Pinkerton never came close to filling that role."

12. Sears, *George B. McClellan*, 103, 134, 176–77, 188; Fishel, 239; Sears, *Civil War Papers*, 275.

13. EHC to GAC, April 18, 1862, Folder 2, Box 1, LAFCC. The staff shared GBM's anger at his enemies; see Slotkin, *Long Road to Antietam*, 45–46, 176–79. Slotkin, 31, writes that GBM believed himself to be engaged in a "two front war to save the Union from the Rebels in front and the Radicals in the rear."

14. "Fair Oaks, Va. Lt. James B. Washington, a Confederate Prisoner, with Capt. George A. Custer of the 5th Cavalry, U.S.A.," James F. Gibson, photographic print, call number LC-B815-428 Lot 4188, Prints and Photographs Division, LOC; Shelby Foote, *The Civil War: A Narrative*, vol. 1: *Fort Sumter to Perryville* (New York: Vintage, 1986 [orig. pub. 1958]), 445–51. The photograph label, provided by the Brady Studio, identifies GAC as a captain, though his official designation as a "Captain and additional aide-de-camp" was dated June 5, 1862, several days later; HR 3328, CRM.

15. Morris Schaff, *The Spirit of Old West Point, 1858–1862* (Boston: Houghton Mifflin, 1908), 142. Washington was a distant nephew of the nation's first president.

16. "Lieut. Washington, a Confederate Prisoner, and Capt. Custer, U.S.A.," photographic print, call number LC-USZ62-109737, Prints and Photographs Division, LOC. EBC would later claim that Washington called for the young contraband to be included, but the photographer used the same young man in at least one other photograph. See Merington, 129–30.

17. Marie Miller to GAC, n.d., Folder 21, Box 1, LAFCC. The letter is undated, but it makes reference to his interest in Nellie Van Wormer and his apparent direct contact with contrabands, which suggests that it was written while he was on the Peninsula. Examples of other letters discussing the sending home of contrabands appear in Nina Silber, *Daughters of the Union: Northern Women Fight the Civil War* (Cambridge, Mass.: Harvard University Press, 2005), 215, 231–32.

18. James Marten, "A Feeling of Restless Anxiety: Loyalty and Race in the Peninsula Campaign and Beyond," in Gary W. Gallagher, ed., *The Richmond Campaign of 1862: The Peninsula and the Seven Days* (Chapel Hill: University of North Carolina Press, 2000), 121–52.

19. Marten, "A Feeling of Restless Anxiety," 121–52; James M. McPherson, *For Cause and Comrades: Why Men Fought in the Civil War* (New York: Oxford University Press, 1997), 118–19; Glenn David Brasher, *The Peninsula Campaign & the Necessity of Emancipation: African Americans and the Fight for Freedom* (Chapel Hill: University of North Carolina Press, 2012), 144–45.

20. McPherson, *For Cause and Comrades*, stresses the practical thinking behind much of the burgeoning antislavery sentiment in the army.

21. Sears, *To the Gates*, 21; Slotkin, *Long Road to Antietam*, 47; GBM to Randolph B. Marcy, August 20, 1865, Roll 36, GBM Papers, LOC.

22. GBM to Samuel L. M. Barlow, November 8, 1861, in Sears, *Civil War Papers*, 127–28.

23. Allan Nevins, ed., *A Diary of Battle: The Personal Journals of Colonel Charles S. Wainwright, 1861–1865* (New York: Da Capo Press, 1998), 9. Throughout *Battle Cry of Freedom*, James M. McPherson offers a clear but nuanced account of Lincoln's handling of slavery as a war aim; see, for example, McPherson, 352–64.

24. James Grant Wilson and John Fiske, eds., *Appleton's Cyclopaedia of American Biography*, vol. 1 (New York: D. Appleton, 1888), 112, 167, 231; Stiles, *First Tycoon*, 176, 192, 281, 322, 326. See also Sears, *George B. McClellan*, 51; Slotkin, *Long Road to Antietam*, 26.

25. Sears, *To the Gates*, 107–08; Sears, *Civil War Papers*, 288, 306; Stiles, *First Tycoon*, 338.

26. François Joinville to Edward Everett, November 9, 1864, Abraham Lincoln Papers, LOC; GAC to Brother and Sister, July 13, 1862, GAC Correspondence, LBH. On GAC's exposure to the conservative-financier wing of the Democratic Party, see Richard Slotkin, *The Fatal Environment: The Myth of the Frontier in the Age of Industrialization, 1800–1890* (Norman: University of Oklahoma Press, 1994 [orig. pub. 1985]), 382.

27. All quotes in Sears, *George B. McClellan*, 203–04. See also Stephen W. Sears, *Landscape Turned Red: The Battle of Antietam* (New Haven, Conn.: Ticknor and Field, 1983), 35–36; Sears, *To the Gates*, 160–61.

28. Sears, *George B. McClellan*, 203–04; Sears, *To the Gates*, 160–61.

29. GAC to Brother and Sister, July 13, 1862, GAC Correspondence, LBH. David Reed and LAR were on the Peninsula as recently as June 23, 1862, when Henry Clay Christiancy noted Reed's visit in his diary; Henry Clay Christiancy Diary, Folder 1, Box 3, Christiancy and Pickett Families' Papers, LOC.

30. GAC to Brother and Sister, July 13, 1862, GAC Correspondence, LBH; Sears, *To the Gates*, 201–03.

31. GAC to Brother and Sister, July 13, 1862, GAC Correspondence, LBH; Sears, *George B. McClellan*, 205–06; Joinville, 63; McPherson, 464; William W. Averell, "With the Cavalry on the Peninsula," *B&L* 2, 430.

32. GAC to Brother and Sister, July 13, 1862, GAC Correspondence, LBH.

33. Sears, *To the Gates*, 202–04; Sears, *George B. McClellan*, 206–09.

34. *OR*, Series 1, Vol. 11, Part 1: 117.

35. Sears, *To the Gates*, 210–11; Sears, *George B. McClellan*, 205–06; McPherson, 464–68; Slotkin, *Long Road to Antietam*, 51–52.

36. Sears, *To the Gates*, 224–35; *OR*, Series 1, Vol. 11, Part 2: 75–76; McPherson, 464–68. Rafuse offers a more generous reading of Confederate numbers, actually claiming a slight Confederate numerical superiority, but even if correct GBM faced nothing like the numbers in his own estimates of enemy strength.

37. *OR*, Series 1, Vol. 11, Part 2: 75–76; GAC to Brother and Sister, July 13, 1862, GAC Correspondence, LBH; Philip St. George Cooke, "The Charge of Cooke's Cavalry at Gaines's Mill," *B&L* 2: 344–46.

38. GAC to Brother and Sister, July 13, 1862, GAC Correspondence, LBH; Entry 1950, Cullum 2: 559.

39. McPherson, 462–72.

40. GAC to Brother and Sister, July 13, 1862, GAC Correspondence, LBH; Slotkin, *Long Road to Antietam*, 54; McPherson, 470.

41. McPherson, 471.

42. GAC to Brother and Sister, July 13, 1862, GAC Correspondence, LBH; GBM, *McClellan's Own Story* (New York: Charles L. Webster and Co., 1887), 364; Entry 1950, Cullum 2: 559.

43. GAC to Brother and Sister, July 13, 1862, GAC Correspondence, LBH.

44. Slotkin, *Long Road to Antietam*, 54–55.

45. Slotkin and McPherson examine this telegram and its repercussions, though the most detailed discussion is by Sears, *George B. McClellan*, 231–15.

46. Slotkin, *Long Road to Antietam*, 57–58; Sears, *George B. McClellan*, 226–28

47. GBM, *McClellan's Own Story*, 487–89.

48. Sears, *Civil War Papers*, 349, 361, 351.

49. McPherson, 499–510; Sears, *George B. McClellan*, 229–34; Chandler quoted in Gary W. Gallagher, "A Civil War Watershed: The 1862 Richmond Campaign in Perspective," in Gary W. Gallagher, ed., *The Richmond Campaign of 1862: The Peninsula and the Seven Days* (Chapel Hill: University of North Carolina Press, 2000), 3–27; GBM quoted in Sears, *Civil War Papers*, 369.

50. Lincoln quoted in McPherson, 504.

51. Whittaker, 128–29.

52. Crary, 214–15.

53. Whittaker, 122–23; Merington, 32–33; *OR*, Series 1, Vol. 11, Part 2: 946–48. GBM wrote to his wife, "Averell went out with 3 squadrons, met & thrashed an entire regiment, drove them to & through their camp, which he captured & leisurely destroyed"; Sears, *Civil War Papers*, 385.

54. *OR*, Series 1, Vol. 11, Part 2: 954–55; Merington, 32–33; Whittaker, 122–23. Merington inaccurately paraphrases the GAC letter quoted here. I rely here on Whittaker, who quoted the entire document, apparently verbatim. For an excellent discussion of killing in the Civil War, see Drew Gilpin Faust, *This Republic of Suffering: Death and the American Civil War* (New York: Alfred A. Knopf, 2008), 32–60.

55. Sears, *Civil War Papers*, 369, 374.

56. Sears, *Civil War Papers*, 379; Slotkin, *Long Road to Antietam*, 45, 99–100, 102, 104, 176, 178. See also Sears, *George B. McClellan*, 237–38.

57. Burnside quoted in Sears, *George B. McClellan*, 241; Kearny quoted in Slotkin, *Long Road to Antietam*, 100.

58. Sears, *George B. McClellan*, 244–47, 253–55; McPherson, 524–33.

59. Sears, *Landscape Turned Red*, 12–14; Slotkin, *Long Road to Antietam*, 131, 135; Sears, *George B. McClellan*, 257–60; McPherson, 533–35; Whittaker, 129.

60. Sears, *Landscape Turned Red*, 15–16; Slotkin, *Long Road to Antietam*, 135–37; Sears, *George B. McClellan*, 257–60; McPherson, 533–35; GBM, *McClellan's Own Story*, 535.

61. *OR*, Series 1, Vol. 19, Part 1: 209–10 and Vol. 19, Part 2: 177; David L. Thompson, "In the Ranks to the Antietam," 557–58, in *B&L* 2, 556–58.

62. McPherson, 537–39; *OR*, Series 1, Vol. 19, Part 1: 209–10 and Vol. 19, Part 2: 177; Sears, *Landscape Turned Red*, 157–58.

63. Stephen W. Sears, *Controversies and Commanders: Dispatches from the Army of the Potomac* (New York: Houghton Mifflin Harcourt, 2000), 134; Slotkin, *Long Road to Antietam*, 135–36, 177–79.

64. McPherson, 537; John Gibbon, *Personal Recollections of the Civil War* (New York: G. P. Putnam's Sons, 1928), 73.
65. Slotkin, *Long Road to Antietam*, 182–83, 217; *OR*, Series 1, Vol. 19, Part 1: 209–10; Sears, *Landscape Turned Red*, 114–50, 157.
66. Starr 1: 313–14; Slotkin, *Long Road to Antietam*, 174.
67. *OR*, Series 1, Vol. 19, Part 1: 209–10; Starr 1: 313–16; R. L. T. Beale, *History of the Ninth Virginia Cavalry in the War Between the States* (Richmond, Va.: B. F. Johnson Publishing, 1899), 39–40; Abner Hard, *History of the Eighth Cavalry Regiment, Illinois Volunteers, During the Great Rebellion* (Aurora, Ill.: n.p., 1868), 178–79.
68. GAC to GBM, September 15, 1862, Roll 32, GBM Papers, LOC; Sears, *Landscape Turned Red*, 150, 157–59; Slotkin, *Long Road to Antietam*, 217.
69. Sears, *Landscape Turned Red*, 158–59; Slotkin, *Long Road to Antietam*, 274; GAC to GBM, September 17 [sic], 1862, Roll 32, GBM Papers, LOC. This note from GAC was misdated by a later archivist as September 17. Sears transcribes "Cartersville" as "Potomac"; close inspection reveals that GAC made a phonetic error in repeating the name of Keedysville.
70. Sears, *Landscape Turned Red*, 160–69.
71. Sears, *George B. McClellan*, 307; Slotkin, *Long Road to Antietam*, 274.
72. McPherson, 539–45; Sears, *Landscape Turned Red*, 303. McPherson, 544, includes the Spanish-American War in the casualty tally topped by Antietam.
73. GAC, "War Memoirs," *Galaxy* (June 1876).
74. Oliver Wendell Holmes, "My Hunt After 'The Captain,'" in *Pages from an Old Volume of Life: A Collection of Essays, 1857–1881* (Boston: Houghton, Mifflin and Company, 1891), 16–77. The essay originally appeared in *Atlantic Monthly* (December 1862).
75. GAC to Sister, September 27, 1862, GAC Correspondence, LBH; James H. Wilson, *Under the Old Flag*, vol. 1 (New York: D. Appleton, 1912), 100–03; Entry 1852, Cullum 2: 498.
76. McPherson, 557–58.
77. Sears, *Civil War Papers*, 481; Slotkin, *Long Road to Antietam*, 371; Sears, *Landscape Turned Red*, 317–20.
78. Sears, *Civil War Papers*, 482.
79. Sears, *Landscape Turned Red*, 319–20; Slotkin, *Long Road to Antietam*, 372, 376–77.
80. Slotkin, *Long Road to Antietam*, 380–83; Sears, *Civil War Papers*, 489–90; GAC to Cousin Augusta, October 3, 1862, transcript copy, GAC Papers, USMA.
81. GAC to Cousin Augusta, October 3, 1862, Transcript Copy, GAC Papers, USMA.
82. Slotkin, *Long Road to Antietam*, 380–83; Sears, *Civil War Papers*, 489–90.
83. GAC to Sister, September 27, 1862, GAC Correspondence, LBH.
84. Entry for November 10, 1862, Henry Clay Christiancy Diary, Folder 3, Box 1, Christiancy and Pickett Families' Papers, LOC; Slotkin, *Long Road to Antietam*, 384–91; McPherson, 568–70; Sears, *George B. McClellan*, 340–43; "Statement of the Military Service of George A. Custer of the United States Army," Adjutant General's Office, June 14, 1922, HR 3328, CRM.

Four: The Prodigy

1. Stiles, *First Tycoon*, 241. The transition from a personal economy to an institutional, organizational one is a major theme of *First Tycoon;* see, for example, 365–69. As noted in chapter 1, Mark R. Wilson writes persuasively of the professionalization and systemization of procedures initiated by the antebellum Quartermaster's Department in the U.S. Army in *The Business of Civil War: Military Mobilization and the State, 1861–1865* (Baltimore, Md.: Johns Hopkins University Press, 2006).
2. GAC to I. P. Christiancy, November 21, 1862, Box 1, GAC Papers, USMA; *Monroe Commercial*, May 29, 1862; Talcott E. Wing, ed., *History of Monroe County Michigan* (New York: Munsell and Co., 1890), 246–48, 260, 268, 277, 566.
3. GAC to I. P. Christiancy, November 21, 1862, Box 1, GAC Papers, USMA. The contents of Christiancy's letter must be deduced from GAC's reply, as no copy has been preserved in publicly accessible archives.
4. GAC to I. P. Christiancy, November 21, 1862, Box 1, GAC Papers, USMA.
5. *Twelfth Annual Catalogue of the Officers and Pupils of the Young Ladies' Seminary and Collegiate Institute at Monroe City, Michigan*, 1862 (Monroe, Mich.: Edward G. Morton, 1862), 4–7, 10–17; Merington, 46–47; Leckie, 22–23.
6. Catherine S. Crary, ed., *Dear Belle: Letters from a Cadet and Officer to His Sweetheart, 1858–1865* (Middletown, Conn.: Wesleyan University Press, 1965), 215.
7. *Twelfth Annual Catalogue*, 7–8; Leckie, 18, 22.
8. Leckie, 22–23; Merington, 46–47; Shirley A. Leckie, "The Civil War Partnership of Elizabeth and George A. Custer," in Carol K. Bleser and Lesley J. Gordon, eds., *Intimate Strategies of the Civil War: Military Commanders and Their Wives* (New York: Oxford University Press, 2001), 178–98 (to be called Leckie, "Partnership").
9. Entry for December 17, 1862, Elizabeth Bacon's Journal, Shirley A. Leckie Notes, Privately Held; Leckie, 25; Frost, *General Custer's Libbie*, 56–58. Leckie relies on EBC's journal for this period, as does Frost. Unfortunately this invaluable document, once owned by the Custer family, apparently has passed into the hands of private collectors. Leckie generously made her handwritten notes on this journal available to me, but I found that almost all material of interest in her notes appears in her published work.
10. Crary, 215; Tully McCrea to GAC, August 13, 1861, GAC Correspondence, LBH. Leckie, "Partnership," 179, speculates that gossip about his early affair with Mollie had traveled from Ohio to Monroe, which I find to be only remotely possible at best.
11. GAC to Sister, May 27, 1863, GAC Correspondence, LBH; *History of Monroe County*, 314; Leckie, 25–26; Frost, *General Custer's Libbie*, 58. Leckie, "Partnership," 179, notes that EBC wrote in her journal about GAC and Fifield, "He, like others, takes all she gives which I sometimes think is *everything*." Frost, 58, quotes the journal as saying, "John Bulkley told Nan [Darrah] that GAC knew Fan as well as any of the boys do!" See also Merington, 48–49, although, as Leckie warns, Merington's account incorrectly accepts EBC's later justification that the Fifield courtship was a fake, concocted to divert gossips from GAC's real love for EBC.
12. Leckie, 24–26; Frost, *General Custer's Libbie*, 59–60.

13. GBM to Adjutant General, December 9, 1862, Roll 35, GBM Papers, LOC; GAC to Sister, April 13, 1863, GAC Correspondence, LBH; Sears, *George B. McClellan*, 345.

14. GAC to Sister, April 13, 1863, GAC Correspondence, LBH; Sears, *George B. McClellan*, 344–47.

15. Edwin G. Burrow and Mike Wallace, *Gotham: A History of New York City to 1898* (New York: Oxford University Press, 1999), 565, 671–72, 974; GAC to Sister, April 13, 1863, GAC Correspondence, LBH.

16. Erving E. Beauregard, *Bingham of the Hills: Politician and Diplomat Extraordinary* (New York: Peter Lang, 1989), 70. See also Tom O'Neil, "Two Men of Ohio: Custer & Bingham," *Research Review: The Journal of the Little Big Horn Associates* 8, no. 1 (January 1994): 10–13. Christiancy shared this letter with Bingham, who reported the contents to an old law partner in the letter quoted here. Unfortunately the private letter collection from which this quote is taken has disappeared from public view, as explained to me by the Harrison County Historical Society of Cadiz, Ohio. Note, however, that more than a decade later Christiancy claimed that Blair could not help GAC merely because "the positions were filled. . . . [We] both regretted that he could not give you a place at the time." See Isaac P. Christiancy to GAC, February 10, 1875, Folder 11, Box 4, MMP. I am not inclined to credit this recollection.

17. Extract of Special Orders No. 169, April 13, 1863, and Invoice of Clothing, Camp, and Garrison Equipage, April 22, 1863, GAC Correspondence, LBH.

18. Stephen W. Sears, *Chancellorsville* (Boston: Houghton Mifflin, 1996), 67–73; Edward G. Longacre, *Lincoln's Cavalrymen: A History of the Mounted Forces of the Army of the Potomac* (Mechanicsburg, Pa.: Stackpole Books, 2000), 127–28.

19. Sears, *Chancellorsville*, 161–62; GAC to GBM, May 6, 1863, Roll 35, GBM Papers, LOC; Longacre, *Lincoln's Cavalrymen*, 111, 140. On GAC and Pleasonton, see, for example, a report of GAC at Pleasonton's side during a skirmish in Virginia on November 4, 1862, in *Maine Farmer*, November 27, 1862. GAC's assignment in late April and early May is difficult to pinpoint. The GAC papers in the LBH collection show that he reached Washington no later than April 22, and was issued field equipment. His letter to GBM, May 6, 1863, clearly shows that he was not with the raid under Stoneman, and was written on the stationery of Pleasonton's division headquarters, yet in it he declared that he commanded a company of the 5th U.S. Cavalry. Of course, he might not have been *with* his company during the raid. On May 16, 1863, he turned in a set of equipment appropriate for a company upon taking up duties as Pleasonton's aide-de-camp, as shown in the GAC papers in the LBH collection.

20. GAC to GBM, May 6, 1863, Roll 35, GBM Papers, LOC; Sears, *Chancellorsville*, 191, 266, 336–38; McPherson, 638–44.

21. GAC to GBM, May 6, 1863, Roll 35, GBM Papers, LOC; Charles Francis Adams Jr. to his mother, May 12, 1863, in Ford, ed., *A Cycle of Adams Letters*, 2: 8.

22. Longacre, *Lincoln's Cavalrymen*, 142, 149–50; Sears, *Chancellorsville*, 439–440; Receipt of Equipment Received by Quartermaster, May 16, 1863, and Receipt for Equipment Received by Ordnance Officer, May 16, 1863, GAC Correspondence, LBH. On Hooker, Stoneman, and Pleasonton, and the transfer of corps command, see GAC to I. P. Christiancy, May 31, 1863, Box 1, GAC Papers, USMA.

23. GAC to Sister, May 16, 1863, GAC Correspondence, LBH.

24. Leckie, 26.

25. GAC to Sister, May 16 and 27, 1863, GAC Correspondence, LBH.

26. GAC to Judge I. P. Christiancy, May 17, 1863, insert in Henry Clay Christiancy Diary, Folder 3, Box 1, Christiancy and Pickett Families' Papers, LOC.

27. *OR*, Series 1, Vol. 25, Part 1: 1116 and Vol. 27, Part 3: 97–98; GAC to Sister, May 27, 1863, GAC Correspondence, LBH; GAC to I. P. Christiancy, May 31, 1863, Box 1, GAC Papers, USMA; GAC to James Barnes, June 22, 1864, Folder 9, Box 1, James Barnes Papers, Naval Historical Society Collection, NYHS; Whittaker, 149–51; Wert, 75–76. On the extent of GAC's authority as aide-de-camp, see also GAC to Capt. Andrew J. Cohen, AAG, Cavalry Corps, May 28, 1863, ni 77, Huntington Library, San Marino, Calif.

28. Samuel Harris, *Personal Reminiscences* (Chicago: Rogerson Press, 1897), 17, 23–24; GAC to I. P. Christiancy, May 31, 1863, Box 1, GAC Papers, USMA. See also GAC to Judge I. P. Christiancy, May 17, 1863, insert, and entry for June 3, 1863, Henry Clay Christiancy Diary, Folder 3, Box 1, Christiancy and Pickett Families' Papers, LOC.

29. GAC to I. P. Christiancy, May 31, 1863, Box 1, GAC Papers, USMA; Whittaker, 148–51.

30. Stephen W. Sears, *Gettysburg* (New York: Houghton Mifflin, 2003), 60–61. The quote was from Hooker's explanation to Lincoln of his orders to Pleasonton.

31. *OR*, Series 1, Vol. 27, Part 1: 1046; Sears, *Gettysburg*, 64–74; Edward G. Longacre, *The Cavalry at Gettysburg: A Tactical Study of Mounted Operations During the Civil War's Pivotal Campaign, 9 June–14 July 1863* (Lincoln: University of Nebraska Press, 1986), 61–64, 69; Wert, 78.

32. Sears, *Gettysburg*, 72–74, 97; Longacre, *Cavalry at Gettysburg*, 66–91.

33. Longacre, *Cavalry at Gettysburg*, 103–9; Sears, *Gettysburg*, 98–99; Whittaker, 157–59.

34. Alfred Pleasonton to General Farnsworth, June 18, 1863, Alfred Pleasonton Papers, LOC. See also Longacre, *Cavalry at Gettysburg*, 109, and *Lincoln's Cavalrymen*, 172–73, which also recounts Pleasonton's relationship with Hooker, 147–73.

35. Sears, *Gettysburg*, 99–101; Longacre, *Lincoln's Cavalrymen*, 172–74; Alfred Pleasonton to General Farnsworth, June 23, 1863, Alfred Pleasonton Papers, LOC.

36. Sears, *Gettysburg*, 121–31.

37. Wert, 80–82; GAC to Judge Christiancy, July 26, 1863, insert in Henry Clay Christiancy Diary, Folder 3, Box 1, Christiancy and Pickett Families' Papers, LOC; *OR*, Series 1, Vol. 27, Part 3: 373; Extract of Special Orders No. 175, June 28, 1863, Special Orders No. 2, June 29, 1863, and GAC to Sister, July 26, 1863, GAC Correspondence, LBH.

38. GAC to Judge Christiancy, July 26, 1863, Christiancy and Pickett Families' Papers, LOC; GAC to Sister, July 26, 1863, GAC Correspondence, LBH; *OR*, Series 1, Vol. 27, Part 3: 373, 376. GAC was not, as he believed, the youngest Union general in the war, but he was certainly one of the youngest.

39. GAC to Sister, July 26, 1863, GAC Correspondence, LBH.

40. Merington, 58–61; Gregory J. W. Urwin, *Custer Victorious: The Civil War Battles of General George Armstrong Custer* (Lincoln: University of Nebraska Press, 1983), 57–58; Whittaker, 169. My analysis echoes that of Wert, to whom much credit belongs, 82–83.

41. Crary, 214.

42. George R. Agassiz, ed., *Meade's Headquarters, 1863–1865: Letters of Colonel Theodore Lyman, from the Wilderness to Appomattox* (Boston: Atlantic Monthly Press, 1922), 14.

43. Entry for June 29, 1863, Henry Clay Christiancy Diary, Folder 3, Box 1, Christiancy and Pickett Families' Papers, LOC.

44. Steven Hahn, *A Nation Under Our Feet: Black Political Struggles in the Rural South from Slavery to the Great Migration* (Cambridge, Mass.: Harvard University Press, 2003), 62–115.

45. Of the many studies of the attitudes of average soldiers, perhaps the best and most accessible is James M. McPherson, *For Cause and Comrades: Why Men Fought in the Civil War* (New York: Oxford University Press, 1997). I base my characterization not only on McPherson's book but on conclusions drawn from soldiers' letters and diaries, newspaper accounts, memoirs, and other sources I have read over the years.

46. Wert, 85–87; Longacre, *Cavalry at Gettysburg*, 172–78; Edward G. Longacre, *Custer and His Wolverines: The Michigan Cavalry Brigade, 1861–1865* (Conshohocken, Pa.: Combined Publishing, 1997), 132–38; Eric J. Wittenberg, ed., *At Custer's Side: The Civil War Writings of James Harvey Kidd* (Kent, Ohio: Kent State University Press, 2001), 6–11; John Robertson, ed., *Michigan in the War: Revised Edition* (Lansing, Mich.: W. S. George and Co., 1882), 583. Quote from Victor E. Comte to Elise, July 7, 1863, Victor E. Comte Papers, Bentley Historical Library, University of Michigan, Ann Arbor, Mich. Comte's quote refers specifically to another battle a few days later, but he was describing the general effect of the Spencer rifle on the Confederates. I have substituted "reload" for "charge" in the translation of Comte's letter, which was written originally in French.

47. William E. Miller, "The Cavalry Battle Near Gettysburg," *B&L* 3: 397–406 (quote on 399).

48. Charles Francis Adams Jr. to his mother, May 12, 1863, Worthington Chauncey Ford, ed., *A Cycle of Adams Letters, 1861–1865*, vol. 2 (Boston: Houghton Mifflin, 1920), 3–5.

49. Longacre, *Cavalry at Gettysburg*, 198–201; Longacre, *Custer and His Wolverines*, 138–42; *Michigan in the War*, 586–87; Wert, 88–89. Troy Hartman, "Hunterstown: North Cavalry Field of Gettysburg," in John P. Hart, ed., *Custer and His Times: Book Five* (Dexter, Mich.: Little Big Horn Associates, 2008), 25–34, argues that GAC charged merely to bait a trap, to draw the Confederate counterattack into the fire of his dismounted men and artillery. I find no evidence of planning a trap at Hunterstown. Deploying a supporting line on foot was standard tactical doctrine by July 1863. And his charge at the head of a handful of men would have seemed suicidal, as it nearly was, if he had had any notion of how many Confederates he faced.

50. Urwin, 68; Longacre, *Cavalry at Gettysburg*, 222–25.

51. GAC's report, August 22, 1863, in *Michigan in the War*, 582–84; *OR*, Series 1, Vol. 27, Part 1: 956–57; Longacre, *Cavalry at Gettysburg*, 222–25. Cress's Ridge is also known as Cress Ridge.

52. GAC's report, August 22, 1863, in *Michigan in the War*, 582–84; *OR*, Series 1, Vol. 27, Part 1: 956–57; Longacre, *Cavalry at Gettysburg*, 222–25; McPherson, 661–62.

53. GAC's report, August 22, 1863, in *Michigan in the War*, 582–84; *OR* Series 1, Vol.

27, Part 1: 956–57; Longacre, *Cavalry at Gettysburg*, 225–39; Longacre, *Custer and His Wolverines*, 147–54; Wert, 91–95.

54. William E. Miller, "The Cavalry Battle Near Gettysburg," *B&L* 3: 397–406.
55. GAC's report, August 22, 1863, in *Michigan in the War*, 582–84; *OR*, Series 1, Vol. 27, Part 1: 956–57; Longacre, *Cavalry at Gettysburg*, 225–39; Longacre, *Custer and His Wolverines*, 147–54; Wert, 91–95.
56. James H. Kidd to Father and Mother, July 9, 1863, James H. Kidd Papers, Bentley Historical Library, University of Michigan, Ann Arbor, Mich.
57. GAC's report, August 22, 1863, in *Michigan in the War*, 582–84; Miller, "The Cavalry Battle Near Gettysburg"; *OR*, Series 1, Vol. 27, Part 1: 956–57; Longacre, *Cavalry at Gettysburg*, 225–39; Longacre, *Custer and His Wolverines*, 147–54; Wert, 91–95.
58. GAC's report, August 22, 1863, in *Michigan in the War*, 582–84; *OR*, Series 1, Vol. 27, Part 1: 956–57; GAC to Sister, May 27 and July 26, 1863, GAC Correspondence, LBH; James H. Kidd to Father and Mother, July 9, 1863, James H. Kidd Papers, Bentley Historical Library, University of Michigan, Ann Arbor, Mich.; Longacre, *Cavalry at Gettysburg*, 225–39; Longacre, *Custer and His Wolverines*, 147–54; Wert, 91–95.
59. GAC's report, August 22, 1863, in *Michigan in the War*, 582–84.
60. Longacre, *Custer and His Wolverines*, 154. See also *OR*, Series 1, Vol. 27, Part 1: 186. GAC's brigade's aggregate losses in the Gettysburg Campaign as a whole, 355, compare to fifty-six for Gregg's entire division.
61. McPherson, 662.
62. Quoted in Wert, 102.

Five: The Women

1. LAR's obituary in the *Monroe Democrat*, July 6, 1906, notes that she was "never very robust. . . . Always deeply religious, quiet, and unostentatious. . . . She cared little for the world's pleasure, but found her chief enjoyment in church." On the role of women as moral and religious guardians, see, for example, Nina Silber, *Daughters of the Union: Northern Women Fight the Civil War* (Cambridge, Mass.: Harvard University Press, 2005), 6, 103. For an image of LAR, see Frost, *General Custer's Libbie*, 31.
2. LAR to GAC, August 13, 1862, Folder 21, Box 1, LAFCC; Whittaker, 122.
3. LAR to GAC, June 23, 1863, Folder 11, Box 2, LAFCC; *Monroe Democrat*, July 6, 1906.
4. GAC to Sister, May 16, 1863, GAC Correspondence, LBH; LAR to GAC, June 23, 1863, Folder 11, Box 2, LAFCC.
5. LAR to GAC, Jul 25, 1863, Folder 11, Box 2, LAFCC; Leckie, 31. Whittaker, 156–59, describes the picture and reproduces the engraving made from the sketch.
6. Leckie, 31.
7. LAR to GAC, Jul 25, 1863, Folder 11, Box 2, LAFCC. David Reed seems to have derived much of his income from farming. He owned a two-horse carriage and had a live-in female domestic servant and a live-in male farmhand. The 1860 census listed him as a "farmer" with $5,000 worth of real estate and a personal estate valued at $3,000. By contrast Daniel Bacon, listed as a "miller," had real estate worth $17,500 and the same-sized personal estate, along with a live-

in domestic servant from Germany. See returns for 1st Ward, City of Monroe, Michigan, 1860 U.S. Census, and Tax Assessment List, Division 10, District 1, Michigan, 1862, Internal Revenue Bureau, NA.

8. LAR to GAC, August 5, 1863, Folder 11, Box 2, LAFCC.

9. LAR to GAC, August 5 and 24, 1863, Folder 11, Box 2, LAFCC.

10. LAR to GAC, August 5 and 24, 1863, Folder 11, Box 2, LAFCC; GAC to LAR, July 25, 1863, GAC Correspondence, LBH.

11. Frost, *General Custer's Libbie*, 62.

12. Nettie Humphrey [Greene] to EBC, December 31, 1863, December 31, 1864, Folder 8, Box 2, LAFCC; Leckie, 6, 16.

13. Leckie makes this point after a thorough reading of EBC's now-unavailable diary—her uncertainty, self-doubt, desire to remain carefree, and fears "that she was useless and idle." She called herself "a little girl." See Leckie, 28–29, 36.

14. Leckie, 6–9; Frost, *General Custer's Libbie*, 5, 15.

15. Leckie, 7, 14–15.

16. Leckie, 9–10.

17. DSB to GAC, October 22, 1863, Folder 1, Box 1, LAFCC.

18. Leckie, 9–11, 15–16; Merington, 38; Frost, *General Custer's Libbie*, 31, 37.

19. DSB to GAC, October 22, 1863, Folder 1, Box 1, LAFCC; Leckie, 16–20; *Governor's Message to the Legislature of the State of Michigan, in Session, January 7, 1868* (Lansing, Mich.: John A. Kerr, 1863), 58–60.

20. EBC to Parents, March 20 [1864], Folder 14, Box 4, MMP; Leckie, 35.

21. Leckie, 14, 20–21.

22. Leckie, 19–20; Silber, 6, 44–46, 19, 168–72.

23. Frost, *General Custer's Libbie*, 39–41; Leckie, 21–22.

24. Leckie, 21–22.

25. *New York Herald*, May 16, 1864, reprinted in *Chicago Tribune*, May 20, 1864.

26. Leckie, 22–23; Nettie Humphrey to EBC, December 31, 1863, Folder 8, Box 2, LAFCC.

27. Leckie, 24–25.

28. DSB to GAC, October 22, 1863, Folder 1, Box 1, NHG to GAC, August 24, 1863, and Nettie Humphrey [Greene] to EBC, December 31, 1863, Folder 8, Box 2, LAFCC.

29. Entry for December 17, 1862, Elizabeth Bacon's Journal, Shirley A. Leckie Notes, Privately Held; Leckie, 25; Frost, *General Custer's Libbie*, 56–58, 62–63.

30. Leckie, 25; Frost, *General Custer's Libbie*, 59.

31. Leckie, 25–26.

32. Leckie, 26. My account of GAC and EBC's budding relationship tracks Leckie's closely. Not only has she written a very fine biography of EBC, but she had access to primary sources that are no longer publicly accessible, especially EBC's diary, as mentioned previously in the notes.

33. Leckie, 27, 36; Frost, *General Custer's Libbie*, 60; Reynolds, 72. On free-love advocacy, see, for example, Austin Kent, *Free Love: Or, a Philosophical Demonstration of the Non-Exclusive Nature of Connubial Love* (Hopkinton, N.Y.: Published by the author, 1857).

34. Frost, *General Custer's Libbie*, 62–63; Leckie, 30–32.

35. *Monroe Commercial*, July 2, 1863.

36. Leckie, 30–32; Frost, *General Custer's Libbie*, 72–74.

37. *Monroe Commercial,* July 23, 1863.

38. Leckie, 30–32; Frost, *General Custer's Libbie,* 72–74. For a photograph of David Reed, see Frost, *General Custer's Libbie,* 32.

39. Steven Hahn, *A Nation Under Our Feet: Black Political Struggles in the Rural South from Slavery to the Great Migration* (Cambridge, Mass.: Belknap Press, 2003), 24–26, 31; Nancy P. Allan, "Standing Up for Liberty: Eliza Brown Davison and the Custers," *Research Review: The Journal of the Little Bighorn Association* 17, no. 1 (winter 2003): 2–12; 1860 United States Census: Rappahannock County, Virginia, 55, and Slave Schedules, 19.

40. 1880 United States Census: District No. 4, Village of Athens, Athens County, Ohio, 17; Allan, "Standing Up"; Brenda E. Stevenson, *Life in Black and White: Family and Community in the Slave South* (New York: Oxford University Press, 1996), 160–61, 182–83.

41. Stevenson, 176–87, 197; Deborah Gray White, "Female Slaves: Sex Roles and Status in the Antebellum Plantation South," in Catherine Clinton, ed., *Half Sisters of History: Southern Women and the American Past* (Durham, N.C.: Duke University Press, 1994), 56–75.

42. Hahn, 16–36, 41–42; Stevenson, 228–29.

43. Hahn, 40–42; Stevenson, 227–39; White, "Female Slaves."

44. Stevenson, 160–61, 203, 205, 227–39, 251.

45. White, "Female Slaves"; Hahn, 14–19; Reynolds, 45–48; EBC, *Tenting on the Plains,* 40. See also Allan, "Standing Up."

46. Reid Mitchell, *Civil War Soldiers* (New York: Penguin, 1988), 162–64; Allan, "Standing Up."

47. Hahn, 15, 41; James M. McPherson, *The Negro's Civil War: How American Negroes Felt and Acted During the War for the Union* (New York: Pantheon, 1965), 62.

48. Victor E. Comte to Elise, July 30, 1863, Victor E. Comte Papers, Bentley Historical Library, University of Michigan, Ann Arbor, Mich.

49. Reporting to Pleasonton, GAC noted the precise time that the division occupied Amissville; *OR,* Series 1, Vol. 27, Part 3: 753.

50. EBC, *Tenting on the Plains,* 40–41. At different times Eliza Brown answered the question of why she fled the Pierce farm with a different emphasis, stressing the lack of food after armies marched through. The two answers are hardly incompatible, but I believe she had learned to tailor her responses to the expectations of white audiences. The exasperation expressed in this quote strikes me as authentic.

51. Reynolds, 45; Hahn, 22. Glenn David Brasher argues effectively that the insistence of the enslaved on seizing freedom altered the course of the war and pressed the issue of emancipation to the point where it became federal policy; see Brasher's *The Peninsula Campaign & the Necessity of Emancipation: African Americans and the Fight for Freedom* (Chapel Hill: University of North Carolina Press, 2012).

52. Edward G. Longacre, *Lincoln's Cavalrymen: A History of the Mounted Forces of the Army of the Potomac* (Mechanicsburg, Pa.: Stackpole Books, 2000), 203–06.

53. Victor E. Comte to Elise, July 7, 1863, Victor E. Comte Papers, Bentley Historical Library, University of Michigan, Ann Arbor, Mich.

54. Eric J. Wittenberg, J. David Petruzzi, and Michael F. Nugent, *One Continu-*

ous Fight: The Retreat from Gettysburg and the Pursuit of Lee's Army of Northern Virginia, July 4–14 (New York: Savas Beatie, 2008), 3–121; Longacre, *Lincoln's Cavalrymen*, 208–12; Longacre, *Custer and His Wolverines*, 156–58.

55. Victor E. Comte to Elise, July 16, 1863, Victor E. Comte Papers, Bentley Historical Library, University of Michigan, Ann Arbor, Mich.; Longacre, *Custer and His Wolverines*, 160–64.

56. James H. Kidd to Father and Mother, July 16, 1863, James H. Kidd Papers, Bentley Historical Library, University of Michigan, Ann Arbor, Mich.; Longacre, *Custer and His Wolverines*, 164–65.

57. Longacre, *Custer and His Wolverines*, 164–65; Wittenberg et al., *One Continuous Fight*, 284–97; Victor E. Comte to Elise, July 16, 1863, Victor E. Comte Papers, Bentley Historical Library, University of Michigan, Ann Arbor, Mich., and James H. Kidd to Father and Mother, July 16, 1863, James H. Kidd Papers, Bentley Historical Library, University of Michigan, Ann Arbor, Mich.

58. *OR*, Series 1, Vol. 27, Part 1: 1001–04 and Part 3: 741, 753–54; Victor E. Comte to Elise, July 20, 1863, Victor E. Comte Papers, Bentley Historical Library, University of Michigan, Ann Arbor, Mich.

59. *OR*, Series 1, Vol. 27, Part 1: 1001–03 and Part 3: 765–66. Longacre, in *Custer and His Wolverines*, 178–80, suggests that GAC hoped to delay the Confederates in time for an infantry attack, which never materialized. Even if this is accurate, GAC does not appear to have coordinated his movements with any other commander.

60. GAC to LAR, July 26, 1863, LBH; *OR*, Series 1, Vol. 27, Part 3: 765–66. On the struggle to refit—in particular, to remount—the cavalry after the Gettysburg Campaign, see Starr 2: 3–19.

61. *OR*, Series 1, Vol. 27, Part 3: 753–54; Victor E. Comte to Elise, July 20 and July 30, 1863, Victor E. Comte Papers, Bentley Historical Library, University of Michigan, Ann Arbor, Mich. I have slightly altered the translation from French in the Comte Papers to provide a more idiomatic reading.

62. *OR*, Series 1, Vol. 27, Part 1: 1001–02, Part 3: 830, Vol. 29, Part 2: 38–39, 63; James I. Christiancy to Father, August 21, 1863, Folder 4, Box 1, Christiancy and Pickett Families' Papers, LOC; Longacre, *Custer and His Wolverines*, 180–81. On the guerrilla war in Missouri, see Part II of Stiles, *Jesse James*.

63. GAC to John Bulkley, August 2, 1863, Folder 9, Box 1, GAC Collection, MCHMA.

64. GAC to Isaac P. Christiancy, July 26, 1863, insert in Henry Clay Christiancy Diary, Christiancy and Pickett Families' Papers, LOC; IPC to GAC, November 8, 1863, Folder 3, and James J. David to S. Thomas, August 4, 1863, Folder 4, Box 1, LAFCC.

65. *OR*, Series 1, Vol. 27, Part 1: 1004 and Vol. 27, Part 3: 775, 792. EBC later recalled hearing Eliza Brown say that she met GAC at Amissville in August; this appears unlikely from official records of the division's movement. See EBC, *Tenting on the Plains*, 40–41.

66. EBC, *Tenting on the Plains*, 40–42; Hahn, 73; Jim Downs, *Sick from Freedom: African-American Illness and Suffering During the Civil War and Reconstruction* (New York: Oxford University Press, 2012), 22–26, 47. EBC's writings, most dating to two or more decades after these events, are our main source on Eliza Brown. It appears that she attempted to reproduce Brown's speech accurately, and so quotations of Brown from EBC's work generally will not

standardize spelling. However EBC, like many nineteenth-century white writ-ers who attempted phonetic transcriptions of African American speech, inex-plicably changed the spelling of some words in a way that did not change their pronunciation—"cum" for "come," "sez" for "says," "wuz" for "was," "wasen't" for "wasn't," to name some examples. Since such spellings strike me as both uninformative and egregiously condescending, I have standardized them in such cases.

67. Hahn, 73–74. Downs, 4–8, 22–28, 46–47, discusses the disruption of support networks caused by mass escapes.
68. EBC, *Tenting on the Plains*, 40–42; Reynolds, 6, 44–45; Downs, 46–47.
69. EBC, *Tenting on the Plains*, 40–42; Reynolds, 45.
70. EBC, *Tenting on the Plains*, 40–42.
71. Reynolds, 48, 59, 70.
72. EBC, *Tenting on the Plains*, 40–42. Decades later, Frederick Benteen would claim that he had heard that GAC did sleep with Brown. Benteen did not know GAC during the Civil War, and hated him at the time he made this claim. His comments cannot be accepted as evidence.
73. *OR*, Series 1, Vol. 27, Part 1: 1004 and Part 3: 792; *Philadelphia Inquirer*, quoted in *Monroe Commercial*, July 23, 1863; Victor E. Comte to Elise, August 1863, Victor E. Comte Papers, Bentley Historical Library, University of Michigan, Ann Arbor, Mich.; Bruce Catton, *The Army of the Potomac: A Stillness at Appo-mattox* (New York: Anchor Books, 1990 [orig. pub. 1953]), 3–5; Longacre, *Lin-coln's Cavalrymen*, 225–26.
74. L. G. Estis to GAC, August 14, 1863, Old Book 89: 15, contained within Vol. 71: 3rd Cavalry Division, Cavalry Corps, Army of the Potomac, Entry 1593: Letters Sent August 1863–June 1865, Part 2, RG 393, NA.
75. *New York Times*, September 20, 1863; *Personal Reminiscences of Samuel Harris* (Chicago: Rogerson Press, 1897), 45–46; Judson Kilpatrick to C. Ross Smith, September 12, 1863, Old Book 89: 42, contained within Vol. 71: 3rd Cavalry Division, Cavalry Corps, Army of the Potomac, Entry 1593: Letters Sent August 1863–June 1865, Part 2, RG 393, NA.
76. Nettie Humphrey [Greene] to GAC, August 24, 1863, Folder 8, Box 2, LAFCC.
77. GAC to LAR, July 26, 1863, LBH.
78. James Christiancy to DSB, August 27, 1863, GAC Correspondence, LBH.
79. GAC to E. B. Parsons, September 5, 1863, CRM; AKR to GAC, August 24, 1863 [concluded on Sept. 4.], Folder 11, Box 2, LAFCC.
80. *OR*, Series 1, Vol. 29, Part 1: 111–19; George R. Agassiz, ed., *Meade's Head-quarters, 1863–1865: Letters of Colonel Theodore Lyman from the Wilderness to Appomattox* (Boston: Massachusetts Historical Society, 1922), 13–17; Longacre, *Custer and His Wolverines*, 183–85; Longacre, *Lincoln's Cavalrymen*, 223–24.
81. GAC to E. B. Parsons, September 13, 1863, Surgeon's Certificate, September 13, 1863, Personnel Files, CRM; *New York Herald*, September 15, 1863.
82. Frost, *General Custer's Libbie*, 75.
83. Frost, *General Custer's Libbie*, 72–73; *New York Tribune*, September 17, 1863.
84. Nettie Humphrey [Greene] to GAC, August 24, 1863, Folder 8, Box 2, LAFCC; *Monroe Monitor*, September 30, 1863; Frost, *General Custer's Libbie*, 75.
85. *Monroe Commercial*, October 1, 1863; Frost, *General Custer's Libbie*, 75.
86. Wert, 113–14; Frost, *General Custer's Libbie*, 76.
87. GAC to EBC, October 6, 1863, quoted in Whittaker, 210–11.

88. Frost, *General Custer's Libbie*, 76–77.
89. GAC to Nettie Humphrey, October 7, 1863, quoted in Whittaker, 211.
90. GAC to Nettie Humphrey, quoted in Whittaker, 213.
91. Whittaker, 214–15; Frost, *General Custer's Libbie*, 76–77.
92. Frost, *General Custer's Libbie*, 76–77.
93. Frost, *General Custer's Libbie*, 76–79; DSB to GAC, October 22, 1863, Folder 1, Box 1, LAFCC.

Six: The General

1. GAC to LAR, October 25, 1863, GAC Correspondence, LBH.
2. This is a generalized observation of evangelical culture in the Civil War North. I have found no discussions of theater in the letters of any of GAC's relatives apart from EBC. See Laurence Senelick, "Introduction," in Senelick, ed., *The American Stage: Writing on Theater from Washington Irving to Tony Kushner* (New York: Library of America, 2010), xvii–xxxi.
3. GAC to LAR, October 25, 1863, GAC Correspondence, LBH.
4. LAR to GAC, August 24, 1863, Folder 11, Box 2; EHC to GAC, October 25 1863, Folder 20, Box 1; Margaret Custer to GAC, October 27, 1863, Folder 2, Box 2, LAFCC.
5. GAC to LAR, November 6, 1863, GAC Correspondence, LBH.
6. GAC to Nettie Humphrey, October 9, 1863, quoted in Whittaker, 212–13; GAC to LAR, October 25, 1863, GAC Correspondence, LBH.
7. Edward G. Longacre, *Lincoln's Cavalrymen: A History of the Mounted Forces of the Army of the Potomac* (Mechanicsburg, Pa.: Stackpole Books, 2000), 226–28; Edward G. Longacre, *Custer and His Wolverines: The Michigan Cavalry Brigade, 1861–1865* (Conshohocken, Pa.: Combined Publishing, 1997), 186–89; Shelby Foote, *The Civil War: A Narrative*, vol. 2: *Fredericksburg to Meridian* (New York: Vintage, 1986 [orig. pub. 1963]), 786–92; Gregory J. W. Urwin, *Custer Victorious: The Civil War Battles of General George Armstrong Custer* (Lincoln: University of Nebraska Press, 1990 [orig. pub. 1983]), 102–03; Wert, 116–17; Starr 2: 23–27; Whittaker, 201–02; *OR*, Series 1, Vol. 29, Part 1: 229–30, 389–90, 393–95; GAC to LAR, October 25, 1863, GAC Correspondence, LBH.
8. Utley, *Cavalier in Buckskin*, 20; Starr 2: 26–27.
9. *OR*, Series 1, Vol. 29, Part 1: 390.
10. GAC to Nettie Humphrey, October 12, 1863, quoted in Whittaker, 213; Merington, 66.
11. See, for example, Thom Hatch, *Glorious War: The Civil War Adventures of George Armstrong Custer* (New York: St. Martin's Press, 2014).
12. *OR*, Series 1, Vol. 29, Part 2: 448. On the bureaucratization of the supply of horses and the disputes over their quality, see Starr 2: 12–19. Victor E. Comte was detailed to obtain remounts, and found fewer than fifty that were "any good" to replace 150 worn-out horses that he brought to the Dismounted Camp. "In the Dismounted Camp there are about 7,000 soldiers who are waiting for arms and horses." See Victor E. Comte to Elise, October 28, 1863, Victor E. Comte Papers, Bentley Historical Library, University of Michigan, Ann Arbor, Mich.
13. Foote 2: 790–802. Foote's massive work offers an excellent narrative, though his sympathies for the Confederacy consistently cloud his conclusions. In the Bris-

toe Station Campaign, Lee suffered more casualties in absolute numbers than Meade, and dramatically more as a percentage of his forces; he was defeated in the battle at Bristoe Station; and his brief advance proved fruitless, leaving him to retreat to his original position, his forces reduced for the effort. Yet Foote 2: 796, deems this a "highly successful" campaign for Lee. The claim is mystifying.

14. GAC to Isaac P. Christiancy, October 29, 1863, Insert in Henry Clay Christiancy Diary, Christiancy and Pickett Families' Papers, LOC; letter fragment, October 29, 1863, GAC Papers, USMA. I believe these two letter fragments are from the same piece of correspondence. The continuity, tone, and reference to "Jim," meaning James Christiancy, strongly point to Judge Christiancy as the recipient of the latter fragment.

15. Whittaker, 196–97; Victor E. Comte to Elise, November 6, 1863, Victor E. Comte Papers, Bentley Historical Library, University of Michigan, Ann Arbor, Mich.

16. GAC to LAR, October 25, 1863, GAC Correspondence, LBH; Thomas Ward to GAC, November 2, 1863, Folder 21, Box 1, LAFCC.

17. *Chicago Tribune*, October 27, 1863; Longacre, *Lincoln's Cavalrymen*, 226–31; Starr 2: 29–30; Wert, 118–20.

18. *OR*, Series 1, Vol. 29, Part 1: 390–92, 462–64; James H. Kidd to Father and Mother, October 26, 1863, James H. Kidd Papers, Bentley Historical Library, University of Michigan, Ann Arbor, Mich.; *New York Evangelist*, November 19, 1863; Longacre, *Lincoln's Cavalrymen*, 226–31; Starr 2: 29–30; Longacre, *Custer and His Wolverines*, 189–91; Wert, 118–20.

19. GAC to Nettie Humphrey, quoted in Whittaker, 214, and Merington, 68–69.

20. James H. Kidd to Father and Mother, October 26, 1863, James H. Kidd Papers, Bentley Historical Library, University of Michigan, Ann Arbor, Mich.

21. *OR*, Series 1, Vol. 29, Part 1: 462–64; Longacre, *Custer and His Wolverines*, 190–91; Wert, 120–21; letter fragment, October 29, 1863, GAC Papers, USMA.

22. GAC to Nettie Humphrey, quoted in Whittaker, 214, and Merington, 68–69. Whittaker seems to have been much more careful in quoting letters than Merington, who freely edited letters without indicating changes or excisions in the text. In this case, both quoted the same letter, but Merington did so at much greater length.

23. Longacre, *Lincoln's Cavalrymen*, 226.

24. Quoted in Merington, 69. References in this letter to heavy losses and refitting and remounting indicate that it was written at the very end of October 1863.

25. EHC to GAC, October 25, 1863, Folder 20, Box 1, LAFCC. On biographers' views of Emmanuel Custer, see, for example, Richard Slotkin, *The Fatal Environment: The Myth of the Frontier in the Age of Industrialization, 1800–1890* (Norman: University of Oklahoma Press, 1995 [orig. pub. 1985]), 374–35; Wert, 18–19.

26. GAC to LAR, October 25, 1863, November 6, 1863, GAC Correspondence, LBH.

27. As with so many general observations of GAC's personality offered in this book, this one is not original. See, for example, Slotkin, *The Fatal Environment*, 371–432.

28. Isaac P. Christiancy to GAC, November 8, 1863, Folder 3, Box 1, LAFCC.

29. Merington, 73–74; Leckie, 34.

30. DSB to GAC, December 12, 1863, Folder 1, Box 1, LAFCC.
31. GAC to DSB, December 18, 1863, Folder 1, Box 4, MMP; GAC to LAR, December 22, 1863, GAC Correspondence, LBH.
32. Merington, 74–80; Leckie, 32–33, 35–37.
33. Merington, 76–77; Leckie, 32–33, 35–37; Wert, 143–45.
34. Merington, 75, 77.
35. Merington, 77; Nettie Humphrey to EBC, December 31, 1863, Folder 8, Box 2, LAFCC.
36. Nettie Humphrey to EBC, December 31, 1863, Folder 8, Box 2, LAFCC.
37. Leckie, 34–35; *New York Times*, November 18, 1863. GAC wrote that he awoke one morning in December to find fifty men from the 7th Michigan Infantry outside his headquarters, hoping to join his command; GAC to LAR, December 7, 1863, GAC Correspondence, LBH. He wrote to Christiancy, apparently, on December 19 that he was to be married in February, noting that James would accompany him home to Monroe. See GAC to Friend, December 19, 1863, GAC Papers, USMA.
38. GAC to Jacob M. Howard, January 4, 1864, reproduced in Hamilton Gay Howard, *Civil War Echoes: Character Sketches and State Secrets* (Washington, D.C.: Howard Publishing, 1907), 304–05; GAC to Senator Zachariah Chandler, January 4, 1864, Roll 1, Zachariah Chandler Papers, LOC; James H. Kidd to Parents, April 16, 1864, James H. Kidd Papers, Bentley Historical Library, University of Michigan, Ann Arbor, Mich. See also Gregory J. W. Urwin, "Custer: The Civil War Years," in Paul Andrew Hutton, ed., *The Custer Reader* (Norman: University of Oklahoma Press, 2004 [orig. pub. 1992]), 7–32.
39. GAC to Friend, January 7, 1864, GAC to Dear Friend, January 7, 1864, GAC Papers, USMA. Both of these appear to be to Isaac Christiancy, the second written after the receipt of new information from Washington.
40. GAC to DSB, January 19, 1864, Folder 2, Box 4, MMP; GAC to Friend, January 20, 1864, GAC Papers, USMA.
41. Reynolds, 45; James H. Kidd to Parents, January 18, 1864, James H. Kidd Papers, Bentley Historical Library, University of Michigan, Ann Arbor, Mich.; Foner, 60–61; GAC to Friend, January 20, 1864, GAC Papers, USMA. For a discussion of this letter and GAC's contrary political convictions, see Slotkin, *The Fatal Environment*, 383–84.
42. GAC to Jacob Howard, January 19, 1864, reproduced in Howard, 306–13.
43. As evidence of the ferocity of his desire to win, see GAC to Emmanuel Custer, October 16, 1864, typescript copy, GAC Papers, USMA.
44. Reynolds, 74.
45. GAC to Jacob Howard, January 19, 1864, reproduced in Howard, 306–13.
46. Leckie, 36–37.
47. GAC to DSB, January 19, 1864, Folder 2, Box 4, MMP.
48. GAC to Friend, January 20, 1864, GAC Papers, USMA. The Senate did not vote on his confirmation until April 1, when it confirmed a large batch of some two dozen brigadier general appointments, including those of Adelbert Ames and Judson Kilpatrick; *New York Times*, April 2, 1864.
49. DSB to Sister, April 13, 1864, Folder 1, Box 1, LAFCC.
50. DSB to Sister, April 13, 1864, DSB to EBC and GAC, n.d., Folder 1, Box 1, LAFCC; *Monroe Commercial*, February 11, 1864; *Monroe Monitor*, February 10, 1864; Merington, 82; Leckie, 37.

51. Merington, 82–83; Frost, 91–93; GAC to Friend, December 19, 1863, GAC Papers, USMA.

52. GAC to EBC, March 30, 1865, Folder 3, Box 4, MMP.

53. Merington, 83; McPherson, 88–91. Frost, *General Custer's Libbie*, 94, writes that the Custers stopped in Buffalo specifically to allow Libbie to see a play for the first time.

54. Merington, 84–85; Leckie, 38; Leckie, "The Civil War Partnership of Elizabeth and George A. Custer," in Carol K. Bleser and Lesley J. Gordon, eds., *Intimate Strategies of the Civil War: Military Commanders and Their Wives* (New York: Oxford University Press, 2001), 178–98.

55. Reynolds, 73–74.

56. Reynolds, 73.

57. GAC to DSB, April 23, 1864, GAC Correspondence, LBH; Merington, 82.

58. GAC to DSB, April 23, 1864, GAC Correspondence, LBH.

59. GAC to S. Williams, February 13, 1864, Alfred Pleasonton to S. Williams, February 16, 1864, Alfred Pleasonton to E. B. Parsons, February 26, 1864, Personnel Files, CRM.

60. Reynolds, 44–45, 48.

61. Reynolds, 44–48, 66; Leckie, 40.

62. Reynolds, 66–67; Leckie, 40.

63. Reynolds, 45–48; Longacre, *Lincoln's Cavalrymen*, 237–245; Stephen W. Sears, *Controversies and Commanders: Dispatches from the Army of the Potomac* (New York: Houghton Mifflin, 1999), 225–52; Wert, 137–42.

64. James H. Kidd to his parents, March 20, 1864, James H. Kidd Papers, Bentley Historical Library, University of Michigan, Ann Arbor, Mich.

65. *OR*, Series 1, Vol. 33: 161–63, 164–66, 171.

66. EBC to her parents, March 20 [n.d.], Folder 14, Box 4, MMP. The letter was written on a Sunday, which narrows the year to 1864.

67. Merington, 86–87; EBC to her parents, March 20 [n.d.], Folder 14, Box 4, MMP; Rebecca Richmond to Aunt, Uncle, and Half-Cousin, March 30, 1864, Folder 18, Box 1, LAFCC; Statement of William Wysham [?], Surgeon in Chief, 2d Brig. 3 Div., March 24, 1864, Personnel Files, CRM.

68. Wert, 142–44; Frost, *General Custer's Libbie*, 96–97. I have located references to this case in the National Archives, but have been unable to find the original documents quoted, which appear in Wert and Frost.

Seven: The Hero

1. EBC to Aunt Eliza, July 3, 1864, GAC Correspondence, LBH; EBC to her parents, March 28, 1864, quoted in Merington, 87.

2. Adams, Meade, and Wainwright quoted in John J. Hennessy, "I Dread the Spring: The Army of the Potomac Prepares for the Overland Campaign," in Gary W. Gallagher, ed., *The Wilderness Campaign* (Chapel Hill: University of North Carolina Press, 1997), 66–105; see also John Keegan, *The Mask of Command* (New York: Viking, 1987), 202; William S. McFeely, *Grant: A Biography* (New York: W. W. Norton, 1982), esp. 58–89; McPherson, 395–96, 588–90, 718.

3. Merington, 87–88.

4. Keegan, 205–12, 232–33 (*New York World* quoted on 208).

5. EBC to Daniel and Rhoda Bacon, April 3, 1864, Folder 2, Box 4, MMP.

6. GAC to EBC, April 16, 1864, GAC to EBC, May 17, 1864, Folder 2, Box 4, GAC to EBC, April 20 [1864], GAC to EBC, undated fragment, Folder 14, Box 4, MMP.

7. Jacob Greene to GAC, March 30, 1864, Folder 2, Box 4, MMP.

8. EBC to Daniel and Rhoda Bacon, April 3, 1864, Folder 2, Box 4, MMP; Francis W. Kellogg to James H. Kidd, June 5, 1864, James H. Kidd Papers, Bentley Historical Library, University of Michigan, Ann Arbor, Mich.; *Boston Herald*, April 2, 1864. On EBC's emerging role as GAC's representative in Washington, see Leckie's perceptive analysis, 43–45.

9. EBC to Daniel and Rhoda Bacon, April 3, 1864, Folder 2, Box 4, MMP; *Harper's Weekly*, March 19, 1864.

10. Jacob Greene to GAC, March 30, 1864, Folder 2, Box 4, MMP; Starr 2: 68–77.

11. Victor Comte to Elise, April 20, 1864, Victor E. Comte Papers, Bentley Historical Library, University of Michigan, Ann Arbor, Mich.

12. James H. Kidd to his parents, April 16, 1864, James H. Kidd Papers; Victor Comte to Elise, April 20, 1864, Victor E. Comte Papers, Bentley Historical Library, University of Michigan, Ann Arbor, Mich; Wert, 148.

13. GAC to DSB, April 23, 1864, GAC Correspondence, LBH.

14. GAC to DSB, April 23, 1864, GAC Correspondence, LBH.

15. GAC to DSB, April 23, 1864, GAC Correspondence, LBH; GAC to EBC, April 16, 1864, Folder 2, Box 4, MMP.

16. Starr 2: 74–75; PHS, *Personal Memoirs of P. H. Sheridan* (New York: Da Capo Press, 1992 [orig. pub. 1888]), 187, 193; Hennessy, "I Dread the Spring," 66–105.

17. GAC to DSB, April 23, 1864, GAC Correspondence, LBH; Sheridan, 194–95; George Gray to James H. Kidd, April 28, 1864, James H. Kidd Papers, Bentley Historical Library, University of Michigan, Ann Arbor, Mich.; Edward G. Longacre, *Lincoln's Cavalrymen: A History of the Mounted Forces of the Army of the Potomac, 1861–1865* (Mechanicsburg, Pa.: Stackpole Books, 2000), 250–56.

18. GAC to EBC, April 20 [1864], Folder 14, Box 4, MMP.

19. GAC to EBC, April 16, 1864, Folder 2, Box 4, MMP. GAC specifically told DSB that he had not informed EBC of his troubles, which is supported by GAC's upbeat letter to her a few days earlier. See GAC to DSB, April 23, 1864, GAC Correspondence, LBH; GAC to EBC, April 16, 1864, Folder 2, Box 4, MMP.

20. Merington, 94.

21. James I. Christiancy to Father, May 3, 1864, Folder 4, Box 1, Christiancy and Pickett Families' Papers, LOC.

22. McPherson, 724–25; Gordon C. Rhea, "Union Cavalry in the Wilderness: The Education of Philip H. Sheridan and James H. Wilson," in Gary W. Gallagher, ed., *The Wilderness Campaign* (Chapel Hill: University of North Carolina Press, 1997), 106–35.

23. McPherson, 725–26; Rhea, "Union Cavalry in the Wilderness."

24. Rhea, "Union Cavalry in the Wilderness"; Wert, 152–53; Edward G. Longacre, *Custer's Wolverines: The Michigan Cavalry Brigade, 1861–1865* (Conshohocken, Pa.: Combined Publishing, 1997), 206–07; Millard K. Bushong and Dean M. Bushong, *Fightin' Tom Rosser, C.S.A.* (Shippensburg, Pa.: Beidel Printing House,

1983), 1–3, 12, 75; William Naylor McDonald, *History of the Laurel Brigade* (Baltimore, Md.: Sun Job Printing Office, 1907), 234–35; *OR*, Series 1, Vol. 36, Part 2: 774. McPherson, 724–28, places initial Union and Confederate strength at 115,000 and 64,000 respectively, and losses at 17,500 and nearly 11,000, though any such tallies can only be approximate.

25. *Circular*, July 11, 1864; *OR*, Series 1, Vol. 36, Part 1: 776–78; *New York Herald*, May 16, 1864, reprinted in *Chicago Tribune*, May 20, 1864; McPherson, 728.

26. Sheridan, 199–201.

27. *Circular*, July 11, 1864; *OR*, Series 1, Vol. 36, Part 1: 776–78; *New York Herald*, May 16, 1864, reprinted in *Chicago Tribune*, May 20, 1864; Sheridan, 204.

28. Sheridan, 205; McPherson, 728.

29. *OR*, Series 1, Vol. 36, Part 1: 817–18; Longacre, *Lincoln's Cavalrymen*, 266–68; Longacre, *Custer's Wolverines*, 210–13; Shelby Foote, *The Civil War: A Narrative*, vol. 3: *Red River to Appomattox* (New York: Vintage, 1986 [orig. pub. 1974), 229–31; James H. Kidd, *Personal Recollections of a Cavalryman* (Ionia, Mich.: Sentinel Press, 1908), 282.

30. *OR*, Series 1, Vol. 36, Part 1: 787–88, 817–18, 828; Kidd, 282, 296–306; Longacre, *Lincoln's Cavalrymen*, 266–68; Longacre, *Custer's Wolverines*, 210–14; Foote 3: 229–31; Wert, 155–57.

31. *Chicago Tribune*, June 1, 1864; *OR*, Series 1, Vol. 36, Part 1: 787–88, 817–18, 828, 834; *New York Herald*, May 16, 1864, reprinted in *Chicago Tribune*, May 20, 1864. The *Tribune* story of June 1 identified the private who shot Stuart as "Dunn," but in other respects it corresponds closely to other reports, including Alger's. Most historians describe Huff as having shot Stuart with a revolver—in many accounts, as the Michigan Brigade was driven back from a charge. I quote the *Tribune* account because it agrees with Alger's report, was printed soon after the event, and makes the most sense: a long-range shot with a Spencer, after dislodging the Confederates from their initial position. However, reporting of such small details of large battles is necessarily inaccurate; certainty is impossible. Stuart may have been shot with a revolver as traditional accounts claim. See, for example, Mark Grimsley, *And Keep Moving On: The Virginia Campaign, May–June 1864* (Lincoln: University of Nebraska Press, 2002), 116.

32. *Chicago Tribune*, June 1, 1864; *OR*, Series 1, Vol. 36, Part 1: 787–88, 817–18, 828, 834; *New York Herald*, May 16, 1864, reprinted in *Chicago Tribune*, May 20, 1864; Foote 3: 231–32; McPherson, 728. Foote's Southern bias comes through clearly in his description of the conclusion of the battle, in which he states that the Confederates restored their line and Sheridan concluded to leave, which was simply not true.

33. GAC to EBC, May 17, 1864, Folder 2, Box 4, MMP.

34. McPherson, 736–41; Grimsley, *And Keep Moving On*, 90–93; Richard Slotkin, *No Quarter: The Battle of the Crater, 1864* (New York: Random House, 2009), 7–17.

35. *New York Herald*, May 16, 1864, reprinted in *Chicago Tribune*, May 20, 1864; *Circular*, July 11, 1864; EBC to her parents, May 1, 1864, quoted in Merington, 94; James H. Kidd to his parents, June 3, 1864, James H. Kidd Papers, Bentley Historical Library, University of Michigan, Ann Arbor, Mich.

36. GAC to EBC, April 23 and May 16, 1864, Merington, 93, 97.

37. EBC to GAC, April 1864, quoted in Merington, 89.

38. Merington, 89–95, 100, 107, 113; EBC to Aunt Eliza, July 3, 1864, GAC Correspondence, LBH.

39. Leckie, 45; Merington, 92, 95; GAC to EBC, May 17, 1864, Folder 2, Box 4, MMP.

40. Leckie, 44; Merington, 93, 100–01; GAC to Judge Christiancy, July 26, 1863, insert in Henry Clay Christiancy Diary, Folder 3, Box 1, Christiancy and Pickett Families' Papers, LOC. See also Shirley Leckie's fine study of the Custer marriage during the war years, "The Civil War Partnership of Elizabeth and George A. Custer," in Carol K. Bleser and Lesley J. Gordon, eds., *Intimate Strategies of the Civil War: Military Commanders and Their Wives* (New York: Oxford University Press, 2001), 178–98.

41. Merington, 90–93 (Merington frequently combines different letters or paraphrases or makes error of transcription without explaining herself, so these quotes may well be from multiple letters); John J. Hennessy, "I Dread the Spring: The Army of the Potomac Prepares for the Overland Campaign," in Gary W. Gallagher, ed., *The Wilderness Campaign* (Chapel Hill: University of North Carolina Press, 1997), 66–105. On May 22, 1863, War Department General Order 143 created the Bureau of Colored Troops; see Walter B. Hill Jr., "Living with the Hydra: The Documentation of Slavery and the Slave Trade in Federal Records, Part 2," *Prologue Magazine* 32, no. 4 (winter 2000).

42. Merington, 90–91; EBC to Aunt Eliza, July 3, 1864, GAC Correspondence, LBH.

43. Merington, 100–01, 113. For an example of Francis Kellogg's brazen trading of favors, see Francis W. Kellogg to James H. Kidd, June 5, 1864, James H. Kidd Papers, Bentley Historical Library, University of Michigan, Ann Arbor, Mich. In it, he promises that Governor Austin Blair will appoint Kidd as colonel of the 6th Michigan Cavalry Regiment, and in return he expects Kidd to appoint Kellogg's designees to his staff.

44. Merington, 101, 106, 108–09; EBC to Aunt Eliza, July 3, 1864, GAC Correspondence, LBH.

45. Grimsley, *And Keep Moving On*, 151–52, 196–221; Merington, 101. For descriptions of Haw's Shop and GAC's behavior there, see James H. Kidd to Parents, June 3, 1864, James H. Kidd Papers, Bentley Historical Library, University of Michigan, Ann Arbor, Mich.; Sheridan, 218–22. John Huff, the trooper who killed Stuart, died at Haw's Shop.

46. Merington, 100–01; EBC to Aunt Eliza, July 3, 1864, GAC Correspondence, LBH.

47. Unidentified Author, Diary, Mss 5:1 W2767:1, Virginia Historical Society, Richmond, Va.

48. Grimsley, *And Keep Moving On*, 135–36.

49. Unidentified Author, Diary, Mss 5:1 W2767:1, Virginia Historical Society, Richmond, Va.

50. Merington, 104; Eric J. Wittenberg, *Glory Enough for All: Sheridan's Second Raid and the Battle of Trevilian Station* (Washington, D.C.: Brassey's, 2001), 22–23. Wittenberg, xviii, notes that Sheridan tended to distort the truth in his reports and memoirs, often using hindsight to claim intent where favorable developments had been, in fact, purely fortuitous; this appears to be the case with the intent of the raid, which Sheridan claimed was designed to draw away Lee's cavalry. And yet, as Wittenberg also notes, such a purpose was consistent

with Grant's strategy, and so in fact may have been an aspect of the original plan.

51. Wittenberg, 37–41, 47, 52–57.
52. Merington, 104; Wittenberg, 97–125, particularly 112–13.
53. David G. Smith, "Race and Retaliation: The Capture of African Americans During the Gettysburg Campaign," in Peter Wallenstein and Bertram Wyatt-Brown, eds., *Virginia's Civil War* (Charlottesville: University of Virginia Press, 2005), 137–51.
54. EBC, *Tenting on the Plains*, 40–42.
55. Merington, 104.
56. Merington, 104–06, 109.
57. Wittenberg, 97–125, particularly 112–13; Merington, 104; *OR*, Series 1, Vol. 36, Part 1: 796, 823; Wittenberg, 59, 98–100. A military rule of thumb states that an attacking force should have a three-to-one advantage to be confident of success. GAC only found the road with the guidance of a local contraband; see his testimony in HR 30, Part IV: 72, 1st Session, 39th Congress.
58. Wittenberg, 71–91; *OR*, Series 1, Vol. 36, Part 1: 823–25.
59. Millard K. Bushong and Dean M. Bushong, *Fightin' Tom Rosser, C.S.A.* (Shippensburg, Pa.: Beidel Printing House, 1983), 1–3, 12, 75; McDonald, *History of the Laurel Brigade*, 234–35.
60. Kidd, *Personal Recollections*, 353; Wittenberg, 102.
61. Wittenberg, 102–25 (Rosser quoted on 123–24); *OR*, Series 1, Vol. 36, Part 1: 823–24; Kidd, *Personal Recollections*, 360–61.
62. Wittenberg, 125, 138.
63. Merington, 104–05; Wittenberg, 117–25; Urwin, 157–64.
64. Wittenberg, 114–15.
65. James H. Kidd to Parents, June 21, 1864, James H. Kidd Papers, Bentley Historical Library, University of Michigan, Ann Arbor, Mich.; Wittenberg, 72–91; 133–36.
66. Wittenberg, 151; *OR*, Series 1, Vol. 36, Part 1: 823–25.
67. Wittenberg, 156–58.
68. Morris Schaff, *The Sunset of the Confederacy* (Boston: John W. Luce and Co., 1912), 179.
69. Schaff, 179–80; Reynolds, 70; Merington, 104.
70. Wittenberg, 183–217.
71. Charles Francis Adams Jr. to Charles Francis Adams, May 29, 1864, Worthington Chauncey Ford, ed., *A Cycle of Adams Letters, 1861–1864*, vol. 2 (Boston: Houghton Mifflin, 1920), 131–34.
72. For an example of GAC using the phrase "Custer luck," see GAC to EBC, February 8, 1869, Folder 7, Box 4, MMP.
73. Merington, 113.
74. Merington, 113–14; EBC to Aunt Eliza, July 3, 1864, GAC Correspondence, LBH.
75. GAC to Zachariah Chandler, June 26, 1864, Zachariah Chandler Papers, LOC.
76. Merington, 113–14; EBC to Aunt Eliza, July 3, 1864, GAC Correspondence, LBH.
77. Acting Surgeon in Chief's Statement, 1 Brig. 1st Div., July 11, 1864, Personnel Files, CRM.

78. James H. Kidd to his parents, July 12, 1864, James H. Kidd Papers, Bentley Historical Library, University of Michigan, Ann Arbor, Mich.

Eight: The Victor

1. Merington, 102, 105. When Merington transcribed this June letter (the original now being unavailable to researchers), she wrote "*double entendu.*" As Merington made various errors of transcription of letters that are available for inspection, the phrase has been rendered correctly here, on the assumption that she made an error in this case.
2. Wert, 167–69; Leckie, 48; Merington, 121. Wert, 34–35, suggests plausibly that GAC's treatment for gonorrhea at West Point may have impaired his fertility. Of course, there may have been other factors that inhibited the couple's ability to produce children.
3. Ida C. Brown, *Michigan Men in the Civil War* (Ann Arbor: University of Michigan Press, 1959), 36; Victor Comte to Elise, November 6, 1863, Victor E. Comte Papers, Bentley Historical Library, University of Michigan, Ann Arbor, Mich.
4. Charles Wainwright, June 14, 1864, Allan Nevins, ed., *A Diary of Battle: The Personal Journals of Colonel Charles S. Wainwright, 1861–1865* (New York: Da Capo Press, 1998 [orig. pub. 1962], 419–20; McPherson, 742–43; Richard Slotkin, *No Quarter: The Battle of the Crater, 1864* (New York: Random House, 2009), 7–15; Mark Grimsley, *And Keep Moving On: The Virginia Campaign, May–June 1864* (Lincoln: University of Nebraska Press, 2002), 90–93, 161.
5. McPherson, 740–43; Grimsley, *And Keep Moving On*, 90–93, 225–39.
6. McPherson, 739, 756–58; Joseph T. Glatthaar, "U. S. Grant and the Union High Command During the 1864 Valley Campaign," in Gary W. Gallagher, ed., *The Shenandoah Valley Campaign of 1864* (Chapel Hill: University of North Carolina Press, 2006), 34–55.
7. McPherson, 756–58.
8. GAC to LAR, August 24, 1864, GAC Correspondence, LBH; Wert, 172–73; Gregory J. W. Urwin, *Custer Victorious: The Civil War Battles of General George Armstrong Custer* (Lincoln: University of Nebraska Press, 1990 [orig. pub. 1983]), 171–74.
9. James H. Kidd to Parents, September 9, 1864, James H. Kidd Papers, Bentley Historical Library, University of Michigan, Ann Arbor, Mich.; GAC to DSB, September 2, 1864, GAC Correspondence, LBH; Jeffry D. Wert, *From Winchester to Cedar Creek: The Shenandoah Campaign of 1864* (New York: Simon and Schuster, 1987), 18–22.
10. Merington, 116.
11. GAC to LAR, August 24, 1864, GAC to DSB, September 2, 1864, GAC to LAR, September 17, 1864, GAC Correspondence, LBH.
12. Reynolds, 46; GAC to LAR, August 24, 1864, GAC Correspondence, LBH.
13. GAC to DSB, September 2, 1864, GAC Correspondence, LBH; EHC to GAC September 1 and 20, 1864, Folder 20, Box 1, LAFCC. Note that the manuscript letter from GAC to DSB refers to DSB only as "My dear Father," which raises the possibility that it was addressed to EHC, not DSB. However, the formality of the letter and contextual references make it clear that it was sent to DSB, whom GAC referred to as "father" after his marriage to EBC.

14. GAC to DSB, September 2, 1864, GAC Correspondence, LBH.
15. *New York Tribune*, August 22, 1864.
16. McPherson, 771; Stephen W. Sears, *George B. McClellan: The Young Napoleon* (New York: Da Capo Press, 1999 [orig. pub. 1988]), 371–77.
17. Merington, 118–19.
18. Reynolds, 77–78.
19. EHC to GAC September 1 and 6, 1864, Folder 20, Box 1, David Reed to GAC, September 14, 1864, Folder 12, Box 2, LAFCC.
20. GAC to Friend, September 16, 1864, GAC Papers, USMA.
21. Wert, 174–75; Jay W. Simson, *Custer and the Port Royal Executions of 1864* (Jefferson, N.C.: McFarland and Co., 2009).
22. GAC to Friend, September 16, 1864, GAC Papers, USMA; *New York Times*, October 27, 1864. The *New York Times* edited the letter somewhat.
23. I. P. Christiancy to GAC, September 21 and 22, 1864, Folder 3, Box 1, LAFCC.
24. EHC to GAC, September 22, 1864, Folder 20, IPC to GAC, September 22, 1864, Folder 3, Box 1, LAFCC.
25. GAC to EHC, October 16, 1864, typescript copy, GAC Papers, USMA; *New York Times*, October 27, 1864.
26. I. P. Christiancy to GAC, September 22, 1864, Folder 3, Box 1, LAFCC.
27. GAC to Amasa E. Dana, September 8, 1864, CW 77, Huntington Library, San Marino, Calif.; Wert, *From Winchester to Cedar Creek*, 41–54, 73.
28. Wert, *From Winchester to Cedar Creek*, 73–74.
29. Wert, *From Winchester to Cedar Creek*, 47–70, 74, 80–94.
30. Wert, *From Winchester to Cedar Creek*, 77–78; *OR*, Series 1, Vol. 43, Part 1: 456.
31. *OR*, Series 1, Vol. 43, Part 1: 456.
32. Wert, *From Winchester to Cedar Creek*, 47–70, 74, 80–94; *OR*, Series 1, Vol. 43, Part 1: 456–57.
33. *OR*, Series 1, Vol. 43, Part 1: 456–57; "Recollections of General Custer at Winchester, Sept. 19, 1864," in W. C. King and W. P. Derby, eds., *Camp-Fire Sketches and Battle-Field Echoes* (Springfield, Mass.: King, Richardson and Co., 1888), 77.
34. Wert, 180–83; Urwin, 178–88; Wert, *From Winchester to Cedar Creek*, 95–97, 103, 106; *OR*, Series 1, Vol. 43, Part 1: 445, 458.
35. Wert, *From Winchester to Cedar Creek*, 144; Edward G. Longacre, *Lincoln's Cavalrymen: A History of the Mounted Forces of the Army of the Potomac* (Mechanicsburg, Pa.: Stackpole Books, 2000), 307–09; Merington, 122; Special Orders No. 42, September 26, 1864, GAC Correspondence, LBH; McPherson, 777; Robert E. L. Krick, "A Stampeede [sic] of Stampeeds [sic]: The Confederate Disaster at Fisher's Hill," in Gary W. Gallagher, ed., *The Shenandoah Valley Campaign of 1864* (Chapel Hill: University of North Carolina Press, 2006), 161–99; William J. Miller, "Never Has There Been a More Complete Victory: The Cavalry Engagement at Tom's Brook, October 9, 1864," in Gary W. Gallagher, ed., *The Shenandoah Valley Campaign of 1864* (Chapel Hill: University of North Carolina Press, 2006), 134–60, esp. 140–41; James H. Kidd to Father, October 21, 1864, James H. Kidd Papers, Bentley Historical Library, University of Michigan, Ann Arbor, Mich.
36. Edward G. Longacre, *Custer and His Wolverines: The Michigan Cavalry Brigade, 1861–1865* (Conshohocken, Pa.: Combined Publishing, 1997), 251; Merington, 119–20; Wert, 186–87; GAC to James H. Kidd, October 3, 1864, James H. Kidd Papers, Bentley Historical Library, University of Michigan, Ann Arbor, Mich.

37. Wert, *From Winchester to Cedar Creek*, 144.
38. Wert, 188–89; Wert, *From Winchester to Cedar Creek*, 144–45; William G. Thomas, "Nothing Ought to Astonish Us: Confederate Civilians in the 1864 Shenandoah Valley Campaign," in Gary W. Gallagher, ed., *The Shenandoah Valley Campaign of 1864* (Chapel Hill: University of North Carolina Press, 2006), 222–56; OR, Series 1, Vol. 43, Part 1: 55–56. On the violence in Missouri, see Stiles, *Jesse James*, 73–143. Mark Grimsley emphasizes the term "hard war" over "total war," noting that space must be preserved for the great difference between the Civil War and the mobilization and mass killing of civilians seen in twentieth-century world wars. He stresses the limits on the destruction, but also shows how emancipation transformed the Civil War, and was the "touchstone of hard war." See Mark Grimsley, *The Hard Hand of War: Union Military Policy Toward Southern Civilians, 1861–1865* (New York: Cambridge University Press, 1995), 120–41, 171–225.
39. Miller, "Never Has There Been a More Complete Victory," 135; Millard Bushong and Dean Bushong, *Fightin' Tom Rosser, C.S.A.* (Shippensburg, PA: Beidel Printing House, 1983), 111–14.
40. Miller, "Never Has There Been a More Complete Victory," 139–41; PSH, *Personal Memoirs of P. H. Sheridan* (New York: Da Capo Press, 1992 [orig. pub. 1888]), 310–11.
41. Miller, "Never Has There Been a More Complete Victory," 139–41; Wert, 190–91; OR, Series 1, Vol. 43, Part 1: 520–22.
42. Miller, "Never Has There Been a More Complete Victory," 139–41; Wert, 190–91; OR, Series 1, Vol. 43, Part 1: 520–22, 527–28; Whittaker, 258.
43. Miller, "Never Has There Been a More Complete Victory," 139–41; Wert, 190–91; OR, Series 1, Vol. 43, Part 1: 520–22, 527–28; Merington, 122. Making fun of Rosser as the "Savior of the Valley" was a popular sport after Tom's Brook, indulged in by Sheridan and James H. Kidd, among others. See James H. Kidd to Father, October 21, 1864, James H. Kidd Papers, Bentley Historical Library, University of Michigan, Ann Arbor, Mich.
44. OR, Series 1, Vol. 43, Part 1: 522–28; EBC, *Tenting on the Plains*, 40–44.
45. *Harper's Weekly*, November 5 and 11, 1864; Wert, 193–97; OR, Series 1, Vol. 43, Part 1: 522–28; William W. Bergen, "The Other Hero of Cedar Creek: The 'Not Especially Ambitious' Horatio G. Wright," in Gary W. Gallagher, ed., *The Shenandoah Valley Campaign of 1864* (Chapel Hill: University of North Carolina Press, 2006), 85–133; Gary W. Gallagher, *Stephen Dodson Ramseur: Lee's Gallant General* (Chapel Hill: University of North Carolina Press, 1985), 164–66.
46. W. H. Seward to General Stevenson, October 22, 1864, Personnel Files, CRM; *New York Times*, October 27, 1864; *Boston Herald*, October 25, 1864; *Harper's Weekly*, November 12, 1864; Merington, 125–26; Leckie, 59–60. GAC was the commander of only about half of the enlisted men taking part in the ceremony.
47. Merington, 127–28.
48. *New York Times*, October 27, 1864.
49. Special Orders No. 340, October 10, 1864, and No. 132, October 23, 1864, GAC Correspondence, LBH; GAC to James H. Kidd, October 3, 1864, James H. Kidd Papers, Bentley Historical Library, University of Michigan, Ann Arbor, Mich.; Carl F. Day, *Tom Custer: Ride to Glory* (Norman: University of Oklahoma Press, 2002), 47.
50. GAC to Samuel Dreck, December 2, 1864, Personnel Files, CRM; GAC to

Judge Bacon, November 20, 1864, EBC to Parents, Folder 2, Box 4, MMP, NYPL; Merington, 129; Wert, 199.

51. Margaret Custer to GAC and EBC, December 2, 1864, Folder 2, Box 2, LAFCC.

52. EBC to Parents, November 20, 1864, and December 4, 1864 (typescript), Folder 2, Box 4, MMP.

53. Diary of Corporal William E. Walsh, Special and Archival Collections, Providence College.

54. GAC to William Russell Jr., February 13, 1865, GAC to F. C. Newhall, February 20, 1865, GAC to William Rupell Jr., February 24, 1865, L. Hubert to A. B. Nettleton, February 24, 1865, GAC to A. C. M. Pennington, February 24, 1865, 3rd Cavalry Division, Cavalry Corps, Army of the Potomac, Entry 1593: Letters Sent August 1863–June 1865, 87–97, RG 393, Part 2, No. 71, NA; A. B. Dyer to GAC, January 4, 1865, GAC Correspondence, LBH; Wert, 199–204.

55. EBC to Parents, November 20, 1864, and December 4, 1864 (typescript), Folder 2, Box 4, MMP, NYPL; Nettie Humphrey to EBC, December 31, 1864, January 8, 1865, Folder 8, Box 2, LAFCC; Merington, 131–36; Wert, 199–204.

56. DSB to GAC, February 8, 1865, DSB to Sister, February 17, 1865, Folder 1, Box 1, LAFCC; Wert, 203–04.

57. EHC to GAC, February 20, 1865, Folder 20, Box 1, LAFCC.

58. DSB to Sister, February 17, 1865, Folder 1, Box 1, LAFCC.

59. GAC to Zachariah Chandler, February 22, 1865, Zachariah Chandler Papers, LOC; Wert, 204–05.

60. *New York Herald* in *Chicago Tribune*, March 14, 1865; *New York Times*, March 26, 1865; Edward G. Longacre, *Lincoln's Cavalrymen: A History of the Mounted Forces of the Army of the Potomac, 1861–1865* (Mechanicsburg, Pa.: Stackpole Books, 2000), 318–19; Wert, 205–10; Urwin, 226–30.

61. GAC to Zachariah Chandler, March 19, 1865, Zachariah Chandler Papers, LOC; Wert, 213. Bingham wrote to Stanton, urging GAC's appointment to the rank of brigadier general in the Regular Army; John A. Bingham to Edwin Stanton, April 3, 1865, Civil War Letters Received, GAC Correspondence, LBH, and Personnel Files, CRM.

62. GAC to EBC, March 30, 1865, Folder 3, Box 4, MMP.

63. McPherson, 563–65. For more than a generation, historical scholarship has stressed the agency of enslaved African Americans. See, for example, Steven Hahn, *A Nation Under Our Feet: Black Political Struggles in the Rural South from Slavery to the Great Migration* (Cambridge, Mass.: Harvard University Press, 2003), 1–127, and Eric Foner, *Reconstruction: America's Unfinished Revolution, 1863–1877* (New York: Harper and Row, 1988), 77–123. On the centrality of slavery to the existence of the Confederate States of America, see for example Section 9 of Article 1 of the Constitution of the Confederate States of America.

64. Mark Grimsley and Brooks D. Simpson, "Introduction," and Mark Grimsley, "Learning to Say 'Enough': Southern Generals and the Final Weeks of the Confederacy," in Mark Grimsley and Brooks D. Simpson, eds., *The Collapse of the Confederacy* (Lincoln: University of Nebraska Press, 2001), 1–12, 40–79.

65. GAC to EBC, March 30 and 31, 1865, Folder 3, Box 4, MMP; *OR*, Series 1, Vol. 46, Part 1: 1129–31; Urwin, 237.

66. *OR*, Series 1, Vol. 46, Part 1: 1129–31; Longacre, *Lincoln's Cavalrymen*, 327–28; Urwin, 239–43; Wert, 216–19; Carl F. Day, *Tom Custer: Ride to Glory* (Norman: University of Oklahoma Press, 2002), 60–65; McPherson, 844–46.

67. McPherson, 846.
68. Urwin, 244; Wert, 218–20; Day, 67–71; *OR*, Series 1, Vol. 46, Part 1: 1131–32.
69. Whittaker, 301–04; Wert, 244–50; 220–21; Day, 71–77; McPherson, 848; *OR*, Series 1, Vol. 46, Part 1: 1132.
70. Wert, 222–23; Whittaker, 306; Urwin, 249–53. For an account of executions of two men for "insulting women," see entry for October 26, 1864, Diary of Corporal William E. Walsh, Special and Archival Collections, Providence College.
71. James Longstreet, *From Manassas to Appomattox: Memoirs of the Civil War in America* (Philadelphia, Pa.: J. B. Lippincott Company, 1908), 627; Wert, 224–25.
72. McPherson, 849.
73. GAC to Sister, April 21, 1865, typescript copy, GAC Papers, USMA.
74. GAC to EBC, April 11, 1865, EBC Papers, Beinecke Library, Yale University, New Haven, Conn.
75. GAC to ECB, April 10, 1865, Folder 3, Box 4, MMP; Frost, *General Custer's Libbie*, 130–32; Wert, 225–26; GAC to the Soldiers of the Third Cavalry Division, April 9, 1865, CRM.
76. Frost, *General Custer's Libbie*, 130–32; Wert, 225–26; PHS to EBC, April 10, 1865, Civil War Letters Received, GAC Correspondence, LBH; HR 338, CRM; S. F. Chalfin to GAC, May 19, 1865, GAC Correspondence, LBH, states that the appointment date was April 3, 1865.
77. The standard estimate for the number of dead in the Civil War has long stood at around 620,000. However a new scholarly consensus of 752,000 to 851,000 has emerged, thanks to J. David Hacker, "A Census-Based Count of the Civil War Dead," *Civil War History* 57, no. 4 (December 2011): 307–48.

PART II

Nine: The Executioner

1. Affidavit of Junius Garland, May 23, 1865, Affidavit of Richard V. Gaines, May 23, 1865, GAC Papers, Receipt, July 1, 1865, Civil War Letters Received, GAC Correspondence, and EBC Notes, EBC Literary Manuscripts and Notes, LBH.
2. Affidavit of C. W. P. Brock, May 23, 1865, GAC Correspondence, LBH.
3. John Keegan, *The Mask of Command* (New York: Penguin, 1988 [orig. pub. 1987]), 233.
4. Rebecca Richmond to Father, March 24, 1865, Civil War Letters Received, GAC Correspondence, LBH.
5. EBC, *Tenting on the Plains*, 40–44; GAC to Sister, April 21, 1865, typescript copy, GAC Papers, USMA; IPC to GAC, May 16, 1865, Folder 3, Box 1, LAFCC; *Baltimore Sun*, May 25, 1865.
6. GAC to Sister, April 21, 1865, typescript copy, GAC Papers, USMA; DSB to Sister, May 20, 1865, Folder 1, Box 1, LAFCC.
7. DSB to Sister, May 20, 1865, Folder 1, Box 1, LAFCC; GAC to Jacob Greene, Washington, D.C., n.d., Jacob Greene Papers, U.S. Army Military History Institute; Whittaker, 310–11; *Harper's Weekly*, June 10, 1865.
8. *Chicago Tribune*, May 24, 1865; *Harper's Weekly*, June 10, 1865; *New York Evangelist*, May 25, 1865; *New York Tribune*, May 24, 1865; *Harrisburg Weekly Patriot and Union*, June 8, 1865.
9. PHS to GAC, May 7 and 17, June 17, 1865, GAC Correspondence, LBH; *OR*,

Series 1, Vol. 48, Part 2: 743; *New York Tribune,* May 25, 1865; *Baltimore Sun,* May 25, 1865; McPherson, 668.

10. *New York Tribune,* June 1, 1865.

11. *Baltimore Sun,* May 25, 1865; *Monroe Commercial,* June 1, 1865.

12. *Monroe Commercial,* June 1, 1865; Marie Miller to GAC, n.d., Folder 21, Box 1, LFCC; EBC, *Tenting on the Plains,* 40–44, 76. See also Nina Silber, *Daughters of the Union: Northern Women Fight the Civil War* (Cambridge, Mass.: Harvard University Press, 2005), 215, 231–32.

13. EBC, *Tenting on the Plains,* 36–38.

14. EBC, *Tenting on the Plains,* 50–66; *New York Tribune,* June 30, 1865.

15. GAC to Brother & Sister, June 23, 1865, typescript copy, GAC Papers, USMA; *OR,* Series 1, Vol. 48, Part 2: 743, 917 and Vol. 53: 608.

16. GAC to Brother & Sister, June 23, 1865, typescript copy, GAC Papers, USMA; EBC, *Tenting on the Plains,* 67–71; Thomas S. Cogley, *History of the Seventh Indiana Cavalry Volunteers* (LaPorte, Ind.: Herald Company, 1876), 162; John F. Marszalek, *Sherman: A Soldier's Passion for Order* (New York: Free Press, 1993), 123–49.

17. Merington, 168.

18. EBC, *Tenting on the Plains,* 76–80; Cogley, 164. On racial stereotypes and Democratic political culture, pertinent to further developments in this chapter, see Jean H. Baker, *Affairs of Party: The Political Culture of Northern Democrats in the Mid-Nineteenth Century* (New York: Fordham University Press, 1998), 212–58.

19. EBC, *Tenting on the Plains,* 76, 106–10; Foner, 77–81, 106–10 (quote on 109); Baker, 177–81; George Frederickson, *The Black Image in the White Mind: The Debate on Afro-American Character and Destiny, 1817–1914* (Middletown, Conn.: Wesleyan University Press, 1987 [orig. pub. 1971]), 63.

20. *Washington Constitutional Union,* July 19, 1865.

21. Foner, 175–93, 199–205.

22. It should be noted that GAC's orders were both controversial and also part of a continuum of military action. On the controversy, see, for example, *San Francisco Bulletin,* August 24, 1865. General Gordon Granger, who occupied Galveston and declared slaves in Texas free on June 19, 1865 (thereafter celebrated as "Juneteenth"), also warned against "idleness," as did Maj. Gen. Oliver O. Howard, the commissioner of the Freedmen's Bureau. Other officers, influenced by white planters, tried to suppress what they saw as "vagrancy." Perhaps most important, from the standpoint of precedent and law, was Gen. Nathaniel Banks's General Orders No. 23, issued in Louisiana. Banks eliminated flogging, allotted plots to allow black families to raise food for themselves, established schools and medical care, and limited work to a ten-hour day; but he also required able-bodied men to take labor contracts, prohibited them from leaving their workplaces, and seized the unemployed as vagrants and put them to work on public works. See William L. Richter, *Overreached on All Sides: The Freedmen's Bureau Administrators in Texas, 1865–1868* (College Station, Tex.: Texas A&M University Press, 1991), 19–27; William L. Richter, *The Army in Texas During Reconstruction: 1865–1870* (College Station, Tex.: Texas A&M University Press, 1987), 14–16.

23. Affidavit of Richard V. Gaines, Affidavit of Junius Garland, Affidavit of C. W. P. Brock, all May 23, 1865, GAC Correspondence, LBH; *Washington Star* in *New York Herald,* June 30, 1865.

24. *New York Times*, June 25, 1865; Receipt, July 1, 1865, GAC Correspondence, LBH; GAC to DSB, fragment, c. July 1865, EBC Papers, Beinecke Library, Yale University, New Haven, Conn.

25. Pedigree of Don Juan, dated April 12, 1866, and Affidavit of GAC, June 19, 1866, GAC Correspondence, LBH.

26. PHS to GAC, October 10, 1865, PHS to Headquarters, Armies of the United States, July 8, 1865, Letters Received, GAC Correspondence, LBH; *OR*, Series 1, Vol. 48, Part 2: 1068.

27. Ulysses S. Grant, *Personal Memoirs of U.S. Grant* (New York: Da Capo Press, 1982 [orig. pub. 1885]), 186.

28. John Keegan, *The Mask of Command* (New York: Viking, 1987), 194.

29. John Y. Simon, ed., *The Papers of Ulysses S. Grant*, vol. 15 (Carbondale, Ill.: Southern Illinois University Press, 1988), 259n; *OR*, Series 1, Vol. 48, Part 2: 917, 1068 and Vol. 53: 608; Charles H. Lothrop, *A History of the First Regiment Iowa Cavalry* (Lyons, Iowa: Beers and Eaton, 1890), 217.

30. John M. Carroll, *Custer in Texas: An Interrupted Narrative* (New York: Sol Lewis, 1975), 32; Cogley, 164; Lothrop, 216; entry 3099: Special Orders Issued, June 1865–January 1866, Vol. 17/48 D Tex, pp. 22–25, 34, No. 198: 2nd Cavalry Division, Department of Texas, RG 393, Part 2.

31. *OR*, Series 1, Vol. 48, Part 2: 1068; Lothrop, 217–18, 226–30; Henry L. Morrill to Henry Albers, July 19, 1865, Folder 2, Box 1, Henry Leighton Morrill Papers, Beinecke Library, Yale University, New Haven, Conn.

32. ECB to Judge Bacon & Wife, August 6, 1865, GAC to Judge & Mrs. Bacon, October 5, 1865, Folder 3, Box 4, MMP; EBC, *Tenting on the Plains*, 81–89, 119; Cogley, 165.

33. Entry 3099: Special Orders Issued, June 1865–January 1866, Vol. 17/48 Department of Texas, pp. 44–45, No. 198, 2nd Cavalry Division, Department of Texas, RG 393, Part 2, NA; Cogley, 164; Carroll, 31.

34. Lothrop, 218–19; Richter, *The Army in Texas*, 13–16.

35. Lothrop, 218–19.

36. Lothrop, 222; Henry L. Morrill to Henry Albers, June 27, 1865, Folder 2, Box 1, Henry Leighton Morrill Papers, Beinecke Library, Yale University, New Haven, Conn.

37. Entry 3099: Special Orders Issued, June 1865–January 1866, Vol. 17/48 Department of Texas, pp. 68–70, No. 198, 2nd Cavalry Division, Department of Texas, RG 393, Part 2, NA.

38. Carroll, 33, 50–51; Cogley, 165–66; Lothrop, 223–24; *Papers of Ulysses S. Grant*, vol. 15: 431–32n; Wert, 233–34. As noted by the 2nd Wisconsin historian, quoted in Carroll, Lancaster was released after a few months and long outlived GAC.

39. Inspector General, Department of the Army, "The Mikolashek Report: Detainee Operations Inspection, July 21, 2004," in Karen J. Greenberg and Joshua L. Dratel, eds., *The Torture Papers: The Road to Abu Ghraib* (New York: Cambridge University Press, 2005), 630–907.

40. Henry L. Morrill to Henry Albers, August 26, 1865, Folder 2, Box 1, Henry Leighton Morrill Papers, Beinecke Library, Yale University, New Haven, Conn.; Lothrop, 290.

41. Lothrop, 290; EBC to her Aunt, Eliza Sabin, September 3, 1865, Folder 3, Box 4, MMP; General Orders No. 15, August 7, 1865, Charles H. Lothrop Papers,

State Historical Society of Iowa; Leckie, 72–76; EBC, *Tenting on the Plains*, 119–30.

42. PHS to GAC, August 15, 1865, GAC Correspondence, LBH; Provost Marshal Lee to George B. Davidson, September 11, 1865, Charles H. Lothrop Papers, State Historical Society of Iowa; Wert, 235; entry 3099: Special Orders Issued, June 1865–January 1866, Vol. 17/48 Department of Texas, pp. 36–37, and Old Book 48: 39, 43, No. 198, 2nd Cavalry Division, Department of Texas, RG 393, Part 2, NA. For commentary on the civilian whipping, see Henry L. Morrill to Henry Albers, September 3, 1865, Folder 1, Box 3, Henry Leighton Morrill Papers, Beinecke Library, Yale University, New Haven, Conn.

43. GAC's reply is typical of his pique in dealing with these resignation attempts. Entry 3099: Special Orders Issued, June 1865–January 1866, Vol. 17/48 Department of Texas, pp. 38–39, 48–49, No. 198, 2nd Cavalry Division, Department of Texas, RG 393, Part 2, NA.

44. Lothrop, 292, 297; EBC, *Tenting on the Plains*, 100–04.

45. Henry L. Morrill to Henry Albers, September 10 and November 6, 1865, Folder 2, Box 1, Henry Leighton Morrill Papers, Beinecke Library, Yale University, New Haven, Conn.; entries for September 1, October 15 and 19, 1865, Vol. 154, Register of Letters Received, Secretary of War, Roll 125, Microfilm Publication M22, NA; Simon 15: 431, 431–32n; *Washington Constitutional Union*, March 22, 1866; Wert, 235.

46. Simon 15: 431, 431–32n; *Des Moines State Register*, July 24, 1868.

47. Henry L. Morrill to Henry Albers, December 1, 1865, Folder 2, Box 1, Henry Leighton Morrill Papers, Beinecke Library, Yale University, New Haven, Conn. Contrast GAC's difficulties with the success of Wesley Merritt on a longer march, Richter, *Army in Texas*, 18–19. See also *New York Times*, March 5, 1866.

48. *Des Moines State Register*, July 24, 1868.

49. M. P. Hanson, Surgeon, 2nd Wisconsin Cavalry, to E. M. Gregory, Superintendent of Freedmen, Refugees, and Abandoned Lands, October 12, 1865, Letters Received, Unregistered, 1865–66, Roll 17, Records of the Assistant Commissioner for the State of Texas, Bureau of Refugees, Freedmen, and Abandoned Lands, 1865–1869, Microfilm Publication M821, NA.

50. McPherson, 174–76, 852.

51. EBC, *Tenting on the Plains*, 160–70, 206–08.

52. EBC, *Tenting on the Plains*, 78–81, 166–68, 179–208, 230–31.

53. Richter, *The Army in Texas*, 33; Richter, *Overreached*, 11.

54. Provisional Governor A. J. Hamilton of Texas to Major General H. G. Wright, September 27, 1865, Letters Received, Unregistered, 1865–66, Roll 17, Records of the Assistant Commissioner for the State of Texas, Bureau of Refugees, Freedmen, and Abandoned Lands, 1865–1869, Microfilm Publication M821, NA; Carl H. Moneyhon, *Texas After the Civil War: The Struggle of Reconstruction* (College Station, Tex.: Texas A&M University Press, 2004), 5–6, 21–37.

55. Maj. General H. G. Wright to Governor A. J. Hamilton, October 10, 1865, Letters Sent by the Department of Texas, the District of Texas, and the 5th Military District, Roll 1, Microfilm Publication M1165, NA.

56. M. P. Hanson, Surgeon, 2nd Wisconsin Cavalry, to E. M. Gregory, Superintendent of Freedmen, Refugees, and Abandoned Lands, October 12, 1865, Letters Received, Unregistered, 1865–66, Roll 17, Records of the Assistant Commis-

sioner for the State of Texas, Bureau of Refugees, Freedmen, and Abandoned Lands, 1865–1869, Microfilm Publication M821, NA.

57. Benjamin L. Brisbane to Thomas W. Conway, September 14, 1865, Letters Received, Unregistered, 1865–66, Roll 17, Records of the Assistant Commissioner for the State of Texas, Bureau of Refugees, Freedmen, and Abandoned Lands, 1865–1869, Microfilm Publication M821, NA.

58. EBC, *Tenting on the Plains*, 245–46, 258.

59. EBC to Rebecca Richmond, November 17, 1865, EBC Correspondence, LBH; EBC, *Tenting on the Plains*, 158–64, 179–82, 216–25, 266.

60. EBC, *Tenting on the Plains*, 232–36.

61. EBC, *Tenting on the Plains*, 179–208; EBC to Rebecca Richmond, June 29, 1865, EBC Correspondence, PHS to GAC, October 10, 1865, GAC Correspondence, LBH; GAC to Brother & Sister, October 15, 1865, typescript copy, GAC Papers, USMA.

62. GAC to Daniel and Rhoda Bacon, October 5, 1865, Folder 3, Box 4, MMP.

63. GAC to Daniel and Rhoda Bacon, October 5, 1865, Folder 3, Box 4, MMP; EBC, *Tenting on the Plains*, 80–81; GAC to Brother & Sister, October 15, 1865, typescript copy, GAC Papers, USMA; Baker, 177–81, 212–58; Frederickson, 71–96, 130–97.

64. George C. Aston [?] to E. M. Gregory, December 16, 1865, Letters Received, Unregistered, 1865–66, Roll 17, Records of the Assistant Commissioner for the State of Texas, Bureau of Refugees, Freedmen, and Abandoned Lands, 1865–1869, Microfilm Publication M821, NA. See also Richter, *Overreached*, 3–75.

65. *New York Times*, March 5, 1866; Special Orders Nos. 7 and 8, Vol. 1, pp. 108–109, Entry 4794: Special Orders Issued, August 1865 to August 1868, Department of Texas and 5th Military District, RG 393, Part 1; GAC to Jacob Greene, January 8, 1866 (three letters of same date), GAC to Jacob Greene, n.d., Jacob Greene Papers, U.S. Military History Institute, Carlisle, Pa.: Richter, *Army in Texas*, 25–28, *Overreached*, 40. See also Major General H. G. Wright to GAC, January 15, 1866, and Regimental Returns, January 9, 1866, Letters Sent by the Department of Texas, the District of Texas, and the 5th Military District, Roll 1, Microfilm Publication M1165, NA.

66. Major General H. G. Wright to Maj. George Lee, January 5, 1866, and Major General H. G. Wright to GAC, January 11, 1866, Letters Sent by the Department of Texas, the District of Texas, and the 5th Military District, Roll 1, Microfilm Publication M1165, NA; Kenneth W. Howell, "Introduction: The Elusive Story of Violence in Reconstruction Texas, 1865–1874," 1–33, and James M. Smallwood, "When the Klan Rode: Terrorism in Reconstruction Texas," 214–42, in Kenneth W. Howell, ed., *Still the Arena of Violence: Violence and Turmoil in Reconstruction Texas, 1865–1874* (Denton, Tex.: University of North Texas Press, 2012).

67. GAC to Zachariah Chandler, January 5, 1866, Thomas W. Custer to Edward M. Stanton, December 29, 1865, PHS and GAC, Endorsement of Application for appointment of Thomas W. Custer as lieutenant in the U.S. Army, January 9, 1864, GAC to Zachariah Chandler, January 24, 1866, Roll 2, Zachariah Chandler Papers, LOC.

68. GAC to Zachariah Chandler, January 8 and 14, 1866, Roll 2, Zachariah Chandler Papers, LOC.

69. GAC to Sister, January 12, 1866, typescript copy, GAC Papers, USMA.

70. C. H. Whittelsey to GAC, January 27, 1866, Letters Sent by the Department of Texas, the District of Texas, and the 5th Military District, Roll 1, Microfilm Publication M1165, NA; GAC to Jacob Greene, January 31, 1866, Jacob Greene Papers, U.S. Military History Institute, Carlisle, Pa.: *New York*, January 10, 1866; EBC, *Tenting on the Plains*, 266–68, 270–80. When the plans to muster out GAC were announced in the press, DSB intervened with Senator Chandler on his son-in-law's behalf, without success. See Zachariah Chandler to DSB, January 17, 1866, and DSB to GAC, January 20, 1866, Folder 1, Box 1, LAFCC. It appears that GAC was initially uncertain of his muster-out, as he sent a telegram to headquarters asking for confirmation; see GAC to Horatio Wright, January 27, 1866, Personnel Files, CRM.

Ten: The Politician

1. EBC, *Tenting on the Plains*, 273–81.
2. GAC to EBC, April 10, 1867, in *Tenting on the Plains*, 552–53.
3. HR 30, Part 4: 72, 1st Session, 39th Congress.
4. See, for example, GAC to Zachariah Chandler, January 8, 1866, Roll 2, Zachariah Chandler Papers, LOC, and Eric L. McKitrick, *Andrew Johnson and Reconstruction* (New York: Oxford University Press, 1988), 145.
5. Foner, 216–19; Henry L. Morrill to Henry Albers, October 9, 1865, Folder 3, Box 1, Henry Leighton Morrill Papers, Beinecke Library, Yale University, New Haven, Conn.
6. Foner, 216–27, 239–40.
7. Foner, 243–49.
8. HR 30, Part 4: 72–78, 1st Session, 39th Congress; *New York Times*, April 1, 1866. For historians' agreement with GAC's assessment, see Kenneth W. Howell, "Introduction: The Elusive Story of Violence in Reconstruction Texas, 1865–1874," 1–33, James M. Smallwood, "When the Klan Rode: Terrorism in Reconstruction Texas," 214–42, and John Gorman, "Reconstruction Violence in the Lower Brazos River Valley," 387–420, in Kenneth W. Howell, ed., *Still the Arena of Civil War: Violence and Turmoil in Reconstruction Texas, 1865–1874* (Denton, Tex.: University of North Texas Press, 2012). On January 25, 1866, while still in Texas, GAC wrote an open letter to the *National Republican* to denounce "the statements and doctrines of the ex(?)-rebels, *whose hostility and opposition to the Government is now as strongly and openly manifested as at any time during the Rebellion!*" See *Philadelphia Inquirer*, March 1, 1866.
9. *Baltimore Sun*, March 22, 1866; *Independent*, March 29, 1866; *New York Times*, April 1, 1866; Foner, 246–47.
10. See Joshua Paddison, "Race, Religion, and Naturalization: How the West Shaped Citizenship Debates in the Reconstruction Congress," in Adam Arenson and Andrew R. Graybill, eds., *Civil War Wests: Testing the Limits of the United States* (Oakland: University of California Press, 2015), 181–201.
11. Foner, 242–51.
12. Merington, 177–81.
13. Merington, 178–79.
14. Merington, 180; Edwin G. Burrows and Mike Wallace, *Gotham: A History of New York City to 1898* (New York: Oxford University Press, 1999), 672; Stiles, *First Tycoon*, 415. I am not the first to note GAC's attraction to New York, nor

his connections to the conservative Democratic financiers associated with Belmont and others. See in particular Richard Slotkin, *The Fatal Environment: The Myth of the Frontier in the Age of Industrialization, 1800–1890* (Norman: University of Oklahoma Press, 1994 [orig. pub. 1985]), 373–76, 389–91, 405–06.

15. Merington, 180–82; Frost, *General Custer's Libbie*, 147–49; Leckie, 82–85; Burrows and Wallace, 955; *Harper's Weekly*, April 14, 1866. See also GAC to EBC, April 17, 1866, Folder 4, Box 4, MMP.

16. Merington, 181; Utley, *Cavalier in Buckskin*, 39; Frost, *General Custer's Libbie*, 147–49.

17. GAC to EBC, April 17, 1866, Folder 4, Box 4, MMP; Pedigree of Don Juan, dated April 12, 1866, and Affidavit of GAC, June 19, 1866, LBH; USG to F. M. Romero, May 16, 1866, USG Papers, USMA; Stiles, *First Tycoon*, 194, 484, 504.

18. Leckie, 85.

19. DSB to GAC, January 20th, 1866, Folder 1, Box 1, LAFCC; Merington, 182–84; Leckie, 85–86.

20. Merington, 182–84; Leckie, 86; Roy Morris Jr., *Sheridan: The Life and Wars of General Phil Sheridan* (New York: Vintage, 1993 [orig. pub. 1992]), 271–72.

21. Utley, *Cavalier in Buckskin*, 39; *Chicago Tribune*, June 25, 1866; *Turf, Field and Farm*, August 11, 1866. Don Juan is buried in Tecumseh, Michigan, where it was lodged at a stud farm. A boulder and plaque marks the site.

22. Coffman, 216–19; GAC to Andrew Johnson, August 13, 1866, Paul A. Bergeron, ed., *The Papers of Andrew Johnson*, vol. 11 (Knoxville: University of Tennessee Press, 1994), 68; McPherson, 769; Paul A. Hutton, *Phil Sheridan and His Army* (Norman: University of Oklahoma Press, 1999), 137.

23. John Y. Simon, ed., *Papers of Ulysses S. Grant*, vol. 16 (Carbondale: Southern Illinois University Press, 1988), 274–75, 75–77n.

24. Simon 16: 276–77n; GAC to Andrew Johnson, August 13, 1866, Bergeron 11: 68.

25. Stiles, *Jesse James*, 175–77; Morris, 272–74; Foner, 261–65.

26. Bingham quoted in *New York Times*, March 1, 1866; Akhil Reed Amar, *America's Constitution: A Biography* (New York: Random House, 2005), 385–88, and *The Bill of Rights: Creation and Reconstruction* (New Haven, Conn.: Yale University Press, 2008); Foner, 267–68.

27. *New York Times*, August 22, 1866.

28. EBC to Rebecca Richmond, August 29, 1866, EBC Correspondence, LBH; Foner, 264–65.

29. Merington, 303; Utley, *Cavalier in Buckskin*, 39; EBC to Rebecca Richmond, August 29, 1866, EBC Correspondence, LBH. For more on the intensity of the politics of this year, see Patrick W. Riddleberger, *1866: The Critical Year Revisited* (Carbondale: Southern Illinois University Press, 1979), and Stiles, *Jesse James*, 175–87.

30. *Philadelphia Wigwam for the Johnson Convention*, lithograph, 1866, Library Company of Philadelphia; *New York Times*, August 12, 13, 17, 18, 1866; Albert Castel, *The Presidency of Andrew Johnson* (Lawrence: University Press of Kansas, 1979), 85–86.

31. *Chicago Tribune*, August 20, 1866.

32. *Chicago Tribune*, August 15, 26, 1866; *New York Times*, August 22, 1866.

33. *New York Times*, August 22, 1866; *New York Tribune*, August 25, 1866; "Custer's Reply to the Atrocious Attempts of the Corrupt Insane Radical Press to Pervert

His Testimony, &c.," *Cleveland Plain Dealer* (Extra), 1866, GAC Papers, Beinecke Library, Yale University, New Haven, Conn.

34. *New York Times*, August 17, 1866.

35. Stiles, *First Tycoon*, 429; Castel, 89–90; Paul H. Bergeron, *Andrew Johnson's Civil War and Reconstruction* (Knoxville: University of Tennessee Press, 2011), 126–29.

36. Jean Edward Smith, *Grant* (New York: Simon and Schuster, 2001), 426; McFeely, 249–52.

37. Garry Boulard, *The Swing Around the Circle: Andrew Johnson and the Train Ride That Destroyed a Presidency* (Bloomington, Ind.: iUniverse, 2008), 75–88, 95–103; Castel, 89–92; Stiles, *Jesse James*, 175–77. See also *Cincinnati Inquirer*, September 14, 1866, *New Hampshire Sentinel*, September 20, 1866.

38. Merington, 188–89.

39. Castel, 90–92; Foner, 264–66.

40. Grant quoted in McFeely, 252; *Chicago Tribune*, September 14, 1866; *Cincinnati Inquirer*, September 19, 1866.

41. *Cincinnati Inquirer*, September 14, 1866.

42. *Detroit Free Press*, in *New York Times*, September 16, 1866.

43. *Chicago Tribune*, September 18, 19, 21, 1866; *New York Times*, September 19, 1866.

44. *Boston Advertiser* in *New Orleans Times*, October 15, 1866.

45. *Monroe Commercial*, September 20, 1866.

46. Ulysses S. Grant to PHS, December 19, 1865, Box 39, PHS Papers, LOC.

47. Simon 16: 277n; *Cleveland Herald* in *Monroe Commercial*, September 27, 1866. I have corrected the spelling of "Riley" in Grant's letter.

48. EBC to Rebecca Richmond, August 29, 1867, EBC Correspondence, LBH.

49. *Chicago Tribune*, October 6, 7, 30, November 14, 16, 1866; *New York Times*, October 8, 1866; *Monroe Commercial*, October 11, November 1, 1866; *Flake's Bulletin*, November 6, 1866; J. Logan Chipman to Andrew Johnson, October 5, 1866, Bergeron 11: 308.

50. GAC to Jacob Howard, December 26, 1866, in Hamilton Gay Howard, *Civil-War Echoes: Character Sketches and State Secrets* (Washington, D.C.: Howard Publishing, 1907), 315–18.

Eleven: The Fallen

1. Lawrence A. Frost, *The Court-Martial of General George Armstrong Custer* (Norman: University of Oklahoma Press, 1968), 96–104; Arthur Brigham Carpenter to Mother, February 10, 1867, Arthur Brigham Carpenter Papers, Beinecke Library, Yale University, New Haven, Conn.; Benjamin Grierson to Alice Grierson, n.d. [September 1867], Benjamin Henry Grierson Papers, Newberry Library. For more on "11worth," see De B. Randolph Keim, *Sheridan's Troopers on the Border: A Winter Campaign on the Plains* (Philadelphia, Pa.: David McKay, 1885), 9–11. I have consulted the records of these proceedings in the National Archives; see the 1867 court-martial file in CRM, and General Court-Martial of Gen. George Armstrong Custer, 1867, Microfilm Publication T-1103. I will cite Frost's published transcription as a convenience to the reader and researcher, but each quotation of the proceedings for which I cite Frost's book may also be found verbatim in these National Archives records.

2. Entry 558, Cullum 1: 347-48; Photograph of William Hoffman, Commissary General of Prisoners, 1865, Call Number LC-B817-7288, and photograph of Benjamin H. Grierson, Call Number LC-USZC4-7991, Prints and Photographs Division, LOC; Benjamin Grierson to Alice Grierson, n.d. [September 1867], Benjamin Henry Grierson Papers, Newberry Library, Chicago, Ill.; William L. Richter, *The Army in Texas During Reconstruction: 1865–1870* (College Station, Tex.: Texas A&M University Press, 1987), 19; Frost, *Court-Martial*, 96–104.

3. GAC to ?, September 26, 1867, Folder 5, Box 4, MMP; Frost, *Court-Martial*, 99–104.

4. Frost, *Court-Martial*, 92; entry 1945, Cullum 2, 556; Merington, 211. For evidence of GAC's involvement in his defense, see, for example, GAC to unknown, September 26, 1867, Folder 5, Box 4, MMP, and I. P. Christiancy to GAC, October 13, 1867, Folder 3, Box 1, LAFCC.

5. Frost, *Court-Martial*, 99–104.

6. E. M. Forster, *Aspects of the Novel* (New York: Harcourt Brace, 1927), 47, 63.

7. Lawrence Barrett, "Personal Recollections of General Custer," in Whittaker, 629–43.

8. Quoted in Leckie, 85.

9. EBC, *Tenting on the Plains*, 328–33, 336–37; Leckie, 89; Anna Darrah to EBC, n.d., Anna Darrah to EBC, October 1864, Folder 9, Box 2, LAFCC.

10. EBC, *Tenting on the Plains*, 336–37.

11. EBC, *Tenting on the Plains*, 339–40; EBC to Rebecca Richmond, December 6, 1866, EBC Correspondence, LBH. Barker helped GAC with the transportation of his horses; see GAC to C. F. Hatch, October 1, 1866, Folder 2, GAC Papers, Beinecke Library, Yale University, New Haven, Conn.

12. EBC to Rebecca Richmond, December 6, 1866, EBC Correspondence, LBH; EBC, *Tenting on the Plains*, 341–46; *Report of the Treasurer of the Missouri Southern Relief Association* (Missouri History Library and Museum: St. Louis, Mo., 1866); Stiles, *Jesse James*, 224; Aaron Astor, *Rebels on the Border: Civil War, Emancipation, and the Reconstruction of Kentucky and Missouri* (Baton Rouge: Louisiana State University Press, 2012), 204.

13. EBC, *Tenting on the Plains*, 343–46; Elwyn A. Barron, *Lawrence Barrett: A Professional Sketch* (Chicago: Knight and Leonard, 1889), frontis, 28–30; Barrett, "Personal Recollections of General Custer," in Whittaker, 629–43; *New York Times*, March 21, 22, 1891.

14. EBC, *Tenting on the Plains*, 343–46; Barrett, "Personal Recollections of General Custer"; EBC to Rebecca Richmond, December 6, 1866, EBC Correspondence, LBH; *New York Times*, March 21, 22, 1891.

15. EBC, *Tenting on the Plains*, 371; Barrett, "Personal Recollections of General Custer."

16. Leo Tolstoy, "Sebastopol in August 1855," in *The Sebastopol Sketches*, trans. David McDuff (New York: Penguin, 1986), 152–53.

17. EBC to Rebecca Richmond, December 6, 1866, EBC Correspondence, LBH; Utley, *Cavalier in Buckskin*, 44–45; Ron Field, *Forts of the American Frontier, 1820–91: Central and Northern Plains* (Oxford, UK: Osprey Publishing, 2005), 22; Elliott West, *The Contested Plains: Indians, Goldseekers, and the Rush to Colorado* (Lawrence: University Press of Kansas, 2005), 120, 273.

18. Utley, *Cavalier in Buckskin*, 44–47; Wert, 244–49; Coffman, 255, 328–39, 350–52; William Y. Chalfant, *Hancock's War: Conflict on the Southern Plains* (Norman: University of Oklahoma Press, 2010), 84.

19. Robert M. Utley, ed., *Life in Custer's Cavalry: Diaries and Letters of Albert and Jennie Barnitz, 1867–1868* (Lincoln: University of Nebraska Press, 1987 [orig. pub. 1977]), 10; Wert, 247–48; Utley, *Cavalier in Buckskin*, 44–47; entry 313, Cullum 2: 168–69; photograph of Alfred Gibbs, reproduction number LC-DIG-cwpb-05859, Prints and Photographs Division, LOC.

20. The 1866 act restructuring and expanding the Regular Army required that all lieutenants in the newly formed regiments come from the ranks of Civil War volunteers, and that all ranks above first lieutenant be staffed with an equal number of West Point graduates and volunteers; Paul Andrew Hutton, *Phil Sheridan and His Army* (Norman: University of Oklahoma Press, 1999 [orig. pub. 1985]), 137; John M. Carroll, *They Rode with Custer: A Biographical Directory of the Men That Rode with General George A. Custer, Revised and Enlarged* (Mattituck, N.Y.: J. M. Carroll and Co., 1993), 260–61; Coffman, 222–23.

21. Frederick Benteen to Frank Blair Jr., September 13, 1866, Frederick Benteen to Adjutant General, U.S. Army, March 14, 1867, Frederick Benteen to Tom Nuell, July 9, 1867, James H. Wilson to Adjutant General, U.S. Army, June 14, 1867, Frederick Benteen Reference Microfilm, NA; Charles K. Mills, *Harvest of Barren Regrets: The Army Career of Frederick William Benteen, 1834–1898* (Glendale, Calif.: Arthur H. Clark Co., 1985), 11, 129–30.

22. Utley, ed., *Life*, 15; Wert, 246.

23. Utley, *Cavalier in Buckskin*, 44–45; entry 976, Cullum 1: 566–67. On Weir's administrative role in the District of the Upper Arkansas, see, for example, GAC to Thomas B. Weir, May 4, 1867, Special Files of Headquarters, Division of the Missouri, Relating to Military Operations and Administration, 1863–1865, Roll 7, Microfilm Publication M1495, NA.

24. GAC passed his examination and a physical examination on December 5; W. Thomson to David Hunter, December 5, 1866, and David Hunter to Adjutant General, December 5, 1866, Personnel Files, CRM. See also Utley, *Cavalier in Buckskin*, 44; Chalfant, 84. EBC wrote from Fort Riley of GAC's absence, as she remained behind; EBC to Rebecca Richmond, December 6, 1866, EBC Correspondence, LBH.

25. Chalfant, 84. Professional examinations would not become routine in the U.S. Army until 1890, but had been instituted for this wave of veterans of the U.S. Volunteers who had been appointed to the Regular Army. An institutional impulse toward professionalization existed as early as the 1820s, but gained momentum in the three decades following the Civil War; see Coffman, 96–103, 269–81.

26. *New York Times*, February 11, 1867, October 10, 1906; EBC to GAC, April 5, 1867, *Tenting on the Plains*, 440–42, 535–37; EBC to Rebecca Richmond, December 6, 1866, EBC Correspondence, LBH.

27. *Harper's New Monthly Magazine*, February 1867; Joseph G. Rosa, *They Called Him Wild Bill: The Life and Adventures of James Butler Hickok* (Norman: University of Oklahoma Press, 1974), 104–07; Richard Maxwell Brown, *No Duty to Retreat: Violence and Values in American History and Society* (New York: Oxford University Press, 1991), 49–51; Wert, 253; Chalfant, 81–89, 175–76.

28. Chalfant, 81–89; Robert M. Utley, *Frontier Regulars: The United States Army and the Indian, 1866–1891* (Lincoln: University of Nebraska Press, 1994 [orig. pub. 1973]), 13–14.

29. W. J. D. Kennedy, ed., *On the Plains with Custer and Hancock: The Journal of Isaac Coates, Army Surgeon* (Boulder, Co.: Johnson Books, 1997), 46–49. I have consulted the original Coates journal—actually a detailed memoir—in the Western history collection of the Denver Public Library, but for ease of reference for those consulting these notes, I am referring to Kennedy's published version, which I find contains very few transcription errors and includes helpful supplementary information.

30. Arthur B. Carpenter to Mother, April 9, 1867, Arthur Brigham Carpenter Papers, Beinecke Library, Yale University, New Haven, Conn.; Utley, ed., *Life*, 28–30; GAC to EBC, March 28, April 3, 1867, GAC to EBC, April 3 1867, *Tenting on the Plains*, 516–19, 524; Kennedy, 49; Barnett, 132.

31. GAC to EBC, March 30, April 10, 1867, *Tenting on the Plains*, 521–22, 552–53.

32. GAC to EBC, April 8, 1867, *Tenting on the Plains*, 525–30.

33. West, 273; Field, 23; Arthur B. Carpenter to Mother, April 9, 1867, Arthur Brigham Carpenter Papers, Beinecke Library, Yale University, New Haven, Conn.; Henry M. Stanley, *My Early Travels and Adventures in America and Asia* (New York: Charles Scribner's Sons, 1895), 27; Kennedy, 55.

34. GAC to EBC, April 8, 1867, *Tenting on the Plains*, 525–30.

35. Stanley, 29–35; Utley, ed., *Life*, 44; Kennedy, 52–60; *New York Tribune*, April 24, 1867; Theodore Davis, "A Summer on the Plains," *Harper's New Monthly Magazine* (February 1868); Chalfant, 135–43.

36. Utley, ed., *Life*, 31; GAC to EBC, April 14, 1867, *Tenting on the Plains*, 556–59; Chalfant, 147–53.

37. Davis, "A Summer on the Plains"; Kennedy, 61–63; Chalfant, 147–55.

38. GAC to EBC, April 14, 1867, *Tenting on the Plains*, 556–59.

39. For an excellent overview and a stress on the disadvantages as well as advantages of the adoption of mounted nomadism, see Pekka Hämäläinen, "The Rise and Fall of Plains Indian Horse Cultures," *Journal of American History* 90, no. 3 (December 2003): 833–62.

40. Pekka Hämäläinen, *The Comanche Empire* (New Haven, Conn.: Yale University Press, 2008), esp. 23–29, 141–43 (to be referred to as "Hämäläinen").

41. West, 63–87. Andrew C. Isenberg, *The Destruction of the Bison* (New York: Cambridge University Press, 2000), 65, emphasizes that the nomadic bison-hunting culture of the high-plains tribes, and the communal ethic it engendered, "was neither timeless nor universal."

42. West, 76–77.

43. West, 76–86, 190–200; Isenberg, 16–29, 69, 94–107; Hämäläinen, 246, 295.

44. H. Craig Miner and William E. Unrau, *The End of Indian Kansas: A Study of Cultural Revolution, 1854–1871* (Lawrence: Regents Press of Kansas, 1978), 1–24.

45. West, 229–309; Hämäläinen, 295; Isenberg, 14–16, 109.

46. Report of Lieutenant General William T. Sherman, Commander of the Military Division of the Missouri, October 1, 1867, HED 1, 2nd Session, 40th Congress; Richard White, *Railroaded: The Transcontinentals and the Making of Modern America* (New York: W. W. Norton and Co., 2011), 455–60.

47. William T. Sherman to Ulysses S. Grant, June 11, 1867, Roll 7, Microfilm Pub-

lication M1495, NA; Robert M. Utley, *The Indian Frontier of the American West, 1846–1890* (Albuquerque: University of New Mexico Press, 1984), 41.

48. West, 284–307.
49. Maj. H. Douglass to Chauncey McKeever, Assistant Adjutant General, Department of the Missouri, February 24, 1867, HED 240, 2nd Session, 41st Congress; SED 13, 1st Session, 40th Congress; Proceedings of Council Held by Major General Hancock with Head Chief "Sa-Tan-Ta" of the Kiowa Tribe of Indians in Kansas, at Fort Larned, May 1, 1867, Headquarters Records of Fort Dodge, Kansas, 1866–1882, Unregistered Letters Received, Roll 11, Microfilm Publication M989, NA.
50. Chalfant, 76–77.
51. GAC to EBC, April 14, 1867, *Tenting on the Plains*, 559–60.
52. GAC, "On the Plains," October 26, 1867, published in *Turf, Field and Farm*, November 9, 1867, reprinted in Brian W. Dippie, ed., *Nomad: George A. Custer in* Turf, Field and Farm (Austin: University of Texas Press, 1980), 20–26; "A Summer on the Plains"; Kennedy, 63–76; Chalfant, 159–70.
53. Chalfant, 170–75; Report of Winfield S. Hancock, April 13 and 15, 1867, List of Property Found in the Camps, HED 240, 2nd Session, 41st Congress.
54. GAC to EBC, April 15, 1867, *Tenting on the Plains*, 560–61; Report of Winfield S. Hancock, April 13 and 15, 1867, HED 240, 2nd Session, 41st Congress.
55. GAC to EBC, April 15, 1867, *Tenting on the Plains*, 560–61; Kennedy, 69; Utley, ed., *Life*, 33–35; William Winer Cooke to Mother, April 20, 1867, William Winer Cooke Papers, USMA; GAC, "On the Plains."
56. Utley, ed., *Life*, 34–35; List of Property Found in the Camps, HED 240, 2nd Session, 41st Congress.
57. J. H. Leavenworth to N. G. Taylor, April 15, 1867, SED 13, 1st Session, 40th Congress; Winfield Scott Hancock to William T. Sherman, April 17, 1867, Special Field Orders No. 12, April 17, 1867; HED 240, 2nd Session, 41st Congress; GAC to EBC, April 15, 1867, *Tenting on the Plains*, 560–61.
58. GAC to Lt. Thomas B. Weir, April 16, 1867, Roll 7, Microfilm Publication M1495, NA.
59. Kennedy, 77–79; Utley, ed., *Life*, 35–37; GAC to Lt. Thomas B. Weir, April 17, 1867, Roll 7, Microfilm Publication M1495, NA.
60. GAC to EBC, April 20, 1867, *Tenting on the Plains*, 562–70; Kennedy, 79; William Winer Cooke to Mother, April 20, 1867, William Winer Cooke Papers, USMA.
61. Utley, ed., *Life*, 35–37; GAC to Lt. Thomas B. Weir, April 17, 1867, Roll 7, Microfilm Publication M1495, NA.
62. GAC to Lt. Thomas B. Weir, April 17 and 19, 1867, Roll 7, Microfilm Publication M1495, NA; Utley, ed., *Life*, 35–37.
63. Utley, ed., *Life*, 37–38; GAC to Lt. Thomas B. Weir, April 19, 1867, Roll 7, Microfilm Publication M1495, NA; Winfield Scott Hancock to William T. Sherman, April 17 and 18, 1867, Special Field Orders No. 12, April 17, 1867, HED 240, 2nd Session, 41st Congress; GAC to Thomas B. Weir, May 4, 1867, Roll 7, Microfilm Publication M1495, NA.
64. EBC, *Tenting on the Plains*, 490–94.
65. EBC, *Tenting on the Plains*, 503–04, 508. In 1869, Congress consolidated the four infantry regiments of black troops, the 38th, 39th, 40th, and 41st, into the 24th and 25th Infantry. The 9th and 10th Cavalry continued as originally

organized. See T. J. Stiles, "Buffalo Soldiers," *Smithsonian Magazine* (December 1998).

66. EBC to GAC, March [n.d.], April 5 and 20, 1867, *Tenting on the Plains*, 503–05, 531–40.

67. EBC, *Tenting on the Plains*, 503–05.

68. Robert M. Utley, *Frontier Regulars: The United States Army and the Indian, 1866–1891* (Lincoln: University of Nebraska Press, 1984 [orig. pub. 1973]), 25–28; see also William H. Leckie, *Buffalo Soldiers: A Narrative of the Negro Cavalry in the West* (Norman: University of Oklahoma Press, 1999), and Stiles, "Buffalo Soldiers."

69. EBC to GAC, March, May 4, 1867, *Tenting on the Plains*, 531–34, 545–46; see also 456, 485, 508–12, and EBC to GAC, April 22, 1867, 540–41; Carl F. Day, *Tom Custer: Ride to Glory* (Norman: University of Oklahoma Press, 2002), 105–07; Leckie, 95.

70. GAC to EBC, April 25 and 30, 1867, *Tenting on the Plains*, 572–74; Leckie, 96.

71. Leckie, 96–97.

72. Leckie, 116.

73. GAC to EBC, April 22, 1867, *Tenting on the Plains*, 570; Leckie, 96–97.

74. Leckie, 97–98; EBC, *Tenting on the Plains*, 600–09; Utley, ed., *Life*, 52.

75. On Barnitz's admiration for GAC during the Civil War, see Barnett, 133–34.

76. Utley, ed., *Life*, 45–50; Winfield S. Hancock to William T. Sherman, April 21, 1867, HED 240, 2nd Session, 41st Congress; Minnie Dubbs Millbrook, "The West Breaks in General Custer," in Paul A. Hutton, ed., *The Custer Reader* (Norman: University of Oklahoma Press, 1992), 116–58. See also GAC to EBC, May 2 and 4, 1867, *Tenting on the Plains*, 576–80, 609.

77. Utley, ed., *Life*, 50–52. Hancock received reports of scurvy among the cavalry at Fort Hays as early as April 21; Winfield S. Hancock to William T. Sherman, April 21, 1867, HED 240, 2nd Session, 41st Congress.

78. Blaine Burkey, *Custer, Come at Once! The Fort Hays Years of George and Elizabeth Custer, 1867–1870* (Hays, Kan.: Society of Friends of Historic Fort Hays, 1991), 20–23; Utley, ed., *Life*, 51–55; EBC, *Tenting on the Plains*, 609–22, 655.

79. Burkey, 31–32; Utley, ed., *Life*, 56–59; EBC, *Tenting on the Plains*, 636–49.

80. On that march, see Frost, *Court-Martial*, 104–06; *Harper's Weekly*, December 19, 1868.

81. Frost, *Court-Martial*, 123–25.

82. Davis, "A Summer on the Plains"; *New York Herald*, July 2, 1867; GAC to Andrew J. Smith, June 15, 1867, GAC Correspondence, LBH; GAC to My Dear Genl, June 12, 1867, Documents Relating to GAC, GAC Papers, Beinecke Library, Yale University, New Haven, Conn.; Millbrook, "The West Breaks in General Custer."

83. GAC to EBC, May 2, 1867, *Tenting on the Plains*, 576–79.

84. William T. Sherman to GAC, June 13, 1867, Other Sources, LBH; Report of Lieutenant General Sherman, October 1, 1867, HED 1, 2nd Session, 40th Congress; William T. Sherman to Ellen Sherman, June 8, 1867, Roll 3, William T. Sherman Family Papers, University of Notre Dame, copy in LOC; William T. Sherman to Edwin M. Stanton, June 17, 1867, Roll 7, Microfilm Publication M1495, NA; William T. Sherman to GAC, June 17, 1867, Documents Relating to GAC, GAC Papers, Beinecke Library, Yale University, New Haven, Conn.

85. Richard White, "The Winning of the West: The Expansion of the Western

Sioux in the Eighteenth and Nineteenth Centuries," *Journal of American History* 65, no. 2 (September 1978): 319–43. See also John D. McDermott, *Red Cloud's War: The Bozeman Trail, 1866–1868*, vols. 1–2 (Norman, Ok.: Arthur H. Clark Company, 2010).

86. Merington, 201; *Harper's Weekly*, August 3, 1867; GAC, "On the Plains," *Turf, Field and Farm*, September 24, 1869, reprinted in Dippie, 44–50 (see 50). On the "frontier imposture," see Louis S. Warren, *Buffalo Bill's America: William Cody and the Wild West Show* (New York: Vintage, 2005), esp. 80, 134.

87. Davis, "A Summer on the Plains"; Millbrook, "The West Breaks in Custer"; Merington, 204–08; Leckie, 100–03; William T. Sherman to Ulysses S. Grant, July 4, 1867, Roll 7, Microfilm Publication M1495, NA; GAC to Winfield S. Hancock, July 10, 1867, Letters Received by the Office of the Adjutant General (Main Series), 1861–1870, Roll 722, Microfilm Publication M619, NA.

88. GAC to EBC, June 22, 1867, EBC to GAC, June 27, 1867, *Tenting on the Plains*, 547–49, 582; *New York Times*, July 1, 1867; *Cincinnati Gazette*, July 2, 1867; William T. Sherman to Ulysses S. Grant, July 4, 1867, Roll 7, Microfilm Publication M1495, NA.

89. *New York Herald*, July 2, 1867; *New York Times*, June 6, 1867; Utley, *Frontier Regulars* 23; Utley, ed., *Life*, 86–88.

90. Frost, *Court-Martial*, 150–55, 159–63, 165–74, 177–92.

91. Davis, "A Summer on the Plains"; GAC, *My Life on the Plains*, 76–78.

92. Utley, ed., *Life*, 88–92; Wert, 260–61. GAC would later claim that Fort Wallace was in "a state of siege," the supplies were gone, and an epidemic of cholera caused deaths on a daily basis. He claimed that he left to retrieve essential supplies, especially medicine. Millbrook, in "The West Breaks In Custer," states, "Not one of these statements was true." She notes that, though cholera did break out in army posts in Kansas that summer, it did not strike the 7th Cavalry until after GAC left Fort Wallace, and there is no evidence that he had yet learned of the first outbreak of cholera at Fort Harker (where EBC was not located in any event). Though some biographers and historians have taken the threat of cholera seriously as a motivation for GAC's departure from Fort Wallace, I am convinced by Millbrook and Leckie's arguments that it played no role in his decision, and have left it out of my narrative. See also Leckie, 102.

93. Frost, *Court-Martial*, 92, 104–14; *Harper's Weekly*, December 19, 1868.

94. Frost, *Court-Martial*, 116–23.

95. Frost, *Court-Martial*, 123–30.

96. Leckie, 102–03, finds reasons to accept these rumors, reported years later by the very hostile Benteen and also Edward Mathey, who did not join the 7th Cavalry until September 1867, and thus had no direct knowledge of these events. Mathey may well have heard this rumor from Benteen himself. I agree with the analysis in Barnett, 138–39, who finds Benteen's claims illogical and extremely doubtful. On Mathey, see Carroll, *They Rode with Custer*, 171–72.

97. Frost, *Court-Martial*, 131–34.

98. Frost, *Court-Martial*, 120, 134–36; Arthur Brigham Carpenter to Mother, August 15, 1867, Arthur Brigham Carpenter Papers, Beinecke Library, Yale University, New Haven, Conn.

99. Frost, *Court-Martial*, 137–47.

100. Frost, *Court-Martial*, 149–50.

101. Frost, *Court-Martial*, 150–55.

102. Frost, *Court-Martial*, 165–74.
103. EBC, *Tenting on the Plains*, 722.
104. Merington, 212; EBC, *Tenting on the Plains*, 702.
105. GAC to unknown, September 26, 1867, Folder 5, Box 4, MMP.
106. GAC, "On the Plains," *Turf, Field and Farm*, September 21 and October 12, 1867, in Dippie, 7–19 (see also ix–6); *Turf, Field and Farm*, December 28, 1867.
107. EBC to Rebecca Richmond [cousin], October 13, 1867, Folder 5, Box 4, MMP.
108. Frost, *Court-Martial*, 164–65, 177–90; Benjamin Grierson to Alice Grierson, September 20, 27, 1867, Benjamin Henry Grierson Papers, Newberry Library.
109. Frost, *Court-Martial*, 214–15.
110. Frost, *Court-Martial*, 226, 216–37.
111. Frost, *Court-Martial*, 237–46.

Twelve: The Indian Killer

1. Foner, 277.
2. Foner, 271–80; William S. McFeely, *Grant: A Biography* (New York: W. W. Norton and Co., 1981), 260–65.
3. Roy Morris Jr., *Sheridan: The Life and Wars of General Phil Sheridan* (New York: Crown, 1992), 273–96; McFeely, 262–63; HED 1, 2nd Session, 40th Congress; *New York Tribune*, August 30, 1867.
4. William T. Sherman to Ulysses S. Grant, August 3, 1867, Joseph Holt to Ulysses S. Grant, August 22, 1867, in John Y. Simon, ed., *The Papers of Ulysses S. Grant*, vol. 17 (Carbondale: Southern Illinois University Press, 1991), 242, 516–17. On Holt, see William Gardner Bell, *Secretaries of War and Secretaries of the Army: Portraits & Biographical Sketches* (Washington, D.C.: Center of Military History, 1992), 68.
5. Joseph Holt to Ulysses S. Grant, November 8, 1867, in Simon 17: 370–72. See also Lawrence A. Frost, *The Court-Martial of General George Armstrong Custer* (Norman: University of Oklahoma Press, 1968), 245–46.
6. Robert M. Utley, *Frontier Regulars: The United States Army and the Indian, 1866–1891* (Lincoln: University of Nebraska Press, 1994 [orig. pub. 1973]), 27.
7. *Leavenworth Bulletin*, November 27, 1867; *New York Times*, November 30, 1867; *Baltimore Sun*, December 2, 1867; Frost, *Court-Martial*, 247; Robert M. Utley, ed., *Life in Custer's Cavalry: Diaries and Letters of Albert and Jennie Barnitz, 1867–1868* (Lincoln: University of Nebraska Press, 1987 [orig. pub. 1977]), 128, 130–31.
8. *New York Times*, December 7, 1867.
9. GAC to "My Dear Friend," December 2, 1867, Folder 5, Box 4, MMP; *Turf, Field and Farm*, December 28, 1867; Wedding Invitation, April 23, 1867, Folder 6, Box 3, LAFCC; *New York Times*, November 18, 1899; Utley, ed., *Life*, 128, 130–31; Leckie, 107.
10. EBC to Rebecca Richmond, October 13, 1867, GAC to "My Dear Friend," December 2, 1867, Folder 5, Box 4, MMP. Leckie, 107, also notes the contrast of the Custers' private reaction and their "outward demeanor."
11. EBC to Rebecca Richmond, October 13, 1867, GAC to "My Dear Friend," December 2, 1867, GAC to unknown, September 26, 1867, Folder 5, Box 4, MMP; Frost, *Court-Martial*, 261–63; entry for January 3, 1868, Rebecca Rich-

mond Diary, Dr. Lawrence A. Frost Collection, MCLS; *Chicago Tribune*, January 17, 1868; *Memphis Avalanche*, January 28, 1868.

12. GAC, "On the Plains," October 26, 1867, published in *Turf, Field and Farm*, November 9, 1867, reprinted in Brian W. Dippie, ed., *Nomad: George A. Custer in* Turf, Field and Farm (Austin: University of Texas Press, 1980), 20–26.

13. GAC, "On the Plains," November 11, 1867, December 15, 1867, published in *Turf, Field and Farm*, November 23, 1867, January 4, 1868, in Dippie, 27–39.

14. *Sandusky* (Ohio) *Register*, December 28, 1867, copy in Dr. Lawrence Frost Collection, MCLS; *New York Tribune*, December 28, 1867; *New York Times*, December 31, 1867. West certainly was an alcoholic; see Captain Barnitz's commentary, Utley, ed., *Life*, 125.

15. Joseph Holt to Ulysses S. Grant, February 14, 1868, in John Y. Simon, ed., *The Papers of Ulysses S. Grant*, vol. 18 (Carbondale: Southern Illinois University Press, 1991), 372–73.

16. McFeely, 264–66.

17. McFeely, 266–73.

18. GAC had taken pains to distance himself publicly from Johnson and the Democrats after the fiasco of the Swing Around the Circle, but he remained a supporter. See GAC to Andrew Johnson, February 2, 1875, in Paul Bergeron, ed., *The Papers of Andrew Johnson*, vol. 16 (Knoxville: University of Tennessee Press, 2000), 695.

19. Paul A. Hutton, *Phil Sheridan and His Army* (Norman: University of Oklahoma Press, 1999 [orig. pub. 1985]), 1. Sheridan did not stay long enough for Colonel Grierson, 10th Cavalry, to pay his respects; Benjamin Grierson to Alice Grierson, n.d. [September 1867], Benjamin Henry Grierson Papers, Newberry Library. On Sheridan's private support for GAC, see GAC to Dear Friend, September 26, December 2, 1867, December 2, Folder 5, Box 4, MMP.

20. PHS to Ulysses S. Grant, April 15, 1868, in Simon 18: 373; Wert, 265.

21. Joseph Holt to Ulysses S. Grant, May 8, 1868, in Simon 18: 560–62.

22. GAC to Doctor, May 2, 1868, typescript copy, GAC Papers, USMA.

23. Wert, 75; Leckie, 107–08; Utley, ed., *Life*, 132–36; Frost, *General Custer's Libbie*, 173; entry for January 1, 1868, Rebecca Richmond Diary, Dr. Lawrence A. Frost Collection, MCLS.

24. EHC to GAC, December 21, 1867, Folder 20, Box 1, LAFCC.

25. Margaret Custer to GAC, August 5, 1867, Folder 2, Box 2, LAFCC.

26. EHC to GAC, December 21, 1867, Folder 20, Box 1, LAFCC.

27. Stiles, *Jesse James*, 202.

28. *New Orleans Picayune*, July 19, 1868; *Des Moines State Register*, July 24, 1868.

29. EBC to Laura, September 18, 1869, EBC Correspondence, LBH.

30. There is a tantalizing possibility that GAC felt he could not publish his war memoirs at this time because it would force him to admit his first court-martial and conviction, as he later would when he began to publish recollections in serial form. See GAC, "War Memoirs: From West Point to the Battlefield," *Galaxy* (April 1876).

31. PHS to GAC, September 24, 25, 1868, Other Sources, LBH.

32. William T. Sherman to Ulysses S. Grant, September 27, 1868, Ulysses S. Grant to John M. Schofield, September 28, 1868, in John Y. Simon, ed., *The Papers of Ulysses S. Grant*, vol. 19 (Carbondale: Southern Illinois University Press, 1995),

45. Note that PHS's telegrams to GAC predated by three days Sherman's correspondence with Grant and Grant's request to Secretary of War Schofield. PHS referred specifically to Sherman in his September 24 message, suggesting that Sherman promised to obtain GAC's release from his sentence before taking it up with Grant.

33. Jerome A. Greene, *Washita: The U.S. Army and the Southern Cheyennes, 1867–1869* (Norman: University of Oklahoma Press, 2004), 34–38; Robert M. Utley, *The Indian Frontier of the American West, 1846–1980* (Albuquerque: University of New Mexico Press, 1984), 108–16.

34. Utley, *Indian Frontier*, 108–16; William T. Sherman to Ulysses S. Grant, July 19, 1867, in Simon 17: 241. On the two factions on the commission agreeing on the goal, see Utley, *Cavalier in Buckskin*, 58.

35. Elliott West, *The Contested Plains: Indians, Goldseekers, and the Rush to Colorado* (Lawrence: University Press of Kansas, 2005), 310; Greene, 35–38.

36. Utley, ed., *Life*, 115; West, 310. For an example of the view that the Cheyennes and others simply had no idea what they were agreeing to, see Utley, *Frontier Regulars*, 143.

37. West, 310–11.

38. William T. Sherman to Ellen Sherman, July 15, 1868, William T. Sherman Family Papers, University of Notre Dame, copy at LOC; Hutton, 35–37.

39. Hutton, 38. In *The Lance and the Shield: The Life and Times of Sitting Bull* (New York: Henry Holt, 1993), 102, Robert M. Utley describes the difficulties the high-plains Indians had finding a sufficient supply of ammunition for repeating rifles, such as the Spencer and Henry, which used metallic cartridges. They would gather up spent cartridges and painstakingly reload them.

40. Interview between Col. E. W. Wynkoop and Little Rock, a Cheyenne Chief, at Fort Larned, Kansas, August 19, 1868, SED 13, 3rd Session, 40th Congress; Hutton, 38; West, 311; Greene, 48–57.

41. Sully's failure in the sand hills gave PHS his specific grounds for obtaining GAC's return to duty. Sherman wrote to Grant, "Sully got among them but I infer he failed in nerve or activity & Sheridan asks for the services of Gen'l Custar [sic]"; William T. Sherman to Ulysses S. Grant, September 27, 1868, in Simon 19: 45; Greene, 61–70.

42. Greene, 61–71, 74; Hutton, 43–49; West, 311–12.

43. Andrew C. Isenberg argues, in *The Destruction of the Bison* (New York: Cambridge University Press, 2000), 129, that "the expansive American economy" caused the destruction of the bison on the Central and Southern Plains, through the introduction of hunters and cattle, leading to the ultimate death of nomadism.

44. Interview between Col. E. W. Wynkoop and Little Rock, a Cheyenne Chief, at Fort Larned, Kansas, August 19, 1868, SED 13, 3rd Session, 40th Congress; Affidavit of Edmund Guerrier, February 9, 1869, Letters Received by the Office of the Adjutant General (Main Series), 1861–1870, Roll 812, Microfilm Publication M619, NA.

45. William T. Sherman to Ulysses S. Grant, July 19, 1867, in Simon 17: 241. Greene, 104–05, 186–90, offers a fine summary of the thinking on the part of Sheridan and the War Department, and the question of collective responsibility for the raids.

46. Interview between Col. E. W. Wynkoop and Little Rock, a Cheyenne Chief,

at Fort Larned, Kansas, August 19, 1868, SED 13, 3rd Session, 40th Congress; Hutton, 51–51; Utley, ed., *Life*, 198–99.

47. GAC to EBC, October 24, November 3, 1868, EBC, *Following the Guidon*, 13–14; Greene, 78–81.

48. *New York Sun*, May 14, 1899, in Richard G. Hardorff, ed., *Washita Memories: Eyewitness Views of Custer's Attack on Black Kettle's Village* (Norman: University of Oklahoma Press, 2006), 202–05.

49. Greene, 80; Utley, ed., *Life*, 204–05; Nathaniel Philbrick, *The Last Stand: Custer, Sitting Bull, and the Battle of the Little Bighorn* (New York: Viking, 2010), 132.

50. GAC, *My Life on the Plains*, 141–42. Ironically, in testimony in the Reno Court of Inquiry (discussed at length in the epilogue of this volume), Benteen illustrated the utility of uniform horse colors when he described how he identified a company by its gray horses as he first glimpsed the battlefield at the Little Bighorn.

51. GAC to EBC, October 18, November 3, 1868, EBC, *Following the Guidon*, 12–13, 14–15; GAC to Kirkland C. Barker, c. October 1868, Folder 5, Box 4, MMP.

52. GAC to Annette (Nettie) Humphrey, November 8, 1868, Folder 6, Box 4, MMP; Greene, 94. The other Osage scouts, as identified by Greene, were Little Buffalo Head, Draw Them Up, Sharp Hair, Patient Man, I Don't Want It, Big Elk, Little Black Bear, Lightning Bug, Little Buffalo, and Straight Line.

53. GAC to J. Schuyler Crosby, October 28, 1868, GAC Letters, 1867–1868, Beinecke Library, Yale University, New Haven, Conn.

54. Greene, 61–62; Utley, *Frontier Regulars*, 147.

55. Utley, *Frontier Regulars*, 150; Greene, 82–85; Hutton, 61–62.

56. Utley, ed., *Life*, 208–10.

57. Greene, 71–72; Hutton, 52–53.

58. Greene, 106–09. For Hazen's account of his actions, and the course of the Kiowas and Comanches, see William B. Hazen, *Some Corrections to "My Life on the Plains"* (St. Paul, Minn.: Ramaley and Cunningham, 1875), Beinecke Library, Yale University, New Haven, Conn.

59. Utley, *Cavalier in Buckskin*, 60; Hutton, 17–18, 185, also 54–55; Greene, 59, 71–72, 86. I would further argue that warfare on the Great Plains was not true guerrilla warfare, as is sometimes claimed. Guerrilla warfare occurs in settled societies; insurgents derive support from a static civilian population. The high-plains nations engaged in raiding warfare, a distinct product of nomadic societies. Both feature hit-and-run tactics, in which the guerrillas or raiders seek tactical superiority under circumstances of strategic inferiority; but nomadic raiders take their populations with them, so to speak, removing them from the enemy's grasp. See for example Archer Jones, *The Art of War in the Western World* (Urbana: University of Illinois Press, 2000).

60. Greene, 86–88.

61. *New York Sun*, May 14, 1899, in Hardorff, ed., 205; Utley, ed., *Life*, 210, 213; Greene, 97.

62. Greene, 94–95; GAC to EBC, February 20, 1869, EBC, *Following the Guidon*, 51–56.

63. Greene, 97; GAC, *My Life on the Plains*, 146.

64. Greene, 97–98; GAC, *My Life on the Plains*, 146–48; Utley, ed., *Life*, 213.

65. Greene, 99; GAC, *My Life on the Plains*, 148; *New York Sun*, May 14, 1899, in Hardorff, ed., 205.

66. Greene, 89, 99; Sandy Barnard, *A Hoosier Quaker Goes to War: The Life and Death of Major Joel H. Elliott, 7th Cavalry* (Wake Forest, N.C.: AST Press, 2010), 145–59.

67. Greene, 100–01, 109; GAC to Mrs. Hamilton, August 29, 1869, in "In Memoriam: Brevet Major Louis McLane Hamilton, Captain 7th U.S. Cavalry," GAC Papers, Beinecke Library, Yale University, New Haven, Conn.

68. Greene, 110.

69. GAC, *My Life on the Plains*, 157; GAC to Mrs. Hamilton, August 29, 1869, in "In Memoriam: Brevet Major Louis McLane Hamilton, Captain 7th U.S. Cavalry," GAC Papers, Beinecke Library, Yale University, New Haven, Conn.; Edward S. Godfrey, "Reminiscences, Including the Washita Battle, November 27, 1868," in Paul Andrew Hutton, ed., *The Custer Reader* (Norman: University of Oklahoma Press, 2004 [orig. pub. 1992]), 159–79; Greene, 110.

70. GAC, *My Life on the Plains*, 157–59; "In Memoriam: Brevet Major Louis McLane Hamilton, Captain 7th U.S. Cavalry," GAC Papers, Beinecke Library, Yale University, New Haven, Conn.; Godfrey, "Reminiscences," in Hutton, ed., *The Custer Reader*, 159–79; Greene, 111.

71. Greene, 111–12; *New York Sun*, May 14, 1899, in Hardorff, ed., 205.

72. Greene, 111–12, 191; *New York Sun*, May 14, 1899, in Hardorff, ed., 205; Utley, ed., *Life*, 214–20.

73. Greene, 112–19; GAC, *My Life on the Plains*, 159–63; Utley, ed., *Life*, 214–20; GAC to Mrs. Hamilton, August 29, 1869, in "In Memoriam: Brevet Major Louis McLane Hamilton, Captain 7th U.S. Cavalry," GAC Papers, Beinecke Library, Yale University, New Haven, Conn.

74. Greene, 105–07; Black Kettle, "Speech," November 20, 1868, in Hardorff, ed., 54–57.

75. Black Kettle, "Speech," November 20, 1868, in Hardorff, ed., 54–57; Greene, 106–07.

76. Greene, 103, 109–10, 119, 128–35.

77. Greene, 129.

78. *New York Sun*, May 14, 1899, *Kansas City Star*, December 4, 1904, and "Interview and Field Notes by Walter M. Camp," October 22, 1910, in Hardorff, ed., 204–34; Greene, 117–19.

79. GAC, *My Life on the Plains*, 167.

80. Greene, 119–29.

81. Godfrey, "Reminiscences."

82. *New York Herald* in *Georgia Weekly Telegraph*, January 8, 1869; *New York Sun*, May 14, 1899, *Kansas City Star*, December 4, 1904, and "Interview and Field Notes by Walter M. Camp"; Greene, 117–28.

83. Godfrey, "Reminiscences"; *New York Sun*, May 14, 1899, *Kansas City Star*, December 4, 1904, and "Interview and Field Notes by Walter M. Camp"; Greene, 117–28.

84. "In Memoriam: Brevet Major Louis McLane Hamilton, Captain 7th U.S. Cavalry," GAC Papers, Beinecke Library, Yale University, New Haven, Conn.; Greene, 135, 162–63, 171–72. Hamilton's remains were later moved. The number of enlisted men with Elliott is variously described as seventeen, eighteen, or nineteen. See Utley, *Cavalier in Buckskin*, 68; Wert, 275.

85. Greene, 173–75; *New York Herald* in *Chicago Tribune*, January 7, 1869.

86. Greene, 135–37; Utley, *Cavalier in Buckskin*, 70–71. Greene, like many

historians—notably Dee Brown in *Bury My Heart at Wounded Knee: An Indian History of the American West* (New York: Henry Holt, 1970)—largely accepts the Cheyenne total. If the true total of dead warriors truly were only 10 percent of GAC's claim, it would have been obvious on the day of the battle and especially when the field was revisited two weeks later. The gap would have been exploited by his enemies, particularly Benteen.

87. *New York Herald* in *Chicago Tribune*, January 7, 1869; *Leavenworth Bulletin*, December 31, 1868; GAC to EBC, December 19, 1868, January 2, 1869, EBC, *Following the Guidon*, 46–47; GAC to My Dear Doctor, January 2, 1869, GAC Correspondence, LBH; Greene, 173–78.

88. GAC to EBC, December 19, 1868, January 2, 1869, EBC, *Following the Guidon*, 46–47; GAC to EBC, February 8, 1869, Folder 7, Box 4, MMP; Greene, 173–78.

89. GAC to EBC, February 8, 1869, EBC, *Following the Guidon*, 49–50; Greene, 178–79.

90. Greene, 179–81; David L. Spotts, *Campaigning with Custer and the Nineteenth Kansas Volunteer Cavalry in the Washita Campaign, 1868–69*, ed. E. A. Brininstool (Lincoln: University of Nebraska Press, 1988 [orig. pub. 1928]), 147–48.

91. Letter from Camp Supply, March 29, 1869, quoted in *New York Times*, May 3, 1869; *New York Tribune*, April 24, 1869; Spotts, 147–48; GAC, *My Life on the Plains*, 232–38; Utley, *Cavalier in Buckskin*, 73–74; Greene, 179–80.

92. Greene, 180–82; Spotts, 151–59; Charles Duncan and Jay Smith, "The Captives," *Research Review: The Journal of the Little Bighorn Associates* 7, no. 2 (June 1993): 3–21, 31; GAC to EBC, March 24, 1869, EBC, *Following the Guidon*, 56–57; GAC, *My Life on the Plains*, 238–51; *New York Times*, May 3, 1869; *New York Tribune*, April 24, 1869. Spotts's account, in the form of a journal, illustrates how GAC's account in *My Life on the Plains* greatly romanticized and simplified the facts.

93. Spotts, 158.

94. Greene, 181–82; West, 312–15; GAC to EBC, March 24, 1869, EBC, *Following the Guidon*, 56–57.

95. Eugene A. Carr to GAC, August 16, 1869, Other Sources, LBH; GAC to EBC, March 24, 1869, in EBC, *Following the Guidon*, 56–57.

96. *New York Observer and Chronicle*, December 24, 1868.

97. *New York Times*, December 4, 13, and 22, 1868; *Baltimore Sun*, December 30, 1868.

98. Greene, 186–87; Richard Slotkin, *The Fatal Environment: The Myth of the Frontier in the Age of Industrialization, 1800–1890* (Norman: University of Oklahoma Press, 1994 [orig. pub. 1985]), 400. For a fine discussion of the moral quandaries of the Washita, and wars against American Indians in general, see Utley, *Cavalier in Buckskin*, 74–78.

99. Alfred Sully to Henning Von Minden, December 23, 1868, Alfred Sully Letters, Beinecke Library, Yale University, New Haven, Conn.; *St. Louis Democrat*, February 9, 1869, in *New York Times*, February 14, 1869; Hutton, *Phil Sheridan and His Army*, 63. See also Barnett, 163–66.

100. As Slotkin notes in *The Fatal Environment*, 400, "Ultimate culpability for the 'massacre' of the Washita must be with the makers of Indian policy."

101. *St. Louis Democrat*, February 9, 1869, in *New York Times*, February 14, 1869, and *Chicago Tribune*, February 15, 1869.

102. *New York Sun*, May 14, 1899, *Kansas City Star*, December 4, 1904, and "Interview and Field Notes by Walter M. Camp"; Wert, 279.

103. Wert, 278–79; Barnett, 160–63; Utley, *Cavalier in Buckskin*, 76–77. It is difficult to find other officers in the 7th Cavalry who shared Benteen's anger, but Sully seized on his letter to support his own grudge against GAC; see Alfred Sully to Henning Von Minden, February 17, 1869, Alfred Sully Letters, Beinecke Library, Yale University, New Haven, Conn. The assessment of GAC's actions presented here echoes Utley's judgments.

104. W. A. Graham, ed., *The Custer Myth: A Source Book of Custeriana* (Mechanicsburg, Pa.: Stackpole Books, 2000 [orig. pub. 1953]), 213; *Seventeenth Annual Reunion of the Association of the Graduates of the United States Military Academy at West Point, New York, June 10th, 1886* (East Saginaw, Mich.: Evening News, 1886), 104–06; Hutton, *Phil Sheridan and His Army*, 96; Roger Darling, *Custer's Seventh Cavalry Comes to Dakota* (El Segundo, Calif: Upton and Sons, 1989), 178–81. I find it impossible to read Benteen's nitpicking defense of his failure to follow orders, recounted in Darling, and imagine that this was an officer who would challenge his commander to personal combat.

105. Henry L. Morrill to Henry Albers, December 1, 1865, Folder 2, Box 1, Henry Leighton Morrill Papers, Beinecke Library, Yale University, New Haven, Conn.; Wert, 278–79; Barnett, 160–63.

106. "Interview and Field Notes by Walter M. Camp"; Wert, 286–88; Barnett, 194–97.

107. GAC to EBC, February 8, 1869, Folder 7, Box 4, MMP; Wert, 288–89.

Thirteen: The Financier

1. Charles Dudley Warner and Mark Twain, *The Gilded Age: A Tale of Today* (New York: Harper and Brothers, 1915), 208.

2. Stiles, *First Tycoon*, 511.

3. Stiles, *First Tycoon*, 398–99.

4. Warner and Twain, 208–09.

5. Blaine Burkey, *Custer, Come at Once! The Fort Hays Years of George and Elizabeth Custer, 1867–1870* (Hays, Kan.: Society of Friends of Historic Fort Hays, 1991), 64–73.

6. Heather Cox Richardson, *West from Appomattox: The Reconstruction of America After the Civil War* (New Haven, Conn.: Yale University Press, 2007), 74–77, 113–15; William S. McFeely, *Grant: A Biography* (New York: W. W. Norton, 1981), 305–18.

7. For the impact of the West's multiracial, multiethnic society on the attempt to define citizenship, see Joshua Paddison, "Race, Religion, and Naturalization: How the West Shaped Citizenship Debates in the Reconstruction Congress," in Adam Arenson and Andrew R. Graybill, eds., *Civil War Wests: Testing the Limits of the United States* (Oakland: University of California Press, 2015), 181–201. Paddison's emphasis on the limitations of the expansion of citizenship is well taken, but, for the purposes of this discussion, it is important to note that even in excluding Chinese and American Indians Congress sought grounds other than race. For an illuminating discussion of the original distinction between *liberty* and *freedom* in the American context, see David Hackett

Fischer, *Liberty and Freedom: A Visual History of America's Founding Ideas* (New York: Oxford University Press, 2005).

8. In 1871 Congress would enact an appropriations bill with a rider stating that "hereafter, no Indian nation or tribe within the United States shall be recognized or acknowledged as an independent nation, tribe, or power with whom the United States may contract by treaty." As Martha Sandweiss notes, "With that [measure], a diplomatic practice stretching back to the earliest days of the republic ended, and a new era of federal Indian policy began." See Martha A. Sandweiss, "Still Picture, Moving Stories: Reconstruction Comes to Indian Country," in Arenson and Graybill, eds., *Civil War Wests*, 158–78.

9. EBC, *Following the Guidon*, 83–91, 102–04, 120–21; Wert, 286–87; see also *New York Herald* in *Georgia Weekly Telegraph*, January 8, 1869.

10. EBC, *Following the Guidon*, 90–91; Barnett, 194–97.

11. *Detroit Free Press*, June 10, 1869, in *New York Times*, June 13, 1869.

12. EBC, *Following the Guidon*, 231.

13. EBC, *Following the Guidon*, 112–14, 120–22, 227–40, 289–98, 314–15.

14. Burkey, 47–63, 81–91; EBC, *Following the Guidon*, 263–77; EBC to Rebecca Richmond, September 17, 1869, EBC to Laura, September 18, 1869, EBC Correspondence, LBH; *Pomeroy's Democrat*, September 22, 1869; PHS to GAC, September 28, 1869, Other Sources, LBH.

15. On GAC playing poker with fellow officers, see, for example, GAC to EBC, May 2, 1867, *Tenting on the Plains*, 576–79.

16. Burkey, 68–79.

17. EBC to Laura, September 18, 1869, EBC to Rebecca Richmond, October 16, n.d., EBC Correspondence, LBH; Burkey, 87, 101.

18. Albert T. Morgan, *Yazoo: Or, On the Picket Line of Freedom in the South* (Washington, D.C.: n.p., 1884).

19. Robert M. Utley, *Frontier Regulars: The United States Army and the Indian, 1866–1891* (Lincoln: University of Nebraska Press, 1994 [orig. pub. 1973]), 15–16; Paul A. Hutton, *Phil Sheridan and His Army* (Norman: University of Oklahoma Press, 1999), 118, 137–41.

20. Entry 1303, Cullum 1: 159–60; Samuel D. Sturgis, endorsement, August 13, 1869, Other Sources, LBH.

21. Grant of Leave, December 2, 1869, Military Division of the Missouri, Other Sources, LBH; GAC to EBC, November 27 and December 16, 1869, Folder 7, Box 4, MMP; Wert, 291–92; Leckie, 122–23.

22. Leckie, 126–27, was the first to grasp that these three fragments comprised the same letter. She placed the date in December 1870. In my private correspondence with Leckie, she argued that late 1869 is the most likely date, which, after my own review of the internal evidence, I accept. See EBC to GAC, letter fragment, Folder 2, EBC Papers, Beinecke Library, Yale University, New Haven, Conn.; GAC to EBC, undated fragments, Folder 14, Box 4, MMP.

23. EBC to GAC, undated letter fragment, Folder 2, EBC Papers, Beinecke Library, Yale University, New Haven, Conn.; GAC to EBC, two undated fragments, Folder 14, Box 4, MMP; Leckie, 126–27.

24. Rebecca Richmond to Mother, March 16 and 21, 1870, Other Sources, LBH; Rebecca Richmond Diary, March 9, 1870, Dr. Lawrence A. Frost Collection, MCLS.

25. John Schofield to GAC, April 30 and May 20, 1870, Other Sources, LBH; H. Craig Miner and William E. Unrau, *The End of Indian Kansas: A Study of Cultural Revolution, 1854–1871* (Lawrence: Regents Press of Kansas, 1978), 139. Miner and Unrau address the fate of the many low-plains nations that lie outside the scope of this biography.

26. *Chicago Tribune*, September 22, 1870; Joseph G. Rosa, *They Called Him Wild Bill: The Life and Adventures of James Butler Hickok* (Norman: University of Oklahoma Press, 1974 [orig. pub. 1964]), 135.

27. Rosa, 135–52; *Leavenworth Bulletin*, June 21, 1870; Richard White, "Animals and Enterprise," and Richard Maxwell Brown, "Violence," in Clyde A. Milner II, Carol A. O'Connor, and Martha A. Sandweiss, eds., *The Oxford History of the American West* (New York: Oxford University Press, 1994), 237–73, 393–425; Richard Maxwell Brown, *No Duty to Retreat: Violence and Values in American History and Society* (New York: Oxford University Press, 1991), 53–58. It should be noted that Terry G. Jordan, in *North American Cattle-Ranching Frontiers: Origins, Diffusion, and Differentiation* (Albuquerque: University of New Mexico Press, 1993), 208–40, argues that Anglo-Texan ranching began in a semitropical coastal zone, and the longhorns were unsuited to the winter conditions farther north on the plains. Yet he also notes that Texas ranching did indeed spread north prior to a collapse in the 1880s, taking root in Kansas as Texans wintered near railheads with access to the crucial Chicago market.

28. Rosa, 140–57; GAC, *My Life on the Plains*, 34.

29. Brian C. Pohanka, ed., *A Summer on the Plains with Custer's 7th Cavalry: The 1870 Diary of Annie Gibson Roberts* (Lynchburg, Va.: Schroeder Publications, 2004), 8–17, 150–51.

30. Pohanka, ed., 35–41, 50–51, 56–60, 66–67.

31. Richard Slotkin, *The Fatal Environment: The Myth of the Frontier in the Age of Industrialization, 1800–1890* (Norman: University of Oklahoma Press, 1994 [orig. pub. 1985]), 373–76, also stresses GAC's attraction to New York, writing, "He consistently elected to go east rather than west in search of opportunity." But I argue that he would fail in the role Slotkin ascribes to him, as "an early type of organization man," whether in New York or in the army. He was attracted to the metropolitan center without truly belonging to it or mastering its ways.

32. *New York Herald*, December 16, 1870; Certification, James M. Millan, February 15, 1871, Other Sources, LBH; GAC to William T. Sherman, May 30, 1870, James Calhoun Records, Dr. Lawrence A. Frost Collection, MCLS; Merington, 232–33; Pohanka, ed., 104–05; Wert, 289–93; Leckie, 125–28.

33. Merington, 232–33.

34. Merington, 232; Edwin G. Burrows and Mike Wallace, *Gotham: A History of New York City to 1898* (New York: Oxford University Press, 1999), 672; GAC to Edward D. Townsend, March 5, 1871, Personnel Files, CRM; Stiles, *First Tycoon*, 515.

35. Stiles, *First Tycoon*, 505–06.

36. Stiles, *First Tycoon*, 127, 363–75.

37. Stiles, *First Tycoon*, 370–507.

38. *New York Times*, November 10, 1866; *Harper's Weekly*, December 15, 1866; *Cleveland Leader*, January 27, 1867; *Round Table*, February 9, 1867; Charles Fran-

cis Adams Jr., "A Chapter of Erie," *North American Review* (July 1869); Stiles, *First Tycoon*, 365–401, 431–45.

39. Stiles, *First Tycoon*, 372–80, 391–98, 487–95.

40. Stiles, *First Tycoon*, 398–99, 421–22, 442–43, 449–65, 521–22; David Nasaw, *Andrew Carnegie* (New York: Penguin, 2006), 61–63.

41. Anthony Trollope, *The Way We Live Now* (New York: Modern Library, 2001), 332.

42. Unknown to GAC, n.d., 1870, Other Sources, LBH; James Grant Wilson and John Fiske, eds., *Appleton's Cyclopaedia of American Biography*, vol. 1 (New York: D. Appleton, 1888), 112, 167, 231; Stiles, *First Tycoon*, 176, 192, 281, 322, 326, 381, 415–16.

43. Slotkin, 405–06; "The Stevens Lode," prospectus, n.d., Broadsides, Clippings, and Memorabilia, LBH; Jairus W. Hall to GAC, November 29, 1870, Other Sources, LBH; Erl H. Ellis and Carrie Scott Ellis, *The Saga of Upper Clear Creek* (Frederick, Colo.: Jende-Hagan, 1983), 96–102; Alexander N. Easton, *The New York Stock Exchange: Its History, Its Contribution to National Prosperity, and Its Relation to American Finance at the Outset of the Twentieth Century* (New York: Stock Exchange Historical Company, 1905), 159. On Jairus W. Hall as colonel of the 4th Michigan Infantry Regiment, see *OR*, Series 1, Vol. 45, Part 2: 584, and *Official Army Register of the Volunteer Force of the United States Army for the Years 1861, '62, '63, '64, '65: Part V, Ohio, Michigan* (Washington, D.C.: Adjutant General's Office, 1865), 298. GAC visited Denver in mid-1870; see entry for September 9, 10, 1870, Winfield S. Harvey Diary, 1868–71, Box 6, Edward S. Godfrey Papers, LOC.

44. "The Stevens Lode," prospectus, n.d., Broadsides, Clippings, and Memorabilia, LBH; Jairus W. Hall to GAC, November 29, 1870, L. P. Morton to Joseph Seligman, February 6, 1871, L. P. Morton to GAC, February 9, 1871, Other Sources, LBH; James Grant Wilson and John Fiske, eds., *Appleton's Cyclopaedia of American Biography*, vol. 4 (New York: D. Appleton, 1900), 431.

45. Frost, *General Custer's Libbie*, 191–92.

46. Special Orders No. 100, March 11, 1871, Special Orders No. 137, April 5, 1871, Special Orders No. 171, April 27, 1871, Special Orders No. 244, June 21, 1871, Other Sources, LBH; Endorsement, March 20, 1871, GAC to Edward D. Townsend, March 22, 28, April 15, 1871, Personnel Files, CRM.

47. L. P. Morton to Joseph Seligman, February 6, 1871, Other Sources, LBH; Frost, *General Custer's Libbie*, 191–92; Leckie, 128.

48. GAC to EBC, April 13, 1871, Folder 8, Box 4, MMP; Merington, 232–39; Stiles, *First Tycoon*, 452, 456, 460–65, 508–09, 522; Maury Klein, *The Life and Legend of Jay Gould* (Baltimore, Md.: Johns Hopkins University Press, 1988), 79–122.

49. *New York Times*, February 28, March 20, 1861, January 17, 1871, May 14, 1916; Merington, 232–35; Leckie, 125–31.

50. Merington, 232–39; Leckie, 125–31.

51. Leckie, 125–26, 128–31; Wert, 291–92.

52. Leckie, 116; Merington, 238–39; L. P. Morton to GAC, February 9, 1871, Other Sources, LBH.

53. Entry for September 7, 1870, Pohanka, ed., 97–98; Frost, *General Custer's Libbie*, 192–93; Leckie, 125–31.

54. Easton, 192–94; Henry Clews, *Twenty-eight Years on Wall Street* (New York:

Irving Publishing, 1888), 407–24; William W. Fowler, *Ten Years in Wall Street: Or, Revelations of Inside Life and Experience on 'Change* (Hartford, Conn.: Worthington, Dustin and Co., 1870), 218–21; Adlai E. Stevenson, *Something of Men I Have Known* (Chicago: A. C. McClurg and Co., 1909), 395–96; Charles E. Trevathan, *The American Thoroughbred* (New York: Macmillan, 1905), 313–14: Stiles, *First Tycoon*, 383–85.

55. "The Stevens Lode," prospectus, n.d., Broadsides, Clippings, and Memorabilia, LBH. For evidence of Travers's close involvement, see Jairus W. Hall to GAC, June 14, July 15, 1872, Other Sources, LBH; Merington, 238–39. On par value of stock, see Stiles, *First Tycoon*, 439–40, 479–82.

56. Stiles, *First Tycoon*, 383–84, 493–95, 516–17, 526–27; John Jacob Astor to GAC, April 7, 1871, Other Sources, LBH.

57. John Jacob Astor to GAC, April 7, 1871, Other Sources, LBH; "The Stevens Lode," prospectus, n.d., Broadsides, Clippings, and Memorabilia, LBH; Easton, 159–60, 269n, 287; Clews, 670–71; Frost, *General Custer's Libbie*, 191–92.

58. Merington, 232, 234. Merington appears to have combined more than one letter under a single date, as she often did. She referred to James H. Banker as "Barker," but I judge this to be a mistake, given my reading of the original documents and Banker's centrality to Wall Street in 1871. Many writers have followed Merington in her error.

59. *New York World*, April 24, 1871, in *Columbus Enquirer*, April 28, 1871; GAC to EBC, [April] 29th, 1871, Folder 8, Box 4, MMP; Jairus W. Hall to GAC, April 20, 27, and 30, 1871, General Orders No. 4, March 8, 1871, Other Sources, LBH; HED 1, Part 2, 2nd Session, 42nd Congress; Endorsement, March 20, 1871, and GAC to Edward D. Townsend, April 15, 1871, Personnel Files, CRM; Merington, 237.

60. *Philadelphia Inquirer*, May 13, 1871; *Kalamazoo Gazette*, May 19, 1871; GAC to EBC, [April] 29, 1871, Folder 8, Box 4, MMP; GAC to Edward D. Townsend, June 10, 1871, Personnel Files, CRM; Frost, *General Custer's Libbie*, 192; Leckie, 130–31.

61. *New York Times*, July 15, 1871; Stiles, *First Tycoon*, 414–25.

62. Francis P. Church to GAC, March 8 [1871], GAC Correspondence, LBH; *New York Times*, May 24, 1917; Leckie, 131; Merington, 238–39.

63. Jairus W. Hall to GAC, April 27, 30, 1871, Other Sources, LBH.

64. Jairus W. Hall to GAC, April 20, 27, 30, 1871, August 8, 1872, Other Sources, LBH; GAC to EBC, [April] 29, 1871, Folder 8, Box 4, MMP.

65. Jairus W. Hall to GAC, April 24, June 6, 14, July 15, August 8, 1872, Other Sources, LBH. On GAC's purchase of his stake on credit, see Jairus W. Hall to GAC, August 19, 1874, same collection.

66. Jairus W. Hall to GAC, July 26, 1872, Other Sources, LBH; Klein, 121–22.

67. Jairus W. Hall to GAC, August 8, 1872, Other Sources, LBH; Slotkin, 405–06.

68. Jairus W. Hall to GAC, August 13, 21, September 23, 1872, Theodore H. Lowe to Jairus W. Hall, August 14, 1872, Other Sources, LBH; Frost, *General Custer's Libbie*, 216. See especially Ellis and Ellis, 96–102, and Jairus W. Hall to William R. Travers, February 23, 1875, Other Sources, LBH.

69. Hall's correspondence with GAC disappears until August 19, 1874, when he wrote a letter that makes it clear that GAC paid little attention to the mine, though he maintained a financial interest in it. See Jairus W. Hall to GAC, August 19, 1874, Other Sources, LBH.

Fourteen: The Writer

1. Theodore J. Crackel, "Custer's Kentucky: General George Armstrong Custer and Elizabethtown, Kentucky, 1871–1873," *Filson Club History Quarterly* 48 (April 1974): 144–55; GAC to EBC, n.d., Folder 14, Box 4, MMP; Merington, 240–41.

2. HED 1, Part 2, 2nd Session, 42nd Congress; Brian W. Dippie, ed., *Nomad: George A. Custer in* Turf, Field and Farm (Austin: University of Texas Press, 1980), 73–81; See also Elizabethtown, Kentucky, Post 198, Vol. 1, Entry 7: Special Orders, Part 5, RG 393, NA; EBC, *Boots and Saddles,* 11.

3. A. B. Cain to Asst. Adj. Gen., Dept. of the South, November 6, 1871, Elizabethtown, Kentucky, Post 198, Vol. 2: 134–35, Entry 1: Letters Sent, Part 5, RG 393, NA.

4. GAC to Margaret Custer, November 29, 1871, Folder 8, Box 4, MMP.

5. Special Orders No. 81, August 18, 1871, Elizabethtown, Kentucky, Post 198, Vol. 1: 55–56, Entry 7: Special Orders, Part 5, RG 393, NA; *New York Times,* September 10, 1874; George C. Wright, *Racial Violence in Kentucky, 1865–1940: Lynchings, Mob Rule, and "Legal Lynchings"* (Baton Rouge: Louisiana State University Press, 1990), 26.

6. Anne E. Marshall, *Creating a Confederate Kentucky: The Lost Cause and Civil War Memory in a Border State* (Chapel Hill: University of North Carolina Press, 2010), 34–72; Aaron Astor, *Rebels on the Border: Civil War, Emancipation, and the Reconstruction of Kentucky and Missouri* (Baton Rouge: Louisiana State University Press, 2012), 156–58, 166, 209–14, 223–30; Wright, 21–25; Patrick A. Lewis, "The Democratic Partisan Militia and the Black Peril: The Kentucky Militia, Racial Violence, and the Fifteenth Amendment, 1870–1873," *Civil War History* 56, no. 2 (June 2010): 145–74; Ross A. Webb, "Kentucky: 'Pariah Among the Elect,'" in Richard O. Curry, ed., *Radicalism, Racism, and Party Realignment: The Border States During Reconstruction* (Baltimore, Md.: Johns Hopkins Press, 1969), 105–45.

7. Wright, 27, 48–58; Lewis, "The Democratic Partisan Militia and the Black Peril."

8. *New York Times,* September 10, 1874; Marshall, 63–64.

9. Foner, 453–54.

10. Foner, 454–55.

11. William S. McFeely, *Grant: A Biography* (New York: W. W. Norton, 1982), 366–69.

12. Benjamin H. Bristow to Amos T. Akerman, telegram August 8, 1871, G. C. Wharton to Benjamin H. Bristow, September 30, 1871, Returns for the Annual Report of the Attorney General, District of Kentucky, January 1, 1872, Letters Received by the Department of Justice from the State of Kentucky, Roll 1, Microfilm Publication M1362, NA II; HED 1, Part 2, 2nd Session, 42nd Congress; Headquarters Circular, Dept. of the South, April 3, 1871, Elizabethtown, Kentucky, Post 198, Vol. 2: 100, Entry 1: Letters Sent, and Post 198, Entry 3: Telegrams Sent and Received, Part 5, RG 393, NA.

13. Special Orders Nos. 113, 115, November 12, 16, 1871, Elizabethtown, Kentucky, Post 198, Vol. 1: 77, 78, Special Orders Nos. 77, 83, June 24, July 12, 1872, Elizabethtown, Kentucky, Post 198, Vol. 2: 3, 7, Entry 7: Special Orders, Part 5, RG 393, NA; Returns for the Annual Report of the Attorney General, Dis-

trict of Kentucky, January 1, 1872, G. C. Wharton to AG George H. Williams, March 27, 1872, Letters Received by the Department of Justice from the State of Kentucky, Roll 1, Microfilm Publication M1362, NA II. See also A. B. Cain to Asst. Adj. Gen., Dept. of the South, March 20, 1872; 1st Lt. Ezekiel to Asst. Adj. Gen., Dept. of the South, May 21, 1872, GAC to Asst. Adj. Gen., Dept. of the South, June 29, 1872; GAC to Asst. Adj. Gen., Dept. of the South, July 22, 1872; all in Elizabethtown, Kentucky, Post 198, Vol. 1: 31, 44, 52, 61, Entry 1: Letters Sent, Part 5, RG 393, NA.

14. Thomas Webb to Ulysses S. Grant, May 12, 1872, Thomas Webb to Ulysses S. Grant, May 12, 1872, W. D. Linkins to Ulysses S. Grant, May 29, 1872, Letters Received by the Department of Justice from the State of Kentucky, Roll 1, Microfilm Publication M1362, NA II.

15. G. C. Wharton to George H. Williams, August 28, 1873, Special Report of H. C. Whitley to the Department of Justice on Outages in Kentucky, September 24, 1873, Letters Received by the Department of Justice from the State of Kentucky, Roll 1, Microfilm Publication M1362, NA II.

16. McFeely, 372–73.

17. Brian W. Dippie, ed., *Nomad: George A. Custer in* Turf, Field and Farm (Austin: University of Texas Press, 1980), 86–87. On the *Louisville Courier-Journal*'s campaign against the KKK, see, for example, the issue of August 25, 1873.

18. Dippie, ed., 73–81; GAC to EBC, n.d., Thomas Custer to EBC, n.d., Folder 14, Box 4, MMP. The *New York Times*, October 28, 1872, reported that GAC spent $2,200 on a thoroughbred. See also Elizabethtown, Kentucky, Post 198, Entry 7, Vols. 1–2: Special Orders, Part 5, RG 393, NA.

19. Paul A. Hutton, *Phil Sheridan and His Army* (Norman: University of Oklahoma Press, 1999), 212–16.

20. *New York Herald* in *Cincinnati Inquirer*, January 18, 1872.

21. *Kansas City Journal of Commerce* in *Chicago Tribune*, January 19, 1872; Hutton, 212–16.

22. *Louisville Courier-Journal* in *Cincinnati Commercial*, February 4, 1872; *Cincinnati Gazette*, February 7, 1872. For an idea of the bond formed between GAC and Alexis, see Baron N. Schilling to EBC, March 25, 1877, Folder 13, Box 4, MMP, which states, "About your heroic husband, . . . the Grand Duke speaks always in terms of the highest esteem and admiration."

23. *New York Times*, August 23, 1872; *New York Tribune*, September 3, 1872; *Atlanta Constitution*, September 3, 1872.

24. A. E. Smith to Asst. Adj. Gen., Dept. of the South, [?] 1871, Elizabethtown, Kentucky, Post 198, Vol. 1: 109, Entry 2: Letters Sent, Part 5, RG 393, NA; Frost, *General Custer's Libbie*, 197.

25. Margaret E. Custer and James Calhoun Marriage License, March 7, 1872, Margaret E. Custer Calhoun to LAR, April 5, 1872, James Calhoun Records, Dr. Lawrence A. Frost Collection, MCLS.

26. Endorsement, June 22, 1872, Elizabethtown, Kentucky, Post 198, Vol. 2: 95, Entry 2: Endorsements, Part 5, RG 393, NA; EBC, *Following the Guidon*, 231–33.

27. A. B. Cain to Asst. Adj. Gen., Dept. of the South, March 20, 1872; 1st Lt. Ezekiel to Asst. Adj. Gen., Dept. of the South, May 21, 1872, GAC to Asst. Adj. Gen., Dept. of the South, June 29, 1872; GAC to Asst. Adj. Gen., Dept. of the South, July 22, 1872; all in Elizabethtown, Kentucky, Post 198, Vol. 1: 31, 44,

52, 61, Entry 1: Letters Sent, Part 5, RG 393, NA; Special Orders Nos. 77, 83, 106, 112, 118, June 24, July 12, September 12, October 2, 22, 1872, Elizabethtown, Kentucky, Post 198, Vol. 2: 3, 7, 19, 23, 26, 29, Entry 7: Special Orders, Part 5, RG 393, NA. On the Alabama mission, see also John M. Carroll, ed., *Custer's Chief of Scouts: The Reminiscences of Charles A. Varnum* (Lincoln: University of Nebraska Press, 1987), 35–37.

28. Samuel R. Graves to GAC, August 18, 1872, J. P. Ainsworth to GAC, January 5, 1873, Other Sources, LBH. On Graves, a member of Parliament for Liverpool, see *Monroe Commercial*, May 11, 1871.

29. GAC to D. B. Sackett, Inspector General, U.S. Army, December 30, 1872, Elizabethtown, Kentucky, Post 198, Vol. 1: 83, Entry 1: Letters Sent, Part 5, RG 393, NA.

30. This sketch of Adelbert Ames, in this paragraph and those that follow, draws from a number of sources, which are cited in detail in Stiles, *Jesse James*, 141–42, 307–35. These sources include Richard Nelson Current, *Those Terrible Carpetbaggers: A Reinterpretation* (New York: Oxford University Press, 1988); Blanche Butler Ames, ed., *Chronicles from the Nineteenth Century: Family Letters of Blanche Butler and Adelbert Ames*, vols. 1–2 (Clinton, Mass.: n.p., 1957); Blanche Butler Ames, *Adelbert Ames, 1835–1933: General, Senator, Governor* (London: MacDonald, 1964); John R. Lynch, *Reminiscences of an Active Life: The Reminiscences of John Roy Lynch* (Chicago: University of Chicago Press, 1970); *Mississippi in 1875: Report of the Select Committee to Inquire into the Mississippi Election of 1875, with the Testimony and Documentary Evidence*, vol. 1 (Washington, D.C.: Government Printing Office, 1876), 1–16; Albert T. Morgan, *Yazoo: Or, On the Picket Line of Freedom in the South, A Personal Narrative* (Washington, D.C.: n.p., 1884); entries for Charles Caldwell and John R. Lynch in Eric Foner, *Freedom's Lawmakers: A Directory of Black Officeholders During Reconstruction* (New York: Oxford University Press, 1993), 36, 138–39.

31. *Chicago Tribune*, December 20, 1871.

32. Dippie, ed., 73–101.

33. Edwin G. Burrow and Mike Wallace, *Gotham: A History of New York City to 1898* (New York: Oxford University Press, 1999), 683–85; George Palmer Putnam, *A Memoir* (New York: G. P. Putnam's Sons, 1912), 171; John William Tebbel and Mary Ellen Zuckerman, *The Magazine in America, 1741–1990* (New York: Oxford University Press, 1991), 3–25. See also Jeffrey L. Pasley, *The Tyranny of Printers: Newspaper Politics in the Early American Republic* (Charlottesville: University of Virginia Press, 2001).

34. Tebbel and Zuckerman, 57–59.

35. GAC, "My Life on the Plains," *Galaxy* (January 1872).

36. Drew Gilpin Faust, *This Republic of Suffering: Death and the American Civil War* (New York: Alfred A. Knopf, 2008), 172–73. On GAC's fascination with fossils and geology, see, for example, GAC to EBC, July 19, 1873, Folder 9, Box 4, MMP. For an important analysis of these articles, see Richard Slotkin, *The Fatal Environment: The Myth of the Frontier in the Age of Industrialization, 1800–1890* (Norman: University of Oklahoma Press, 1994 [orig. pub. 1985]), 409–12.

37. GAC, "My Life on the Plains," *Galaxy* (January 1872).

38. Louis Menand, *The Metaphysical Club* (New York: Farrar, Straus and Giroux, 2001), 97–114.

39. GAC, "My Life on the Plains: Origin and Decay of the Indians," *Galaxy* (February 1872). Richard Slotkin writes that GAC "here applies the orthodox tests of racialist science," *The Fatal Environment*, 410–11, though I do not believe our analyses are identical.

40. *Independent*, January 4, 1872; *San Francisco Chronicle*, January 30, 1872.

41. *Literary World*, March 1, 1872; *New York Tribune*, July 13, 1872; *Turf, Field and Farm*, March 22, 1872; *Massachusetts Ploughman*, March 23, 1872; *Chicago Tribune*, March 25, 1872.

42. Tebbel and Zuckerman, 61.

43. GAC, "My Life on the Plains," *Galaxy* (January 1872); GAC to EBC, September 10, 1873, Folder 9, Box 4, MMP.

44. GAC, "My Life on the Plains," *Galaxy* (April 1872).

45. GAC, *My Life on the Plains*, 244–51. See also Barnett's fine analysis, 194–97.

46. Faust, 185–96.

47. Faust, 196–200; Edmund Wilson, *Patriotic Gore: Studies in the Literature of the American Civil War* (New York: W. W. Norton, 1994 [orig. pub. 1962]), 617–34; Ambrose Bierce, "On a Mountain," in S. T. Joshi, ed., *Ambrose Bierce: The Devil's Dictionary, Tales, & Memoirs* (New York: Library of America, 2011), 655–59.

48. Menand, 56–69.

49. Charles Francis Adams Jr. to his mother, May 12, 1863, in Worthington Chauncey Ford, ed., *A Cycle of Adams Letters, 1861–1865*, vol. 2 (Boston: Houghton Mifflin, 1920), 3–5; Edward Chase Kirkland, *Charles Francis Adams Jr., 1835–1915: The Patrician at Bay* (Cambridge, Mass.: Harvard University Press, 1965), 28–31.

50. Charles Francis Adams Jr., "A Chapter of Erie," *North American Review* (July 1869); Kirkland, 34–64; Stiles, *First Tycoon*, 467–70, 496–501.

51. Faust, 200.

52. Lawrence Barrett to GAC, September 23, 1872, Other Sources, LBH; GAC to Zachariah Chandler, January 16, 1873, Roll 3, Zachariah Chandler Papers, LOC; *Turf, Field and Farm*, March 7, 1873; GAC to O. D. Greene, February 15, 25, 1873, Letters Received, Department of Dakota, Roll 14, Microfilm Publication M1734, NA.

53. Special Orders No. 13, 15, 50, February 25, March 11, 13, 1873, Other Sources, LBH; GAC to O. D. Greene, February 15, 25, 1873, Letters Received, Department of Dakota, Roll 14, Microfilm Publication M1734, NA.

Fifteen: The Enemy

1. Lawrence Barrett to GAC, March 23 [1873], Folder 3, EBC Papers, Beinecke Library, Yale University, New Haven, Conn.

2. Leckie, 154.

3. Lawrence Barrett to GAC, March 23 [1873], Folder 3, EBC Papers, Beinecke Library, Yale University, New Haven, Conn.; EBC, *Boots and Saddles*, 11; GAC to EBC, n.d., Folder 14, Box 4, MMP.

4. GAC to EBC, c. 1873, Folder 2, EBC Papers, Beinecke Library, Yale University, New Haven, Conn.

5. EBC, *Boots and Saddles*, 19–33; C. W. Foster to O. D. Greene, April 14, 1873, GAC to O. D. Greene, April 16, 1873, Special Files of Headquarters, Division of the Missouri, Relating to Military Operations and Administration, Roll 1,

Microfilm Publication M1495, NA; *New York Times*, April 23, 1873. The 7th Cavalry's movement to Yankton and on to Fort Rice is massively documented in Roger Darling, *Custer's Seventh Cavalry Comes to Dakota* (El Segundo, Calif.: Upton and Sons, 1989). Drawing upon a newspaper printing of GAC's telegram concerning the effects of the blizzard, which identified the recipient as the War Department in Washington, Darling, 71–97, speculates that the failure to wire Department of Dakota headquarters, rather than the War Department, angered General Alfred Terry, and polluted their relationship, leading eventually to Col. Samuel Sturgis's temporary assignment to Yankton. In fact, the telegrams reproduced in NA Microfilm Publication M1495 show that GAC reported to department headquarters in St. Paul, so Darling's speculation is misplaced. Other factors, discussed below, troubled his official relationship with the chain of command.

6. Charles W. Larned to Mother, April 19, 1873, Charles William Larned Papers, USMA; entry 2339, Cullum 3: 154.

7. Charles W. Larned to Mother, April 12, 19, 25, June 11, 1873, Charles William Larned Papers, USMA; *Sioux City Journal*, April 26, 1873.

8. Charles W. Larned to Mother, April 25, 1873, Charles William Larned Papers, USMA.

9. Charles W. Larned to Mother, April 19, 30, May 24, 1873, Charles William Larned Papers, USMA.

10. *New York Tribune*, September 8, 1873; M. John Lubetkin, *Jay Cooke's Gamble: The Northern Pacific Railroad, the Sioux, and the Panic of 1873* (Norman: University of Oklahoma Press, 2006), 193. Larned complained of the constant duties assigned to the men without reflecting that work kept them busy and in camp; he himself collected men who slipped into Yankton to get drunk. See Charles W. Larned to Mother, May 9, 1873, and entry for June 25, 1873, Diary, Charles William Larned Papers, USMA.

11. Charles W. Larned to Mother, April 30, June 11, 1873, Charles William Larned Papers, USMA.

12. Reynolds, 72–73.

13. Alfred H. Terry to O. D. Greene, April 19, 26, 1873, GAC to O. D. Greene, April 25, 26, 1873, O. D. Greene to Alfred H. Terry, April 26, 1873, C. W. Forster to O. D. Greene, May 3, 1873, O. D. Greene to GAC, April 27, 1873, Samuel D. Sturgis to O. D. Greene, May 3, 1873, Special Files of Headquarters, Division of the Missouri, Relating to Military Operations and Administration, Roll 1, Microfilm Publication M1495, NA; Lubetkin, 49, 147. GAC also complained about other things, including the variety of carbines issued to the 7th Cavalry, only to be told that records showed that the regiment "is substantially armed with Sharp's improved carbine—a few other patterns being distributed in three troops for experimental trial on just such an expedition as you are going on. In view of this fact your application is deemed singular, and is not well understood." See GAC to O. D. Greene, April 26, 1873, O. D. Greene to GAC, April 27, 1873, Telegram, Roll 1, Microfilm Publication M1495, NA.

14. Leckie, 155–56.

15. *Chicago Tribune*, July 19, 1873; David S. Stanley, *Personal Memoirs of Major-General D. S. Stanley* (Cambridge, Mass.: Harvard University Press, 1917), 244–55; Charles W. Larned to Mother, June 25–26, 1873, Charles William Larned Papers, USMA.

16. Entry 1544, Cullum 2: 309–10; Charles W. Larned to Mother, June 11, 1873, Charles William Larned Papers, USMA; Lubetkin, 95–98, 148–53.

17. GAC to EBC, July 19, 1873, GAC to Kirkland Barker, September 6, 1873, Folder 9, Box 4, MMP; Charles W. Larned to Mother, June 25–26, 1873, Charles William Larned Papers, USMA; *Boston Globe*, July 14, 1873; *Chicago Tribune*, July 19, 1873; Stanley, *Personal Memoirs*, 244–45; Leckie, 156, 161.

18. *Chicago Tribune*, July 19, 1873; *Boston Globe*, July 14, 1873; *Arizona Miner*, September 13, 1873.

19. Stanley, *Personal Memoirs*, 239–40. It's important to note that GAC himself did not see any general dislike for him in his regiment. He wrote to EBC during the expedition, "With the exception of one officer I . . . would be glad to have every one of the officers now with me stationed at my post. My relations with them personal & official are extremely agreable. They are all counting on going with me to [Fort] Lincoln," though only six companies were to be posted there. However, he wrote this after the regiment's two battles during this expedition, and the battles seem to have changed the sentiment toward him, as discussed below. See GAC to EBC, July 19, 1873, Folder 9, Box 4, MMP.

20. Merington, 251–52.

21. Lubetkin, 54–55, 189–92; *Arizona Miner*, September 13, 1873.

22. *Indianapolis Sentinel*, September 6, 1873; Lubetkin, 191–95.

23. Lubetkin, 195; GAC to EBC, September 10, 1873, Folder 9, Box 4, MMP; Stanley, *Personal Memoirs*, 240. Larned wrote, "Stanley is under the whiskey curse and gets on periodical tears of two or three days duration during which time he manages to disgrace himself and insult every one who happens to displease him." Even Larned agreed that Stanley arrested GAC over a trivial matter. See Charles W. Larned to Mother, July 28, 1873, Charles William Larned Papers, USMA.

24. GAC to EBC, July 19, 1873, Folder 9, Box 4, MMP. Though this letter is dated July 19, Custer added to it daily, through July 27.

25. GAC to EBC, July 19, September 6, 10, 1873, Folder 9, and fragments, n.d., Folder 14, Box 4, MMP; Stanley, *Personal Memoirs*, 240–42; Charles W. Larned to Mother, June 25–26, 1873, Charles William Larned Papers, USMA.

26. GAC to EBC, fragments, n.d., Folder 14, Box 4, MMP; Lubetkin, 197–99.

27. A. Baliran to D. S. Stanley, July 24, 1873, Letters Received by Headquarters, Department of Dakota, 1866–1877, Roll 14, Microfilm Publication M1734, NA; Stanley, *Personal Memoirs*, 239; *Chicago Tribune*, August 19, 1873; GAC to EBC, September 10, 1873, Folder 9, Box 4, MMP; Lubetkin, 194, 198.

28. Stiles, *First Tycoon*, 526; *Railroad Gazette*, March 16, 1872, June 28, 1873. On Union Pacific's travails under presidents who paid little attention to managing it, among other things, see Maury Klein, *Union Pacific*, vol. 1 (Minneapolis: University of Minnesota Press, 2006). On Carnegie and the Pennsylvania Railroad's management team's speculative Union Pacific maneuver, see David Nasaw, *Andrew Carnegie* (New York: Penguin, 2007), 123–24. This discussion of the transcontinentals owes much not only to the work that went into *The First Tycoon*, but also to Richard White, *Railroaded: The Transcontinentals and the Making of Modern America* (New York: W. W. Norton, 2011), esp. 1–87. White's prosecutorial tone invites debate, yet his massively researched work provides an essential corrective to the tradition of celebratory writing about the transcontinental railroads. As White notes, men such as Vanderbilt, who understood how

to make railroad operations profitable, tended to stay away from the transcontinental lines in their early years, when they were more often run by political manipulators and financial buccaneers. In time, as Klein notes, Jay Gould made serious efforts to reform Union Pacific, and James J. Hill constructed the Great Northern Railway without federal land grants, but Northern Pacific certainly began in the class of government-supported enterprises that included the Central Pacific/Union Pacific line.

29. Stiles, *First Tycoon*, 467–70, 496–501; Mark Wahlgren Summers, *The Era of Good Stealings* (New York: Oxford University Press, 1993), 46–54; White, *Railroaded*, 26–28, 31–35.

30. *New York Herald*, September 19, 1873; White, *Railroaded*, 23–24; Lubetkin, 57–79, 162–74.

31. An excellent guide to the financial integration of the nation through financial markets and federal banking laws, which caused regional bank reserves to pyramid in New York, can be found in Richard Franklin Bensel, *Yankee Leviathan: The Origins of Central State Authority in America, 1859–1877* (New York: Cambridge University Press, 1990), esp. 124, 152–53, 162–63, 238–81.

32. Nicolas Barreyre, "The Politics of Economic Crises: The Panic of 1873, the End of Reconstruction, and the Realignment of American Politics," and Scott Reynolds Nelson, "A Storm of Cheap Goods: New American Commodities and the Panic of 1873," *Journal of the Gilded Age and Progressive Era* 10, no. 4 (October 2011): 403–23, 447–53; Stiles, *First Tycoon*, 533–36; Lubetkin, esp. 57–79, 162–74.

33. Robert M. Utley, *The Lance and the Shield: The Life and Times of Sitting Bull* (New York: Henry Holt, 1993), 111.

34. Richard White, "The Winning of the West: The Expansion of the Western Sioux in the Eighteenth and Nineteenth Centuries," *Journal of American History* 65, no. 2 (September 1978): 319–43.

35. White, "Winning of the West"; Utley, *The Lance and the Shield*, 3–5. As White notes, all the Lakota tribes but the Oglala and Brulé originated in an earlier body, the Saones.

36. White, "Winning of the West"; Elliott West, *The Contested Plains: Indians, Goldseekers, and the Rush to Colorado* (Lawrence: University Press of Kansas, 2005), 76–77; Pekka Hämäläinen, "The Rise and Fall of Plains Indian Horse Cultures," *Journal of American History* 90, no. 3 (December 2003): 833–62; Andrew C. Isenberg, *The Destruction of the Bison* (New York: Cambridge University Press, 2000), 111; Utley, *The Lance and the Shield*, 45; *New York Tribune*, August 27, 1873.

37. Utley, *The Lance and the Shield*, 10–42.

38. Thomas Powers, *The Killing of Crazy Horse* (New York: Alfred A. Knopf, 2010), 3–17; Robert M. Utley, *Frontier Regulars: The United States Army and the Indian, 1866–1891* (Lincoln: University of Nebraska Press, 1984 [orig. pub. 1973]), 93–107.

39. Utley, *Frontier Regulars*, 134–37; transcript of Fort Laramie Treaty, Avalon Project, Lillian Goldman Law Library, Yale University, available at http://avalon.law.yale.edu/19th_century/ntoo1.asp.

40. White, "The Winning of the West"; Utley, *Frontier Regulars*, 237–42; Utley, *The Lance and the Shield*, 84–88.

41. Utley, *Frontier Regulars*, 236–42; Utley, *The Lance and the Shield*, 3–105.

42. Utley, *The Lance and the Shield*, 112; White, *Railroaded*, 25. Isenberg, 125, notes that the undefined northern boundary of the unceded territory invited the conflict that ensued over the Northern Pacific Railroad.

43. Utley, *The Lance and the Shield*, 112.

44. GAC to EBC, n.d., Folder 14, Box 4, MMP.

45. *New York Tribune*, September 8, 1873; Stanley, 248–49; Lubetkin, 241–44.

46. *New York Tribune*, September 8, 9, 1873; GAC, "Battling with the Sioux on the Yellowstone," *Galaxy* (July 1876): 91–102; Ami Frank Mulford, *Fighting Indians in the 7th United States Cavalry: Custer's Favorite Regiment* (Corning, N.Y.: Paul Lindsley Mulford, 1879), 136; Robert W. Larson, *Gall: Lakota War Chief* (Norman: University of Oklahoma Press, 2007), 35, 55–56; Lubetkin, 126.

47. This account of the fighting on the Yellowstone on August 4, 1873 is based on *New York Tribune*, September 8, 9, 1873; GAC, "Battling with the Sioux on the Yellowstone"; Mulford, 134–44; Lubetkin, 244–52.

48. *New York Tribune*, September 8, 9, 1873; GAC, "Battling with the Sioux on the Yellowstone"; "Official Report of General Custer," August 15, 1873, in Mulford, 134–44; Lubetkin, 244–52.

49. *New York Tribune*, September 8, 1873; Lubetkin, 248–50.

50. *New York Tribune*, September 9, 1873; Utley, *The Lance and the Shield*, 112; Lubetkin, 253–55. Apparently few Oglalas joined Sitting Bull; they were engaged in a major offensive against the Pawnees, which resulted in the devastating attack on the Pawnee hunting party on the Republican mentioned earlier. See *Chicago Tribune*, October 29, 1873. Lubetkin theorizes that GAC subconsciously wished to fail in his pursuit, citing as evidence the fact that he brought along cattle to slaughter for food. In fact, GAC covered forty miles in about twenty-four hours in intense heat, an extremely fast pace. Cavalry rarely moved faster than a walk on the march, particularly under such poor conditions.

51. The account that follows of the battle of August 11, 1873, is drawn throughout from a variety of sources, including *New York Tribune*, August 25, September 6 and 9, 1873; "Official Report" in Mulford, 134–44; Utley, *The Lance and the Shield*, 112–15; Lubetkin, 253–67; Larson, 87–92.

52. *New York Tribune*, August 25, September 6 and 9, 1873; "Official Report" in Mulford, 134–44; Utley, *The Lance and the Shield*, 112–15; Lubetkin, 253–67; Larson, 87–92.

53. Charles W. Larned to Mother, September 6, 1873, Charles William Larned Papers, USMA; GAC to EBC, September 10, 1873, Folder 9, Box 4, MMP. Contrast Larned's September 6 letter with that of July 28, in which he wrote, "I keep away from him altogether as I have no taste for court circles and very little desire to be of use there."

54. EBC, *Tenting on the Plains*, 433. GAC wrote, "With the exception of one officer I . . . would be glad to have every one of the officers now with me stationed at my post. My relations with them personal & official are extremely agreable." See GAC to EBC, July 19, 1873, Folder 9, Box 4, MMP.

55. Stanley, *Personal Memoirs*, 240–42.

56. GAC to EBC, September 21, 23, 1873, Folder 9, Box 4, MMP. On the battle, casualties, and its repercussions, see *New York Tribune*, August 25, September 6 and 9, 1873; "Official Report" in Mulford, 134–44; Utley, *The Lance and the Shield*, 112–15; Lubetkin, 253–67; Larson, 87–92. A third-hand claim from the Lakotas, reported in the *Chicago Tribune*, October 29, 1873, stated that the

Lakotas suffered only four dead and twelve wounded total in the two engagements. That count is unquestionably too low. The veracity of this report—really a report of a report of a report—is doubtful; for example, it also stated that "very few" Hunkpapas joined in the second fight, and Sitting Bull refused to participate, an assertion that is clearly false. GAC's claims for the casualties he inflicted were quite modest—only a few in the first battle, and forty in the second—though they should be taken as the upper limit. Larson, Gall's biographer, believes the troops inflicted thirty or so casualties in the second battle.

57. GAC to EBC, September 10, 1873, Folder 9, and GAC to EBC, n.d., Folder 14, Box 4, MMP.

58. Leckie, 158, 133; EBC, *Boots and Saddles*, 93. The quotations are from letters once held by Brice C. W. Custer, which as mentioned before appear to have passed into a private collector's hands. I quote them because I trust Leckie's scholarship; these letters have also been examined and quoted by such authorities as Robert Utley.

59. Leckie, 158–59.

60. Leckie, 158–60, 164; Heather Cox Richardson, *West from Appomattox: The Reconstruction of America After the Civil War* (New Haven, Conn.: Yale University Press, 2007), 81–82, 111–13. A great abundance of literature exists on Elizabeth Cady Stanton, Susan B. Anthony, and the women's suffrage movement. On Victoria Woodhull, see Stiles, *First Tycoon*, 484–85, 501–05, 555–56, 668 n107; Mary Gabriel, *Notorious Victoria: The Life of Victoria Woodhull, Uncensored* (Chapel Hill, N.C.: Algonquin Books of Chapel Hill, 1998); Louis Beachy Underhill, *The Woman Who Ran for President: The Many Lives of Victoria Woodhull* (Bridgehampton, N.Y.: Bridge Works Publishing, 1995); Helen Lefkowitz Horowitz, "Victoria Woodhull, Anthony Comstock, and Conflict over Sex in the United States in the 1870s," *Journal of American History* 87, no. 2 (September 2000): 403–34; "A Victoria Woodhull for the 1990s," *Reviews in American History* 27, no. 1 (1999): 87–97.

61. Leckie, 32–33, 158–59.

62. Leckie, 161–62; *Chicago Tribune*, October 17, 1873; *Leslie's Illustrated Newspaper* in *Atlanta Constitution*, November 8, 1873; *Cincinnati Gazette*, October 16, 17, 1873; *Pomeroy's Democrat*, October 25, 1873.

63. EBC, *Boots and Saddles*, 93.

64. GAC to William P. Carlin, February 6, 1874, Folder 10, Box 4, MMP; Leckie, 155, 162. Darling, 50–200, shows that the march from Yankton to Fort Rice was much more troubled than EBC suggests in *Boots and Saddles*, with insubordination by Benteen, disputes with steamboat operators, and conflict with Indian villages encountered along the way.

65. *New York Times*, September 19, 1873.

66. Barreyre, "The Politics of Economic Crises"; White, *Railroaded*, 81–84; Stiles, *First Tycoon*, 536–40.

67. *New York Times*, September 3, 1875; Lubetkin, 63, 82; White, *Railroaded*, 81–84; Leckie, 160; Finding Aid, Unregistered Letters Received and Related Records, undated and 1864–1876, Northern Pacific Railway Company, Microfilm Publication M459, Minnesota Historical Society, St. Paul, Minn.

68. Thomas A. Rosser to GAC, February 16, 1874, Other Sources, LBH; Edward S. Cooper, *William Babcock Hazen: The Best Hated Man* (Madison, N.J.: Fairleigh Dickinson University Press, 2005), 239–41.

69. Hutton, *Phil Sheridan and His Army*, 56–60, 83–94, 148–49, 169–74.

70. *The Northern Pacific Railroad: Character and Climate of the Country It Traverses* (Northern Pacific Railroad Co., 1874), GAC Papers, Beinecke Library, Yale University, New Haven, Conn.; A. B. Nettleton to GAC, March 19, 1874, Other Sources, LBH; Slotkin, *The Fatal Environment*, 413–14.

71. William B. Hazen, *Some Corrections to "My Life on the Plains"* (St. Paul, Minn.: Ramaley and Cunningham, 1875), GAC Papers, Beinecke Library, Yale University, New Haven, Conn.

72. *Independent*, September 11, 1873.

73. *New York Times*, July 1, 26, 1875; White, *Railroaded*, 81–84.

74. Barnett, 249; Leckie, 163–66; Louis S. Warren, *Buffalo Bill's America: William Cody and the Wild West Show* (New York: Vintage, 2005), esp. 80, 134.

75. GAC to Jairus W. Hall, April 14, 1874, Folder 10, Box 4, MMP; Jairus W. Hall to GAC, August 19, 1874, Other Sources, LBH; Erl H. Ellis and Carrie Scott Ellis, *The Saga of Upper Clear Creek* (Frederick, Colo.: Jende-Hagan, 1983), 96–102; Richardson, 163.

Sixteen: The Accuser

1. William T. Sherman to Ulysses S. Grant, June 11, 1867, Special Files of Headquarters, Division of the Missouri, Relating to Military Operations and Administration, 1863–1865, Roll 7, Microfilm Publication M1495, NA.

2. Paul A. Hutton, *Phil Sheridan and His Army* (Norman: University of Oklahoma Press, 1999), 280–81.

3. The American belief in the necessity of violently conquering the natural West is a prevailing theme in much of the historiography. See in particular Richard Slotkin's seminal trilogy on the nineteenth-century West, *Gunfighter Nation, Regeneration Through Violence*, and especially *The Fatal Environment: The Myth of the Frontier in the Age of Industrialization, 1800–1890* (Norman: University of Oklahoma Press, 1998 [orig. pub. 1985]), 401 and throughout.

4. Hutton, *Phil Sheridan and His Army*, 245–61; Andrew C. Isenberg, *The Destruction of the Bison* (New York: Cambridge University Press, 2000), 10, 106, 134–36. Sheridan and Sherman were not the only generals who believed that bison were going extinct and that it was desirable. Winfield S. Hancock expressed the same thoughts during his councils with Cheyenne and Kiowa leaders during his 1867 expedition. See *New York Tribune*, April 24, 1867; Theodore Davis, "A Summer on the Plains," *Harper's New Monthly Magazine* (February 1868); Henry M. Stanley, *My Early Travels and Adventures in America and Asia* (New York: Charles Scribner's Sons, 1895), 29–35.

5. Hutton, *Phil Sheridan and His Army*, 286–87.

6. Hutton, *Phil Sheridan and His Army*, 287–90, 295–97.

7. PHS to Jonathan Wheeler, November 24, 1874, Roll 6, PHS Papers, LOC; Hutton, *Phil Sheridan and His Army*, 287–90; Utley, *Cavalier in Buckskin*, 132–33.

8. GAC to Lawrence Barrett, May 19, 1874, GAC Miscellaneous Manuscripts, LOC; Tom O'Neil, ed., *Letters from Boston Custer* (Brooklyn, N.Y.: Arrow and Trooper, 1993); Hutton, *Phil Sheridan and His Army*, 167.

9. Lawrence Barrett to GAC, April 24, June 3, 1874, Other Sources, LBH.

10. *Sioux City Journal*, May 14, 29, 1874; *Bismarck Tribune*, May 27, 1874, in *Sioux City Journal*, June 2, 1874. See also *Baltimore Sun*, July 25, 1874.

11. *Chicago Inter-Ocean*, July 9, 1874.

12. *Forest and Stream*, June 4, 1874; Merington, 271. Hutton, *Phil Sheridan and His Army*, 163–68.

13. *Baltimore Sun*, July 25, 1874; *Chicago Tribune*, July 2 and 3, 1874; *Boston Advertiser*, September 3, 1874.

14. *Chicago Inter-Ocean*, August 27, 1874; *Yankton Press and Dakotaian*, August 13, 1874; GAC to EBC, July 15, August 15, 1874, Folder 10, Box 4, MMP; GAC Report, August 2, 1874, SED 32, 2nd Session, 43rd Congress.

15. *Bismarck Tribune* in *Philadelphia Inquirer*, September 10, 1874.

16. GAC Report, August 15, 1874, SED 32, 43rd Congress, 2nd Session; Patricia Nelson Limerick, *The Legacy of Conquest: The Unbroken Past of the American West* (New York: W. W. Norton and Co., 1987), 105–18.

17. *Chicago Inter-Ocean*, September 1, 1874. Official records show that the army made serious efforts to capture and remove trespassers in the Black Hills. Captain Benteen, for example, caught forty-five miners late in 1875; Frederick W. Benteen to Assistant Adjutant General, Department of Dakota, September 16, 1875, Roll 2, Microfilm Publication M1495, NA.

18. *Independent*, November 5, 1874; *Indianapolis Sentinel*, September 18, 1874; *Cincinnati Gazette*, September 18, 1874; *New York Herald*, October 20, 1874; *Chicago Inter-Ocean*, September 18, October 14, 20, 1874; *Sioux City Journal*, October 21, 1874.

19. William S. McFeely, *Grant: A Biography* (New York: W. W. Norton, 1981), 305–41, 356–79; George Boutwell, *Reminiscences of Sixty Years in Public Affairs*, vol. 2 (Boston: McClure, Phillips, and Co., 1902), 251.

20. McFeely, 20, 51, 55, 87, 157, 287–331, 336–51; Jean Edward Smith, *Grant* (New York: Simon and Schuster, 2001), 499–506; Nicholas Guyatt, "America's Conservatory: Race, Reconstruction, and the Santo Domingo Debate," *Journal of American History* (March 2011): 974–1000; Stiles, *First Tycoon*, 187–88.

21. McFeely, 336–51, 393–97; Stiles, *First Tycoon*, 538–39; Nicolas Barreyre, "The Politics of Economic Crises: The Panic of 1873, the End of Reconstruction, and the Realignment of American Politics," *Journal of the Gilded Age and Progressive Era* 10, no. 4 (October 2011): 403–23.

22. Stiles, *First Tycoon*, 350–51.

23. On the deflationary impact of the gold standard in the nineteenth century—at least until the use of cyanide for more efficient refining and the introduction of South African gold into the world economy—see Milton Friedman and Anna Jacobson Schwartz, *A Monetary History of the United States, 1867–1960* (Princeton, N.J.: Princeton University Press, 1963).

24. Stiles, *First Tycoon*, 466–67, 542–47; Mark T. Kanazawa and Roger G. Noll, "The Origins of State Railroad Regulation: The Illinois Constitution of 1870," in Claudia Goldin and Gary D. Libecap, eds., *The Regulated Economy: A Historical Approach to Political Economy* (Chicago: University of Chicago Press, 1994), 13–54. Barreyre, "The Politics of Economic Crises," stresses the centrality of the currency question in the economic debate. Irwin Unger's classic *The Greenback Era: A Social and Political History of American Finance, 1865–1879* (Princeton, N.J.: Princeton University Press, 1965) and Richard Bensel's *Yankee Leviathan: The Origins of Central State Authority in America, 1859–1877* (New York: Cambridge University Press, 1991) have been very important sources for my discussion here. Smith, 578–82, presents a positive view of the veto of the

so-called "inflation bill" and the 1875 Resumption Act, which restored the gold standard. Smith repeats the conventional wisdom of financial leaders of the era in his embrace of the gold standard, as he acknowledges, and does not discuss the economic and political costs.

25. Barreyre, "The Politics of Economic Crises."
26. Foner, 546–75.
27. Quoted in Utley, *Cavalier in Buckskin*, 150.
28. GAC to Andrew Johnson, February 2, 1875, in Paul H. Bergeron, ed., *Papers of Andrew Johnson*, vol. 16 (Knoxville: University of Tennessee Press, 2000), 695.
29. David S. Stanley to Assistant Adjutant General, Department of Dakota, March 1, 1874, Letters Received, Office of the Adjutant General, 1871–1889, Roll 122, Microfilm Publication M666, NA.
30. GAC to Alfred Terry, December 7 and 16, 1874, Roll 122, Microfilm Publication M666, NA.
31. *Chicago Inter-Ocean*, January 12, 1875; GAC to Alfred Terry, December 16, 1874, George Yates to Assistant Adjutant General, Department of Dakota, April 23, 1875, Roll 122, Microfilm Publication M666, NA.
32. GAC to Alfred Terry, December 18 and 19, 1874, Roll 122, Microfilm Publication M666, NA; Utley, *Cavalier in Buckskin*, 144–45.
33. Isaac P. Christiancy to GAC, February 10, 1875, Folder 11, Box 4, MMP; Foner, 554.
34. *Chicago Inter-Ocean*, January 5, 1875; *Chicago Tribune*, January 8, 1875.
35. Jairus W. Hall to William R. Travers, February 23, 1875, Jairus W. Hall to GAC, April and June 3, 1875, Other Sources, LBH; Erl H. Ellis and Carrie Scott Ellis, *The Saga of Upper Clear Creek* (Frederick, Colo.: Jende-Hagan, 1983), 96–102; See also Slotkin, *The Fatal Environment*, 405–06.
36. James P. McClure, "The Epizootic of 1872: Horses and Disease in a Nation in Motion," *New York History* 79, no. 1 (January 1998): 5–22; Stiles, *First Tycoon*, 528; Brian W. Dippie, ed., *Nomad: George A. Custer in Turf, Field and Farm* (Austin: University of Texas Press, 1980), 74–75.
37. GAC to EBC, c. 1873, Folder 2, EBC Papers, Beinecke Library, Yale University, New Haven, Conn.
38. F. A. Allen to GAC, January 25, 1875, Robert B. Roosevelt to GAC, March 28, 1875, Other Sources, LBH; Edwin G. Burrows and Mike Wallace, *Gotham: A History of New York City to 1898* (New York: Oxford University Press, 1999), 639, 1083, 1101.
39. Hampton Sides, *In the Kingdom of Ice: The Grand Terrible Polar Voyage of the U.S.S. Jeannette* (New York: Doubleday, 2014), 64–76; Burrows and Wallace, 677, 954–55, 996–98, 1151–54; James McGrath Morris, *Pulitzer: A Life in Politics, Print, and Power* (New York: Harper, 2010), 80–174; James G. Bennett Jr. to GAC, April 1, 1875, Other Sources, LBH. On the rise of newspaper-driven politics in America, see Jeffrey L. Pasley, *The Tyranny of Printers: Newspaper Politics in the Early American Republic* (Charlottesville: University Press of Virginia, 2001).
40. James G. Bennett Jr. to GAC, April 1, 1875, Other Sources, LBH.
41. GAC to Augusta Ward, August 18, 1875, typescript copy, GAC Papers, USMA; *New York Tribune*, May 22, 1875.
42. Leckie, 171.
43. James G. Wilson and John Fiske, eds., *Appleton's Cyclopaedia of American Biog-*

raphy, vol. 5 (New York: D. Appleton and Co., 1888), 431; Montgomery Schuyler to GAC, May 13, 1875, Ralph Meeker to GAC, September 17, 1875, Other Sources, LBH; Burrows and Wallace, 1151.

44. Amelia Ransome Neville, "The Apollo Balls," in Malcolm E. Barker, ed., *More San Francisco Memoirs: 1852–1899: The Ripening Years* (San Francisco: Londonborn, 1996), 104; *Banker's Magazine and Statistical Register*, February 1864; *Latter-Day Saints' Millennial Star*, February 9, 1867; *New York Times*, December 18, 1883.

45. "Emil Justh v. Benjamin Holliday [sic]," *Reports of Cases Argued and Adjudged in the Supreme Court of the District of Columbia, Sitting in General Term, from May 25, 1882, to October 29, 1883* (Washington, D.C.: John L. Ginck, 1884), 346–60 (to be cited hereafter as "Justh v. Holliday").

46. "Justh v. Holliday"; *New York Times*, May 18 and 20, 1875.

47. "Justh v. Holliday"; Stiles, *First Tycoon*, 168–69, 376–77.

48. "Justh v. Holliday."

49. Leckie, 168.

50. Robert S. Eckley, *Lincoln's Forgotten Friend, Leonard Swett* (Carbondale: Southern Illinois University Press, 2012), 169–74; Leonard Herbert Swett to Laura Swett, May 30, 1875, HM 68695, Leonard Herbert Swett to Leonard Swett and Laura Swett, June 4 and 6, 1875, HM 68697 and 68698, Leonard Herbert Swett Papers, Huntington Library, San Marino, Calif.

51. Leonard Herbert Swett to Laura Swett, May 30, June 16, 1875, HM 68695 and 68701, Leonard Herbert Swett to Leonard Swett and Laura Swett, June 4 and 6, 1875, HM 68697 and 68698, Leonard Herbert Swett Papers, Huntington Library, San Marino, Calif.

52. Leonard Swett to GAC, June 13, 1875, Other Sources, LBH; Leonard Herbert Swett to Laura Swett, June 14, 28, 30, July 4, 1875, HM 68700, 68705, 68706, and 68707, Leonard Herbert Swett to Laura Swett and Leonard Swett, June 6, 1875, HM 68698, Leonard Herbert Swett Papers, Huntington Library, San Marino, Calif.

53. *New York Tribune*, August 16, 1875; see, among other reports in the same source, Frederick W. Benteen to Assistant Adjutant General, Department of Dakota, September 16, 1875, Roll 2, Microfilm Publication M1495, NA.

54. McFeely, 55, 157, 340, 343; E. Kimbark MacColl, *The Shaping of a City: Business and Politics in Portland, Oregon, 1885–1915* (Portland, Ore.: Georgian Press Company, 1976), 39–43. Holladay and Ingalls were close friends, so much so that Holladay's widow asked the courts to appoint Ingalls as one of the executors of her husband's estate; *New York Times*, October 15, 1887.

55. Rufus Ingalls to GAC, August 22, 1875, Other Sources, LBH; *New York Times*, May 24, June 11, 1875, February 10, April 3, 1876; Slotkin, *The Fatal Environment*, 421–24. Slotkin argues that GAC was fully engaged in the Holladay and Ingalls plot, arguing further that its failure led GAC and Holladay to speculate in the stock market together. However, GAC's speculations with Justh predated Ingalls's letter. Holladay's endorsement of a promissory note does not ipso facto indicate a joint stock operation, nor is there any evidence of a connection with a Black Hills scheme. Leckie, 173, discusses Benteen's allegation that GAC took kickbacks from sutlers, but given that there is no evidence for his claims, and that he hated GAC, and that the army generated rampant and frequently inaccurate rumors, I feel compelled to discount Benteen's claim.

56. Edward S. Cooper, *William Worth Belknap: An American Disgrace* (Madison, N.J.: Fairleigh Dickinson University Press, 2003), 19–21, 204–06, 217–18; McFeely, 426–29; Hutton, *Phil Sheridan and His Army*, 295–97; Leckie, 174–75; Slotkin, *The Fatal Environment*, 424–25; GAC testimony, March 29, 1876, HR 799, 1st Session, 44th Congress.

57. GAC testimony, March 29, 1876, HR 799, 1st Session, 44th Congress; Cooper, 204–07, 217–18.

58. *New York Times*, October 1, 1875; *New York Herald*, October 2, 1875; Ralph Meeker to GAC, September 17, October 5, 1875, Jonathan Russell Garry to GAC, December 22, 1875, Other Sources, LBH.

59. Leckie, 175; "Justh v. Holliday"; "Delia F. Sheldon v. Isaac E. Sheldon, et al.," Charles H. Mills, ed., *New York State Reporter*, vol. 65 (Albany, N.Y.: W. C. Little and Co., 1895), 693–95.

60. GAC Deposition, October 8, 1875, Atlantic Publishing Company v. GAC, EG Box 13, Huntington Library, San Marino, Calif.; Isaac E. Sheldon to GAC, November 11, 1875, Other Sources, LBH. Despite extensive searches during past research for the records of the Marine Court, I have been unable to locate them, possibly because the cases only dealt with small sums.

61. Merington, 176–77; Burrows and Wallace, 1149.

62. Leonard Herbert Swett to Leonard Swett and Laura Swett, January 15, 1876, Leonard Herbert Swett to Laura Swett, January 20, 1876, HM0361, Swett Family Correspondence, Huntington Library, San Marino, Calif.

63. Ralph Meeker to GAC, December 30, 1875, Other Sources, LBH.

64. J. R. Pond to GAC, February 7, 1876, Folder 13, GAC letter fragment, Folder 14, Box 4, MMP.

65. "Justh v. Holliday."

66. McFeely, 429.

67. Mark Wahlgren Summers, *The Era of Good Stealings* (New York: Oxford University Press, 1993), 16–29, 61, 181–99; Mark Wahlgren Summers, *The Plundering Generation: Corruption and the Crisis of the Union, 1849–1861* (New York: Oxford University Press, 1987); Mark Wahlgren Summers, "'To Make the Wheels Revolve We Must Have Grease': Barrel Politics in the Gilded Age," *Journal of Policy History* 14, no. 1 (2002): 49–72; Stiles, *First Tycoon*, 174–84, 257–64, 372–79, 393–401, 458–70. It has often been claimed that corruption after the Civil War emerged from a new obsession with money; see, for example, James Donovan, *A Terrible Glory: Custer and the Little Bighorn—the Last Great Battle of the American West* (New York: Little, Brown, 2008), 101–02. A look at the preceding decades shows that moneymaking had long defined American culture; see, for example, Part 1 of Stiles, *First Tycoon*.

68. Smith, 577–78, 582–84; McFeely, 405–11.

69. McFeely, 405–11; Smith, 583–85, 590–93. See also John McDonald, *Secrets of the Great Whiskey Ring* (Chicago: Belford, Clarke and Co., 1880), an entertaining account for the historically informed, though self-serving and not to be trusted on all points.

70. McFeely, 430–34; Smith, 586–87.

71. Hutton, *Phil Sheridan and His Army*, 292–300; Utley, *The Lance and the Shield*, 115–16, 125–28. Isenberg, 141, attributes the decline of the bison in the north less to hunting than to drought and the spread of ranching.

72. Report of E. C. Watkins, November 9, 1875, enclosed in Edward P. Smith,

Commissioner, Department of the Interior, Office of Indian Affairs, to the Secretary of the Interior, November 27, 1875, Container 91, PHS Papers, Manuscripts Division, LOC; Hutton, *Phil Sheridan and His Army*, 299–301.

73. McFeely, 405–11. Smith, 590–93, entertains the possibility that Babcock was innocent. An important element in the Whiskey Ring, according to ring member John McDonald, 36–49, 315, was that it used its proceeds for partisan purposes, particularly to buy influence with key newspapers, a credible assertion given the state of political corruption and a possible explanation for Babcock's modest lifestyle. McDonald's claims of Grant's knowledge of such activities are much less credible.

74. *New York Herald*, February 9, 10, 1876; Cooper, 17–35; Slotkin, *The Fatal Environment*, 441.

75. Cooper, 29–39; Hiester Clymer Poster, 1866, LOCLC-USZ62-32498, Prints and Photographs Division, LOC.

76. Cooper, 29–39; McFeely, 432–34.

77. HR 799, 1st Session, 44th Congress.

78. GAC to EBC, April 1, 1876, Folder 12, Box 4, MMP; Utley, *Cavalier in Buckskin*, 156–59; EBC, *Boots and Saddles*, 253–59.

79. *Chicago Tribune*, February 14, 1876.

80. Utley, *Cavalier in Buckskin*, 159; Slotkin, *The Fatal Environment*, 425–26.

81. HR 799, 1st Session, 44th Congress.

82. GAC to EBC, April 10, 1876, Folder 12, Box 4, MMP; *New York Herald*, March 31, 1876; *Chicago Inter-Ocean*, April 14, 1876; HR 799, 1st Session, 44th Congress; Utley, *Cavalier in Buckskin*, 159; Slotkin, *The Fatal Environment*, 425–26.

83. GAC to EBC, April 1, 8, 1876, typescript copy, April 10, 1876, GAC to EBC, fragment, n.d., Folder 12, Box 4, MMP; *Washington Critic*, April 19, 1876; *Cincinnati Gazette*, April 19, 1876; *New York Times*, April 5, 19, 1876; Slotkin, *The Fatal Environment*, 425–26; Utley, *Cavalier in Buckskin*, 131, 158–59. A story circulated that F. W. Rice, mentioned by GAC as the intermediary of the payoff given to Belknap, published a card calling GAC a liar, and GAC saw him in the street and gave him a severe beating with a cane. Rice publicly denied the story; *Cincinnati Enquirer*, April 11, 1876.

84. Hutton, *Phil Sheridan and His Army*, 301–11.

85. GAC to EBC, April 1, 8, 10, 1876, Folder 12, Box 4, MMP; *Chicago Times*, April 9, 1876.

86. GAC to Augusta Ward, April 25, 1876, typescript copy, GAC Papers, USMA; Utley, *Cavalier in Buckskin*, 159–61.

87. PHS to Edward D. Townsend, April 27, 1876, Roll 7, PHS Papers, LOC; GAC to EBC, April 8, 1876, typescript copy, GAC to EBC, April 10, 1876, Folder 12, Box 4, MMP; *Washington Critic*, April 13, 1876; Testimony of Orvil Grant, March 9, 1876, and James W. Forsyth to William W. Belknap, April 5, 10, 1876, reprinted in John Y. Simon, ed., *The Papers of Ulysses S. Grant*, vol. 27 (Carbondale: Southern Illinois University Press, 2005), 67, 71; Utley, *Cavalier in Buckskin*, 160–61.

88. William T. Sherman to PHS, April 28, 1876; William T. Sherman to Ulysses S. Grant Jr., May 4, 1876; reprinted in Simon 27: 71–72.

89. William T. Sherman to Ulysses S. Grant Jr., May 4, 1876, reprinted in Simon 27: 71–73; GAC to EBC, April 8, 1876, typescript copy, April 10, 1876, Folder 12, Box 4, MMP.

90. William T. Sherman to PHS, April 28, May 2, 1876; PHS to William T. Sherman, April 29, 1876; GAC to Ulysses S. Grant, May 1, 1876; Ulysses S. Grant Jr. to William T. Sherman, May 4, 1876; William T. Sherman to Ulysses S. Grant Jr., May 4, 1876; Alphonso Taft to Ulysses S. Grant Jr., May 4, 1876; all reprinted in Simon 27: 72–74; Utley, *Cavalier in Buckskin*, 161–63. Note that GAC appears to have drafted another article in Chicago; what sounds very much like newspaper copy, referring to GAC in the third person but written in his hand, appears in GAC letter, May 5, 1876, GAC Correspondence, LBH.

91. GAC to William T. Sherman, May 4, 1876 (two telegrams); William T. Sherman to GAC, May 4, 1876; PHS to Edward D. Townsend, May 7, 1876 (Alfred Terry to PHS, May 6, 1876, enclosed); all reprinted in Simon 27: 73–74. Utley, *Cavalier in Buckskin*, 162, cites Terry's recollections in writing that Terry "dictated a telegram to send" over GAC's signature. Likely he advised GAC to write the message and (unlike GAC's previous telegrams to Sherman) to send it up the chain of command in proper fashion; but the wording of the letter echoes GAC's prior appeal for clemency in 1861 so closely that it seems unlikely that Terry "dictated" it, even if he did influence its composition.

92. William T. Sherman to Alfred Terry, May 7, 1876, Letters Received by Headquarters, Department of Dakota, 1866–1877, Roll 17, Microfilm Publication M1734, NA.

93. Utley, *Cavalier in Buckskin*, 163; Merington, 303.

94. PHS to Alfred Terry, May 16, 1876, Roll 17, Microfilm Publication M1734, NA; Wert, 327.

95. Utley, *Cavalier in Buckskin*, 165–67; Wert, 327–28.

Epilogue

1. *The Reno Court of Inquiry: The Chicago Times Account* (Fort Collins, Tex.: Old Army Press, 1972), 2–6 (to be called *Times Account*); Special Orders No. 255, November 25, 1878, and First Day Minutes, January 13, 1879, both in Proceedings of a Court of Inquiry Concerning the Conduct of Major Marcus A. Reno at the Battle of the Little Big Horn River on June 25 and 26, 1876, Roll 1, Microfilm Publication M592, NA.

2. *Times Account*, 2–6, 37; First and Second Day Minutes, January 13, 14, 1879, Roll 1, Microfilm Publication M592, NA; Ronald H. Nichols, *In Custer's Shadow: Major Marcus Reno* (Norman: University of Oklahoma, 2000), 263–84.

3. *Times Account*, 39; Second Day Minutes, January 14, 1879, Roll 1, Microfilm Publication M592, NA.

4. Utley, *Cavalier in Buckskin*, 169–77; James Donovan, *A Terrible Glory: Custer and the Little Bighorn—the Last Great Battle of the American West* (New York: Little, Brown, 2008), 172–76. For an example of a hammer-and-anvil operation during the Civil War, see Stiles, *Jesse James*, 86–87. There have been decades of debate over every aspect of the Little Bighorn Campaign, some of it centering on the question of whether GAC had authority to attack without awaiting Gibbon's arrival from the north. Rather than relitigate this often-disputed question, I have simply stated in the narrative my view of the plans for this operation. I agree with Utley that Terry intended to grant GAC discretion to attack when he found an opportunity. Indeed, it would have been extraordinary if Terry

had believed that two columns approaching from opposite directions and lacking any means of communication with each other, secure or otherwise, could execute a simultaneous attack without prior discovery by the Lakotas.

5. Donovan, 191; Second Day Minutes, January 14, 1879, Roll 1, Microfilm Publication M592, NA.

6. *Times Account*, 46–47; Nichols, 284.

7. Wallace's testimony has been drawn from Third Day Minutes, January 15, 1879, Roll 1, Microfilm Publication M592, NA.

8. Third Day Minutes, January 15, 1879, Roll 1, Microfilm Publication M592, NA. On Wallace's dishonesty, see for example Donovan, 306, 361–63.

9. Fourth and Fifth Day Minutes, January 16, 17, 1879, Roll 1, Microfilm Publication M592, NA.

10. Donovan, 363; *Times Account*, 64–65, 112–13; Fifth Day Minutes, January 17, 1879, Roll 1, Microfilm Publication M592, NA.

11. Fifth Day Minutes, January 17, 1879, Roll 1, Microfilm Publication M592, NA. On the Battle of the Rosebud, see Neil C. Mangum, *Battle of the Rosebud: Prelude to the Little Bighorn* (El Segundo, Calif.: Upton and Sons, 1996); John F. Finerty, *War-Path and Bivouac, or, The Conquest of the Sioux* (Norman: University of Oklahoma Press, 1977 [orig. pub. 1890]); Donovan, 214.

12. Fifth and Seventh Day Minutes, January 17, 20, 1879, Roll 1, Microfilm Publication M592, NA; James E. Mueller, *Shooting Arrows and Slinging Mud: Custer, the Press, and the Little Bighorn* (Norman: University of Oklahoma Press, 2013), 22.

13. Fifth and Seventh Day Minutes, January 17, 20, 1879, Roll 1, Microfilm Publication M592, NA; Donovan, 237–41.

14. Sixth Day Minutes, January 18, 1879, Roll 1, Microfilm Publication M592, NA.

15. Donovan, 344–82; Nichols, 239–90.

16. Donovan, 307–11.

17. I have represented this order as it was actually written, not as it was recorded in the transcript of the hearing. See Utley, *Cavalier in Buckskin*, 186, and 18th Day Minutes, February 1, 1879, Roll 2, Microfilm Publication M592, NA.

18. 18th Day Minutes, February 1, 1879, Roll 2, Microfilm Publication M592, NA.

19. Frederick Benteen to Robert N. Price, March 6, 1879, in W. A. Graham, ed., *The Custer Myth: A Source Book of Custeriana* (Mechanicsburg, Pa.: Stackpole Books, 2000 [orig. pub. 1953]), 325–26. The number of enlisted men with Elliott at the Battle of the Washita is variously described as seventeen, eighteen, and nineteen. See Utley, *Cavalier in Buckskin*, 68; Wert, 275.

20. W. M. Dunn, Judge Advocate General, to George W. McCrary, February 21, 1879, Roll 1, Microfilm Publication M592, NA.

21. Mueller, 44; Utley, *Cavalier in Buckskin*, 196–97.

22. Utley, *Cavalier in Buckskin*, 194–212. Note that I make no claim to originality in any of my assessments of the battle.

23. Mueller, 43–45, 56–64; Donovan, 324–25.

24. Utley, *Cavalier in Buckskin*, 194.

25. See Utley, *The Lance and the Shield*; Thomas Powers, *The Killing of Crazy Horse* (New York: Alfred A. Knopf, 2010).

26. Eliza Brown Davison to EBC, October 24 [1885], Other Sources, LBH.

27. Nancy P. Allan, "Standing Up for Liberty: Eliza Brown Davison and the

Custers," *Research Review: The Journal of the Little Big Horn Associates* 17: 1 (winter 2003), 2–12; Eliza Brown Davison to EBC, June 6, 1886, Other Sources, LBH.

28. EBC, *Boots and Saddles*; *New York Times*, December 18, 1883; Probate Court Inventory, Petition to Probate Court by Emil Justh, and GAC Will, Folder 1, Box 9, GAC Collection, MCHMA; "Emil Justh v. Benjamin Holliday [sic]," *Reports of Cases Argued and Adjudged in the Supreme Court of the District of Columbia, Sitting in General Term, from May 25, 1882, to October 29, 1883* (Washington, D.C.: John L. Ginck, 1884), 346–60; Leckie, 198–212, 234.

29. Leckie, 233–49.

30. EBC, *Tenting on the Plains*, 44–48, 480–83. As noted previously, when quoting EBC's rendering of Eliza Brown Davison's speech, I have standardized nonstandard spellings that provide no real information about vocalization and tend to belittle Davison's speech (e.g., "wuz").

31. Leckie, 198–249; Shirley Leckie correspondence with the author. See also Frost, *General Custer's Libbie*, 244–325.

Primary Source Bibliography

UNPUBLISHED MANUSCRIPT AND MICROFILM COLLECTIONS

Miscellaneous Collections

James Barnes Papers, Naval Historical Society Collection, New-York Historical Society, New York, N.Y.

Isaac Coates Journal, Denver Public Library, Denver, Co.

Elizabeth Bacon Custer Collection, Microfilm Publication, Little Bighorn National Battlefield, Crow Agency, Mont.

George Armstrong Custer Collection, L. Tom Perry Special Collections, Harold B. Lee Library, Brigham Young University, Provo, Utah

Dr. Lawrence A. Frost Collection, Monroe County Library System, Monroe, Mich.

Jacob Greene Papers, U.S. Army Military History Institute, Carlisle, Pa.

Benjamin Henry Grierson Papers, Newberry Library, Chicago, Ill.

Charles H. Lothrop Papers, State Historical Society of Iowa, Iowa City, Iowa

Shirley A. Leckie Notes, Elizabeth Bacon Journal, privately held

Northern Pacific Railway Collection, Minnesota Historical Society, St. Paul, Minn.

Unidentified Author, Diary, Mss 5:1 W2767:1, Virginia Historical Society, Richmond, Va.

William E. Walsh Diary, Special and Archival Collections, Philips Memorial Library, Providence College, Providence, R.I.

Libraries and Archives with Multiple Collections

Huntington Library, San Marino, Calif.
    George Armstrong Custer Deposition, October 8, 1875, *Atlantic Publishing Company v. George Armstrong Custer*
    George Armstrong Custer to Capt. Andrew J. Cohen, AAG, Cavalry Corps, May 28, 1863, ni 77
    George Armstrong Custer to Amasa E. Dana, September 8, 1864, CW 77
    Samuel L. M. Barlow Papers
    Leonard Herbert Swett Papers
    Swett Family Correspondence
Manuscript Division, Library of Congress, Washington, D.C.
    Zachariah Chandler Papers
    Christiancy and Pickett Families' Papers
    George Armstrong Custer Miscellaneous Manuscripts
    Edward S. Godfrey Papers

Abraham Lincoln Papers
George B. McClellan Papers
Alfred Pleasonton Papers
Philip H. Sheridan Papers
William T. Sherman Family Papers. Copy of Original at University of Notre
    Dame
Alfred H. Terry Papers
Monroe County Historical Museum Archives, Monroe, Mich.
    General George Armtrong Custer Collection
    Dr. Lawrence A. Frost Collection of Custeriana
National Archives, College Park, Md.
    Department of Justice, Letters Received from the State of Kentucky, Roll 1,
        Microfilm Publication M1362
National Archives, Washington, D.C.
    Manuscripts:
    Record Group 393:
        Entry 1: Post 198, Elizabethtown, Kentucky, Vol. 2: Letters Sent, Part 5
        Entry 2: Post 198, Elizabethtown, Kentucky, Vol. 2: Endorsements, Part 5
        Entry 3: Post 198, Elizabethtown, Kentucky: Telegrams Sent and Received,
            Part 5
        Entry 7: Post 198, Elizabethtown, Kentucky, Vols. 1–2: Special Orders,
            Part 5
        Entry 1593: 3rd Cavalry Division, Cavalry Corps, Army of the Potomac,
            Letters Sent August 1863–June 1865, containing Old Book 89, No. 71,
            Part 2
        Entry 3099: Special Orders Issued, June 1865–January 1866, containing
            Old Book 48, Volume 17/48, DTex, 2nd Cavalry Division, Department
            of Texas, No. 198, Part 2
        Entry 4794: Special Orders Issued, August 1865 to August 1868, Depart-
            ment of Texas and 5th Military District, No. 1, Part 1
    Microfilm Publications:
    Frederick Benteen Reference Microfilm
    George Armstrong Custer Reference Microfilm:
        House Report 3328
        George A. Custer Application Papers to the U.S. Military Academy,
            Records of the Adjutant General's Office, 1783–1917, Record Group 94
        1861 Court-Martial Trial of George Armstrong Custer, Records of the
            Office of Judge Advocate General, Record Group 153
        1867 Court-Martial Trial of George Armstrong Custer, Records of the
            Office of Judge Advocate General, Record Group 153
        Personnel Files, Office of the Adjutant General, Record Group 407
    Marcus Reno Reference Microfilm
    Secretary of War, Register of Letters Received, Roll 125, Microfilm Publication
        M22
    Proceedings of a Court of Inquiry Concerning the Conduct of Major Marcus A.
        Reno at the Battle of the Little Big Horn River on June 25 and 26, 1876, Rolls
        1–2, Microfilm Publication M592
    Office of the Adjutant General (Main Series), Letters Received, 1861–1870, Roll
        722, Microfilm Publication M619

Office of the Adjutant General, Letters Received: 1871–1889, Roll 122, Microfilm Publication M666

Records of the Assistant Commissioner for the State of Texas, Bureau of Refugees, Freedmen, and Abandoned Lands, 1865–1869, Unregistered Letters Received, 1865–66, Roll 17, Microfilm Publication M821

Headquarters Records of Fort Dodge, Kansas, 1866–1882, Unregistered Letters Received, Roll 11, Microfilm Publication M989, NA

Department of Texas, the District of Texas, and the 5th Military District, Letters Sent, Roll 1, Microfilm Publication M1165

Division of the Missouri, Special Files of Headquarters Relating to Military Operations and Administration, Rolls 1, 7, Microfilm Publication M1495

Department of Dakota, Letters Received, Rolls 14, 17, Microfilm Publication M1734

General Court Martial of General George Armstrong Custer, 1867, Microfilm Publication T-1103

Eighth Census of the United States, 1860

Ninth Census of the United States, 1870

Tenth Census of the United States, 1880

Tax Assessment List, Division 10, District 1, Michigan, 1862, Internal Revenue Bureau

Manuscripts and Archives Division, New York Public Library, Astor Lenox, and Tilden Foundations, New York, N.Y.

Robert S. Ellison Collection

Marguerite Merington Papers

Samuel J. Tilden Papers

Bentley Historical Library, University of Michigan, Ann Arbor, Mich.

Austin Blair Papers

Victor E. Comte Papers

James H. Kidd Papers

Special Collections and Archives, United States Military Academy, West Point, N.Y.

William Winer Cooke Papers

George Armstrong Custer Papers

Register of Delinquencies, 1856–1861

Ulysses S. Grant Papers

Charles William Larned Papers

Beinecke Rare Book and Manuscript Library, Yale University, New Haven, Conn.

Arthur Brigham Carpenter Papers

Elizabeth Bacon Custer Papers

George Armstrong Custer Letters to "Dear Mollie"

George Armstrong Custer Papers

Henry Leighton Morrill Papers

Alfred Sully Letters

PUBLISHED PRIMARY SOURCES

Congressional Reports and Executive Documents

House of Representatives Report 30, 1st Session, 39th Congress

———. Report 799, 1st Session, 44th Congress

———. Executive Document 1, 2nd Session, 40th Congress

———. Executive Document 1, 2nd Session, 41st Congress
———. Executive Document 240, 2nd Session, 41st Congress
———. Executive Document 1, 2nd Session, 42nd Congress
Senate Report 59, 2nd Session, 41st Congress
Senate Executive Document 13, 1st Session, 40th Congress
———. 13, 3rd Session, 40th Congress
———. 18, 3rd Session, 40th Congress
———. 36, 3rd Session, 40th Congress
———. 40, 3rd Session, 40th Congress
———. 32, 2nd Session, 43rd Congress

Books and Articles

Agassiz, George R. ed. *Meade's Headquarters, 1863–1865: Letters of Colonel Theodore Lyman, from the Wilderness to Appomattox.* Boston: Atlantic Monthly Press, 1922.

Ames, Blanche Butler, ed. *Chronicles from the Nineteenth Century: Family Letters of Blanche Butler and Adelbert Ames.* Vols. 1–2. Clinton, Mass.: n.p., 1957.

Barker, Malcolm E., ed. *More San Francisco Memoirs: 1852–1899: The Ripening Years.* San Francisco: Londonborn, 1996.

Barnard, John G. *The Peninsular Campaign and Its Antecedents.* New York: D. Van Nostrand, 1864.

Barrett, Lawrence. "Personal Recollections of General Custer," in Frederick Whittaker, *A Complete Life of Gen. George A. Custer: Major-General of Volunteers Brevet Major-General U.S. Army, and Lieutenant-Colonel Seventh U.S. Cavalry.* New York: Sheldon and Co., 1876, 629–43.

Beale, R. L. T. *History of the Ninth Virginia Cavalry in the War Between the States.* Richmond, Va.: B. F. Johnson Publishing , 1899.

Bergeron, Paul A., ed. *The Papers of Andrew Johnson.* Vols. 11, 16. Knoxville: University of Tennessee Press, 1994, 2000.

Boutwell, George. *Reminiscences of Sixty Years in Public Affairs.* Vol. 2. Boston: McClure, Phillips, and Co., 1902.

Boynton, Edward C. *History of West Point, and Its Military Importance During the American Revolution and the Origins and Progress of the United States Military Academy.* London: Sampson Low, Son, and Marston, 1864.

Brininstool, E. A., ed., and David L. Spotts. *Campaigning with Custer and the Nineteenth Kansas Volunteer Cavalry in the Washita Campaign, 1868–69.* Lincoln: University of Nebraska Press, 1988 [orig. pub. 1928].

Carroll, John M. *Custer in Texas: An Interrupted Narrative.* New York: Sol Lewis, 1975.

Carroll, John M., ed. *The Benteen-Goldin Letters on Custer and His Last Battle.* Lincoln: University of Nebraska Press, 1991 [orig. pub. 1974].

———. *Custer's Chief of Scouts: The Reminiscences of Charles A. Varnum.* Lincoln: University of Nebraska Press, 1987.

Clews, Henry. *Twenty-eight Years on Wall Street.* New York: Irving Publishing, 1888.

Cogley, Thomas S. *History of the Seventh Indiana Cavalry Volunteers.* LaPorte, Ind.: Herald Company, 1876.

Crary, Catherine S., ed. *Dear Belle: Letters from a Cadet and Officer to His Sweetheart, 1858–1865.* Middletown, Conn.: Wesleyan University Press, 1965.

Custer, Elizabeth Bacon. *"Boots and Saddles," or Life in Dakota with General Custer.* New York: Harper and Brothers, 1885.

———. *Following the Guidon.* New York: Harper and Brothers, 1890.

———. *Tenting on the Plains, or General Custer in Kansas and Texas.* New York: Harper and Brothers, 1887.

Custer, George Armstrong. *My Life on the Plains, or Personal Experiences with the Indians.* New York: Sheldon and Co., 1874.

———. Correspondence, in Frederick Whittaker, *A Complete Life of Gen. George A. Custer: Major-General of Volunteers Brevet Major-General U.S. Army, and Lieutenant-Colonel Seventh U.S. Cavalry.* New York: Sheldon and Co., 1876.

Dippie, Brian W., ed. *Nomad: George A. Custer in* Turf, Field and Farm. Austin: University of Texas Press, 1980.

Easton, Alexander N. *The New York Stock Exchange: Its History, Its Contribution to National Prosperity, and Its Relation to American Finance at the Outset of the Twentieth Century.* New York: Stock Exchange Historical Company, 1905.

Finerty, John F. *War-Path and Bivouac, or, The Conquest of the Sioux.* Norman: University of Oklahoma Press, 1977 [orig. pub. 1890].

Ford, Worthington Chauncey, ed. *A Cycle of Adams Letters, 1861–1865.* Vols. 1–2. Boston: Houghton Mifflin, 1920.

Fowler, William W. *Ten Years in Wall Street: Or, Revelations of Inside Life and Experience on 'Change.* Hartford, Conn.: Worthington, Dustin and Co., 1870.

Frost, Lawrence A. *The Court-Martial of General George Armstrong Custer.* Norman: University of Oklahoma Press, 1968.

Gibbon, John. *Personal Recollections of the Civil War.* New York: G. P. Putnam's Sons, 1928.

Governor's Message to the Legislature of the State of Michigan, in Session, January 7, 1868. Lansing, Mich.: John A. Kerr, 1863.

Graham, W. A., ed. *The Custer Myth: A Source Book of Custeriana.* Mechanicsburg, Pa.: Stackpole Books, 2000 [orig. pub. 1953].

Grant, Ulysses S. *Personal Memoirs of U.S. Grant.* New York: Da Capo Press, 1982 [orig. pub. 1885].

Greenberg, Karen J., and Joshua L. Dratel, eds. *The Torture Papers: The Road to Abu Ghraib.* New York: Cambridge University Press, 2005.

Hard, Abner. *History of the Eighth Cavalry Regiment, Illinois Volunteers, During the Great Rebellion.* Aurora, Ill.: n.p., 1868.

Hardorff, Richard G., ed. *Washita Memories: Eyewitness Views of Custer's Attack on Black Kettle's Village.* Norman: University of Oklahoma Press, 2006.

Harris, Samuel. *Personal Reminiscences.* Chicago: Rogerson Press, 1897.

Hazen, William B. *Some Corrections to "My Life on the Plains."* St. Paul: Ramaley and Cunningham, 1875.

Holmes, Oliver Wendell. "My Hunt After 'The Captain,'" *Atlantic Monthly,* December 1862.

———. *Pages from an Old Volume of Life: A Collection of Essays, 1857–1881.* Boston: Houghton, Mifflin and Company, 1891.

Howard, Hamilton Gay. *Civil War Echoes: Character Sketches and State Secrets.* Washington, D.C.: Howard Publishing, 1907.

Hutton, Paul Andrew, ed. *The Custer Reader.* Norman: University of Oklahoma Press, 2004 [orig. pub. 1992].

Johnson, Robert Underwood, and Clarence Clough Buel, eds. *Battles and Leaders of the Civil War*. Vols. 1–4. New York: Century Company, 1884–88.

Joinville, François, Prince de. *The Army of the Potomac: Its Organization, Its Commander, and Its Campaign*. Trans. William Henry Hurlbut. New York: Anson D. F. Randolph, 1862.

Joshi, S. T., ed. *Ambrose Bierce: The Devil's Dictionary, Tales, & Memoirs*. New York: Library of America, 2011.

Keim, De B. Randolph. *Sheridan's Troopers on the Border: A Winter Campaign on the Plains*. Philadelphia: David McKay, 1885.

Kennedy, W. J. D., ed. *On the Plains with Custer and Hancock: The Journal of Isaac Coates, Army Surgeon*. Boulder, Colo.: Johnson Books, 1997.

Kent, Austin. *Free Love: Or, a Philosophical Demonstration of the Non-Exclusive Nature of Connubial Love*. Hopkinton, N.Y.: n.p., 1857.

Kidd, James H. *Personal Recollections of a Cavalryman*. Ionia, Mich.: Sentinel Press, 1908.

King, W. C., and W. P. Derby, eds. *Camp-Fire Sketches and Battle-Field Echoes*. Springfield, Mass.: King, Richardson and Co., 1888.

Longstreet, James. *From Manassas to Appomattox: Memoirs of the Civil War in America*. Philadelphia: J. B. Lippincott Company, 1908.

Lothrop, Charles H. *A History of the First Regiment Iowa Cavalry*. Lyons, Iowa.: Beers and Eaton, 1890.

Lynch, John R. *Reminiscences of an Active Life: The Reminiscences of John Roy Lynch*. Chicago: University of Chicago Press, 1970.

McClellan, George B. *McClellan's Own Story*. New York: Charles L. Webster and Co., 1887.

McDonald, John. *Secrets of the Great Whiskey Ring*. Chicago: Belford, Clarke and Co., 1880.

McDonald, William Naylor. *History of the Laurel Brigade*. Baltimore, Md.: Sun Job Printing Office, 1907.

Merington, Marguerite. *The Custer Story: The Life and Intimate Letters of General George A. Custer and His Wife Elizabeth*. Lincoln: University of Nebraska Press, 1987 [orig. pub. 1950].

Michie, Peter. "Reminiscences of Cadet and Army Service," in A. Noel Blakeman, ed., *Personal Recollections of the War of the Rebellion: Second Series*. New York: G. P. Putnam's Sons, 1897.

Mills, Charles H., ed. *The New York State Reporter*. Vol. 65. Albany, N.Y.: W. C. Little and Co., 1895.

Mississippi in 1875: Report of the Select Committee to Inquire into the Mississippi Election of 1875, with the Testimony and Documentary Evidence. Vol. 1. Washington, D.C.: Government Printing Office, 1876.

Morgan, Albert T. *Yazoo: Or, On the Picket Line of Freedom in the South*. Washington, D.C.: N.p., 1884.

Mulford, Ami Frank. *Fighting Indians in the 7th United States Cavalry: Custer's Favorite Regiment*. Corning, N.Y.: Paul Lindsley Mulford, 1879.

Nevins, Allan, ed. *A Diary of Battle: The Personal Journals of Colonel Charles S. Wainwright, 1861–1865*. New York: Da Capo, 1998.

Nevins, Allan, and Milton Halsey Thomas, eds. *The Diary of George Templeton Strong*. Vol. 2. New York: Macmillan, 1952.

Official Army Register of the Volunteer Force of the United States Army for the Years 1861,

'62, '63, '64, '65: Part V, Ohio, Michigan. Washington, D.C.: Adjutant General's Office, 1865.

O'Neil, Tom, ed. *Letters from Boston Custer.* Brooklyn: Arrow and Trooper, 1993.

Pohanka, Brian C., ed. *A Summer on the Plains with Custer's 7th Cavalry: The 1870 Diary of Annie Gibson Roberts.* Lynchburg, Va.: Schroeder Publications, 2004.

Putnam, George Palmer. *A Memoir.* New York: G. P. Putnam's Sons, 1912.

The Reno Court of Inquiry: The Chicago Times Account. Fort Collins, Colo.: Old Army Press, 1972.

Report of the Treasurer of the Missouri Southern Relief Association. Missouri History Library and Museum: St. Louis, Mo., 1866.

Reports of Cases Argued and Adjudged in the Supreme Court of the District of Columbia, Sitting in General Term, from May 25, 1882, to October 29, 1883. Washington, D.C.: John L. Ginck, 1884.

Reynolds, Arlene, ed. *The Civil War Memories of Elizabeth Bacon Custer: Reconstructed from Her Diaries and Notes.* Austin: University of Texas Press, 1994.

Robertson, John, ed. *Michigan in the War.* Rev. ed. Lansing, Mich.: W. S. George and Co., 1882.

Rowland, Thomas. "Letters of a Virginia Cadet at West Point, 1859–1861." *South Atlantic Quarterly* 15, no. 4 (October 1915): 330–47.

Russell, William Howard. *My Diary: North and South.* Vol. 1. London: Bradbury and Evans, 1863.

Schaff, Morris. *The Spirit of Old West Point: 1858–1862.* Boston: Houghton Mifflin, 1912.

———. *The Sunset of the Confederacy.* Boston: John W. Luce and Co., 1912.

Sears, Stephen W., ed. *The Civil War Papers of George B. McClellan: Selected Correspondence, 1860–1865.* New York: Da Capo Press, 1992.

Seventeenth Annual Reunion of the Association of the Graduates of the United States Military Academy at West Point, New York, June 10th, 1886. East Saginaw, Mich.: Evening News, 1886.

Sheridan, Philip H. *Personal Memoirs of P. H. Sheridan.* New York: Da Capo Press, 1992 [orig. pub. 1888].

Simon, John. Y., ed. *The Papers of Ulysses S. Grant.* Vols. 15–27. Carbondale, Ill.: Southern Illinois University Press, 1988–2005.

Stanley, David S. *Personal Memoirs of Major-General D. S. Stanley.* Cambridge, Mass.: Harvard University Press, 1917.

Stanley, Henry M. *My Early Travels and Adventures in America and Asia.* New York: Charles Scribner's Sons, 1895.

Stevenson, Adlai E. *Something of Men I Have Known.* Chicago: A. C. McClurg and Co., 1909.

Strong, George C. *Cadet Life at West Point.* Boston: T. O. H. P. Burnham, 1862.

Trevathan, Charles E. *The American Thoroughbred.* New York: Macmillan, 1905.

Twelfth Annual Catalogue of the Officers and Pupils of the Young Ladies' Seminary and Collegiate Institute at Monroe City, Michigan, 1862. Monroe, Mich: Edward G. Morton, 1862.

Utley, Robert M., ed. *Life in Custer's Cavalry: Diaries and Letters of Albert and Jennie Barnitz, 1867–1868.* Lincoln: University of Nebraska Press, 1987 [orig. pub. 1977].

The War of the Rebellion: A Compilation of the Official Records of the Union and Confederate Armies. Washington, D.C.: Government Printing Office, 1880–1901.

Wilson, James Grant, and John Fiske, eds. *Appleton's Cyclopaedia of American Biography*. Vol. 1. New York: D. Appleton, 1888.
Wilson, James H. *Under the Old Flag*. Vol. 1. New York: D. Appleton, 1912.

Newspapers and Magazines

Advance
Arizona Miner
Atlanta Constitution
Atlantic Monthly
Baltimore Sun
Banker's Magazine and Statistical Register
Bismarck Tribune
Boston Advertiser
Boston Globe
Boston Herald
Chicago Inter-Ocean
Chicago Times
Chicago Tribune
Cincinnati Enquirer
Cincinnati Gazette
Circular
Cleveland Leader
Columbus Enquirer
Des Moines State Register
Detroit Free Press
Flake's Bulletin
Forest and Stream
Frank Leslie's Illustrated Newspaper
Galaxy
Georgia Weekly Telegraph
Harper's New Monthly Magazine
Harper's Weekly
Harrisburg Weekly Patriot and Union
Hartford Courant
Independent
Indianapolis Sentinel
Kalamazoo Gazette

Kansas City Journal of Commerce
Kansas City Star
Latter-Day Saints' Millenial Star
Leavenworth Bulletin
Literary World
Louisville Courier-Journal
Maine Farmer
Massachusetts Ploughman
Monroe [Mich.] *Commercial*
Monroe [Mich.] *Democrat*
Monroe [Mich.] *Monitor*
New Orleans Picayune
New Orleans Times
New York Evangelist
New York Herald
New York Observer and Chronicle
New York Sun
New York Times
New York Tribune
New York World
North American Review
Philadelphia Inquirer
Pomeroy's Democrat
Railroad Gazette
Round Table
St. Louis Democrat
San Francisco Bulletin
San Francisco Chronicle
Sioux City Journal
Turf, Field and Farm
Washington Critic
Washington Constitutional Union
Yankton Press and Dakotaian

Index

Page numbers in *italics* refer to maps.

A Note About the Author

T. J. Stiles is the author of *The First Tycoon: The Epic Life of Cornelius Vanderbilt*, winner of the Pulitzer Prize for Biography and the National Book Award for Nonfiction, and *Jesse James: Last Rebel of the Civil War*, which received the Ambassador Book Award and the Peter Seaborg Award for Civil War Scholarship, and was a finalist for the *Los Angeles Times* Book Prize. An elected member of the Society of American Historians and a member of the board of the Authors Guild, he was a 2011 fellow of the John Simon Guggenheim Memorial Foundation, a 2004 Gilder Lehrman Fellow in American History at the New York Public Library's Dorothy and Lewis B. Cullman Center for Scholars and Writers, and a member of the 2014 faculty of the World Economic Forum. He lives in Berkeley, California, with his wife and two children.

A Note on the Type

This book was set in Janson, a typeface long thought to have been made by the Dutchman Anton Janson, who was a practicing typefounder in Leipzig during the years 1668–1687. However, it has been conclusively demonstrated that these types are actually the work of Nicholas Kis (1650–1702), a Hungarian, who most probably learned his trade from the master Dutch typefounder Dirk Voskens. The type is an excellent example of the influential and sturdy Dutch types that prevailed in England up to the time William Caslon (1692–1766) developed his own incomparable designs from them.

Composed by North Market Street Graphics
Lancaster, Pennsylvania

Printed and Bound by Berryville Graphics
Berryville, Virginia

Designed by M. Kristen Bearse